DIVING PIONEERS AND INNOVATORS

A SERIES OF IN-DEPTH INTERVIEWS

BRET GILLIAM

Contributors
Fred Garth, Eric Hanauer, Lina Hitchcock,
Douglas David Seifert, Michel Gilbert & Danielle Alary

New World Publications, Inc.
Jacksonville, Florida USA

in association with
Oceans Media Inc.
Arrowsic, Maine USA & British Virgin Islands

Printed
By
D2Print Pte Limited.
Singapore

ISBN: 978-1-878348-42-5

DEDICATED TO

Dick Anderson | Paul Tzimoulis | Peter Gimbel | Ron Church

Sheck Exley | Mike Kevorkian | Frank Scalli | E. R. Cross

Bill Meistrell | John Cronin | Rob Palmer | Jack McKenney

Bill Turbeville | Cliff Simoneau | Larry Smith | Dr. Bob Dill

This book captures some of the diving industries' most interesting characters in their own words. I'm glad that I had the chance to get Peter Benchley's interview done before he passed away in February 2006. But I missed the chance to preserve the life stories of others who should have been part of this project. Their untimely passing was mourned by all who knew them… as well as those who didn't, but benefited from their contributions to diving. To those eternal personalities, this book is dedicated.

THE INSPIRATION FOR THIS BOOK CAME FROM Eric Hanauer. Over 15 years ago we both were doing a series of books for Watersport Publishing in San Diego. I was writing weighty tomes on technical diving and Eric had done a travel book on the Red Sea. In 1994 I visited the offices for some editing meetings and found a preliminary layout for a book called, you guessed it, *Diving Pioneers*. I saw Eric's name on the thing and knew that it would be worth my time. I meant to sit down and peruse it for a few minutes and ended up reading the whole thing in one sitting. I had to tell publisher Ken Loyst that we'd pick up our meeting the next day. After that he learned never to leave anything out that would distract me when I flew in for a visit.

Eric's book was about 250 pages and profiled 22 people in short chapters and a collection of black and white photos. It was heavily biased toward California divers from the 1940s and 1950s era but everyone included was a legitimate "pioneer" and I found it fascinating. It sparked my idea to take off where Eric had stopped and do a series of lengthy interviews with other compelling diving figures. I started the interviews two years later in *Deep Tech* magazine with Bev Morgan. Up until then, the diving press limited interviews to a few pages of mostly formulaic stock question scripts and rarely did an interview subject reveal much about the person. The response to Morgan's piece was a bit overwhelming and we got swamped by readers asking for more. Others followed in *Deep Tech* and I expanded the

series later in *Fathoms* magazine. When I sold out in 2005 I made plans to turn those dialogues into a book and widen the content by including more of diving's movers and shakers.

Deciding on the final lineup was tough. Certainly this does not include all who should be in such a book. And that's why I already have plans for a Volume II. But it does represent an interesting cross section of the first two generations of diving with filmmakers, manufacturers, authors, explorers, publishers, photographers, and entrepreneurs. I expanded Eric's original title to include "Innovators" and felt it fit the group pretty well. Some are now retired, one (Peter Benchley) is tragically deceased, and many are still making history. I think you'll find it to be an interesting bunch to hang out with, albeit vicariously from the pages. But it's their story in their own words.

A book like this cannot succeed without the complete cooperation and trust of the folks included as interview subjects. It requires quite a long process to get the initial Q&A over and then a committed excavation of photo archives to resurrect the images necessary to bring the dialogue to life. I think some of the photos we worked with may have been originally taken by Matthew Brady with a massive daguerreotype on a tripod hewn from whole oak. (Is that Stan Waterman in the back row of the Union army at Gettysburg?) No matter whether recorded on old dusty glass plates, 35mm slides, prints, or today's digital files… someone had to go dig for them. And I appreciate the effort. So my first "shout out" of thanks goes straight to the characters profiled. It was a pleasure working with each one of you.

I also very much appreciate the stellar contributions of my co-authors Fred Garth, Douglas Seifert, and Michel Gilbert & Danielle Alary who captured the interviews I couldn't squeeze in myself. Thanks especially to Lina Hitchcock who drew the unenviable task of interviewing me. Of course, Eric Hanauer predictably joins the crew and I thank him again for setting the concept.

My longtime collaborator Kim Barry gets all the credit for designing the book and carefully melding images and dialogue into a cohesive and interesting package. Kim, none of the magazines and book projects I've done since 2000 would have been possible without your creative skill and steady hand. And you cook like a deranged gourmet, as well.

Sue Drafahl rounded up the images for Zale Parry when a lot of that material would have been lost. Dr. Gregg Gaylord, Hugh Duncan, and Ned Deloach helped with critical and much needed input on content and style. Eric Riesch at New World Publications was invaluable helping coordinate the project with the printers and liaison all the details of getting this monster from a digital file, to press, and back from Singapore.

Thanks to my wife Gretchen for helping in so many ways and playing hostess and "hotelier" to so many of the interviewees and other various degenerates and swashbucklers who like to drop in and stay awhile. (Please see if Mike deGruy is still in the hot tub.)

I'd also like to thank all the readers of my magazines, articles, and books who encouraged me to put together this special edition of conversations with diving's most interesting people. You guys were right: There wasn't another book like this and it was long overdue. I hope it can help preserve a true "oral history" of diving and let you share in the intimacy and fun of sitting down with some great story-tellers and just letting them rip. Some of these interviews were fueled by coffee. Others were helped along by some fine wines. All were driven by a great combination of camaraderie and a bit of adrenalin generated by recalling pivotal career moments… whether tragic, exciting or just plain fun. But our intent was to bring the reader right into the conversation and encourage you to pull up a chair and listen in.

We hope you enjoy yourself and come away a bit better for the experience. There's a lot of water under the collective keels of the divers you're going to read about. Capturing these stories was a project spanning a decade. We all hope it's a fun ride for you to share.

Even better would be to say hi in person. So don't be shy about introducing yourself to anyone we interviewed if your paths cross at a dive program, a movie screening, or even better, on a dive boat somewhere.

Just explain that you were already introduced… and then buy the first round!

Bret Gilliam, June 2007

Bret Gilliam

IT HAPPENS THAT I HAD NEVER DIVED WITH Bret Gilliam. I knew his name. His reputation as a preeminently successful entrepreneur in the diving world, a veteran participant and pioneer in almost every facet of the industry, was known to me as it was to almost every one, old and new, who had joined his or her life to the sea and diving.

We met many years ago at one of those raucous, salubrious cocktail receptions by the Boston Sea Rovers. I joined a circle that had formed around a booming, resonant deep voice. When I could get close enough to look around the heads I focused on the storyteller. Not only did he have the full attention of his audience, he had them body and soul.

We became friends. We often shared the stage at film festivals and gatherings. I have a few stories to tell myself. I ultimately tried to precede Bret with the best story I could uncork and have now learned to avoid ever following his act.

When, in 2001, Bret decided to turn his hand again to publishing and editing a dive journal he asked me to contribute an essay to each issue. I was happy to do so and more than pleased to provide

the grist for an interview with the unique and very sensible provision that I write freely - any length of my choosing – in response to a series of questions posed by him as my interrogator. The collected interviews that compose the main substance of this book are lengthy, intimate and provide a fascinating autobiography of the interviewee. I believe that this open-ended written interview style is unique in the world of diving journalism.

Many of the persons interviewed were my good friends or colleagues or both. Some I had never met (wreck explorer John Chatterton and filmmaker Greg MacGillivray). At least one, Peter Benchley, had a name familiar internationally. All were major achievers, their currency high and respected among divers. Since mine was one of the early interviews, I must confess that I probably rated the honor by having been in the business so long that I had been labeled a "Pioneer". I'll let it go at that. The bottom line is that I was, indeed, honored to be included.

All of the interviews are a "good read". Peter Benchley was my friend, an intimate of frequent family dinners (we were neighbors and had worked together on television network shows for many years). His interview revealed intimate experiences in his life that were entirely new to me. Ron and Valerie Taylor joined me on that infamous voyage that produced *Blue Water, White Death* so many years ago. Some of my first forays into big time Hollywood film jobs were with Al Giddings and Chuck Nicklin. The same holds true for Howard and Michele Hall. I had worked with them in their early days, their seminal periods in underwater camera work from which they would immerge as top underwater cameramen in the world and later producers of network series and IMAX productions. I knew why they had reached that preeminence – because they were both enterprising and good – but many of the accounts of adventures and perilous experiences along the way were fresh for me. Bret is a master of the interview craft precisely because of the detailed research he does in advance, as well as his personal relationship with so many of the subjects.

As I scroll down the names of those interviewed my brain neurons, though numbed by excessive use of strong drink, still drag back from yesteryear remembrances of camaraderie and shared experiences from long ago. Bob Ballard, a young researcher, was working on his doctorial degree at Woods Hole when I met him years ago. He was a member of the Boston Sea Rovers, a brotherhood of enthusiastic divers in the Boston area, all dedicated to lobster feasts and riotous good times. His achievements as the programmer for the famous submersible, *Alvin*, began to impress us but hardly stirred the world outside of the marine science community. Then the discovery of the *Titanic* projected him into world recognition. The full story of his rise to preeminence could only best be told by his own recollections. The interview format provides that vehicle.

From the beginning, Bret told me, "I made a commitment to giving interviews considerable space and really letting the interviewees tell their stories". One after another the interviews have fulfilled that purpose. The names are legends in their time: Zale Parry, a true lady pioneer who starred in *Sea Hunt* and dozens of other television and movie roles; Wes Skiles, world renowned cave explorer; the infamous Bev Morgan who changed commercial diving equipment forever; innovative filmmaker Mike deGruy; Bob Hollis and Dick Bonin, pioneers and giants in the manufacture of sport diving equipment; Paul Humann, lawyer turned prolific author/publisher of marine animal identification books; and legendary photographer Ernie Brooks... all those interviewed in the body of this articulate and often delightfully personal book represent two generations of divers who were dynamically part of the sport's evolution and growth.

In speaking of this project Bret said, "I want this book to be a way of preserving an oral history of diving, directly from the mouths of those responsible for shaping the sport from so many different segments". Most of this book's readers will not have personally known the famous men and women whose interviews compose the text. By giving each the time to marshal his or her thoughts, reach back into the experiences and adventures that became the very fabric of their growths, a window into the life of each is opened for the reader. I did know most personally. I still found the words of each a page-turner.

In this book's original draft, one most-wished-for interview was missing, that of the author. With a career that spans over 35 years Bret has logged over 17,000 dives. His business activities took him into almost every aspect of the diving world, both sport and commercial. I am acquainted with no one more discerningly qualified to select a representative group of pioneers, many of whom are still "cutting the mustard" with fresh productivity. When I pointed out this conspicuous absence, Bret dismissed including himself. But eventually he caved in and sat for his own interview session so I now consider the volume complete.

For myself, having survived into my eighties (with no thanks to prudence or world-shaking achievement) the very fact that I started diving in the 1930s before mask, fins and snorkels appeared and have miraculously survived to continue diving into my eighties seems to make me a "pioneer". I won't argue.

I am writing this foreword on the liveaboard dive boat, *Nai'a*, in Fiji waters. When I reach home again Susy, my wife of fifty-six years, will shout, "Never mind that pioneer stuff; get busy right here! The recyclables and garbage have to go out for tomorrow's pick up."

With that stirring call, I am back to reality.

Stan Waterman, December 2006

13

::

BRET GILLIAM | **principal author**

In a career spanning 35 years in professional diving, Gilliam has logged more than 17,000 dives in military, commercial, scientific, filming, and technical diving operations. He was one diving's most successful entrepreneurs with investments in publishing, training agencies, manufacturing, resorts, dive vessels, cruise ships, and film support companies. Author of over 600 articles and dozens of formal medical and scientific papers, he has been published worldwide. Bret was a senior editor with *Scuba Times*, Rodale's *Scuba Diving*, and *Diving Adventure* magazines as well as publisher of *Deep Tech* and founder/publisher of *Fathoms*. He is the principal author or contributor to 27 books. He was elected to the Explorers Club and the Boston Sea Rovers. Bret lives on an island in Maine now after 25 years running diving operations in the Caribbean, Atlantic and Pacific regions. **www.bretgilliam.com**

FRED GARTH | **contributor: Wes Skiles Interview**

A professional journalist since 1980, Garth has been published in numerous magazines and newspapers for more than 25 years. From 1986-1998 he served as editor and publisher of *Scuba Times* magazine and subsequently held editor positions at *Deep Tech*, *Skin Diver*, *Southern Diver* and *Dive Report*. In 1995, Garth helped create the Internet's first diving e-magazine, *Scuba Times Online*, which was acquired by *Skin Diver* in 1999 along with *Scuba Times* and *Deep Tech*. In early 2001, Garth and Bret Gilliam launched *Fathoms*, a magazine dedicated to the serious dive enthusiast. He is a technical diving instructor, rebreather instructor and a diver of more than 30 years. A full-time writer and editor, Garth lives in Pensacola, Florida with his wife, two daughters and bunny, Hoppy. His third novel, *Perdido*, is scheduled for publication in early 2007. **www.fredgarth.com**

LINA HITCHCOCK | **contributor: Bret Gilliam Interview**

Lina began diving in 1977 in the Virgin Islands. She joined the staff of Bret Gilliam's V. I. Divers Ltd. that same year and became Operations Manager in 1980. She worked as a film support technician and model, both topside and underwater, with Gilliam and Stephen Frink spanning three decades. Her diving has taken her to the Red Sea, Micronesia, the Solomon Islands, Indonesia, Cocos Island, the Caribbean, Bahamas, Melanesia, and Papua New Guinea on modeling and film work. As a model, she has appeared in scores of published articles and the giant Kodak photo-mural in Grand Central Station. She is a Senior Manager with Veeder-Root CMS in charge of Environmental Compliance programs. She lives in Houston, Texas.

KIM BARRY | **art director**

A native Mainer and ironically a non-diver, Kim has been a graphic designer for two decades. She established her design studio, Mayvrik Design, in 2000 and a year later was introduced to Gilliam. She has since been viewing the underwater world vicariously through his many entertaining stories, beautiful imagery and nutty acquaintances. She now splits her time between clients and her recent senior design position in Phoenix, Arizona. Though Gilliam has repeatedly offered to certify her in diving, she stands firm in her conviction that she has been qualified as "certifiable" – as is evident from her recent move across the country from Maine to the desert, where she has traded in her down jacket for an asbestos suit.

14

DOUGLAS DAVID SEIFERT | contributor: Ron & Valerie Taylor Interview
Douglas David Seifert began his diving career in 1974 in West Palm Beach, collecting unlucky tropical fish for his many aquariums. In 1994, he turned to writing and published his first feature, on sperm whales, in *Ocean Realm*, then followed it up with extensive features on whale sharks and manatees. He was hired away by *DIVE International* in London and has been working for them ever since. He was Editor-in-chief of *Oceans Illustrated* and continues to write for *DIVE* magazine and, as Contributing Editor, has published dozens of features. His underwater photographic images have been published in books, newspapers and magazines around the world, including *The New York Times*, *The International Herald-Tribune*, *Men's Journal*, *Esquire*, *Forbes*, *FYI*, *Outside*, *GQ*, *Reader's Digest*, *Sports Afield*, *Nature's Best* and most of the dive magazines. He calls Jupiter, Florida, home when he is not on boats somewhere hard to find on a map. **www.douglasseifert.com**

ERIC HANAUER | contributor: Chuck Nicklin Interview
Although Eric made his first dives in Chicago's lakes and quarries in 1959, he didn't focus primarily on diving until 15 years later. In the meantime he was a successful swimming coach at Morgan Park High School and at California State University Fullerton. He developed the grab start, which is now used by swimmers worldwide. Hanauer founded the scuba program at Cal State Fullerton and when he moved from coaching into teaching began shooting pictures underwater instead of shooting fish. He introduced thousands of students to the underwater world over a 35 year career. In 1977, he broke into a new field with his first article in *Skin Diver* magazine. Over the past 30 years, his work has been published in magazines, books, posters, and CDs worldwide. He has written guidebooks to the Red Sea and Micronesia, as well as an oral history of diving. Recently Hanauer began shooting underwater video, and his films have been selected for showing in festivals and on the Internet. **www.ehanauer.com**

DANIELLE ALARY & MICHEL GILBERT | contributors: Ernie Brooks Interview
Award-winning, lecturers, photography and multimedia producers, Michel and Danielle have been exploring the underwater environment for more than 25 years. Authors of more than 500 articles related to diving, travel and sailing, they are underwater photography columnists for *Diver* magazine. Their work is sold worldwide by various agencies. They regularly lecture and give workshops at dive shows in North America and abroad. They have received numerous awards including: Canadian Diving Achievement Award (1991), Diver of the Year Award for the Arts (Beneath the Sea, 1995). Silver Diver Award (Antibes World Festival of Underwater Images, 1997). Grand Prize from the Ministry of Tourism of Québec (2002), Our World Underwater Award (Chicago 2007). Danielle is a member of the Women Divers Hall Of Fame. Michel and Danielle chair and participate in various juries at renowned underwater film and photography competitions, including numerous participations in the elite jurors at the World Festival of Underwater images held in Antibes, on the Côte d'Azur. **www.sub-images.com**

Connie Morgan

Leslie Leaney and early American diving helmet.
Scripps Instution of Oceanography, La Jolla, California

GRAINY BLACK AND WHITE IMAGES FLICKERED
across the length of the auditorium. The audience
fell silent as the screen showed an athletically built
young man standing on the swaying deck of a
small boat. With a deep tan and sun-bleached hair
and beard he looked like a sea gypsy. Assisted by
a bearded crewman, he placed a navy submarine
escape apparatus over his head, put on his nose
clip, mask, and fins. And then, without pause, he
took a step off the deck of the boat, and into the
sea. The images then moved underwater as the
young man gleefully swam around the seabed in a
lengthy series of maneuvers reminiscent of a solo
aerobatic display. Somersaults, loops and rolls.
Liberated in a three-dimensional world, he instantly
became a fish among the fishes. He was free at last!
It was a surreal moment in the sea.

In the front rows of the sold-out auditorium

headliner speakers James Cameron, Stan Waterman,
Ernie Brooks, John Chatterton, Bret Gilliam and
others sat in revered silence. You could hear a pin
drop. Seated on the auditorium stage in the silent
darkness, an elegant older couple sat holding hands.
The gentleman turned his head to the screen slightly
and nodded as if to reassure himself of a fact. Could
what he was seeing really have been 64 years ago
and half a world away? Could it?

What the audience was witnessing was the
original footage of what most historians consider the
dive that launched scuba diving as we know it. The
fact that the actual diver who made it was sitting on
the stage in front of them with his wife Lotte, made
the whole experience even more surreal.

The step that Austria's Hans Hass took on July
12,1942, at the Greek island of Ari Ronisi, heralded
the dawn of recreational and scientific scuba diving. A
threshold had been crossed. Twenty-seven years later
America's Neil Armstrong stepped across another
threshold. "One small step for man, a giant leap for
mankind." The whole world knows Armstrong's first
step. Only a handful of divers know of Hass' first step.
That too was also a giant leap for mankind.

Hans Hass' 1942 step was but the first of
millions that were to follow, as humans discovered
the thrill of scuba diving. Less than a year later
Cousteau and Gagnan invented the Aqua-Lung
and full French production of the unit would follow
within three years. By 1948 the Aqua-Lung was
available in the United States and the sport of
recreational diving started to develop.

In the years that have followed, numerous
sea lovers tried to make a career out their passion

for diving. Then, as now, it proved to be a difficult thing to do. Those that were able to convert the intoxication of this new adventure into a meaningful career became the pioneers of the sport. However, scant attention was given to the historical relevance of what was being invented, discovered, and photographed or filmed. Few participants thought what they were doing would qualify for the designation of "historic." But some of it was.

In 1992 I co-founded the Historical Diving Society of America to help record and preserve some of this early history, partly because the first wave of pioneers were reaching their very senior years. Even with the assistance of recognized scuba historians such as Nick Icorn, Eric Hanauer, Philippe Rousseau, Nyle Monday, Peter Jackson, Kent Rockwell, and Michael Jung, it has proven to be an extremely challenging task. This is partly because, unlike almost every other sport, we divers do not enter a competition with each other to provide a set of winners and losers. Consequently, we do not provide victors who become sports heroes, nor Most Valuable Players that are recognizable to the general public. The way divers generally get any recognition is by overall consistent career accomplishments displayed in a body of work and in service. It is here we find our heroes and MVPs.

In the pages that follow you will get to meet, via interview, a very select group whose work in the underwater realm has elevated them to MVP status. Stan Waterman gives you an introduction to these divers, but let me endorse that they are some of the most interesting creatures swimming in our oceans today. By granting practically unlimited editorial space to each, the interviews have captured not only the history of these careers but also the essence of the subject's character. Each interview provides a personal link in the chain of diving history that connects us all to the birth of our sport, and it also records some of the milestones they created along the way.

Perhaps the most appealing element of this book is that it is easy to imagine that you are actually sitting opposite the divers as they tell their story. For me it felt like I could have been relaxing on the back of a dive boat and watching the sun set listening to someone who has had a measurable influence on the overall culture of diving. Very rare air indeed.

Since Hans' early step of 1942, the world has accumulated an increasing archive of imagery and words that record many individual contributions to the culture of diving. But the pristine world that some of these pioneers have seen may no longer be available to their grandchildren. As we now all face the environmental uncertainties of the future, it is important to know from where we have come. The divers interviewed here present some illumination to that historic path which includes the discoveries of their personal journey. Theirs has been a unique experience and I am delighted that this book gives these special characters a chance to share some of their adventures, and enables them leave their indelible fin-prints in the historical sands of time.

Leslie Leaney, President
The Historical Diving Society, USA
Santa Barbara, California
June 2007

The Historical Diving Society
www.hds.org

THE HISTORICAL DIVING SOCIETY OF USA WAS founded in 1992 to record and preserve the history of diving. It is a registered 501 (c) 3 not-for-profit corporation professionally governed by an elected Board of Directors and administered by appointed officers. The Society is supported by a broad international membership base and the majority of divers interviewed in this book are members. There are no special requirements for membership. The HDS is open to anyone with an interest in diving history. Sponsorship opportunities are also available.

To service the Society's educational mission statement of "Preservation Through Education," the Society publishes the quarterly magazine *Historical Diver* which is mailed to members in over 40 countries. The Society provides members with a regular supply of international book titles on diving history and hosts an annual Conference that presents papers on diving history. The Society produces four major awards that are presented at the annual Awards Banquet on the same night as the Conference. It exhibits at every major diving show in America and is used as an historical resource by numerous publishers, museums, and television and film producers.

The Society enjoys the support of an Advisory Board currently consisting of the following members who have distinguished themselves in their chosen underwater field.

Bob Barth, Dr. George Bass, Dr. Peter B. Bennett, Dick Bonin, Ernest H. Brooks III, Jim Caldwell, James Cameron, Scott Carpenter, Jean-Michel Cousteau, Henri Delauze (France), Dr. Sylvia Earle, Bernard Eaton (UK), Rodney Fox (Australia), André Galerne, Lad Handelman, Professor Hans Hass (Austria), Lotte Hass (Austria), Dr. Christian J. Lambertsen, Jack Lavanchy (Switzerland), Dick Long, Joseph MacInnis M.D. (Canada), Bob Meistrell, Daniel Mercier (France), J. Thomas Millington, M.D., Bev Morgan, Phil Nuytten (Canada) Torrance Parker, Zale Parry, Surgeon Vice-Admiral Sir John Rawlins (UK), Ross Saxon, Robert Sténuit (Belgium), Ron Taylor (Australia), Valerie Taylor (Australia), and Stan Waterman.

For their service to the Society we recognize our friends: E.R. Cross (1913-2000), Billy Meistrell (1928-2006), and Andreas B. Rechnitzer (1924-2005)

The Society is grateful to our member Bret Gilliam for allowing us to present our mission and history on the pages of this book, which we consider a most valuable contribution to the oral history of diving.

If you would like to join Bret and the many other notable divers listed here who are members, please contact the Society at hds@hds.org or visit us on the web at www.hds.org.

We look forward to sharing the adventures of diving history with you.

The Board of Directors
The Historical Diving Society, USA
Santa Barbara, California.
www.hds.com

CREDITS

Art Director: Kim Barry
First Edition: September 2007

ISBN: 978-1-878348-42-5
Copyright:
New World Publications Inc. and Oceans Media Inc.

Cover Photo
Legendary commercial diver
Bev Morgan in hard hat dress, 1973

PUBLISHERS

New World Publications Inc.,
1861 Cornell Rd., Jacksonville, FL 32207
(904) 737-6558
www.fishid.com | eric@fishid.com

Oceans Media Inc.,
54 Stonetree Rd., Arrowsic, ME 04530
(207) 442-0998
www.bretgilliam.com | bretgilliam@gwi.net

Portions of these interviews were previously published

Giddings, Morgan, Howard Hall in *Deep Tech* magazine
Gilliam in *Deep Tech*, *Unterwasser*, *Dive New Zealand* magazines
Brooks in *Diver* magazine
Chatterton in *Diving Adventure* magazine
Waterman, Morgan, Nicklin, Benchley, Bonin,
Skiles, Ballard, deGruy, MacGillivray,
Giddings, Howard Hall in *Fathoms* magazine

Gretchen Gilliam

I NEVER THOUGHT THAT DIVING WOULD BE MY career. It was always something I loved to do so it was hard to look at going underwater as work. I originally thought I was going to be a schoolteacher. Okay, stop chuckling. With a bit of hindsight, that seems a fairly unrealistic goal as I very much doubt that my independent nature would have fit well into a regimented and inflexible system that required me to actually adopt a modicum of temperate behavior. When I finished up my work diving for the navy in 1971, I decided to hang out in the Caribbean and see if I could make a little money in diving outside military projects. When my mother's friends would ask her what her son did for a living, she'd always say, "Anything to avoid a real job." She was uniquely blessed with the gift of clarity. And she knew I would never do anything that required me to wear a tie or uncomfortable shoes. I'm still a tee shirt & shorts guy and barefoot is my preferred fashion statement. It worked out pretty well and I got sucked in… for over 35 years. I'm still infused with the same passion.

I survived a shark attack, four cases of bends, two aircraft crashes, a hotel bombing, a shopping list of interesting tropical bites, stings, and abrasions… as well as some strange mushrooms Jimmy Buffett gave me in Tortola in 1975 that had me pretty damned confused for about a week. Over the years my work has introduced me to some colorful and crazy people… from politicians, movie

and television personalities, rock stars, and other assorted characters. And the partying we did back in the Caribbean days fueled by liquor, controlled substances, and semi-religious herbs would probably have euthanized a more highly evolved organism.

Diving also took me away to distant places for long periods of time at sea, on film locations, and on expedition explorations. I'm the ultimate frequent flyer. Every airline counter agent knows me (and the mounds of gear with me) on sight. But eventually months on the road off in the back of beyond for most of the last three decades takes its toll on the mind and body. Not to mention my hairline. I used to have a forehead… now I've got a fivehead.

In the last few years I also came to the harsh reality of losing too many friends, far too early. And it finally caught up with me. I knew I wanted to spend more time with the things that mattered most: close friends, my wife Gretchen, and my adoring dog Pete. Then recently I was diagnosed with a severe case of a disease that has been named after me: "Gilliam's Posterior Vocational Glaucoma." That's when you get up and just can't see your ass going to work that day. I'm sure that many of you have experienced the same symptoms.

So I decided to sell the last of my companies and retire while I was still young enough to enjoy diving in its purity and allow more time for other interests that had been put on the back burner. Like this book and others to follow.

But I would never have gotten my start in business without the initial help of my semi-deranged accountant mentor, Frank Majnerich. The legendary Dave Coston taught me to stay alive in commercial diving and introduced me to the science of breath hold diving and hunting underwater. Dick Bonin, President of Scubapro, took a chance on me by giving my fledgling company the franchise in 1973 and all my downstream successes grew from that initial start. Bill Walker joined me as Vice President of V. I. Divers Ltd. in St. Croix in 1974 and provided the "yin" to my "yang" as he helped me build the company from a tiny cubbyhole on Company Street to the largest diving operation in the Virgin Islands. Mark Shurilla, Kevin Bonnie, Dan Farrar and Lina

Hitchcock shared some great times on ships and yachts in far flung anchorages over the years.

I owe a lot to attorney Joel Holt who kept me focused on business, out of police custody (for the most part), and was always there as a friend during the wild days in St. Croix. Joe Giacinto and I met in 1972 at an instructor program. He lived on tiny Marina Cay in the British Virgin Islands and managed that unique resort. We've shared a few tragedies, a few monumental paydays, a lot of time on my yachts, and a lifetime of fun out on the edge. I'm tempted to reflect, "There ought to be a law against having that good a time," but there actually were plenty of laws addressing our misadventures. We just chose to ignore them. As his late brother Mike once told us, "If you're not living on the edge, then you're taking up too much space!"

My photography benefited from the stellar help of my models Lois Leonard, Lina Hitchcock, Lynn Hendrickson, Cathryn Castle Whitman, and my wife Gretchen. You ladies are the best!

Blake Hendrickson introduced me to the modern Mac/Apple computer and changed my life as a writer previously shackled to the confines of a typewriter. Fred Garth and I shared the same passion for making journalism fun and never underestimated the intellect of our readers. He stood shoulder-to-shoulder with me when we were threatened by loss of advertising revenue when we dared to print the truth about nitrox, dive computers, technical diving, and other controversial topics. Ethics in diving journalism? What a foreign concept. It worked pretty well for us and we had some fun along the way.

Thanks to visionary dive operators and friends like Dan Ruth, Peter Hughes, Lenny Kolczynski, Avi Klapfer, and Tony Rhodes. The modern liveaboard industry is a better place for all divers because of your vessels. David Sipperly and Miguel Sanchez also were valued dive partners who epitomized professionalism, courage and leadership.

A big part of my legal business has been consulting in litigation and risk management. In most cases this would be about as dull as dinner with a life insurance salesman. But not with characters like Rick Lesser, Michele Bass, Peter Meyer, Dr. Tom Neuman,

and our late friend and colleague Bill Turbeville. It's been a good posse to roll with and we certainly kept the wine merchants in business over the years.

My sincerest appreciation to friends Howard & Michele Hall and Stan Waterman for bringing their class acts to my publishing ventures. And a nod to Brian Carney who came to work for me right out of college, later bought TDI/SDI, and proved to be the only person that seems to know how to run one of my companies successfully after I sell them. Go get 'em, kid! I'd like to thank all the great writers and photographers that I've worked with and published over the years.

Music has been a huge part of my life and I've been lucky enough to share times, private concerts, and friendships with some of the defining artists that made music that mattered. Thanks to Jonathan Edwards, Chris Smither, Dave Mallett, Chuck Kruger, and the best damn band out of Texas: Wheatfield (Connie Mims Pinkerton, Craig Calvert and Ezra Idlet). Thanks guys, you made our lives better with your extraordinary talent.

A parting wave to Jim Graham, my primary bad influence, and a true friend over more than three decades. Remember: a "good friend" answers your phone call and bails you out of jail after a night of inspired debauchery. But a "true friend" sits handcuffed next to you in the back seat of the squad car and says, "Shit man, that was one helluva good time!"

But most of all, I'd like to thank you. I would never have enjoyed the success I did if you hadn't been customers of my diving operations, taken training with my certification agencies (TDI & SDI), bought equipment that I manufactured, or welcomed me into your homes by reading my magazines, articles, and books. It's been my deepest honor and privilege and I can't imagine a more meaningful reward than your support.

For over 35 years I got paid far too well to go diving and visit the most exotic places in the world with some of the best people anyone could call friends. Many are profiled in this book. It's a pleasure I cannot adequately express. My sincerest and heartfelt thanks to you all.

Bret Gilliam, June 2007

"It's not the critic who counts,

not the man who points out how the strong man stumbled,

or where the doer of deeds could have done them better.

The credit belongs to the man who is actually in the arena,

whose face is marred by dust and sweat and blood,

who strives valiantly, who errs and who comes up short again and again,

who knows great enthusiasms, the great devotions

and spends himself in a worthy cause,

who at the best knows the triumphs of high achievement,

and who at the worst, if he fails, at least fails while daring greatly,

so that his place shall never be among those cold and timid souls

who know neither pity or defeat."

President Theodore Roosevelt

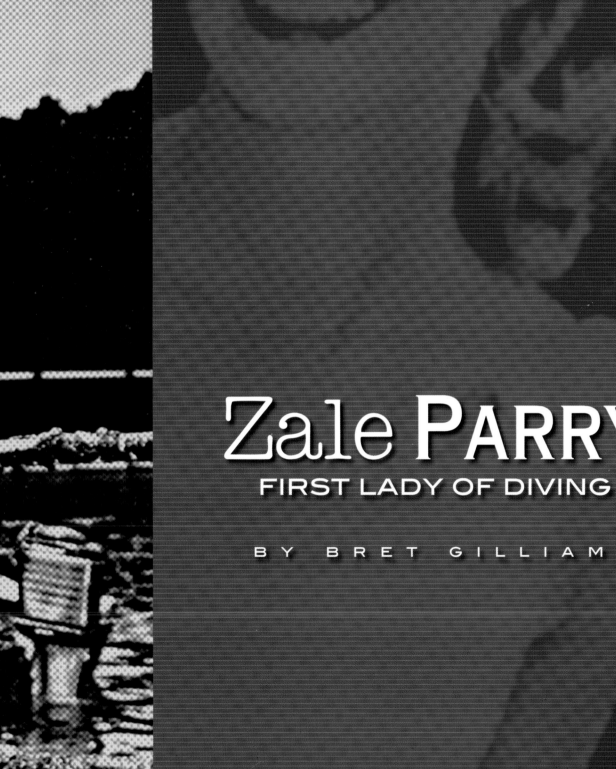

Zale PARRY
FIRST LADY OF DIVING

BY BRET GILLIAM

"ZALE PARRY GIVES OFF AN AURA OF PRINCESS GRACE OF MONACO: GRACE KELLY THE MOVIE STAR,

too pretty and nice to be more than just window dressing. But this lasting icon of sports diving history is make of steel and hard working parts. Nobody helps her put her diving gear on although every male in sight is eager to do just that. No dive is out of her range. »

Good lord, I don't dare tell you the experimental stuff her brilliant first husband, Parry Bivens, M.D., set up for her to "guinea pig" through. She pushed into the unknown of diving in those early days while most of us scuba pioneers were wallowing in the shallows. Zale broke the scuba depth record and surfaced to become the prettiest woman ever to grace the cover of Sports Illustrated. She was the first bathing suit issue."

Al Tillman, diving pioneer

Zale Parry is a true icon. She literally was the "face" of scuba diving for millions of people who first began to notice the emerging sport in the 1950s. She was one of the very first diving instructors, a champion competitive swimmer and veteran of the grand "swim show circuit", a test diver for new equipment, pioneer in underwater photography, and the "go to" actress for just about every movie and television production that had a diving or water theme for over a decade.

1. Diving in California, 1962 2. The celebrated *Sports Illustrated* cover, May 1955 3. Zale and Lloyd Bridges, 1958

I remember Zale from the very first time I saw her. It was one of her never-ending "damsel in distress" roles as co-star with Lloyd Bridges in the blockbuster television series *Sea Hunt* that captured the interest of the entire nation and gave a weekly glimpse into the then foreign world of scuba diving. The series combined underwater action with one of the earliest environmental and conservation themes. It gave Bridges his signature role as Mike Nelson, diver detective. And Zale became the sex symbol that everyone wanted to give CPR to.

Al Tillman notes that Zale had the "aura" of Grace Kelly. True enough, but she also was a dead-ringer for her. Her diving skills allowed her to set an international women's depth record in 1954 but her natural beauty put her on the cover of *Sports Illustrated* and launched her acting career that continues to this day. If she wasn't handling her own starring roles, she was backstopping other leading actresses as their stunt doubles. She even doubled for Sophia Loren in her breakout role in *Boy On A Dolphin*. There's an impossible choice for admiring male movie fans: Sophia or Zale? Call it a draw…

I met Zale originally when I was researching my book *Deep Diving: An Advanced Guide to Physiology, Procedures and Systems* back in 1991. The opening chapter was on the history of deep diving and I had to track down some images of Zale's record dive. I cornered her at a diving show where I was introduced. She recalled the dive, nearly 40 years prior, as if it were yesterday and steered me to a source for archived photos. I was struck not only by her keen sense of diving's heritage but also her striking allure. Years later when I asked her about being interviewed for this book, she immediately embraced the idea and gave me her fullest cooperation as the long process took place over the course of several months.

Recently she was the MC of *Beneath the Sea's* 2007 Saturday Evening Film Program. Sharing the stage with Stan Waterman, Rodney Fox, Ron & Valerie Taylor, John Chatterton, Richie Kohler, Ernie Brooks, and myself, she brought down the house with a film clip from one of her roles in *Sea Hunt*. Most of the audience wasn't born when the program originally aired, but as the black & white footage splashed across the two jumbo-screens behind her she held them in the palm of her hand and was greeted with a standing ovation to close the evening.

But she's used to that. And the acclaim is well deserved. She helped give diving its identity. She is a pioneer in the truest sense. And a grand lady. ■

1. Zale in Wisconsin, age 10, 1943
2. Underwater photography system, 1960

Tell us about your early years and how you got interested in the water and acting. »I was born on March 19, 1933 in Milwaukee at my grandparents' house. The snow was falling fast and high when I came into the world and the heirloom cradle that I was supposed to go in was still in storage. My dad quickly emptied a dresser drawer to hold me when the doctor handed me over. The world of water was a natural for me. We moved to Pewaukee Lake, 30 miles outside the city when I was only three weeks old and my formative years were spent in and around the water. My parents were athletic and strong swimmers who encouraged me since I was a child. My dad made the U.S. Olympic Team in Track and Field. The fruit is always close to the tree as the old adage proclaims. I became an ardent dedicated swimmer. By time I was eight, I was skin diving without a face mask or fins. I followed the turtles when they appeared and watched the nasty muskrats swim away after they left their calling card on the top step of the pier ladder. With bare feet, I walked along the shoreline to turn over the rocks and nooks to catch crawdads, frogs and fat toads. My strength was built with my feet pressed against the tackle box while rowing the boat

along the shore beneath huge willow trees while Daddy cast for Northern Pike and Black Bass. Fishing was a marvelous way to procure a fine meal.

During high school from 1947 to 1951, I joined the swim team in breaststroke and Australian crawl events. I was the water ballet president during my senior year. Speech and drama were intermingled with the usual study courses. I was popular due to my unabashed outgoing personality and became Homecoming Queen as a junior. During those four years of high school, I attended fourteen formal dances and fell in love with every escort even though they were advised to bring me home immediately afterward. And only with a short kiss at the door. Nothing more since my Mother was waiting in the doorway!

In October 1951, I got a job at Douglas Aircraft Santa Monica as a stenographer. That same month I met Parry Bivens on a blind date and learned of our mutual interest in the waters around us. During this same period of time, I began teaching swimming classes in the evenings twice a week for the Santa Monica Red Cross Chapter utilizing and alternating the indoor swimming pools in The Chase Hotel, The Deauville Hotel and the Kabat-Kaiser Hotel along the beaches. The Kabat-Kaiser Hotel was similar to a rehabilitation center for the victims of poliomyelitis, the dominant crippling disease of the 1940s and 1950s. Some of the stronger victims, who could remain out of the helpful lung-chamber a while, would be lowered by a special lift into the swimming pool for aquatic exercise. I'd be in the water to release and balance the victims as they tried to move with their arms only. There were teenagers to middle-aged people who were as eager and determined to beat their wrap of paralysis, as I was to help them.

I stayed with the Red Cross Swim Program for several years. Of course, after class one evening, I tried one of Parry's tanks and regulator in a pool when he came to watch me volunteer teaching. His only instructions were, "Don't hold your breath and surface slowly." To be underwater and breathe there was remarkable... a wish to behold.

Who else was around in the diving scene then and how did they regard a woman's interest in the sport? »You know, it's incredible but true, no one but the media was inquisitive about a woman's interest in that so-called "man's sport" of diving. Furthermore, in that era women stayed at home as housewives with

Los Angeles County Underwater Instructor Life Recognition Award »

FILMS | **AWARDS** | HONORS ::

children. I considered that a backbreaking, 24-hour position. The men were the breadwinners. One way they could include a seafood meal and enjoy a free sport of skin diving was with a spear. It was a keen scheme to add pleasure during tough times after WWII.

Al and Norma Hansen lived out at Avalon on Catalina Island. They were workhorses of the sea doing moorings, search and rescue, that sort of thing. E. R. Cross had his Sparling School of Diving; Mel Fisher and his wife Deo had a compressed air station on his mother's chicken farm or we could get fills at René Bussoz's sporting goods store. Courtney Brown was there and later became Lloyd Bridges' double on *Sea Hunt*.

There were a bunch of real characters from the early days including Rory Page (of Hope-Page non-return mouthpiece fame), Phil Jackson, Paul

Streate, "Cap" Perkins, Dick Anderson, Jim Auxier and Chuck Blakeslee who founded *Skin Diver* magazine, Commander Doug Fane, Johnny Weissmuller (*Tarzan*), Buster Crabbe (Olympic champion swimmer and actor), all the members of The Bottom Scratchers Club of San Diego, Connie Limbaugh from Scripps, Al Tillman, Bob and Bill Meistrell (Body Glove), Bev Morgan (commercial diving manufacturer), Paul Stater, Fred Zindar. Norma Hansen was the first woman I knew who did hardhat-helmet and scuba diving.

You also were a professional swimmer and toured the country in that role. What was that like?》Childhood choices affect our adult lives. An advertisement in the *Milwaukee Journal* in May of 1947 was a call for an audition to perform in the Sam Howard Aqua Follies. I became what I am today on a whim to earn my own allowance doing what I loved... swimming while entertaining.

I auditioned and was accepted to join the troupe of performers. In competition for the water production circuits were the three "biggies": Buster Crabbe, Johnny Weissmuller and Sam Howard who had the Mid-West Sportsmen Shows, State Fairs and County Fairs. So I began show business at fourteen. All performances were during the summer time and during Easter vacation so as not to interfere with school studies. All six female swimmers traveled in Helen Howard's (always) new Lincoln Continental. Sam drove the 18-wheeler with the stage, the huge deep swimming pool, diving platform and guide wires. It was the big grandstand show.

Life was exciting. World War II was over. Fashion and fabrics changed. The pizzazz of color appeared copied from the electric raspberry and chartreuse shades used for bailout military emergency gear, as in "find me quickly". Our swimsuits for the show were costumed in black with front panels of the hot pink or green slippery fabrics. Our bathing caps, gloves and ribbons laced around our big toes and criss-crossed up our ankles matched the colored panels of the swimsuit. We practiced the water ballet routines until we were perfect since we performed with black light and full, live orchestra music. Swim movements in error would be a neon sign. And we'd be "payroll sanctioned" if dignitaries were in the audience and we screwed up. Modeling the swim wear, precision swimming, and surface diving to Big Band Era music provided a colossal show. We were Hollywood in miniature. We knew it!

My popularity and ability in the water were soon noticed by several manufacturing companies, and by 1948 I was appearing in advertisements for Mercury and Evinrude outboard motors, as well as for Harley-Davidson motorcycles.

How about the old days for equipment? »You'll be surprised, but no modifications were needed with the early diving equipment for me. Any size person could easily fit the Jack Browne DESCO Diving Gear of full-face mask with adjustable straps, hose and compressor-combo. The compressor was placed on the stern thwart of the skiff, so the operator had room to work it. Many times the compressor quit. Free ascents were commonplace, two or more a day. We knew to continue to exhale until we reached the surface. Simple, no fuss. Diving was all easy.

Early air tanks were thin and small. All had the medical K-valve that needed a slot-wrench to open and close the airflow. The purged fire extinguisher cylinders were chubby and slightly heavier on deck but

1. Ready for dive at Marineland, 1955
2. Early dive promo shot at Silver Springs, 1956

underwater made no cumbersome effect. Tanks were longer in size and circumference when the new swing of all same-size air tanks came on the market in 1953-1954 by U.S. Divers. Pressed Steel tanks had the ICC stamp manufactured out of Milwaukee, Wisconsin. PST tanks had a short wing-nut-on/off valve, easy to operate without the valve wrench. My hair became tangled in the wing nut unless I used a bathing cap or clipped my hair with a barrette. Since the tanks were longer in size, they rode high on an angle on a small person.

Safety regulations came slowly for the diver and for the equipment. The tank was one of the legislative items. No longer did one see divers using fire extinguishers. In 1951-1952 some divers yoked two tanks together. Some of the Scripps Oceanographic Institution divers used these smaller tanks. Later the Pressed Steel tank company produced this size bottle with the ICC stamp for a while. One would recognize these tanks if viewing a *Sea Hunt* episode where they were frequently used. Many times I used my own smaller tanks for diving when I was working on a movie set.

The choice of masks was limited. We called them "face plates". By the way, much of the nomenclature for skin and scuba diving came from the books used for hardhat-helmet diving better known as the *U.S.*

35

Navy Manual. Face plates were modeled by U.S. Navy Frogmen or the popular French Squale mask priced at $4.95. It was smart looking and fit well. Or for a short while the Italian Cressi "death-trap" kind were on the market. These were a full-faced mask with a single or double built-in snorkels each topped with automatic closure of a light ping-pong ball sized cup.

Gustav Dalla Valle arrived in America in 1954 representing Italian lines with the new look of the face plate. In his cache of diving equipment were the Pinocchio goggles with a molded nose to pinch by the diver who needed to clear ears. Today various versions of this formed shaped goggle are popular throughout the underwater community.

Parry and I went to the Army-Navy Surplus Stores to shop for military stuff… as in khaki itchy garments and used double woolen sweaters to keep from shivering. We looked like urchins of the streets in our "thermal" wear. It didn't matter until Dr. Hugh Bradner, a friend of Parry's from Berkeley, came up with the invention of the true neoprene unicellular wet suit and created EDCO Engineering Development Corporation. We were having fun until play turned to pay very soon.

Weren't you one of the first female diving instructors? Yes, I was the third woman out of the Los Angeles County Underwater Instructors Course. Dottie Frazier was the first. Barbara Allen was the second.

1. Return from world record dive with husband
Dr. Parry Bivens (far right in above image), 1954
2. Husband (holding daughter Margaret) and Zale, 1960

Did you have thermal suits? No, rubber suits did not arrive until about 1953. The all-rubber dry suits came from Italy and France. If it fit properly, one would wear full long underwear beneath. A heavier rubber, supposedly dry suit, called the Pescasport from Italy was worn by only those who could afford it. By 1954 U.S. Divers Corporation, formerly René's Sports, sold the Pirelli rubber dry suit used by the frogmen for a while. It came with a hood for $70.00. Expensive, as all equipment for diving was. I never owned or wore one.

Other people in my class, who had already been teaching or life guarding, but needed a certification card (like a license), were Dick Anderson, Mel Fisher, Bob and Bill Meistrell. Al Tillman was our leader and creator of the course at the Los Angeles County Underwater Unit.

You also did test diving for some manufacturers. What did this entail and what kinds of gear did they want you to try out? I was associated with the Scientific Underwater Research Enterprises (SURE). This company had a very competent and experienced diving team of which I was a member. The team was composed of engineers, geologists, scientists, ichthyologists, water sports experts and plain old deep sea divers. It was the best group of this type to have been formed thus far. It was the aim of the group to found and develop into practicality, a sort of "underwriters approval" for underwater equipment. We would test, prove, and submit redesigns for products that are placed on the market for sale to the consumer. We were able to furnish manufacturers with information from practical tests and analysis by people who are not only qualified to dive, but who had the technical range

2

to suggest practical redesign. This way the product would be made safe before a user loses his life finding out, or maybe never discovering, the weakness or error.

SURE's team was compiled of (my future husband) Parry Bivens, research engineer; Phil Jackson, geologist, oceanographer from Scripps Institution of Oceanography, "Cap" Perkins and Paul Streate, underwater specialists for search and rescue from Avalon, Santa Catalina Island. I was the stenographer, business executive, and a lead diver.

In 1954 you set a record for deep diving. Tell us about that. »It was on Sunday, the 22nd of August 1954, at Avalon Bay, Catalina. I set a new world's record for women with a dive to 209 feet, exceeding the old record set by Esther Lorenz at Avalon Bay the same year by 24 feet. Esther's brother, Bob Lorenz, was attempting deep dives approaching 300 feet during that year. Depth diving seemed to be popular what with the new diving gear and the guts of the new divers to explorer the sea deeper and deeper. But a record was not really the purpose of my dive.

Rory Page was the engineer of the Hope-Page non-return valve. He wanted a test on his mouthpiece with a non-return valve design to allow air to enter on an inhale from the right side of a double hose regulator and exit on the exhale that followed without permitting water to enter where we could accidentally breathe or swallow it. This new arrival on the dive market was the true reason for the deep dive to 200 feet. The valve worked. From that date forward all dive regulator manufacturers changed the mouthpiece design. It was a "Safety First" non-return valve that stopped water from entering the breathing hoses. There was no more panic from losing your mouthpiece because the valve allowed replacement and continued breathing with no additional effort. One need not lift the right intake hose, tilt the head, and blow hard to remove any water that entered it. There was no more gurgling from water that had seeped in around the mouthpiece into the breathing hoses while underwater.

René Bussoz, President of U.S. Divers Corporation, who were the makers of the famed Aqua-Lung furnished us with all the equipment we desired. Of course, all of the regulators had the mouthpiece removed and replaced with the Hope-Page value mouthpiece. No one on the team suffered equipment trouble at any time during the entire dive.

The day before the record dive, the entire team made a practice dive to 165 feet. We prepared and coordinated signals and methods to be used. They were also smiling and making crazy signs about the slight narcosis they all had experienced. I wasn't having any trouble with narcosis.

We gathered together Carl Bailey, who was Mr. Big of KBIG radio fame, Ensign John Stein of the U.S. Coast Guard and Bill Gressman, Restaurateur of Avalon as witnesses as we proceeded. Parry, Phil and Rory prepared the diving course, time and decompression.

Phil moved the vessel that we were diving from out into deeper water while the remaining team members prepared the diving equipment. I rested in one of the top bunks nurturing menstrual cramps. Parry lowered the diving line and things were beginning to take shape fast. When the witnesses arrived the diving line was pulled up and examined by them, and after fastening a plastic slate to the bottom of the diving line, it was again put over the side hand-over-hand. The team then began to suit up to dive.

It was decided that Parry and Phil would accompany me to the bottom. Parry would keep a constant vigilance on me and Phil would guide the other two to the bottom. We would drop one diver at the 100-foot level and another at the 150-ft. level with an extra Aqua-Lung in the event anyone ran into any trouble. Rory acted as safety man, not descending below a level where he would be required to decompress, in case he had to ascend in a hurry to secure other equipment or help. This was the dive plan.

Just before the dive at zero hour, I came out on deck and joined the rest of the team in preparing for the dive. All divers were treated equally. No special treatment, not even for the test of a new piece of equipment. I wore a swimming suit, a suit of long khaki underwear, three sweaters, and a two-piece dry rubber suit made especially for me by Bel Aqua. The dry rubber suit was a free-flowing water outfit. Water entered at the neck, wrists and ankles and was pushed out by my movements. Yes, of course, I was toasty warm.

The entire team then donned their gear and at 3:00 P.M. we entered the water. We assembled at the surface and started the dive immediately. The water temperature on top was 68 degrees and before we reached the 100-ft. level, the water temperature had dropped nearly 16 degrees. As we left the 100-ft. level, the water was beginning to get a little dark. On arriving at the bottom, Parry watched me while I signed my name on the slate with the red crayon I had brought with me. Phil picked up a couple of starfish directly below the guideline, and then we started our ascent.

They reported the bottom temperature at 50 degrees, an 18-degree drop. Visibility was about like a dimly lit room. It had taken approximately two and half minutes to make the descent, and three and half minutes to ascend to the first decompression stage.

I wrote on a slate that I was okay but cold. We were all trying to talk with our hands and eyes. When

1. Glamour shot, 1957
2. Zale in pre-production for *Kingdom of the Sea*, 1955

decompression was over, we exited the water. Everyone was cold, elated and excited. The dive was complete; the non-return value mouthpieces worked like a charm, and a new record was set. The total time underwater was 23 minutes. I had a big satisfied grin on my face and then a laugh and a wave for everyone. The dive had gone off like clockwork. Everyone had done a perfect job.

Interestingly, the group, excepting me, had experienced slight nitrogen narcosis from 160 feet down. They were all very curious about this problem and were preparing to do extensive research to try and analyze it more thoroughly. The intention was to prepare a technical paper on the subject of nitrogen narcosis since we could not find enough subject matter. We wanted to give a good true picture of what happens.

The event changed my life. All it took was three miles off the shores of Avalon, Santa Catalina Island with a slight afternoon chop and a dive to 209 feet to a sandy rippled bottom with a strand of Bull Kelp and one discarded Schlitz beer can… From there on the radio, television, newspapers and magazines had agents calling for interviews and fun game shows.

It was fantastic to successfully complete an equipment test. But little did I know that my new identity, "Girl Skin Diver", as *Sports Illustrated* called me, would be in prominent demand. The dive shot me into the limelight. At first, this interruption of life was disturbing. Every interviewer didn't know "oxygen" in the dive tanks would kill after a certain depth. They misused the nomenclature and it wasn't always possible to catch the writer before the story went into print. I was teaching diving procedures with each inquirer. After a while the routine of being questioned in person or over the telephone became a plateau in life I accepted.

We were married in July 1955 and immediately honeymooned on location in Baja, California for the television production, *Kingdom Of The Sea*.

Parry was a graduate in Structural Engineering from Berkeley in 1947. He was a reader, a visionary, a genius in all ways. He experimented with his wild dreams, challenging himself and the marketed diving equipment in the sea. He worked a slide rule quicker than a wink and studied all the available books mostly

2

Can you tell us about your husband who was quite a notable intellect? Parry and I had a blind date in October 1951. We stuck together like peanut butter and jelly for all the experiments and diving. Even finished a boat together. I lived at home with my family, worked at Douglas Aircraft in Santa Monica and he went back to school to complete a medical degree. Jumping into the ocean in those early days was shear bliss especially since we were in love and had projects we could work together. Many times we dived with Mel and Deo Fisher who were made of the same ingredients.

from the U.S. Navy's Experimental Diving Unit. He communicated with Dr. Ed End at St. Luke's Hospital in Milwaukee, with Dr. Ed Lamphier, Dr. Christian Lambertson, long before they became common names in the diving community. He queried E. R. Cross for comparison of thoughts on hard-hat helmet diving equipment and chamber dives. He worked out new solutions of numbers with his every-ready slide rule. His mental and physical library of technical information on everything from cybernetics to cryogenetics to Einstein to quantum physics, to psychopharmacology was extensive. He was all of that and much more. Parry was ahead of his own future, a genius that wanted to change the world's thinking. Never satisfied with the status quo, he became friends with Dr. Linus Pauling and Aldus Huxley when he was 29 years old.

He cared a lot for the indigent and the homeless. One Saturday morning when I returned from grocery shopping, I found Parry kneeling on one knee next

truth. Our home was home to medical students and visitors from faraway lands that Parry met through his associates. Some stayed longer than most. One visitor from India stayed a week. He made a comment about all the conveniences I had compared to his family without a toaster, washing machine and vacuum cleaner. "A woman's work is appalling in America", he softly whispered.

to a stranger who was sitting in the living room on the sofa. The stranger was a peddler who was selling fresh strawberries, had all the signs of an alcoholic. I noticed the entire crate of twelve boxes of berries on the kitchen sink. Parry very kindly talked with the man for a short while, paid for the berries and handed him a bottle of multi-vitamins. Then he led the man to the door with the verbal prescription to "take one of these pills once a day and get some needed sleep. You will feel better." I'll never forget the day or the scene. Furthermore, I visualized a stream of outsiders coming to the door. The thought was not too far from the

He encouraged your interest in acting as well, right? »Parry was my guiding light, my incubator for all I know today. He encouraged my enthusiasm for learning. Through him I met actor Dick Powell, June Allison's husband. Dick in turn introduced me as a student to Agnes Moorehead's 20th Century Fox classes. I attended evenings twice a week for one year. Miss Moorehead taught theater, period dances, fencing and quick improvisations. She was a delight! Next I entered UCLA's Theater Arts class. My teacher, Mr. McGowen, was Jimmy Cagney's brother-in-law. Sometimes Jeanne Cagney, teacher's wife, was our substitute.

1. Zale at controls of SURE recompression chamber, 1954
2. Back roll entry, 1959

Parry designed some early underwater camera systems, didn't he? »One Sunday drive late in the afternoon on our way home after diving, Parry stopped at a large junkyard in Torrance, California, to purchase a cylinder of steel big enough to arrange a 16mm gun camera in it. The configuration of the placement and outside trigger, port and welding to seal the ends were measured. He took his blueprint to an outside steel malleable company for completion. (Later this same company, Butane Tank, produced our three chambers.) Parry had his own underwater movie camera, used it and sold footage to the up and coming underwater television and motion picture producers. Some footage was sold to Disney Studios who paid $20.00 a foot of film at the time.

He also designed portable recompression chambers. How were they marketed and used? »The underwater camera housing was the beginning of his work with decompression/recompression chambers. The first chamber was a small one for small sized dive equipment and large enough to place three guinea pigs in it for a 1000-ft. deep dive on air. They made the dive successfully while munching lettuce unabashed. Wristwatches and depth gauges were most popular dive equipment for testing.

Water-filled kettles from my kitchen were used to place the items tested to certain depths in this first chamber. In 1957 Gustav Dalla Valle purchased the small chamber for the laboratory used at Sportsways to save the company money for the outside service we provided.

By 1955 the first civilian single-lock chamber was built. It was large enough for one victim and technician-operator sitting Indian style or victim lying down with technician-operator on the outside controls. It had a medical lock (used for food, medicine or lavatory transfer). The unique feature was that the chamber was portable. It could be trailered and had the steel eye o-rings on top for easy lifting aboard ships or dockside.

In this chamber we easily tested the breathing ease or difficulty at different depths of almost all the regulators by all the manufacturers existing in the era of 1953 to 1959. The same for more wristwatches, depth gauges, all sorts. I did a 307-ft. dive on air in this chamber. With me was a portable typewriter, paper, pencils and complicated metal puzzles. It was a test of brain and brawn. Successfully completed, I might add!

As important as the chambers were to a diver, we had little success in attracting any clients. Every single communication we wrote to military facilities and main hospitals in the nation's cities was ignored. One person in our search for buyers finally accepted our invitation to visit us. He was Commander Francis Douglas Fane who became a terrific colleague and friend. Fane was the Commander of the Underwater Demolition Team Unit One on Coronado Island in the San Diego area. He had the finest, toughest UDT Frogmen in all the U.S. Navy. He was as tough. They called him "Red Dog".

Commander Fane contacted his bosses in Washington, D.C. and the U.S. Navy Experimental Diving Unit. He wanted a chamber for his Unit One Frogmen. But he couldn't convince the U.S. Government Procuring Department for the need of a chamber. They never bought one despite Fane's insistent efforts. Here we had a vital piece of safety equipment and no interest from the people who probably could have best utilized it. We were too early in the conception of the sport of diving.

In 1957, we received a telephone call from The United States Atomic Energy Commission Office. The gentleman calling represented the U.S. Navy, too. Interested in the chamber, he asked to visit. Our hearts leaped. Finally, a buyer. The chamber was shipped to Eniwetok Atoll. Sailors were skin and scuba diving on their R & R leaves. The chamber would be a safety factor for any bends-related situation. The first single-lock SURE chamber we supplied is still in operation today. The second and last chamber built was a double-lock, longer in length. It was sold to an oil drilling company in Maracaibo, Venezuela in 1959. It, too, is still used today.

Parry got involved with some "mind-bending" research experiments later. »After the chamber business, Parry concentrated on medicine. As a physician and surgeon, he was developing his research in pharmopsychology. He worked with Dr. Sydney Cohen, Dr. Keith Ditman, and Dr. Oscar Janiger with patients from UCLA and The Los Angeles County Hospital. The patients suffered from schizophrenia or incurable alcoholism. A new drug for America from Sandoz Pharmaceutical in Switzerland was delivered to our address and shared with the other doctors on the first run of experiments with the patients. The state of a human mind after administering the drug changed drastically, sometimes for the better and sometimes for the worse. It was a promising experiment for healing.

But as time went on artists, writers, musicians, screen actors including Cary Grant, Aldus Huxley, *Time-Life* founder Henry Luce and wife, Clare Boothe Luce, and others were eager to have the drug administered to them individually under a watchful eye for the many hours it took to wear off. "The Doors Of Perception" as Huxley wrote were opened. Slowly the medical world and the government played with the drug: d-Lysergic Acid. It was more often known by the acronym "LSD". By now there were other hallucination ingredients available. Peyote, marijuana, psilocybin and a list of such derivatives became popular. Soon the college inmates and street people became acquainted with these medical instruments without control. This was a classic example of how a meaningful cure turned into the horrors of abuse and misuse.

This came to a tragic conclusion. »Life was out of control for the world, Parry saw it coming. Also, his father, a wealthy contractor, had constructed a beautiful medical building that we understood was to be given to Parry as a gift. After all, his parents did treat him as the Golden Child. But the medical building instead was sold to a corporation. Other doctors rented the offices. This was the *coup de grace*, the end of Parry's hope to have his own practice. As it was, he was employed by

the Ross Loos Hospital in Santa Monica as a physician and surgeon. He was healthy and strong, yet depression took over. He took his own life with a .357 Magnum. The coroner's report listed cause of death as simply "gun shot." No drugs were found in the body.

1. Marineland, 1962
2. Lloyd Bridges and Zale on *Sea Hunt* set, 1958

You were featured in a dramatic cover shot for *Sports Illustrated* in 1955. How did that come to be? »The cover shot for *Sports Illustrated* came about because of the international record deep dive I did the year before. They were fascinated by a "girl skin diver". The magazine, an offshoot of *Life* and *Time* was brand new. A female diver really wasn't publicized except in the few diving newsletters. The story was ripe and the photography of girl in a scanty bathing suit was a good draw. A celebration dinner for four of the *SI* cover people was held at the famous Tail of the Cock Restaurant on Sunset Boulevard in Hollywood. Our surprise guests were Mr. and Mrs. Charles Alden Black... none other than the gracious Shirley Temple and hubby. What a treat!

So you were the inspiration for their annual swimsuit issue? ⟫I think they would tell you so. I did some more appearances in the magazine later. The 35th anniversary issue with all the covers appeared in 1990. *Catching Up With Zale Parry, Diver May 23, 1955* was a feature in the Swim Suit Issue, Winter 1999.

Your role as "girl skin diver" attracted a lot of other attention from newspapers and magazines in the mid-1950s. Were you surprised at the fascination the press had for you in this lunatic fringe sport? ⟫The press was in lunatic thinking in those days. No different than in today's media. Yes,

I appeared in quite a few more magazines. *Argosy* made a wonderful fuss. Even my hometown *Milwaukee Journal* told the tale. I was surprised and overwhelmed. I still have those feelings when I am approached today by someone with a copy of the real issue from 50 years ago. I get asked to autograph a lot of those by the collectors. It's great fun and an honor to be remembered so fondly.

Many credit you as the face of a new sport and in advancing it beyond the exclusive status as something only for the hardiest macho types. What's your memory of the era? »Women *are*

hardy and in some respects have less back problems than men. We can tolerate pain in greater and longer sessions than men, too. If you remember in my story of the record dive, I needed no help to gear-up and I didn't pout or ask for assistance. Enjoy the whole of the sport. Servants do not increase bliss. My memory of the era is simply that the sport of diving was for everyone. It is an enhancement of richness for the knowledge of the sea.

Your publicity also led to a lot of public appearances and lectures. »Wow, I did hundreds of medical meetings, Rotary Clubs, Lions Clubs, grade school classes, diving clubs. Hilo Hatti arrived in town

Cameraman Lamar Boren with Zale sets up underwater sequence
on *Sea Hunt* episode, Silver Springs, Florida, 1959

and I appeared with her for a publicity gathering. The list is long including the National Sporting Goods Convention where I represented Healthways Products in Chicago 1955. Evel Knievel with his stunt bike and appeared with me in my dive gear at the Seattle Space Needle Convention Center for a sports event. Publicity shows continued for the opening of resorts and guest speaking gigs with a display of diving gear and my shell collection.

At this present time, I appeared in my little town of Tillamook's Chamber of Commerce Meeting

and have latched unto the Tillamook Estuaries and Watershed Partnership programs. The next appearance is April 10th, 2007 for the Children's Clean Water Festival. Busloads of fourth graders from seven cities of Tillamook County will have their water festival about the importance of one drop of water. There will be my exhibit with explanation of plastic debris in the waterways that lead to the sea and what happens to it when it gets there. Appearances never stop. I love the people… they are so enchanted and interested in diving adventures.

At some point, television beckoned. Share with us those early experiences. ⟫Jack Douglas Productions presented a television series of adventures. They were *Seven League Boots*, *Golden Voyage*, and *I Search For Adventure*. Jack Douglas had a legendary traveler and underwater pro, Colonel John D. Craig, as his guest presenter often. At a production meeting one day, Jack asked Col. Craig whether he would like to include a series of his own and he agreed. Before we knew it, *Kingdom Of The Sea* was conceived. The end of each episode would be a live three-minute demonstration of diving techniques. They wanted to get some diver to perform in a tank on the live stage set. This was a daunting thought. Who would be the diver with the knowledge and stage presence? The discussion of ideas for demonstrations became more crucial when a name of a skin and scuba diver was not instantly perceived.

Now the publicity director for Jack Douglas Productions was Jerry Ross and my parents' next-door neighbor. He attended this meeting listening to the dilemma. Then interjected, "The kid next door is swimming and diving all the time. But…she's a girl!"

That evening Jerry told my folks to have me call Jack Douglas the next day. "He needs a diver to perform in a new series," he mentioned. So I called and made arrangements to meet after work thinking it was another one of a string of free appearances. It was my first introduction to Colonel Craig who became a friend forever with wife, Mildred, and two gorgeous daughters, Sharon and Kathy. Jack Douglas wanted to take me home with him even though he had a beautiful wife. Everyone was pleased and a television contract was drawn and I signed it without even getting wet.

Our first assignment coincided with the opening date of Marineland Of The Pacific Oceanarium in Pacific Palisades, California. It was May 1955. The television program went underwater. We wore Scott Hydropak diving gear with a microphone inside of the full-face mask enabling us to talk to the television audience and the throng of observers outside the aquarium windows. We took turns pointing out fish life at the bottom of the main tank. There were a variety of common sea creatures for us to point out and explain where they live and what they eat. We had to fight a swift current as we settled to the sandy bottom. First day opening was a continued test for the structure's plumbing that brought the seawater directly into the tank from the ocean close-by. The fish-feeding diver had double weights to help him walk. We were free swimming with diving gear.

Kingdom Of The Sea premiered on Saturday, June 4, 1955. This was the first program of this type produced for television that was devoted entirely to the underwater adventure. Verne Pedersen and Colonel Craig did the underwater photography with cameras on tripods. By now, my husband Parry owned and used his Sampson-Hall 16mm camera to shoot other angles and stock footage of fish and kelp.

Each filmed episode consisted of an adventure experienced by us or one by Colonel Craig. The studio had set up a special water tank for the purpose of showing and demonstrating safety in skin diving and underwater equipment of various types by me in a timed three-minute segment as a closure... and we did it all live.

I can vividly remember seeing you in episodes of *Sea Hunt*. How did that involvement come about? »As *Kingdom Of The Sea* was coming to an end, actor and associate director George Wilhelm called me in 1956 and told me about a new underwater series being discussed by filmmaker Ivan Tors. The series was to be modeled after Tors's feature film, *Underwater Warrior*, a movie loosely based on the exploits of Commander Francis Douglas Fane, the decorated commander of the Underwater Demolition Team Unit One during World War II. Fane had once confided to Tors that he would like to get a boat for search and salvage and go into the diving business after the war was over. This new program was to follow that concept.

George told me they were looking for someone to co-star with Lloyd Bridges in this new show to be called *Sea Hunt*. I met with Ivan, and he said in his very thick Hungarian accent, "Vell, you look okay. I vant you to do

Zale poses for cameraman Lamar Boren, *Sea Hunt,* 1959

the show." Then he said that he also wanted me to help his secretary with the technical aspects of the program.

At the time, Westerns were popular and Lloyd Bridges had the opportunity to do a Western. But Ivan convinced him to do *Sea Hunt* instead. In actuality, the show was like an underwater Western. The bad guys always wore the black wet suits and the good guys always wore the gray wet suits. You have to realize, too, the dynamics... the technology, the equipment, everything in diving in those days was so primitive. We had no idea what was going to happen next. We were all very powerful swimmers because you had to be. For example, I'd be dropped off a helicopter quite a ways

from the camera boat and then the camera boat would simply come in and try to find me. No GPS for divers or even automobiles at that time.

During the production of *Sea Hunt*, I worked in numerous capacities. I performed all of the underwater work and stunts for other actresses, and starred in 12 episodes, portraying a variety of characters both underwater and on the surface, except for the last two months of my pregnancy. Between shootings, I oftentimes scouted locations, applied for permits, or did whatever else a script might call for. I often traveled from one location to another since Unit One, with Lloyd Bridges was in Los Angeles, and Unit Two was on location along the California Channel Islands,

Marineland, or in Silver Springs, Florida, the Bahamas or wherever else a scene might dictate.

While the days could be long and the water cold at times, I had the opportunity to work with some of the best divers and watermen of the era. Courtney Brown played Mike Nelson, Bridges's character in all underwater scenes except close-ups. Ricou Browning, who won acclaim by playing the *Creature From The Black Lagoon*, usually played the villain. Another villain was played by Jon Lindbergh (son of famed aviator Charles Lindbergh), a former frogman. Chief underwater cameraman, Lamar Boren, led the underwater crew with Paul Stater as underwater director. A number of the actors we used in the series achieved a grand degree

of stardom later. They were Victor Buono, Robert Conrad, Ken Curtis, Bruce Dern, Anthony George, Larry Hagman, Ted Knight, Ross Martin, Jack Nicholson, Leonard Nimoy, and Robert Quarry.

What was Lloyd Bridges like? »He was a well-seasoned Shakespearean actor and the true "actors' actor" as the industry labels people. He played stage summer stock whenever he could. Lloyd, "Bud" to his close friends, was a genuine gentleman… handsome, kind, considerate, physically fit and eager to learn to do the proper action with this new equipment. After all, he was used to the props of a holster and pistol and was an excellent swimmer. Diving gear was a lot different. He was a caring family man with sons Beau, Jeff and daughter, Lucinda. Later Beau and Jeff were placed in the cast for some episodes. Dorothy was the teacher for the children's theatrical prowess and a Rock of Gibraltar beautiful wife.

He had to be trained in scuba for the role, right? »We didn't really have time for that in the beginning so his training was everyday on the set although Courtney Brown and I had him in a swimming pool for quick lessons at first. Lloyd was an expert at copying a character and mimicked Courtney's flutter kick to perfection. It wasn't until the end of the series, that Lloyd came to Bob Meistrell and told him that he would like to take the full scuba course so that he would be considered a Certified Diver.

So you were more experienced as a diver than the man who single-handedly came to be *the* figurehead for diving for many? »That's true. I had a lot of experience diving but he really made the character of Mike Nelson come alive for audiences. He was a great actor and a great friend.

There is a great story that comes to mind, though. After the *Sea Hunt* series was over, Lloyd wanted to some diving on his own, purely for his own enjoyment. He arranged for Dick Anderson to accompany him. Dick, of course, had done just about everything in diving from commercial work, stuntman, filming, equipment design, etc. They get out to Catalina and Lloyd says, "Dick, I want to make it clear that I'm really a beginner. I'm not Mike Nelson."

Dick replied, "Don't worry, I am!"

For those of our readers who became collectors of the series, what were some of your favorite appearances?》That's one of those impossible things to answer. Each one is a favorite.

1. Zale on underwater wreck set, 1961
2. With actor Dan Dailey on set of *Underwater Warrior*, 1957

It seemed that the guys always got to wear wet suits but you always were in a swimsuit. Didn't you get cold? 》Guys did wear wet suits much of the time. However if possible, I wore a wet suit. But because of my early swimming days with the Aqua Follies and with *Kingdom* demonstrations in cold water pumped into the performance tanks by the fire departments, I didn't shiver as much as the men. Lamar Boren wore a wet suit… once. As our main cameraman on the set much of the time (and Jordon

Klein, another pro camera man on the East Coast) balancing to steady a large 35mm camera housing was easier in his blue satin swim shorts.

I heard that one time you had to do some re-shooting of scenes, originally done in Florida or the Bahamas, in California. And the director let the guys wear wet suits but you had to stay in your skin. How about that? 》What can I say? There was no complaining. I knew I had to wear whatever the script called for. And for re-shoots to maintain continuity, I had to wear the same outfit we originally shot the scenes in. So, yes, there were times when it got pretty chilly for me and the guys had a better deal in wet suits.

Your television work led to mainstream Hollywood films as well. Was that much of a transition? 》No, it was fairly easy from television to motion picture work. It's all sort of the same rules and procedures.

What films were you in and what actors did you work with? 》*Underwater Warrior*, an Ivan Tors-MGM production, was a wonderful experience. Dan Dailey played the lead character of real-life navy veteran Commander Doug Fane. I played his wife underwater.

Another great film was *Boy On A Dolphin*. It was a good story by 20th Century Fox studio. I was the double for Sophia Loren underwater. It was difficult. All breath hold diving from surface to the 22-ft. deep underwater set. She had that famous wet shirt scene in that film. It almost caused a scandal. She was years ahead of Jackie Bissett when she did her similar scene in *The Deep*!

Tell us about the film *Underwater Warrior*? 》That film was put together before the *Sea Hunt* series aired. The cast, crew and six of Commander Fane's top frogmen flew to Hawaii on a United Air Lines DC-7 Hawaiian Mainliner, a 4-engine propeller airplane. It took eight hours to get to Honolulu on September 27, 1957. The entire airplane was treated as First Class. On our return, we were on a Pan American Stratacruiser with a piano bar on the main level and sleeping quarters with a ladder to get into them. Our first location was the Hawaiian Village Hotel, the tallest building at that time along Waikiki Beach. Contractors were starting the 5th floor while we were there.

Commander Fane appropriated a Pacific Fleet minesweeper. Next he made an appointment with the Admiral at the U.S. Navy Base at Barber's Point for approval before having me play Fane's wife underwater in the film and living aboard the ship with the remaining cast and crew of men.

"No woman was going to sink the U.S. Navy's Pacific Fleet" were the undertones. I was presented to the Admiral for inspection, thoroughly interviewed, and checked out in the Barber's Point Dive Tower. A military diver accompanied me in the tall tank of fresh water. The two of us wore swimsuits and nose clips... no masks or fins. From the surface near the ladder we took a deep breath, feet-first, pointed toes and descended with a swoop of our arms overhead with precision. It was a quick drop. The sides of the tank clearly labeled the depth. We went to 70 feet when the military diver touched my shoulder and gave the signal to stop. We kicked to the surface. As we broke the water, I could see the catwalk balcony around the tank with uniformed men, the Admiral and Doug Fane resting their elbows on the rail watching intently. This was my test to be with the film crew or be flown back to the mainland. The Admiral gave the "thumbs up" sign. I passed. I was the first female to dive the tower.

The minesweeper carried all the UDT equipment, rubber rafts, scuba gear, crew and cast. The first officer assigned to that ship was given leave to allow accommodations for "the girl" on board. The month of September and weeks into October were practically used up with underwater and topside filming using almost every Hawaiian island.

For one of the shots, a submarine joined us for a full day's shooting. We were in 60 feet of water off the Island of Molokai for that one. The submarine submerged very slowly while cameraman Lamar Boren captured every angle. The star, Dan Dailey, performed well in the submarine escape hatch sequence. When we finished the day's work, we were allowed to stand on the deck of the sub while it surfaced very, very slowly. An eerie experience. When we were ankle-deep in water, Dailey performed a Broadway stage soft-shoe-shuffle while still wearing UDT garb with fins and those of us next to him joined the dance. This was serious fun!

When filming was complete, arrangements were made for Fane and his personal choice of UDT men with Lamar Boren boarded an airplane to the Marshal Islands to find and film sharks. These were to be the stock footage of the live shark scenes not only for *Underwater Warrior* but also for the upcoming *Sea Hunt* television series.

What kind of guy was Fane? ⟫ Doug Fane was a brilliant Scotchman. World traveler. A great entertainer as a dinner guest. He knew lyrics to a book of clever musical ditties. Sang them with a good voice. He relished eating unborn eels and raw fish of certain sorts… a real connoisseur of gourmet delights. He had wit. He enjoyed our company and the best Scotch Whiskey. It has been said by him that he had six wives… I'm not so sure about the truth of that. He was a Commander and a strong one. A top notched diver with and without diving gear. I know. I dived with him. He had command of the English language as an author and wrote well. Everyone called him "Red Dog".

In addition to the famed Ivan Tors, you also worked with Lamar Boren. Share some insight on these two pioneers. ⟫ There is only one Ivan Tors. Ivan was a treasure. Intelligent in all living ways and clever. A Hungarian by birth, brilliant mind, science fiction writer for the *Science Fiction Theater*. When the Russians' *Sputnik* shot to fame into space, no broadcasting company had any staff scientist to draw a diagram of what *Sputnik* was and how it worked. In one of Ivan Tors earlier writings for the *SFT* program, he had the workings of a spacecraft drawn and filmed in it. The broadcasting companies were issued a piece of the story to portray the news properly. It was Ivan's imagination that created the true picture.

He loved animals and created Africa USA with his friend, Ralph Helfer, in the Santa Clarita Valley, California, before it became a city. He had big animals and later arranged for Collette Martine to establish a home and hospital for them. He was so caring with tender warmth, everyone loved him. Frequently, he and his family went to Africa to enjoy the safari. His oldest son, Steve, eventually stayed in Africa to become the youngest ranger on the plains. Peter and David remained in America.

Lamar Boren was a huge teddy bear that at one time had a growing photography studio in La Jolla, California, where he lived in a gorgeous house on the beach. He was part of the Bottom Scratcher Club, active with the group and of course, had housings

1. Early scuba diving in California, 1951
2. Dick Anderson and Zale rode this underwater submarine vehicle from San Diego to Catalina, a distance of 26 miles, 1955

for his cameras. He was honored as Underwater Photographer of the Year at one of the International Underwater Film Festivals that Albert Tillman and I put together for 17 years as producers and directors.

Lamar was the photographer chosen to film the movie *Underwater* with Jane Russell. Lamar knew still and motion picture photography better than most because it was his business and career. I liked Lamar. He had a constant watchful eye on what was going on through the camera lens especially for the safety of the "damsel in distress". That was frequently me. He saw everything before the safety diver could move in to help anyone if needed.

How deep did you work on the television and movie shoots? 》We worked where the ambient light was the best for underwater photography. For most of the underwater movie shoots, we did not need to go

any further than the depth of Marineland's tank (22 feet) or the depth of Silver Springs (60 feet). Off shore, in preferably clear water, we were no more than 30 feet deep. Sometimes we worked through a few scenes in a row. In the shallow waters for practical reasons we stayed under a long time to finish the direction. This was long enough to run out of air. A signal to a stand-by safety diver would deliver a fresh tank. Frequently, tanks were replaced while we were underwater. Naturally, those who had more swimming or fighting action used air quicker than stand-by safety divers. Lloyd Bridges used a small tank of water on stage for the close-ups.

Did you use stunt doubles? 》There was never a stunt double for me. For the other characters in a story, stunt doubles were used. I took pride in doing my own stunts.

What do you consider the hardest role you had to play? 》None of the roles were too difficult. Although, I do remember one where the damsel in distress was actually rolling in the surf and being tossed by the strong waves. That's where you can lose control.

51

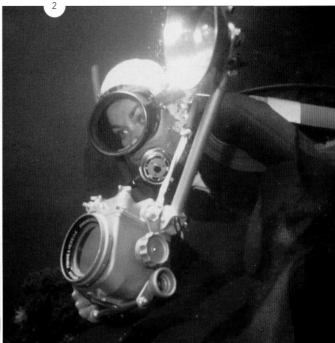

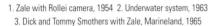
1. Zale with Rollei camera, 1954 2. Underwater system, 1963
3. Dick and Tommy Smothers with Zale, Marineland, 1965
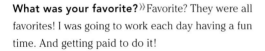

What was your favorite? » Favorite? They were all favorites! I was going to work each day having a fun time. And getting paid to do it!

Any close calls? » Maybe one when I wanted to make a free accent during a scene, because the regular was feeding water instead of air. Lamar held me in position by the strap of my swimsuit and another regulator was given to me to breathe air… instead of water.

Your work as an actress spanned a huge breadth of parts. Didn't you even do westerns? » *Wagon Train* was fun. Sometimes the costume of a period made the acting interesting. And, Andy Devine was divine...marvelous.

For some years you had always been on the other side of a camera, but you developed an interest in photography yourself. What was the gear like then? » My mother had an ancient fold-out bellows type Kodak camera that used 616 film with eight exposures. I was given permission to use it when I wanted but mother would want it returned in the place I found it. For my high school graduation gift, my parents presented a Brownie Camera to me. My first and very own. I used it on everyone, every flower, and everything. When I met Parry, he gave his older 35mm

Kodak camera to me. Jack Douglas knew my interest and gave me a Leica with a Zeiss lens he wasn't using any longer. When I was on the Groucho Marx show, I won enough money to purchase the first, or at least the next to first, Rolleimarin underwater housing with a 3.5 lens Rollei to fit into it. Later I purchased another Rollei with a 2.5 lens. The Weston II Light Meter was used with a housing for underwater, too. But after a while, I got to know a reading of the light… ambient, sun, part sun, without a meter. The setting F11 worked well in most places in clear Caribbean waters or F8 to F5.3 for California waters. The Rolleimarin had the flash and all the filters. It was the dream still camera to have early on with one snag. It only had twelve exposures.

Everyone was taking pictures underwater. Everyone had photos stored in shoeboxes or dresser drawers. Al Tillman and I originated the Underwater Photographic Society in 1957. It developed into the idea for the International Underwater Film Festivals. The Society is now called the Los Angeles Chapter. Many underwater photographic clubs grew from then on. We were the whale… and the minnows slid off our back.

You share my interest in preserving the history of diving. Please tell us about your own journalistic work in this regard. ⟩⟩Since 1978, Al Tillman and I researched the human history of the sport of diving and the defining events that occurred during its golden era. *Scuba America Volume One* premiered in the year 2000. It's now out of print but I'm working on *Volume Two*.

You now live in Oregon. What attracted you to that spot? ⟩⟩Tillamook, Oregon… my home in Fernwood Forest is serene, peaceful and beautiful. No comparison to California where I spent a chunk of my years. Without shoveling much snow and suffering severe cold weather, Tillamook reminds me of my childhood days of Wisconsin. I had lived alone for almost 10 years. Three of those years I was on a hunt to find a new, delightful place to enjoy the rest of my journey.

I checked out the land and homes in Al Giddings's neighborhood in Pray, Livingston and Billings, Montana. I checked up and down the California Coastline from San Diego to Big Sur. Anacortes, Fedilgo Island and Orcas Island, where Al Tillman had his roots, were other places I studied. Then when Sue and Jack Drafahl realized I was seeking to move, they suggested Cape Meares, Oregon, where they live in a beautiful home on the beach. Another "seek and find" trip took me to their home. From Cape Meares to the foothills of Tillamook, I found Fernwood Forest.

I understand that you've been working on a movie project called *Tillamook Treasure*? Can you share with us what that's about? ⟩⟩It's a wonderful family film set in the beautiful coast village of Manzanita, Oregon. Manzanita is about 45 minutes north from my home. The movie is based on an Indian legend about a treasure buried on Neahkahnie Mountain by Spanish sailors in the 1600s. This is the story of a 14-year old girl's discovery of what is important in life. Bright Light Studio, an independent, used the Sony HDW-F900 (High Definition) technology pioneered by Lucasfilm for its *Star Wars* series. *Tillamook Treasure* is digital cinema from front to back. The film will be distributed digitally directly to theaters, by-passing the need to go to film. The process opens the doors of feature film making to low budget independent films and reduces the cost so that high production values are within the budget of independent filmmakers. It is a new world of picture making with the highest quality digital filming, edited digitally, and released to theaters digitally.

News appeared in our once-a-week Wednesday *Headlight Herald* about a Hollywood company coming to town with the list of characters to be cast. I e-mailed the producers to audition for the grandmother's part. A reply came from Jane Beaumont Hall by telephone that evening. Jane said, "We know who you are, Zale. You are too young to be the grandmother. But we'll find a place for you." They did. I was cast as the hardware store owner where the girl shops with her dad to buy the tools for excavating the buried treasure. The movie has won the Outstanding Family Award in a number of Film Festivals.

Do you still dive? ⟩⟩Of course. Diving is like bicycling. My next outing is in July 2007 on the *Nautilus Explorer* on a dive trip through the Alaskan Straits where the cruise ships cannot squeeze through the narrow passages. Then in October, I'm off for a caged Great White Shark adventure at Guadalupe Island.

Who are your personal heroes in diving? ⟩⟩First, my dear Parry who was my love and hero from the start. He went beyond any other. Then E. R. Cross is another hero. I worked with him one day as buddy-inspector on

the Standard Oil pipeline off Barbers Point, Oahu. Dick Anderson had been working with him for several weeks before I arrived and his other worker was ill for a day. I was staying with Cross and Diana while researching dive stores and diving in Hawaii. I needed to interview Cross, too, for my writing. He asked if I would like to help him for a day. Cross was an amazing person with an incredible diving history. Fun to be around. Others would be Valerie Taylor and Dr. Eugenie Clark. I never dived with these special women, but I would have liked a day or two with them with their adventures. They are honored as I am in the Women Divers Hall of Fame and of course, hold the "Oscar" of the underwater community, the NOGI, as a fellow of The Academy

of Underwater Arts and Sciences. Dr. Eugenie Clark's book, *Lady With A Spear* was one of the first gifts I received from Parry.

Has the growth of diving met your expectations? 》 No one was expecting the sport of diving to take off into the splendor it has when I began diving. Water was cold, sometimes rough, and the equipment was not for ignorant sissies. The early divers were lifeguards or water-proofed with water safety certification. They were strong swimmers first and foremost.

How can diving best attract newcomers? 》I believe the scuba shows around the world have offered so many

amenities, treats of exhibits, resorts and liveaboards with comforts of home and film festivals to entice the young and old to join the experience. At the same time, diving groups are encouraging the young people to make a career out of studying the creatures of the sea, protecting them and in turn protecting us for the future.

Our Tillamook Estuaries Partnership and Oregon States educational institutions are spilling over with sea

1. Courtney Brown, the stunt double for Lloyd Bridges and Zale, filming wreck dive sequence, *Sea Hunt*, 1959
2. Bev Morgan, Zale and Bobby Meistrell, 2006
3. Zale, Stan Waterman and Jacque Cousteau, 1963
4. Zale at DEMA, Orlando Florida, 2006

lab programs. The Northwest is earnest in protecting the sea and getting the sea programs injected into the school curriculum beginning in grade school. I'm delighted to be a part of this.

If you had one choice of a place to go diving right now, where would that be?» I believe I will be happy with Alaska and Narwhals. But I'm always looking forward to the next dive no matter where. ∎

ALL PHOTOS FROM STAN WATERMAN COLLECTION EXCEPT AS NOTED

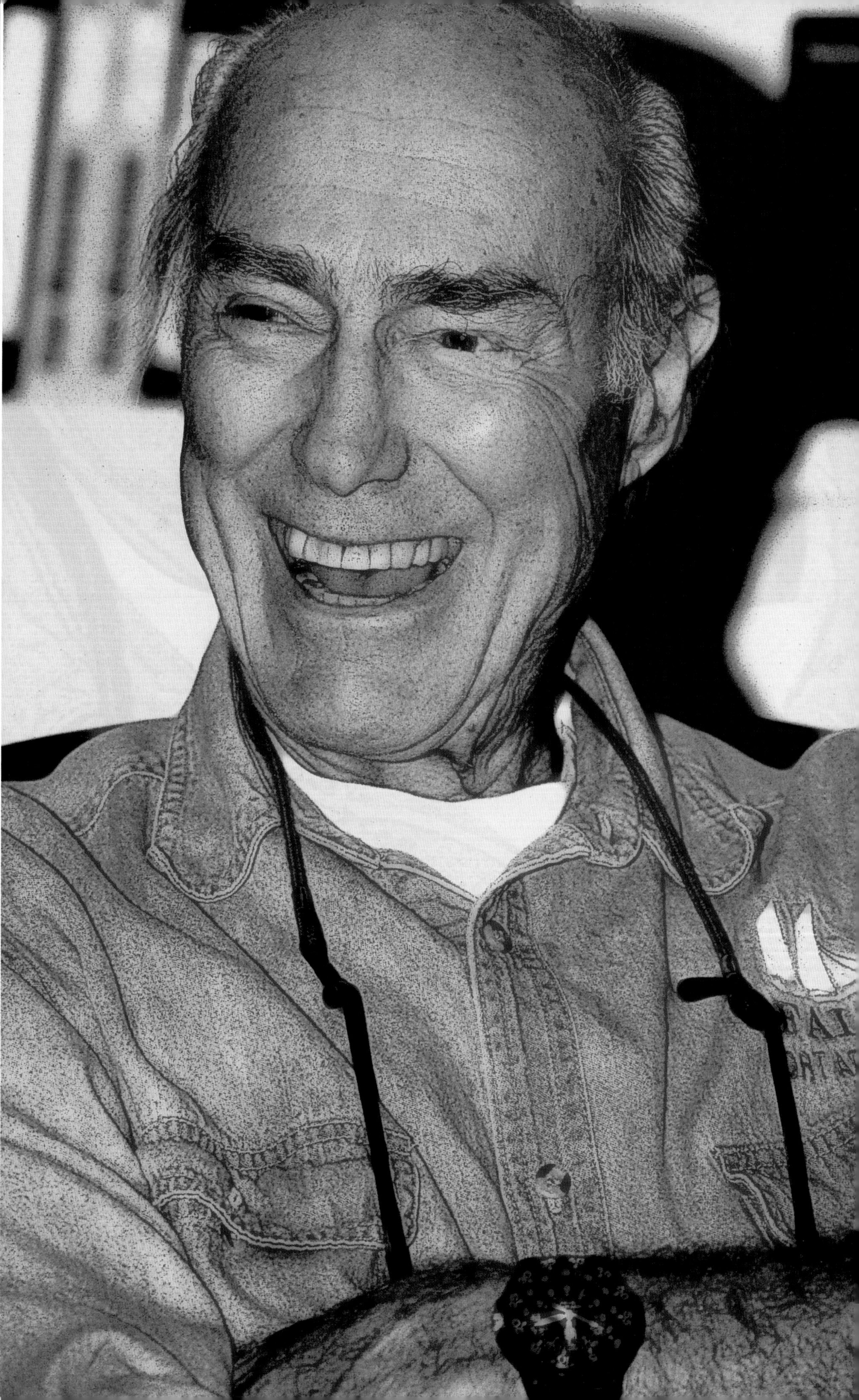

Stan Waterman
DIVING'S GRAND AMBASSADOR

BY BRET GILLIAM

1. On location, 1993 2. Age 6
3. Track star at Dartmouth

IT'S A SAFE BET THAT MOST FOLKS WILL HAVE NAME RECOGNITION FOR THE LIKES OF JACQUES COUSTEAU

or Lloyd Bridges who brought television's diving hero Mike Nelson to life in *Sea Hunt*. But for divers, the one person most likely to hit 100 percent recognition, popular approval, and appreciation scales simultaneously is, of course, none other than diving's eloquent ambassador, Stan Waterman. »

It's also worth noting that he began diving well before either Cousteau or Bridges first dipped their faces beneath the ocean. Stan's contribution to the popularity and initial recognition of scuba diving is virtually unequaled. Indeed, he has survived longer than any other diving pioneers (except Hans & Lotte Hass) and continues to spark audiences with his graceful charm and quick wit.

From a humble beginning as a blueberry farmer in coastal Maine, he was inspired to start one of the first pure diving operations in the Bahamas. Chafing at confinement to one locale, he indulged his passion for diving by teaching himself the art of motion picture photography and producing some of diving's earliest films. His first documentary in 1954, *Water World*, set the hook in the young adventurer and he widely toured the U.S. personally narrating the show to astounded viewers.

In 1959 Waterman participated in the first underwater archaeological expedition to Asia Minor to film a Bronze Age shipwreck. The resulting film, *3,000 Years Under the Sea*, was a hit. His third effort in 1963, *Man Looks to the Sea*, won numerous awards including top honors at the United Kingdom International Film Festival. Following that success, he packed his entire family off with him to Polynesia for a year working on a film that became a *National Geographic* special.

But one film was singularly most responsible for launching him into the consciousness of divers and the generally terrified viewing public: the astonishing epic *Blue Water, White Death*. Released in theaters in late 1970 after nearly two years in filming, the movie induced a primal gut reaction for most audiences that combined horror and fear with fascination. No one before had ever left the safety of cages to swim in open water with pelagic sharks. Waterman (with Peter Gimbel and Ron & Valerie Taylor) blew everyone away by leaving the cages to swim with hundreds of feeding sharks... at night. The film's dramatic conclusion, featuring the first Great White shark footage ever presented, left an indelible impression on millions and firmly established Waterman's reputation.

Following the popularity of the movie *Jaws* release in 1975, ABC latched on to Waterman to film an *American Sportsman* segment with author Peter Benchley. A year later Hollywood came calling to ask him to co-direct the underwater unit for *The Deep*.

Over the years Stan has mentored and guided such current luminaries as Howard Hall, Marty Snyderman, and Bob Cranston while becoming a confidant and close personal friend of Benchley. They got together on the phone or in person almost weekly until Benchely passed away in early 2006. Stan will be 84 by the time this book comes off the press and still keeps to a diving and speaking schedule that would daunt persons the age of his grandchildren.

Don't miss his excellent book of essays titled *Sea Salt* (also put out by New World Publications). This fascinating book recounts his career in a series of autobiographical chapters and others that simply relate stories of great diving adventures spanning seven decades.

Stan and I have been friends for years. I stay over at his house in Maine and he visits mine. Lately I've been cruising over to his waterfront estate near Deer Island on beautiful Eggemoggin Reach. I anchor my motor yacht *Encore* in his snug harbor known as The Punch Bowl and we get together to share strong drink and tell stories. We've shared many stages over the years as well in Chicago, New York, and Boston and I always look forward to hanging out with a true American legend. There will never be a grander or more articulate spokesperson and ambassador for diving... or a better friend. ∎

59

Bret Gilliam

Everyone has to start somewhere, what led you into diving originally? While on Christmas holiday in Florida with my family in 1934 a lady who had just returned from Japan gave me a curiosity. The curiosity was a Japanese Ama diver's mask. The Ama were the lady divers who breath-hold dived to harvest the seabeds around Japan.

Their handcrafted full face masks preceded by many years the first appearance of face masks for divers in the Western World. I swam out with it along the breakwater in front of the Breakers Hotel in Palm Beach, dove down, opened my eyes and was hooked for the rest of my life. I was 11 years old then. That was 73 years ago. It could have been yesterday. It is still fresh in my memory.

My father was a successful cigar manufacturer. Cigars were still king in the early 1930s when I was grown enough to relate with joy to the sea. My summers were divided with half going to my divorced mother at Rehoboth Beach, Del. The other half on the Maine coast at my father's summer home. With ocean on three sides of the house, Maine was tidal pools, a first small sailboat for exploring the coast within sight of the house, and finally a tough Herreshoff sloop. I rigged a small outboard on the stern and sailed far out to the cod fishing grounds, often returning after dark. At Rehoboth Beach I body surfed every day with my gang and challenged the big waves in storm time. We were all as agile and unafraid as seals. So the sea was with me almost from the beginning.

You did time in the Navy? During the war – that's WWII – the one that would supposedly end all wars, I was stationed with a Naval Air Station in the Canal Zone. I trained as an aviation radioman gunner in SBD dive-bombers. There were California "ab" and "bug" divers in my squadron. We had acquired the new fins, masks and snorkels along with pole guns for spear fishing. The whole sport was so new that I actually corresponded with Owen Churchill. The year was 1943. He had invented the first fins for market in the U.S. They were called "frog feet". With an order that he sent he pitched in a cork-handled knife in a wooden scabbard and asked for an opinion on its use. I can't recall what I wrote to him. The knife was entirely ridiculous. But I made common cause with the California divers. We had a couple of motorcycles with sidecars and snuck off base to dive from isolated parts of the shore and spear anything that moved. We bartered the fish at the Ships Service. The local girls who worked there were delighted to take the fish home. We were delighted with free shakes and burgers.

After the war, a grateful government put me through college on the G.I. Bill of Rights. The gratitude was top-heavy on my side. I had never fired a shot in anger or faced an enemy during my four years in service. I had as fine a liberal arts education as one may have in this country. At Dartmouth I majored in English, focusing on Shakespeare. I studied with Robert Frost. I was a big enough athletic cheese (two mile and cross-country) to enjoy status. I started wooing my present wife of 58 years, a summer romance aided and abetted by her wonderful family taking me in. Both my mother and father had died early during the war. The only home I had when I emerged from college was the summer house in Maine. I wanted to live there. I married Susy two weeks after graduation. We took up residence in Maine, winterizing a part of the old house and I went to work as a blueberry farmer. Three economies dominate Maine (aside from tourism): lobstering, lumbering and blueberries.

What was your first scuba gear? 》During the second year the Aqua-lung arrived in the U.S. Two Frenchmen, Rene Bussoz and Paul Arnold had the foresighted enterprise to buy the U.S. marketing rights for the Aqua-Lung from Cousteau for $10,000. I heard that Cousteau quickly realized his mistake and bought the company – called U.S. Divers – back, supposedly for a cool million

1. Stan and wife Susy on honeymoon, 1950 2. Inset: Stan and Susy in Maine, 2002 3. Joyce Stirling and Stan on *Zingaro*, Bahamas, 1955

dollars. I have always thought there was considerable hyperbole in that story. Whatever, I purchased my first Aqua-Lung from the first U.S. Divers Co.

Cornelius made the only portable compressor available then and suitable for high-pressure breathing air. They made compressors for filling airplane tires. I acquired the 25th. The Aqua-Lung was probably the first in the state of Maine. Bill Barrada, of *Skin Diver* magazine, marketed a latex rubber, back or neck entry dry suit to be worn over heavy underwear for

Maine waters. It was never dry. The crotch squeeze was excruciating; but I could take to the water with it. I charged $25 for my services, recovered scallop drags and moorings, unfouled propellers and for the grand sum of $125, threaded cables under the hull of a big work tug that had gone down in 70 feet of water within sight of our house. I even dove from the pontoon of a seaplane that flew me into a Maine lake to search for and recover a half dozen expensive rifles that had been lost when the hunters capsized their canoe.

The adventure was supreme. My system was the only game in town. I eventually hooked up with a wholesaler in Ardmore, PA. who marketed Healthways line of equipment along with U.S. Divers scuba gear. I retailed a half dozen full sets of equipment to adventurous friends in the area. None of them stayed with us but they all avoided death. In hindsight I realize how lucky that was.

One of your first forays into diving as a profession led you to take a converted Maine lobster boat to the Bahamas to run dive charters. What was the market then and who were your customers? 》In 1953 I was inspired by Hans Hass and Cousteau to design a lobster boat hull especially for diving, helped to build it at a local boat yard and in 1954 took the 40-ft. *Zingaro* from Maine to Nassau. There I set up shop as the first liveaboard dive boat in business. Back then few people went to the Bahamas during the summer months.

Winter had the worst weather. Summer was the best time for diving. But the tourists did not know that. I hedged my bets, not being at all sure how this new enterprise would pan out, stored my boat each May up the New River in Fort Lauderdale and headed up to Maine to get the crew working on the blueberry land. In November, when the blueberry land was burned and put to bed for the winter, I would take the boat across the Gulf Stream, over the Little Bahama Banks and over The Tongue Of the Ocean to Nassau and start the diving season. We had good friends in Nassau, all divers and spearfishermen. They were my mentors in learning about navigating reefs.

How did you start in underwater filming? 》The diving just barely broke even. But I had started shooting 16mm film with an early Fenjohn housing, then a Rebikoff housing, then my own plexiglass housings and commenced lecturing with my first film, *Water World* during my off-seasons at home. That led to another dimension and my own particular evolution in the business.

Guests on my boat were the genesis of my extended reach beyond the Bahamas. I was invited to join expeditions in return for shooting and editing a 16mm documentary record. *Zingaro* circumscribed the range of my activities. I certainly could have dived the Bahamas for the rest of my life, but I wanted very much to see and dive in other parts of the world's oceans. After three years of charter boating divers in the Bahamas I sold *Zingaro* and

made my move. I planned to work with expeditions in the late spring and summer. The experiences would provide fresh material for lecturing during a season that generally ran from fall to April. My first economically viable season was 1959. An agent had picked up my act. For the princely fee of $125 per show I commenced a film lecture tour. Remember, television had not yet appeared on the scene. So called "Armchair Adventure" and – in New England – Athenium Lecture Series provided live entertainment for communities across the country. The speakers projected their films and narrated them live from the stage. I added music from a tape recorder that I cued from the podium. Three agents and three years later I was making $350 per date, doing block bookings across the U.S. and Canada plus the Hawaiian Islands. One exhausting, peak year I did 162 speaking dates.

I called it "Gum Shoeing In the Bible Belt". I was on the road for three weeks to a month at a time, one-night stands in little towns and big cities as well. Big cities might have audiences of 2,000. Little towns - like Scarlet, Nebraska might have 350, almost the total population. For many small communities the lecture series were the only game in town. Most of the shows ran along the line of *Norway: Land of Contrast*, *Exotic Hawaii*, *The Four Seasons of Scandinavia*. My underwater shows were a total anomaly. I tried to make them entertaining and exciting. The hyperbole that attended shark and moray eel footage was outrageous but gratifying.

Sounds like you were away a lot? Susy was practically a single mother. We had three children then, Gordy, Susy-dell and Gar in that order. Maine was too isolated for a family with an absent father much of the time. The schools were rated the third worst in the country. I looked for a community that had good schools, a cultural matrix for Susy's receptive

1. The family on the cover of *Sports Illustrated*, 1965
2. The 1965 Christmas card from Tahiti 3. While it made good headlines, Stan recovered quickly from a bends accident in 1965
4. Hangin' with the locals in the Tuamutu Islands 1964 5. Filming the hermit who lived at the southern end of Tahihi, 1963

mind and fine intelligence. I found it in Princeton, a university town with old friends to help us settle. More important, Susy's wonderful, supportive family lived only two and a half hours away in Pennsylvania. Important for me was a reliable major airport just an hour away. My old airport in Bangor, Maine was fogged in as often as not.

You have always tried to include your family in your adventures. What did they think when you hauled them off to Tahiti and Bora Bora for a year? 》When I decided to take my family to French Polynesia for a whole year I had already been to Tahiti twice on contract, shooting underwater footage for other documentary filmmakers. So I had some friends and connections there to help me plan the real logistics of spending a year. Susy and I both wanted to have a family adventure together while the children were still young. Kenneth Graham wrote in *The Wind In the Willows*, "…for the days pass and never return." We wanted that experience before the children were out of the nest and gone from us. They were then 10, 12, and 14. As they became full teenagers I used to take one with me each summer on whatever expedition I was documenting. One-on-one, we got to know one another. Those experiences forged a bond between Susy and me and the children that has never lost strength. The Tahiti year, as I call it, especially engendered a family esprit, the most valuable move we made in those formative years. So the children have never moved away. All three live in Connecticut about two hours away. One or more call almost daily. We share all the major holidays. Gordy is 56 this year.

Share with us some of the other destinations and films you chose to feature in your early career. 》There were some fine adventures I lucked out with as professional contacts, new friends and acquaintances generated during my three years in the Bahamas made the new experiences available. They were the grist for my lecture mill. Essentially I evolved from charter boating to working with others' boats and facilities, expanding my range beyond the Bahamas. I hoped to produce a fresh lecture film each year, shooting in the summer and fall, then lecturing through winter and spring to amortize my costs and keep a roof over our heads. Thus my friendship with Drayton Cochran, a customer on *Zingaro* when I was still in the Bahamas, led to a trip through Europe on the rivers and canals from the North Sea to the Mediterranean in his 71-ft motor sailor, *Little Vigilant*. For my third cruise with Drayton I did the advance planning for a trip through the Aegean Islands, finally focusing on a rough archaeological survey of wrecks along the coast of Asia Minor. Ultimately we located a wreck off the Turkish coast opposite Rhodes that proved – at that time – to be the oldest wreck found. The clue had come from scraps of bronze found by Turkish sponge divers and heard about by an amateur underwater archaeologist, Peter Throckmorton, who came with us.

The wreck was from the late Bronze Age, about 1300 BC. We raised copper ingots, bronze weapons and tools. A professor at Princeton University identified the age when I showed him a bronze dagger blade and double-bitted axe head that we had smuggled back with us. By that time I had moved my family to Princeton for better schools and a bright academic community for

Susy when I was away so much. The lecture film that I edited was entitled *3000 Years Under the Sea*.

Didn't you do some early work in South America as well? »Another expedition took me up the Amazon for the first attempt to capture and bring back alive the two species of fresh-water dolphins, *Innia* and *Sotalia*. The goals were achieved. The Niagara Falls Aquarium was the sponsor. We flew to Manaus, 1,000 miles up the Amazon, the last civilization, and from there went up river with a wood-burning steamboat – the last on the river – one barge for our hammocks and cuisine – another barge that we filled with water to transport the dolphins and Indian guides. It was an epic experience and totally successful. The dolphins were safely flown back to the States, introduced to three major aquaria and the first to be seen in the U.S.

I have lost touch with them (that was about 45 years ago) but I believe that the originals mostly prospered and bred to start new generations.

To make up the 90-minute format required for the stand-up film lectures I produced a three-part program that I named *The Call Of the Running Tide*. Part 1 was on the first women's team to go into saturation in an underwater habitat. The exercise was called *Tektite II*. Dr. Sylvia Earl was the leader. Part 2 focused on the first deep divers for black coral in the Hawaiian Islands. Part 3 was about the life and times of a New England harbor seal, Andre.

When I was shooting *3000 Years Under the Sea* I wanted some background shots of the Bay of Salamis where, in 480 BC, the Greek navy annihilated the superior fleet of the Persian king, Xerxes. I was guided by a young naval officer who assured me he knew a fine spot at the top of a long, high hill that overlooked

the bay. We climbed for what seemed hours in the unrelenting Aegean sun, lugging tripod, camera case and other paraphernalia. Reaching the top we discovered no view at all. Higher hills lay between us and the historic bay. I ended up shooting one of those wonderful illustrations in *National Geographic* magazine. It showed Xerxes, himself, seated on a golden throne at the top of the right hill, watching his fleet go down the tubes.

What was it like slogging away on the speaking tours then? »There were so many hilarious (in hindsight) experiences that I had during my years on the lecture circuit that I couldn't begin to recount all of them. So many of the dates were in the Midwest that I got to know the grass roots parts of the U.S. that my eastern education could never have provided. In Sioux City, Iowa my program was in a church with a complex beamed structure high above the audience. Shortly after I started my introductory talk several bats awakened and started swooping down over the heads of the audience. Some women whimpered and clutched their men. I thought to put a spin on the growing panic

1. Close encounter with White shark, Dangerous Reef, South Australia, 1970
2. Support vessell *Terrier Eight* off South Africa, 1969
3. Updating his journal in his cabin aboard the ship, 1969
4. Out of the cage for the first time and filming Oceanic Whitetips feeding on dead whale carcass above, off South Africa, 1969

by alluding to Count Dracula and Transylvania.

At length I thought it best to call for lights out and get the film on the screen. I had not anticipated the result. When the bats flew in front of the projector light path they appeared on the screen as big as pterodactyls. There were screams. Some unfortunate cases of the "vapors" with an exodus by a less hardy segment of the audience. I finished the show, declined an invitation for pie and coffee at the home of a sponsor and – as S.J. Pearlman used to do – "repaired to a dark clinic with a sympathetic intern."

Blue Water, White Death was a stunning film for many reasons. How did you get involved initially? »I knew Peter Gimbel. We were friends. He visited with us in Maine during the summer of 1964. There, in the evenings by the fire in the living room we planned the outline for the production of *Blue Water, White Death*. It was originally planned that I would co-produce the film with Peter. However, Peter had the connections with CBS for the sponsorship and the money and time to start the physical preparations for the production. I was still on the lecture circuit and soon after (1965-'66) took my family away for the year in French Polynesia. That left Peter with the entire load. When I returned I demoted myself to Associate Producer and Underwater Cameraman. On Peter's shoulders fell the full burden of forming the team, designing the special cages and camera systems. He threw himself into the project with total dedication and personal enthusiasm. It was Peter's show. His energy and enterprise made it happen.

How was the rest of the team selected? »The rest of the team was composed in part of personal friends and professionals like Ron and Val Taylor, Jim Lipscomb for topside camera and Stuart Cody for electronics and equipment maintenance. Peter signed them on by their reputations.

What were they like to work with on such an extended project? »The project took almost a full year in the field and another year for preparation. The group was remarkably compatible. Of course there were some dust ups. The most benign family could hardly avoid times of lost patience and personal

"BLUE WATER, WHITE DEATH"
The hunt for the Great White Shark

differences living on a small ship for weeks and months on end. I think we came off very well. Peter led by example. He was fearless at times. Most often prudent. Every member had at least some sense of humor and that is a great leavening force.

Why did Gimbel choose to locate in South Africa instead of looking for the Great White shark in Australia as the Taylors suggested? »I do not recall why Peter did his major reconnaissance to South Africa instead of South Australia, a known haunt for the Great White and an area of White shark encounters, pioneered by the Taylors. In

South Africa he was advised by the Union Whaling Co. that their whalers encountered legions of Great White sharks that fed on the whale carcasses before they could retrieve them. The Union Whaling Co. was shore-based in Durban. They could provide a retired whale hunting ship, the *Terrier Eight*, to join their fleet, provide a base for our team, and cooperate with us to the fullest. That looked good to Peter. One misunderstanding proved critical and only evident when we were on location there. The sharks guaranteed by the whaling company were Oceanic Whitetips, not Great Whites. As it turned out the experiences we had with the Oceanic Whitetips

(*Charcrinus longimanous*) were the most dramatic and certainly the most harrowing in our months of diving.

Valerie Taylor's diary shares some frustration at the film process and at Gimbel. What was your perspective as the oldest member of the principal crew and a producer? »Gimbel was strong-willed, so is Valerie. I remember incidents that occasioned strong differences and tempers on edge. I would rather not reflect on them or review them. In my many years of experience and among those I most value, being a part of that splendid adventure is at the top. I would not have missed a day of it. I prefer to remember it that way and, indeed, I do.

1. Ron Taylor and Stan filming shark frenzy 2. Movie Poster for film's release, 1970 3. Thirty year reunion with crew, Rodney Fox, Stan Waterman and Ron and Valerie Taylor, 2000

You and Gimbel actually gave up your salaries at one point to get the company to complete the film. How did that come about and did the final result make it up to you both? »There was a clause in our contract with Cinema Center films that was, in fact, quite standard for productions. It specified – as I generally recall – that if a certain amount of the production was not completed in a time proscribed by the contract, further budget money would be withheld. Peter and I agreed to forfeit our salaries until the film was completed as a show of faith. That placated the backers. We were ultimately recompensed.

No diver had ever left the safety of a cage with large numbers of sharks back then. You guys swam out into hundreds of feeding sharks. Who made that call and why? »Our first day on location with the sharks next to a sperm whale carcass was spent inside the two cages. Peter and Valerie shared

one cage. Ron and I were in the other. It was evident that shooting from the cages was cumbersome, the action much circumscribed. On the second day Peter exited his cage without any forewarning that he was going to do that. I thought it was dangerous for him to be so exposed in the open with a large number of the big Oceanic sharks cruising about. I exited my cage, thinking to cover him. I was, in fact, scared to death. Peter admitted later that he was, too. But it was the right thing to do. We soon discovered that we could not cover one another but must fend for ourselves, shooting toward one another as the sharks bumped and rubbed against us. They did not bite. We fended them off on frontal approaches with the cameras. But we were just as often nosed from behind. We could not keep track of their movements. There were too many. It was a mind-blowing experience. The footage was terrific. We subsequently decided that we would all exit the cages and shoot against one another. The action was just as compelling. With three cameras going and Valerie tearing about to bop sharks on the head as they were nudging us the footage proved to be even more dramatic than our ultimate encounter with the Great Whites in South Australia, all filmed from inside the cages.

While the movie earned lavish critical praise, it has largely been unavailable since the early 1970s for the next generation of divers to view. What happened to the rights and how can someone see it today? »*Blue Water, White Death* vanished from view and never was marketed as a video cassette. The reason: Cinema Center Films, the producer, sold their entire library to Paramount Studios. That library included a John Wayne feature, another with Dustin Hoffman, and several others that were recycled in video sales. Paramount put our feature in storage where it still remains. Efforts to buy the TV rights have come to nothing. Paramount is uninterested.

It's been over 35 years since it was first released. Has any diving film ever equaled its break-through sequences since in your opinion? »Hans Hass and Cousteau produced theater-released features that certainly had the impact of *Blue Water, White Death* on the public. That I know of there have been no feature productions the equal of it since for theater presentation. There have been a number of fine

Stan and 55-ft. Whale shark

Marjorie Bank

documentary series produced for television. The latest, *The Blue Planet*, is more than a match for anything we did. Howard and Michele Hall's marine animal series, *Secrets of the Ocean Realm*, is without peer.

What would you have done to make it better today? » The action and the range of the story make it unique both then and now. Cameras and optics have advanced, of course, and there are exciting marine life subjects that have emerged since our time. Had we known about the Great White shark scene in South Africa off Cape Town we would certainly have included that. But we were breaking ground, bringing that magnificent, supreme predator to the public eye for the first time. That perspective would be hard to beat today. Incidentally, we were on the island of Grand Comoro off the east coast of Africa in 1969 when we heard that the U.S. had put a man on the moon. That certainly beat any scenario we could come up with.

Moving to another subject, I noticed that you supplied many of the photos for the book about the orphaned harbor seal, Andre. How did you come to meet Harry Goodrich and Andre? » Harry Goodrich lived in Rockport, Maine. I lived diagonally eastward across Penobscot Bay. I had a fast boat. With easy weather I could make it to Rockport in a little over an hour. Harry and I were among the very few who had Aqua-Lungs in Maine. I can't recall how we met. I am sure I sought Harry out. We became good friends, dove together, and had family visits. Harry's wife, Thalis, made pies that caused strong men to sob aloud. I would shamelessly telephone that I was going to run over by boat and thought I would be there in time for lunch. I was with Harry when he caught Andre, in a long-handled crab net by the ledges off Rockport. Andre was raised with the family, actually had his pad on the kitchen floor during the winter months while he was still a pup. The whole scene was so compellingly charming that I shot a segment of one of my magazine format lecture films about Andre and the Goodrich family. Andre not only made Harry famous but also provided him with satisfying, compelling purpose and self-esteem that his profession as a tree surgeon could not provide. With Andre, Harry achieved celebrity status. Hollywood some years later made a film about the Andre story and shot it on the West Coast with a sea lion. Andre was, of course, an honest New England harbor seal. I never saw the movie but I know that the publicity afforded great pleasure to the Goodrich family.

When Hollywood took on the daunting project of making Peter Benchley's *The Deep* into a movie, how did you get involved? »Peter and I became good friends when he moved to Princeton after the publishing of *Jaws*. Our houses were within a few blocks of each other and we had many adventures working together for *ABC, The American Sportsman* show. So it was natural that Peter would introduce me to Peter Guber, the producer of *The Deep* and urge I be contracted to do the underwater camera work. I was accepted and brought Al Giddings in with me and he accepted on the condition that we equally share the credits.

You and Al Giddings were designated as co-underwater directors. Did that work? »Al was an old friend with whom I had stayed many times in Berkeley when I was lecturing in the San Francisco area. I knew his capabilities. He was far better qualified for bringing together a support team and preparing the cameras, lights and diving equipment than I was. He took charge of the logistical preparation for the shoot, designing the housings for the 35mm cameras as well as the lights. Al, with enterprise, initiative, creative energy and a capacity for taking charge way beyond my range, did – indeed – take over. Chuck Nicklin and I in effect became second cameramen. Of course, I was personally injured and humiliated (laughing). At the same time there is no question that the better man for the job seized the reins. My input hardly justified sharing the same credits with Al.

Peter Yates, the movie's director, had made such action films as *Bullitt* with Steve McQueen that became the standard for action films and car chases. How did a non-diver get on with you two when he couldn't actually direct or even see the film's most exciting sequences as they occurred underwater? »Peter Yates was an excellent director. And became a good friend. He quickly learned to dive and very soon into the production was personally present on the underwater sets. He was hard-wired for communication to the surface with his directions relayed to us through a transponder. Thus he extended his direction into

1. Relaxing with his pipe on location 2. Stan being held above Robert Shaw to film air-lift escape sequence, *The Deep*, 1976
3. Jackie Bissett, Robert Shaw and Nick Nolte, *The Deep*, 1976

the underwater second unit. Only when we went to Australia and on to the Coral Sea to shoot the shark sequence with doubles were we on our own. Al, of course, took over direction.

Jackie Bissett and some of the other actors were not divers before filming began. How did you get around that obstacle? »Lou Gosset was an experienced diver and had a fine time diving with a local dive operator when he was not scheduled to be on-camera. In fact it was Lou who returned from a day of diving on the wreck of the *Constellation* and showed us a bag full of morphine ampules he had fanned out of the sand. Nick was certified already and athletic enough to be easy in the water. Jackie had never dived, was not athletic at all or into that sort of macho sport. But she did not lack for determination. We gave her a quick course with the vital essentials. Then on every dive with her we used two safely divers to watch her closely. To her great credit and the benefit of the production she took to the water like a beautiful swan, began to enjoy the experience. We had to insist that her double, Jackie Kilbride, do some of the heavy scenes (i.e. being slammed into the wreck by the giant eel).

Robert Shaw was a notorious character that never hid his love for whiskey, on and off the set. What was it like to work with him? »Robert Shaw came to the production with the largest celebrity status. No one begrudged his special housing. That comes with stardom. He was certainly an alcoholic and we were aware of delays in the shooting because of that. We only encountered his temper once. He had his own trailer on the set and used it during the day. My son

Gordy, was an underwater grip, making more money on the Hollywood budget than he had ever dreamed of. At the same time he was reluctant to use the very liberal room and board per diem that enabled most of us to stay at the South Hampton Princess Hotel. So he eyeballed Robert Shaw's empty trailer, discovered he had access to it after dark and so nested down there. I had no idea he was doing that or later how long he gotten away with it. One morning he overslept and was discovered by the great man. Shaw would have the cheeky grip fired from the production. Cooler heads prevailed. A bit of nepotism also helped.

How did you like filming on the 1867 wreck of the *Rhone* in the British Virgin Islands? »I knew the *Rhone* well, having dived and filmed there previously. Parts of it were wonderfully photogenic and readily accessible. All other divers and commercial dive operations were restricted from diving on the *Rhone* while we were working there. Since our production there lasted over three weeks you may imagine the local divers would have liked to nuke us all.

Dealing with currents and varying visibility conditions must have been a challenge? »The *Rhone* is so popular as a dive sight that it is hard-worn today, not just by the legions of divers but by storms as well. When we were on it we generally had excellent visibility and calm seas. The forward part of the wreck which provided our interior takes was deeper than we might have wished, requiring long decompression times that found us hanging off after dark. All the close action interior takes were, of course, done in the underwater set at Bermuda.

Did you find the underwater set built in Bermuda to be as easy to work as it looked? »The underwater set in Bermuda provided the only physical structure in which we could light, prepare and shoot the complicated scenes. Toward the finish of the shooting, which lasted almost a month, the plastic composition used to seal the walls of the million-gallon tank that had been created started to disintegrate. The marine life that had been introduced as props began to die. The water become so toxic, despite renewal from the sea, that we all developed ear infections. Our second unit part of the production was a "wrap" just in time before the set totally deteriorated.

71

Howard Hall credits you with getting him started in professional underwater filming. Who mentored and influenced you? »I was certainly influenced by Hans Hass and Jacques Cousteau. I picked up Hass's book, *Diving To Adventure*, right after I mustered out of the Navy in 1946 and was much fired by it. That was the opening shot. But it was Cousteau's Red Sea article in *National Geographic* that was the catalyst for me to try the sea and diving as a vocation. I was a farmer in Maine at the time. The year was 1953. I was bored with farming and still too young to spend the long winters making birdhouses in my workshop. That article started me thinking about taking a chance, making a move. Shakespeare had something to do with it too. In *Hamlet* he wrote, "There is a tide in the affairs of men that taken at the flood leads on to fortune. Omitted, all the journeys of their lives are bound in shallows and in miseries. You must take the current when it serves or lose the venture". So I re-mortgaged, shot my wad on building a boat that I designed for diving and set up in the Bahamas. The Bahamas years (from 1954 to '59) hardly broke even. But they were the foundation for a vocation that I have never regretted.

There have been many evolutions in diving equipment over the last 50 years. What do you consider to be some of the most important innovations? »Way back when it was the lowly o-ring that was a major advance in equipment. It enabled us to make our own Plexiglas housings with watertight control lever into the sides of the housings. Hi-8 emancipated me from 16mm film. It was not broadcast quality but was a dream for the small non-broadcast videos that I produced. Then along came digital as well as better optics for the housings and big improvements in lights and batteries. Howard Hall is now shooting high definition; very wisely building his stock footage for the near future when top broadcast productions will demand that quality. Being long of tooth and no longer in the market for broadcast level shooting contracts, I will never reach the high-definition level. That market has been pre-empted by a younger generation, all old friends who have come into their own. That is the way it should be.

Do you dive with nitrox or rebreathers now? » All the dive boats I work with now have nitrox. I subscribe to it entirely and only return to air if I want to go deeper for some reason. The reasons seldom

appear. I use the standard Dräger rebreather only occasionally. I am certified for it and will use it when I return to Cocos Island. I should use it more, especially since animal behavior is my major focus. I probably will in the future.

When you started the Nikonos had never been released. And underwater motion picture systems were both primitive and bulky. Share some perspective on the benefits of modern cameras and the advent of digital imaging. »When I started 16mm film was the medium for sports and documentary

1. Stan is up-ended for Boston Sea Rovers *Diver of the Year* 2. Stan and best friend Peter Benchly on location, 1993 3. Stan, Mimi and Mike deGruy, Michele and Howard Hall at Hans Hass award ceremony, Santa Barbara, 1998 4. The Diving Legacy Foundation selection board dons eye patches in Stan's honor announcing Pioneer Award 2007, L to R: Bret Gilliam, Stan Waterman, Sylvia Earle, Douglas Seifert, Phil Nuytten 5. Stan exults with sculptor Viktor as Gilliam announces $25,000 check

productions. Film stocks had such low ASA levels that big lights were required. That meant 1,000-watt lights with cables to a surface generator. The cameras at best carried 400-ft. magazines that provided 12 minutes of shooting. Light values were meter read; f-stops and focus were manually adjusted. When all the variables were right the Eastman Color Negative stock produced

Gretchen Gilliam

Gretchen Gilliam

a beautiful finished print. Hi-8 could not compete for quality but fit into a housing perhaps a 2/3 smaller than the 16mm housings. So little light was required that cables were no longer necessary. Lights and batteries mounted on the housing. Settings were electronically automated with manual options. But Hi-8 tape stock was vulnerable to drop outs and abrasion from too much reuse. Digital cameras again reduced the size of the housing, increased the effectiveness of the electronic controls, and produced an image with better color balance and definition. There is, of course, a difference in the finished product from a one-chip camera and a three-chip camera. Even at the consumer level the three-chip can turn out a broadcast quality video

You are still actively diving and sharing the experience with fellow divers by leading custom tours. Where are your favorite dive locations and what are your favorite liveaboards? My favorite dive areas are New Guinea, Malaysia, Indonesia and Fiji. I also return almost every year to Palau and love

74

France at the age of 124 the press had interviewed her the previous year. When asked what she had to say about her future, she said, "Not much!"

If a shark eats me on my next round I will be sorry to pack it up but grateful for what the sea has given me during a long, productive and satisfying career. Tennyson wrote of *Ulysses*, "How dull it is

1. In his Maine boathouse, 2003 2. Stan with Diving Legacy Foundation award statue 2007 3. On German television with Hans Hass, 1978 4. Boston Sea Rovers 50th Anniversary Film Program presenters:
Front: Philippe Cousteau, Dave Morton, Smokey Roberts
Back: Nick Caloyianis, Ernie Brooks, Emory Kristoff, Joe McInnis, Bob Ballard, Stan Waterman, Brian Skerry, Bret Gilliam

diving there. Those areas have yielded the most exciting macro encounters, and macro is my favorite subject these days. The Lembeh Strait at the northeast end of Sulawesi in Indonesia and the Kungkungan Bay Resort that serves it is the most exciting dive location I have encountered. I will decline rating liveaboard dive boats with which I work. They are all excellent with fine crews. The locations vary in their appeal to me but I am pleased with all the boats I work with.

You'll be 84 years old in early 2007. Any plans to slow down or take up golf? » I will give up diving when I no longer enjoy it. It will almost surely be when I am no longer physically able to dive comfortably and safely. Leni Riefenstahl, the "super woman" survivor of the Third Reich was diving at the age of 91. If I start main-lining Geritol I may make it. When the oldest living human with a certified birth certificate died in

to pause, to rust unburnished, not to shine in use as though to breathe were life."

In March of 2007 at the Beneath the Sea diving show, Stan was honored as a "Diving Legend" with the entire weekend devoted to a celebration of his astounding career. In addition to those honors, I was privileged to present him with the Pioneer Award from the Diving Legacy Foundation. Along with Selection Board members (Jim Clark, Sylvia Earle, Phil Nuytten, and Douglas Seifert) we took the stage for the Saturday evening program and presented him with a trophy and an 1800-lb. granite statue depicting him with his movie camera. The award was accompanied by a $25,000 honorarium check, the largest ever presented in the diving industry. Stan received two standing ovations from the audience during the ceremony, justly fitting as diving's grand ambassador. ■

Sea Salt

Reviewed by Bret Gilliam

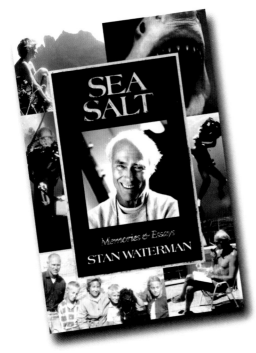

FOR ANYONE LUCKY ENOUGH TO CATCH ONE of Stan Waterman's personal appearances, you undoubtedly came away with a lasting impression of his wonderful speaking presence and gift for oration. I remember my own feelings after seeing him for the first time some thirty-five years ago: it was like listening to Lincoln or Churchill... but with a better vocabulary. And Stan talked about diving, my passion, in a way that no one else could.

Stan, of course, is the U.S.'s first pioneer of diving. Someone once suggested that he was the "Jacques Cousteau of American diving" and was promptly corrected by an observer to note that "Cousteau was actually more like the Stan Waterman of France." It's a fair statement.

Over the years, Stan has been a prolific filmmaker winning multiple Emmys and gaining his first international fame in the iconic 1971 release of *Blue Water, White Death*. Collaborating with Peter Gimbel, he co-produced, filmed and starred in this groundbreaking documentary about their quest to find and film the Great White shark in its natural element. Five years later he joined Al Giddings as co-director of underwater photography on the Hollywood blockbuster hit *The Deep*. In 1994 the Discovery Channel honored him with a feature two-hour special aptly named *The Man Who Loves Sharks*. The September 12, 2005 issue of *Sports Illustrated* has a profile of Stan remembering his first appearance in the magazine on its cover in January 1958. It's hard to find a serious diver who has not been touched in some way by this gentle and eloquent man's creative works.

But Stan is truly in his element when you discover him through his writings. That's not hard to believe when you consider that he actually studied under Robert Frost at Dartmouth. Throughout his lengthy career, he has carefully chronicled his underwater rites of passage in a widely published series of articles, features, anecdotal musings, and interviews. Now for the first time, a nearly complete body of that work is available in one book spanning his earliest youth to the present.

For years, Stan's friends have urged him to release just such a collection and I'm glad to note that he finally capitulated. New World Publications, the brainchild of Ned DeLoach and Paul Humann, made their reputation with the superb series of marine life and coral identification books. *Sea Salt* is their first offering in this genre.

Opening with forewords by Peter Benchley and Howard Hall, the reader is treated to a series of chapters in the book's first half that unveil Waterman's earliest development as his interest in diving and the sea awakens. The second half of the book contains the essay series originally begun with *Ocean Realm* magazine in the 1980s and that I continued with *Fathoms*.

I consider myself something of a Waterman aficionado and still was surprised to discover original works contained here that I had missed over the years. At 288 pages with 72 photos, the hardback tome has a rich treasure of adventure, opinions, shared observations on interesting friends and companions, the thrills of behind the scenes happenings on film and dive projects, as well as soul-baring reflections on his family and the strains that he sometimes brought them due his globe-trotting zeal in pursuit of his diving muse.

References are often made to the skill of master photographers who "paint with light." Waterman goes far beyond that. He paints a richly diverse canvass of life experiences with only words. One of the most poignant memories he shares describes an outing off Corsica in 1950 when the motivation for many early underwater explorers was to hunt fish:

"I entered the Mediterranean with mask, fins, snorkel and Arbalete speargun, my first dive on the old world side of the Atlantic. The recollection is so clear that it might have been yesterday. I was immediately surrounded by a great school of silver jacks. They flashed in the sun as they turned in unison, circling around me. They were friendly, curious, beautiful ambassadors of the Mediterranean world. And how did I greet them? I fired into the middle of the school, wounding one and frightening away the entire lot. And such was my fear of sharks and the unknown in the deep blue water beyond my reach that I nervously swam for the jetty and scrambled out of the water, happy to have escaped alive from this daring adventure. There was no shame in having violated that peaceful world into which I had intruded. I was rather proud of myself for having at least winged a fish. Yet the memory of that violent, thoughtless act still evokes an unpleasant sense of shame today."

Sea Salt is a magnificent volume. It will excite, sadden, thrill and mesmerize the reader with tales of a singular life by an extraordinary man who has emerged as diving's most articulate and sensitive spokesperson.

You can obtain yours by contacting: New World Publications 904-737-6558 or by ordering direct from their web site: www.fishid.com

ALL PHOTOS FROM BEV MORGAN COLLECTION EXCEPT AS NOTED

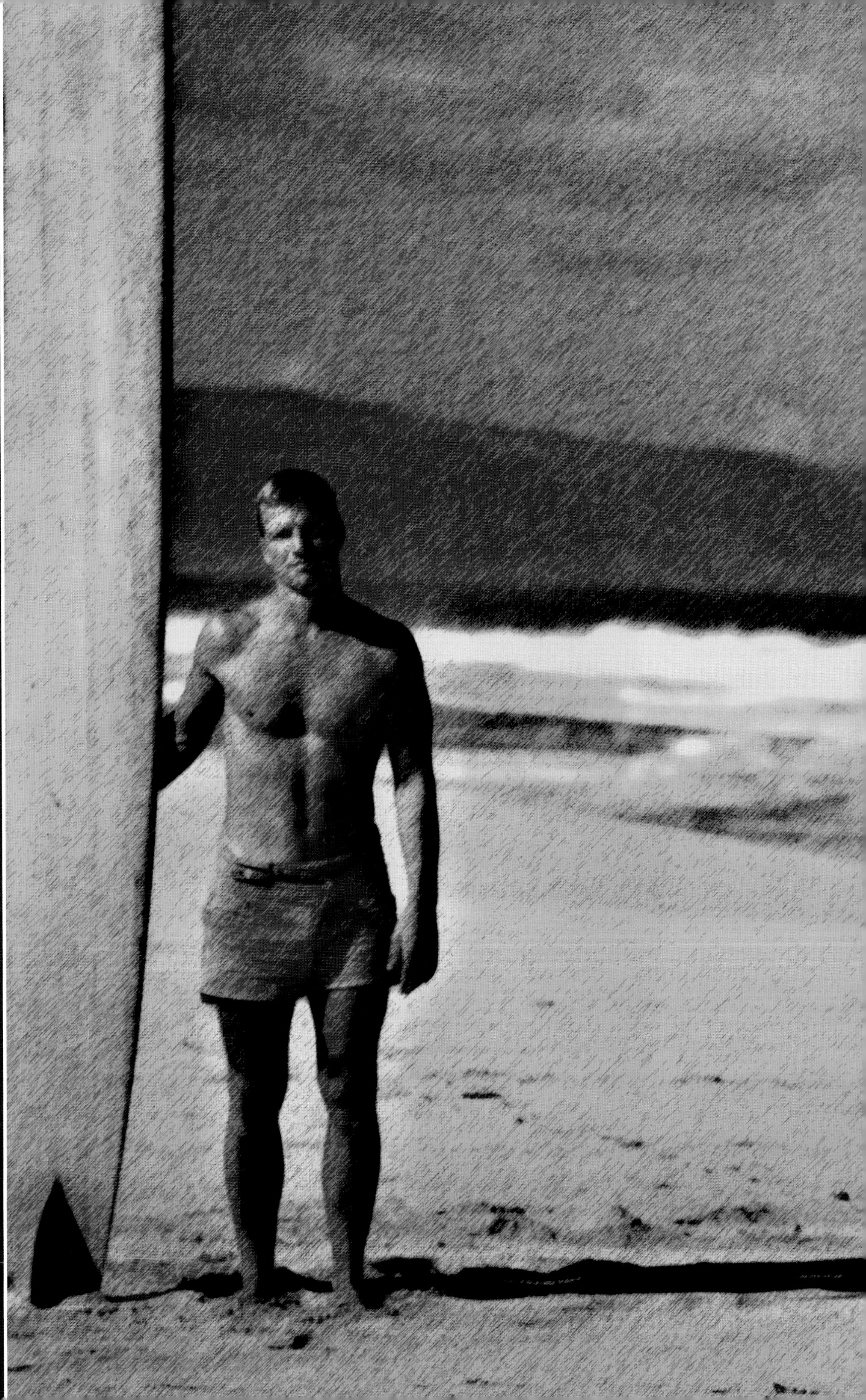

BEV MORGAN

Pioneer, Pirate
Photographer
Entrepreneur

BY BRET GILLIAM

1

2

IT WOULD
BE DIFFICULT
TO IMAGINE
A MAN MORE
DESERVING OF THE
MONIKER "PIONEER" ...

than legendary commercial diver and manufacturer Bev Morgan. In a professional career spanning nearly six decades, Morgan has managed to leave his mark on diving in so many ways that the accomplishments of others pale in comparrison. »

From a modest start as a lifeguard, he'd go on to amass considerable wealth as the founder of Diving Systems International, the world's largest manufacturer of commercial dive gear. Along the way he helped originate the first dive training programs in the U.S., started the company that became the multi-million grossing wetsuit conglomerate Body Glove, indulged himself in a variety of hedonistic (and sometimes scientific) voyages of discovery to the South Pacific and beyond, and ended up as soul mate and confidant to rock musician David Crosby. Honored by DEMA as one of its first inductees into diving's Hall of Fame, Morgan remains an intensely private man who has shunned the limelight in spite of his considerable successes.

I originally trained to dive in 1959 using Morgan's book, *Underwater Safety*, and he's been a hero of mine ever since. Although he is the stuff of legend in diving and surfing, in real life he's even larger. While standing well south of six feet in stature, he towers above most when you simply consider the contributions he has made to diving. And surfing for that matter. One of the things I've most enjoyed about Bev is his refreshing candor and point blank way of speaking. Ask him why he was first interested in diving

commercial diving professionals he enjoys a reputation as "da man" and the "go to" guy for whatever piece of gear or methodology necessary to get the job done. When Hollywood needs impossible special equipment designed for underwater films, the solution is always, "Get Morgan on the phone!" And then there's a few assignments he's accepted from our government that he really can't talk about... at least not when the tape recorder is running.

He's a hell raiser in every sense of the

3

81

and he'll tell you straight off that it looked like a good way of getting girls at the beach. For a guy who never went to college, he will leave you simultaneously amazed and educated with the most complex engineering explanation you could hope for. Differential mixed gas formula equations? He'll solve them from both ends and never spill his drink. Ask him for an opinion? You'll get it "no holds barred" and with none of the expletives deleted. Among military and

word. That's another quality I most admire about him. Bev is going to make sure a good time is had along the way. He'll take care of business, but he's not going to miss the party. His sense of humor is also the stuff of legend. A decade or so ago, we were having dinner in a swank restaurant in Texas when a member of our party began choking on a piece of steak that went down the wrong way. I jumped up to administer the Heimlich Maneuver to our gasping

1. Morgan (center in photo) with lobster-smuggling desperados, armed and dangerous, Mexico, 1957 2. Morgan (at left in photo) and associates loading fuel aboard airplane used to smuggle lobsters from Baja, 1957 3. Morgan surfing at San Onofre, 1953

Bev Morgan

dinner companion and Bev watched with interest... never missing a bite of his own meal as pandemonium briefly reigned. On my third attempt, the piece of meat departed from the man's clogged airway and sailed in a high arc across the table to land inches from Bev's plate. He drained his wine glass, stabbed the offending morsel with his salad fork, and inquired calmly, "Are you done with this?' The whole room exploded in laughter and relief.

Since he's been around long enough to pioneer both diving and surfing, he's something of a cross-over cult figure. Bev built dive gear. And he built surfboards. He practically invented the scuba certification programs of the 1950s. He was the first to grasp the market for wet suits in both sports and overcame the initial disdain that

surfers cast on any type of thermal wear by showing the retailers that it was good business. You see, in spite of Bev's frequent departures from the entanglements of various enterprises to embark on sailing adventures leaving behind a long list of serial relationships with girlfriends and a revolving door of wives, he had the inherent "business gene" that so very few possess. He was an instinctive entrepreneur who managed to make his avocations a career that made him staggeringly wealthy in markets notorious for financial failure. Surfing? Diving? When Morgan got involved originally these weren't business ventures; they were bad habits.

He sailed across the Pacific exploring places that few white men had been in centuries. He helped "renew" the shallow gene pool on Pitcairn Island where the *Bounty* mutineers had settled in virtual isolation. He was one of the first to dive Cocos Island and Polynesia. When the lure of Hawaii's infamous North Shore big surf was being ridden for the first time, it was Morgan standing tall with characters like Greg Noll, Ricky Grigg, Buzzy Trent, and other water rats with

more guts than common sense who tackled Waimea and the Pipeline. He excelled as a photographer and his library of images chronicling surfing and diving from the early days to the modern era is a monument of captured history. He was a senior editor and writer for both *Surfer* and *Skin Diver* magazines in their start-ups. He smuggled lobster from Mexico into the U.S. along with a few other commodities that NAFTA didn't figure on.

But most of all he changed the way men worked underwater by creating the revolutionary lightweight commercial gear that freed divers from the cumbersome hard hat dress that had dominated the piers, ships and waterfronts for nearly a century. That probably will be his legacy. The George Washington of the commercial diving industry.

What can I say? Morgan is a character of so many dimensions. World class businessman, world class *bon vivant.* And one hell of a guy to hang with. This interview came about over the course of three sessions from 1996 to 2004. The first

time we let the tape recorder run was at his hillside home in Santa Barbara. We continued again later in his waterfront offices. Finally, I tracked him down at his new home in the Santa Ynez valley, just over the mountains. His pal David Crosby lived just down the road and helped him find the place. (Now he's moved again back to Santa Barbara. I wish I was his real estate agent...) Each time he greeted me warmly and we settled in for lengthy dialogues. I asked him to reminisce about his phenomenal career and the adventures that cropped up. ■

1. Morgan with yellowtail, 1953 2. Local beauty on the beach in Tahiti, 1956

Tell us about how you first got involved in this. »As a kid, I didn't know much about the water or any of those things, then one day, I drove by the beach and there were a lot of girls. So, I started going to the beach to look at the pretty girls. It turned out to be a neat environment.

1. Morgan in classic hardhat dress, 1973 2. The start of Dive 'N Surf, circa 1955. It is probably the oldest dive store in the world. Shown from left to right: Dale Velzy, Hap Jacobs, Bill Meistrell and Bev Morgan

What year was this? »I'd say around 1946. One day I was surfing in San Diego. It was a flat day and some divers went by. They were getting a lot of abalone and lobster. That got me real interested. They invited me over for a cookout on the beach. Turned out it was Connie Limbaugh, Jim Stewart, Andy Rechnitzer who were going to Scripps, back in the early days. It looked like a real fun deal to get food out of the ocean. This

chance meeting turned into a long friendship. A little later I was working with two fellows named Rex Guthrie and Tom King up at Los Angeles County Life Guards. They took a World War II frogman's mask and put a tilt valve regulator in it from a B-29 bomber oxygen unit. We breathed in through the nose and out through the mouth and the damned thing worked pretty good. When the Aqua-Lung came along it worked better so we bought a couple.

When? »That was probably 1949 or 1950. We bought the Aqua-Lungs in 1951 or '52 and began diving with them. As a lifeguard for the County Guards, I worked on their only boat at the time, named the *Baywatch*. One of the jobs was body recovery from the boat. We started recovering scuba divers because nobody knew how to dive and they were renting or buying the equipment with no training. The only instruction the Aqua-Lung manual gave was not to hold your breath when you come up.

In those days there was no formalized training program, was there? »Well, no. There was really only the YMCA. A guy named Fred Swankowski ran a diving class at the YMCA pool in Long Beach. I attended either the first or second class. At the time, the Los Angeles County Board of Supervisors was seeking to make it illegal to dive with scuba equipment due to the high accident rate. Back then, five or six out of 100 people diving would lose their lives; that was a pretty high percentage. My idea, along with Limbaugh and E.R. Cross, was to organize a board of advisors. The Board of Supervisors recommended that we start a diving instruction program, so they provided us with a budget. So I, along with Ramsey Parks, who was my diving partner at the time, put one together and it became the Los Angeles County dive instruction program.

What time frame are we talking about? »We put it together in 1953. The following year we taught about 1,000 students in the LA County pools. We quickly realized that there was no way we could teach all the people in Los Angeles County, let alone everyone else interested in scuba diving. So, at the end of the summer of 1954 we put together an instructor's program and began developing a manual on how to instruct scuba divers. At that point it became obvious to me that this diving program should not be a government-controlled or dive club-controlled operation. I felt very strongly

that it should be a dive shop-associated training program. My concept was a dive shop with a pool, classroom, workshop and showroom.

In those days, how many dive shops are we talking about in the Southern California area? » Two! But the enthusiasm for the sport was overwhelming. *The Los Angeles Times* was very generous in giving article space and write-ups. We were in the sports section at least twice a month with good full-page features. At that time there was only one manufacturer in the United States and that was U.S. Divers. In those days there was no PADI or NAUI. Al Tillman, one of the fellows who had helped us start the LA County Instructor program, went on to start NAUI a few years later. It all grew out of that original little L.A. County course we started.

Didn't you decided to try your hand at retailing around then? » In 1955 I started a shop called Dive 'n Surf and later brought in Bill and Bob Meistrell. We sold the complete U.S. Divers line since they were the only company manufacturing dive gear in those days. They had the Aqua-lung. There was no other scuba available.

Did you have suits in those days? » Before I opened the shop I went to the Scripps library and ran across a report from a fellow named Hugh Bradner who recommended the use of foam neoprene for military divers to keep them warm. The insulation was in the material itself so the diver got wet but stayed warm. He called his new suit a "wet suit." I read the report and it gave a source on where to buy the material. I bought a sheet of it and made myself a suit. It worked very well. I then made suits for all my diving buddies and that's how Dive 'n Surf began as a suit manufacturer.

Who was using these suits? » Scuba divers.

What about surfers? » No, not surfers. Surfers considered it chicken to put on a rubber suit so we couldn't break into that market, no matter what we did in those days. I remained with Dive 'n Surf until 1957 then I sold out to the Meistrells. We dove most of the time. We'd get up at 4:00 a.m. and go diving, then open the shop at 9:00 a.m. They were great partners but I decided to go adventure sailing and diving aboard a 61-ft. ketch named *Chiriqui*, so I sold out to them. I went down to the South Pacific with a crew of dive buddies for a couple of years. We did a lot of filming, 16mm stuff and lots of still pictures.

but sure enough, when we pulled into Chatham Bay and dropped the hook, we heard all this crunching. We thought we were dragging across rock or coral. When we looked, we actually saw that it was a bunch of sharks chewing on the anchor chain! As we let it out we thought, "Geez, we better rethink this." We didn't know if we were going to dive there or not. But, we found a

1. Morgan with black sea bass, 1955 2. Tom Carlin, Byron Kough and Bev Morgan show the typical diving equipment for commercial abalone diving in California during the 1950s

Tell us about some of the places you visited. Did you dive while you were there? »Yeah, had a compressor on board and a bunch of bottles, dove our brains out. It started out in Long Beach, went down along the coast of Mexico. We dove all the way down. We spent a month at Tres Marias, a group of islands off of Mazatlan. From there we sailed to Acapulco continuing to dive all the way down to Cocos Island. It was untouched in 1957, nobody had ever collected fish there. We offered to do a collection for Scripps. We soon found out the reason why no one had put together a fish collection there. There were a lot of sharks. A lot of sharks. Before we arrived in Cocos we read that the reef sharks chewed on the anchor chain when it was let out. I just laughed thinking it was a joke,

place the next day where we could get our back against a vertical drop and jump in the water.

Sharks came at us right away. While in Mexico, we encountered quite a few sharks so we made "shark billys," poke sticks about two feet long and made of ironwood. They were heavier than water so if it was knocked from your hand it sunk to the bottom, and the bottom was a much better place to be than mid-water to recover your "billy." We didn't go in the water without those shark billies. When the sharks swam up to you, you'd hit them in the nose and they would go away. We'd dive back to back, usually three men to a

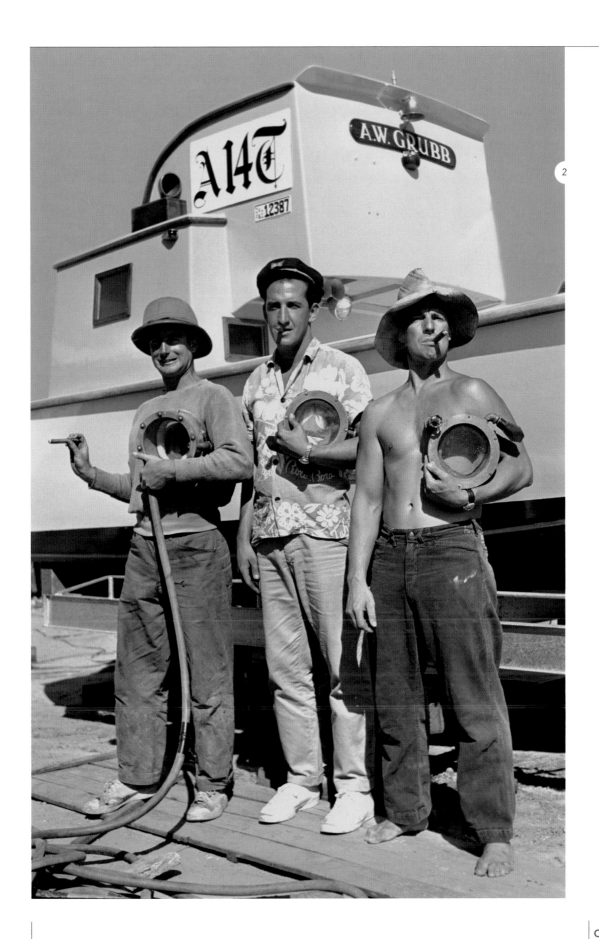

team. Two guys back to back, one guy fish collecting or whatever you are up to. We'd never spear too many fish unless we were next to the boat and could hand up the gun then jump in the boat after the fish was speared, and let somebody else haul the fish in. You might only get half of it in otherwise.

Our final day of diving at Cocos was out in the blue at the edge of a drop-off. Three of us had just dropped into the water from our 14-ft. skiff. Two very large sharks, not reef sharks, came slowly towards us. One guy, Lowell, froze. Ramsey Parks and I looked at him, then at each other. Lowell just hung there not moving. Ramsey and I had our shark billies at the poke position towards the two approaching big boys. When they were about 20 feet away they separated and split off to the side. We soon realized why. A third shark was approaching slowly behind them. This guy was really, really huge. I couldn't really see how long it was and that didn't matter. What mattered was how big around he was. He continued swimming slowly toward Lowell who remained frozen in mid-water. His mouth was slowly opening. This monster shark was going to eat Lowell and his mouth was big enough to do the job in one easy gulp. It was as if the shark detected which of us was more scared. When the shark was about 10 feet away Ramsey and I swam toward it and started poking its nose with the billies. It broke off the approach and kicked its tail, which tumbled us as it swam away. Ramsey and I grabbed each side of Lowell and began shoving him into the boat. I don't recall how all three of us got into the boat, but somehow we were all in the boat when the three sharks returned and started to bump against the bottom as if trying to dump us out. Ramsey fired up the outboard and took off at high speed back to the safety of the big boat. There was silence as we secured everything and set out to sea to find a better island to dive.

Where did you go after that? ›› We went to the Galapagos and we spent two months going through those islands. That was real interesting down there. We would see an occasional fish boat but no yachts. We were only the second yacht to ever go to Easter Island. There were many rumors about the big statues and roads into the ocean as well as the submerged cities. Much speculation was made about the statues in those days coming from the moon, because the experts couldn't figure out where the quarry was or where they had been made.

Had anybody been there before with any diving equipment? ›› I don't think so. We were the first to dive there. Thor Heyerdahl had been there six months prior to our arrival. He had a big expedition, *Kon-Tiki*, and all that. He explored the island and when he came out with his book, his information was more accurate than any expert's previously. He even discovered a few atypical statues from the big-lipped ones.

Did you continue on to the West Pacific? ›› We went to Pitcairn Island and dove on what was left of the *Bounty*. The mutineers ended up there after taking the ship from Captain Bligh and leaving Tahiti. The remains of the wreck are up in the surf line, but we got a few pieces of anchor chain. Kind of neat to have a piece of that history.

Every other person there must have been named Christian. ›› Well, there are about six common names: Christian, Adams and a couple of others. But that leads to an interesting point. Due to the fact that there are not many visitors, there was a lot of in-breeding on several of the remote islands including Pitcairn. They needed fresh genes, new blood. There were five of us young guys on the boat at that point. They would meet us with a reception committee and match up who was going to be with who.

Well, I guess you could say we did our duty. It kind of wore us out to stop at any particular island. So I guess there's more than a few Morgans out there now widening the gene pool. I like to think I did my part

Bev Morgan

1. The schooner *Constellation* rides at the quay in Papeete, Tahiti on an adventure through the Society Islands 2. One of the local girls. Was Tahiti really thatched roofs, party time and everything that one hears about the "old days?" YES, and then some!

to ensure that the future generations of some of these remote Pacific islands remain healthy. And maybe they won't all look like Prince Charles.

From Pitcairn we went to Minerva Reef. We had read that German pearlers worked there in the last century and got a lot of pearl shell. The visibility was the clearest I've ever seen in the world, anywhere.

How clear?》Well, I could see a hazy outline of the boat when I was standing on the anchor and we had the 300-feet of chain out. It was clearer than anything I've seen since, absolutely clear water.

Probably only a handful of white people have ever visited there. What was your reception like from the natives?》Very positive, everybody thought we were wonderful. For them, California was where all the movies were made and before we left we stocked up the boat with a lot of film. One of the guys on the crew had been to the South Pacific many times and he told us how they loved action movies, so we went up to Hollywood and picked up footage from fight scenes, we had two hours of nothing but violence. Fighting, riders getting shot off of horses – cowboys and Indians mainly. We spliced it together and made a feature film out of it with no story line, nothing, just violence. It was nothing but action, fighting, and crashes.

Probably be a hit movie today.》We'd set up a projector and screen in the most godforsaken island in the South Pacific and show this film. It was interesting, the natives would just yell and howl, they loved it. Anyway, they thought we were really unique creatures.

How far out did you get into the Pacific?》Tahiti. As many boat trips do, it all kind of fell apart in Tahiti. Before we arrived, we mutinied. A fellow by the name of Lowell Thomson was the majority owner of the boat, but we all had a share. He was a character. He had a mine in Idaho. He got hooked on diving. When we got to Easter Island, Lowell started acting weird, as people on sailboats do after a certain amount of time. All of a sudden we had a bunch of guns on the boat missing. We found out that Lowell had retrieved all of the guns and put them in his cabin. We didn't exactly know what he had in mind but it wasn't good. Somewhere between Pitcairn and Tahiti he brandished a gun at one of the crew. We found an old rusty shotgun in the bow of the boat that one of the guys had stored there. We threw a few shells in it then cornered Lowell with the shotgun and told him he'd be toast if he didn't behave.

He was confined to his cabin for nine days. We'd let him out with armed guards to eat and go pee over the side of the boat. We feared he'd shoot us. When we got to port in Papeete, he turned us into the authorities and we turned him in. The French were used to it – just another mutiny. We each went our separate ways in Tahiti. He sailed to Hawaii without our services, and the crew on that voyage also planned mutiny. So we weren't the only guys.

Was it sometime after that when you began making gear?》Actually, back when we had Dive 'n Surf, I tried my hand at some garage engineering. U.S. Divers had come out with a regulator called the Mistral. It was a nice venturi-assisted regulator. Single stage regulator, two hose. It worked fine on the workbench but once in the ocean, it would squirt water right on the choke center in the middle of your throat. So I fiddled around with it and got it to work properly by redesigning the damn thing. And wouldn't you know, the company actually incorporated my stuff and changed the regulator. I called them up a few months later and said, "Hey, that was all my idea, what's the deal? You never paid me for any of that."

So the guy at U.S. Divers says, "Well, I tell you

what, you have a pickup truck?" I said, "Yeah, so what?" He says, "How about if I give you everything you can put in your pickup truck out of my warehouse and we'll call it even?" I said, "You've got a deal!"

So I told the Meistrells about it and we all ended up in the damn truck. We got there and loaded that truck down to its axles. Everything they had, regulators and tanks, then drove off. I was happy and he was happy, it worked out fine. At any rate, it that was the first time I realized that I could fool around and come up with stuff.

After I came back from the South Pacific, about 1960 I began doing commercial abalone diving. There were times when the surf was up and we couldn't dive so I had time on my hands and worked on getting surf suits accepted by surfers. I've always worn a wetsuit surfing. I could care less whether or not it was chicken. I made 100 suits for surfers. They were called "short johns." They came down to the middle of your thigh with a Farmer John kind of upper. We sold them for $15.

So I contacted my surfer buddies like Hobie Alter and the other board makers. They all had surf teams. I convinced their top 10 team riders to wear this wetsuit. First they said it was chicken and they weren't going to wear it. I told them if the profit off your wetsuit sales doesn't pay your rent, I'll pay your rent for you. Well, they all said that's different, it's not chicken to pay the rent. They all agreed to it. So I had 100 of the top surfers on the coast wear a wet suit all in the same week. They were warm and it wasn't chicken because all of the other good surfers were wearing them and all the younger folks, beginners and all, thought the surfing wet suit was great from then on.

We had somewhere in the neighborhood of 1,000 orders that first week. So I'm knocking myself out to produce these things and my partners say, "Look this is little old lady work – we're not going to make these wetsuits." I tell them, "Guys you only have to work for about a month, then it's retirement city!" They said, "No, we are not making wetsuits, especially surfer wetsuits. It's beneath us, we're divers and we're not going to do it."

So, I packed the whole thing up on the truck and I drove up to the Meistrells and said, "Look, I want to sell you my new surfing wetsuit business." They weren't making surf suits at that time because nobody knew how to crack that market, except for O'Neil up north because of the cold water. Anyway, I took a sewing

machine, a batch of rubber and by then 2,000 orders to Billy, and he said, "I don't know." I wanted $3,000 for the whole package, business and all. He ended up buying it. They called me a couple of months later to say they were making a $5,000 profit a day each on this deal.

And that's how Body Glove started? »That was the deal. Those guys made a nice bit of change over the years from that load of stuff in my pickup. As soon as I unloaded the rubber, the sewing machine and everything else, I drove straight to *Surfer Magazine* and got hooked up to edit the publication with John Severson for a year. At the end of the year though, the old dive itch just got to me. Danny Wilson had put his first bell together and had made his first helium dive in Santa Barbara so I just packed up and came to Santa Barbara and asked Danny for a job. Danny says, "Well, I tell you what, I don't know if you're qualified for this commercial diving." I said, "Let's not hear that again. This is a new deal, it's working out of the bell. You're not even going to use heavy gear."

"Well," he said, "you've got to pass the qualifications." He whips out two fifths of vodka and puts one in front of me. He then takes one himself and says, "You've got to keep up with me. If you can make it through the whole bottle you're hired."

So we sat down and talked diving and we talked drinking and we each drank, right out of the bottle… a fifth of vodka each. I woke up in the morning with my head in his toilet. His wife, taking pity on me, gave me a wet towel and said, "You've got the job."

How about manufacturing commercial gear? » When I went into the abalone business I had a difficult time finding a mask, so I built one instead. Being a surfboard glasser, I built the mold and made it out of fiberglass. It worked really good so when I got into petroleum diving, I just kept tinkering with the design. Many of the abalone divers graduated to petroleum diving when the oil companies started doing offshore work. Prior to that, the only people the oil companies would employ were heavy gear divers who wore big metal helmets because they had always had bad luck with scuba divers.

Most scuba divers weren't journeymen plumbers and that's what they needed, so you had to be a hard hat diver to get any work in that business. I was a mask diver on the end of the hose, but not hard hat. I had

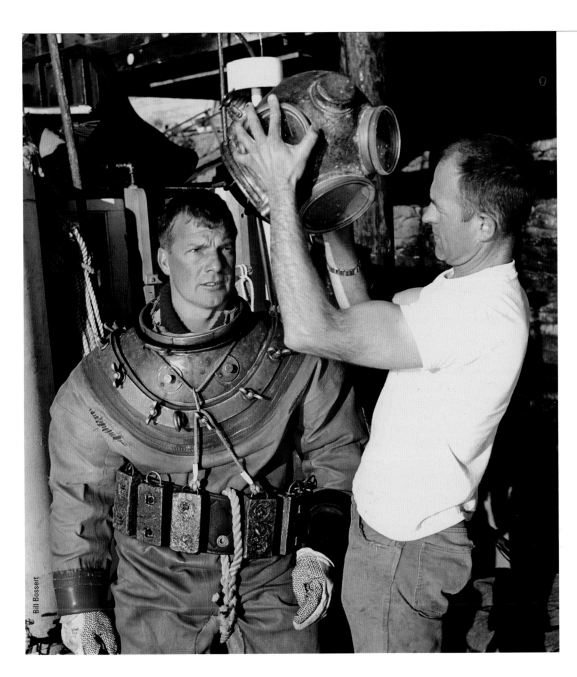

Bill Bossert

Bob Christiansen places the standard gear helmet on Morgan during additional construction on the Trans-Pacific telephone cable, 1964

to buy a hard hat and learn how to use it to get into the petroleum business. I then had the opportunity to design equipment that was more advantageous than the big metal helmets.

But in those days there was considerable resistance to trying to simplify this gear. ⟩⟩ Yes, there was. Standard heavy gear had gone unchanged for 150 years. Very little had changed, a metal helmet covered your head and it married to a dry dress and you wore woolen underwear under it to stay dry. You jump into the water and walk over to the job site and do your job.

But three-dimensional gear in which you could have the same communications that you have in heavy gear and you could walk on the bottom if you want and you can swim if you want – that is better gear. In addition to that, equipment you can put on by yourself is more efficient. Also, in most emergencies, you can take care of yourself. The primary advantage is the shorter training needed with the newer gear.

Morgan on Hawaii's North
Shore, Banzai Pipeline, 1956

John Elwell

But probably the biggest single change that came up that you couldn't do in heavy gear was the dive bell. You couldn't dive out of it with heavy gear; it wouldn't fit through the hatch. So the guys had to switch to a lighter weight gear. I was getting nowhere trying to get any new type of helmets sold, so I went into business with Bob Kirby building heavy gear. Kirby was a metal smith and we built some beautiful copper helmets. We were spinning the domes and working the metal, putting ports in. As far as heavy gear is concerned, we built the best diving helmets in the world. That was 1964. Everybody came to us for those helmets and then we said, yeah, but this little helmet here is better. There was no way for them to counter.

You'd already established your credibility? 》
Yeah, but it took seven years for them to accept the lightweight fiberglass helmets. At that point, there were less than 100 commercial divers and the petroleum companies projected that they'd need 5,000 for all the upcoming offshore work.

Where were these guys going to come from? 》
Well, there was only one base of divers – scuba divers. You can't go to the plumbers union and say we need 5,000 plumbers who like diving. You're going to have to go out and get divers who are willing to learn plumbing and that's what we did. We started schools to teach diving and one of them was here in Santa Barbara. The Santa Barbara Marine Technology Program. Another one started, Commercial Diving Center, (CDC) turned into the College of Oceaneering in San Pedro.

The schools trained scuba divers to be commercial divers. The most they could have trained using standard helmets (heavy gear or copper hats) in the time allotted would have been about 300 or 400 divers, so we came up with the Band Mask. This design enabled any scuba diver to do a couple hours training and be fairly comfortable in this umbilical mask and have full communications. Now all they had to do was learn the trade of underwater plumbing and they didn't have to relearn diving. Within five years they were able to train 5,000 qualified divers because of this equipment. That put Kirby and me on the map. Kirby and I built a lot of equipment and supplied all of those divers.

That was also at a time when they switched from the concept of living underwater and working, to living on deck and taking an elevator down to do the work. These guys were stored at working pressure. They were put back in the bell and transported to the job site where they did the work, then moved back topside to sleep and eat.

How long could some of these missions be? 》
When they got into sat diving, there were 20-day dives. You put in your six-hour day on the bottom, so the guys would work three shifts with a couple hours going and coming.

How deep did these divers get? 》 They did good solid working dives around 800-1,000 feet in that area. A few did 1,200 feet, in test diving, of course, Comex had some guys go 2,000 feet,

It's interesting, in an industry where no one manufacturer has ever achieved dominance, your company has achieved a market share that most people can only dream of. How did that happen? What do you estimate your market share to be? 》 Oh, I have no idea, but it is a high number.

It has been variously reported as high as 85 percent to 95 percent or more of the world market. Do you think that is accurate? 》 It could be. I just have no idea. I started building the first commercial fiberglass helmets around 1960, then got set back and had to build metal helmets for a while. In essence, that makes 47 years we've been working with commercial stuff. Thirty of those years have been in intense manufacturing and development. I even dabbled in some sport scuba gear. For instance, I showed Gustav Dalla Valle (co-founder of Scubapro) the adjustable regulators that we've had on our unit since 1957. Six months later he came out with their adjustable second stage, even though he told me they weren't interested in it.

Did he present you with the offer to back your truck up to his place? 》 Nope, Gustav was tighter than the other guys. I never got anything out of him but a couple of great lunches and some wine.

What trends do you see now in commercial diving? Is it growing or is it flat? 》 Well, right now commercial diving is flat as far as the number of divers working, but there is always a chance it will expand. We're going through a lot of work right now. Many divers are busy maintaining the offshore towers. The way it works is when gasoline is high, the price of oil is high, of course, and the oil companies do all their maintenance because they have the cash flow to do the offshore maintenance. When it's lower, they pull back on the maintenance until the cash flow gets good. Well, you can imagine at nearly $60 a barrel, which is where it is now, they want to get all the work possible done offshore, so all the divers are working but there are now fewer divers than there were 10 years ago.

A decade ago, people hypothesized that the diver itself might eventually become obsolete and be replaced by ROVs or divers in one-atmosphere suits. Do you envision that happening? »In water down to 150 feet, I don't think they'll ever replace the diver because they can still get more done and are still more economical than an ROV. The one-atmosphere suit is too clumsy, too expensive and too much work for that depth. What I'm finding is the ROVs actually create work for divers. For instance, there are cross girders and things on offshore platforms that have completely disappeared and nobody knew about it for a few years until the divers finally did their inspection. Now, ROVs go down and inspect anytime they feel like it. And what they find creates work for divers.

Interesting. Beyond 150 feet, what would you consider a practical alternative to a diver? »Zero to 150-165 feet is common air diving. Beyond that, you need mixed gas. In Europe, you must have a closed-bottom bell that can be pressurized and brought on deck, so the price goes up quite a bit as soon as you hit 165 feet plus. In the North Sea you contend with cold, rough water – big seas, and it makes sense to have a closed bell. In the Gulf of Mexico, however, where you have warm, clear still water, you can dive using mixed gas with a "come home" open-bottom bell – a dome is all it is, you can descend to 220 feet. But beyond 220 feet, even in calm, still water, you should use a closed-bottom bell. Many projects are made more efficient when using a closed-bottom bell in 400-600 feet of water. Beyond that, saturation diving begins when you take a crew of divers and put them

in a pressure vessel for 10 or 20 days of diving, the whole support gets very expensive.

Are there as many saturation projects going on now as there were a decade ago? »Yes, there are because they're saturating for shallower jobs. A few years ago when they did saturation, it was usually

at 800 feet or so and now they'll saturate for a 200-ft. dive if it makes sense. The way it's done is you pencil out so many hours a day for sat diving and so much decompression and somewhere around 300-400 feet, it becomes economical. So there's actually more sat diving in shallower water now than there used to be.

If you put a diver in sat with the hatch depth around 400 feet, it still gives him the excursion capability to go below that to what, another couple hundred feet or so with no decompression and return to storage? »You can always cut your pressure in half without decompressing. So if you're stored at 400 feet, you can go to 800 feet. It depends on

1. With California lobster, 1970
2. In his office holding sketch of diving helmet, 2004

the logistics of support. You know, do they have a bell that will go that deep? Are the cables set up properly? Does the job require that many hours? Then there's the safety factor. So instead of storing the guys at 400 and making 800-ft. runs, the companies prefer to store the guys a little deeper so you don't have any chance of getting the bends.

Your company gained a tremendous reputation early on with your lightweight divers' helmets. What other products are you making to support this? Are you actually designing suits and bells, things like this? »No. We work with the suit manufacturers to marry the suits to the helmets, but we don't actually build the suits themselves. We build a few scuba-diving suits since we're going to have a neoprene department anyway, but no, we stick mainly to helmets and avoid chambers and plumbing and stuff like that.

Has the old brass helmet been completely retired at this point? »No. Many people still use them. A fiberglass version of the old metal helmet that operates the same way, with a breastplate and all, is still made. Some of the guys prefer it and it is good gear. It still has its place but it's not as convenient as the stuff we make.

A few years back, you were working on a new split full-face mask that would be adaptable to a lot of uses. »Well, the whole idea was to make a full-face mask with a trap door over the mouth – we call that a pod, and when you remove the mouth pod, it attaches very simply and easily underwater or on surface. So you can put on your mask and all your gear and still breathe air but not breathe your tanks down and then snap this in place. And because the pod provides a little dry area, you can take the mouthpiece out and communicate. Since then, we've also discovered that it's very comfortable to have your mouth in air. You've got the mouthpiece in place but there's no water on your mouth and it's more convenient – and feels better too. For a rebreather diver, it's very important because it's one more barrier to the water getting into the system. You don't want to get your chemical absorbent or your bags wet. We find the military divers like this mask because it gives them that extra barrier. If they pass out, they don't flood. If they pass out, they don't drop the mouthpiece. Their buddy has time to go over and get him, and dry drowning is always better than wet drowning for bringing guys back.

In addition to your commercial interests, you also have a significant amount of military clients, don't you? »Yes. We sell more or less to all the navies of the world; they're predominantly ships husbandry diving gear as opposed to swimming gear and now that we're getting into the new mask for swimmers, we find we're now getting more calls from all the foreign navies too.

You've done some movie stuff, like *The Wreck of the Mary Deare* with Gary Cooper back in the '50s and now you've recently expanded into Hollywood support for they're underwater needs. Tell us about some of the movie productions you've worked on. »*Sphere* was a film we did in 1997 with Warner Bros. It was a lot of fun and very interesting to work with the movie people again. We designed the

95

equipment to work in front of the camera. The whole idea was to allow the camera to see the diver's face in full – from the side and front view. We worked on the microphones to get studio-quality voice communication underwater. That was really tricky because you have backpressure resistance. All underwater breathing apparatus, including our helmets, have backpressure. We designed it so that when the actor divers talked on camera, we could tap off their microphone so that the production soundmen could take the sound directly from the helmet microphones. It was the first time the quality of sound was there and it didn't have to be dubbed in. We lowered the resistance for exhalation to the point of where they could act and enunciate and have no forced breathing resistance or forced vocal resistance. It made a big change.

Now, I remember from working on movies like *The Deep* back in 1976, in those days, it was a real transition to get these actors in the water and to make them basically be able to function down there. You were working with Samuel L. Jackson, Sharon Stone, Dustin Hoffman and some others. How did they do?» They did great. We set up with Director Barry Levinson and told him we wanted to have the right instructors as well as the time to teach them properly in the swimming pool. The filming was done in tanks, but the movie was supposed to take place at a 1,000-ft. depth. They did a lot of trick stuff to get the water the right darkness and then we spent a month with the diving crew and the actors. By the time we finished with the new helmets and had broken them in, the actors were as comfortable as I've ever seen. On the first day of shooting, they went into an enclosed cave. Even though it was a fabricated cave, it was still a cave. It was about 50 feet long and I get nervous as heck when there's an overhead problem with novices. Well, these guys were beyond being novices by then. They went in there, played the part like troopers, and never had any trouble. It went off without a hitch and was a good shoot all the way through. No safety problems whatsoever.

What are you concentrating on next?» We're working on making the helmets lighter, which means making them less buoyant. We're also trying to bring the price down. The commercial market needs equipment at lower cost and we're working on production methods for doing that. So that's one of the challenges.

What interests you most in diving today?» A very lightweight, low-priced set of gear that will do everything our heavier stuff does. It's interesting that we called our helmets SuperLites. Though they are lighter than the older helmets, the SuperLites weigh 27 pounds average and that's not very light by today's standards. But nobody has yet made a lighter one. We've got them down to 20 pounds but they floated off your head. A true 10-lb. helmet that works well would really be needed but it's a difficult design to undertake and make economical for now. So I'd say that would be the biggest challenge. Another large challenge is to make breathing equipment that breathes so easily you'll never outbreathe it and you don't even know it's in your mouth.

When diving began back in that era, there really wasn't much difference between commercial and sport; it was sort of all the same animal. Now we've seen tremendous jumps develop in sport diving equipment. Do you align yourself with any of these manufacturers, or do you take the best elements of that and design it yourself?» There's a lot of looking at everybody else's equipment to see how they achieve better breathing. I look closely at Scubapro and Oceanic every year when they come out with their new lines. I also look at Atomic and U.S. Divers. All of those regulators are so good, it's incredible. If you come out with a super fine-tuned regulator and it only works once, that's no good. Commercial divers would line up to shoot us if we turned out something like that, because reliability is more important than anything.

Your manufacturing facility has been in Santa Barbara, California for years but I know that you recently established offices in Panama City to put you at close proximity to the Navy Experimental Diving Unit. When did you make this move and how is this working out for you?» Well, we started about seven years ago. We hired one man and had a small shop and we've grown over time. We've got five acres of ground and 10,000 square feet of buildings. It's testing, research and development only, no manufacturing. We're now an official testing body for

CE marking for the European market. We're one of the only dive test houses in the U.S. that can do that.

You have a unique relationship with the Navy. I can't think of another government contractor in a similar industry segment that has had the same side-by-side relationship. 》The Navy changes personnel every two years – they rotate, and you have to get along with the new guys. It's not so much creating and maintaining the relationship, though we do

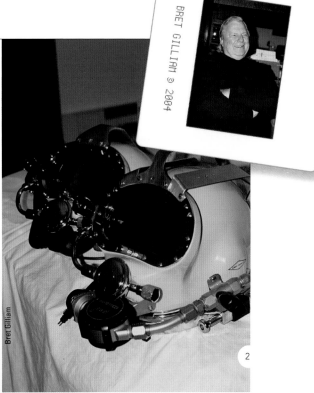

1. Gilliam and Morgan during interview session, 2004
2. The helmet used worldwide by naval, commercial and scientific divers

that, it's more that our focus has always been to provide our Navy with the best equipment possible in the world. By working very closely with them we always know what they need next.

In addition to knowing what they need next, do you ever suggest what they need next? 》Oh, sure. That's working together.

You've been doing this for 50-some years now. What do you think has been the biggest innovation in commercial gear? 》You have to realize that the original Dean Siebe Gorman design of heavy gear helmet – the old metal and copper helmets, dominated commercial diving for 150 years. Though there were diving schools, training was done through apprenticeships, serving as tenders first, then working your way into diving over many years. The biggest factor that changed all that was offshore oil. The offshore oil companies met with commercial divers, myself included, and asked how many commercial divers there were in the United States. We estimated that there might be 400, part-time divers included. This was in the early 60s. They said they

needed 5,000 divers over a ten-year span. The first thing that had to be done was to transition from the heavy gear – which took two to three years to learn, into something that scuba divers could quickly learn to use. So we set up the schools and the equipment to teach these folks. For years we had the market all to ourselves because we had patents on our basic designs in place so that they could not be copied. We're still patenting new things, but now we've got serious competition for the first time. It's good; it's gotten us off our butts. We're working our fannies off trying to stay ahead of the competition.

Let's face it, you can go along with a good piece of equipment you have patents on, then when the patents run out, the competition can come in, take your equipment, reverse engineer it and start right where you are. They paid nothing for engineering so they're able to sell their copies of your product cheaper. This takes away, or at least reduces your market share. That's where we are now. We're busting our rears to develop new innovations to beat the competition and as a result, there are some interesting paths opening up to us. I mean, how does one improve something that's already working very well?

97

For instance, the diver's telephone. Instead of sending your voice messages back and forth on wire, you line the diver with the same wire and heat the diver with that same power source. It's those kinds of things that are in the future. Companies fight change because they don't want to inventory a new set of gear. Divers, however, are pretty innovative. If you've got a new gimmick or gadget, they'll go for it if it assists them on the job. Therein lies my paradox. I couldn't introduce something new when we had an iron grip on the market with our patents because nobody wanted change. Now that there's competition, divers are becoming more interested in new innovations – from me as well as the competition. It'll be interesting to see what direction this all goes.

Six or seven years ago, there was a tremendous interest in rebreathers within the sport and tech communities, it's interesting that they really didn't go anywhere. We've seen almost an even dozen rebreather manufacturers, of which maybe only two or three are left. What do you think happened? ⟫ Historically, though easy to use, rebreathers have always been a lot of work to maintain and prepare, whereas open circuit rigs require so little work it's incredible. They've even improved and become easier to use. You can throw them in the bilge and they still work. All you need to do is get somebody to fill the tank and you can just keep diving. If there's any maintenance at all, it's only once or twice a year when you take them in for a tune-up – replace the o-rings and stuff. That's far, far simpler than tearing down your rig and putting Sodasorb in it, or whatever you're using for absorbent, then making sure your bags are dry and on and on and on. So for the casual sport diver, they're discouraged by the amount of maintenance involved. First, they're intrigued. They expect more bottom time. They expect quieter diving. And they get that but pay for it in maintenance, and they pay for it in money, whereas open circuit scuba, you can go anywhere in the world and get your tank filled. You don't even have to take a tank with you. They've got tanks. All you've got to do is show up and they'll outfit you where you go. You can't do that with a rebreather. We've made a few – strictly for the military.

At one point there were many boutique-like rebreather companies but the only major player

to ever really set their foot firmly in that market was Dräger. They did their own distribution for a couple of years, but eventually dropped that and handed it off to U.S. Divers, who apparently didn't even want it. They actually had the best semi-closed circuit rebreather out there. A lot of people still use them. It's too bad, it's a good product but it's not getting any support. ⟫ Well, Dräger, you've got to understand, is an old line company that has been around for years and I really don't know whether they have any enthusiastic divers left on their payroll.

Schooner *Mayan* outbound for the islands with David Crosby at the helm.

Bev Morgan

That brings up another interesting note. When you got into this sport, it seemed that all the manufacturers were original first-generation divers. There were you, Dick Long, Dick Bonin, Gustaf Dalla Valle and Bob Hollis. Nowadays, it appears that many of these companies have been absorbed into other public companies and I wonder what you think about the leadership here? Can corporate suit bean-counters really lead diving innovation? » Apparently not. I'll probably get skinned alive and roasted for saying that.

Big companies have a lot going for them. They have big budgets, big money and mass production. They can buy things so much cheaper than the little guy. The little guy gets out priced by the big guy. In the beginning, when I got into the business, the big guys didn't even know what I was doing. I now sometimes wonder if the big guys even understand what the sport is about. They've got money, but will they continue to come up with innovations? Well, whoever comes up with the innovations, if the big companies are quick enough to either buy them out, absorb them, make a

deal with them or make their own version, then they'll continue to dominate the market. Where are the young entrepreneurs? Well, I've got a young fellow in my business from Poland who's willing to work 17 hours a day and bust his rear. He can start out seeing my stuff, which is fine, there's nothing wrong with that, and he's willing to invest the time to try and improve it and he is doing a good job. For the first time, I'm looking over my shoulder at competition. So what's going to get Scubapro, U.S. Divers and Mares to look over their shoulders and think the new guys are gaining on them?

The guys at Atomic have done a pretty good job about making them look over their shoulder. 》They sure have. Here's where you had somebody in the business working as employees who pulled out and went off on their own and did well. Are we going to see more

of that? Sure, but I bet the suits at Scubapro won't like it. Letting Doug and Dean go (the founders of Atomic) had to be one of dumbest things Scubapro ever did!

As a photographer, you've been chronicling the sport of diving and surfing for half a century, I'm interested in what you think of the new digital camera systems. Is this going to have applications in commercial diving as it is in the filming industry and everything else? 》Oh, sure. Digital photography is creeping up on us like a monster. You know those pictures you hate to throw away but keep anyway? You look at them every now and then and go, "No, that one's not good enough." Now I can manipulate whatever was technically wrong with those photographs and restore them digitally. Recently, I've been interested in murals and the printed

David Crosby steers the schooner
Mayan while Morgan looks on

We've also seen the same revolution come along in motion picture video. Now you can buy a digital sport camera, toss it in a housing for a fraction of what it used to cost, and produce better stuff than we did in professional broadcast systems even 15 years ago. 》I recently spoke with Al Giddings, he's now got an outfit that can digitize and improve the stuff he used to shoot as A quality. It's just phenomenal. Yeah, the motion picture thing is growing too.

Maybe some day we too can run ourselves through one of these things and rejuvenate our tired bodies. How old are you now, Bev? 》Seventy-six. Inside, I feel 20, but there are certain things that are more difficult to do nowadays.

It looks to me like you'll continue going strong for a long time yet. As I told my wife, "If you pass away before me, I'll throw you a lavish funeral... and I'll bring a date!" You've managed to go through the turnstile of marriage quite a few times. How many wives have you had? 》I've had three wives... and I've lost three expensive houses.

So you're probably happier just leasing rather than owning, I take it? 》Houses or women? I'm always open.

One of your best friends over the years has been David Crosby, of *Crosby, Stills & Nash* fame, who is actually a rabid diver as well. 》I had come back from a trip to Palau when a friend of mine invited me to Maui to photograph whales. He was the skipper on Crosby's boat, *Mayan*. So I went over and got on the boat and met David. You know I really enjoyed his music and it turned out he was an avid diver. He loved the diving and so we had a great time. He had this big old Alden schooner and he used it to get away from the crazy side of the record business and concert tours. It worked out well; I had a lot of underwater camera gear and time to break away to do things. Crosby had a great sailboat set up for diving, enjoyed diving and was a good guy. The boat always also seemed to have a lot of very good-looking girls aboard. Lets see now: big sailboat, lots of dive gear, lots of camera gear, good food, good music, good friends, lots of money, time enough between concerts and work to go anywhere we

word on a photograph in combination with enormous photographs. I've got photographs that I make wall-size, four foot by eight foot. I can stand back and almost feel as if I could walk into the picture. It's almost like *Dorian Gray* in reverse, my pictures aren't getting old, I am. But I can actually visualize walking into these prints and the bigger they get, the more I can see it and the more I can have a sense of being there now. I'm getting older and many of my friends are croaking so it's really neat to have a wall of photographs of friends – living and dead. I can vividly walk right into that picture and remember the details of the time. Well, I couldn't do that before. I had a wet darkroom but to make a big print took an enormous amount of labor and help. Now, I can clean up the picture or leave it as is and print it out at any size I want – well actually, I can print eight to a hundred feet. I can do it all myself.

wanted. That started some 30 years ago.

We'd take off, go through the Panama Canal and over to the Bahamas and go diving for a few months. Fly home to work and then meet the *Mayan* at some new place. Sometimes in Tahiti, sometimes Hawaii, sometimes California. It sure has been fun. Actually, I guess that might be an understatement. Trust me, we didn't get bored. We're still at it.

deck and took him home. Now, that's pretty dedicated! He's also a dedicated sailor. And a damned good one too.

Jay Leno had a great riff about Crosby's liver. He said that Crosby might have been pretty wild and crazy but was a pretty good businessman. But this time he might have made a big mistake. His transplant cost about

David is a serious diver and I've known many divers in my life. He's probably the most dedicated diver I know. I'm not saying he's the best diver in the world, but I don't know anyone who enjoys diving more. Let me put it this way: He had a liver transplant, he couldn't walk and his wounds were not quite healed, but he wanted to go diving so badly that he called me up. He wanted to do one more dive in case he croaked in the middle of his liver replacement recovery. I dressed him in a wetsuit that I built specially for him. I took him out on the boat and we winched him into the water, pulled him around underwater then winched him back out, put him on

$40,000 but the liver they took out of him had a "street value" of over a hundred grand! Hell, it might have been worth three times that!

At one point you preserved his boat for him when he had to go away for a while. Yeah, I bought the boat from him to protect it when he had some legal and health problems. It's a nice boat. Wooden Alden schooner, built in 1947 if my memory serves. She's been rebuilt a couple of times. David actually just got through rebuilding her for 10 times the amount of money I could buy an equal fiberglass one. I keep telling him let me get at it with my fiberglass and you won't have to rebuild it again.

1. Crosby and Morgan, Santa Barbara harbor, 2003
2. Schooner *Mayan* under full sail

That would probably violate his "wooden ships" ethic. »Absolutely. It's all in jest because he loves that boat and he wants to make one more go at the South Pacific so he'll probably do it.

You guys think you might have a little fun along the way? »I'm sure that we can find what it takes.

I interviewed Greg McGillivray, the IMAX film director and producer, when he was doing *Coral Reef Adventure* about a year-and-a-half or so ago. He finally decided that the perfect music for the film was going to be a lot of the original music of *Crosby, Stills & Nash* and was delighted to discover that David was a diver and willingly lent their efforts to this project. »I didn't know that.

As good a friends as we are, we give each other a lot of space. For instance, by the time you go to print on this it will be old news, but David had some trouble back east recently (busted for possession of marijuana, but later acquitted). And instead of me calling him up and going, "Oh, my God, what happened?" I figure if he needs my help, he'd call me. Let him slay his own dragons. I've got my dragons, he's got his.

David Crosby in trouble with the law for smoking grass? Who would believe it? »Well, I don't think the latest incident was too big a shocker!

Aside from being one of the musical geniuses of the era, he's managed to remain current and cutting edge from – well, from all the way back to the days of the *Byrds* to what they're still doing now, but he hasn't exactly been the poster child for clean living. »He's one of the brightest guys I've ever known. I mean, I've known a lot of Ph.D.s that couldn't hold a candle to that guy's brain. It's just one of those things. And like he says, when somebody asks, "Are you really David Crosby?" he just says, "Somebody's gotta be."

You've always had this trademark mustache, now I see a respectable, clean-shaven face. Will we see another launch of this mustache? »Oh, of course. The last mask I developed has a pod that comes off on the lower end that seals across your upper lip and for someone with a reasonable mustache such as yours; it's not a problem. Mine however, was so big and bushy that when I put on the mask and tried to get the regulator through the hair, I'd get a mouthful of it.

You've been the driving force in your company for all these years, but didn't you bring one of your kids into the business? »Right. Connie, my youngest daughter, got interested in the business and came in. She's learning the business end of things and doing a great job.

Back in the days when you were trying to convince commercial diving companies to go from heavyweight brass hats to lightweight commercial gear, did you ever envision that someday, an attractive, beautiful lady would be running the world's largest commercial diving company? »No, I got pegged for that a few times. ■

ALL PHOTOS FROM CHUCK NICKLIN COLLECTION EXCEPT AS NOTED

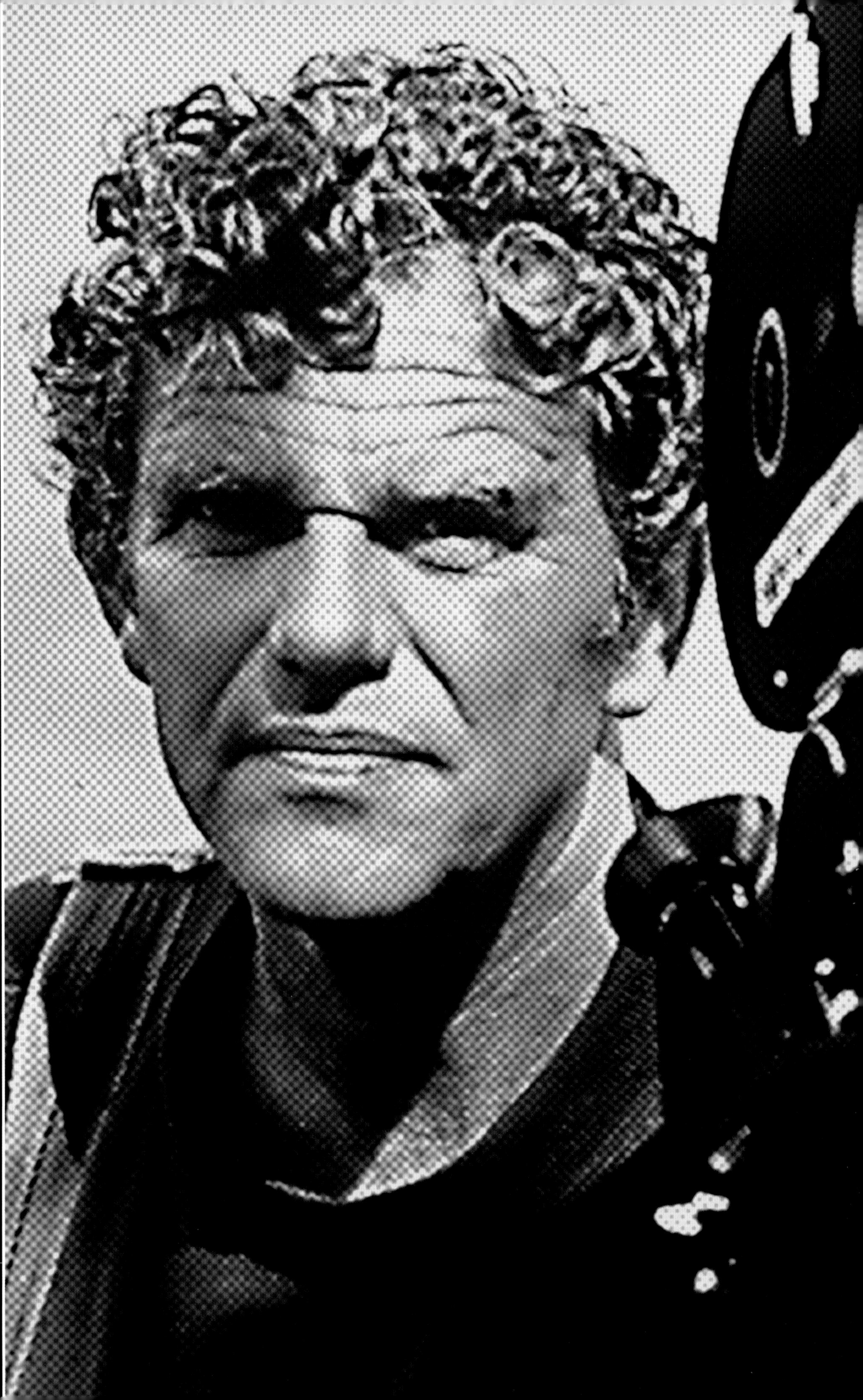

Chuck Nicklin

RETAIL PIONEER
AND FILMMAKER

BY ERIC HANAUER

BASEBALL HALL OF FAMER LEO DUROCHER ONCE SAID, "NICE GUY'S FINISH LAST

The first time I met Chuck, I was presenting a slide show on the Red Sea to a tough audience from the San Diego Underwater Photographic Society. At the time they were putting on the most prestigious underwater film festival on the west coast. »

For two days every year they filled the giant civic opera house for their shows. I was a carpetbagger from Orange County trying to get my slideshow accepted in the show, and felt about as welcome as Bill Clinton at the Fox News studios. When I finished the presentation, I looked at the frowning faces of the judges. But Chuck walked up to me and said, "Congratulations. That was the best show we've seen here in a long time." I was blown away that Chuck Nicklin, world renowned photographer, cinematographer, and diving pioneer, would make the effort to encourage a nobody like me.

Chuck has encouraged a lot of nobodies who later became somebodies.

Some of today's leading underwater shooters, including Howard Hall, Marty Snyderman, and his son, Flip, got their start working for Chuck at the Diving Locker. Unlike photographers who feel threatened by newcomers, Chuck is secure in his own ability to keep raising the bar. And he's still raising that bar as he approaches his 80th birthday.

Most divers of the pioneer era have hung up their fins or moved on to the great coral reef in the sky. Chuck is still at the top of his game, traveling the world and capturing the action in high definition video, and leading trips to exotic locations with his wife, Roz. He has been an underwater shooter for nearly 60 years, ranging from stills in *National Geographic* to Hollywood movies, television, and IMAX films. Beginning as a breath-hold spearfisherman before the introduction of scuba, Chuck opened one of the west coast's first dive shops, the San Diego Diving Locker. He learned from some of the early legends: Jim Stewart, Connie Limbaugh, and Ron Church; then helped the next generation get started.

During the years he owned the Diving Locker, it became a Mecca for traveling diving dignitaries coming through San Diego. Marty Snyderman recalls, "I don't know if it was design or by good luck. But there wasn't another store anywhere in the world that I'm aware of that had that kind of body of energy about photography at that time. Chuck was certainly the leader of all that."

Mary Lynn Price, a rising star in underwater video, is another shooter who credits Nicklin with getting her started. In 1995 she went with his group on her first foreign dive trip, to the Bahamas. In the middle of a shark feed, Chuck handed her his Hi-8 video camera and signaled her to start shooting.

"Chuck has been my underwater mentor ever since," she said. Mary Lynn, in turn, has been his mentor in editing on computers. "He made the transition to the computer age before many of us did, and is one of the most computer comfortable people I've met," she concluded.

Nicklin is constantly on the move to exotic places, organizing and running trips. He keeps threatening to retire, but several friends have been on "Chuck's last trip" four or five times. His media of choice today is high definition video, and he hasn't lost that magic touch. The hardest thing in underwater video is shooting macro subjects without camera movement. Nicklin is a master at that, despite never using a tripod. He's still setting the standard for people half his age. ∎

Q+A

How did you get interested in diving? »When I first moved here from Massachusetts, I'd look down the cliffs at the ocean and thought that's really neat. After I got out of the Navy I went down to La Jolla Cove one day because I just had this urge for the beach. There was a kid in the water with a diving mask. I asked his father, "What is that?" He asked if I wanted to borrow it. So I used this little kid's mask, one of those round, hard ones by Sea Dive. I looked around and said, "This is for

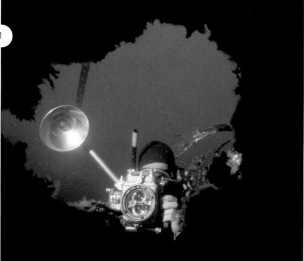

1. With Rolleimarine camera system, 1956
2. Killing time on a deco hang with an apple and a magazine
3. Spearfishing yellowtail, 1958

me." A relative in the Navy bought me a pair of black Owen Churchill UDT fins. My Sea Dive mask came from a local sporting goods store; its hard rubber edge had to be sanded to make a seal. An old Navy sweater kept me from freezing on free dives for lobsters and abalone.

Do you remember your first scuba dive? »The first time I ever went underwater and breathed off anything, it was a gas mask and a little bottle of oxygen... I went to Mission Bay with my father and he put a rope on me. I said, "If you see me stop moving around, pull me in." I turned this thing on to take a breath, held it, turned it off. This was repeated for every breath... for maybe five minutes. I thought there's got to be a better way.

I was in the small grocery business, too poor to buy one of these fancy Aqua-Lungs. The first day of abalone season, it was a tradition to go to Bird Rock in our wool sweaters. I scammed a short Pirelli dry suit, with a band around the waist. Over the top of that I would wear a long john top and bottom. It looked weird, but was necessary to protect the suit. I spent

all my free time talking diving. In the back room of the grocery store I had pictures of diving on the wall, I had scrapbooks, and was gung ho for diving.

When did you start on the Aqua-Lung? »In 1953. I had a friend, Bob Casebolt, who was working at Convair. They had a dive club, Delta Divers, and half dozen tanks. Bob wanted to learn how to dive and so did I. So I joined the club even though I didn't work at Convair. My instructor was George Zorilla. He was an Olympic swimmer out of Argentina, was in the swimming business for a long time, and taught my sons, Flip and Terry, how to swim. All the course consisted of was talking about it for a while, putting on those little weenie 38 cubic foot tanks, a double hose regulator, and making a dive at the shores. I didn't really get a C-card till I started the Diving Locker and took a quick course through the city of San Diego to be an instructor.

We did some weird things, makes we wonder how we got through it. I remember being on the bottom with a bag of ten abalone, the legal limit in those days... I

was starting to breathe hard, kicking away and starting up, and all of a sudden my feet hit the bottom. I hadn't moved at all... was scared to death and dropped the abalone. I couldn't drop the weight belt; it was a cartridge belt with lead in the pockets.

We used to dive in the north canyon and shoot rockfish at about 140 feet, deep enough so their eyes would pop. We knew we should be decompressing, but weren't quite sure how the whole thing worked. So we would take little 38s and lie down at the bottom of the pool at Buena Vista Gardens, thinking we were decompressing. This was probably 45 minutes after we got out of the water. I was a hunter in the early days. The last black sea bass I speared weighed 376 pounds. They would dive down and wrap themselves in the kelp; you're free diving 60, 80 feet to cut them out. Get

that line wrapped around you and you're in a lot of trouble. I did all that and feel sorry about it now.

For ten years I spent any free time at the ocean, free diving and spear fishing. And that's how I met Connie Limbaugh (diving officer at Scripps) and Jim Stewart (Limbaugh's successor) and all those guys, through free diving.

Do you remember how you met Connie? ›› A friend of mine, Homer Rydell, was a salesman for Gallo wine, and he invited me to his house to meet Connie, and we went lobster diving at the cove before it was a preserve. Later we went on an overnight Baja trip together along with Elizabeth Taylor's brother, Howard, and over time became close friends. Limbaugh, Stewart, Andy Rechnitzer, and Wheeler North (researchers from Scripps Institution of Oceanography) were partners in a part-time consulting business, doing their research out of the back room of what would become the Diving Locker. In 1959, a contract on testing the offshore sewage outfall brought in enough money to expand the business into a dive shop. The problem was that they all were graduate students, and had neither the time nor the retailing expertise to run the shop. Rydell recommended me. I was in a small business, knew when the checks would clear and all that stuff; that's good training for running a dive shop. They had a choice of Ron Church or me. They finally decided I would be the manager and Ron would work with me.

The Diving Locker opened on June 15, 1959. I'll remember the date forever. June 14, 1959, was the only authenticated shark attack off San Diego, the day before we opened. Business was really slow. Our entire budget of $5,000 was spent on a Rix compressor. But because of Limbaugh's reputation and his connection with Rene Bussoz (Aqua-Lung), the manufacturers stocked us on credit. Jimmy (Stewart) and Andy (Rechnitzer) and those guys did more than just help running the store. Their reputation made our store a sort of scientific headquarters. Anyone in San Diego on a scientific mission went to the Diving Locker and that helped us get started. Many a day we had a lot of empty boxes on display... because we just didn't have the capital we needed. When Bev Morgan was closing his surf shop, he came down and taught me how to make wet suits. I was a one-man show for a while, made my first suit on the floor of my house. I would sell them the suit, cut it, glue it, try it on them, and take their money.

During our first class, Jacques Cousteau was in town. The class was in the back room, and we introduced him. He said, "This is your introduction to the ocean, I hope it's as good for you as it is for me." Every once in a while someone from that class staggers through the door and asks, "Do you remember when Cousteau welcomed us to the ocean?"

What was it like to run a retail dive shop in those days? » The main reason for diving was to gather abalone, halibut, and all that. That was the basis of our business. The main lines in those days were US Divers, Swimaster with Duck Feet fins, Waterlung, the first serious single hose regulator, and Voit was in it then. Mike Nelson on *Sea Hunt* used to use Voit. In those days we had a sort of crane-like device outside the store. When people shot big fish we'd take a picture and the newspaper was just eager to have that kind of stuff. Rollo Williams was the outdoor editor of the San Diego newspaper, and we'd talk to him a couple times

a week about the water temperature, the halibut are in, that kind of stuff. There's always word of mouth but in those days there were so few divers, the ones that were there got lots of attention.

How big did you guys become? How many stores did you have? » At one time we had four. We bought out Dick Long's retail business and ran that for a while. We didn't make a lot of money but we had a lot of fun; there were a lot of things going on.

When were you at your peak? » Probably in the mid 1970s.

What happened? » The biggest thing that happened was Flip decided he wanted to be a photographer. And Terry was sort of interested, and I was gone all the time. We had some poor management. I think the reason the Diving Locker finally was sold is that I didn't want to do it any more, and neither did Terry. It's tough on guys now that want to be in the business. Werner Kurn (Ocean Enterprises' owner) is complaining about the Internet. He told me about five people that came in, a family. Looked at all the suits, tried the fins on, checked out the regulators, and were there for three hours talking to his employees. When Werner asked, "Can we start to write this up?" the guy said, "We're going to buy it on the Internet." What happens is that guys in business these days stock the equipment, set up a location, hire the employees, and don't get to make the sale. Service and classes and travel are going to be a bigger part of the business as sales go south.

One of the things they have to do is make people realize diving is fun. It was so stupid and I talked about it many times; start classes that had their lectures and pool sessions in San Diego and then take them to someplace warm. Those people will stay in diving. To

1. Showing off the days catch (Nicklin in middle) in front of the first Diving Locker retail store, San Diego, 1959
2. Diving Locker retail store, 1971

take people, especially those who are older and have a little money, and put them in that restrictive wet suit and throw them in that dirty water and in the surf, that doesn't make customers. Then you've got to make it a little jazzy for the kids. They want something extreme.

What's your opinion of the tech movement? ⟩⟩I think there's a place for it. It's not enough to make the sport grow. I had four friends who were good tech divers but they didn't make it.

What about today's equipment? ⟩⟩One of the things that makes it tough on the diving business is that equipment lasts too long. If you're in the camera business you got to get your shoes on because it's changing so fast. But in diving, there's not a lot of reason to buy stuff. Things don't change much.

How did you get started in underwater photography? ⟩⟩Connie and those guys picked Ron Church to run a film section at the store. Ron was the photographer for Convair; I think his early background was aerial photography. We used to go out with an old Rolleimarine with 12 exposures. He'd shoot while I looked for a subject, then I'd shoot while he'd look for a subject and we'd come in with six pictures apiece. Now you can go down and shoot 350 pictures if you want. Ron and I got along pretty well. It was his idea to start Underwater Photographic Society (UPS). He built a darkroom in the back of the store. That was our aim: to build a business out the Diving Locker name.

When Connie Limbaugh died in a diving accident, his wife, Nan, asked if I wanted his camera gear. So all of a sudden I had a fairly sophisticated 16mm camera and a Rolleimarine. I had a base. I had the wonderful friendship of guys like Wheeler and Jimmy that would steer photography to me. I had Ron to help me, and could get away, because after a couple of years there were other employees. It was a big advantage to be able to get away. When a job came up, a lot of other fellows couldn't do it because they worked five days a week. Convair would call with their submarine stuff and I would get involved. At first I was scraping money together to buy a roll of film. Later it was, I just sold a picture so I can buy some more film.

Your big break came on a whale shoot, didn't it? ⟩⟩That's right. One day in the early 1960s, we were diving off La Jolla on Al Santmeyer's boat, *Duchess*. Heading across the bay, we spotted a whale spouting. It was a Bryde's whale caught in a net, the ropes digging into its flukes. It was weak from trying to breathe and barely struggling. Bill De Court and I jumped in, dived to 20 feet, and cut the whale loose… shooting pictures all the time. It was just one of these things that hit at the right time. Nobody knew anything about whales then. Our pictures were

111

in the paper, in *Time* magazine; people were calling from everywhere to interview us because we rode a whale. So this got a lot of publicity. I was getting a lot of calls, "You're the guy who shot the whale, can you shoot this?" So the first thing you know, I was doing more of that kind of thing.

What was your first movie assignment? » It was a Hollywood B-film called *Chubasco*. The producer director was a friend of Wheeler's and he suggested me. They wanted shots of local tuna boats at water level, in the net with the tuna and sharks. I said, "Yeah, I can do that." They said, "Bring diving gear. We'll supply the camera; meet us at the boat in San Diego." So I got on the boat and they pointed, "Well, this is the camera." I said, "Oh my God!" It was the first big Panavision 70mm, about the size of a steamer trunk. It weighed 300 pounds and they had to put it in the water with a crane. And I had been shooting 16mm. I had no idea what it was, or how to load it, and had never even seen a roll of 70mm film. They introduced me to my camera assistant. After the producer walked off, I asked him, "What do you know about this thing?" He said, "'I know everything." I relaxed, "We are going to be a great team." So all I had to do was take it in the water and point it.

At one point I was in the net with the camera, all sorts of skipjack screaming around. A stunt man was supposed to fall in and the other actor was going to jump in and save him. So I'm in the water, the guy falls in, sinks about two feet, and panics. He can't swim. He wanted the job so badly and figured he would learn to swim when the time comes.

It was an easy time to be a photographer. Very few people were doing it. Red starfish pictures were a big deal. In the early days I did a lot of still photography. Ron Church, Chet Tussey, and I and some of the other early photographers started the Underwater Photographic Society. They used to have contests and a friend of mine, Ginny Kellogg, won with a picture of a red starfish. Even if it wasn't in focus, it was a winner.

I did the first diving on the Deep Submergence Rescue Vehicle (DSRV) built by Lockheed. Until they turned it over to the Navy, I did a lot of the photography. When they made their first deep dive, everybody got a dive on it and a plaque stating that they had ridden in it. On my plaque, they put "outside the DSRV" because I had always been on the outside to shoot it.

1. Nicklin with Ocean Eye housing and Subsea strobe, 1971
2. With Jacques Cousteau, 1968 3. Lloyd Bridges and Nicklin, 1971

How did you get started with *National Geographic*? » Bates Littlehales was a staff photographer and we had become friends during a gray whale shoot in San Diego. He was assigned to go to Turkey and shoot George Bass's expedition on a Bronze Age shipwreck. But he ruptured an eardrum on assignment in the Bahamas and recommended me to take his place. They flew me back to Washington, said to throw away all my large format film cameras, handed me a Calypso, a Seahawk housing with a Leica and a 20mm lens, and a couple of Edgerton strobes that hardly ever worked. For three days they gave me Nikons with black and white film and I'd go off and shoot in Washington. They'd process that night then tell me what they liked. They gave me the little booklet on how to shoot for *Geographic*: You need a sunset, you need a scenic with a little animal or a person, you need so many close-ups... a long list.

So I went off to Turkey and shot this story. We had a bell and a submersible decompression chamber. We swam into it at 20 feet and then they brought you up to 10 feet for the rest of your decompression. We also decompressed on a line. They had a bucket with books in it. As long as you kept the books wet they would hold together and you

That seems to be your motto now. »The "once" is getting shorter. (laughs)

16mm was expensive in those days. »That's why not many people did it. Through Scripps I'd end up with extra film, donations. People knew I was interested in it and but primarily if you wanted to shoot 16mm you

SeaCraft

had to have someone who was willing to pay for it. It wasn't like buying a one-hour videotape. I just started doing commercial things and that gave me a chance to improve my skills and learn the business.

could read underwater. We also did that on *The Deep* because we had such long decompressions.

You and Al Giddings have collaborated for many years. How did that begin? »I first met Al at the Pacific Coast spearfishing championships. Afterwards we were sitting around at Ron Church's house and he says, "I'm going to Cozumel to shoot a film with the backing of US Divers." I said, "That sounds like fun." He said, "Come on along; we'll shoot together." I replied, "I can't. I'm in business, it's hard to get away." A short time later Al was down here showing his first film, *The Painted Reefs of Honduras*, at a film festival. When he was up on the stage he said, "You all know Chuck Nicklin who owns Diving Locker. He's going to shoot with me in Cozumel." I told him, "I can't do that; I've got no money." A few days later he called and said, "This is your last chance." So I talked to my wife, Gloria, and said, "I'd really like to do this." And she said, "You only go around once."

What other kind of commercial things were you doing? »All kinds of stuff. I did a US Steel thing on FLIP (a Scripps research ship that flips vertically to do ocean measurements.) I did a beer commercial for a Mexican company, an Olympic commercial in a pool with synchronized swimmers. I did a lot of weird things. It was a very small group of people in those days, and what made it tough for new people was that the pioneers all helped each other. If Al had a job and didn't have time to do it, he'd call me. If I couldn't do it, I'd call Jack McKenney. It was a "good old boys" network. Al and Jack were the heavies. Bernie Campoli was in the Navy and he was one of the early guys. And Stan Waterman, of course.

What was it like shooting Hollywood films? »That was always fun. Some of them were sort of crazy and some of them we were more proud of than others. Everything I did in Hollywood was with Al. He and

I had a good situation in that he wanted to be the producer, director, editor, seller... he wanted to be everything. All I wanted to be was a shooter. I wasn't real competition to him. He'd do all the work, then call and say, "Chuck, your ticket's in the mail." I'd get on a plane and go somewhere in the world for a week or up to four months as a cinematographer, and when the film was over, I'd get on a plane and go home. Al would spend the next two years editing and selling

and promoting it. Al made more money but I had more fun. Al is really aggressive in the business; he's a hard worker. I was a little more independent than some of the others that worked for him, so I didn't have to take some of the hardcore rules that he would come up with. Often I was sort of the interface between the crew and Al. It always seemed to work. We worked together with Stan Waterman on *The Deep*. Al and Stan were the co-directors underwater; I was just an underwater

They told Al and Stan to come right back down to talk about the shoot tomorrow. And I had a date with Jackie Bissett that night. Maybe there is something to just being a cameraman.

Tell me more about *The Deep*. 》We were in the British Virgin Islands about a month. Peter Island was a great place. We had great parties. It was a really fun time. It wasn't tough diving, but we did a lot of dives. It was 90 feet to some parts of the wreck of the *Rhone*, and when you make five dives a day like you do when you're working with Al, we'd have an hour and half deco at the end of the day.

1. Primary underwater film crew for *The Deep*: Stan Waterman, Al Giddings and Nicklin, 1976 2. With Jackie Bissett

Were you using tables to control the dive exposures? 》No, we were using the old SOS deco-meters from Scubapro. They had an analog screen and part of the display just spelled out SURFACE. We just moved the needle up the letters slowly for safety factors.

Were any of the actors there on the *Rhone* dives? 》Oh yeah. They slipped in there for their close-ups. And Jackie did more diving than she would have. She didn't match up well with her diving stunt double. She didn't like the way that girl looked on film. So she did more of the underwater thing than she would have as a rule. Waterman and Al were the co-directors and the big shooters. I was the third cameraman. When they were shooting Jackie in the tee shirt, I was just there with my mouth hanging open. She didn't want to do it and she wasn't happy

cameraman. Peter Yates, the director, would say, "Al, you get the long shot. Stan you get the eyes. And Chuck, get something good." So I had a lot of time to go anywhere I wanted, shooting through holes and when the rushes came up I'd get a lot of comment because my shots were so different. One night we came back from the rushes in Bermuda, Yates and Peter Guber (the movie's producer) were standing in the lobby of the Southampton Princess Hotel when we got off the bus.

1. On location, 1976 2. South Pacific, 1994

with it. Peter Guber talked her into it. But she sure looked good.

What were the actors like to work with? 》Nick Nolte was crazy. He'd come in the morning just wiped out and lay on a table somewhere half asleep. But when it came time to work, he worked. Jack McKenney was his stunt double. A lot of things he did on his own too, because he wanted more in the film than just his face. In one scene when we had to swim through a wreck section to get to the jewelry, he had to hold his breath for long period. And he did it. But that night he'd be off crazy somewhere and he'd come in and look like he'd been dragged behind a car. But when it came time to film, he worked.

Robert Shaw wasn't around very much. He was friends with a lot of people in Bermuda. The last shot we had of him, where the eel came out and bites the head off the bad guy, they'd kept him all day in his hut and he was pissed. He kept drinking with one of his buddies while he waited and he was pretty wiped. I remember him sitting there just chatting while

Yates, Guber and Giddings were deciding whether it was safe to put him in the water. Al turned to me and said, "Chuck, we really got to do this. I gotta have this close-up." So Al took him by the hand and tangled him up in the line that was supposed to have entrapped him and I took the camera. In the scene he really looks distressed. Because he was distressed. He did it in five minutes. We put him in the car and sent him home and that's the last we saw of him.

And Jackie was good. She didn't like to be in the water and it was cold, but she'd get in, smile, and do what she had to do. She was really a neat lady. All three of them were all right. They're movie stars. They just go in and have their pictures taken.

What about the *James Bond* films? 》The one I felt I accomplished the most on was *For Your Eyes Only*. We worked on that movie for four months in the Bahamas. It was a nice film photographically. It was a bit hokey, but most films are a bit hokey. What we did with the cameras underwater is something I can be proud of. I've also done a bunch of funky little things where we did one or two scenes, falling into a pool or a raft. You get paid, it's part of the job, but nobody ever hears about it.

Then there's the time I spit in Sean Connery's mask. We did *Never Say Never* and there was a scene in a cave out in the Exumas. Sean was only going to be in there for his close-up but his mask wouldn't clear. In that cave there was an air space where you could get out of the water. Al and I could communicate just by looking at each other. So he looked at me waved his hand, pointed at the mask, and signaled, "get him out of here." We swam up so we could get our heads out of the water. I said, "Sean, I'm sorry but I've got to do this." He said, "Whatever it is, I really need my close-up." So I spit in his mask, put it back on his face, we went down, and got the shot.

You worked on the *Ocean Quest* television series that wasn't very well received by the diving community. How come? »They thought it was going to be the Cousteau series. It wasn't Cousteau; it was Hollywood. It could have been a lot better but it lost direction. Shawn Weatherly (Miss Universe) was a pretty lady, nice to work with, and she and I hit it off. I had time to spend with her without trying to hustle her. It was supposed to be this pretty girl having adventures, and it turned out to be this macho guy (Al Giddings) taking this pretty girl on a trip. And that's what screwed it up. Al wanted to be the hero. It could have been really great, but it turned out to be a little hokier because of the way it went.

Was Al's bends hit real or staged? »I think he had an embolism. We were diving side by side at 130 feet at San Clemente Island. We took decompression and all that. The difference was he jumped in a hot shower right after the dive. We called the Coast Guard and they were going to send a chopper, but the bubble passed and he was OK. A couple of hours later he was having dinner. But he was in big trouble for a while, and we were nervous. What was staged was Shawn crying when she didn't want to go back in the shark cage. She'd enjoyed watching the sharks. But the director told her to cry.

How long was the shoot and where did you go? »Ten months all together. We went to Antarctic, Truk, Cuba, Baja, and Newfoundland. Lots of memorable things happened. The director had a big black Zodiac with a big engine and he shipped it all the way to Newfoundland. He was proud of it. It took

the guys two days to make a trailer for it. We got it to the docks and he asked a fisherman, "Did you ever see anything like this?" He said, "Yeah, we have two or three of them in back." He could have rented one. Then we burned our hot air balloon. It caught fire in Truk. We took it all the way to Antarctica and never put it up. Shawn was great and she didn't get a very good deal out of it. It didn't help her career because she wasn't portrayed well in the film.

Several of your protégés have gone on to bigger and better things. »The best is Howard Hall. I think he's the best underwater photographer out there, period. For the kind of things Howard does like deep stuff, 3D cameras, and that stuff, he's the best. He was an employee at Diving Locker and was very interested in photography and diving. He was interested in sharks and went with me on some of the early stuff with Blue sharks when we still thought they'd bite. We were putting together the crew for *The Deep* to go to film the shark sequences in Australia. Al said we needed someone who isn't afraid to shoot some fish and attract

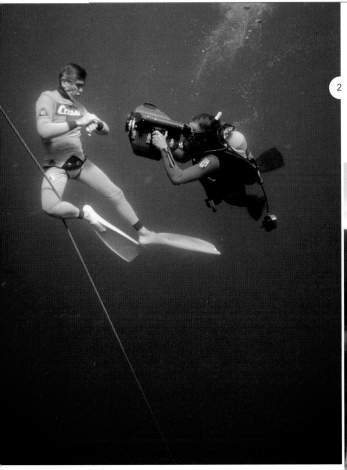

When did you realize Flip had that drive and talent and was going to be so good? »I was doing a job for Sea World, shooting Panavision film in the shark tank and Flip was shooting stills for them at that time. When he was in my way I'd be yelling and screaming and when I was in his way he'd be yelling and screaming. It got to the point when I said, "Goddam

1. Relaxing on dive boat, 1999 2. Filming breathhold diving champion, Jacques Mayol, 1988 3. Nicklin, Sylvia Earle and Al Giddings find a new use for a flooded camera dome, 1979

the sharks. I said, "I know just the guy." Howard hit it off really good with Stan Waterman. Stan took him under his wing and got him on *Wild Kingdom*. He worked on that a long time and built his ability and reputation as a professional. My only part was that I got him out there where he might get bit by a shark.

Of course there's Marty Snyderman, another guy working in the shop as an instructor. I'd come back from a trip with lots of stories and a little bit of money. And he said that's what he wanted to do. I think they were all shooting with Nikonos and the old Oceanic 35mm housing. One of my favorite people who came out of the diving locker is my son, Flip. There's some new guys, too. Mark Thurlow worked for us in the Escondido store at one time. Lance Millbrand worked as my assistant on a couple of jobs with *BBC* and he's worked really hard getting into the business.

it, this is my job," and he said, "All right, now get out of the way." That's when I realized he's serious. He's going to be tough and he wanted to be a photographer.

How about your IMAX films? »John Stoneman was the director of *Nomads of the Deep*. We did that with humpback whales and Blue sharks in Hawaii and in the Red Sea. There was a lot of competition as to who would have his hands on the IMAX camera. Flip was the still photographer on that. He shot his first humpback pictures in Hawaii and that gave him a base for going back to *National Geographic* to eventually get an assignment. I did a couple of other IMAX shoots as well, just doing scenes on location. When we shot the stuff for *Nomads of the Deep*, the first pictures of the singing whales and all that, we used scuba tanks and got away with it. But now they didn't want you to use

tanks because it would scare the whales. It would be a definite advantage to have a rebreather or a small tank.

I've heard Flip say that it's easier to shoot whales now than when he started. »It only makes sense. There's generations of them, especially in Hawaii, and their parents and grandparents are used to divers. They don't have that fear of boats and motors they used to have when everybody they saw was trying to stick a harpoon in them. Flip says some of them hang out there. You could even lay on top of them if you wanted to. Flip says while free diving, he can lay right by the pectoral fin. Sometimes what you are looking for is an inquisitive calf that hangs around while the mother is just saying, "Come on kid, we've got to go."

Do you have any strong opinions on shark feeding? »If you don't feed sharks… there won't be any left. Look at the places where they feed sharks: they are protected. And where they don't… they are fishing

them for fins. It's made people more aware and realistic about sharks and their behavior. I don't see where it does any harm. Even at Cocos, it seemed like the shark populations were getting less and less until they started protecting them.

Out of all your films, what stands out most in your mind? »I like the stuff we shot on *For Your Eyes Only* on the sunken ancient city set. That was done in the ocean, not in a tank. They laid the tile floor and the whole thing. That was also when I blew up my condo. We all had condos up there in the Bahamas. One day I was sleeping on the side of the boat because I wasn't needed until the next scene when someone woke me up and said, "You're wanted on the radio." The message was that my condo just blew up. We'd had a party the previous night and somebody left the propane on. When I left for the day and closed the condo up, the propane filled the room and a burner set it off. It blew out all the big glass doors.

Speaking of sleeping, you have the reputation of being able to sleep anywhere. ⟩⟩ My father always used to say, "Don't stand when you can sit, don't sit when you can lie down, don't stay awake when you can sleep." In the film business there is so much down time that you learn to take a break when you can because you may be diving for the next three hours.

Howard Rosenstein from Red Sea Divers out of Sharm el Sheikh in the Red Sea. It was late, the boat was loaded with too much stuff, it was rough and looked like it might sink any minute. Howard said, "What are you doing?" I'd put all my stuff into my net bag and put on my BC, and laid down and went to sleep. There was nothing I could do; if we were going in the water I was ready.

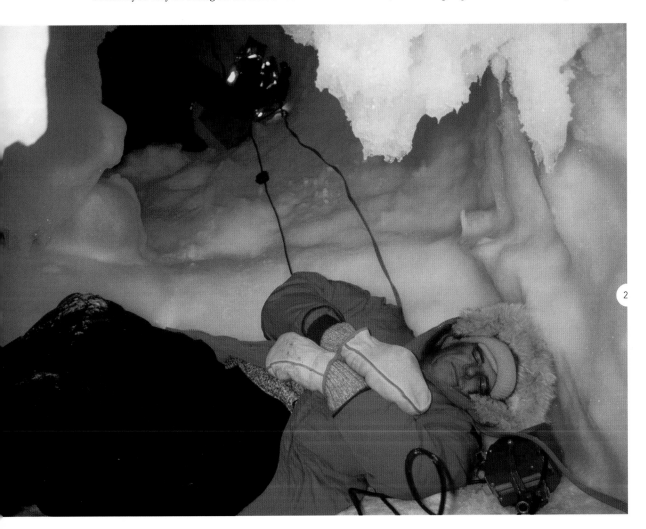

1. Grabbing "forty winks" on location 2. Sleeping in ice cave

I've always been lucky that if there's a space I can squeeze my body into, I can go to sleep. I'd crawl in on a shelf under the camera table that was covered with a blanket and go to sleep. Whenever Peter Guber or any of the big guns on *The Deep* showed up to start the day's activities, a camera assistant would pound on the table and I'd crawl out.

One time I was diving with David Doubilet and

In all those years, you must have had some close calls. ⟩⟩ The closest call, and I think the most dangerous diving I ever did, was on the *Andrea Doria*. I was with Al and Jack McKenney. We were diving air and wreck deck is about 170, 180 feet. It was really dirty and cold, and if you miss the ascent line, you'd be in trouble because of deco and current. We got to the bottom and I was using the K100 (movie camera). It was a hand wind and the trouble was that if you wound it too far it would stick. We hit the deck and started off and

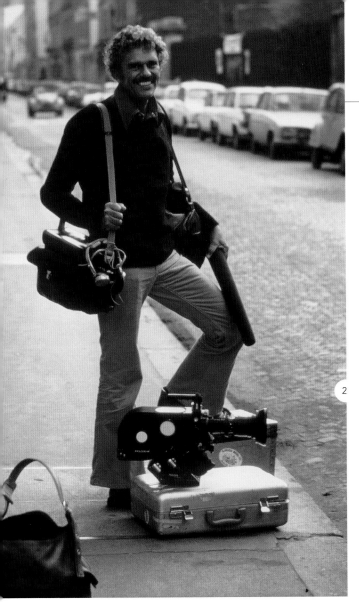

1. Filming a river dolphin up the Amazon, 1994
2. Waiting for a ride in Paris, 1971

I signaled, "My camera isn't working." They signaled back, "See you later." So I pounded on the camera and got it working and filmed the ghost nets where lots of fish got trapped and died. I sort of kept track of where the ascent line was. Then Al and Jack showed up and we started up the line. Jack was right in front of me and all of a sudden kicked my mask off. So my mask is down around my throat, I've got a camera in one hand, a light in the other and I'm saying, "Oh, I've got to get this stuff together." Putting the light under my arm, getting the mask going…

Another thing that happened on one of those *Doria* dives is that Al and I were very competitive. On one of those dives he found a plaque that said "2nd class cabin" in three languages and he thought that was hot. On the next dive I found the plaque that said

"1st class cabin" in three languages. It was a plastic thing on a piece of wood and I stuck it in inside my wetsuit. When we got to the deco stop, I signaled Al, "Look at this," and I reached inside my suit and pulled out just the wood. I'd lost all the stuff with the printing on it.

How about close calls with animals? I got nailed by that lionfish in Lembeh last year. I've never been bit, never been bent. In Vanuatu one time I rolled off the boat on to a Silvertip shark and really spooked it. It came in on me and I had to beat it off with the camera. But considering all the things I've done and all the places I've been, the most pain I had was that lionfish a few months ago. But I only missed one dive.

When did you make the transition to video? I always wanted to do the next new thing. I had one of the first video systems around here, an old JVC unit with a separate deck. The housing was a round thing that looked like a porcupine. Being new to video, I thought that I'd do it all down there; shoot and edit. Well, you don't. You shoot it and edit later. It gave me a chance to shoot more on my own without a budget because the price of tape was so much more reasonable than film. I've always been on the forefront of the people shooting video. Even now, as soon as they came out with high def that was in my price range, I jumped on it.

My idea of making a film is to do it on iMovie sort of like offline, hand it to Mary Lynn Price and have her clean it up. I'm not too excited about spending the rest of my life editing. I'd like to spend the rest of my life shooting. If I can get away with editing simply I'll do it. When I get caught up. (laughs)

Why did you start the San Diego Video club? I felt that some of the still photographers hadn't accepted the idea that video was here to stay. There wasn't much support for video through the traditional photo groups. We were having meetings at the Diving Locker and I thought we ought to discuss video. It sort of outgrew that and we started picking up people who were interested in video. Mary Lynn really pushed for it and that sort of got it started. Then I started thinking we ought to have a way to share it. And that was the idea of the San Diego Undersea Film Exhibition: to share the stuff

Off Hawaii, 2006

we worked so hard on and give more people an opportunity to present stuff because all they needed was five minutes. The first one was at the San Diego Zoo's auditorium and that wasn't quite big enough. With the new theater at the Natural History Museum, it's become a successful and very rewarding thing. It encourages a lot of people not only to do video, but to have more respect for the ocean. It not only shares our chance to show what we're doing but also shares how important the ocean is and how it should be protected.

I really reflect on the old shit I used as camera equipment. What I use now I can hold in the palm of my hand. I can carry it on the plane in my shoulder bag. With my old Arriflex and stuff, I used to fill four Igloos. It's really great. Not only has being a cinematographer become easier, but the quality is so much better. I'm shooting stuff that's so sharp and so exciting that I can't wait to go into the water. That's why I'm going to New Guinea. I didn't have anything going on and said, "I've got to go somewhere." And when I take the stuff I shot with my high def camera and plug it into my high def video, I get so excited I can hardly stand it. I say, "Oh, I've got to do more of this." I think that's why I've always been in the forefront because I always wanted new challenges and wanted to make it better.

What do you see in the future of diving? »Pretty soon it's going to be a travel business with a little diving. The tail is wagging the dog. They've got to make it fun and still make it exciting. There's no excitement anymore. We're too careful. I think the best thing that's happened is some of the shark feeds and stuff. Just to look at Garibaldi fish isn't enough. People want excitement, especially the kids. Thank god, there's photography. Otherwise there wouldn't be any growth in diving. Everybody's got an underwater camera now. You don't have to be big-time any more. When the Nikonos came along, all of a sudden there was a push into photography. Now the same thing is happening with the digital point & shoots. Roz has this eight-megapixel camera in a housing and the whole thing is $400. It's not underwater photography any more: it's photography underwater. Photography is bigger than the underwater. Does that make sense? It's become more important than the diving.

How does that translate into growth for diving? »Some of my travel customers are going back to stills. It's so easy to handle the stills compared to taking a piece of videotape and making it into something people want to see.

Since the death of Jacques Cousteau, there doesn't seem to be a figurehead for diving. Do you see anybody on the horizon? »Howard Hall could be great, but isn't the kind of guy that wants to be. Someone could promote him and make him into the diving god. He looks good; he is good. But he isn't interested. He'd rather fly his airplane.

Do you dive locally any more? »I dove cold water for many years and I used it all up. I don't do any cold water diving any more. Been there and done that. Unfortunately 90 percent of the US is cold. It's not a good place to dive unless you get on an airplane and go someplace warm like Florida. You've got to get people in the water without making them miserable. Instead of trying to get them to take another course, get them in the water and let them count fish.

As you approach the age of 80, what accommodations are you making for your age while diving? »One of the first things I do when I get on a dive boat is tell the crew, "You know, I'm getting sort of long in the tooth and I don't want to carry all this heavy stuff. So I'll swim to the back of the boat and hand up my gear. That's the bad news. The good news is that I'm a big tipper."

That's one of the things that's important to understand. You've only got so much energy and you should use it most effectively. I use it most effectively when I'm in the water. I realize I'm not as agile as I once was, but in the water I'm as comfortable as I ever was. I might be a little more conservative as far as decompression. I'm aware age may have something to do with it and I don't want to take the chance. The youngsters sometimes look at us gray-haired guys and wonder what we're going to do. But then there's a surface current and they are busting their neck, and you're hugging the bottom, passing them by and waving.

Seldom do I get excited in talking about the past. I'd rather talk about plans for the future. I'm much better at looking ahead. I'm going to be 80 real quick and I want to accomplish as much as I can while I still can. And I can. ∎

Ron&Valerie Taylor

A PAIR OF ACES FROM DOWN-UNDER

BY DOUGLAS DAVID SEIFERT

AT SEA ON A BOAT'S DECK SOMEWHERE IN THE WORLD, A TRIED AND TRUE FORMULA IS UNDERWAY.

A man suits up in diving gear and checks his video camera to make certain it is functioning properly. Once satisfied, he signals to his partner, whom, in addition to being his dive buddy, is also his model and his wife. »

She wears a bright pink wetsuit and her waist-long blonde hair is braided and tied into a ponytail with a bright pink ribbon. She, too, checks her camera, which she uses to take still pictures to compliment her husband's moving pictures, and when she is ready, she puts her regulator into her mouth and nods. Together, they jump over the side of the boat and enter the water with the purpose of documenting some aspect of the underwater wilderness. Odds are, most likely, the subject will be sharks.

Why sharks? Because this couple produces underwater documentary films and sharks sell very well. Sharks are what the public wants to see. And the reason that the public wants to see sharks and to see more sharks and more sharks is because this Australian couple has put sharks into people's living rooms for nearly 50 years. Also, they happen to have an affinity for sharks. Which is a good thing because, to the casual observer, it would appear that the husband, Ron Taylor, is trying to get the shark to attack his wife -- which is, and most will deny it, many a husband's occasional, fleeting, deep, dark, secret fantasy.

When asked by me one time, "What it's like, feeding your wife to sharks on a regular basis?" Ron says, "I know Valerie is very capable. She understands them. Valerie's had a few little nips and I've had a nip also. But it's always been our fault. We don't blame the sharks at all. Valerie's very capable with sharks."

Capable, is an understatement, even for Australians, for whom understatement seems part of the genetic makeup and national character. And referring to shark bites as "nips" is typical of Ron. Quiet, soft-spoken, patient… he defines grace under pressure. Nothing fazes him. He sometimes seems detached from, what to others would be, panic situations. He sees problems and solutions; possibilities and outcomes in very real events. For example, when Valerie was bitten by a Blue shark off San Diego many years ago, it was captured on film. The scene is instructive: Valerie lies flat on the boat deck in a great deal of pain. As crewmen try to comfort her, blood from the wound hidden beneath her wetsuit forms a large pool around her on the deck. Ron leans over her and peels back the leg of her wetsuit. What was but a single slice along neoprene is, in the flesh, a gash long, deep

and nasty, leaving her leg looking much like raw steak. He assesses the damage and says simply, very matter-of-factly, "Oh yeah, that's a bad one. A bad cut. That'll have to be stitched." And that's all Ron says.

Valerie, by contrast, can exhibit equal *sang froid* but is notorious for speaking her mind. Describing her as outspoken would be – and often is – an understatement. While she lay on the deck waiting for medical assistance, Howard Hall offered to

Camera discussion in Australia, 1962

stitch up the bite wound. She politely, but emphatically (and you are never, ever left in an ambiguous position of possible doubt about how Valerie feels about something), declined, stating she would instead wait for a proper competent plastic surgeon. In the meantime, she waited… in pain, on camera, bleeding upon the deck.

As if being bitten by a shark might not be serious. Still, the term "nips" does not do justice to the notion of a shark's bite. Take the incident that occurred when the Taylors were experimenting with a chain-mail mesh suit in 1981. The shark "merely" wrapped its mouth, jaws and teeth around Valerie's head. Its teeth in its lower jaw punctured her chin -- the only part of her anatomy that stuck out of the protection offered by the chain mail. Valerie was again in pain, but the extent of the damage seemed to be that she found it hard to chew for a few days. She did not realize that the shark's teeth had actually broken off and had lodged in the bones of her chin until she visited the dentist's office months later. The teeth were revealed, quite prominently, in her set of x-rays made as part of the annual visit. Again, the most important thing was Ron had captured "the action" on film.

They are true diving pioneers: working professionals that have neither stopped nor stalled in a nearly 50 year (so far) career. The story of their life together and their life in the sea is both the history of scuba diving and a mirror to hold up to the now-popular world of scuba diving today. In the world of diving, if you think you've invented something, odds are Ron and Valerie Taylor did it first and did it a long time ago.

For instance: if you're a male photographer trying to meet a pretty girl at a dive club by using the "Won't you model for my camera?" ploy, nice try. But Ron (quiet, mild-mannered, shy Ron!) invented that trick when he met Valerie at the St. Georges Spearfishing Club, back in 1958.

You want to go photograph a Great White shark in South Australia? Sorry, Ron Taylor was the first person to try (and succeed) at that in 1965 and, by the way, without the benefit of a cage. The still frame blow-ups from that movie footage remain their most successful and best-selling image.

Doing a bit of macro photography with extension tubes and framers? Ron

made Valerie the first-ever set in the early seventies. She parlayed her pictures into a cover feature in *National Geographic.*

Fancy exploring the ocean, discovering new dive locations and reefs? A casual perusal of the names of dive sites on the Great Barrier Reef, in Papua New Guinea, in Indonesia and throughout the South Pacific reveal a frequency of places named "Valerie's Reef."

Are you a scuba instructor scheming to teach the rich and famous? During a cruise in Indonesia, Valerie Taylor did teach a man listed on the ship's passenger manifest as "Michael Jagger" how to scuba dive. She called him Michael even though he kept insisting, "Everyone calls me Mick." Well, Mick, "You Can't Always Get What You Want".

The list goes on and on.

On March 30, 1969, Ron and Valerie arrived in Durban, South Africa, to begin a six-month, 12,000-mile odyssey that Valerie describes as "the greatest adventure of my life." The film project was *Blue Water, White Death.*

In 1974, the Taylors were approached by Hollywood producers Darryl Zanuck and David Brown. They were making a movie of the book *Jaws* and it was being directed by a young guy named Steven Spielberg. Ron flew to Hollywood and met with the production designers. They were building three mechanical sharks for their location shooting on Martha's Vineyard and the fake sharks were very realistic-looking. But the producers knew that they could only use fleeting glimpses of the mechanical shark and for the scene where the shark attacks the cage holding marine biologist Matt Hooper, they'd have to use the real animal. So, they designed half-sized cages and had

The Taylors preparing to dive during filming of *Blue Water, White Death*, 1969

to find a half-sized man for the live action. Because, in the movie, the shark was 26 feet in length and the real sharks would be around 13 feet. Again, Ron and Valerie and Rodney Fox set out to South Australia to work with Great Whites in the wild.

The shooting was difficult because of the weather although ultimately, the shark action was the fiercest the Taylors had ever witnessed. The sharks smashed up the small cage pretty well and thrashed the support boat to such a degree that the half-sized man, a midget named Carlo, hid from the Taylors when he was supposed to be getting in the cage. They were lucky to get two or three shots per day since the production required that no boat or cage bars be seen on camera.

Jaws was released in 1975 and was received unlike any movie ever. It produced a phenomenal interest in sharks, initially to the sharks' detriment, but ultimately to a new appreciation for them as animals in the sea. It also led to greater interest in the Taylors and they were besieged with book projects, television projects, public speaking appearances and further film work. As a result, they ended up handling the underwater sequences for *Gallipoli* and *The Year of Living Dangerously* with Mel Gibson; *The Blue Lagoon* and *The Return to the Blue Lagoon*, *Orca*, *Honeymoon in Vegas*, and the third re-make of *The Island of Dr. Moreau* with Marlon Brando.

In recognition of her role in the field of marine conservation – and the protection of the Potato Cod, in particular – Valerie was summoned to Soestdijk Palace in Holland in October 1986. His Royal Highness, Prince Bernhard of the Netherlands honored her by presenting Valerie with a Knighthood in the Order of the Golden Ark.

It's been my good fortune to know the Taylors as friends for some time. When Bret Gilliam suggested I interview them for this book, I jumped at the chance. The tape recorder rolled for hours as we discussed their fascinating careers and lives together. ∎

Q+A

Well, how did it all start?»**RON**: Oh, that was back in 1951 for me, when I found a facemask that had been lost and I put it on and the underwater world became clear. I was fascinated; I was hooked. I took up the sport of spearfishing and at the same time I was interested in photography, so I made my own underwater housing for a still camera. I started to get good still photos and a friend of mine had a 16mm movie camera and I built an underwater housing for that and started shooting news clips for television when it first came to Australia in 1965. Of course, everybody wanted to see *sharks*. From my spearfishing experience, I knew how to attract sharks. The best way to is to spear a fish and have the vibrations and the blood and it brings the sharks around. All of my hands-on experience came from my spearfishing days but I gave that up in 1969 and was shooting with a camera. I was able to turn my hobby and my sport into a business and I've been fascinated

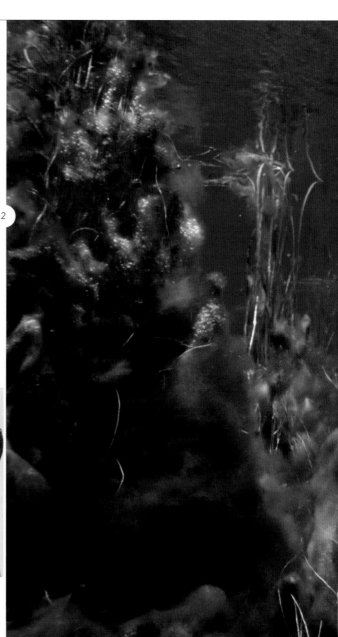

1. Ron with housing he made for Bolex 16mm camera, 1957
2. Valerie swimming through weeds in fresh water sink hole, Piccaninny Ponds, South Australia

ever since. **VALERIE:** My parents had a waterfront home near Sydney. My brother and I used to snorkel and spearfish for our father, who had stomach ulcers and could always eat fish. The man next door was a ship's chandler and he got some sample dive gear right back in the early days. From America it came and he didn't want it so he gave it to us. My brother and I started experimenting with scuba diving – and it wasn't called "scuba" then, it was called "aqua-lunging." We didn't go any deeper than, say, 10 or 15 feet, which is probably the only reason I'm still here today. Because

we'd never heard of the bends; we'd never heard of narcosis; we'd never heard of any of that – embolisms – it was just that we were so nervous that we took our time. And eventually, because I was quite good at spearfishing by this stage, I joined the same club that Ron belonged to. **RON**: I was still experimenting with my 16mm camera at that time and saw this pretty blonde girl in the club and I asked her if she'd pose for my camera underwater and that's how we got together. I got some nice images of Valerie and then we went to the Great Barrier Reef and made a film called

132

Skin Diving Paradise that the Queensland government bought. Then we made a film about sharks, called *Shark Hunters* that the *NBC* network in America bought. So that gave us a terrific boost and I thought, "Wow, this is great. I'll try to make a living out of filming." And that's what we've been doing ever since.

Valerie, when did you start into photography?»
VALERIE: Oh, I fiddled around with still cameras for a while, but I didn't do anything very good. I was mostly the model until *Blue Water, White Death* and I started

taking photographs there. All of which, except one roll, ended up with Peter Gimbel. I never actually even saw the end result. But that got me going. And Ron invented "the prongs." He thought, "If you put a ring behind a camera lens above water for macro, why not do it underwater?" And he got on his lathe and he made me three different rings and put these prongs out and he said, "Don't let anyone see this. You'll be able to do macro underwater and everybody will wonder how you did it." Well, the first people to really wonder were *National Geographic*. They wrote me a letter and said,

"We've seen some of your macro in the wild" – because before that, it was all done in tanks with a camera on a tripod – "and we'd like to see some more. Could you bring it over?" I flew first class to Washington and I took a suitcase that was full to the top with close–ups. And that's how I got my first job with *National Geographic*. They put me on the cover holding the little camera that Ron had made the prongs for. About two or three years later in the American *Skin Diver* magazine someone else came out with the idea. And Ron mused, "Isn't that amazing at the same time someone

else thought of it and marketed it." But that gave me a great leap forward because no one else could do that sort of photography at that time.

Back in these early days diving was considered "a man's sport." Certainly your contribution softened that image. »**VALERIE**: I never ever thought of it as a man's sport. I was frequently the only female, but I thought that was because most women didn't like getting around looking like a drowned rat. Most of the girls who snorkeled or scuba dived or spearfished had

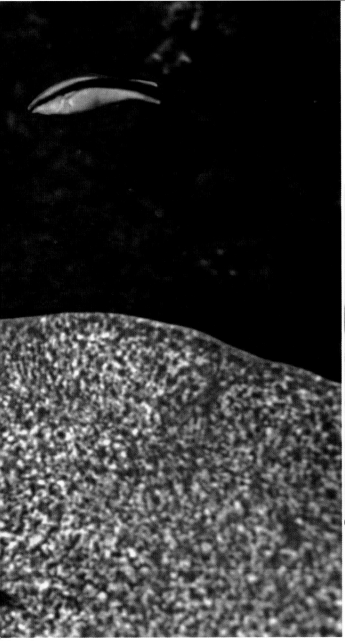

Ron, what's it like to film your wife in the clutches of sharks all the time? 》**RON**: I know Valerie is very capable and if ever the situation got very dangerous, then I'd rush in and beat the shark off. But she's got a lot of guts, as they say, and she can handle sharks as well as anybody. She understands them. And so far, we've got out of it pretty lightly. Valerie's had a few little nips and I've had a nip also. But it's always been our

2

1. Valerie with Harry, a moray eel she befriended at Heron Island bommie in 1970. Harry went on to become a TV star and still lives in the same area where he is quite a tourist attraction, Great Barrier Reef. Australia 2. Ron as an Air Force cadet, National Service, age 18, 1952

boyfriends or husbands who did it. And they did it to keep them company. I was very aware of the fact that if they had just had their hair done there was no way they were going to go into the water. I think nowadays it's much more fashionable and acceptable for women to, you know, look a bit scraggy and look like they're out there fighting the elements. Certainly, I know when I've been diving I don't look particularly attractive because I'm just such a mess. And I don't think it was that it was such a man's sport. I think that it was that women didn't like looking awful.

fault. We've had baits in the water. We don't blame the sharks at all. Valerie's very capable with them.

How do you feel that attitudes towards sharks have changed over the years? 》**VALERIE**: I think that the younger generation sees sharks in a more realistic light. It's the old-time fishermen that still want them to be the monsters of the sea – you know, the vicious animal out there to get you. They justify killing sharks by saying, "Well, it's me or it, you know, and I'm not going to let it get me." When sharks get pulled up along the boat – I've been there – they're screaming out, "Look at the thing! It's trying to get us! Watch it! It's going to get one of us! It's after us!" All the shark is doing is fighting for its own life. It's not trying to get anybody. But they don't like to hear you say that. Makes them sound awful. But it's the truth.

What changes have you noticed in the oceans over the last nearly 50-some years? »**VALERIE**: The changes are huge in all the oceans that I've ever been in. A diver who starts today will never ever know how it really should be or how it really was. And I don't think that the oceans will ever recover from the disastrous impact of man. I think we've done a huge damage and they will recover to a certain extent but they'll never go back to being that wonderful untouched wilderness – a kaleidoscope of fish and color. They were not afraid of you, because marine creatures had evolved without an instinctive fear of man. So when we started spearfishing, it was really easy. They just took no notice of you. I think we've done a lot of damage and we're still doing it. I don't think we're going to stop until it's no longer viable. That's sad. **RON**: The life is not there. The spearfishing and other fishing pressures have reduced the numbers of fish life. It's just not there. And the sharks have lost all their aggression. You go to the Great Barrier Reef, Coral Sea diving, see the same old fish swimming around. The sharks and all the coral trout and most of the tuna are gone. There's so much I never filmed because we thought it would always be as it was. We thought it was limitless. At the end of the 60s, we could start to see that wouldn't be the case.

Val, what would you have done for a living if you didn't dive? »**VALERIE**: I'm an artist by profession and I guess that's my talent. But I love to dive. Diving is addictive. Adventure is addictive. Once you get into adventure and risking your life and skirting on the edge, you just want to go further and further and further. I'll be a little old lady on crutches and I'll be out there doing it and I know it. One day I may never come back. But don't worry about it because I've had a great life.

Is it the animals, is it the environment? »**VALERIE**: It is the adventure of entering the unknown. You can go into the same body of water every day and it's different. You do not know what waits for you beyond the vision – or the limitation of your vision. You do not know what

1. Valerie, 2004 2. Ron won the 1965 World Spearfishing Championships in Tahiti. This fish was the largest speared in the competition 3. A curious Australian sealion checks out Ron, South Australia, 1994

living in it. We've loved it, hated it, but it's everything to us. And I've had many great experiences. One of them happened just about 15 years ago. We had a place in the Coral Sea called Coralita Pass, which wasn't on the charts, where we had 26 sharks that were friendly; they were "our sharks." One day, we were down there working with our sharks and we had Scott Johnson, a

3

scientist from the American Navy, with us. He was there to do tests on sharks to determine what would turn them and what would bring them to you. We put down our table, we put down our baits, we had our frenzy – our sharks frenzying with blood and everything – and we're standing there, the bait's gone, and this big Tiger shark just cruises in. And she's just swimming around. I hold up my fish. I wave it nicely and I say, "Hi, hello, sweetheart, come here, come on, I love you, come on."

They do not know what you say; they know what you think. They know what you feel. They know if something's wrong. They pick up your fear from your heart; they pick up your love from your heart. And this giant creature, 16 feet long, swam over and from my hand, took this little fish, and took it so nicely. I patted her on the head. I said to her, "You're such a good girl."

Our message to the diver on the surface to get more bait was to pat our heads. We knew there was more bait in our dinghy. But he was petrified, he couldn't move. It took him ages to get the bait and when he did – we used frozen tuna, whole tuna, frozen – he brought the tuna out and he was too frightened to swim the tuna down. He dropped it and I saw this tuna floating down. My nephew was with us and we both swam over and chained it to what we called "the table" and we had that Tiger shark for the entire dive. And Ron ran out of film. I stood on the bottom and held my arms outstretched and she would swim between them and I would run my hands along her body and she would come back. And I felt no fear. She was a honey.

And five years later, the finners moved into Coralita Pass and they took all the sharks. They took her too. So, never be afraid of Tiger sharks. Look them in the eye; put out your hand. They eat people. They kill – more people in Australia than Great Whites but they also have a sort of a soul. I'm very fond of them.

How does it feel to be so accepted by such a different world? »**VALERIE**: I never thought of myself as being accepted by the marine world. I think I'm a privileged visitor. I go in gently and I touch softly and I speak to all the animals. They don't know what I say; but I'm sure they know what I think. And I've had some wonderful relationships with marine animals, all different types. I realized that they are no different from land animals. They like to be touched softly. They like to be treated with respect. They enjoy interacting with people just as they enjoy interacting with each other.

We are just as mysterious to them as they are to us. We're both curious. And, if you have the right attitude, you can get so much more from the marine world, than, say a spearfisherman can.

What's your favorite animal in the ocean? »**VALERIE**: My favorite animal in the ocean is the Australian sea lion because he's just loveable, beautiful, gorgeous, sweet, gentle, huggable, kissable, warm. He's everything that I could ever want a creature to be – and he's wild. And, he accepts you.

Ron filming Great White shark from swim platform
with 16mm camera, South Australia, 1966

Ron, did you ever have a normal job? ⟩⟩**RON:** I
spent 10 years as an apprentice in the printing industry
learning photo engraving, making printing plates. I was
interested in photography before that, I think probably
because my father was a photographer.

**You did some early films like _Ron Taylor's Shark
Fighters_ that showed divers stabbing sharks
and creating general mayhem. At some point,
your attitude changed?** ⟩⟩**RON:** About 1965 I just
got sick and tired of spearfishing. When you become

an experienced spearfisherman, there's no spark in
it. The fish just commit suicide. Because you've got
the techniques and you can kill every one of them.
I'd already won many championships. On one hand,
I was killing them and the next dive, I was down
with a camera appreciating their beauty and their
characteristics and getting a rapport with them. It was
sort of a conflict of interests and I just got sickened by
the killing, particularly competitions, where you would
kill fish that are of no use, no good to eat.

I was in a competition one day and it was murky.

It was over at Long Reef and it was cold and murky and I was killing these poor, little, defenseless fish and I just thought to myself, "What the hell am I doing down here, murdering these poor, defenseless fish?" So I just got into my boat, went back, didn't even weigh the fish in, went home and never ever went to another competition again. Just dropped out of it completely, just like that.

When did you first photograph White sharks underwater?》**RON**: After the Australian spearfishing championships at San Reval in Victoria, that's where I met Rodney Fox, Brian Roger and Henri Bource. We actually went over to Lady Julia Percy Island after the championships. That's where Henri Bource lost his leg. We baited for sharks there, that's an island off the Victorian coast. We didn't get any White sharks there but then we got the idea of "Why not get Alf Dean to take us off South Australia". So, that would have been about 1966, would have been the very first expedition. We had a cage, but I found it more convenient to hang over the back because it was on a tuna boat. They had that rack right down at water's level and I would just hang over the top, part of my body in the water with my feet hooked into the tuna rack and so when the shark would come too close, I'd just pull myself out of the water. That's how I got the sequence with the shark opening his mouth and I blew up the frames and it's been our most successful still photo ever. They used it in *Blue Water, White Death* for the poster and in *Jaws* and in just about every book on sharks you'll see that shot.

Any close calls doing that?》**RON**: There was always somebody on deck to tell me if the shark was coming from the side. When you've got a facemask on, you can't see out the sides. The only danger is the shark you can't see.

How did your first films start up?》**RON**: I teamed up with Ben Cropp. I worked with him for a couple of years. We had a company called Taylor & Cropp Underwater. With Valerie, we made a black and white film. I shot it all and Cropp was the actor in it with Valerie. *Shark Hunters* it was called. It was to do with killing sharks and sea snakes and spearfishing and shark drugging. It was all down with sharks and it was very successful because eventually NBC bought it. But then I split up with Cropp because he was a very difficult guy to get along with.

Who else was making underwater movies in Australia when you started in the sixties?》**RON**: As soon as I split up with Ben Cropp, he started in himself. He didn't even have a movie camera when I was with him. I did all the photography. It's interesting that he got the *International Underwater Photographer of the Year* award for that film at Santa Monica in 1964 or 65 – I think it was – but I did all the photography. Incredible! He must have implied that he did it because it was on NBC and it was shown round the place and he was in it. They must have assumed it was his film but actually I did 99 percent of the photography. The market was wide open in those days. Nobody else was doing it, except a couple of stills photographers.

I think you should tell the story about how you nearly got killed.》**RON**: Which time? Actually, I have been bitten by a shark, but it was a wobbegong shark. They're carpet sharks and it was because Valerie and another guy were harassing it and I was fiddling with

up in a couple of weeks' time. But that's nothing.

The closest I think I've ever gone into getting into real trouble was during *Blue Water, White Death* back in 1969. Peter Gimbel, Stan Waterman, Valerie and myself were the four main characters. Now the search was for the Great White shark, "white death" being another name for them. We started off in South Africa, out of Durban, going out into the Indian Ocean, on a whale catcher. We were following the whaling fleet while they were hunting sperm whales. We went with the fleet and when they killed a sperm whale, they would pump air into it, put a buoy on it, then they'd go off hunting the other whales in the pod. Within minutes, sharks would come and start feeding on the whale carcass: Blue sharks and Oceanic Whitetips and a few duskies. But within an hour or two, there would be hundreds of sharks all around. Peter Gimbel made special aluminum cages, which could raise and lower, and we tied those cages to the whale. We'd hang about 30 feet underneath the whale. I was a cameraman with a 35mm movie

1. Peter Gimbel, Val Taylor, Ron Taylor and Stan Waterman board *Terrier* off South Africa, *Blue Water, White Death*, 1969
2. Whitey makes his appearance for the first time, Dangerous Reef, South Australia, 1970

a still camera not paying attention. I felt a bang on the elbow. I looked over and this wobbegong had bitten me. I could see this green blood coming out. I was down about 30 feet and I didn't know how bad it was. I went up to the surface and pulled my wetsuit off and there were puncture marks in my elbow. Well, it healed

camera as were Stan and Peter. Valerie was a safety. She'd carry a short bang stick that was really ineffective. It was very difficult to make the bang stick explode against the shark. In any case, we were not trying to kill the sharks, but we had a particularly wild time that day. Hundreds, you couldn't see them all. **VALERIE**:

It was just incredible. The strangest thing happened. When Gimbel said, "Let's do this, let's go." Ron agreed, of course. Stan wasn't too keen. I said nothing. I just thought, "I'll probably die in there." Peter said, "You don't have to come if you don't want to, Valerie." I didn't hesitate to say, "No, I'm coming. You just go out of the cage first, I want to see what happens." I thought, "If he gets into trouble I'm going to have go out and find him, help him." So, anyway, he swam out of his cage first, and he spun that big camera in its big metal housing around and around, knocking the sharks, all zeroed in on him, bash, bash, then he turned around, came back and got me.

And I swam out with the sharks, bang stick in one hand, and my other on Peter's tank. In the film, everybody thinks I've got my hand on Ron's tank, but it's Peter's tank. Then he swam away from me and I started this tremendous battle with the sharks. All the things above water that I'd said goodbye to and thought I'd never see again… I didn't even mind. Just one single thing happens: you revert to your primeval instincts. You enter a primeval world that hasn't changed in 20 million years, maybe 200 million years, I don't know. Great predators of the deep come to feed on the dead whale and it's been like this for a long time. Certainly when there were dinosaurs roaming the world, long before man. And you revert. You only have one thought: survival. You go out there and you fight for it. There's no fear. There's just the most brilliant, exhilarating excitement. I love it. I'd do it again tomorrow. I'd pay to do it. I loved it. **RON**: We eventually got out of our cages and were swimming with these Oceanic sharks. But we had to be careful. Oceanic Whitetips had a very annoying and potentially dangerous characteristic: it bumps. And we found we had to bump the shark back. We had to be aggressive back towards them. Interestingly enough, they didn't bite immediately. We noticed they did this to the whale carcass. They would go and bump into the whale. They'd rub the underneath of their snout – which is their sensory system – against the whale, go around, do the same thing again, and eventually they'd come back and take a bite and shake. They'd shake a big chunk out of the whale carcass. So we knew that these Oceanic Whitetips were potentially dangerous, so we banged them. If ever we saw an Oceanic Whitetip going to one of our friends, we'd swim over and hit it with a big camera. But this particular day was just enormous; sharks everywhere. I had run out of film

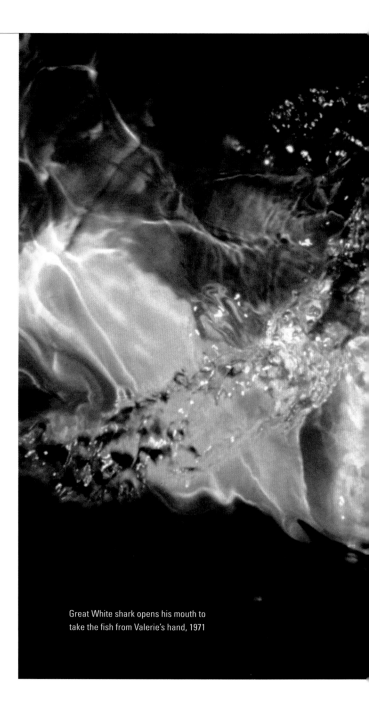

Great White shark opens his mouth to take the fish from Valerie's hand, 1971

and went up and sat on top of the cage, just watching this incredible scene of Oceanic Whitetips, Blue sharks, Silkies swimming around. Valerie, Stan and Peter were still down there, all surrounded.

I was just sitting on the cage with this big camera, just watching, fascinated, and then, all of the sudden, bang! I got hit, here, on the side of my head, and my vision started to narrow. I felt limp, my mouthpiece started coming out of my mouth; I could feel cold water running into my mouth. I knew I was going unconscious. I thought,

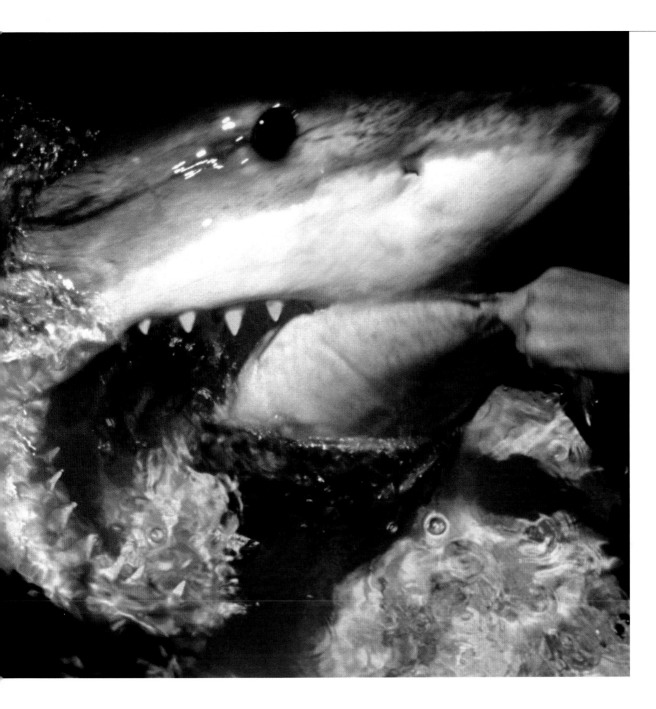

"I've got to hang on, I've got to remain conscious."
Fortunately, I did, because I'm here. But if I'd fallen, the
sharks were watching. I'm sure that I would have started
breathing water and they probably would have noticed
me go off into the depths helpless. They would have taken
me. **VALERIE**: It was two miles deep. **RON**: It was very,
very deep water. We were 50 or 60 miles out in the Indian
Ocean. And the shark didn't try to bite me; it just simply
hit me, just on the critical part on the side of my head. It's
the closest I think I've come to a bad end.

What kind of a man was Peter Gimbel?》**VALERIE**:
Peter was a very unusual man. He had been an
identical twin. He was the son of a very wealthy family,
they owned Gimbel's department stores; they owned
Saks Fifth Avenue, God knows what else. His twin
brother died of cancer. Peter got cancer as well but
survived. I think he always felt that he should have died,
too. He seemed to have a bit of a death wish. But he
was kind, generous, considerate, polite decent human
being and I liked him very much.

What inspired him to do this adventure, do you think? »**VALERIE**: Peter's father was a very wealthy New York Jew, played the stock market extremely well, a very clever man where money was concerned. And I have a feeling that Peter wasn't. He wasn't a "money man". He was an adventurer in his heart. He wanted to go and do outrageous things. He wanted to be admired, not for making money, but for climbing Everest, for diving deepest. He was desperate to make

his mark in a different way altogether from his father. And I think that's what drove him.

Do you think the success of *Blue Water, White Death* validated him? »**VALERIE**: When *Blue Water, White Death* came out it was the second biggest money maker that year! It was a gigantic success… and it was a documentary! In feature films, *Love Story* had the biggest gross, but this was a

Making friends with a Potato Cod
on the Great Barrier Reef, 1982

nature film about sharks. It was just beyond anyone's dreams that a film like that could do that kind of box office revenues. But his father was already dead. His father never knew that his son had finally been a great success. Peter was really sad that his dad wasn't around to see what he had accomplished. It was all a bit ironic… to strive for your dad's attention your whole life and finally achieve a pinnacle of recognition. And then he wasn't there to see it.

Were there ever plans for a follow-up? VALERIE: There was never any talk about a sequel. I think there is a place for something similar. A feature-length *cinema verite* documentary and I'm sure it would be very successful if it's done right. You've got to realize, when we did *Blue Water, White Death* very few divers knew anything about sharks. Diving was still very young, and we went and did something that was totally outrageous. And it was an interesting group of people. It was Gimbel, the rich man from New York, Stan Waterman, a berry-picker from Maine, and Ron and me. Ron was the world's spearfishing champion at the time. The only reason we were invited was because, at that stage, Ron was the only person in the world who had ever filmed a Great White underwater. And I added some flair as a woman in with these guys.

What was the morale like on the boat, from month one until the end of the shooting? VALERIE: We lived on the whale catcher for five months. Things were not easy. It was an old whale catcher and there was a tremendous problem with food. A lot of the colored crew had to be taken off in Sri Lanka, it was called Ceylon back then because they were seasick. Coming back out then, we all had to stand watches. And on whale catchers, it was a big wheel out in the open, in the elements. There were always two of us. Morale was high, extremely high. Ron and I always knew where they could get Great Whites. When we were working out of Durban looking for Whites, we wanted to go south. If we had, we would have got them because we would have gone to Dyer Island. Ron was already looking at those islands, way back then. But we went north and I'm glad we did because it was a great adventure. I loved it. It was fantastic with all the wonderful people on board; Ron and I are still friends with the ones that are still alive. You don't do something like that and walk away from the people you've been with when you do something like that.

During the production, you all ran into some problems, right? RON: Well, they spent a lot of money in America before they came to South Africa because they built these cages. They took the cages and all the people involved to the Caribbean to test them. That sort of surprised me a bit. They didn't take us but all the Americans involved. They had a pretty good time I guess, found that the cages worked and they took the whole lot to South Africa. Chartered the whale catcher, loaded food on board. When we got on board it was in very good condition. But unfortunately, the deep freeze used to freeze up and they'd have to take all the food out and put it on the deck while they defrosted it and chipped out the ice. You could get away with that in fairly cold waters – it was Norwegian – so it would stand on the deck in a cold climate, but we were working around the equator and the food used to defrost. And then it would get frozen again. Every couple of weeks, out it would come, sit on the deck, defrost, while they cleaned out the freezer and go back. And the raw stuff was bad ever since. The production manager was sent off to hospital after terrible, serious stomach problems and we never saw him again. Valerie seemed to have the cast iron stomach. Stan and Peter got through it, but the rest had problems.

The production halted after Sri Lanka? »**VALERIE**: It did. We had to bring the vessel back to South Africa. We had some problems, huge seas, and had to be back there for 10 days and when we finally made land it was Diego Suarez in Madagascar. And the French wouldn't give us any fuel and we had to barter. It took Peter a lot of time and a lot of sweet talk to get the French to sell us fuel so we could sail back to South Africa. But it was good for Ron and me. We managed to get a look around Madagascar. I've been back since and seen huge changes since the French gave up the colony. Ron and I went back to Australia and we started work on a 39 part series called *Barrier Reef*. We were working away on that but in our contract with Peter we'd agreed to be available until the end of the shoot. When they came back out to Australia, we had to leave the job we were working on and go to South Australia with them. We hired Rodney Fox to organize the chum. And we went out on a boat called the *Satori*. There were White sharks out there! As everyone knows who's seen the movie.

That was filmed at Dangerous Reef? »**RON**: Yes. Back then, the water was a lot clearer around here. We went to Wedge, we went to a lot of islands. The first five days Gimbel wouldn't stay still. He was sort of in a state of panic or something. I explained, "You've got to just go and anchor and chum." Finally went to Dangerous Reef and he anchored. We started chumming and on the second day, we got our sharks. We got five all in the one afternoon.

And had he known about the sharks of South Australia before he started the trip in Africa? »**VALERIE**: He absolutely did because he saw Ron's footage that he had shot. He'd seen the film we did called *Hunt for the Great White Shark*. Peter knew that Ron had worked with them before and that was one of the reasons that he was hired. Of course, Ron wouldn't go without me and that was that.

After the film ended, you started doing some shark tours? »**VALERIE**: We used to come down here with Carl Roessler, but then again it was my idea to run trips out. I contacted Dewey Bergman at Sea & See Travel and suggested that we do it. Dewey came to our house and I called Rodney and said, "Come over and speak to this guy". They got something going and we made a documentary about the first trip we did and sold it to American television, taking tourists out to see Great Whites. They didn't live on the boat; they lived on land. We lived on the small boat and when we got the Whites, they just came out on a fast boat. We were working Dangerous Reef at that time. The tourists could go diving elsewhere but they would keep in radio contact all the time. When we got sharks, they just came zooming in. At that particular stage, it worked very well. We started doing White shark tours about 1971 - 1972, I'd say. It was very early in the 70s. In the beginning we only had the one cage. Then we did a film called *Ron and the Great White Shark*s – a Bruno Valotti film. He had two cages made that we used for many years. **RON**: In the 1970s, we started shark feeding: tying baits to reef tables. Our gray reef sharks would go into tremendous frenzies. We found we had a good market for that type of film, but back then they used to dramatize it for sale to television as dangerous creatures. We found that we were doing harm to the sharks to that extent, so we changed our tactics. We went on the talk shows and began showing how we could swim with the sharks and we eventually changed direction with our films and to show how we could go in amongst a feeding frenzy in virtual safety.

Some people didn't like that. There was one guy in particular, named Vic Hisslop – he's well known as a "shark hunter" in Australia – and he did a media release that the Taylors were training Great White sharks to attack people. Because we were putting baits in the water and divers in cages and the sharks were associating divers with food, supposedly creating a

Ron with Gray Reef shark,
French Polynesia, 1985

Giant Jellyfish, Seal Rocks,
NSW, Australia, 1988

dangerous situation. And he got a lot of press coverage because of that. The press didn't want to know about the real story. They wanted to accelerate this "danger." Period. And we got on and said, "When the Great White sharks come around our cages, it's not a particularly pleasant experience for them because generally they go away with all their teeth broken off. Because the Great Whites come up and they bite everything they can see. They bite the cage, the hull of the boat, and their teeth all get broken off." And I note that it's not a particularly pleasant experience for the shark. That characteristic, by the way, is what makes the Great White the most dangerous of all sharks. If it's attracted to food in the water, its behavior is to check everything out by biting it. They don't particularly bite it very hard, but they dig the bottom teeth in that are longer and more pointed. And if it's soft and edible, they'll bring the big triangular teeth down and start shaking. Unfortunate, if you're swimming or happen to be divers…

They normally don't eat people. They generally bite and they see that we're not a marine mammal. Somehow they can tell that humans are not what they've evolved over millions of years to prey upon. Fortunately, they let people go… like Rodney Fox, Henri Bource, Brian Roger. They all survived Great White attacks.

You've done out of the cage work with Great Whites. »RON: We have. We've used the electronic repelling device. And, after you've shocked them quite a few times with this repelling device, it will keep them off. In 1991, we saw on a news clip about this electronic repelling device developed by the Natal Sharks Board in South Africa. We were doing a series for *National Geographic* at the time called *Blue Wilderness*. So we went to South Africa and went to the Natal Sharks Board. That's a government-funded organization that puts the mesh nets along the surfing beaches because South Africa has had a lot of problems with shark attacks on surfing beaches. One of their scientists developed this electronic device that emits a pulsing electric field in the water. It irritates the shark's electro-receptors, probably the ampullae of Lorenzini that are the little black pits you see on these sharks close-up. This really does irritate the sharks and even though the Natal Sharks Board has two very good shark researchers, they haven't had a lot of practical experience swimming with wild sharks. They know how many vertebrae they've got and all the technical details

about sharks. Much, much more than what Valerie or I know. But they really hadn't been in with them.

So, we thought, "This is fantastic! If they can get an electronic device to repel sharks, they'll be able to do away with all these mesh nets." You're probably aware that these mesh nets catch sharks very well but they capture other harmless marine creatures, too – turtles, dolphins, whales, dugongs, fish, tuna, everything. And these things die in the nets. We've still got them because the authorities in Australia are reluctant to take these mesh nets away in case somebody gets bitten by sharks. So we have this electronic device and we jump into the pool in Durban where there are two big Bull sharks. The week before, they had this giant grouper and these Bull sharks devoured it; there were just scales left lying on the bottom. They were just terrified that Valerie and I were going to get devoured by these two Bull sharks in this aquarium that was about the size of a dining room. As soon as we went in, the Bull sharks had a look at us, then went on their way. When they came close, Valerie had the electronic device and I had the video camera, and as soon as she switched it on, you could see a definite repulsion. We were convinced they really had something that would work.

Then we went down south to Cape Town and I asked them if there were any islands around with sea lions. They said yes, about 50 miles away on Dyer Island. We went out there with Leonard Compagno, an American shark researcher who works with Cape Town University. We camped on Dyer Island, which is now a very famous White shark location with a half-dozen guys out baiting for sharks. People pay to go down in cages and look through very, very murky water at Great White sharks. We tested with Whites and, sure enough, it repelled them. Then a big storm came up and washed the cage off the side of the boat and it was lost. What we didn't have on film and what we really wanted was Valerie and I down among the Great White sharks repelling them. We had no cage for safety, so what we had to do, was simply go into the water without any cage, although we did have two very experienced South African spearfishermen with us and they had poles.

But prior to that, I had noticed that we had been shocking them with the electronic device for a couple of hours on that particular day and I felt that those sharks were not aggressive. So I felt it would be fairly safe to go down onto the bottom without the safety of a cage and we didn't have an underwater shocker. We only had a shocker that was working from the boat, so we stayed underneath the boat. And, in theory, the guys up top were going to repel the sharks if they saw them coming too close to us. I would be very reluctant to go in the water with baited Great White sharks without some electronic repelling device or a cage. **VALERIE**: There were five sharks swimming around us. They kept a certain distance away. Sharks are not stupid. They would have known because they could see quite well that the humans were doing something they didn't like. We weren't actually hurting the sharks – permanently – we were giving them little pinpricks – and they got some *respect*.

Did they manage to finally declare the Great White a protected species? »**VALERIE**: I'm not sure they ever really did.

What's the attraction to White sharks? »**RON**: They're so big; they're so exciting. You never know what they're going to do. It's the anticipation of the unexpected. They're always bigger than 10 feet. Average size is about 13-14 feet. And some of them can be very aggressive… biting around the platform, onto the cages, onto the hull of the boat. And it's very exciting when they come around.

I think people are interested in sharks because they are potentially very dangerous. Great White sharks in particular, kill people, so our instinct for self-preservation makes us very aware and very interested in them. When a White shark comes around, it arouses primitive instincts of self-preservation. When I saw my first Great White, the hair stuck up on the back of my neck. Some primitive instinct told me that was a very dangerous creature. I had better be pretty careful. **VALERIE**: I think people are interested in all monsters. Anything that's out there big and dangerous fascinates them. I guess, 100 years or even less ago, they had witches, dragons, all sorts of monsters. But now we know that none of those monsters exist, except in our imaginations, so we've had to find new ones. I guess our desire for a monster has sort of narrowed down to something we can see like the shark. I enjoy working with sharks – all the different species – though I prefer the more dangerous sharks because of that element of risk and a little bit of excitement. It's an achievement to get a good photograph of a shark. It's far easier

"Bruce" the mechanical White shark, used in the film *Jaws*. Martha's Vineyard, 1975

to go and photograph a lion or a tiger. You can sit in a car and change your lenses, stay there for days, if necessary. With sharks, there's a lot of luck and skill. I enjoy the challenge. Also, pictures of sharks sell very well. I guess that's because not too many people do it.

How many White sharks would you say you've seen in your career? »**RON**: I've never counted the number of White sharks I've seen, but I would guess, I'd say 100,

200, something like that. I saw my first Great White shark in these waters nearly 50 years ago. I've been coming back just about every year since, sometimes twice a year.

VALERIE: The first Great White I saw for any length of time was in Memory Cove. I saw a fisherman's 44-gallon drum going under and we went over and had a look. It had a White shark on it… a giant, a female, and the hook had just gone through the lip. She was swimming around and around. We were wondering how to approach this creature and we were in a small abalone boat just looking. Suddenly, a second Great White, equally as large, appeared and ripped open the first shark's stomach. It tore out her liver and ate it. The water was filled with blood. It all happened very quickly and when the blood cleared, our very alive Great White shark was now a very dead one, still hanging by the hook in her lip. After half an hour, I said, "I'm going in the water." So, Ron and I went in the water and did some photography

Val with scaled-down version of shark cage and dummy stand-in for midget stunt double during 2nd Unit live shark sequences for *Jaws*

with her. That was my first Great White. I saw two in one go. We didn't have a cage in the beginning. The first cage that Ron ever filmed out of was, I think, Peter Gimbel's cage in *Blue Water, White Death*.

Valerie, what would you describe as your worst experience underwater and your best experience underwater? 》**VALERIE**: My worst experience was being sucked down a whirlpool. My best experience, there have been so many of them actually, that I can't put my finger on it, on any absolute, best experience. Maybe getting out of the cage in 1969 under the whale in the Indian Ocean, 100 miles offshore, swimming free in the water with maybe 200 large and dangerous sharks – and living to tell the tale. I think that's the best.

How did you come to work on Jaws? 》**RON**: The producers saw *Blue Water, White Death* and so did Peter Benchley who was inspired to write *Jaws*. They later asked Peter Gimbel, producer of *Blue Water, White Death* if he would do the camera work for *Jaws*

and he said, "No, I'm not an underwater cameraman; I'm a producer, a director." Universal said, "Oh, we've already got a director, a young guy by the name of Steven Spielberg." Peter was adamant, "Sorry, I won't do the camera work, but contact the Taylors in Australia. They might do the live shark sequences for *Jaws*." And that's what they did. We read the galley proofs. I flew to Hollywood and met Steve Spielberg, Joe Alves and the team there. We designed half-sized cages. They sent over a half-sized man (a stunt midget) to work with our half-sized sharks – because the movie shark was 26 feet long and our Great Whites were only 13 feet long, so it worked out fine.

Not much of the footage ended up being used in the final film. 》**RON**: No, there were only about a half-dozen shots of the real live shark and there's a shot where the shark appears to be smashing the cage. In fact, it was tangled in the steel cables on the cage. They changed the storyboard for the shoot to accommodate that dramatic sequence.

Do you think there's been a change in the numbers of White sharks here? »**VALERIE**: It would appear to me there's been a huge change in the numbers of Great White sharks in this area. Because 30-some years ago, you'd come out and have four or five right away. It wouldn't be unusual to have 10-12 sharks in just two or three days. Sometimes we'd see even more. Now, it's commonplace to get no sharks at all. If you get one, you're lucky and if you get two, you're elated.

Have you ever had any life-threatening experiences with White sharks? »**VALERIE**: I don't think a Great White has ever threatened my life. We have been in the water swimming with sea lions and had a White shark come and circle us. That was at Hopkins Island, it wasn't very deep, I guess it was 15 feet. Ron and I knew the shark was coming. There was no doubt about that because the sea lions just scattered. They made this funny sort of clucking noise as they went through the water, it must have been their fins hitting the water. We had a filmmaker from the U.S. with us, Bruno Valotti, and he had his head up in the air. I had my mouthpiece out and I'm screaming, "Shark! Shark!" I couldn't see it but I knew it was coming. And he turned around saw Ron lying flat on the kelp. We both flattened down and the shark just came around, very fast, circled twice, and swam away. The sea lions came back and we swam to a little rock – about the size of that shark cage or smaller – and we all climbed out onto it. We could see the boat, way off in the distance at the mooring. The skipper wouldn't come get us because of rocks. And we knew we had to swim back.

Well, I'm pretty good in the water and I didn't have a camera. Ron had his camera and is a very strong swimmer. Bruno was a lot older than us. Lets' just say he was a motivated swimmer. Well, he beat us by back to the boat by a good 10 yards or more! It must have been a 100 yards to swim. But we knew that if the shark was around, the sea lions would let us know. They swam with us as we all swam back to the boat. Bruno's men were on board. They pulled him and his camera out and I was saying, "Hey, help me out. I've got to get out of here!" They were ignoring Ron and I completely. That was the same trip when the shark got tangled in the steel trace on the cage. It was a very sharky trip that one.

Departing from the Whites for a minute, what other species of sharks has caused you moments of anxiety? »**VALERIE**: I was very anxious once off the coast of California when I felt a large bump to my leg and I looked down and saw my leg in a shark's mouth. I didn't really have time to feel anxious because I knew I had to stop the shark from moving its head, which I grabbed. But afterwards, when I was lying in this huge pool of blood on the deck of the boat I thought I might be dead. Actually in the water I thought I might be dead. But I stopped bleeding in a few seconds. At first it was like a tap turned on. It just started squirting out and it sort of flowing away. There was a lot of blood because the bite had cut some arteries. That was a blue shark and there were a lot of blues in the water. Howard Hall had just gone in to check things out and he came back and said, "There's a lot of hungry sharks down there; I sure hope someone's not going to get bit." I said, "Ah, well, it won't be me." Famous last words.

Weren't you also bitten when you were experimenting with the chain mail suit? »**VALERIE**: I was bitten in Australia when I had the chain mail suit in the Coral Sea and that was just sheer accident. We were doing the mesh suit test and we had a nice frenzy going at Action Point at Marion Reef. I had a mackerel or something, a piece of tuna, in my hand and the idea, of course, was to get the sharks to bite me in the suit. So I swam into the frenzy which I felt fairly confident about, but a shark turned towards me and it bit me on the face. And I heard all the teeth going into the mesh – sort of crunch, crunch, crunch – unfortunately it went in under my chin, because my chin sticks out of the suit. And my mask got flooded and my regulator got pulled away. I thought it was bitten off. Actually, I didn't know where it had gone to and I was down pretty deep. I really thought I was going to drown. I knew I was bleeding. Afterwards, when we looked at the footage – Ron was filming – it was four frames from where the shark turned until it hit me. So, people said, "Why didn't you put your mesh hands up over your face?" You can't think that fast. Afterwards, I had a very sore jaw. I couldn't chew anything for a few days. **RON**: When we were doing experiments with the mesh suit, I used to get concerned because Valerie was enticing the sharks to bite onto her body by using baits. Even though we were only using medium sized sharks, they've got razor-sharp teeth and we didn't really know whether the mesh would be

100 percent protective. So that was quite a concern on some occasions, when the sharks were feeding violently on Valerie's arm, for instance.

You've been working with Ron quite a few years. How do you communicate underwater? »**VALERIE**: Ron and I communicate very well because we're both photographers. Generally speaking, if I'm on-camera, I do what I'd want a model to do for me. Occasionally, of course, I get into trouble for presenting my behind or swimming out of frame when I shouldn't or not noticing something. But I also can talk underwater. Ron doesn't even try. But I can talk, tell him things and even when I can't see him, I have a method of calling him that he can hear. We'd do much better if he didn't wear a

hood with his suit, but we do okay. I pretty much know what he wants. **RON**: We both use signals. When I'm working with Valerie, she knows what to do. I know what position to get into and she knows what position to get into. And if we see a potential sequence, we automatically get into the right position. We don't need to do much communicating underwater; both of us know what we need to do to achieve the best film.

Did you think any animals are attracted to colors? »**VALERIE**: No, I never really thought any animals were attracted to any of my wetsuits. I noticed sometimes working in the Coral Sea, sharks like my blue fins. I used to have a blue Farallon flash and they used to be attracted by that, if it floated up they'd bite at it, but

Valerie being bitten by a Blue shark off San Diego while testing the steel mesh suit. Ron first had the idea of protecting divers with the same stainless steel mesh that protects butchers while they carve up animals with razor sharp knives, 1988

hours and hours. The shark bumped it, pushed it, never bit it. We put an orange buoyancy jacket on. In five seconds, it had grabbed it around the jacket. Of course, the dummy's tied to the boat. We managed to get it back, stitched it all up and threw it out again. In five seconds, it attacked it again – on the orange jacket. **VALERIE**: So then we painted our shark cages yellow and I really do think that we got our best bites on the cages on the yellow floats and you'll notice in our photographs we have yellow gloves. We'd hang out the cage waving at the Great White and it would turn. Every time it would come. We tried all sorts of things. Ron used to take an orange lift bag in the cage with him so there was a big orange blob in there to attract the shark. And it appeared to work. We didn't do it enough to say we scientifically tested it or anything but it appeared to work.

You've dived with White sharks in South Australia, Western Australia and South Africa. Do you notice any difference between them in different regions? 》**VALERIE**: I don't think there's any difference between the Great Whites in South Australia or Western Australia. They certainly look the same to me. In South Africa they had a different look. They're still Whites. But they have sort of a longer look with bigger fins and they certainly had a different behavior pattern. There was no doubt at all. Different behavior pattern. The South African Whites didn't put their heads above the water like the South Australian sharks do, to investigate the unusual or just to see what's going on. They didn't like to take a bait at all. They refused to take a bait off the back of the boat. They didn't come and chew around the back of the boat. I have no recollection of them biting on the cage. And when we got in the water with them, they were very wary. There were five of them swimming around us and I'd say the closest one came would be eight feet. It was fairly close, but mostly they seemed to stay 10 to 15 feet away. Certainly we didn't feel threatened at any time.

Any advice for the non-diver or the casual swimmer who worries about sharks? 》**VALERIE**: Swim in a swimming pool, then you don't have any more worries! If you're concerned about sharks, why go down where you might meet one? It's very unlikely but why go around being worried? There are plenty of places to swim where there are no sharks.

we did color tests with Great Whites and there was no doubt whatsoever that they liked the color orange.

Isn't that the color they make life jackets out of? 》**RON**: Yes, that's absolutely correct. We did very extensive tests on orange and red. What made us start doing it, we had a White shark back feeding doing very nicely and Rodney accidentally knocked over a petrol can that was orange with yellow writing. And our shark disappeared over the horizon trying to bite that petrol can. Left the baits. We thought, "Now that's interesting." So we did these tests with a dummy – and everybody thinks we had fish in them, we didn't – we just stuffed it with sheets. We floated out the black dummy. It floated for hours and

What is the thing you're most proud of filming underwater? »**RON**: I think our experiences in *Blue Water, White Death*. It was an adventure, really pushing the frontier of shark encounters. What we achieved then was very satisfying. But the most famous piece of filming I've been involved in was shooting the live shark sequences for *Jaws*.

Where's your favorite place to dive anywhere in the world? »**RON**: I haven't got any one favorite place. I've got several. Because no one place has got everything. Just like here in South Australia, we only come here for Great White sharks, which used to be very, very exciting. For reef sharks, we go to the

Ron filming Great Hammerheads, 1972
Valerie and Ron Taylor Bahamas, 2006

Coral Sea; for critters we go to Papua New Guinea or Indonesia; for schooling hammerheads we go way over to the Eastern Pacific. I've just recently been to the Bahamas where we had a great experience with Caribbean Reef sharks. All these different locations are interesting in themselves, but there's no one place where everything is all in one place.

Any location you'd like to go that you haven't been so far? »**RON**: I'd like to do some more Oceanic work, ya know, offshore sharks. But the last time I went offshore near Sydney I got seasick for the second time

in my life after nearly 50 years of ocean experience. That wasn't very pleasant. I'd like open ocean shark work or large marine creature work in good conditions and usually where the best action is, it's all calm.

Valerie, I noticed something interesting as I've questioned you: you talk about adventure and

156

157

you talk about risk. **Do you consider yourself a risk-taker or a thrill-seeker, because they're not the same.** »**VALERIE:** I like adventure very much. The more you do it, the more you want to do it. It's addictive. Most people don't get enough. My dreams are all about wild adventure. I don't want to venture into outer space or chasing ghosts, I want real adventure.

Do you think if you'd grown up in Africa you'd have been in the bush instead of in the ocean? »**VALERIE:** Absolutely. Damn good at it too, I reckon. I don't know what makes me tick.

What makes Ron tick? »**VALERIE:** Not a clue. except he likes dinner at six o'clock on the dot! ■

Peter Benchley

THE FATHER OF JAWS AND OTHER TALES OF THE DEEP

BY BRET GILLIAM

:: peter benchley

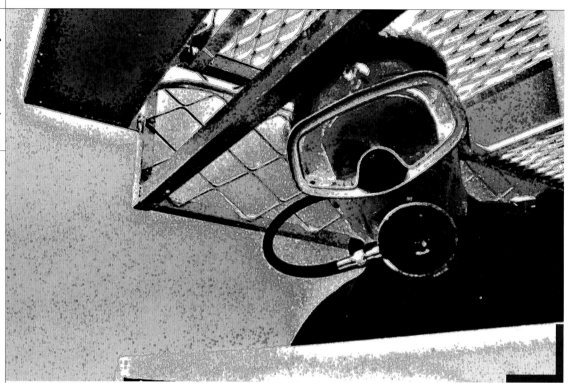

THE GREAT FISH MOVED SILENTLY THROUGH THE NIGHT WATER,

propelled by short sweeps of its crescent tail. The mouth was open just enough to permit a rush of water over its gills... The eyes were sightless in the black, and the other senses transmitted nothing extraordinary to the small primitive brain. »

The land seemed almost as dark as the water, for there was no moon. All that separated sea from shore was a long straight stretch of beach, so white it shone. From a house behind the grass-splotched dunes, lights cast yellow glimmers on the sand.

The front door to the house opened, and a man and woman stepped out onto the wooden front porch, they stood for a moment staring at the sea, embraced quickly, and scrambled down the few steps onto the sand. The man was drunk, and he stumbled on the bottom step. The woman laughed and took his hand, and together they ran to the beach.

"First a swim," said the woman, "to clear your head." □

Is there even one amongst you who doesn't recognize the infamous opening paragraphs of the most terrifying novel of the sea ever written? Without reading one more sentence we all knew that this particular moonlight swim would not end well. The subsequent release of *Jaws* the movie in 1975 created the genre of summer blockbuster films, set director Steven Spielberg on his road to Hollywood immortality, and memorably changed the life of a young struggling novelist named Peter Benchley.

The movie also forever twisted the psyche of hundreds of millions of people in their awareness of sharks and profoundly affected the collective perspective of simply going to the beach. In short, Benchley scared the wits out of a generation and we're still getting over it.

He followed with another successful tale, this one about deep sea treasure, diving and bad guys — *The Deep*. And Jackie Bissett forever earned a place in history for "Most Compelling Use of Large Breasts in a Wet T-Shirt" when the movie was released in 1977. For Benchley, a series of other fine adventure novels, all with a link to the ocean would follow establishing him as a one-man cottage industry of Hollywood and television fodder for decades.

His last book, *Shark Trouble*, was released in the summer of 2002 and I decided it was the perfect time to track him down and get him to talk about his own diving experiences, the writing process, dealing with the movie industry, marine conservation, his buddy Stan Waterman, and how he feels about being branded (unfairly) by some as the man singularly responsible for a global fear of sharks. ∎

Peter Benchley's book jacket photo for the release of *Jaws*, 1974

Okay, so how did a nice boy with a Harvard degree who worked as one of President Lyndon Johnson's speechwriters end up inspired to write the definitive shark terror novel? »I had been carrying around in my pocket for years a 1964 clipping about a fisherman who had harpooned a 4,550-lb. Great White shark somewhere off Montauk, L.I. To someone who'd been fascinated by sharks all my life – I believe implicitly that all male children are fascinated by sharks or dinosaurs, and I chose sharks because they actually exist, I could see their fins slicing the oil-calm surface of the sea on warm summer days – the mere idea that a critter that huge could exist was thrilling. Immediately, I thought to myself: what would happen if one of those monsters came into a resort community and wouldn't go away? The idea of a "rogue" shark hadn't been discredited by then. So little was known about sharks in general, and Great White sharks in particular, that almost any assumption was fair game.

Anyway, I carried the clipping around as a sort of relic, and more than once it proved useful. I was the radio/TV editor of *Newsweek* at the time, and all magazine writers and editors were occasionally courted by publishers on the lookout for fresh book ideas. I kept two arrows in my quiver: the shark idea for a novel and some thoughts about a history of pirates as a non-fiction book. I had them ready to pull out at any free lunch to which I was treated by a publisher. The shark idea always generated interest, and several publishers encouraged me to write it, but I never did. I

had neither the time nor the interest to write a novel; I was satisfied with the free lunches.

Then, in 1971, an editor from Doubleday, Tom Congdon, heard the idea, was taken with it and did what no other editor or publisher had ever done: he offered me money! A thousand dollars for four chapters. If he and Doubleday liked the four chapters, they'd sign me to a contract providing for the balance of the advance: a grand total of $7,500 for a completed, acceptable manuscript. I took the thousand dollars and promptly set about doing ... nothing. I spent the money and continued to work at *Newsweek*.

A couple of months went by, and my agent called to ask where the four chapters were; it seemed that the publishers were insistent on getting either the four chapters or their thousand dollars back. Well, I'd long since spent the dough, of course, so I had no choice. I had a wife and two small children in a tiny house in Pennington, N.J., and I couldn't possibly work there, so I rented (for $50 a month) the back room of a furnace-supply company in downtown Pennington and – amid the clang and clank of hammers on sheet metal, of welders and riveters – wrote down the words, "The great fish moved silently through the night water, propelled by short sweeps of its crescent tail." Then, right away, I was stuck; I had a problem. I phoned my father, who lived in Nantucket, and asked him, "What would happen if you cut a body in two? Would any of it float, and if so, which parts?"

"Depends," he said. "If you cut it above the air sacs, the bottom half would float, if below the air sacs, the top half would float .... What are you up to?"

"Writing a story about a fish."

"What, a fish that bites people in two?"

"Uh-huh."

"That's some fish."

"Yup."

"Well, have a good time with it."

We hung up, I wrote the first four chapters and sent them to Tom Congdon, who ... hated them. In a moment of lunacy, I had decided to try to tell the story as a comedy, and the story was a mess, an unsatisfactory blend of unfunny humor and unthrilling thriller. Tom sent me back to the typewriter.

A month or so later, I had the four chapters. Tom liked them, with reservations, and after we edited the four chapters and agreed on a course for the rest of the story, I repaired to the back room of the furnace-supply company and completed the first draft. Tom and his assistant Kate Medina, criticized, and I rewrote, and rewrote again, and after a total elapsed time of perhaps a year and a half, Doubleday had a completed, acceptable manuscript, and I had the $7,500, minus the thousand already paid.

Your father, Nathaniel Benchley, was a prolific writer himself including a wonderful novel called *The Off Islanders*. Hollywood eventually made that story into a successful movie titled *The Russians Are Coming! The Russians Are Coming!* Did he offer any advice on your early decision to be a novelist? »My father's novel was about Nantucket (and other islands, too, I'm sure) and was a put-down of anyone who wasn't born on the island. If anything, my father discouraged me from becoming a writer. His father had been a writer and actor, Robert Benchley; he himself had been a reporter and a critic and was now a freelance writer, and he knew all too well how hard it was to make a living as a writer. He scratched for every dollar and was barely able to pay my tuitions. I worked at a more-or-less full-time job while I was at college, to earn my own walking-around money.

But once he saw that I was interested in writing, he did a wonderful thing. For two summers, when I was 15 and 16, he paid me the going wage I might make as a gardener or a soda jerk or a club attendant, and my only duty was to sit alone in a room with a typewriter for four hours every day, or until I produced a thousand words, whichever came first. He didn't want to read it; I never had to do anything with it. But I had to produce it. He wanted me to experience both the solitude and the discipline that are requisites of a writing life, to see if I could tolerate them. If I couldn't, he said, I'd better start looking in another direction.

As things turned out, I not only tolerated discipline and isolation, I liked them, and so, at the age of 17, I became half a professional writer: I say half because although I sent story after story to *The New Yorker* and other magazines, none of the stories sold. So I was a professional in that I wrote to make money, but I wasn't a professional in that I never made any. I sold my first freelance journalism at 18, and my first fiction at 21, to *Vogue* magazine.

Did he have any suggestions for making the connection from novel to movies? »Several of my father's books were sold to movies and television, but he never participated in the production of any of them, even though he had been a full-time screenwriter in the mid-1950s. His advice was: take the money and run.

***Jaws* was such a runaway best seller that it surprised most folks in the staid publishing world. How did your publishers initially view the book? When *Jaws* was released as a novel in 1974, it was probably difficult to imagine that Hollywood could come up with the technology to make a mechanical shark feasible.** »Nobody thought *Jaws* would be a success. It was a first novel, and nobody reads first novels. It was a novel about a fish, for God's sake, and who cared about fish? Finally, we all knew it couldn't be made into a movie, because it was a given that no one could catch and train a Great White shark, and everyone involved thought that Hollywood's special-effects technology was nowhere near advanced enough to build a credible mechanical shark.

I understand that you went through a considerable process just to come up with the title? »The title was one of a thousand lucky breaks that happened to the book and the movie. Tom and I labored through about 125 titles, pretentious titles like *A Stillness In The Water* and *Leviathan Rising*, down-market titles like *The Jaws Of Death* and (from my father) *What's That Noshin' On My Laig?* At last, with 20 minutes left before the book had to go into production, I said to Tom, "Look, we can't agree on a title. In fact, the only word we both like is 'jaws.' Why don't we call the bloody thing '*Jaws*'?"

He said, "*Jaws*? What does it mean?"

"Who knows?" I said. "At least it's short."

That was most everyone's reaction." *Jaws*? What does it mean?" And always the response, "Who knows? At least it's short."

It turned out, of course, to be the perfect title: mysterious, dangerous, a little oblique rather than dead-on. And, yes, short, so it fit on a book cover and a movie-house marquee in gigantic letters.

There was nothing subtle about *Jaws* in terms of invoking an almost visceral fear response in the reader. Did you expect that it would have the impact on the public that it did? »No one, least of all I, had any hope that it would have any impact on anyone at all. I was trying to see if I could write a novel. Period.

You wrote with surprising accuracy for a layperson on shark behavior at the time. How did you do your research on the Great White? »Come with me back to the early 1970s. The environmental movement was in its infancy. Earth Day was only a couple of years old. The prevailing attitude about the sea was that it was infinite and invulnerable to anything and everything humans could do to it. Very few people knew anything at all about sharks, and even fewer knew anything about Great Whites. I did all the research I possibly could, which was very little. In addition to reading the accepted texts on sharks, such as *Shadows In The Sea*, Cousteau's shark book and David Davies' *Sharks And Sharks Attacks*, I watched *Blue Water, White Death* as many times as I could and read Peter Matthiessen's account of the odyssey, *Blue Meridian*. By then, I felt I knew pretty much everything that was generally known at the time... not as much as Perry Gilbert or Eugenie Clark, certainly, but as much as any layman.

Were you a diver at the time? Tell us a bit about your early dive experiences. »I had been a diver since 1961, when I was in the south of France and had tried this new sport in the waters off Antibes. The only instruction we received (in French) was, "Don't hold your breath on the way up." Not until after the dive did I realize we had been pitched overboard in 110 feet of water. The assumption of the divemaster was that we'd come up when we ran out of air. There weren't even J-valves on the tanks. After that, I dove whenever I could, but I didn't get certified until 1969 or '70, when I wrote a piece for Holiday magazine on the training course at UNEXSO on Grand Bahama.

Did you have any aspirations to sell the rights for a movie? »A sale to the movies never occurred to me until the book began to have extraordinary pre-publication success: book clubs, paperback sales, foreign sales, etc.

Who courted you for the rights? »Nobody courted me. The manuscript was circulated among the studios by my agents. The "coverage" – meaning the reaction by professional readers – was favorable; in part because the property was what was (and is) called "high concept," i.e. the story could be encapsulated into one sentence. Only the readers ever read the entire manuscript. They put a one-or-two-page synopsis on top of the pile of

1. With Richard Dreyfuss on the set 2. Steven Spielberg preparing Benchley for his scene in *Jaws* 3. Wife Wendy and son Clayton, with the author and Roy Scheider on *Jaws* set

paper. On top of that went a one-paragraph synopsis and a recommendation. Finally, on top of that went a letter grade – A, B, C, D. No executive ever looked at even the two-pager if the grade wasn't at least a high 'B.'

Universal was late in bidding on *Jaws*, or so I heard, because the final reader had meant to put an 'A' on the paper but had used a lower-case letter 'a' which he didn't fully close. As written, it looked like a 'c.' Only after several studios were buzzing about the book did Dick Zanuck and David Brown, the excellent producers, wonder what the hoo-hah was all about and look at the coverage. They then joined the bidding.

What did they offer as compensation? »I have no idea how the bidding went – if there was actual bidding – but the final offer from Universal was $150,000 for the

"Sequel rights!?" shouted I. "I don't care about sequels; who'll ever want to make a sequel to a movie about a fish? Sell them the rights to anything they want ... my life as an astronaut, ANYthing. I need money!"

"Nay," said she. "This is important. Be patient."

And so I was, eating paint and serving sawdust to the kids. As things turned out, of course, she was right. In turn for relinquishing all rights to any sequels – save for a one-time payment of $70,000 for each one – John Ptak secured a doubling of my participation in the original, which was the only one that made substantial profits.

But you'd never done a screenplay? 》David Brown, one of the most gracious, kindly, generous and thoughtful producers ever to work in the fetid swamps of Hollywood, convinced me that I must write the screenplay because only I had the knowledge and the creative genius to do it justice. Naïf that I was, I bathed happily in the ridiculous praise. Not till much later did I discover that the only reason I was permitted to lay a finger on the screenplay was that there was at the time a threat of a craft strike – writers, actors, electricians, I don't remember which – that would have shut down the industry. Because I had never written a screenplay, I wasn't yet a member of the Writers Guild of America, West, so I could continue to work even if a strike did occur. The producers would, therefore, be assured of getting 120 pages that would, at least, be in English and from which they could begin to build the movie.

Jaws ended up with a rookie director named Steven Spielberg. What was your first impression of him? 》As I understand it, Steven was the choice of Sidney Scheinberg, then the president of Universal. Zanuck and Brown – and I, sort of – had interviewed several possible directors, including one who said (out loud), "I've always wanted to do a movie about a whale." Spielberg wasn't a rookie; he had done two movies, a TV movie called *Duel*, about a malevolent truck, and *Sugarland Express*, with Goldie Hawn, and Scheinberg already recognized his genius. With a proposed budget of only $2.5 million, what did Universal have to lose? My first impression – and my lasting impression – was of a young man knowledgeable far beyond his 26 years, a veritable encyclopedia of film, utterly confident, certain of exactly the movie he wanted to make, very pleasant, tolerant of my stupendous ignorance, willing to help me even though he knew (which I didn't) why I had been hired and he had very little reason to believe that I'd turn in anything remotely usable.

Were you satisfied with the movie? 》Absolutely. The only serious, ongoing argument Steven and I had was about the ending. I said that his ending was absurd, couldn't happen, wouldn't be believable, blah, blah, blah. He said, in effect, "I don't care; if I've got the audience hooked for the first two hours, I can do anything I want in the last three minutes and they'll stick with me."

He felt that my ending, the one in the book, was a downer for the movie. He wanted his audience on their feet, screaming and cheering at the end, not wallowing in gloom. He was right, of course... for the movie. It all goes back to William Goldman's old dictate: in film, truth is beautiful, reality is wonderful, but neither of them is worth a dime compared to believability. And contrary to what I knew, Steven had, indeed, lured his audience into believing what he wanted them to at the end.

The other significant changes – losing the Mafia stuff, the romance between Hooper and Ellen, the death of Hooper, etc. – were known to me from the beginning, and I was easy with them. Dick Zanuck's first instruction to me was to "lose all the backstories. I want this to be an A to Z adventure story, a straight line from beginning to end." One of the many, many enriching things Steven gave the A to Z story was the texture, all the little details that fleshed out the characters, like the wonderful scene between Brody and his little son when they make faces at each other, and the drinking scene on the boat at night, which ends with Quint's by-now-classic speech about the sinking of the *Indianapolis*.

How did you come to play a bit role as the news guy on the beach in the film? »David Brown knew I had worked in television as a writer, reporter and anchor, so the role would be second nature for me ... i.e., wouldn't need any acting. *Jaws* and I were getting so much

publicity that he knew that to cast me would give the press something new to write about. Steven had no objection; if I stunk up the place, he could always cut me out.

Did you get your SAG card? »Yes, indeed. So when, later on, I was offered tiny roles in *The Deep*, *Mrs. Parker & The Vicious Circle* and *Creature* (aka *White Shark*). I was already a card-carrying, legal member of SAG.

When *Jaws* was released in the summer of 1975 it opened to huge business and then kept getting bigger. Did you expect that kind of box office success? »No one could have anticipated the phenomenon that *Jaws* became. We had evidence – from screenings, previews and cards that audiences at those events filled out – that people liked the movie a lot, but the prospect of it becoming, albeit briefly, the largest-grossing movie in history was the farthest thing from anyone's mind.

People were afraid to go in the water at the beach. Did you ever dream that you could influence the behavior of millions like that? »Never. Nor had I any ambition to do so.

Many remember the chaos that *Jaws* caused to the infant sport diving business. Diving courses fell off nearly 50 percent and stayed depressed for over a year. Did you ever experience any negativity directed at yourself when you came in contact with dive operators? »Sure. I got hostile letters, messages,

phone calls and press from dive operators, Cousteau and quite a few marine environmentalists (though there weren't very many back then).

Your notoriety from the *Jaws* fame led you into a series of diving adventures of your own. Can you tell us about those and what it was like to confront a Great White yourself the first time? »*Shark Trouble* contains most of the more memorable ones, and I haven't the time, nor you the space, to recount them. I have never, thank God, had any experience even remotely resembling your horrible day in 1972 on the north shore of St. Croix that you tell so well in *Great Shark Adventures*. I hope I never do. *(editor's note: Bret Gilliam survived a fierce attack by two Oceanic Whitetip sharks that killed his dive buddy. The incident is related in detail in the book Benchley refers to, available from Key Porter Books, Canada, edited by Marty Snyderman.)*

More than death-defying adventure, what *Jaws* gave me and my family was the opportunity to gain experience and, most important, education about the sea and its inhabitants. I was able to grow alongside the marine-environmental movement itself. From the first shark show I did for ABC's *The American Sportsman* in 1974 – diving with Tigers, Bronze Whalers and Great Whites in Australia – through nearly three decades of working with *National Geographic Magazine* and various television entities, right up to the present (I leave for South Africa in ten days' time to dive with Whitey for a show called – I kid you not – *The New American Sportsman*), I've been blessed with wonderful opportunities to learn, first-hand, about the

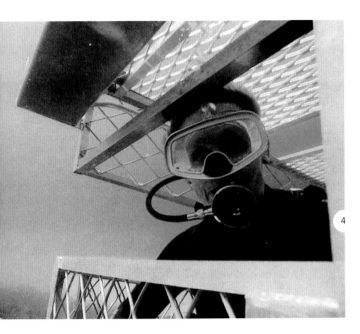

1. With best friend, Stan Waterman 2. Face-off with Oceanic Whitetip during filming of *The American Sportsman* 3. Benchley in cage during ABC special in South Africa, 1999 4. Shark's-eye-view of Benchley as he views the first Great White he ever saw off South Australia in 1976

sea. Looking back on the range of animals I've been privileged to dive with – from all kinds of sharks to orcas to giant octopuses to mantis shrimp, sea snakes and sperm whales – I find only one word that fits: luck. I have been amazingly (and eternally gratefully) lucky.

The very first time I saw a Great White underwater was totally by accident. It was late in 1974, and Stan Waterman and I were just beginning the ABC show. We had arrived on the Barrier Reef, directly off Townesville, where we knew there were no White sharks. Stan went overboard to test his empty 16 mm housing for leaks. I, with nothing better to do, went with him.

As soon as we hit the water, before we could even clear our masks, Stan pointed downward. Rising at us like a slow-motion torpedo from the bottom maybe

40 feet away, was a Great White shark – not very big, perhaps 10 feet max, but a White shark nevertheless. As everyone who has seen Whitey underwater knows, it is an animal unlike any other, instantly recognizable. I had no idea what to do. I knew only that I shouldn't turn and scramble to get back on the boat. So I froze.

Stan didn't. One of the few people on the planet who had ever been in the water with Whitey, Stan knew that the proper thing to do was to appear, as much as possible, like a big, healthy, fearless animal. So, with his housing held out in front of him like a monstrous eye and with me beside (but mostly behind) him, he kicked slowly down, directly at the shark. The shark did precisely what it was supposed to: it kept coming until the distance between us had closed to maybe 10 feet, then it slowly arced downward, swam beneath us and disappeared. Stan checked his housing for leaks, and then – slowly and with forced (on my part) calm – we swam back to the boat.

"By Gregory!" Stan thundered as soon as his mask was off. "Wasn't he a stunner? Wonderful!"

I, wondering whether or not to vomit, had nothing to add.

Blue Water, White Death **was a remarkable documentary on Peter Gimbel's search for the Great White shark. Released in early 1971, had you seen the film and was it an influence on the creation of** *Jaws?* It certainly was. Stan Waterman came to be a close friend and diving advisor. As Stan tells it, in early 1974 he saw the cover of *The New York Times Magazine*, a picture of me in front of a Richard Ellis painting of a Great White shark. The cover story was called something like, "The making of a bestseller." It was a cynical, superior, semi-accurate story about *Jaws*, which was soon to be published. Stan says his immediate reaction was, 'Hey, who's intruding on my territory? I'm the shark expert around here.' He saw in the magazine that I lived nearby, so he sent me a photograph of him in a cage facing Whitey from *Blue Water...* accompanied by a nice note suggesting that we meet. We did.

I noticed that your most recent book, *Shark Trouble*, **is dedicated to Stan. Was that a surprise for him?** A surprise? I suppose so. I gave the book to him in galley proofs and showed him the dedication. He reacted as you would expect: with gratitude and infinite grace. Undoubtedly, he said something that only he would know how to say, but I can't remember it.

Do you still keep in touch and go diving together? We're in touch all the time. He lives only five miles from me, so whenever he's home, we get together for lunch or dinner quite often. We haven't had an opportunity to dive together since … well, I can't remember when, but it's been a while.

gallon underwater set. He was even in the movie, as the dockmaster who barks at Coffin (Eli Wallach).

Once again, the movie production broke a lot of new ground with nearly half the film being shot underwater. Were you involved on the sets during production? One of my lasting regrets is that *The Deep* wasn't recognized publicly (by the Academy or any other group) for its truly groundbreaking

On the set of *The Deep* in Bermuda, 1976, Nick Nolte, Benchley and Jacqueline Bissett

You followed *Jaws* with another blockbuster in *The Deep*. This time the villains were human bad guys and diving was part of the adventure. I understand that Robert Shaw's character was patterned on Bermuda wreck diving legend, Teddy Tucker. How did you come to know him? In 1970 or '71, *National Geographic* offered me a choice of two stories: poisonous sea snakes in the Coral Sea or the history of Bermuda as told by the shipwrecks around it. Thank heavens, I chose the latter. The magazine sent the late Ken MacLeish, an old friend of Teddy and Edna's, down with me to make introductions, for Teddy was known to be prickly about the people he worked with. I spent six weeks diving with him, and we've been fast friends ever since.

Did Tucker like his reincarnation as Treece? He's never said so directly, but I believe so. Teddy worked very closely on the movie. His was the workboat, the mother ship, the camera platform, the ferry, the cafeteria and home base whenever the crew was at sea. His were the decisions about whether or not to go to sea, where to go to accommodate the wind and weather, and whence and how to stock the two-million-

underwater cinematography. Al Giddings, Stan, Chuck Nicklin, Tony Masters (Art Director), Peter Yates and a lot of others accomplished marvels that have never been attempted, let alone duplicated, since. They worked for endless hours in horrible conditions and produced a feature film unlike any other. I don't know why the real world of underwater – as opposed to the fantasy world created in pictures like *The Abyss* – has been so neglected, but it has.

Once again, I wrote three drafts of the screenplay. It was rewritten by a couple of others, and then returned and was re-re-written almost daily on location. I was in Bermuda for most, but not all, of the shoot, and, once again, I was in the movie. Where, you might well ask? I'm in the beginning of the re-edited expanded TV version, playing an officer on the bridge of the *Goliath* as she runs onto the reefs. Extra scenes had to be shot, to make the movie long enough to fill two two-hour slots on TV. Al Giddings was in the TV version, too, as was Cameron Mitchell.

***The Deep* had a bunch of memorable characters involved including Peter Yates as the director and Peter Guber as the producer. What were they like**

to work with?** »Peter Yates, the director, a gracious, low-keyed Englishman, was a delight. He had had a huge success with *Bullitt*, and he plunged into these unknown waters with intelligence and enthusiasm. He had never dived before, yet by the middle of the production he was completely comfortable in the water: standing on the bottom, for example, in jeans and a shortie neoprene top, both arms over his head to hold Stan steady so he could shoot down at Robert Shaw's character digging in the sand. He endured with a smile all the normal perils of movie-making – the anxious studio people, the occasionally difficult cast and crew members, the frenetic producer desperate to bring his picture in on time and on budget – plus all the added horrors of shooting hours and hours of film under water. As calm as his exterior seemed, however, I noticed that by the end of the shoot a nurse was by his side at all times.

Peter Guber, the producer, was like a genius on speed. He worked and talked and talked and worked nonstop, 18 hours a day, generating ideas every five seconds, discarding most of them at the first sign of disagreement, keeping the ones that worked. He was a presence everywhere and always, even when he wasn't around. He was nervous, and justifiably so: this picture could be his passport to a good career as an independent producer, or his ticket back to the relative anonymity of the law or business (he had graduate degrees in both law and business).

He marketed the picture brilliantly, opening it in hundreds of theaters all at once – standard practice today, of course, but pretty new back then – and earning huge receipts in the first two weeks. I've heard it said that *The Deep* saved Columbia Pictures from financial ruin. Whatever the truth of that, Peter Guber certainly used its success as a springboard for his remarkable career. I have no idea what he made on it – a few million dollars, I guess – but he parlayed those bucks into a fortune of hundreds and hundreds of millions.

Your old pal Stan Waterman and Al Giddings teamed up as co-directors of the underwater unit. That must have been satisfying. Did you dive on the film production? »I dove whenever I wanted to, but after touring the underwater set and watching a few days' shooting, there wasn't much to see. To quote another of William Goldman's truisms, "The first day on a movie set is the most exciting day of your life; the second day is the most boring." I didn't join the crew in Tortola (the wreck of the *Rhone*) or join the second unit in Australia, where the shark sequences were filmed. I was enormously pleased that Stan and Al were involved, and I take a measure of credit for suggesting them to Yates and Guber and introducing them all. They did a terrific job.

Who came up with the idea to put Jackie Bissett in a wet t-shirt? »I have no idea, but I'd guess it was one of the two Peters ... Guber or Yates.

How did she feel about that? »She was a very game and gutsy lady. She had never dived – Stan taught her – and she became competent and very willing. I know she wasn't happy with the wet-T-shirt scenes: she felt her gorgeous body was being exploited, which, of course, it was. But she never complained in public (to my knowledge), and she was savvy enough to realize that all the attention she received for her ample endowments could not but help make her a movie star.

The film's second unit also included the young Howard Hall as a support diver who speared fish to start the shark frenzy scene. You've since done some other film work with Howard and Michele. What's it like to work with them? »Howard and Michele are now, and always have been in the more than 20 years I've known them, wonderful. No other word fits. They're not only supremely gifted, but they work like demons and produce (in my opinion) many of the finest underwater films in the world. They're enormously strong – both of them – very smart and ingenious. They have wonderful senses of humor, they're helpful to the ignorant and tolerant of the inept (I speak from personal experience here), and they're as excellent shipmates as anyone could wish for.

I understand that Michele was your inspiration for *The Girl of the Sea of Cortez*? How did that come about? »True. The story's much too long to recount here, so I refer you to the account in *Shark Trouble*. Anything to drive my book sales…

Considering that you were responsible for giving Robert Shaw two of the best parts in his movie career, how was it he didn't end up in your next movie, *The Island*? »In the first place, he wouldn't have been right for the lead. In the second, I never heard his name suggested. In the third place, I have no idea that he would have accepted the part had it been offered to him.

The Island may not have done the box office of Jaws and The Deep but Michael Caine gave a credible performance. Why haven't we seen Beast or White Shark rolled out for the big screen? »Both have been on the small screen. *Beast* was sold to Universal as a feature, but, after receiving scripts from both me and John Carpenter, the studio deemed it too expensive – around $30 million, which doesn't seem like much today, when the average movie costs something like $74 million to make and market, but it stopped them back then. It ended up as a two-part miniseries on NBC in 1996, and I gather it got good ratings.

White Shark was optioned for a feature in 1994, but, again, various studios thought it would be too expensive. So it languished for a while and was finally made into a miniseries for ABC. Were the producers faithful to the book? Why, certainly: they kept everything but the title (it was renamed *Creature*), the location, the good guys, the bad guys, the monster and the story. I don't remember what year it was broadcast, but I heard that it did okay. It starred Craig T. Nelson and Kim Cattrall – long before her *Sex And The City* triumph.

Your latest book, Shark Trouble, might be interpreted as something of a mea culpa. You've spent a lot of time in recent years working to better educate the public about the need for shark conservation and helping to bring some reality to the discussion of sharks as predators of man. How did you feel about the sensationalized stories last summer about shark attacks? »*Shark Trouble* was not intended at all as a *mea culpa*, for several reasons. I don't feel a bit of guilt about *Jaws*. The book made use of the best information that was available 30 years ago. It was as realistic as I could make it. Great White sharks had done every single thing that happened in the book, though not all at once and certainly not one single shark. Over the years, *Jaws* has brought a great deal of positive attention to the plight of sharks and the ocean. I still get about a thousand letters a year from kids who weren't alive when the book was published or the movie released, and they all express fascination and adoration for sharks. The conservation work I've done since – and do still – is the result of education and growth: mine. I've grown up with the environmental movement, and with what I – we all – know now, I couldn't possibly write *Jaws* today. Last summer's hysteria was dumb, hideous and downright wrong! I campaigned against it all summer, and in the fall it became the genesis of *Shark Trouble*. I wanted to write something that set the record straight and pointed out how the Internet makes us all vulnerable to distortions, wild exaggerations, and outright lies.

Are you and your family still active divers? »Oh yes. My two grown kids work in New York and don't have much chance to dive, but Wendy and I and 15-year-old Christopher dive as often as we can. We three took long trips to Polynesia and Galapagos for the *Geographic*, and Christopher has learned from Teddy Tucker how to be a discerning bottle collector. His favorite pastime is diving for old bottles in Bermuda.

What are your favorite places to dive? »That depends on what we're looking for. For White sharks: South Africa. For shipwrecks: Bermuda. For sheer beauty: the Barrier Reef. I've never, though, been to the Philippines, which I hear is spectacular. For variety, beauty and WWII relics: New Guinea. For pristine wildlife and (relatively) untouched reefs in this hemisphere: The Gardens of the Queen, off the southeast coast of Cuba.

Any bad encounters with sharks yourself? »I've had some exciting encounters – all detailed in *Shark Trouble* – but I've never been bitten nor witnessed anyone being bitten. I repeat: I feel awkward even speaking about shark problems in your presence. Your ghastly day near St. Croix is worse than anything I can imagine.

Do you think that sharks are getting a better reputation from the efforts of those like yourself who can use celebrity as a bully pulpit? »I hope so, I think so, but it's hard to know for sure. Certainly, the devastation that's happening to shark populations has nothing to do with fear of sharks: it's all due to human greed.

How do you feel about Florida's ban on shark feeding for divers? »I think it's overkill. Some shark-feeding enterprises – most, in fact – are well run, safe and genuinely educational for the public. A few aren't. I don't think the entire industry needed to be shut down.

What marine life do you find most fascinating? Since I don't take photographs and thus don't know much about the macro creatures that David Doubilet and Stan and others know so well, I still gravitate toward big animals. Sharks are endlessly fascinating to me.

What more should we be doing to further the conservation efforts for sharks and other marine species? It sounds banal, but the answers really are: education and lobbying. I recently spent a day in Washington, lobbying four Senators and two Congressmen on issues like IFQs (Individual Fishing Quotas) and MPAs (Marine Protected Areas), which, in my opinion, are the best solutions currently available to the problem of depletion of species.

Pardon me, but I have to ask, were you involved in the later movie editions in the *Jaws* series? They weren't exactly *Citizen Kane* material. I had nothing to do with any of the sequels. I didn't even see them. I took my fee for each one, and ran like a rabbit.

How many copies of your novels are in print circulation? I haven't the faintest idea. The generally accepted figure for *Jaws* has for years been 20 million, but since it's still in print all around the world, that figure must have grown. Curiously, Bantam let it go out of print here in the U.S., so when the rights reverted to me, I sold them (for a mere pittance) to one of the divisions of Random House, which has kept a paperback in print ever since. I'm told it sells about a 1,000 copies a year – no bestseller, for sure, but worth keeping around. Needless to say, the other books haven't sold nearly as many copies, and most of them are out of print in the U.S.

The royalties will probably put your great grandchildren through Harvard, right? Ah, if only. I receive a few hundred dollars a year from book royalties and a few thousand from the movies of *Jaws* and *The Deep*. I'm not complaining, mind you; I've been very lucky. But if the markets keep plummeting, everything may vanish like my lap when I stand up.

As one who has read and kept first editions of all your novels, what can we look forward to next? I never know what I'm going to write next. What I'm doing next – now and for the foreseeable future – is traveling and speaking on behalf of environmental groups. And, in collaboration with Teddy Tucker and Dr. Greg Stone of the New England Aquarium and the Bermuda Underwater Exploration Institute, I make short films about ocean issues that are given away, free, to any aquarium or museum – or school, for that matter – that wants them. Since no money's involved, success is measured only by how many institutions keep asking for more and how many awards they win. By those standards, the films seem to be doing pretty well.

Will they save the oceans? No. Will I? Not a chance. But if we don't keep hoping and trying, coming up with ideas like IFQs and MPAs and buckets of other acronymic experiments, we might as well retire to the back room with a bottle of gin, and wait for night to fall.

We concluded the interview then and Peter departed off to a dive trip. When the piece was published in Fathoms magazine a few months later, he sent me a note, "Bret, your interview with me is my favorite of all the ones I've done. It has one incontrovertible asset that few, if any others have had: absolute fidelity. The words are mine: no more, no less, no editing, no illusions… and if someone has a bone to pick with them, he or she can come directly to me. In short, it's what an interview should be (and so few are): dead-on accurate."

Peter passed away in February 2006. The entire world mourned his passing. A wave of articles and obituary features poured forth and I was surprised to see many pieces from this interview excerpted to shed a more personal light on him through his own words that we shared.

I think what I appreciated most about Peter was his wicked sense of humor. I had kept original hardback editions of his books in my collection for years and had him sign them for me when we did the interview. His inscription in Jaws reads, "To my friend Bret who publishes the best diving magazine in the world. I see that this is a first edition that you paid $6.95 for. That's a bargain!" He then scrawled a little rendition of a shark over his signature.

I will always treasure the collection but the best bargain I made was in sharing time with the fascinating man who wrote them. ∎

:: dick bonin

ALL PHOTOS FROM DICK BONIN COLLECTION EXCEPT AS NOTED

Dick Bonin

FOUNDER OF SCUBAPRO

BY BRET GILLIAM

SCUBAPRO

WHEN I ORIGINALLY STARTED THE INTERVIEW SERIES MANY YEARS AGO IN DEEP TECH MAGAZINE,

the people chosen were relatively high-profile individuals – most with a background in filming or photojournalism excellence. But this series would have been woefully incomplete if I had failed to profile one of diving's most innovative leaders and pioneers in manufacturing. »

Dick Bonin, the co-founder of Scubapro, has been responsible for some of the most technically advanced equipment lines the industry has ever seen. For those who started diving in the late 1960s or early 1970s, the Scubapro line was revered as the Rolls-Royce of scuba diving. Virtually all other manufacturers were viewed as "also rans" who played second fiddle to the stuff that was stamped with the memorable "S" logo and marked a person as a

serious, committed diver.

The list of diving notables who swore by the Scubapro brand included Stan Waterman, Paul Tzimoulis, Dick Anderson, Jack McKenney, Dr. George Benjamin, Tom Mount, Ann Kristovitch, Sheck Exley, Jim Bowden, Wes Skiles, Hal Watts, Rob Palmer, Howard & Michele Hall, Marty Snyderman, Bob Talbot, Jimmy Stewart, Chuck Nicklin, Dr. Sylia Earle, myself and just about every Caribbean and Pacific divemaster who knew that the gear from Dick Bonin would endure just about every abuse and still bring them back alive. It was a brand built from the outset on the reputations of Bonin and his staff who promised high performance and reliability without compromise. Bonin also took the unprecedented step of offering a lifetime guarantee on his equipment including parts!

In addition to earning the respect of hundreds of thousands of divers who bought his gear, Bonin became a mentor and father figure to his loyal retailers who showcased his line and his philosophy of diving excellence. Bonin was the first to offer business counseling and focused marketing programs to help the dive stores of long ago realize their profit potential. He stood shoulder to shoulder with them in delivering and supporting a brand that became the "gold standard" of diving for nearly three decades.

Think back a moment to some of the "firsts" that Bonin's Scubapro company brought to the industry: the enduring flow-through piston design of his regulators beginning with the immortal Mark V introduced in 1970, the first low-pressure BC inflator, the first back-mounted BC for widespread distribution, the first silicone mask, the first jacket style BC (the infamous Stabilizing Jacket), the shotgun snorkel incorporating an exhaust valve that made clearing effortless, the first integrated inflator/second stage regulator called the AIR II, the first analog decompression meter, the first pilot valve assisted second stage called the AIR I, and last but not least, the celebrated Jet Fin that forever changed the design of what used to be called "flippers." It's a legacy unequaled to this day and perhaps forever.

Dick's passion for providing great equipment that constantly pushed the envelope in design and practicality along with the best dealer support in the industry made him almost a mythical character to those who had a chance to work with him. Above all, Dick was, first and foremost, a real diver who personally evaluated, tested and approved every item his company brought to market. He surrounded himself with the brightest minds in the industry and pushed his research and development engineers to produce the next great piece of diving gear that no serious diver could be without… every year for what seemed an eternity in the short history of the burgeoning diving business.

Bonin got his start as a Navy officer assigned to some of the earliest dive teams and cut his teeth testing gear and blowing up beach approaches in some of the most distant locations in the world. When his Navy hitch was up, he decided to take a stab at selling dive gear for some early manufacturers before realizing that the only way he was going to get the kind of equipment and the company policies he believed in was to do it himself. A partnership with another diving pioneer, Gustav Dalla Valle, led to the start of their own company in 1963. Both men were working for the soon-to-be-bankrupt Healthways company. Dick had been brought in to manage a new division for diving equipment that would be sold only through professional dive stores under the name Scubapro. When the parent company bit the dust, Gustav bought the rights to the name and got its earnest hard-charging manager as well. He paid the princely sum of one dollar!

Dick has noted ruefully, "Gustav bought Scubapro for a dollar and got me with it. He always said he overpaid."

Well, if he did overpay, these two oddly matched entrepreneurs quickly turned that investment into one of the largest success stories in diving history. They built their company into diving's premier brand and then attracted a plethora of corporate conglomerates that wanted to acquire them for their continued growth history and ever-increasing profits. Finally, against Bonin's wishes as the minority shareholder, Dalla Valle sold the company to Johnson Worldwide Associates for a then unprecedented multi-million dollar sum. The following year Johnson forced Dalla Valle out but Bonin continued as President and directed the company's growth and continued profitability until 1991 when he parted ways and retired.

Typically, Dick is discreet about the controversy surrounding leaving the company he founded and nurtured to such success. Ever the gentleman and loath to stoop to the level of those who, in his opinion, have not met his standard of professionalism, he declines to comment on his abrupt exit. However, insiders confirm that his independence and refusal to compromise on issues of product quality and business ethics eventually made him *persona non grata* with the corporate suits that seemed only to care about bottom lines on the balance sheet with little regard to sustaining the brand in the long term. Whatever actually took place will probably remain shrouded in confidentiality agreements and other legalese. But consider the aftermath: a revolving door of inconsistent and oft times inept management making poor decisions doomed the once proud Scubapro line to shrinking market share and a virtual halt to new product innovation. Currently

(2003) mired in a series of product recalls and litigation alleging product defects, the Johnson stock price has dropped and Mamdouh Ashour, the head of its diving division (Scubapro and Uwatec), a man Bonin once banished from the U.S. operation, has taken refuge in Europe in the face of pending lawsuits and possible criminal charges. In the ultimate irony, Johnson Worldwide is also suing Ashour, its own ex-chief executive of diving.

It's hard to imagine anything of the sort taking place under the leadership of Bonin.

There was no problem getting access to Dick. I've been friends with him since 1971 when I helped persuade the U.S. Navy to officially add Scubapro to its list of equipment for Navy divers for the first time. I later became one of Scubapro's top dealers through my Caribbean operation known as V. I. Divers. I visited Dick at his home in Huntington Beach, California in July 2003 to conduct the interview.

I vividly remember meeting Dick the first time at one of the old National Sporting Goods Association shows during a freezing 1972 winter snowstorm in Chicago. Back then, before the DEMA Show, diving manufacturers exhibited to dealers at this mammoth trade show and tended to get lost in the endless aisles of tennis rackets, basketballs, footballs, and snow ski apparatus. Wandering the massive McCormick Place Convention Center, I finally found the tiny Scubapro exhibit and was wrapped in the firm grip of Bonin who seemed to instinctively recognize his far-flung dealers. We talked about our common Navy heritage and I was thrilled to finally see the entire line of gear after previously only knowing some items from the catalog. By

1. Bret Gilliam, Bonin and Bill Walker in front of V.I. Divers original store, St. Croix, Virgin Islands, 1973
2. Gilliam and Bonin, 30 years later, 2003

the time I left Chicago, I felt like Dick was a surrogate father and he promised to visit me in the Virgin Islands some time in the future.

Yeah, right. I figured I had about as much chance of seeing Dick in St. Croix as I did of seeing it snow there. But sure enough, he arrived a year or so later and cut a swath through the island's social scene as though a movie matinee idol had appeared. You have to remember that back then there were only about 7,000 expatriate Americans living there and it seemed that every one of them either snorkeled or dived and I'd outfitted every last one of them in Scubapro gear from my dive store. Dick was in his early 40s then and looked like an action movie hero. Every day we went diving and talked diving business. Then at night we took in dinner and closed down most of the popular bars in the wee hours. He won a series of arm wrestling matches in a particularly tough late night watering hole, including defeating a guy twice his size and half his age. When the vanquished opponent asked the name of his better, Dick replied, "Anthony Stunning" and they're probably still talking about this mysterious character even today.

Dick Bonin was a mentor, friend, fellow diver, and the single best example of how to conduct yourself in business that I ever met. Ask any of his dealers from that era and they'll tell you the same thing. The man exuded honesty, enthusiasm, and an ingrained sense of what was right and what was wrong… along with an unbridled energy for the sport of diving. He oozed integrity. I began my first business as a Scubapro dealer when Dick picked me to distribute his gear over a much bigger established company. He saw a future for

diving in me as a gung-ho 22-year-old that transcended the hefty wallet of the larger company. It paid off for both of us. He got a dealer that bought hundreds of thousands of dollars worth of Scubapro gear over the next 15 years and I used that to springboard my tiny dive store operation into a series of successful corporations. Dick provided the initial opportunity to launch me in business and I owe everything I have today in business to him. There is no one that I have more respect for and I only hope that I can live up to the example he set for all of us.

When I met Dick he was 42 years old and was the toughest guy I ever met. Today (2003) at 73, he looks like he can still kick my ass and those of anyone else who might challenge him. He's still an active free diver and spearfisherman who regularly lands trophy fish in the company of other top divers young enough to be his grandchildren.

If there is ever a Mount Rushmore for divers, I know Stan Waterman will hold the space for George Washington, and Dick Bonin will stand in for Teddy Roosevelt. The other two spots are still up for grabs in my book.

Dick and I settled in with full coffee cups and let the tape recorder run. ■

177

How does a guy from Chicago end up diving? »I grew up in the Midwest, always loved water, swam on the high school swim team. I went to college on an athletic scholarship.

What did you play? »Basically everything, but the scholarship was for football, boxing, baseball, and swimming. Then, when the Korean War broke out, I enlisted in the Navy and they sent me to OCS. There was inter-company swimming, and an officer came over to me one day – I remember that he had a scar on his cheek – and asked if I liked sports. I said yes. "Do you like swimming?" Yeah. "When you finish OCS – you get a few choices, Destroyer, Carrier or UDT" (underwater demolition teams) – so I chose UDT.

Where did they send you? »I was at Little Creek, Virginia in January of 1953. The Korean War was on. I went through all the training. There were 137 of us when we started, 19 when we finished. When I qualified I was sent to extensive underwater training in New London and, in three months time, the Caribbean. Subsequently, I was appointed as a Submersible Operations Officer. There were two teams on the East Coast then, and three teams on the West Coast. Just 500 guys in the whole country! Each team was 100 men, with one diving officer on each team. I was appointed Diving Officer on the East Coast.

How'd you like the Navy? »It was great. I was an Ensign. Early on, our executive officer got a call from Chicago, from a fellow that ran a retail/ wholesale diving business, one of the very first. He was distributing E.R. Cross's mail order study course, *Diving for Fun and Profit*. It was written by Cross, and was a classic. He wanted someone in the Navy to read and okay what Cross was writing. So I was designated for the job. When it was time for me to get out of the Navy, the fellow in Chicago that had the retail/ wholesale operation said, "You're from Chicago, so why don't you come here and see about a job?"

Before we get to that, tell me some of the stuff you were doing in the Navy diving. They actually based you out in the Arctic or something, right? »Well, the first assignment I had was an operation up in the Arctic, blowing and surveying approaches to bring in supplies for the Far Distant Warning Stations. We

1. College football player, 1950 2. Bonin, far left, in UDT drills, 1953 3. Lt. Bonin, circa 1955 4. Blowing beach approaches with UDT divers, 1953

would go from bay to bay. They would bring us in – there were about 12-15 men beside myself – and we would do a survey and then blast it out, so there was nothing left to tear up the landing craft bringing in the supplies. We did that for about three months. Way up north, I don't remember all of the places. It was dull as hell, except when we were operating.

It must have been cold as hell? »We were working in the summertime, but the water was cold, just above freezing.

How did you stay warm? »We had good dry suits. They were made by U.S. Rubber. They were functional but you had to make sure you took care of them and wore a couple of pairs of long johns under them. You couldn't stay in the water for long, but long enough to get the job done. And we would go in and do it as

4

fast as we could. It was pretty simple. You go into a bay, do recon, and then come back the next day with explosives and lay them out, and blast the approach.

Let me tell you a story. I was just an Ensign then, too. We really wanted to do a good job, so we came in and we surveyed one of our first approaches. I said to the men, "Okay, we have to do a thorough job, so this is what we're going to do. We're going to use this much C3 explosive to be sure. That's going a little heavy." So we swim in, set a heavy checkerboard pattern, and we blew that baby sky high! Rocks and debris are coming down all over the fleet! So we go back and the fleet's skipper is waiting there, and asks, "Is it always like this?" I gulped and said, "Yeah, you've got to blast big when it's a tough job." He said, "Well, maybe I'll anchor out a little further then next time." We had a lot of exciting things up there. We shot a polar bear on one swim because, when you are in the water up there, you look like lunch.

Was it making some moves on you? Oh, of course! But we always had a boat, a landing craft or an inflatable, with one armed crewman on board. And, you know, polar bears hunt man. Outside of that, when we worked, it was exciting. But the rest of the time was boring. We read the same books over and over; showed only certain parts of movies because we knew the movies so well. Of course, there was no TV and no newspapers either.

Where did they house you? I bet it was some horrible Quonset hut or something? No, we were on an LSD (Landing Ship Dock) ship. The first ship we were on hit an iceberg on our way to the next site. The skipper of the LSD was in tactical command because he was senior to the captain of the icebreaker in front of us leading the way. A significant iceberg came around the icebreaker in front of us and hit our ship because we were steaming too fast in 70 percent ice coverage. It tore a hole about 10-14 feet high and 22 feet long. I was below when it hit and it knocked me over. I ran topside and there was complete panic. The ship was heeling over fast. It was a hell of a hole. One engineer saved the ship all by himself by his fast action. He got compartments sealed off before it got to the boiler room. We would have all been dead because, without protective suits, you had maybe 30 seconds in the water to survive. He saved the ship and us. They sent a helicopter in to pick up the skipper off of our ship and take him away. It's safe to assume they weren't bringing him in to give him a promotion!

Not to a ticker tape parade, either. 》No! Then they transferred us to another LSD and we finished our work up there. So, we had some exciting incidents in three months aboard.

I remember reading somewhere that you guys were testing some equipment and had a failure on something 250 feet deep or so. 》I was in about my third year as a Submersible Operations officer. We were using three open-circuit units, the Aqua Lung, the Northill and the Scott Air Pak. Do you remember the Scott?

Yes, certainly. 》We had been using it for a number of years, and a directive came down from the Bureau of Ships that they wanted us to do deep-water tests on those three units. I guess, for some reason, they were going to buy new equipment or something. So the Submersible Operations Platoon got on board a submarine rescue ship and we went out off of North Carolina to do deep-water tests. They wanted us to do 200 feet plus. Most of our diving was not really deep. There wasn't that much call to do much over 100 feet. We anchored overnight and put down lines the next day. Officer and chief go first so I had the Northill, and Chief Foster took the Scott. We got down pretty deep and I started taking water in and I cleared it out. Went a little further down, and took more water in, cleared it out. And I got to about somewhere over 200 feet. Anyway, I got to the point where I couldn't clear the water out and I said to myself, "You've bought the farm. You've got two minutes left in your life, and now all you can do is what you were trained for, and go up that line and whistle *Dixie* – ya know, blowing out the expanding air." So, that's just what I did, I went up that line, hand over hand and whistled *Dixie*. It seemed like forever before I got to the decompression stage. But I did get there!

How deep was the deco stage? 》Twenty-30 feet. And there we had regulators you could breathe off. "Jack Brown's" (full face masks w/surface supply hoses). The topside support staff didn't know what was going on because there was no communication, but they knew the line was going slack. And the night before, they had thrown garbage off the fantail that attracted sharks.

1. In the Arctic Ocean ice fields 2. Bonin in UDT gear, circa 1953

There were hammerheads all over, circling the deco stage and the aft end of the ship. It was spectacular, but probably not really that dangerous in retrospect. Later the Navy sent down a representative to talk to me because it was one of the deepest free ascents ever. They had the submarine rescues with the old Momsen Lungs, but this was one of the very first unaided free ascents of significant depth.

Of course, in those days you had the old UDT vests, but that's not going to be any good coming up. What were you kicking with on your feet? Duck Feet? 》Yeah, we went to Duck Feet while I was Sub-Ops officer. But on this ascent, I went hand over hand on the line. I just did what I was trained to do and it worked. What had happened is that the Northill had an exhaust valve right in the middle of the diaphragm, and it would invert under a certain amount of pressure.

You weren't going to resolve that underwater either. 》No. Later on we sent another diver down shallower and it did the same thing. It was pretty exciting in retrospect, I guess.

Now after you survived all of this stuff in the Navy, you're getting out and going back to Chicago

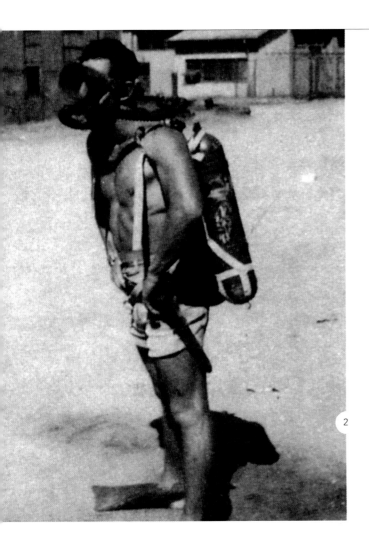

because you reviewed this diving program by E.R. Cross. Was the idea that you were going to take a look at a sport diving industry vocation? »I had no idea. I had always figured I wanted to be a salesman. I never really knew, even when I was in school. I took some accounting but I majored in economics and sports. I just always felt I should get into sales. And they offered me this job. It was a very humble beginning because it was in the early days of diving, and it was a little dive shop. Big for those days, but small by today's standards.

What year was this? »This was when I got out of the Navy, so about 1956. I said to myself, "If I like to sell, I'm going to sell something I like." So I went to work for almost no money and started selling diving equipment. I met all the original pioneers, including Cross, who was one of the most impressive men I'd ever met in my life. I worked there a little over a year. Swimaster had just started with a company called Pacific Moulded

Products in Los Angeles. They had bought some fin molds and masks, but it didn't work. So they bought a spearfishing company that included Duck Feet, wide-view masks, and a couple of other things. They had a fellow by the name of Arthur Brown, a former engineer, one of the truly smartest guys, product-wise, ever in the history of diving equipment. He developed Duck Feet. Swimaster bought the company from Brown, who was actually in this town, Huntington Beach. We used Duck Feet in UDT, and the West Coast teams had them first. When I saw them, I brought them out to the East Coast. We were using Voit fins before that. Well, Swimaster sent out a marketing consultant scouring the country to find someone to run the company, because they were only doing $200,000 in sales or less annually. He picked me and I was thrilled. So, I left the shop in Chicago, and came out to Swimaster, and took over running things. We developed it into a tremendous little company.

But when you got there, you probably only had just rubber goods, right? »Yeah, you're right, when I got there, their inventory was all rubber goods. We had more inventory than their sales, so I came in and said, "Okay, we're going to introduce the professional store theory." Because of having worked for two years in the dive shop, I learned that the demand was created by the pro in the dive shop, and the instructor who teaches you how to dive. So, I set up the distribution strictly through dive shops. We had the Duck Feet and we put a foam rubber edge on the wide view mask. It was just me and the production manager, Jorge Calderon.

That was the whole company, the two of you? »There were lots of other people in assembly but, yeah, it was basically the two of us running things. We brought out the first flexible snorkel. In Chicago, they used to sell surplus aircraft parts so I took a hose and put it on a snorkel tube, and I never forgot that. Swimaster priced it at $2.95 and everyone said we were out of our minds, but we sold them like crazy.

By the way, do you know they sell snorkels now for almost $75 and they have music built into some of them? »That's incredible! Well, later I met Jack Prodanovich and saw the guns that he was custom making. I took them and we made the first American spear guns, and sold the hell out of them. At Swimaster, it was just one continuous product break after another.

The focus of the sport in those days was geared to spearfishing, wasn't it? »Mostly, but not completely. You had a lot of competitions and people then were more inclined to be looking for power fins. There weren't many women in the sport. Everything we introduced was a quality product and it was good. We had the best masks, fins, snorkels, spearguns of that era.

What were you doing for hardware, like regulators and valves? »We really didn't have that stuff then. We did make weight belts. We made the first stainless steel quick release buckles. I never messed around with the regulators because the big boys were in the regulator business and there was just the two of us. I started experimenting with a silicone mask. We studied it. They make specialized aircraft parts out of silicone. This was when silicone was hardly known. It looked like silicone was magic. The chemist I worked with kept trying to make me a silicone mask because I figured if we were successful, it would last forever. We could never get it clear enough or pliable enough. We kept trying, but I eventually filed that idea away. Then later at Scubapro we had a rubber plant, and I went back to that project and we made the first silicone mask. If you think about it, the silicone mask is probably the most commonly used product out there. It was my dream but I didn't call it a silicone mask – I called it a "hypo-allergenic mask."

Before we jump ahead of ourselves, you were still at Swimaster, right? What year are we in? »Yes, I was at Swimaster for about three years and not making much money. It was about 1959. Sportsways was having problems, so they approached me to come and run their company.

Where were they based at that point? »They were in Paramount, California. They were owned by an automotive company. I don't know if you remember Dick Kline from the earlier days, but he was the original Sportsways founder. They were having serious problems so they approached me and offered me more money. Since it didn't look like I was going to make much where I was, I left for Sportsways. It was a good experience, but a mistake. I soon discovered I didn't like the way they did business. I had the privilege of working with Sam Lecocq, who was a truly gifted designer and that was very rewarding, but

there was a lot of nepotism in the company. Eventually I told one of the owners what I thought of him, and he fired me. But while I was at Sportsways with Sam, we established the single hose regulator. We made that a major breakthrough. With his engineering and our marketing, we made the single hose regulator number one in the country.

Didn't you guys also introduce the original submersible pressure gauges? »It wasn't the original gauge, but it was the first one put out by an established diving company. We made the first successful one. We also did the first O-ring seals and specialized tank valves. It was a good start but we all had trouble with the owners.

When you left, what happened with Sam? »Sam remained and the company went on for a couple more years, then Sportsways went bankrupt. In fact, they went down so deep they had to hold a public auction to sell off the tooling. I then went to work with a marketing consultant who hired me for Swimaster for a while. He had some fishing companies and recreational accounts. U.S. Divers, Healthways, Voit, Dacor, and Swimaster – they were the original five diving manufacturers. Healthways, a mass merchandiser, sold to everybody. They decided that they wanted a professional line, like I had done at Swimaster, so they brought me in to develop that concept. At the time, Healthways had Gustav Dalla Valle as their R&D Department head, which meant a European connection for obtaining diving products. So they paired me with him and said, "Develop a line for a new company." It was to be called Scubapro.

Did you guys come up with that name? »No, an advertising guy came up with that name. I wish I could take credit, but I can't. So, it was going to be Scubapro. I got on the phone and started calling our old dealer network, began putting things together, working with Gustav on products. Then the day after Christmas in 1962 the owners called us into the office and said, "We're in Chapter 11." So that was the end of Scubapro.

What was Gustav's reaction? »Well, he wasn't really surprised because he knew it was coming. He had a little garage warehouse, so we went there and said we were going to do it ourselves somehow. Gustav had a little money, not much.

Wasn't he an Italian count or something? 》Gustav was one of the most colorful men ever, maybe the most colorful man in diving history. He was the son of a count who cornered the silk market in Italy at one time. Gustav was given a fortune when he was a young man and blew most of it. He was well educated and had studied architecture. A very cultured guy. He was a *bon vivant* in the fullest sense of the word. Finally, he took

When you guys ended up at Healthways, was this a natural sort of teaming? I mean, you guys are so different. Gustav is so emotional and crazy, and you are so solid and controlled. 》Surprisingly, we got along fine. Gustav was fun to work with. Every day was something new. People used to say that Gustav was not a businessman, but that's not true. He was a very good businessman, intelligent and shrewd. Anyway, we were

© 1972 BY SCUBAPRO

DICK BONIN
President and General Manager Scubapro,
Vice President Under Sea Industries

GUSTAV DELLA VALLE
President, Under Sea Industries

Della Valle and Bonin from the
1972 Scubapro catalog

what money he had left and went to Haiti, and started a little glass-bottom boat business.

This was back in the day of Papa Doc? 》He got there just before. He'd take people out in a glass-bottom boat and demonstrate snorkeling and spearfishing. Then Papa Doc came to power. Gustav was also involved in a gambling casino down there, so he had to get out of Haiti fast. With the new regime taking over, Gustav got out of town and migrated, actually he escaped, to Miami. He started up a business importing dive gear from Europe. His first account was Abercrombie & Fitch. Then he signed with Healthways and had them under contract for a lot of his European lines.

thrown together and just happened to compliment each other and we worked together well. We used to fight a lot but in the best interests of the company. He used to take care of the finances and the purchasing. He couldn't handle the interaction of accounts and staff. I did that and the marketing. We worked on the products together. He bought the name Scubapro for $1 and got me, too. And, 'til the day he died, he said he paid too much.

Paid too much for both of you, huh? 》Yeah! So we started out and it was tough. This was January 3, 1963.

Was that the acorn of the Scubapro company? 》That was it. We opened up the garage door and said, "Let's go to work."

What was your first product? » Well, whatever Gustav could get from Europe on credit. Gustav had some money, but not much. Maybe $20,000 or so. And I had none. Anything he could get on credit we would bring in. For example, we brought in Squale masks that were *passé* even then. I would call the dealers and say, "Here's what I've got. Help me out and we will build a line for you." I called it "sympathy selling." That's how we started. The dealers gave us as much business as they could, not much, but whatever we could get. Then we made a regulator. This was a big step. We brought in a couple of part-time engineers that had done some work for Healthways.

Was one of these guys Dick Anderson? » Right. He came in, never really worked for us full time but gave us a hand. Dave Denis, who became our production manager and Bob Roberts, who we eventually hired, also came in. We developed the first reliable piston regulator. The first regulator we made was a true success. It was a workhorse and it was a winner. Then a little product by the name of Jet Fins came along. In the beginning, we couldn't pay the bills. Gustav and I couldn't take a salary. We couldn't pay the phone bill. We made that unforgettable mistake of bouncing the check for the taxes. I don't really know how we got through it. Every day Gustav would take the sales invoices and go to the loan shark. We did that for I don't know how long. But we finally turned the corner after about two years.

Oh, so you guys were floating loans against your sales? » We were existing off the receivables. We didn't take salaries or anything, but we made it. All of a sudden we started developing more products and adding to the distribution. Now all we had to do was get new products to the dealers out there, because I had the network built. And we did! Then we started growing so fast that we couldn't believe it.

What year did you finally develop your distinctive logo, the "S"? » That was right from the beginning. It's an enduring logo. Memorable. Classic. I changed it by adding the black and the silver. They had the "S" shape and the name when I came there. It was a wonderful name and a wonderful logo.

The company is so well remembered for its initial regulator and the Jet Fins. You guys were getting

them from France, right? » Rene Beauchat invented the Jet Fin. Beauchat was a good friend of Gustav, and was a very successful manufacturer of European diving equipment – spearguns, masks, fins, snorkels, very good stuff. He asked Gustav if he could get Jet Fins started in the United States. Gustav brought them to me, and he said "Dick can you sell these things?" And I said, "Gustav, these are the ugliest fins I've ever seen, but I'll take them to the trade show and see what

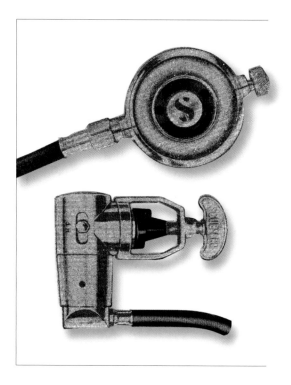

happens." I had never used them. It was a cardinal mistake because I should have. Anyway, we went to the show. We were only a couple of years old when Jet Fins came out, maybe three or four years. I took a bunch to the show and I sold some. The dealers would laugh initially and buy some samples. Then, all of a sudden, the phone calls started coming in wanting to know if we had any more of those "ugly fins." I didn't even like the name. They said, "These fins aren't bad." That taught me a big lesson. After that, I tested everything that came to Scubapro. Jet Fins just took off. I've never seen a product accelerate as quickly. As a matter of fact, I think they are still popular today.

Listen, I just got back from a month at sea at Cocos Island, and four of the divers, professional

photographers out there with me, are still using the 352 Jet Fin, the extra large Jet Fin. Frankly, I don't think they've ever built fins better than that original design. It gave you all the power you could possibly need, and none of the frills and nonsense associated with some of the designs today. I still have a pair of my original ones from 1971 that I keep on the wall in my office. I used them exclusively for, I think, 25

The revolutionary Jet fin and the Mark V regulator, enduring classics

years. 》It was a remarkable product. I understand that there are also still some of our original regulators working out there.

I can assure you that there are a lot of your original regulators in the Caribbean. 》I'm now starting to get calls from memorabilia buffs. I received a letter just last week from a fella looking for our original Scubapro manifold. He's a commercial diver. I get these calls from people all the time who want to talk about the "golden days" of Scubapro. He mentioned in the letter, "I paid $160 for a copy of the 1970 Scubapro catalog."

It's history. You guys were not only the most innovative equipment product company, but also brought a breath of innovation to your marketing.

Now, I can't remember the year but I'm going to take a stab and say it was 1973 or 1974 when you came out with that catalog with all of Dick Anderson's poetry in it. 》We have a couple of catalogs that were classics. Dick Anderson's limericks. One with recipes in it and another with nautical poetry.

I remember one of them to this day. It was from the Dick Anderson catalog and it was in the watch section. It said, "A diver wears a watch to tell what sport is his. The secondary function is to tell what time it is." I never forgot it. 》Those catalogs and the advertising campaign came from Roy Brizz. Roy is gone now.

Yeah, that particular piece was one of his innovative marketing ideas. 》I'll look for some of the catalogs, and I may have a couple of them. Well, I hear they are extremely valuable now. A complete set is priceless. But I don't know if there is a complete set anywhere.

That's one thing I really regret. I had the complete set of catalogs for the entire time that I was a dealer, 18 years, and I lost them in a boat fire in 1993. I had kept them all religiously for all those years. 》They had to be worth a fortune.

Now we are coming into the early 1970s, and you guys have really made your niche. Your concept of the development of a product like this through a pro dive store distribution network was so revolutionary. Now you are really starting to get products that no one else had even conceived of. Things like, the Mark V regulator. How did that come about? 》The Mark V was just really a product by committee. Our engineers, Gustav and I would brainstorm a product then construct an operating prototype and test the hell out of it. We had product meetings and were a diving company. We actually dove our stuff! We dove a lot. The whole company was divers. Our engineers were all divers. Our salesmen were too, of course. We spent more money on R&D than any other company. We hired the best engineers we could find. Some of them were instructors as well as divers. And we all tested our potential products for performance, for durability, for convenience, you name it.

When did you get Sam Ichikawa? »Sam came to Scubapro maybe two or three years after we started. Sam had worked with me at Sportsways. Sam worked for me longer than anybody else.

He taught me my original Scubapro repair clinic in 1971. »Sam was first in his field and did repair seminars all over the world. We picked out people like Sam for every department. We had the distribution and just needed new products and top people. Eventually we created the stabilizing jacket that revolutionized diving safety and convenience. The first time I saw that buoyancy theory being used was with Ed Brawley, when he was teaching diving. As it turns out, everybody I know took credit for the stabilizing jacket. As best I can remember, it was Mike Brock that first suggested, "Why don't we make a wrap-around version of this BC?"

As successful as the stabilizing jacket was, you preceded it in 1973 with the buoyancy compensating pack – which was the first production back-mounted unit to achieve widespread market acceptance. »We did pretty well with that. But although we gained a lot of notoriety with the BCP, the guys at At-Pac were originals with the first back-inflation style BC.

When the BCP came out in 1973, you had all these nutcase conservatives saying this is a terrible design because it's going to float you face down if you are unconscious and all this nonsense. And yet, leap ahead 20 years from there and everybody went back to back-inflated devices because it trimmed you better in the water. All the technical divers, all the cave divers, everybody that was doing wreck penetrations, they all went back to those designs. And they still dominate today; virtually the same as you guys built it back in 1973. »You know, I understand that there's not much new on the market anymore. Too bad.

There was another product you guys came out with that, in a way, revolutionized things – the shotgun snorkel. »That was Joe Schuch's idea.

That was an astounding product. It was so simple and, yet, so effective. »That was from having good people. That came from Joe Schuch, our sales manager.

The stabilizing jacket idea came from Mike Brock, a salesman. These guys were in the water all the time. There were so many new products that I'm sure all the patents put together in the entire diving industry wouldn't equal what we did at Scubapro.

I don't think they've built a better snorkel yet. I still use one myself, and I've got one of the old rubber ones. You can hardly find those anymore. I remember when you brought that out. I think that snorkel sold for $20. And you were worried about selling a $2.95 retail snorkel a few years before then. When we first got them in my store, all we had to do was give it to customers once and it changed their lives. You know what a shotgun snorkel sells for today? I think it's over $50. Fifty dollars! When we started, you could buy a whole set of scuba gear for that. »We had ideas like that. Actually, the idea for the first inflator came from a retailer in the valley, a couple of young fellows, and we said, "Hey that's a good idea. Okay, guys, we want this. What do you want, royalties or cash?" They said, "Give us the cash." So we did. In fact, we gave them more than they asked for.

Probably one of the best deals you've ever made. How many 562 Inflators did you sell? You can tell I'm an oldie. I even know the catalog numbers. I used to have them all in my head. »Gosh, I don't know but it was a lot. It was just a natural evolution and it just went like that all the way down the line. We actually dominated in a lot of categories. The more technical the category was, usually, the stronger we were.

Well, you guys owned the regulator market for almost two decades. No one could compete with you. »And with the stabilizing jackets. The Jet Fins were amazing, and snorkels. Then, when we came out with the first silicone masks, we dominated masks. But after a while everybody had silicone masks. But for a while, we were king.

We have a section in *Fathoms* magazine called the Panel of Experts and we get different questions every issue. One of the ones we asked them a few issues back was what was their original equipment and what was the most innovative equipment that they've seen along the way. Your stuff from the 1970s and 1980s so totally dominated the responses that it looked like a sales hype. Between Howard Hall, Michele Hall,

As president of Scubapro, circa 1970

Marty Snyderman, Chris Newbert, Lina Hitchcock, Stan Waterman, everybody that came down the pike and went through that era, they all seemed to be outfitted with a stabilizing jacket and other Scubapro gear.

That's fantastic, that's a pretty good crowd to be in.

You guys were riding so high, what motivated you to consider selling the company? ⟩⟩ In 1973, Gustav decided that he wanted to cash out. He thought it was time for him to get some security because we never did take big salaries for ourselves. So he wanted to sell. I was adamantly opposed. I was the minority shareholder. When we started I had 20 percent, because I didn't have any money and Gustav provided all the capital. He had control as the majority shareholder. So, I couldn't talk him out of it, and we had close to fistfights over it. Anyways, he put the company up for sale, and we had every major corporation around trying to buy it, because we were very profitable, technically we were a cash cow. And we had glamour… we were THE diving company! So we had everybody, including some of the world's largest corporations, out to see us. Wining

and dining us. Including S.C. Johnson. Ultimately we ended up selling to them in 1974, basically because it was cash. All the other companies wanted to give us stock. This was cash in our fists.

I don't know if you want to talk about it, this would be a matter of public record, but what did the company sell for? ⟩⟩ Let's just say millions, but not enough when you look back on it.

A big payday in 1974. ⟩⟩ A big payday in those days, and it was a steal. Gustav wanted the cash-out and I couldn't stop him, and he sold out. Now it gets delicate, because they "retired" him fast.

You guys had been so independent, running this innovative company and basically lavishing stuff on your R&D department. Scubapro was five years ahead of the rest of the industry for so long. With coming into the Johnson fold now, did this immediately impact the growth of the company? I know that the cash must have been nice, but were you also still free to do the innovative stuff that you wanted to do? ⟩⟩ Yeah, we were doing so well – I wouldn't say that they left us alone but, in the early days, we had less interference.

What prompted their motivation to ease Gustav out? ⟩⟩ For some reason they decided it was time for him to retire. They never did explain their thinking. I suspect it was basic economics, typical big corporate behavior.

I gotta tell you though, I'd have liked to have been there the day they tried to fire Gustav. That must have been an interesting little play. ⟩⟩ Well, it really wasn't as bad as you think. They did it delicately and I suspect he knew it was coming. I warned him before we sold, "The company will never be the same, Gustav, and they are going to get rid of all of us."

Just as an anecdotal aside here, Gustav had a reputation not only for his flamboyancy but, also, for his rather explosive emotions at times. I remember when I first met him, in 1973 or something like that, at your offices, he had a chopping block on his desk with one of your diving stilettos on it. Somebody told me the story about how one day he accidentally stabbed

somebody through the hand with it. 》Almost, actually. One of the vendors who was selling us metal parts let us down, and Gustav took the knife and went 'whack,' and it was left there swaying with about half the blade buried… right between his fingers. The guy about had a heart attack. Gustav was volatile but, let me tell you, it was all controlled. He was in complete control – but he knew when to use fear and he was very good at it. It was usually justified when he did it.

When they finally did decide to let Gustav go, how did he take it? 》He handled it well as he was no longer committed to being involved in the company. And he'd already made his payday. He made a lot of money. A lot!

And that's when he moved up to Northern California and got the wine place? 》Shortly after. He went through a divorce and his wife took half the money. He then bought the place in Mustique in the Caribbean, where his neighbors were Mick Jagger,

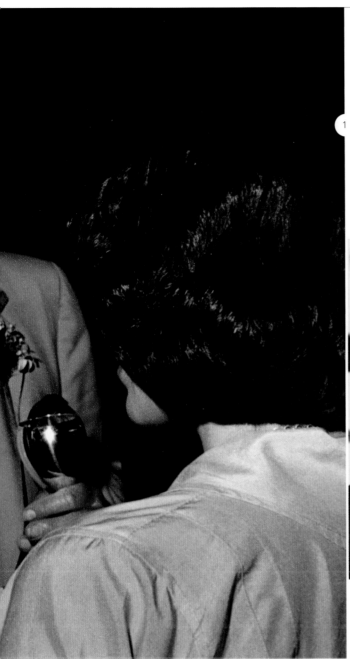

Well, let's take a twist here for a minute. You guys at Scubapro were such strong supporters of your dealers; there are probably more millionaires in the diving industry that came out of being Scubapro retailers than any other segment of the industry. You taught us about business and how to handle our money. That was a foreign concept then: to support and do sales within a professional network like that and not just throw the products everywhere they would go. You fought all sorts of battles**

1. Bonin and Gustav at Scubapro's 25th anniversary, 1988
2. Alone at the top of Scubapro after the sale to Johnson in 1974

Princess Margaret, and all that lot. Eventually, he got tired of it, and came back and bought a vineyard in Napa and developed it into a first-class winery. His wine is sold out now, year after year production is pre-sold.

He passed away what, four or five years ago? He did. He was about 75 or 76. He died of prostate cancer. I think Gustav packed an awful lot of living into the time that he had. I could make a movie on Gustav. He was the most colorful man I ever knew.

along the way with, for instance, *Skin Diver* magazine and their mail-order ads. That's got to have some colorful history to it. Actually, it always astounded me that nobody else did the same. Because it was apparent to me when I started out in a dive shop: Who created the demand for diving equipment? It was very simple, the fellow behind the counter and the fellow that teaches diving lessons. I put that into practice at Swimaster and it worked. Worked like a charm. It was not a complex theory. Basically it was sort of a takeoff on "The Golden Rule" but for business. It was pretty simple economics

SCUBAPRO DIVES

(left to right) **MIKE BROCK** / MIDWEST REGIONAL MANAGER; **JOE SCHUCH** / EASTERN REGIONAL MANAGER; **GUSTAV DELLA VALLE** / PRESIDENT, UNDER SEA INDUSTRIES; **DICK BONIN** / PRESIDENT AND GENERAL MANAGER SCUAPRO, VICE PRESIDENT UNDER SEA INDUSTRIES; **JIM CHRISTIANSEN** / VICE PRESIDENT SCUBAPRO AND WESTERN REGIONAL MANAGER; Not shown is **SAM ICHIKAWA** / TECHINICAL SERVICE MANAGER, for the simple reason that he hadn't come up yet.

to me. Then down the line in my travels, there was a dive shop in Milwaukee owned by Ralph West, who was also in the ski business, and he introduced me to the Head ski system. At that time, they did basically the same thing with extra flourishes. They had professional franchises and I picked up a lot of inspiration looking at Head Skis philosophy in those days. We did have a lot of political battles, because nobody agreed with us. Our beef with the magazines was simple, too: we felt that, ethically, diving equipment should be sold by people that can teach you how to use it and ensure that you are using it correctly. And could also tell you where to dive and provide that extra service to get folks stoked about diving. We did not agree with the magazines that would allow mail order. I felt that someone who doesn't know how to dive, writing from 1,000 miles away to get equipment, was just wrong. So we went for a long time not advertising in magazines that accepted mail order. But we didn't have a lot of support except for our dealer network.

Ultimately you were proven to be dramatically correct, because the stores that were Scubapro dealers not only developed very quickly with reputations as the pro stores, they also had the best equipment. In the 1970s and 1980s, if you didn't have Scubapro as a line, you were already eight steps behind the competition. What were you going to sell? With the junk that was out there, it just was no contest. If you had Scubapro you were automatically the Mercedes dealer of everything in diving. Now it's always amused me, looking back with almost 30 years of retrospect here, that Paul Tzimoulis (the editor & publisher of *Skin Diver* magazine then), who was a very innovative guy in a lot of ways, used to appear in his editorial picture with a Scubapro regulator around his neck and a Scubapro stabilizing jacket. And yet, this was exactly the guy who you had to do battle with to try to resolve issues at that level regarding magazine mail order. ⟩⟩ Yeah, that's a surprise. I didn't know he had our regulators.

The entire time that I knew Paul, and I met him originally in 1974 or something like that, he was always a Scubapro guy from top to bottom. 》Well, that's a compliment. I didn't know that. Our later relationship with *Skin Diver* was really bad. There were some companies that came along that did agree with our philosophy, like John Gaffney's NASDS, but they were short-lived.

There's an interesting name that comes up, Gaffney. Here was a guy who with the NASDS concept – which was also so closely linked to Scubapro, that many people in those days thought you guys were all under the same ownership. The innovative things that NASDS was doing dovetailed so nicely with the innovative things that Scubapro was doing. Back then NASDS probably was one of the most successful training systems compared to the likes of NAUI, YMCA, etc. They were the first to embrace the concept of octopuses, although they called them something else. NASDS always had a great name for things. A compass couldn't be a compass; it had to be a "direction monitor." A regulator couldn't be a regulator; it had to be an "air delivery system." If there were a way to make it more complicated, they would do it. In the early 1970s probably 80 percent your dealers were affiliated with NASDS. 》No, not quite. Remember you were a NAUI guy then and wanted nothing to do with them. Actually, NASDS, Gaffney and I had a long history. He was a hell of a free diver and was doing some work for *Skin Diver* magazine. That's where I met him. He was working for the founding publishers, Chuck Blakeslee and Jim Auxier. We immediately hit it off, and came to discover that we basically had the same philosophy. He started NASDS after leaving the magazine. It's a parallel story, it started after Scubapro, but it's the same type of history. A dealer supported him, and he built it up, and was quite successful. And we actually encouraged our dealers to join NASDS because of that cooperation and jointly held philosophy of how diving could be a business. We had a tremendous relationship with our dealers, but sometimes they looked at their supplier and said, "Why are you telling me how to run my business?" But if NASDS told them the same good principles, they were more likely to accept them.

Well, there were a lot of good principles there. I remember when you convinced me to go to a NASDS clinic in 1973, and I had a choice of going to someplace up in the Puget Sound, or Pensacola, Florida. I went to Pensacola and I'm glad I did. That's where I met Tom Allen (co-host of the television series *Wild Kingdom* and soon to be the southeast sales manager of Scubapro). He and I went through the same NASDS program in September of 1973. The other thing that really distinguished your company is that your sales representatives ended up being some of the most successful guys out there in helping the dive stores actually make coherent decisions about what they were going to do. Some of these guys really went on to have tremendous success stories. 》The first was actually Jim Christiansen. When we started we couldn't afford anybody and I traveled everywhere, including all of the U.S., Canada and the Caribbean. We hired Jim, who was a fireman then and one of the top free divers in the world. We brought him in and trained him, and he worked for us part-time. Eventually, we said, "You've got to make a decision between us and the fire department." He came with us. Next I got Joe Schuch, because I'd always been impressed with Joe and his approach towards business. And I kept finding guys who were avid divers, who loved the sport, had some retail experience, instructional background, and a sense of humor. Then we worked together. We collectively trained each other. So, we all had the same principles, and they all put themselves behind the counter at the dealer's, so they thought like a dealer. They also knew our products inside out from a repair standpoint, a maintenance standpoint, and this was unheard of at the time too. They were all technically trained by Sam. He was the best.

That's right. I remember the first time that Tom Allen came in to us and could run, right there on the premises, a full repair clinic seminar. It was unbelievable for us. That took all the expense out of having to send people to California from the Caribbean. Plus, they were always going to take us to lunch or dinner, which was something we had never heard of either, which was great. Scubapro was now the premier dive manufacturer. As you got into the 1980s and more manufacturers began to pop up, all of a

sudden instead of having the original five dive manufacturers, now we have 24 manufacturers, or something like that. How did you see some of that evolution?»It was good. It kept you on your toes and I actually learned from some of them. Ralph Osterhut (originally Ralph Shamlian), who founded Farallon, I thought was a very sharp guy, a very imaginative guy. I watched and learned from them all. Ralph was an expert on the splash and sizzle. The one evolution that I was kind of tough on was colors. Colors came in and products became just a plethora of color. I was a little reluctant and I had this fixation on "professional black." I still do but I decided that you have to give in here a little bit. But I never went so far as to go into the yellows and pinks.

Pink? I'm trying to imagine Dick Bonin in pink and it conjures up an image that I'm not comfortable with.»I finally compromised and we went with teal.

Well, by the time the 1990s rolled around, with the whole technical diving thing sort of coming out of the closet, everything went back to black again. You can't buy a piece of technical equipment that's not black.»See, I was right, and they all were wrong!

With all of the innovative products that you have built, and put out there, and have stood the test of time, because they have remained largely unchanged to this day – did you ever produce a product that you aren't proud of?»Oh, yes. We developed a regulator and we had a recall. Actually, it wasn't our design and it was in our very early years, before we even had salesmen. We developed a product that had a piston, but the seat was halfway up the piston, instead of a flow-through piston. The seat, in certain cases, could become unlodged and stick and cut off the regulator. Fortunately, we didn't have a great number out there, but that was a close call and really taught us a lesson. It had been out there for a while before we ran into the problem. It wasn't because it hadn't been tested; the problem developed over time and long-term use.

So what did you do when you found out?»We got every one back. This was in the days before there were official recalls. But we got every one back. We had a

couple of other things. We had the Aqua Bomber. The Aqua Bomber was a little craft that looked like a plane, and you got in and peddled. It was a little submarine; it was really a laugh. One of our dealers developed it and I didn't have the heart to say no. I brought a couple to show and our own salesmen razzed me unmercifully. It was a joke. Eventually I sold them to a quiz show.

You guys came out with one of the most enduring regulators in history, the Mark V. I can tell you right now, there are still thousands out there in use. And anybody who can get their hands on a Mark VII is grabbing those, because they have become real collector's items.»Mark VII, Air 1. They've all become highly sought-after collection pieces.

Now, were you still with the company when Doug Toth and Dean Garraffa were hired?»I hired them. In my tenure we had three different Chief Engineers, the last being Jim Dexter, who was a very talented young man. We looked for engineers that had a lot of diving experience, and really loved it, and we came up with Doug and Dean. Dean had done some work for Healthways after it had been resurrected from Chapter 11. Doug was actually a diving instructor. After the interviews it became apparent that these guys fit. They were with us until I left, and they started the Atomic company.

There is a lot of irony here. You left the company in 1991. Doug and Dean exited not too long after that and went off to start a company that competes directly with Scubapro.»There's only one person left at Scubapro that I know. All the engineers are gone. Doug and Dean started Atomic and their regulators are wonderful.

I use them myself.»I've been told they are the best.

Let me ask you this. The Jet Fin, in its era, was such a revolutionary product that everybody used them. Have you had a chance to try out these new split fins?»Yes, I have a pair. I like them. I got them last year. I do mostly free diving and they perform well.

Whose split fins do you use?»Atomic. I'm the old mossback guy. I dive with a lot of industry people, guys I worked with like Doug, Dean, and Dexter. They came on board my boat one day, and I took them out diving. They said, "You're going to try these things." They are very efficient fins.

But somewhere you've got to have a pair of Jet Fins sitting around. »Of course!

You retired from Scubapro in 1991. I know you did some really great work through DEMA and, also, with Ocean Futures after that. But are you retired now? »I am completely retired. I'm 73 (2003).

Seventy-three years young. You are, of course, one of diving's first generation. I've known you

Spearfishing trophy, 2003

for over 30 years now. You look to me like you could go out tomorrow, run a marathon, and still close the bar that night. Do you stay in touch much with what's going on in the diving industry? »No. My communications are basically with the fellows that used to work with me that are still in the diving industry. That's pretty much it. The salesmen all still call, and I talk to them, and they are more up to date than I am. I'll be called for the occasional humor, to see how things are, or somebody like you. I'll ask what's going on but, really, I'm not up-to-date. Generally, I'll hear people say, "You wouldn't like this, but..."

Could you ever imagine back in 1959, though, that the diving industry would grow into the multi-billion dollar industry that it is today? Did you see that? »I always thought so. We went through periods of fast growth, but like any other business, that's an exception. You build it up and battle to survive. Whether it's diving, golf or software, it's all the same. But I always thought it would grow, and then a lot of things happened that you don't anticipate. Diving went through stages, the travel boom, and I guess the latest thing is the technical diving. That started just when I was running DEMA. I remember being asked if I thought it was here to stay. Most people said no, but I thought it was. Divers like a challenge.

It's very surprising how technical diving and nitrox became the largest profit-center in diving in the past decade. There was more profit in those segments of the sport and a renewed interest for divers who wanted to stretch out their limits. But a lot of the conservatives didn't want to have anybody daring to breach what they thought were absolute limits: no decompression diving, no diving below 130 feet, don't do this, don't do that. But then, again, if you think back, it's the same guys that didn't like dive computers. They didn't like inflators. They didn't like BCs. They didn't like wetsuits that weren't black. Whoops, I might be throwing you in that category, though. There is a segment of our industry that has always resisted change and innovation, and being the innovative guy you are, I guess you would be leading the charge today if you were still running things. »You just have to look at the changes, flow and rhythm, and try to get ahead of them. I remember the first time I was asked about technical diving at a seminar and I could just see all of the eyes peering, wondering what I was going to say. I said, "It's here to stay." And that's based on what I know about the people of diving and the people who like to dive. These are people who want to do adventurous things and they're going to try it. They are going to try cave diving, deep wreck diving, rebreathers, free diving. These are people who like adventure.

You're in your early 70s now, you still actively free dive, experiment a bit. Do you see any signs of stopping that? »I see the signs, but I'm ignoring them. ∎

Wes Skiles
CAVE DWELLER

BY FRED GARTH

YOU COULD CALL WES SKILES A CELLULOID TROGLODYTE...

– a cave dweller devoted to filming the earth's underwater Swiss cheese. A lifelong resident of a dot on the map called High Springs, in the heart of Central Florida's cave region, he can slip in and out of the Redneck role like a well-tailored pair of overalls. »

For instance, if you offered Wes a turtle-neck on a cool day in New England, he'd probably think it was something to make soup with.

But he can also smooth talk the Editorial Board of *National Geographic* and get mucho dinero funding approved to blast off to the Antarctic wilderness under icebergs. First and foremost, Wes is a world-class explorer and filmmaker. He's been the friend and understudy of caving legends like Sheck Exley and Parker Turner, both of whom died in their element while riding the razor's edge. He's helped to invent dive gear we use commonly today and has created other contraptions like an underwater decompression habitat for one of the world's most ambitious cave exploration projects.

As a kid Wes made surf films then moved into diving where he's crafted numerous movies, including a critically acclaimed IMAX film, *Amazing Caves*, with Howard Hall. He's been the first to dive ice caves in the world's largest iceberg and he's been known to hang out with likes of the *Grateful Dead*. All this and the man's still in his 40s. There's probably no one on the planet who knows more about diving in cave systems, what rebreather to use, and how to record it all on film.

Skiles is uniquely successful in the decidedly niche market of cave diving. It's a bit of a strange community. All the participants barely tally the number of divers on the Cayman dive boats off the west end any afternoon. Yet it seems that at any given time, there are bitter rivalries and feuds that make the Sunnis and the Shiites look like kissing cousins. It's a bit hard to fathom that such a small group can frequently display such dysfunctional behavior. Wes, on the other hand, rises above the fray and distinguishes himself with his talent... both as an exploration cave diver and as filmmaker/photographer that captures the pure adventure.

Cave diving is not for the faint of heart. It's also not for most people in their right minds. It's dangerous. When you're a few thousand feet back in an underwater cave system and you have a problem... well, generally it's a long friggin' way to get out. There's no option for a free ascent since there's hard ceiling over your head and the only way out is the way you came in. And that may be more than an hour or so away. Lots of cave divers have tempted fate and lost. Some of the best explorers in the world have fallen victim. Skiles has managed, not only to survive, but to thrive in that harsh and unforgiving environment. He also brings a sly sense of humor to his work. Anyone who's seen his act with the filthy false teeth and backwoods Billy-Bob dialect can't possibly stifle a laugh. He even did that to Howard Hall on the IMAX set. (This perhaps cemented Howard's long-held suspicion that cave divers inhabit a very special trailer park out on the lunatic fringe. Wes, by the way, has a double-wide.)

For those that have seen his images and his films, there is no question that Wes is the premier master of his subterranean craft. In person, he's funny, erudite, and a well-informed conservationist who has a deep passion for preservation of the fragile cave systems that have made his career. In the spring of 2002, I corralled him for this interview. So hang on to your scooters while he takes us on a personal tour of his life and insights into the fascinating world of underwater caves. And a few deviations along the way. ■

How long had you been certified before venturing into caves? »Well, I really started going into caves before I was even certified. The springs around here were accessible to us and the nature of it just lead us into caves. Luckily I somehow instinctually knew to stay near the entrance and survived all that. I did my first open-water check-out dive when I was 13 where the grate is now at Ginnie Springs. That's the way they taught scuba diving back then. We didn't think anything about going back that far into a cave to take our mask off and buddy breathe and do ditches and dons all in an overhead environment.

When did you go from fresh water to salt water? »Right after we were certified we were ready to start down to the Keys and to West Palm and off Jacksonville and all that so I've been diving in those places since 1973 or 1974.

Did you ever think that High Springs would become the cave diving Mecca of the world? »Ha Ha. Well, I don't think I would have ever ventured to guess back then that this place would become the heart of technical diving and the cave diving capital of the world. It was just a place down a country road where there were some remarkable natural areas to go diving. And, back then, around every corner was a new discovery. I just don't think we ever expected how the cave community would develop.

How much does the area's popularity have to do with the natural resource and how much does it have to do with the people, such as yourself, who have promoted the region? »I hope I've never promoted the area in a way that would be negative to it. Hopefully, the efforts I've made have been an education to help people survive the experience around here and protect the resource. But I think it's just a natural process, that in teaching cave diving, the area gets promoted. People cut their teeth on cave diving down here and it's the first place they're going to return to try out new skills and new equipment. And it's just a remarkable place. So with all of those factors you get a real charmed environment for people to flock to.

What is your favorite dive near your home? »Always a difficult question, the favorite dive. Since I continue to plug away at exploring virgin caves around my neighborhood, I would have to say that my favorite dive is the exploration I'm working on right now.

That's a good diplomatic answer. »Yeah it is. Certainly as far as falling into a springs, Ginnie Springs and the Devil's Eye is my longest love affair and the reason I live right here next to them.

So you're still able to find virgin springs, even today? »Oh yeah.

How much virgin territory is out there yet to explore? »Did I say there are still virgin springs and caves? I'm sorry I made a terrible mistake just then (laughs). No, there's nothing left for the next generation to explore. That's our philosophy, leave nothing for the next generations (laughs again). No, seriously, there's always something new to be explored out here. There's always new territory. Technology and knowledge put together will always carry us to new distances inside of our favorite caves and help us find new places we haven't discovered before.

So you're not talking about new entrances but simply further exploration of existing cave systems. »Oh no, no. New entrances. I mean, in the last 10 years our team has explored probably 60 to 80 new cave systems from the entrance. It comes from a collective knowledge that you can only get from living here. I've been right here in the middle of this thing quietly looking around with my friends. We're out on the river every weekend we can, kicking around and checking systematically every square inch. So for someone else to step in and look at this area, it's mind-boggling. There are thousands of miles of rivers and nooks and crannies and sloughs and you just couldn't begin right now and catch up with us because we've been going at it for 20 years.

Are you finding these new caves along the river banks, rather than back in the woods or around swamps and so on? »I decline to answer that question.

So you don't want a lot of people poking around looking for caves. Is that it? »No, they're welcome to come explore the area. That's not the point. Anybody that's an explorer will find stuff. But I'm not going to sit here in this interview and provide a list of how to find

Skiles' photo captured Nancy Morris examining
Mastadon bone during 1987 Wakulla Project

Wes Skiles

caves the way we're finding them. I don't want to be rude about it. It's just that we love our exploration.

It's kind of like keeping the secret of a good fishing hole, huh? »Exactly. When people ask me where I've been diving, I just say the Withalaswanta Fe or Chataholawithchee. And, they'll go, "Oh yeah, okay. I think I've heard of that." And they'll walk away scratching their heads and hope to find it on a map. Which, of course, they won't.

I remember the first article I edited for *Scuba Times* in 1986. It was a piece you wrote about recovering a body in a cave. How did you get into that? »The first recovery I ever did was in 1976, right after I had met Bob Wray. I was working at Steve Matheny's dive shop in Orange Park, Florida and Bob had seen my cave systems maps and had said, "Wow, you've been all through these caves." About two weeks later a drowning occurred at Ginnie and he told the authorities that he knew somebody who had mapped all these caves. So Bob contacted me. When I got there that evening the lights were flashing in the woods and the officer said, "There's nothing down here for you young man. Get out of here." And Bob Wray said, "No, no, this is the guy I called."

There were group of divers there including Lewis Sollenberger and Mary Melton and a few others and we went in and found the first body. Later on the next day we found the second and that was my introduction to it. I was still in high school at the time and it was a real eye-opening experience.

What did that do to your psyche? »Well, I was probably mortified at the thought. It really scared me because I didn't know how I would react. So leading up to that first recovery was by far the hardest thing. I mean my heart was racing and I was wondering why I was doing this. Then when I saw that body lying there covered in silt I was still calm. I went, "Okay, there's the body," you know, and nothing happened and I was okay. Of course, I sat bolt upright in bed three or four times a nights after that, impacted by that fact that I'd seen such a grizzly thing. It was my first dealing with death. No one had died in my life and there it was in this sport I loved. But, you know, two, three, four, five, 15, 25 or 30 recoveries later, it was something that I had really adapted to. I felt it was an important

Mark and Annette Long approach the "lock-out" chamber during the Wakulla II Project, 1998.

part of cave diving's responsibility to the public and to the communities and these counties that owned these springs that we carry off a responsible duty and demonstrate that we can do it safely.

That *Scuba Times* article also had some outstanding images. What got you into photography? »I was always into it actually, from a very young age. I had land cameras as a kid then when I was 14, I bought a Nikonos. I saved up lawn mowing money for it. But I always had a fascination for photography. I was a photographer on the yearbook staff in high school and did all of my own processing and developing so I had a real love for that early on.

When did you make the leap to moving pictures? »Well, movies actually came first. My brother and I made surf movies before I got into diving. We were big into surfing and I was his editor. So we would go out and film and bring home 8mm and super 8 movies and put them together. So through that I got into claymation and stop-action photography and did a

Wes Skiles

bunch of animated things in film. So I had that passion for it and my brother had a friend in Hollywood who was into filmmaking and I learned a lot from him. And then, all of our camera gear was stolen. It wasn't conceivable that we could replace it. Our parents had helped us buy it all and they weren't going to buy new stuff for us. So, I sort of got out of the motion picture stuff and dove into still photography.

But as some point you jumped back into film. 》 Yeah, I was giving a presentation at a dive show and a guy from Sony saw one of my multi-projector shows. His name was Ira Freidman and he said, "You know, you should be doing your style of story telling in motion. And we'd like to sponsor you for a year with Sony equipment." I said, "Okay" and he gave me two complete set ups of their 8mm equipment. And that was the beginning of the Sony 8mm format that eventually evolved into the DV format.

And what sort of housing did you use? 》 Well, Sony had a housing which was sort of a yellow round

thing. But that same weekend I met Val Renetkins who would turn out to be a lifetime friend and partner. Val had a little thing called a Capsule 8 he'd built for the same camera. Just like Ira Freidman, Val offered me a housing. He said, "This is what you need. It has better optics, it's a smaller package and has a wider angle lens and so on." So, just like that, I had a complete system.

Val Renetkins founded Amphibico, right? 》 Yes. He started with *National Geographic* and then developed Aqua Vision, which became Aquatica. Then he started Amphibico.

Are you using his High Definition housings now? 》 I am. My philosophy has evolved and I'm now conscious and aware that what we do and see is unique and sometimes priceless. Knowing this, it's important to capture our experience in the highest quality format available. High Definition is redefining how we look at the world. It's an amazing technology that makes you feel like you're actually there.

So what was the first underwater footage that you sold? 》 About two months after I got the video equipment I bought a film camera from one of Howard Hall's old buddies, Larry Cochran. Howard, Larry, Bill Lovin and even Cousteau had been using this design of tube camera. I started shooting film with that and I did the piece that *National Geographic* bought. So that was my first sale. Then the next two sales were to CBS and CNN with the Wakulla Springs Project.

So you started at the top and stayed there. 》 Well, I kind of always said I came in through the exit door from inside of an underwater cave. That was an environment that nobody was filming then so at that time I was the only show in town and it was easy to bamboozle people.

You mentioned the Wakulla Project, which I recall was in 1987. Tell us how that came to pass. 》 In 1985 I had written a thing called *The Future of Cave Diving* in which I drew a bunch of possible inventions: a habitat that you could weight down or anchor into a cave that you could bring air in and decompress inside of. Dr. Bill Stone was at that presentation. It was an AAUS meeting in Tallahassee and he told me about the things he was working on – the rebreather and other stuff for

201

1. Mike Madden pushing through restriction during
8,000-foot penetration into Nahoch Nachich system, 1995
2. Mexican Yucatan pack horses during 8km trek into "Far Point Station"
during filming of *Most Dangerous Science*

his cave projects – and he wanted to see if we could get together on all of these inventions for a project in Wakulla. So after a year of preparation, Bill's amazing engineering, and our collective vision of building these things (certainly all at Bill's hands as far as the designing and engineering) we put together the Wakulla Project, sponsored among others, by *National Geographic*.

For those who don't know, Wakulla is one of the world's largest cave systems and it's also located near High Springs. »Well, not too far away. It's a Florida State Park so we needed special permits and so on. They gave us two months to do the project.

What were some of the goals? »Deep penetration as well as developing a lot of technical diving techniques. I mean up until that point in time, people had never even postulated about the possibilities of doing what we set ourselves up to do. For the first time ever, we had a real cache of mixed gas and the help of Dr. Bill Hamilton, through Parker Turner I might add. We had a set of tables that would allow us to do some remarkable dives. This was prior to decompression computers, prior to people doing

these types of mixed-gas dives. We brought in German-made scooters because the scooter revolution had not begun and AquaZepp scooters were the best deal to get us far back in the cave very quickly. And so it was really a three-way show between Sheck Exley and Paul DeLoach doing a series of dives, Bill developing the rebreather, and our team of divers who, were filming the scientific work and pushing the exploration. It got to be quite an adventure where we were proving good things and bad things about diving at 300-ft. depths.

202

And we learned the hard way to let go of our old ways and accept the new. Even while we were tuned into that idea it was hard to make changes because for many, many years things had been done a certain way and it required a lot of mind bending and flexing to step into this new arena of diving.

But it was by far, at that time, the most adventuresome cave diving ever done. In the end, Tom Morris, Paul Heinerth, and I made it 4,176 feet into the B Tunnel, which at that depth, no one had even contemplated going that far. It was a 14-hour dive including decompression. We had our portable habitat, the *Habitent*, so at least decompression was semi-dry.

The Wakulla Project kind of gets glazed over by a lot of people in today's time. But if you look very carefully you'll see that was the project that changed the whole world of technical diving: the way scooters were used, the way equipment was combined together, the way staging techniques were developed, the way gas mixtures were laid out in formal style for deco mixes - from the deep water deco nitrox mixes to O2 and then the deep water trimix and heliox gases we were diving. That was the beginning, the moment in time in which a big project verified and quantified that it could be done. And Bill Hamiliton's superb book kind of laid out the blueprint. From there, guys like Jim King stood up and went right into it with the Eagle's Nest project and then we started to see it just balloon one after the other.

So besides kicking off the technical diving revolution, what was the coolest thing you discovered? »That the cave just kept going and going. It was the dream and the hope, I mean, when I was getting ready for that project I remember laying in bed and dreaming about endless big tunnels and passageways going everywhere and the sensation of flying and that's exactly what we found. When we left it was still going so it was that big dream fulfilled. Flying through those big rooms and being able to film it all was incredible. I shot a lot of 16mm film and stills during that project. For me, the really exciting part was making history and being able to document it all.

As I recall you made history of a few cameras as well. »Yeah, we had a couple of things happen. One time the camera was tilted inside of the housing

so we shot an entire day's worth of footage and it was all blurred. Then we had the Benthos camera, which was used on the *Titanic* expedition. It had just come off of that project and was given to us by *National Geographic*. Two of the magazine's long-time photographers, Al Chandler and Emory Kristoff, were there when that camera was passed on to me. And so I'm kind of boasting, "I'm using the camera that was used on the *Titanic*." I was pretty proud. When I asked them about maintenance they said, "No, no, don't do anything." And I'm thinking, "Boy that doesn't sound right. I don't know that they understand how sandy and silty our environment is."

But I wanted to do exactly what they told me so I didn't do anything. On one of the next dives the camera flooded. But Bill Stone, being infinitely resourceful, somehow cleaned it up and put it back together. So I took it on the next dive and this time it caught on fire. We were at 300 feet and basically had a bomb on our hands. It was smoking and I could see sparks flying around inside the housing. So I literally dumped it off. We were loaded up with line and since we couldn't do any photography, I said, "Yahoo let's go" and that ended up being the deepest penetration we did on the project. So it's kind of a bittersweet story.

How has your luck been in getting more loaner cameras from Emory Kristoff? »Pretty good, really. We recovered the camera and I made a big impression when I sent it back with a note inside that just said, "Oops."

Was the camera flood the freakiest thing that happened? »No, there were several close calls all related to gas management. I built this sled that held tanks to the bottom of the AquaZepp and one time I just ran flat out of gas. As I was trying to figure it out, I kind of fell calmly all the way to the bottom into the silt at about 300 feet. We were back about 1,200 feet in the tunnel and that was real scary for my partner on that dive, Clark Pitcairn. He watched me go down into the silt and he was kind of like, "Come on Wes, come on Wes, get out of there." When we got back to the *Habitent*, he told me that he was going to get out of the project. He said, "When I saw you falling down there I realized that I didn't have it in me to help you. I have kids and I didn't want to die." I said, "Hey man, I respect that completely and I understand and embrace that." I didn't have any ill feelings at all.

Wait a minute, you said you ran flat out of gas and fell into the silt but how'd you get out? »Oh, did I glaze over that? I was able to switch to my back mounted gas and I ended up having plenty of gas. It was just a matter of getting used to the equipment.

Sheck and Paul had a problem too, right? »Yeah, they were still trying to hang on to their old traditional trimix gases. They both fell into a narcosis and oxygen problem. The scooters failed on them and they got tangled into some line and we were all cognizant that they were very late. There were some tense moments but through Sheck's perseverance and Paul keeping his head, in what was a real mind-numbing experience for them, they were able to make it back. They ended up going through the various safety bottles we'd left behind. And they made it from stop to stop and finally back to the surface. At that point we drew a line in the sand and said there's no more old-style diving with trimix.

What was the problem with trimix? »It wasn't a problem with trimix, just the mixture that they choose to dive. Essentially they were diving with too much nitrogen and oxygen in their mix and it was almost lethal. We were using an 86/14 heliox, which totally eliminated nitrogen so the narcotic effect was gone and we took the oxygen down to a level that reduced the risk of oxygen toxicity. So that's what we all used from there on out.

How did you know to use that mix? »Well, at first we were trying to use the navy tables and my friend Parker Turner came to us and said, "Hey guys, you're going to kill yourselves trying to do this with navy tables. You've got to meet this guy Bill Hamilton." Parker had been out of cave diving for about a decade but was getting back into it. Anyway, he arranged a meeting with Hamilton right at the beginning of the project. So Bill came in and cut us a custom set of tables and off we went.

I know that was a blow to you when Parker had his accident. What happened? »It was a few years after Wakulla, and Parker had continued to perfect his cave diving skills. The best we could ever tell was that the sand and rock slope above the opening at Indian Springs began to avalanche during their dive. So it closed the small hole they would normally have come through. On the way out, he and Bill Gavin found nothing. They just saw their line going into sand and rock. From there it's real sketchy as to what happened. Bill somehow made it through only to find that Parker had already made it through but had drowned just a few feet shy of getting to some extra bottles.

What about Wakulla II? »That was like the next generation literally. The gear had made quantum leaps. We had the rebreather working well and Bill just thought it was time to take the next step. Wakulla II represented the future of what was possible. Like Wakulla I, this project marked the beginning of a new world of possibilities. The centerpiece of the project was a fully operational saturation diving rig brought in from the oil fields. With his usual inventive flair, Bill engineered a way to make it all work in the confines of the spring. For the first time ever, divers were doing four and five hours at 300-ft. depths on rebreathers without a care in the world. It was really incredible. After a dive, the team would simply enter a lockout capsule on the bottom, and then be transported to the surface habitat. Using this concept, divers in the future will be able to perform a week's worth of exploration and only decompress once. Another very exciting development was the 3D mapper Dr. Bill Stone and Barbara Am Ende invented and proved during the project. For the first time we had true representations of the places we explored instead of the crude stick maps I'm famous for.

What about the WKPP? What's up with them? »Well, I doubt most of your readers know who they are, but they are the Woodville Karst Plain Project. They're a highly disciplined group of cave divers who have made a career out of diving mostly one major cave system. In doing so they have become the best at doing a certain type of hybrid technical deep cave diving. I really don't think that anyone's done it better than those guys. They're quite extraordinary. Unfortunately, their current leader, who speaks for the group, is George Irvine. I've dealt with his type lots when I was in junior high school, ya know, the schoolyard bully. He likes to pick on, and attempt to demoralize anyone who doesn't follow his rules and conventions. Basically, he's a real dick, a total asshole. The way I look at it is people like him tend to come and go from this sport. One day the cave diving community will wake up and he'll be gone, maybe on to another sport to pick on.

The rest of the core of the WKPP has some really talented guys. They'll probably always have an elitist type of attitude that they are better than anyone else but I guess that's okay. So, I wait with my fingers crossed that those guys who are truly leading the WKPP will one day step up and take the helm and bring their group and technology and their incredible knowledge and experience into the community as a partnership

What about the Mike Madden/Steve Gerrard battle that's been waged in Mexico's cave system? That's definitely real. 》Yeah, but that's what happens. That's a good example. Those were individuals who were in different groups. It's really between those two guys rather than the organizations themselves. The hearts of those organizations are dedicated to great things: education, conservations, protection of the environment and outreach.

Wes Skiles

Mike Madden and Eric Hutcheson during the Nahoch Project to connect Nahoch and Dos Ojos, 1995.

where they can be functional. But until they do that, they're kind of a group on their own, is my attitude.

Does cave diving make people antagonists? You've got the WKPP and then all the infighting between the National Association of Cave Divers (NACD) and the National Speleological Society-Cave Diving Section (NSS-CDS). What's up with all that? 》I think a lot of it is perception. People naturally congregate in different groups. The NACD and NSS-CDS offer different things so naturally you get different personalities. But the leaders of those groups get along. I know what you're talking about but I really don't think it's real. Like I said, a lot of it is perception.

On a more positive note, tell us about the accomplishments in Mexico at the Dos Ojos and Nahoch Nachich cave systems. 》First of all it's just a fascinating wonderland down there. I mean we're able to do some big-time swims, some 18,000-ft. penetrations, where we're blending film making with exploration. Plus, I was fortunate enough to be part of the team that ultimately connected Nahoch to the ocean. And then a couple of years later it was time to do the IMAX film. We were scouting locations and had the challenge of unbelievable logistics of pulling off an IMAX film in an underwater cave in a jungle. So we had a very tough decision. I was like, "We have to do it in Nahoch to work with Mike Madden and everything." But the logistics just forbade it. There was no way we could helicopter everything in. There was no road in there at the time and I had to face reality that this Dos Ojos cave was better. And as I did that, I recognized that it was a great cave. I really started falling in love with Dos Ojos.

Has there been much competition between the caving groups to keep pushing further and further in order to make "their" cave the longest? »Oh yeah. Back in 1996 and before, there were lots of explorations competitions going on. Dos Ojos and Nahoch were at the peak of their potential connection and there were bands of cave divers working projects simultaneously just mere yards form each other in underwater distances but thousands and thousands of feet from the nearest entrances. The competition and the goals of who was going to connect what, got pretty heated. It got to its lowest point when the Mexican military was out hunting Mike Madden with guns and they had us cornered in one of the holes on the Ejido property. We were there, I guess I'll say, improperly. We were informed that they were going to arrest us when we came out of the woods so our determination was to just stay in the woods. So we stayed in there for like 10 days eking out every scrap of food we had and kept on diving. When we finally came out there was no one there to arrest us… so I guess we just outlasted them. But eventually all of that settled down and we were able to laugh about it.

Being so close to one another, are Nahoch NaChich and Dos Ojos similar? »No, they're remarkably different for being geologically so similar. There's no doubt they're related somehow or another but they appear to be within their own regime. So the big-picture geology that sort of controls how caves are formed and the past water level stands all made similar structured caves. Their orientations and their patterns are all laid out side by side. But their differences are quite remarkable in what must be the chemistry of the water in the two caves and therefore their appearance.

So what are those remarkable differences? » Nahoch is a much more consistently white, very clean laid out cave and Dos Ojos has a lot more mineralization and darkness in color and black walls in places and speleothemes that are various colors. Both are amazing in their own way and when you

dive both systems you go, "Yeah, this is cool." I mean, you could drop me blindfolded into either systems and even though most people wouldn't know, I could immediately tell which cave I was in.

Aren't they both competing to be the world's longest caves? »They were back and forth Guinness World Record's longest caves. I think Nahoch held it the longest just because Mike and his team was diligent about pushing farther and farther and keeping it in the record books. But they still have not been connected yet. They still remain spitting distance from each other but not connected. Hope's not given up. It's funny. Here recently a lot of us joined together. It's kind of like two bands, like *Bad Company* and *Foreigner*, breaking up and then reforming a new group. Paul and Jill Heinerth were on a lot of the big pushes on Dos Ojos along with Gary and Kay Walton, and since then some of our Nahoch crowd has started diving with those

Grateful Dead drummer Bill Kreutzmann and Skiles during filming of *Ocean Spirit*.

and there I had the advantage. But as far as Howard's expertise and knowledge as an IMAX cameraman there was no question that we were getting a dream team: to have me in control of directing and lighting the film and Howard coming in with the camera to film. All I can say is great things about the relationships that were formed when we got down there and how things laid out. It was an amazing team project and quite funny at times. And it was mind-boggling as far as the logistics and technology required to get 18,000 watts of permanent light into the cave and developing the illusion of cave exploration and discovery with such huge cameras that are so light hungry.

Were you satisfied with the film? »I was thrilled, sort of. I think it's a great film but as a purist there are always things that you see. I would have liked to see the cave-diving segment longer and I remember a lot of scenes that we shot that must have been awfully good that they passed on to go after the more glorified elements of the film. But, all in all, I was very pleased. It was a difficult but great team effort and I'm glad Howard enjoyed my serenading him so much.

Let's jump backwards in time to the film you made with *Grateful Dead* drummer Bill Kreutzmann. How'd you land that gig? »That evolved from one of the great women divers in our sport, Marjorie Bank. She and I were best friends and she called me one day and said, "Wes, have you ever heard of the *Grateful Dead*?" And, I just laughed. This was 1991, basically at the peak of their career, and she'd never heard of them. I couldn't believe it. And she asks me what she should wear. She says, "I'm going to their concert and there's this guy, Bruce Hornsby, coming to pick me up." And, I'm like, "Bruce Hornsby is coming to pick you up?" And she says, "Yeah, he's one of the players." So I say, "The keyboard player?" And she goes, "Yeah, I think that's it." So I'm just sitting there aghast that Marjorie is going to a *Grateful Dead* concert because she and the *Dead* are like oil and water.

So I come to find out the she and Billy Kreutzmann had been on a liveaboard together and they had this run-in at the beginning of the trip about who would get the nicest cabin. Finally it settled out and Marjorie determines that this guy was just a "lovely fellow." But that's the way she was. So we were coming back from the Underwater Canada show and she asks

guys. Buddy Quattlebaum put on a trip recently where we all went out there to Pet Cemetery to look at the possibilities of taking what was left of the two old teams and giving it one more whack at making the connection between the two systems.

Pet Cemetery? »That's one of the territorial entrances of the two cave systems. Actually it has a dry connection of the two caves. But it's not a real cemetery. I guess it just has that appearance.

Then you were down there again in 1998 and 1999 doing the IMAX with Howard Hall, right? »Correct. Yeah, I was surprised to read that Howard thought I would be threatened to have him coming in. I really didn't think that at all. Sure, I will give him that I was disappointed when I heard he would be filming because I believed cave divers would be the best people to film underwater cave environments me to come to Atlanta with her to see the *Dead*. We went straight in with our backstage passes and we met Jerry and Billy and Bobby and Phil and the whole group. And, of course, Jerry and Bob and Bill were all big into scuba diving. They had already seen a bunch of my films so they were like, "Tell us about this and what about that." So Billy came down to High Springs about two weeks later with some Betacam gear and wanted me to show him how to use it.

After a couple days of playing around with the camera in the springs he says, "I'm not really getting this, am I?" And I said, "Hey you don't just grab this stuff and start using it. It's taken me 18 years to get halfway competent and you don't just learn it in two or three days." So he goes, "Well why don't you come with me on this expedition. I'm going to take a sailboat 1,800 miles from San Francisco down to these islands, the Revillagigedos." So we jumped on this sailboat in San Francisco on what would become an epic journey.

And what was the goal of the expedition? »It was really about exploration in the spirit of cave diving but to go down and document and map and tell a story of the Sea of Cortez – stopping in fishing villages and meeting people and checking out marine life and filming and ultimately heading down to this group of island which have now become very popular. But back then hardly anybody had been there. So we dove Socorro and Benedicto and updated maps and drawings...

And taking a little LSD on the side? »No, (laughing) no LSD on that trip!

What was the film called and how did it play? »It was called *Ocean Spirit* and it was received extremely well and a well-done film. It's a very different kind of film.

How do we get a copy? »I think it's available on the *Grateful Dead* website.

Let's jump into gear. Are rebreathers passing us by? Are we relegated to cylinders until the end of time or will Joe Diver ever use a rebreather? »I believe we're marching quickly toward the ultimate evolution of rebreathers entering the diving market. I know people don't see it that way but it's coming. From my point of view, having been one of the first guys to ever dive a rebreather in a cave environment, they

1. Ice Crystal Palace and Camp Patience, Ice Island Expedition, 2001 2. Paul and Jill Heinerth surface after a close call in Ice Island Cave

are now commonplace here. I mean, people are diving Megladons and Cis-Lunars. You see Buddy Inspirations and all kinds of incarnations in between. It's just a lot more prevalent. Photographers like Tom Campbell are diving rebreathers and filming in High Def. Howard Hall is doing it and I'm doing it. We're out there on the cutting edge in open water and technical environments using this technology. As history shows, when we do it, it becomes a permanent part of the sport.

Sheck and a small band of people decided to drill some holes in the first stage of a regulator. Back when I was a kid, I would go into this machine shop in Jacksonville and I would see chrome shaved off of regulator housings down to the brass. Joseph Califino, who was this old machinist, would be drilling holes in regulators where holes had never been and tapping in new hoses. We now all dive with octopuses and safe seconds and inflators. Those things were developments out of needs for more efficiencies and more safety in cave diving, that ultimately became a permanent part of diving equipment. The Stabilizing Jacket, what is now the common design for buoyancy, came from Court Smith and me mixing buoyancy compensators and inner tubes and horse collars together and creating things that became a permanent part of better diving. So, I think it's at that point now with rebreathers. They're permeating all levels and one day we'll have hybrids. I think that's where we're headed, toward some hybrid like cars are going now. They still use gasoline but they also have battery power. I think we're going to find ourselves diving semi-closed rebreathers that are packed down so we're not diving 80s or 72s anymore. We'll be diving 30s or 40s and getting four or five times longer than a single tank allows us to dive. It's all good.

Except for Dräger's sporadic support, none of the mainstream manufacturers have embraced rebreathers. Why do you think that is so? »I think it hasn't gotten there economically and ergonomically yet. People are still putting them together with plumbing supplies and PVC and they're still garage-built things. What's going to happen is that one manufacturer will get a foothold firmly enough that the money will come and they'll overcome the liabilities and step into the big time. And that's forthcoming.

Do you see any other major gear developments coming down the pipe? »From a photography points of view, certainly digital image making and High Definition. I'm right there now working on these hybrid projects for *National Geographic*. We're now using digital image making in the pages of the magazine.

Digital still cameras? »Yeah. And I did the first ever, all digital presentation to the *National Geographic* editors. It was the first time a slide projector was not in the room showing images for a final presentation. Up until that point all the presentations had gone, ka-plunk, ka-plunk, ka-plunk. And they all stopped and turned

around and went, "Have we ever done this before?" And they all said, "No." And then they said, "Well this is a first. I guess we're going into the new millennium with this." And one of 'em said, "It better be good, Skiles."

It was a presentation on Antarctica and I did it all with my laptop and a projector and showed scans and frame grabs from three different formats: from regular traditional still photography with emulsion, from digital photography, and then from actual frame grabs off my High Def camera. This evolution is leading to a sort of hybrid world in which you can grab publishable photographs from motion picture frames and we'll be seeing more developments along the lines of digital matrix photography, which starts to truly compete with film emulsions. And when that happens, that's another evolutionary step for our sport because it just opens up a world of possibilities.

Are you're still shooting with still film? »Yeah, I'm going out this weekend and shooting with 70mm, 2 x 2 stuff. I still love the old traditional quality you get with film but there's nothing like the quick feedback that digital photography gives you.

How does High Def and IMAX cross? Are they two different graphs or do the lines cross somewhere? »Well, I think the lines will eventually cross and maybe trip each other up at the same time. There's a lot happening very quickly in the world of High Def and the most prominent area of High Def crossing over to IMAX is in the use of this equipment in 3D. They take two High Def cameras and stereo them together and shoot what is truly High Def, IMAX quality 3D film by doubling up on the images of two High Def cameras. When you put just a single High Def camera in the housing and say this is shooting the same as 70mm film is shooting, that's just a joke. There's no way that it's there yet. It's the same as saying that the best digital still camera is shooting as good or better than film is. It's not there yet but it doesn't have to be.

We're going in the wrong direction. We're asking digital to become film. But what digital does much better than film is its own thing, digital. It should be kept in the digital domain and projected digitally. So what I think we're going to see is this split personality battle. I think we're going to see High Def theatres. We'll see what I call Digital IMAX theatres that can be built in half the size and a tenth the money. They'll give people similar experiences - the big images, the surround sound, the big action – so that now they'll be in museums and aquariums and special education outreach facilities and theme parks can have very specialized films. This is an area I'm very excited to be working in. I've just gotten a major contract with the State of Florida with the Department of Environmental Protection to create the first even High Def film on the Florida aquifer and the explorations inside the springs and caves to help share with the world the value of those resources. Initially, we're building a Welcome Center in Icheutucnee Springs State Park, which will show it in High Def with 6.1 surround sound. Ultimately, we hope this will be the flagship model for other facilities in Florida.

Stepping back, how did the whole digital presentation on Antarctica go? I got the hair-brained idea to go to Antarctica, with some suggestions from Emory Kristoff. He told me that he knew about a ship that was going down there and that *National Geographic* wanted to hear a new idea from me so he thought I should go down. It was already one of my goals because I had always wanted to go down into that hostile environment and try out some state-of-the-art technology. So I went up to Washington, D.C. to give a presentation. And the night before, Emory told me that I hadn't told him anything convincing. He said, "This thing better be good or you're dead meat." I was like, "Thanks Emory." And so I attempted to go to bed and really didn't have a strong story idea.

So, I decided to browse around on the Internet and stumbled on the fact that just two days prior to the meeting, the world's largest iceberg had broken off of the Ross ice shelf. I logged on and got into the conversation between two guys, Dr. Doug McAyeal and Matthew Lazarra, and they were talking about what was going on from their different disciplines. And I'm thinking, "This is it." So, I pinged those guys and asked them a little about it and went in the next day and said, "We're going to go to the largest iceberg in recorded history and we're going to go diving inside of it."

And that did it. So from that point on we put together a program to take rebreathers and High Definition equipment and a vessel capable of getting

us there with a helicopter on the deck so that we could navigate and shoot aerials and explore that world. About eight months later we were off. We set ourselves up for certainly what would become one of the most difficult expeditions in modern time in that we left out of Wellington, New Zealand on a 120-ft. boat with a 2,400-mile, one-way journey just to get there. We crossed what is the most violent sea on the planet, the Southern Ocean. On about the sixth day into the trip we hit 40 to 50 foot seas and I just got trashed for days on end. When we battled through that, at one point, rolled and thought we weren't going to come up. It was getting pretty ugly. We finally got a break in the weather and then got caught in a Katibotic storm, which is like a hurricane-force storm.

So we hid behind icebergs to get away from that, then we got trapped in the pack ice and we're all just trying to get near this iceberg. It was one thing after another that kept knocking us back. We finally decided we weren't going to make it to the iceberg and we retreated a little bit after being trapped in the pack ice for about five days. We set up base camp on an iceberg and got our wits about us and decided to give it one more try. During that time we were doing our forays into the water with our rebreathers and the rest of the equipment. And ultimately, we still fell shy of getting to the iceberg. Finally the helicopter pilot, Laurie Prouting, a really amazing New Zealand bloke, and I hatched this hair-brained plan to fly the helicopter, hop-skipping it across icebergs and carrying in extra fuel on the skids and camping gear and physically fly to B-15. And that's what we did. We flew there and were the first human beings to land on the largest iceberg in recorded history and plant the flag. There's nothing to prepare you for the magnitude and the immensity of it.

So how big is it? It's huge, 170 miles by 40 miles. It's about the size of Jamaica. And it's 2,200 feet thick on average so it's 2,000 feet deep under this thing since 10 percent of an iceberg sticks out of the water.

What else did you learn about it, besides the fact that it was really big? The science we learned was quite remarkable. Through aerial photography and a few basic studies that we were given by the scientists on our ship, we were able to document some really profound things about the way B-15 was impacting the

San Augustin cave entrance, Huatatla, 1994
(Inset) Skiles in early cave diving rig, 1975

Wes Skiles

entire Ross Sea. Eventually we returned to the ship, we retreated from that area to find a new area of icebergs, and started diving inside the caves. It was ethereal to go inside the ice caves. Again I'm with Jill and Paul Heinerth, who were remarkable divers on this thing pioneering the use of Cis-Lunar rebreathers and using this technology to dive further and longer than any human being had ever done.

Where did you go after you left B-15? » We went around to a place called Cape Hallet on the mainland, which is a little tamer, and we found a group of really nice icebergs to explore.

How did you find the caves? » We started probing around and boating around. Basically, we looked for caves like we would look for springs in Florida. We would systematically start exploring icebergs. We'd fly around and say, "Hey, there's an iceberg that looks like it has geology." Or I guess you'd call it iceology. And we'd find cracks and folds in the ice. Finally we found a place that had a huge crevasse in it. I wanted to film the first-ever attempt from above water and make sure that Paul and Jill took underwater cameras with them. So they entered the crevasse and while they were in there, I was left in the boat. All of a sudden there was this gut-wrenching sound and this chunk of ice about the size of a house turned and our boat got thrown about 18 feet into the air. We came down, almost tipped over and looked down and the crevasse was gone.

From our vantage it was closed. Sealed completely with them trapped inside. For the next 45 minutes we backed out of this thing because it was continuing to fall apart. We realized right then how unstable these environments were. The whole time we were thinking that Paul and Jill had been killed. Then they showed back up somewhere else. They hadn't experienced what we had and didn't even realize anything had happened.

After we got over that incident, we went back and continued exploring farther and farther back into these caves. We were using Oceanic drysuits, Patco suit heaters and the rebreathers with their warmer air so we were able to stay down much longer than people can normally stay in those kinds of waters. You've got to remember this water is 28 degrees Fahrenheit, only a tenth of a degree from turning

into ice. We finally reached a point where we were a thousand feet inside this cave, which we called Ice Island Cave Number 4. Suddenly we found ourselves in a violent current situation, which was totally unexpected. We started trying to swim out and were making no progress. The thing that was holding me back was the High Definition camera and I was like, "I'm going to die before I drop this camera."

The rebreathers were really getting taxed. By the way, we had tried to do some open circuit stuff before and every time it failed miserably. Anyway, so here we were, down at 130 feet inside of an iceberg being pulled in by a siphon current. We were at 82 minutes and I remember thinking that we were really deep in shit. Luckily we were able to persevere. Paul got along side of me and we found some areas where the current wasn't so strong and somehow we were able to work our way out. When we reached the entrance we had a lot of decompression but not near as bad as if we had been on open circuit. During decompression, I realized that Bill Stone's Cis-Lunar rebreather had kept us alive in what would have been no-survivable conditions otherwise.

Sounds like Antarctica was one helluva a trip. » Yeah it was. We had the hellacious crossing and several near-death experiences. But overall it was another incredible adventure. The film is called *Ice Island* and will be released on PBS later in 2002. You can get copies through my company, Karst Productions.

What are some of the other most memorable projects you've worked on? » Well, several other projects immediately come to mind largely because of the drama that unfolded on each. The first was the expedition to Nullarbor in Australia. It was during that expedition that a freak storm collapsed a massive cave entrance. Thirteen unlucky individuals, including myself, were buried underground. It was one of the most horrifying experiences you could ever imagine. Fortunately, we were able to escape to a chamber where we were able to regroup. Over the next two days, Dirks Stoffels, the late Rob Palmer and I explored our way partially out of the cave. We were literally crawling and climbing in places where solid wall existed just hours before. Miraculously, a friend and fellow caver, Vicki Bonwick had managed to explore down from the surface and we met her on an unstable ledge somewhere in the middle of the new cave. Everyone managed to escape unharmed but I lost a vast quantity of filming equipment.

The next would be trips I made to South Africa to film White sharks. No one had really started working there yet, so I built some really poor shark cages and literally hitch-hiked around from bay to bay exploring and filming. I had lost my first cage in a really violent storm so I built another that I thought would allow me more freedom to get really good shots of pointers without the cage. It ended up almost being my undoing. On one particular pass, a 14-ft. female hit the cage just right and it pried open like a Gary Larson cartoon.

The shark literally crashed into me and began to seriously trash me. My only defense was my 16mm film camera and it was a really good thing I had it. I kept screaming, "This is it, this is it." If you ever wonder what you might say when you think you're really going down that might be it. The shark swam us deep before it came to the end of the rope tied to the boat. When we stopped, the shark stopped struggling for a second and the foam blocks pulled us to the surface. For the people in the boat it was evidently an eerie and frightening site seeing this massive tail rise up out of the water. When that happened, the shark's position changed and I started pushing it away from me with my camera. As fast as it had happened, the shark popped out of the cage and swam off. When I surfaced one of the crew threw up on me because they thought I had been eaten.

Deciding I should leave that type of filmmaking up to Howard Hall, I retreated back to caves and joined up with my old friend Bill Stone for what would become one of the most extreme descents into the earth ever attempted. The place is called Huatatla in Southern Mexico and is poised to be the deepest cave on earth. I went down there to photograph it for *National Geographic*. I arrived to the news that a good friend of mine, Ian Roland, was dead... nearly 5,000 feet beneath the surface. A week later, after we got Ian out, Sheck Exley drowned on his depth record attempt in Northern Mexico. It was an extremely tough time in my life. Not only did I feel like I had been playing dodge ball with the Grim Reaper, but now all of my friends were getting taken out - unable to dodge the ball in the ultimate game of life on the edge. To make matters worse, a

week later I found myself trapped again, this time by floodwaters that came without warning. We were trapped for five days with no possible rescue or help from above. When the floodwaters finally receded I decided I'd had enough. It took me 18 hours to ascend on rope out of the cave system. On the surface, life never had seemed so beautiful.

Skiles self-portrait during filming of *African Shark Safari*, 1992

Wes Skiles

What else is in store for you in the near or distant future? Surviving is pretty much on the top of my list, but I pretty much plan on continuing to do what I have always have done which is to pursue adventures in exploration and filmmaking. It's a nice combination for me. I hope to continue to help encourage and advance technological tools to allow us to trek into the unknown and make images along the way. I would also really love to see the rebreather and one-atmosphere diving concepts reach their prime during my tenure as an explorer. With that in mind, I would like to think there are some more unthinkable projects out there for our team to crack. ■

Photo: Bret Gilliam

Bob Ballard

DEEP OCEAN EXPLORER

BY BRET GILLIAM

MOST OF THE PREVIOUS INTERVIEW SUBJECTS HAVE BEEN WITH PURE DIVERS WHO...

made their mark in film, manufacturing, writing and photography. This interview however, is with famed oceanographer Dr. Bob Ballard, discoverer of the *Titanic* and *Bismarck* wrecks and leader of over a hundred other memorable expeditions. »

Ballard's offices are located at the Institute For Exploration (IFE) at the Mystic Aquarium in Mystic, Connecticut. As summer crowds of eager visitors thronged through the turnstiles of the IFE exhibits at the rate of nearly a 1,000 an hour, I navigated my way past a full-sized replica of a support ship with a full-scale submersible on its aft deck "floating" in its own massive water basin. I then rendezvoused with an eager staff member who shuttled me into a private elevator and up to Ballard's inner sanctum.

Catching up with Dr. Bob Ballard, probably the world's apex ocean explorer, is roughly akin to attempting to lasso a tornado. The man moves at the manic pace of a Jack Russell terrier that had way too many cups of coffee. It's not hard to see how he maintains an athletic frame well into late middle age. Since both of us were on a tight schedule that day (he was off for a horseback riding vacation in Jackson Hole, Wyoming and I had to depart for Cocos Island to ride sharks), I outlined what I needed for some photo opportunities before settling down for the interview Q&A. Before the last words were out of my mouth, Ballard was off with the urgent stride of an Omaha insurance salesman late for his first lap dance at a Las Vegas convention.

I streamed behind in the turbulence of his wake as we set up shots in his office, by the submersible exhibits, at a control console for some of his many remote video streams from cameras in the wild, and on a sprinting slalom course through the fascinating museum of oceanography he has put together. In less than 20 minutes, I'd seen the entire Institute For Exploration, burned four rolls of film, met about a dozen staff and assistants, climbed over the exhibits including re-created models of *Titanic*'s radio room, *PT-109*'s bridge, and probably lost five pounds through perspiration alone.

We ended up in Ballard's spacious office suite dominated on one wall by a 30-ft. long map of the world and an opposite wall of glass overlooking the outside exhibits. As he sat at his desk politely answering my questions and reflecting on his unique career, a large plasma TV screen streamed a live video from a rocky kelp bed off California where two kayakers were ogling a sea lion colony. Aside from being a fascinating intellect, Ballard is perhaps the premier "gadget guy" I've ever met. He views advances in imaging technology as the ultimate tools for exploration. He's also a font of insightful quotes that help the layperson find some perspective between hype and science.

"Exploration is a discipline," explains Ballard. "Look at Charles Darwin, Christopher Columbus, and one of my heroes, Capt. James Cook. They were sent forth as disciplined observers. Adventure is bungee jumping off a bridge; exploring is mapping the canyon under the water of that bridge."

This perspective dovetails nicely with the IFE's mission statement: "To inspire people everywhere to care about and protect our ocean by exploring and sharing their biological, ecological, and cultural treasures."

Ballard's just the guy to make all that happen. He has a Ph.D. in marine geology and geophysics from the University of Rhode Island. He spent three decades at Woods Hole Oceanographic Institute where he helped refine and develop the use of manned submersibles and remotely

217

With *Titanic* model

operated vehicles (ROVs) for marine exploration. With 13 honorary degrees, the rank of commander in the Naval Reserves, and a litany of cutting edge research expeditions that have rightly established him as "da man" in the niche of modern ocean exploration, Ballard had already made a career's worth of marks when he made himself a household name with the discovery of *Titanic's* wreck over two miles deep in 1985.

He notes ruefully, "After I found the ship, I got some 16,000 letters from children." This may have been the richest treasure he has discovered: the imagination of a whole new generation of potential scientists, explorers, ecologists, etc. that is growing up in a new age of information and access.

Ballard has been involved in over 110 expeditions that included break-through research in proving the theory of plate tectonics, the discovery of hydrothermal hot water vents, the pioneering use of submersibles and ROVs as scientific tools, and a host of other pure science accomplishments that should have left a footprint in the public's consciousness along the way.

"No child had ever said to me, 'that's cool!' about my work," he reflects. "But as soon as I find an old rusty ship, I'm inundated."

Go figure.

Ballard's Jason project now allows nearly two million students and 33,000 teachers to join him in his work through the modern miracle of telepresence... each year! His new facility in Mystic carries that educational mission a notch farther and his imagination continues to grow.

"When I first arrived in 1967, the best way of getting to work was submarines. So I was a pioneer in using submarines to explore the deep sea. During the course of that work, it became glaringly obvious that physically going to the ocean floor was not going to work. With the average depth of the ocean at 12,000 feet, it used to take me two and a half hours just to do the descents. That's a five hour commute round trip! My average bottom time was three and half hours and I could only explore about a mile. It was ludicrous.

"Since 71 percent of the planet is under water, and there are only five submarines in the world that can go to that depth, and each of them can only carry three people... this means that on a really good day, you might have 15 people exploring. So I got out of submarines after decades of diving, and went to Stanford, circa 1979, and taught geophysics."

While there teaching, Ballard saw the acorn of a technology advance that would grow into Silicon Valley. The rest would prove to be historic for him and the ocean science community. He was on a roll and I let him go.

"What I was most interested in was fiber optics. You know in the movie *The Graduate* where the guy whispers to Dustin Hoffman's character: 'It's plastics.'

Well, I'll tell you, it's fiber optics! I could see the logical breakthrough in my world because of fiber optics."

This forever relieved explorers of the need to physically dive the depths of the ocean and deal with the limitations of time, not to mention the associated hazards. Physically, he could be relieved of the need to travel to the work site if an underwater robot observer could communicate what it was 'seeing' effectively. This led to the development of the *Argo-Jason* concept.

"*Argo-Jason* was named in honor of Jason and the Argonauts, the first explorers of western civilization. This allowed us to put robots under the ocean and leave them there, around the clock. Instead of three hours, we now had 24 hours, and could do 10 times the work. Instead of three people crammed into this little metal ball, freezing to death with the angst of 'we could all die down here,' the idea was to build a control center and do it all by telepresence. Now I can turn on a monitor, and I'm under the ocean, the TV monitors are my windows. More importantly, I can have 20 other people with me. So when something swims by, there is all this mental intellect gathered together, plus a satellite link. Say the world's expert on something is fishing in Montana, we can go get them online, then ask, hey, take a look at this!"

With that opener, we began talking about what got him started along this path. ∎

1. Full-scale model at the Mystic Aquarium in Connecticut.
2. Artist's rendering of *Alvin* 3. ROV *Jason Jr.* peering into one
of *Titanc's* starboard side cabins

You began as a geologist in physical sciences then went on a career path to becoming a classic scientist. Did you perceive a change to oceanography when you did graduate work at the University of Hawaii? »The change came much later when I was asked by the Navy to survey the sunken remains of the *U.S.S. Thresher* and *Scorpion*, followed then by my search for and investigation of the *RMS Titanic*. That changed my career direction from geological oceanography to archaeological and historical oceanography.

When and where did you learn to scuba dive? »I learned to scuba dive in Southern California in 1958-59. I was certified by the L.A. County Fire Department, if I recall correctly, since back then that was the only organization that could certify divers.

You spent time in Hawaii as a dolphin trainer and later commented that you felt the dolphins were training you. »It was interesting working with an intelligent animal. I discovered that kindness and affection was as powerful a motivator as food.

You earned an ROTC commission as an Army officer but ended up being transferred to the Navy. How did that come about? »I was a graduate student pursuing a Ph.D. in Oceanography at the University of Hawaii and went down to the Navy Recruiting Office at Pearl Harbor to inquire about transferring. The Navy needed oceanographers so they took me.

Tell us about your first experience with deep submersibles at the Ocean Systems Group in 1966. »I was working for Dr. Andy Rechnitzer and Dr. Richard Terry. They were designing and building the *Beaver Mark IV* lock-in, lock-out submersible for Mobile Oil and wanted to use it for scientific as well as commercial purposes. My job was to dream up operational requirements for geological exploration and observe how that translated into the design.

What was it like to work with Dr. Rechnitzer? » Great. He and Dr. Terry were both dreamers.

The Navy threw a wrench in your academic path when they suddenly called you up for duty. What was that like being uprooted from sunny California and landing in the snowy northeast? »I loathed it at first, it was quite a culture shock but it proved to be a critical turning point in my career.

The Navy assignment was your first introduction to Woods Hole Oceanographic Institution (WHOI). How did you fit in? »I had helped in the original design of *Alvin* while working for Rechnitzer and Terry, therefore knew a lot about similar submersibles. I was also going to graduate school at USC and working for the Oceans Systems Group. The head of the Geology

NATIONAL GEOGRAPHIC
COLLECTOR'S EDITION

SECRETS OF THE
TITANIC

A LEGEND SURRENDERS HER MYSTERIES.

Davis Meltzer

3

Group at Woods Hole was Dr. K.O. Emery who founded the Graduate School of Marine Geology at USC, so both groups accepted me and I was quickly put to work. Later it was Dr. Emery and Bill Rainnie who made it possible for me to return to graduate school at Rhode Island to receive my Ph.D. while making a living with the *Alvin Group*.

Was this your first experience with intense competition between various academics for funding? » That came later. At first I worked for the *Alvin Group* with the Office of Naval Research (ONR) funding.

Originally it was the WHOI that brought you and the Alvin deep submersible together. What was Alvin's history and mission at that time? » There was quite the buzz when I arrived at WHOI in March of 1967. *Alvin* had just found the H-bomb off Spain. As submersibles were still considered scientifically

untested, the science community did not take them seriously. *Alvin* was also unable to dive deeper than 6,000 feet; therefore it was confined to dives on the continental margin while many other findings were happening in the deeper mid-ocean ridge.

What projects had Alvin participated in? » Besides the bomb search, *Alvin* was doing dives for geologists and biologists but nothing earth shaking.

1. *Alvin's* divers communicate with support ship *A-II* before the sub begins a dive on *Titanic* 2. Artist's rendering of "black smoker" being investigated by *Alvin*

Can you share with us some of the first research projects you were involved in at WHOI? »At first, I went to sea with K.O. Emery and one of his previous graduate students from USC, Dr. Al Uchupi. They taught me a great deal about continental margin geology, submarine canyons, and the complex geology of the Gulf of Maine and its relationship to the newly emerging science of plate tectonics.

You had to deal with some raging egos that infiltrated some of your cruises and affected morale. What did you learn from those Ph.D. types that seemed to lack leadership? »Intelligence is not a substitute for leadership. In fact, the scientific community tends to produce poor leaders.

Alvin and the NR-1 represented different approaches to submersible design, compared to older craft like Trieste. Did you see the exploration potential right away? »Not so much an exploration potential in the case of *Alvin* as it can only cover a limited amount of terrain, but what made it

unique was its ability to go to complex geologic settings and figure out the science associated with it. The *NR-1* had exploration potential but it was highly classified, very expensive, and very uncomfortable to use.

Alvin sank in 1968. What happened? »They were lowering the sub in its cradle with the hatch open when the forward cables snapped, throwing the sub into the water with enough force to send it underwater and flood the pressure sphere. They were lucky to get out alive before she sank.

What was your first dive in *Alvin* like? »I had dove in Ben *Franklin* the previous year. The *Franklin* was very comfortable and could stay down for three-to-five days. My first dive in *Alvin* was in the Gulf of Maine and it was very frustrating because visibility was so poor.

While you were in New England you hooked up with the Boston Sea Rovers. »I was a young Ensign in the Navy when I went to my first Sea Rovers Clinic. Cousteau, Waterman, Giddings, and many others were there. It was the greatest collection of diving egos you could ever hope to meet. The annual gathering was full of energy and excitement, but as I would later learn, the focus of these clinics was not necessarily about the science of the sea, but rather the art of diving.

I understand that one of your first discussions about *Titanic* originated at a lobster bake with the Sea Rovers. Did you envision then that such a dive in a submersible was possible? »Yes. The project was named *Titanius*, not far off from *Titanic*. *Alvin's* steel hull was about to be replaced with one made of titanium. The new hull would allow for an increase in diving depth. This meant *Alvin* could now reach the *Titanic* for the first time.

Eventually you were forced to make a decision between a Navy career and pursuing your Ph.D. as a scientist. Was that a difficult choice for you? »No, I knew I had to pursue a Ph.D. Without one you can't lead. You have to work under someone else and always play second fiddle.

How did you become the designated fundraiser for the *Alvin* projects? »In 1970, ONR told Bill Rainnie he had three years to replace ONR's funding with new, non-military funding sources. I was convinced it could be done so Bill hired me to do it and I did.

Describe your feelings upon first viewing the deep water Jonah crabs from a submersible. »It was on my first *Ben Franklin* dive. We had dropped a bait can to attract life and when I saw the 55-gallon drum completely covered by hundreds if not thousands of feeding crabs... I decided never to be buried at sea.

Later you became embroiled in the debate among scientists over the theory of "continental drift." These differing opinions sparked heated and sometimes rancorous discussion, didn't **they?** »That was a very exciting and heady time which truly demonstrated how exciting science really is and that diving should be more than just a great story at a Sea Rover clinic.

Didn't *Alvin* help to confirm your theory about continental drift? »Yes, but only in a supporting role to a lot of other tools.

You changed the way *Alvin* and other submersibles were utilized by trying to pinpoint their focus on specific marine areas. »During *Project Famous*, *Alvin* demonstrated that having human eyes and hands on the bottom of the ocean was the ultimate final step in underwater science.

On one of your earlier *Alvin* dives you were nearly crushed by a huge boulder? How deep were you and how did that happen? »It was 1976 and we were diving in the Cayman Trough. We were working at the base of a giant cliff pulling rocks out of the rock face. As we moved up the face, we realized that the rocks we were trying to pry loose were holding up a massive boulder just above us. That was a scary moment. Thank God we were unsuccessful in prying them loose!

Alvin was originally only designed to go to 6,000 feet. You pushed for the submersible to be certified to twice that depth. How did you accomplish that? »The Navy wanted to build and test a new titanium sphere so we convinced them to use Alvin as a test bed for that program.

Tell us about the pioneering work you did on *Famous*? »*Famous* was the turning point in deep submergence science. We were under scrutiny by the entire oceanographic community and they were convinced it would fail. Fortunately, the critical science could be done over a very small area, ideally suited for *Alvin*. The rift valley of the mid-ocean ridge along the plate boundary was rugged and complex, yet less than one mile across.

You also had a narrow escape when a fire started on a deep dive. What caused that and how did you deal with it? »I was diving in the French bathyscaph *Archimede* in 1973, a year before we used *Alvin*, on a series of preliminary dives in the *Famous* area. We were on the bottom at 9,000 feet when an electrical fire broke out inside the pressure sphere. The sphere quickly filled with toxic black insulation smoke. Our eyes and lungs were burning as we dropped out weights and headed up. It took one and a half hours to surface. I was sick with strep throat, which only compounded my misery, but it was a historic dive.

Did you feel vindicated when finally earning your Ph.D. after all the challenges to your work? » Getting my Ph.D. was the end of one phase in my life and beginning of a new one. Without it, too many doors were locked.

How did *Angus* come about? » *Angus* was developed by Dr. Bill Bryan and Dr. Joe Phillips at WHOI for *Famous* to conduct a series of film runs across the rift valley floor. I went on to perfect it as a search tool for *Alvin*. We used it in 1977 to find the first active hydrothermal vents and in 1979 to find the first "Black Smokers."

You discovered publicity aided funding for your exploration projects. But this also brought criticism from the old school academics. How did you deal with that element? » Working for *National Geographic* was a blessing and a curse. Every Sea Rover loved *National Geographic* while most oceanographers thought doing anything with them was a waste of time. I later discovered it was much more complex than that. The fact was most oceanographers were doing things that the public and *National Geographic* had no interest in. To make matters more difficult, the press, *National Geographic* included, portrayed science as an "I" profession when in reality, it's an "us" (it's a collective scientific effort). The press would single out an individual and make them a hero. This made some rightfully angry and others wrongly jealous.

The discovery of the hydrothermal vents off the Galapagos was another landmark. » It was a great expedition and it was clearly the result of much hard work by many great scientists.

Didn't you also nearly have an accident by approaching a hot water chimney vent? » We

didn't realize at the time how hot the vent water was until Alvin returned to the surface and we saw the heat damage. It had melted down to the foam, close to the viewport on the port side of the sub. We then became very careful when working around black smokers on future dives. It could have been a disaster had we let the hot fluid hit our view ports inches away.

Although you were a huge advocate of deep submersibles, you eventually favored a different means of observation in deep ocean zones by utilizing unmanned vehicles. Did this cause a rift between your ideas and the manned submersible factions? » My conversion to remotely operated vehicles made me a traitor in the eyes of the deep submergence community. It was a fraternity that felt I

1. Diver inspects *Alvin's* ascent and descent weights
2. Artist's rendering of *Argo* illuminating the giant swastika on the bow of the German battleship *Bismarck*

had deserted them. The physical act of diving was such a part of deep submergence that not doing it, or worse yet, replacing it with robots threatened to emasculate those who utilized remotely operated submersibles. I was more interested in why I was diving as opposed to the pure act of diving. Diving was becoming "old hat" for me and I saw so many people continuing to "pound their chests" about the dangers of diving when in reality air travel took more lives. People would return from a dive then talk about it but never tell me anything interesting about what they saw. It was too macho a world for me to live up to the rest of my life – a Sea Rovers Clinic gone to the extreme.

2

the accepted theories and why? »Prior to that experience, the standard way to look for something on the bottom was to use a side-scan sonar. But in complex bottom terrain with many targets, deep canyons and narrow ridges, a side-scan sonar can quickly become difficult to use. In such terrain, only the largest of targets can be seen and then you have to be on top of them before they're detected. The *Thresher* was destroyed by a powerful implosion creating a vast debris field that stretched out over several square kilometers. A side-scan was unable to tell the difference between debris and the millions of

You were left to conceive, design and build the *Argo-Jason* system. »In 1979, we returned from the Galapagos Rift with the first biologists to see the exotic marine life living around the vents. We mounted a new digital color camera on *Alvin's* arm to test. I had my back turned to the view ports and was looking at a TV monitor when I noticed the biologist was doing the same. A light went off in my mind. Why were we down here if the biologist thought the view on the screen was better than looking out of the sub's viewport? That year, I took a sabbatical to Stanford and began to dream up the *Argo/Jason* system. The idea was to use the newly emerging technology of fiber optics to move the sub's window to the surface so we could achieve more bottom time. Bottom time is so short in a submersible, particularly when you make a deep dive. It takes too long to get down, surface, and then recharge the batteries. With an ROV, our bottom time could be 24-hours a day. Again I was more interested in why I was diving than the act itself. I was willing to give up the chest-pounding heroics to get more time on the bottom and learn more about the wonders of the underwater world.

In searching for the wreck of the submarine *Thresher* you had an epiphany about the trajectory and trace debris left on the bottom that changed your methodology for looking for wrecks. Can you explain how you changed

glacial stones (erratics) dropped by melting icebergs years before, but a camera could.

The discovery of the *Titanic*, sunk to a depth of more than 12,000 feet, etched your reputation for all time. »Finding the *Titanic* was a mixed bag. It made me famous, it made me enemies for life and it totally changed my life and career. I often wonder where I would be today had I not found the *Titanic*. I am very happy where I am today, thanks in a large degree to the *Titanic*. I'm doing things that never would have been possible. Clearly, however, finding the *Titanic* was not the most important project I have ever done. My biggest disappointment concerning the *Titanic* project was the conflict that erupted between the French and Woods Hole over credit for the discovery, as well as the subsequent salvaging of

the *Titanic* by the French after the discovery. I'm convinced that had there been a diplomatic solution, both sides would have protected the *Titanic*, and she would look just like she did when we first found her.

Although many artifacts of the *Titanic* are nearly perfectly preserved, there are no traces of human remains. Why? »Remember the Jonah crabs? People are eaten and their bones are exposed. The deep sea is undersaturated in calcium carbonates that make up bones. As a result, bones dissolve quickly leaving only the inedible shoes behind. Inside wrecks you'll find bodies and skeletons, but not outside unless you are in the Black Sea, which has no oxygen.

What are your thoughts on the practice of taking laypersons on submersible dives to the *Titanic* if they ante up the fee? »I think visiting the *Titanic* by lay people is wonderful. It's no different from going to see the *Arizona* in Pearl Harbor. My concern is for the damage to her decks that will

result from the subs that land there and leave things behind. I'll give you an update next summer when I go back for the first time since finding her.

Did you like Jim Cameron's movie *Titanic*? »Yes. Great movie!

You and I are both members of the prestigious Explorers Club. Cameron was just inducted and given a special award, how does this sit with you? »I think Jim is a great moviemaker and an innovator of filming technology. I wish I had his cameras, lights and his budgets.

You've had a long relationship with the National Geographic Society and produced some great articles and films for them. You've had your differences along the way including a ruckus over the first press conferences following *Titanic's* discovery in 1985. How do you balance the relationship with sponsors? »I have a wonderful relationship with the National Geographic Society. I am one of their Explorers-in-Residence and receive more support from them now than I have ever received in the past. I hope it goes on forever. National Geographic management stood with me during the *Titanic* press flap with the French and our sub-sequent return to the *Titanic* the following year, others didn't.

Please enlighten us on the discovery of the *Bismarck*. Was it a similar project to *Titanic*? »
Same visual-search strategy just a larger area and with another sunken ship close by that threw us off the first year, we recovered the second year and found her. Before one can explore a ship, one needs to find it, and that is the hard part. Exploring a wreck site is the reward one is given after the hunt ends. And finding the German battleship Bismarck was not easy. In fact, it was the most difficult hunt I have ever conducted,

1. Celebrating *Titanic's* discovery with sparkling wine in paper cups in *Argo's* control van 2. The moment of discovering *Bismarck*.

and that includes finding the *RMS Titanic*, the *USS Yorktown*, and *PT-109*.

What made the search for *Bismarck* difficult was the depth at which the ship lies—more than 14,500 feet of water—the uncertainty of its location, the terrain in which it had come to rest, and the avalanche it set off on impact with the seafloor. Unlike other seekers of shipwrecks, I adopted a hunt strategy for finding shipwrecks in the deep that involved constant visual contact with the bottom. My colleagues questioned this

strategy, relying instead upon the age-old technique of using a side-scan sonar to search. Operating in total darkness, video cameras can only see a short distance, 30 meters at best, while 100 kHz side-scan sonars can reach out more than 400 meters to a side. Why would I want to search with a camera?

Back in 1984, the U.S. Navy was thinking about disposing of the nuclear containment vessel that housed the reactors in retired nuclear submarines. We were concerned about the adverse affects the reactors might have on the deep benthic environment. For that reason, the Navy wanted to investigate the nuclear reactors of the *USS Thresher* and *USS Scorpion* that have been lost and still never found, in the 1960s. I was called in to see if I could find them using my new camera sled *Argo*.

While mapping the wreck sites, I made a fundamental discovery. Shortly after sinking, both subs imploded catastrophically thousands of feet above the sea floor, creating a mass of debris of all weights and sizes. As this material sank, underwater currents carried the lighter debris more than one mile away from the heavier objects, creating a long trail of wreckage. More importantly, side-scan sonars were unable to detect these light objects while a camera could.

Both *Titanic* and *Bismarck* released a tremendous quantity of debris into the water at their moment of sinking. Knowing the currents in the area, I could predict the direction in which the debris would have drifted and lay out search patterns that crossed the debris field at one-mile intervals. This made it possible to move through the area very quickly. For *Titanic*, this strategy worked fantastically. Once I located the debris field, I was able to follow it to the shipwreck. For *Bismarck*, however, the method proved more difficult. During the 1988 search, I picked up a debris trail that led to another ship, a larger wooden schooner that had sunk years before. The summer search window was lost.

The following year, I picked up another debris field but it led to a large depression with nothing in it. Had *Bismarck* been buried by its own impact? No, *Bismarck's* impact with the seafloor had set off a giant landslide, carrying the ship downslope, requiring more time to finally locate her. As I got close, I saw its skid marks on the bottom, surrounded by hundreds of German boots.

Except for a small portion of the stern, the ship was upright, intact and in an amazing state of preservation. The swastikas on her bow and stern decks were still there. We examined the mighty armor belt looking for signs of damage. We found none. As I wrote in my 1990 book, the *Discovery of the Bismarck*, "alongside the hull we could see evidence of hits from the British secondary guns. In some cases, the shells had splattered like bugs on a windshield, seeming to leave the armor intact."

But what struck us most as we returned to port was the absence of implosive damage to her hull like that on the stern of *Titanic*, the result of a ship sinking before being fully flooded. From the integrity of the wreck, it would seem that *Bismarck* sank well after her watertight compartments had been blown open to speed her final journey to the ocean floor. The first question I was asked by the British press was, "Did we sink her or was she scuttled?" To their horror, I answered, "I believe she was scuttled." But only after further exploration would we know for sure.

You've extensively explored the shipwrecks of the Solomon Islands' Iron Bottom Sound. You later turned your attention to locating the wreckage of John Kennedy's *PT-109* off Gizo in the northern Solomons. How did that search differ from your hunt for other wrecks? 》*PT-109* was a true needle in a haystack. It wasn't where everyone thought, so what's new? And we didn't have much time to find her. The bottom currents were very strong and she was mostly buried by drifting sand dunes.

How did the Kennedy family feel about your expedition? 》The Kennedy family was great and fun to work with, particularly Max Kennedy who went on the expedition with us. Our strongest support came from Senator Edward Kennedy and his great staff.

You've also been conducting explorations in the Mediterranean for ancient shipwrecks. 》After finding many contemporary shipwrecks like *Titanic*, *Bismarck*, *PT-109*, *Yorktown*, etc. I began to wonder about the fate of older and potentially more important ancient shipwrecks. This thought has now set me on a new path. I'm now convinced that the deep sea contains more ancient history than all of the museums in the world combined and I want to help unlock that underwater museum for the world to enjoy and learn from.

Do you believe that, as a society, we are spending too much money on space exploration and not enough on marine and ocean exploration? 》I think space exploration is something our nation should do including putting humans on Mars. I simply think we, as a society, should be spending a similar amount on ocean exploration.

What's your opinion on the state of manned submersible and ROV units today and what would you like to see next? 》The Ocean Science Board of the National Academy of Science has been asked by the National Science Foundation to deal with the furtherance of deep submergence technology. That study is underway and I've made a specific series of recommendations to the group but time (less than a few months) will tell. Their hearings are ongoing.

program. This year alone, one and a half million students are doing *Jason* and 33,000 pre-college science teachers are using our web-based curriculum and annual "live" expedition.

Let's touch on an item of controversy. Are wrecks graveyards to be left undisturbed or are they fair game for archaeological study? »It depends. There are wrecks… and there are wrecks. Some are important and many are not. I draw a line between a recent wreck and an ancient wreck. Recent wrecks have living survivors and living relatives of the dead. They need to be treated with respect for the feelings of the living individuals left behind. I draw a line between wrecks that are historical and ones that are not. I draw a line between wrecks that are fascinating and/or beautiful to visit and ones that are not. In other words, if you find a wreck that is historically or archaeologically important, a wreck that is enjoyable or beautiful to visit, what gives you the right to take something from that wreck that makes it less important, less

1. WWII PT boat display, Institute for Exploration, Mystic Aquarium
2. Entrance of *PT-109* show, Mystic Aquarium

Graham Hawks' *Deep Flight* submersible has gotten a lot of press. It exudes sizzle and sex appeal but do you feel it will it prove to be a useful tool for science? »I think it will provide people, particularly the lay public, with a wonderful opportunity to fly in the underwater world. I don't think it will result in a great deal of compelling science, but that doesn't mean *Deep Flight* submersibles shouldn't be built with private money.

Since you founded *Jason* in 1989 it has greatly expanded. Bring us up to date on its current programs and where you see this going. »The Jason Foundation for Education is entering its 15th year. More than five million students and teachers have been involved in its annual educational

enjoyable, or less beautiful for those who follow. Just because you can take something from a wreck does not mean you should. I think objects taken from a ship lessen the object and lessen the ship. Once found, a ship is no longer lost. Modern technology is making it easier and easier for others to visit that ship in person or with telepresence technology. Again, I think salvage is a form of macho thinking that needs to change. It demonstrates lack of integrity to rip something off a shipwreck and it proves nothing. It takes much more character to leave it as you find it.

Bret Gilliam

Should artifacts be studied and left underwater or brought up and preserved? » If there is something to be learned scientifically or archaeologically, then recovery is justified. Many of the ancient shipwrecks I found were commercial carriers with large quantities of the same object and in some cases, these objects are still preserved underwater. In such cases, only a few need to be recovered. The remainder is not going anywhere and is easy to locate should scientists need another sample. I think underwater museums should be created. It's very expensive to conserve, guard and protect ancient artifacts forever. Forever is a long time!

What about the ships themselves, such as the Civil War ironclad *Monitor*? » In some cases, bringing shipwrecks to the surface, particularly small ones, is the best way to preserve them for others to enjoy and that action is justifiable. But in the case of the *Titanic*, removing artifacts, particularly artifacts that can remain underwater for thousands of years (i.e. glass, ceramics, etc.) lessens the experience of others who follow. I think technology will soon make it possible to stop further degradation, in fact, even reverse it.

What's this new project you've got going at the Mystic Aquarium? » It is the Institute For Exploration (IFE)/Mystic Aquarium and it has no endowment. Wish it did. Donations are accepted. IFE is dependent upon many sources including federal grants from the Office of Naval Research, NOAA, in particular, Office of Ocean Exploration, National Geographic Society, private donations, and 750,000 visitors that come to our exhibit center every year.

For most of your career, you've had to chase funding from the Navy, *National Geographic*, National Science Foundation, etc. Will your new Institute make your exploration projects easier now? » The need to raise funds to chase your dreams will never go away. Columbus had to do it. Lewis and Clark had to do it. Peary had to do it and I, along with other explorers, am no exception. It's a rite of passage.

You've recently embarked on a project for semi-submersible oceanic habitats. Do you see floating cities in our future? Is *Waterworld* just around the corner? » I don't think a large number of people will live beneath the sea in ambient pressure habitats. That's great for science and for industry but too expensive for the masses. I do believe that more people will move out onto the sea. They already are doing it on offshore platforms of the oil and gas industry. Tens of thousands of us do it each day. I foresee a time when families will begin to do it on vertical spar buoys like Scripps' FLIP. It's a matter of time and dropping costs.

You've managed to carve out a fascinating career as an underwater equivalent of *Indiana Jones*. What advice might you give young people who'd like to pursue a similar path in ocean exploration? » I always tell young people to follow their dreams. Not their mother's, father's, or teacher's dreams but their own. You need the passion of your dreams to get you back up on your feet when society knocks you down.

What are your new dreams? » I have always lived in two worlds. The world of deep submergence technology and the world of deep submergence science. It goes back to my upbringing by Andy Rechnitzer and Dick Terry and later by K.O. Emery and Bill Rainnie. In the world of deep submergence technology, I want to go to the next level in telepresence this summer when I begin the process of moving the diver to the beach so one can have infinite "bottom time." Just think, if you come to Mystic in July and August, for 24 hours a day for 30 days you can be underwater in the Black Sea and Eastern Mediterranean diving on a series of ancient shipwrecks, working with those at sea as if you were there. In the world of deep submergence science, I want to begin a new field of research in deep-water archaeology. Just last year, I accepted a full professorship at my alma mater, the Graduate School of Oceanography at the University of Rhode Island where I received my Ph.D. in the summer of 1974, just before going to sea on *Project Famous*.

I am now director of the Institute for Archaeological Oceanography and starting next year we begin offering a dual degree with the University's History Department. New graduate students in this program will receive a Ph.D. in Oceanography and a Masters in Marine Archaeology. Using our newly developed vehicle systems (*Echo, Argus, Little Herc*, and *Hercules*), we hope to pioneer this new field of research and uncover lost chapters of human history while the world looks on. ■

ALL PHOTOS FROM MIKE DEGRUY COLLECTION EXCEPT AS NOTED

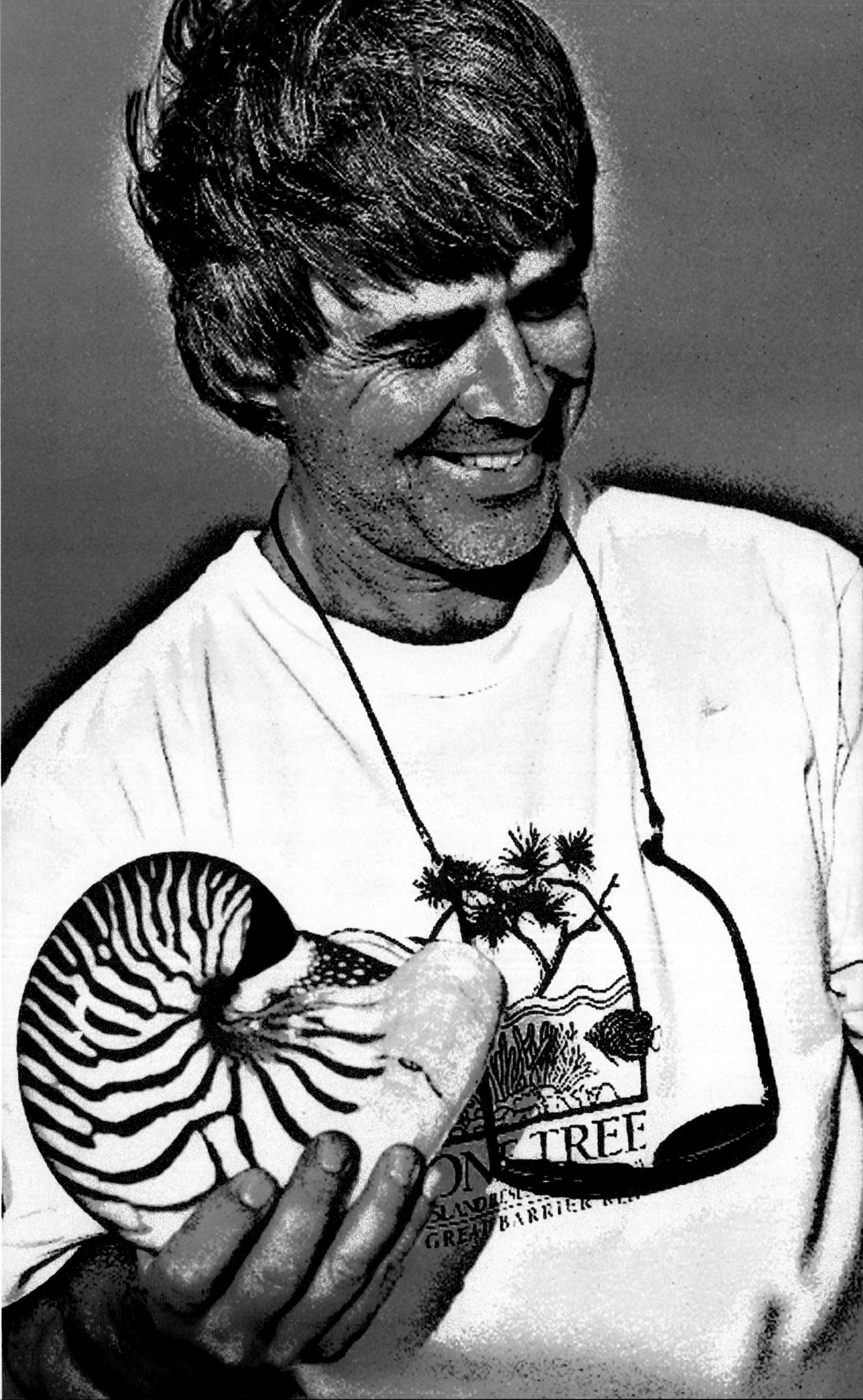

Mike deGruy
LITTLE BIG MAN

BY BRET GILLIAM

Eddy O'Connor

AS A HIGHLY SUCCESSFUL FILMMAKER FOR OVER 25 YEARS,

Mike deGruy has had his ups and downs. He's won dozens of awards both domestically and abroad and his work has appeared everywhere, BBC, PBS, TBS and National Geographic Television. But along the way he's spent a few nights in Heartbreak Hotel. »

Early in his career, deGruy was viciously attacked by a shark and narrowly escaped death. He's lost over a half a million dollars worth of filming equipment due to circumstances beyond his control in the field. And he's even had his support ship sink out from under him into 2,000 feet of water. Yet, like a true pro Mike has always come back with the footage. From his dramatic images of orcas snatching sea lion pups from the beach to his elaborately detailed studio sets, deGruy's career has taken him to the world's most remote and spectacular locations.

Although a bit "vertically challenged", at about five and a half feet in height, Mike is also perhaps the most boundlessly enthusiastic person in diving. Whether onstage narrating a film segment or appearing in his numerous documentary productions, there is no mistaking when he makes his appearance. Audiences are snapped to attention. Children crane their necks to get a better view. Even dogs and cats strain to figure out what all the ruckus is about. The man is like a Tasmanian Devil on speed. And once he get's going... well, it's best to just get out of the way.

We met in February 1996 while we were both working on a *National Geographic Explorer* documentary on humpback whales out on the Silver Bank, north of the Dominican Republic. He was the Director of Photography and I was the designated "whale expert" whose mission was to shepherd host Boyd Matson into camera frame with the leviathans and, hopefully, bring him back alive. I also had to train all the film crew to dive on rebreathers, a product that was new to most divers at the

time. We've been close friends ever since.

Our trip started out steeped in humor and only got funnier. In an article I wrote back then called *On the Road with National Geographic* I noted our departure from Grand Turk in rough seas:

"I knew right away that Mike deGruy and I were going to get along as we both stifled laughter observing the rest of the *National Geographic Explorer* film crew trying to cope with seasickness. Mike is one of the world's top nature cameramen both above and below water. And he's spent his fair share of time bouncing around boats in various ends of the earth. He even had a shark try to chew off his arm a few years back leaving enough scars to win any bar

room contest of diver stories. So I didn't expect the 10 foot seas we were battling today to bother him too much.

But Boyd Matson, the show's host and resident talking head, was a bit less experienced. When he boarded the expedition vessel at 5:00 AM that morning, I had already placed him under "fashion arrest" for carrying more that 50 lbs. of hair

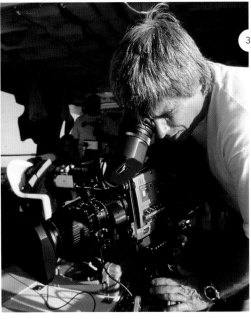

care products in his luggage. Boyd has hosted the *National Geographic Explorer* series for about a year now and he's got to be one of the nicest guys you'll ever meet. He kind of looks like a Nordic cross between Robert Redford and Huck Finn with a tousled head of blond hair right out of the J. Crew catalog. For a balding guy like me, it was disgusting.

But seasickness had Boyd's full attention. Right now he was wiping the fruits of his last "heave ho" out of that million-dollar hairdo and working on his best thousand yard stare while silently

1. *National Geographic Explorer* film crew on location, Silver Bank for humpback whales, (Left to right), Peck Euwer, Boyd Matson, Fred Garth, deGruy and Bret Gilliam 2. Humpback whale cavorting for photographers. 3. deGruy at work

Photos: Bret Gilliam

1

Photos: Bret Gilliam

to bring back some gut-wrenching hang gliding footage. So I guess, we *should have* cut him some slack when he showed up to learn to dive with rebreathers... and 60 ton whales... in the open ocean... in one day. But, of course, we didn't.

Mike, being a professional diver, got used to rebreathers in a heartbeat. Boyd's learning curve was a bit steeper. Think of looking back on Everest's north face route and that might put it in perspective. But sort of like an eager golden retriever, Boyd would try anything and keep going at it until he *almost* got it right. I swear I contemplated tossing a Frisbee off the stern of the boat once just to see if he would fetch it."

When I launched *Fathoms* magazine in 2001, I asked Mike to be our first interview subject. He agreed, "As long as we don't have to discuss that hot tub incident at your house during the snowstorm."

In the dialogue that followed, Mike spoke frankly about his life, filmmaking, and what it's like to take a deep submersible into the ocean's depths. His encounter with my treacherous hot tub remains forever sealed. ■

praying that the damn boat would stop rocking. Lined up next to him in white-knuckled angst were producer Claire Van dePolder and sound technician Eddy O'Connor. Both were engaged in spirited Technicolor projectile vomiting. As Mike and I turned away giggling inanely, Eddy flashed me a look that said, "Who do I have to screw to get out of this movie?"

Yeah, we were off to a good start. And before you could say "Sasoon Herbal Cream Conditioner", Boyd and his cosmetics were on the way to the whale petting zoo.

All kidding aside, Boyd's got a pretty tough job. He basically has to learn a new extreme sport every week and try to look good doing it. The week before he had been traveling by dog sled in mid-winter blizzards in Minnesota and then was shipped off to be hurled off some high altitude mountain peak

237

1. Fifty-foot female Humpback whale dives inches away from Gilliam's camera during *National Geographic Explorer* television shoot
2. Shipwreck stranded on Silver Bank, film support vessels anchor nearby in the lee
3. Rebreather diver Lynn Hendrickson and whale 4. Male Humpback waves to film crew

Mike, we've found out that you're originally from Mobile, Alabama. How did a Southerner make it in the California film scene? »Hmmm... That's a bit strong. Certainly I have not made it in Hollywood. I may have lucked into a few dollars and filmmaking opportunities in my little natural history documentary world, but after 20 years, who wouldn't? Mobile was important to what I do today. I grew up, on and in the water in the many rivers around Mobile Bay and the Gulf. I had a mad obsession of flying and since I couldn't afford a plane, I bought a regulator. It's the same thing really, only you're flying underwater, and much cheaper. School and the urge to see and study coral reefs took me away from the South and to Hawaii. I never left the Pacific.

Kidding aside, how'd you get started in filmmaking and not, say, lumberjacking? »Let's get something straight here: kidding is never an aside. Okay, here's the brief scoop: while I was a lowly grad student at the University of Hawaii, thinking I was headed for a career in Marine Biology, fighting my friends for tenure at some plum spot in the tropics, teaching Zoo 101 the rest of my life, I met a madman who sent me, Bruce Carlson (current Director of the Waikiki Aquarium) and Paul and Gracie Atkins (who took the same career path as me) to Palau to collect live chambered nautilus (my research animal at UH). At the last minute he threw a couple of old Arriflex S cameras at us and said, "Make a movie of this."

So we did. It had to be the worst piece of crap you'd ever seen, but it was a blast to do and upon returning I immediately dropped out of school and started making films. I never told anybody I didn't know what I was doing, so I kept getting hired. I have to say, however, that splitting logs was a close second.

How long were you in the Marshall Islands? »I lived in the Marshalls for three years as the resident manager of a marine lab. This was a wild period of my life. I took a year off from school for the job and after three years made that trip to Palau and, well, never returned to UH. I was in my mid-20s, had free run of a spectacular atoll, managed about 10 boats, had full diving facilities and dove my butt off in some of the most spectacular waters and reefs I have ever seen. Never mind that little shark thing.

Speaking of that, what's it like having a reef shark chewing on your arm like it was a chicken wing? »Grey Reef sharks just have no sense of humor. What's it like? What the hell do you think it was like? Well, that's not entirely fair since you have experienced a shark attack first hand as well. You know, between the two of us and friends like Al Giddings, Rodney Fox, Jimmy Stewart... we ought to start our own club for shark survivors. That would be a neat little fraternity.

But back to my own personal little *Jaws* incident. I innocently took a picture of a shark that was some 20 feet away, admittedly it was in a threat posture, but jeez... and the little five footer shot right in and ripped off the top of my arm! I couldn't believe it! At first everything was happening in super slow motion

vanished… a bad sign. Out of the deep came a rather large Silvertip shark, about 10 feet long. I pulled out my trusty powerhead, which was only about two feet long, and watched as the shark cruised right at us and passed straight over my head. I literally had to back up to keep from being scraped. I couldn't believe this… my first dive back, into THIS! Of course, Al just kept filming.

But to answer your question, I still react differently to sharks. Before my incident, I never really thought about them, except as photographic subjects, as well

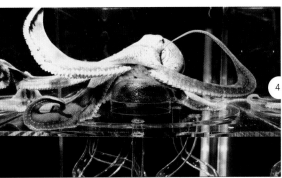

1. Face to face with a half a ton of blubber 2. In a protective mobile shark cage deGruy designed and built, deGruy filmed sharks in the Marshall Islands for a BBC and *National Geographic* film, *Sharks on their Best Behavior* 3. Filming for the BBC series *Live in the Freezer,* Antarctica 4. This tank was used to simulate a coral head by prompting the octopus to probe the curly tubes for food as they do on natural coral reefs

and I watched with unbelieving eyes. The shark's head approached, brushed my camera aside, and at the very last nanosecond, opened its mouth and engulfed my right forearm. After the mouth closed and it began shaking like some rabid dog, things sped up really fast and I was being jerked around like a rag in a mad dog's mouth. It ripped off the top of my arm, did a loop, and attacked again from below. As I futilely kicked at it, thinking "aloha world," it grabbed my fin rather than my lower thigh, again shook like a paint shaker and tore out a semi-circle of rubber. This, apparently it didn't like, as it spat it out and went after Phil Light, my diving partner. I'd never imagined I would be happy to see someone attacked by a shark, but I sure was then! Phil was cut, but okay.

After the accident, how long did it take before you could go back into the water without getting the willies? » I had 11 operations over a two-year period, but got back into the water after about a year. Interestingly, one of my first, if not the first, dives was again in the same place with this little-known cameraman named Al Giddings. We were on the dropoff near the Deep Passage and Al was filming Grey Reef sharks. Suddenly I noticed the Greys had

as marveling at their unique and awesome beauty. After nearly getting killed by one, I am acutely aware of them and swimming around in shallow water at night is no longer fun. And swimming in your hot tub after dark is pretty conflicting, too!

After the Marshall Islands, what direction did your career take? » The Marshalls were literally a life-changing experience. Almost from life to death, in fact. I officially wrote off school and the career that a Ph.D. would have given me. I left everything I had trained for (Marine Biology) entirely. This was a tad intimidating, but must speak volumes about how much I loved that collecting/filming trip to Palau. Paul Atkins and I both quit graduate school and along with his now wife, Gracie, managed to twice return to Palau and finish the film we started on the chambered nautilus. We sold it to PBS and the BBC and never turned back. I became a freelance cameraman for the BBC working extensively on major series like *Trials of Life*, *The Living Planet*, *Life in the Freezer*, and began producing my own films shortly thereafter. I got hired by this foxy little lass at *Turner Broadcasting* in Atlanta for a shoot in Samoa and ended up marrying her. Mimi and I now produce a film about every three years.

2000 Int'l Electronic Cinema Festival – Astrolabium Award for Cinematography | 1997 Valle d'Aosta Int'l Film Festival – Airone Prize | 1996 CINE Golden Eagle »   Q+A »

AWARDS I RECOGNITIONS I NOMINATIONS ::

239

What are your current projects and where will they be taking you? »I am travelling to Punta Norte in Patagonia to film killer whales literally rushing out of the water to grab hapless sea lion pups from the dry beach. I filmed this some eight years ago for *The Trials of Life* and have to say I still get a lot of comments about that sequence. Of all the natural history phenomenon I have filmed, or even witnessed,

this has to be right at the top. When you are laying in the surf zone, wearing a wetsuit and a camera and 40-ft. whales are screaming out of the water right next to you, grabbing scurrying sea lions and violently slapping them back and forth, ripping them apart, then returning to sea where they flip them 30 feet into the air with their tails… well, this has a lasting memory. So I return, this time with a 35mm movie camera for an upcoming feature film on whales. Wish me luck.

When and how did you get started filming from deep submarines? »Maui Divers is a jewelry manufacturer in Hawaii, who uses exotic corals as stones. To acquire these precious corals, they owned and operated a little submarine, the *Star II*. I was a diver helping launch and recover the sub and had several opportunities to dive in it as well. I had experienced nothing like this before. At 1,200 feet in Hawaii's beautiful blue Pacific, there was a dim moonlight glow over the bottom. Surrounding us were huge bushy gold coral trees that sparkled like Christmas decorations with their bioluminescence. Then there were the bamboo corals – as you might imagine from the name, these spectacular creatures had a skeleton beginning at the bottom of about an inch thick. But what most impressed me was

their bioluminescence. If you gently nudged these corals with the sub, a ring of blue-green light appeared at their base and traveled right up the stalk, took the 90 degree turn and spiraled its way off the tip. Spectacular! This was the seed that took 20 years to germinate.

Four years ago I got a call from the BBC, who were producing a film for *The Discovery Channel* on a search for the giant squid. They told me they were taking a one-man sub to New Zealand to try to film a giant squid, and was I interested in going to Kaikura for a month, learning how to drive the sub and be the pilot/photographer! At this point I just have to ask… is this a great job or what?! Anyway,

I said I didn't know, I'd check my schedule and get back to them in a month. Right. Needless to say, I signed on and that turned out to be a defining moment for me. I am totally and completely hooked on small submersibles and expect the rest of my life to revolve around them.

---

1. deGruy looks through a plexiglass octopus tube for his film, *The Octopus Show*, co-produced by *National Geographic* and *Nature* 2. deGruy packed in the cabin of Wood's Hole's submersible, *Alvin* 3. The one-man *Deep Rover* sub made by Phil Nuytten's company, Nuytco, is one of deGruy's favorite filming platforms

3

What's the deepest stuff you've filmed? »The deepest stuff I have filmed is off Panama, on the mid-ocean ridge. These dives were just over 10,000 feet and I did four or five of them from the Woods Hole sub, *Alvin*. We were diving on the hot vents, characterized by extraordinary black smokers, towering underwater volcanoes violently belching what looks everything in the world like thick black smoke from a 1950 steel mill stack gone bad. It is a place of extremes. Extreme conditions, needless to say, as there is no light, great pressure, you do the math (some 4,500 psi), and near

freezing conditions. Not to mention very little oxygen. But the greatest extreme has to be the contrasts. The vents are dispersed along the East Pacific Rise, part of the submarine mountain range encircling the earth. It is now generally agreed that these rift zones produce the earth we now drive and grow tomatoes on. Anyway, the hot spots are ephemeral and seem to have about a 20-year life span, then they quit spewing – like terrestrial volcanoes, just a different time scale.

As you cruise along the bottom, your porthole reveals lava. Huge fields of black lava which looks exactly like the lava fields in Hawaii. Nothing seems to live there, just bleak, stark basalt with the occasional rattail, sea cucumber or bizarrofish oozing by. Then you start seeing tiny white specks on the bottom. These specks increase in number and soon you recognize them as crabs and funny looking lobster. Within 30 feet from starkness, you hear a "Holy shit, there it is!" from the pilot (he has the best view) and out of your little window emerges an entire community of creatures thriving on the noxious gases and chemicals super heated by the earth's molten core. Masses of tube worms, 12-feet long, pure white with brilliant red plumes hide many species of fish, gastropods, other types of worms, crustaceans of all sizes and shapes and perhaps my favorite, octopus like you've never seen before. What a place that is. Perhaps what made it so special was the equipment I was using on the *Alvin*. Woods Hole has invested a substantial amount of money toward superb imaging and we rigged the sub with high definition camera systems. We saw details of this unique community that had never been seen before.

What's the most interesting subject you've filmed? »That's a tough one. So many elements are involved in making a place interesting, the animals, the conditions, the physical elements… But as far as subjects go, I have to say that the phenomenon I am about to embark on again has to be right up there. In Patagonia, a group of killer whales have cued in on the "fledging" of a population of sea lion pups, which are just learning to swim. I was there with Paul Atkins, who was also filming the event and perhaps the busiest Assistant Cameraman known to man, Keith Turner. Keith was loading magazines for the both of us, and running roll after roll of film at 150 frames/second kept the poor guy mighty busy. Several things impressed me about this extraordinary phenomenon; the whales

1996 US Int'l Film Festival, Gold Camera Award | 1996 Missoula Int'l Film Festival, Cinematography Award | 1995 BAFTA Award for Cinematography »   Q+A »

AWARDS | RECOGNITIONS | NOMINATIONS ::

were not there except for the two weeks when the pups dared to enter the water, then they showed up right on cue. How did they know the pups were ringing that dinner bell? The same whales return year after year, at exactly the right time, so they must be cueing in on something – certainly not the calendar. Then the behavior itself is amazing, if not downright morbid. The big males hunt individually, while the smaller females hunt in an organized pack.

There is a break in the reef about 100-feet wide and even at this break the whales can only make it over at high tide. So they wait, as did I. At high tide, when the pups foolishly enter this "dead zone," they are history – better frame up your shot and start rolling because the black and white freight train is coming through. Their speed and inertia bring them literally out of the water and up onto the beach, where they grab an unsuspecting pup. With a violent shaking of their head and bodies they slam the little sea lion time and time again against the beach while they work their hulk back into the water. But it doesn't end there. They take the pups out to sea and release them offshore. This is the morbid part – they breach on top of them, take them in their mouths and sling them 30-to-40 yards across the water and swim beneath them and flip them 50 feet into the air with their tails. The pups are still alive during this punishment, which may go on for 10-to-15 minutes. Then the telltale blood arrives at the surface and it's over. This cycle repeats itself for over a week.

1. Mike used Harbor Branch's Johnson *Sea-Link* sub to film cold water seeps and brine lakes in the Gulf of Mexico in "shallow" depths between 2,000 and 2,500 feet 2. The actors in wildlife can be as fickle as anyone in Hollywood. Sadly, this sea lion pup was starving to death because of a seasonal lack of food

How did you make the *National Geographic* connection? »In 1989, my lovely bride and I produced a film on sharks called *Sharks on Their Best Behavior* for the Hawaiian PBS station, KHET. About a year into the three-year project, *Geographic* bought into it and I have worked on and off with them ever since.

Weren't you competing against Boyd Matson for that hosting spot? »How embarrassing. I'd hardly saying I was competing with Boyd, because he clearly is perfect for that *Explorer* position and obviously I was no competition as they chose him, but I did audition. We were considering moving to Annapolis, Maryland at the time and the *Explorer* spot seemed a reasonable idea. Fortunately, I came to my senses and moved to Santa Barbara instead, a city that I love living in.

After they picked him over you, didn't you ended up shooting him repeatedly - photographically that is? »Yeah, for a while I was shooting quite a few of the openings and links for *Explorer*. That was back in the days when they were still using film and we had an absolute blast travelling all over the world doing three-minute pieces. Then they went to video and after one of those video jobs I never heard from them again! I guess that speaks for itself… I still shoot film.

Besides yourself, who are your favorite underwater filmmakers? »I can't possibly answer that. This is such a small world and everybody knows each other and to single out one of two without naming the whole lot would be, well, I just can't do that. I can say this, however, as far as watching programs in an auditorium setting and listening to the filmmaker narrate their

1995 De Cine Submarino, Premio Especial Award | 1994 BAFTA Award for Cinematography | 1993 The New York Festivals, Bronze Award »

AWARDS | RECOGNITIONS | NOMINATIONS ::

footage, I have never heard anyone come close to Stan Waterman. That man is elegant, funny and totally entertaining. I also have to mention Peter Scoones. Now here is a cowboy. He's got to be in his mid 60s by now, still diving 300 days a year, builds all his own housings, takes Sony's $70,000 cameras and turns them into a stream of screws, circuit boards and glass on his bench, reconstructs them inside a slick little bit of metal he turned on his lathe, designs his own ports and optics, installs that and goes out and shoots the most beautiful pictures you can imagine with these contraptions that are truly one-of-a-kind. Although I did catch him once with an off-the-shelf still housing.

inexpensive video cameras that produce "broadcast" images, there are a hundred people out there making films where 10 years ago there were two. So the competition for an hour of broadcast time has skyrocketed, which, in general, I think is good. This proliferation of filmmakers, especially the younger ones, adds an edge to the programs that the older gang just does not.

Having said that, I personally think there has also been a proliferation of crap being broadcast and this is, in large part, is directly related to the budgets these new filmmakers agree to make programs for. A typical high-end natural history film, like a BBC or

2

Early in my career, a filmmaker once told me that shooting pictures is all about light but isn't it really all about money? »Sure, it's all about light and exposure if you don't want to eat, take lovely cruises through Greece, drink nice wine and live where you want. Seriously though, in this business, especially today with the explosion of extremely

National Geographic special, has a budget of around a million bucks. So here you have a new cable channel offering $100-150 thousand for an hour film and there are 50 people standing in line for that slot! At one-tenth of the budget, what do you think you get for the product? Yeah, it is about the light, but certainly the money helps.

1993 Missoula Int'l Film Festival, 2 Merit Awards | 1991 BAFTA Award for Cinematography | 1989 National EMMY Nominee »

AWARDS | RECOGNITIONS | NOMINATIONS ::

Let's talk about filmmaking gear. There's been a lot of buzz about High Definition camera systems. Are you using them? What do you think the next big breakthrough will be? In a nutshell, I am still a firm believer in the image that film delivers over anything I have seen in video. However, I now have serious conditions to that statement that I did not have five years ago. Video is making huge strides toward looking at life the way humans see it. I think this has as much to do with the myriad customizing capabilities on the new cameras as it does with the vastly improved image quality itself. My biggest complaint with video has been its poor ability to handle contrast ratios – shooting in the tropics with harsh sunlit subjects with dark shadows and heaps of bright highlights has always produced a video image that looks like crap to me – blocked up shadows and blown out skies, etc. Film has trouble with these harsh subjects as well, but does a far better job than video.

1. Filming a television commercial for Chevron Oil titled, *People Do*, deGruy used California's kelp forests with a Pace housing to illustrate the program 2. When working in the Marshall Islands, deGruy used whatever was available to house his research subjects. This Boston Whaler shark aquarium is also a great way to keep people from borrowing your boat

However, you put yourself at 150 feet in the murky Galapagos, at four in the afternoon, and a different picture emerges, pun intended. This is the world, low light, low contrast situations where I think I'd rather have a nice video camera over my trusty Arri. In the last two years I have been using High Definition video and have learned to love it in some situations. Still, on that beach in Rangiaroa, give me my Arriflex. But low contrasty situations underwater, especially at thousands of feet where I have been working with it lately, high def is the only way to go.

I swear, when I first saw Billy Lang's camera system at the hot vents, the jumbo octopus, screaming black smokers and masses of vibrant tube worms, for the first time I felt the technology had been removed from the television system. I saw little or no difference from my high def monitor to my view out the porthole. It was astonishing and I'd never felt that emotion delivered from video before. Then it grew better and better as I was able to fill the frame with fingernail-sized creatures and see them in far greater detail than they have been seen in before, not to mention from out of a little porthole.

The major drawbacks of this new technology are that it is inherently complicated and expensive to use and maintain. And in many ways it is old technology polished up. By this I mean the cameras are still plastic things with funky viewfinders, they are large, heavy and

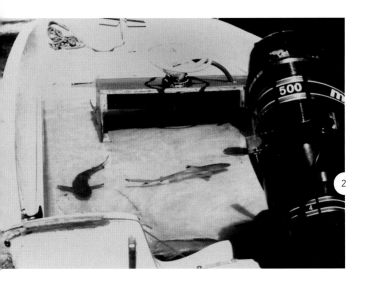

still fragile and susceptible to environmental elements. I'd like to see them beefed up physically, sealed better and feel more like their price. Then there are the recorders. A high def camcorder is about $90,000 and a good studio deck costs more than that. Why do we still have to record on such electronically and mechanically sophisticated machines, not to mention large and heavy and finicky? I anxiously wait for the "chip" recorders that have to be in the near future.

Even with the proliferation of cable and satellite channels is there consistently enough market for well-produced, high-end documentaries? In a word, no. Not in the natural history genre that I tend to dwell in anyway. I remember clearly when the cable explosion began, a lot of people began rubbing their

hands together thinking there would be heaps more work to go around. In a sense they were right, but one minor detail slipped off the radar screen. There were heaps of new outlets all right, but the pot of money stayed the same. So what happened is that the budgets began to shrink across the board because to fill all the new slots, broadcasters began to put more money into quantity rather than quality. For a while this had little effect on the people who were producing the high end "blue chip" films as there were still the same outlets for those, but the economics of those programs, which take a long time to make and therefore are expensive, began to make less and less sense to the funders. They have a hard time getting their money back, as the various outlets they sold to internationally, became cheaper and cheaper as well.

Since camera gear is obviously foremost on your list of necessities, what about the support equipment you need to wear while you dive to get you in position for your shots? What type of scuba system do you employ? Are you into rebreathers? Nitrox? Inflatable doll lift bags? We spend long stretches in the field, so inflatable dolls are a necessity, of course. And they better be good looking! As for dive gear, it varies greatly according to the shoot. About six years ago we bought three rebreathers, the Biomarine CCR500s. I think Al Giddings took delivery of the first two and I got the next three. I don't know Al's experiences, but mine was less than pleasant. I sent them back three years ago for changes and upgrades and one came back a year later and I have never seen the other two again. After literally a hundred calls and faxes I can only speculate on what happened to them. Anyway, before the manufacturer stole them, we used them very effectively on a film shot extensively in the California kelp forests. What they brought to us above all else was time underwater.

I tend to light extensively, but well away from the camera, creating strong back and highlights, but try to be subtle enough to make the lighting invisible. To accomplish this, I may use up to 10, 1200 watt HMIs and a couple larger and a few smaller ones. This scheme can be maddening when you are diving in kelp, as you might imagine, considering these are all AC lights with cables to the support boat. The rebreathers gave us four hours at 60 feet to set up all this, with no decompression required. No bubbles are

nice and the air is warm but the time is what I liked best. Anything that gives you more time, whether it is a good drysuit, nitrox or rebreathers get my vote. When you are paying for a boat, full crew and there is something great happening beneath you, an hour underwater just doesn't cut it.

Al Giddings once told me he refers to you as "Black Cloud deGruy," a thinly veiled reference to the misfortunes that have sometimes accompanied your work. In addition to having survived a shark attack, tell us about the time you had the unique experience of watching your own support vessel sink in front of your eyes in Palau. »Thanks Al, I really needed that. I seem to have lost three Arriflex SR's, three underwater housings for them, two full stills packages and then there was that pesky little boat thing. What do they say? "Shit happens?" Maybe the reputation is deserved, but I feel pretty good about some of the stuff we've pulled off, and if a little gear goes here and there, well that's better than lives! I've been diving in subs a lot recently

1. For his film, *Tempest From the Deep*, deGruy employed this 30-ft. Jimmy Jib boom to film elephant seals 2. Gearing up for dive making *The Octopus Show*, off Vancouver Island
3. Down she goes! During a shoot in Palau for the BBC's *Nature*, deGruy's 40-ft. support vessel sank taking all of the filming equipment with it

and I remember a funny feeling I got in New Zealand while about 1,000 feet down in the one-man sub, *Deep Rover*. I wondered how I'd get out of the thing if, on my way back to the surface during inclement weather, I saw our boat on its way down. Maybe it was the Palau experience that put that thought in my head.

We were shooting for a film on cephalopods called *Incredible Suckers*. That was a name I gave it as a joke about the guys who funded the project, and somehow it stuck. I had studied the chambered nautilus, captured many with traps, but never had seen them *in situ*. So we rented a ROV from Harbor Branch and flew it to Palau with a tech and pilot named Jerry Neeley. As often happens, on the very last day of filming: Viola! Nautilus! We were nailing the sequence,

1985 Missoula Int'l Wildlife Film Festival | 1985 American Film Festival, Red Ribbon | 1985 Missoula Int'l Film Festival, Merit Award ■

AWARDS I RECOGNITIONS I NOMINATIONS ::

shooting them against the vertical reef at 900 feet and I was in the control room of the 40-ft. boat we chartered screaming with delight. Then Peck Euwer, my assistant cameraman, stuck his head in the door and said, "Hey Mike, there's a lot of water on the back deck."

"Water??!" I jumped up and to my horror saw scuba tanks and diving gear sloshing around on the afterdeck. I pulled open the cover to the engine room and it was half full. The captain yelled to "Lose the ROV" and I went into the cabin and told Jerry. He was calmly filming away with the ROV and said, "Okay." So we disconnected the ROV and threw the cable overboard. Within 10 minutes the boat was resting at her new home at 1,000 feet. Dang. Never knew why.

In addition to your reputation as a cameraman and director, you're also widely sought after as a commentator and color man in underwater documentaries. In fact, in 1999's *Discovery*

Bret Gilliam

Channel live broadcast from Bikini Atoll during *Shark Week,* you actually stole the spotlight from Giddings. What's it like to have to work with the pressure of live TV with millions in the international viewing audience? »When you are live, there is an intimidation factor that I have felt in no other situation. The moment you screw up, the world sees it, so there is obviously an edge. The first time I did a live broadcast, I was the host and we were in the Red Sea broadcasting from a

ear, ..."Mike... uh.. cover for a bit while we sort this one...." Cover! Hell, I had never done anything like this in my life and suddenly everyone was looking at me, all cameras on me and all I could think of was... nothing! I yabbered on a bit and thank God Eugenie Clark was there to talk to.

You're living in Santa Barbara with an interesting collection of dive pros. How do you like this compared to your old digs in LA?》Santa Barbara is great. Bev and Connie Morgan and the DSI gang are there, Bob Kirby, and a lot of stills and filmmaker types. It really is hot spot for diving innovation and filmmaking. Brooks Institute is there, the Marine Tech Dept. at City College is fantastic, UCSB has a great diving

1. Mike editing film stock in his Santa Barbara studio, 2001
2. Bret Gilliam, Stan Waterman and deGruy at the
2005 Boston Sea Rovers. Mike was honored as *Diver of the Year*

program and now we're getting a pretty good influx of Hollywood. It is a beautiful city with fantastic support for diving. We have the Santa Barbara Channel which is brimming with cetaceans, pinnipeds, kelp forests, then there are the Channel Islands offshore where I swear, when the conditions are right, is the most beautiful diving I have ever done. I love that place. I know quite a few people working over there and am impressed with some of their programs, especially the educational elements they bring to ours and other communities.

Finally, at a whopping five-foot-seven-inches tall, tell us once and for all, does size really matter?》Nope. ■

ship. I was talking to Martha Holmes from the BBC while she was 40 feet down and wearing a bobble helmet. Ten minutes into the 30-minute broadcast, she surfaced with a helmet half full of water; there goes the show! So I get this stuttering whisper in my

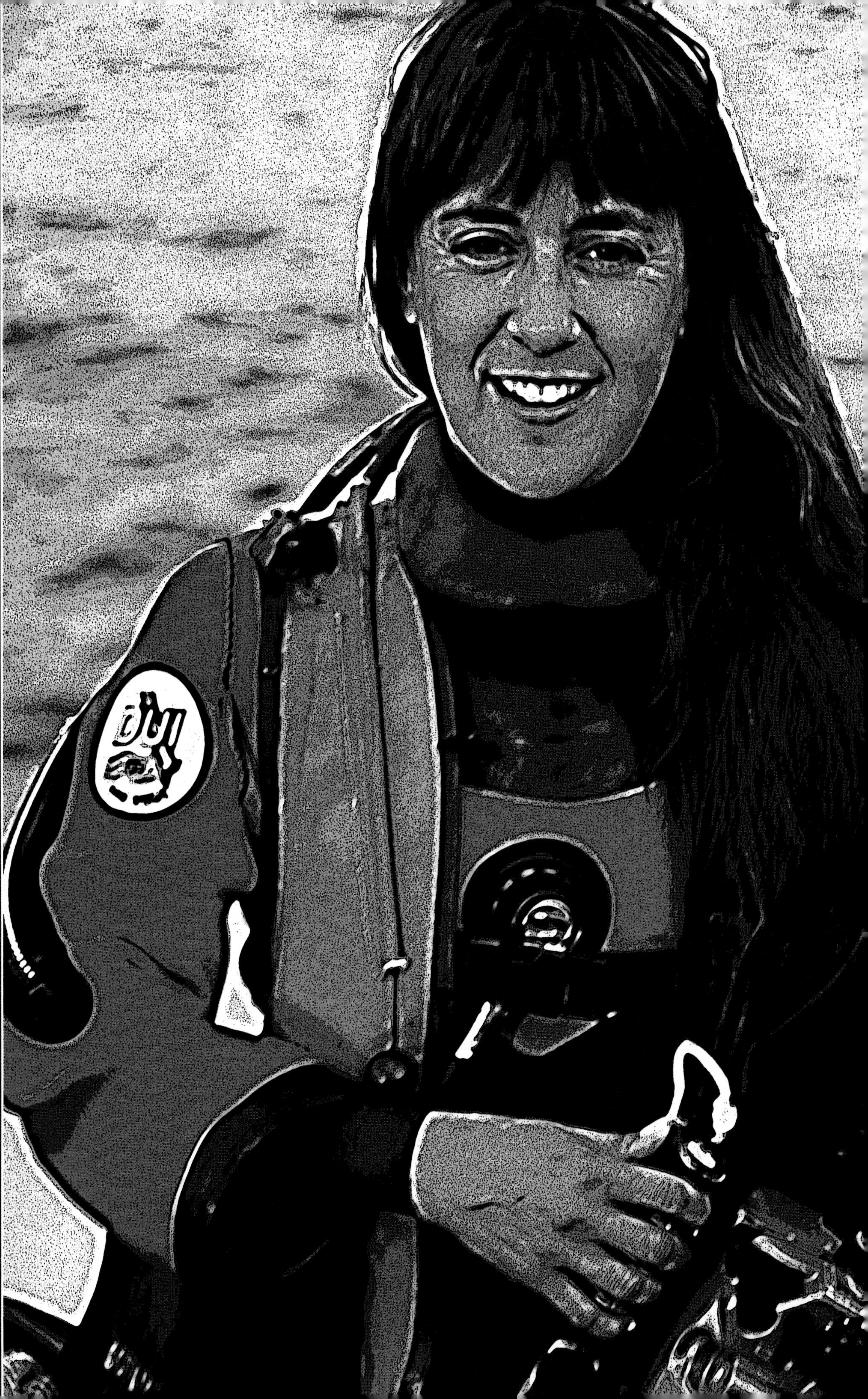

ALL PHOTOS FROM MICHELE HALL COLLECTION EXCEPT AS NOTED

Michele Hall

MEDICAL PROFESSIONAL TO MOVIE PRODUCER

BY BRET GILLIAM

GUESS WHO OUR MYSTERY GUEST IS: A DIVER WHO BECAME ONE OF THE TOP PRODUCERS OF...

documentary and IMAX films; one who made a significant mark as a professional photographer. This is a person whose business cards simply identify them as "boss" and no one doubts for a second the authority wielded. »

In short, a no-nonsense industry pro who is preposterously successful, the recipient of multiple Emmys and awards, and is still aggressively negotiating the next big project when dozens of other filmmakers can't even get their pitches past the secretary at the desk. And did I mention that all this talent and intellect is contained in a barely five-foot-something package of head-turning natural beauty? No, it's not Al Giddings.

It's Michele Hall, wife and business partner of Howard Hall. The "twin towers" of underwater filmmaking in the 21st Century have managed to reach the pinnacle of professional achievement in a decidedly niche market by the simple formula of hard work, incredible talent, and a focused commitment to achievement that should be a model for all. And they're nice folks. In today's cutthroat business

world you'd think that last attribute would probably be a liability. But for anyone who knows them, their genuine charm and warm personalities stand out. It's impossible to find anyone, from little children to grandparents, who doesn't instantly like and admire the Halls.

Although it's Howard behind the camera, it's Michele who's handling the details… coordinating the production crew, liaisoning with the studio and financial backers, contracting the deal, and cashing the checks. Imagine the infamous Weinstein brothers at Miramax… but with personality bypasses. And the Halls look a whole lot better in bathing suits.

Professional diving, in all facets, is dominated by men. While there may be plenty of instructors and resort dive guides that are women, most of those spots are relatively short-term careers and the chance to really make a lasting mark is fleeting. Indeed, the best-known women in diving probably are Sylvia Earle and Genie Clark, both distinguished scientists who use diving as the vehicle for their studies. But inside the everyday real world of the diving industry, there are but a handful of women

that have achieved notoriety and individual distinction. When deciding the persons to profile in this book though, our decision was easy. Zale Parry and Valerie Taylor from diving's first generation were obvious. And Michele Hall rounded out the tribunal of diving's first ladies. It's a special group.

Michele was a nursing professional who moved to California and got sidetracked by a handsome dive instructor. They married and she finally pushed him into the film business fulltime. She even assumed the role of principal breadwinner as her income from nursing allowed Howard the independence to get his film career going. Once established, Michele gave up nursing to assume the mantel of producer for Howard Hall Productions. It was the perfect match, both of marriage and careers. Michele even became the inspiration for one of Peter Benchley's novels. The rest, as the cliché goes, is history. ∎

How did a nice east coast girl end up over there in the southern California land of the infidels? I grew up a city girl, born to city folks. My idea of an outdoor adventure was a Sunday walk in a city park or sun bathing at a hotel swimming pool. As a child we didn't visit national parks, and I traveled only once outside the continental United States - on a short trip to a Bahamas' resort. (I believe that was to the Jack Tarr Hotel Resort, which I had the chance to see again 45 or so years later while on location for a film project. Imagine my dismay to see a holiday resort from my childhood, now little more than a pile of rubble!). My Dad's work in the retail business prompted us to move numerous times while I was growing up. By the time I graduated high school in Kansas City, I'd lived in 15 cities – mostly in the mid-west and on the east coast, but also a couple of times in South Florida (where I actually gave surfing a try during a summer vacation when I was 14!). Once out of high school I stayed in Kansas City to attend nursing school. After another year of humid summers and winter's ice storms, California sounded appealing and so I moved west.

What prompted your first interest in diving? In 1975 I was dating one of the surgery Fellows I'd met while working in the Pediatric Intensive Care Unit at University Hospital in San Diego. I'd briefly thought about taking SCUBA lessons the year before. So, when I realized that he was a sport diver, I decided to learn to dive.

But have I told you about the first opportunity I had to try SCUBA – which I flatly turned down?? It was while on my senior trip in nursing school, in the Ozarks in Missouri. We were offered the chance to try breathing off a tank in a swimming pool at the hotel. I staunchly refused to give it a go. My stubborn mind-set was that there was no way I was going to be dependant on a metal bottle filled with air strapped to my back for my life support! My old nursing school buddies sure get a kick out of teasing me about that now! I mentioned this to the audience at the opening of one of our IMAX films (*Coral Reef Adventure*) in Kansas City in 2003. A reporter included the anecdote in his review, citing that the young girl who wouldn't take an introductory pool SCUBA session was a now a diver and producer of underwater films, and was being featured on the big screen, allowing cleaner shrimp to crawl in her mouth!

Okay, right up front, is it true that you married your dive instructor? And does that make you a filthy whore? Yes. And no!

How did you enjoy California diving initially? I LOVED IT!!! I was hooked from my first open water dive, in May 1975. I was so enthralled with the experience and the environment that I don't recall being cold, even though the water temperature was probably in the 60s and I wore a rental wetsuit, which was too big. While I continued to wear a wetsuit for a few years, I eventually switched to a dry suit. Though my enthusiasm eventually gave way enough to become more sensitive to the chilly elements, my passion for the sea hasn't faded.

You were a full-time nursing professional. I understand this provided the financial stability to let Howard indulge his burgeoning career as filmmaker. How long did you continue medical practice before joining him full time in the film business? My 19-year nursing career began in 1972. Howard and I met in 1975 (yes – when he was my diving instructor!). By the way, imagine my parents' reaction upon discovering that my romantic attentions had drifted away from a doctor and future plastic surgeon, and toward a diving instructor! Following my heart, we married in 1981.

1. Michele and Howard, Sea of Cortez, 1981
2. Michele on the beach in Queensland, Australia, 1978

Howard's primary source of income when we met was teaching diving and working at Chuck Nicklin's Diving Locker. He left the dive shop in 1978 and began working as 'have-camera-will-travel' - in other words, as a cameraman for hire for others' productions. A decade later, in 1988, he began producing his own films. By the fall of 1990, as he was completing one production and beginning pre-production on another, it was apparent that he needed to either hire an assistant or I needed to switch gears and professions. We opted for the latter.

It's a very tough world out there for most diving filmmakers. Did you think back in the 1970s that this could be a career for both of you? »No, in the 1970s I didn't think that underwater photography could support us, and I couldn't envision that I would want it to be my career. It's true that occasionally during the early 1980s Howard and I fantasized about working together. But I loved the work I was doing as a pediatric nurse, and after working so hard to get to the point I was at in my career, I had no real desire to give it up.

After starting my nursing career in the operating room at a general hospital, I began to specialize in pediatrics, first with another job in a pediatric O.R., and then in a pediatric Intensive Care Unit. During the last 10 years of my nursing career, as the Coordinator of a Genetic Newborn Screening Program for the California State Department of Health Services, I was involved in cutting edge diagnosis, research and treatment of newborns with metabolic and genetic disorders. And because I loved the work so much and found it so rewarding, for many years I was reluctant to leave medicine.

Share with us some early film work projects. How long before these could start paying the bills? »Howard's first paying job as a cameraman for hire was on a shark film for *Survival Anglia* with Stan Waterman. A few years prior to that Chuck Nicklin had facilitated his being hired to go to South Australia as the "shark wrangler" with the Second Unit team for the feature film *The Deep* – a Peter Yates film made from Peter Benchley's novel. Working on *The Deep* was the beginning of Howard's introduction to filmmaking work and a turning point in his life and career. Virtually everyone whom he worked with on that project eventually became dear friends, including Peter, Stan, Jack McKenney and Al Giddings. In the 1980s he went on to work on some 18 episodes of Mutual of Omaha's *Wild Kingdom*, various episodes of the PBS series *Nature*, and many other documentaries for US, British and German television. He was so good at what he did, so well liked, and so easy to get along with that he was in high demand. The bills were being paid. The contacts he made, the things he learned about filmmaking, and his knowledge of and love for marine wildlife led to the award-winning *Seasons of the Sea*, the first film he produced, directed and wrote on his own.

What do you perceive now as the big career break for you guys? »There's a *Catch 22* in getting the financing to produce a film. No one wants to trust you with the funds required to make a film until you prove that you can manage the production. And you can't prove that you can manage a production until and unless you're given the funds to do so! So, in 1988 when David Healy, former Executive Producer at WNET *Nature*, was willing to give Howard a contract to make what turned into the television program *Seasons in the Sea*, -- well, that was a huge break and turning point. Especially when you realize that the reputation he earned from *Seasons* led to a career in making IMAX films.

Howard is an extremely talented still photographer. But you also wield a camera with coveted skill. How did you get started? »Most of the people I dived with when I was first certified were taking underwater photos. During my early months of diving I modeled for many of them, Howard included. Before long I decided to give photography a try so that I could show my non-diving friends what intrigued me about the underwater world.

What systems were you using then? »I have small hands, and when I tried a few of the housed systems that were available at the time I found they were just too big and cumbersome for me to manage. So for my first underwater camera system I used a Nikonos III with a 35mm lens and extension tubes. I was very happy with that system for quite some time.

How would you compare those early editions to what has evolved and is available now? »Eventually smaller housings were developed and as my diving skills improved I became more comfortable handling the gear. Though I still loved and continued to use my Nikonos III with the 15mm lens for wide-angle shots.

Do you still shoot stills on your motion picture projects? »As our film projects have become more complex (large format/IMAX films vs. television productions) and hence my responsibilities to the production more time consuming, I have less time for photography. But I still shoot behind-the-scenes production stills, and I continue to enjoy documenting the beauty of our seas and animal behavior when I can.

Have you transitioned from film to digital? »I – somewhat reluctantly - made the switch to digital

in August 2004. Why was I reluctant? The change required more than just a commitment of funds for new equipment. I had to make a commitment of time, not only to learn to use a new camera system and new techniques and parameters, but to learn how to deal with the images after taking them! Gone were the days of sitting in a darkened room for an evening or two after returning from a dive trip to look at slides and fill up a trashcan with the rejects!

Howard Hall

1

What system are you shooting? »I used Nikon cameras for years to shoot slide film. Prior to switching to digital for my still photography, Howard had developed a way to shoot time lapse for our high definition stock footage video library using a digital still camera. At the time Canon was considered to have superior digital cameras. So we switched, and are now so invested in cameras, lenses and housings that we've stuck with it, even though Nikon cameras have reached parity.

Howard Hall

1. On location at Catalina Island, California during filming of *Into The Deep*, 1994 2. Up close and personal with green moray, Grand Cayman, circa 1980

Give us your perspective on film versus digital. 》 I have a real love/hate relationship with digital photography. I love not being limited to taking 36 images on a dive. I love the immediate gratification that comes with looking at my images after a dive, learning from my mistakes while on location, and having the chance to go back and give it another try. But I resent the amount of time I must spend editing, processing and to catalog the images. It's so easy to fall behind when I'm on location that I now feel compelled to spend every spare moment dealing with images. And I still have trouble keeping up with it all. Gone are the days of enjoying bits of quiet time to relax with a book.

How did you and Howard make the jump to IMAX productions? 》 Howard received a call in October 1992 from Graeme Ferguson, one of the co-founders of IMAX Corporation. Graeme was in pre-production for on IMAX's first underwater 3D film. Howard's reputation as producer, director and cameraman of the award winning television program

Seasons in the Sea led to his being recommended as the director and cameraman for this exciting new project. At first we thought the phone call was a prank – a joke being played on us by one of our buddies. But when Graeme actually came to town a few weeks later for a meeting with Howard, and then asked him to fly to Toronto to consult on designing the underwater housing, we started taking the project seriously. That film, and its subsequent tremendous success, of course opened the door to other projects.

From a sheer size standpoint, putting a standard IMAX system in the water must be daunting? 》 The underwater 16mm film camera system we used in the 1980s and 1990s weighed in at 48 pounds. Mark Conlin, our AC (assistant cameraman) for our television documentaries, used to hand off that 16mm system to Howard by holding it over the edge of the boat's swim step or the side of the inflatable or skiff. In contrast, the IMAX 3D system (camera, housing and accessories) weighs 1,300 pounds. The housing measures 4 feet by 4 feet by 3 feet – big enough for me to crawl inside! Placing it in the water requires a crane or A-frame capable of handling loads of at least 2,500 pounds. Even the standard 2D IMAX system, weighing 250 pounds, requires, at minimum, a davit to hoist it.

Michele in the Coral Sea with
giant sea fan, shooting macro, 1978

258

Howard Hall

Any close calls with that thing? ≫ Safety is a major concern when dealing with this massive system, and three situations come to mind. We avoid getting into strong currents that would hamper getting the camera back to the boat, and are prepared to either hook up a tow line directly from the camera to the boat or have a skiff on stand-by to tow it back.

If the housing were to leak, the added weight as it took on water could make retrieval impossible. An early housing design included placing the camera in a neoprene bag to minimize damage should there be a leak. But sometimes attempts at too much safety can be as bad as not enough! The bag got caught in the o-ring seal, causing a slight leak. Luckily the water-sensor alarm alerted Howard of the need to return to the surface before the housing got heavy and any damage was caused. The bag-system was immediately retired.

Then… there was the night of terror. It was 2a.m., we were drifting in the open ocean in the Sea of Cortez, and we were bringing the camera system back aboard the *Solmar V* during a night of filming Humboldt squid feeding. The seas were rough. The camera was hooked to the boat's crane and was being lifted to the upper deck. The boat took a swell. About eight of us were on the upper deck as the 1300-lb. system started swinging violently out of control. I recall yelling, "DUCK!!!" as the housing swung across the deck, and then watched in awe as it swung back out and over the side and our skilled crane operator released the brake. Luckily no one on the upper deck was hurt, and no one was in the water when the housing hit the surface. The only harm done was the need to run an extra load of soiled laundry.

You've done critically praised IMAX projects in both 2D and 3D. Which do you prefer? ≫ I enjoy working in the IMAX format – whether it's 2D or 3D. Both are challenging and result in a film that's shown on the big screen. I don't really have a preference.

For motion picture work, where does the future lie: film or HD video? ≫ The future is certainly digital. Few people are shooting television documentaries in film any more, and ever more features are being shot in digital. The 70mm IMAX film image has been estimated to have a resolution of between 8 and 12K. As I write this, no digital motion picture system is capable of producing image resolution beyond 4K, but they get closer every day.

The Halls must have one of the best film stock libraries in existence. How do you manage that resource? Have you used any of the new technology to upgrade your own footage from 4x3 to 16x9 format? ≫ From the time Howard began producing his own films in 1988, we began acquiring footage for our 16mm film stock footage library. For years we marketed that footage for use in exhibits and other television productions. By 1999 we'd accumulated 145 hours of footage and decided to sell the library. After buying our Sony HDW 900 Cine Alta camera in 2000 and designing and building its underwater housing, we began capturing a new library in high definition format in July 2001. We represent our footage for licensing, and as well as having contracts with a few agents.

Over the years, you have developed a pretty tightly knit group that works on your films. Tell us about them and how those relationships came about? ≫ We've been fortunate to work with a wonderful group of guys over the years in our film productions. We tend to spend weeks at a time in the field, usually on liveaboard boats. So it's really important that everyone is easy-going and compatible. No prima donnas allowed. And they have to believe that chocolate is one of the major food groups. Some of our crewmembers have worked with us since the early 1980s, and others came on board as our films got more complicated and the requirements for more divers and technical talents grew.

You and Howard have also spent a record amount of time aboard Avi Klapfer's vessels. Tell us about those films and why you chose that operator? ≫ Our first dive trip to Cocos Island, Costa Rica was aboard the *Undersea Hunter*, and after experiencing their wonderful operation it was only natural to continue our association with them when filming there. Since that first trip, Avi, his wife Orly, their business partner Yosy, and many of the office staff have become good friends. Their expertise is superb.

We made our 2D IMAX feature *Island of the Sharks* at Cocos aboard the *Undersea Hunter*. The vessel met our needs so well that when we were in pre-production with Greg MacGillivray on *Coral Reef Adventure* we talked with Avi and Yosy about taking her to Fiji and Tahiti. By the time *CRA* was complete, I'd calculated that we'd spent more than a year aboard the *Undersea*

1. Michele, Howard, Bob Cranston and Mark Thurlow on location at Cocos for *Island of the Sharks*, 1998 2. Michele and Howard with IMAX 3D camera system in the Bahamas shooting *Deep Sea 3D*, 2005

Hunter. There was a time when Avi posted a plaque on the cabin that had become our home-away-from-home that read "The Hall's Cabin"!

Your work has taken you into some of the remotest locations possible. What's it like to stage a multi-million dollar shoot with no outside support, either for equipment repair or medical emergencies? Time is of the essence when we're on location filming. In other words, time is money. Our daily production costs while at sea making a 3D film can run $14,000 or more. And that's before we shoot even a single frame of film, and doesn't account for airfare and shipping costs to get us to location. So, we need to be prepared to fend for ourselves as much as possible in remote locations.

As was the case when making *Into the Deep*, at times just 30 miles off California's coast, we know there would be lost time and money if equipment failed and we didn't have back-ups. So, we travel with redundancy – a second camera, back-up lenses, and crewmembers that can stand-in for each other if someone gets sick. We don't have a second underwater housing - so a major flood of the housing would be a real problem.

Still, the potential of difficulties and the need to access assistance is one of the reasons we didn't go father from shore than California's Channel Islands for *Into the Deep*. In fact, we did run into some technical difficulties and called for one of IMAX's camera technicians to leave his home base in IMAX's Camera Department in Toronto and join the crew on location. He came on board for what he thought would be a day or two of repairs. As this was the first time the housing had been in the field and it was experiencing some glitches, we were reluctant to let him go home. We kept him on board for the duration of the expedition… during the month of January… when we were enjoying unusually nice weather… and his wife was home with two toddlers… enduring bitterly cold temperatures. Talk about having torn feelings about needing to be on location!!

With the experience of *Into the Deep* under our belts, we ventured father offshore for *Deep Sea 3D*, and we'll really push the envelope when we head to South Australia and the Indo-Pacific for our next IMAX 3D film.

Medical emergencies are another story. A good first aid kit and having plans in place for treating various emergencies have helped us to stay on the job. While making *Coral Reef Adventure*, when Howard realized he had a case of decompression illness, we immediately implemented our emergency plan for in-water-recompression. Four hours later once he was back on-board, the boat cruised to the closest recompression chamber (10 hours away) where he underwent four subsequent precautionary treatments. He came through all of it without any residual affects. But I'm convinced that if we hadn't been prepared with a plan for in-water recompression, that would not have been the case and the outcome would not have been so rosey. And you wonder why I have some gray hair?

Tell us about your latest release *Deep Sea 3D*. How did that come about and where were you shooting? » *Into the Deep* was an immediate success when it was released in the fall of 1994. Within the

Peter Cragh

year IMAX theater operators began asking us when we might begin another. We were eager, but, as we've often said, the most difficult part of making a film is raising the money. It took some 12 years to put together the finances. Our enthusiasm for another IMAX 3D project never waned, but in the meantime we made programs for television - including the PBS series *Secrets of the Ocean Realm*, an episode of the PBS series *Nature*, and programming for Tokyo Broadcasting Systems (TBS). And we worked on a few other IMAX films - including *Island of the Sharks* and *Coral Reef Adventure*. Renewed interest for another 3D film in late 2003 led to writing a treatment and a new fund-raising campaign.

Then in the spring of 2004, when Warner Bros. saw the success of their collaboration with IMAX Corporation on *NASCAR The IMAX Experience*, they expressed interest in partnering on another 3D film. We got the green light for *Deep Sea 3D* that June (2004). When the call came in, it seemed to me that timing couldn't be worse!

They wanted us to deliver the finished film in March 2006 (less than 2 years away then), which meant being in the field shooting that September – an unprecedented short pre-production period for us. Even if we didn't have anything else on our plate for the coming months, the challenges of getting the team together, chartering seven boats, getting film and work permits for the first expedition (in Mexico, only three months later), and gear sorted out and to location would have been monumental. But... the call actually came while we were out of the office for a few days, in Houston presenting *Coral Reef Adventure* at Sea Space's Film Festival. Howard was leaving straight away for a 2-week filming expedition to the Marshall Islands, so he wouldn't be available to participate in the early stages of planning. On top of it, we were in production on an episode for TBS and in post-production on the *Nature* episode *Shark Mountain*.

But after waiting so long for the chance to make another IMAX 3D film, we didn't want to pass up the opportunity. So, as terrible as the timing was, we pulled out all the stops. And by September 15th my ground crew was driving a truck across the California/Mexico border on the way to Santa Rosalia with 7,000 pounds of equipment. The next day the rest of us flew to Loreto and a bus was waiting to take us to Santa Rosalia where we boarded the *Solmar V*. Then Hurricane Javier bore

its way across the Baja Peninsula. We were caught up in the adventures of film production!

Your business card used to simply identify you as "boss". You are billed most often as "producer" on your projects. What does that entail? » Ah!! The famed business cards! Actually, these were a gift from Howard when I left my last nursing job. And I still use them – though I have some that don't say "Boss" that I

Tracey Medway and Michele with giant Potato Cod off Australia's Great Barrier Reef during filming of *Coral Reef Adventure*, 2001

give to people who might not understand the humor. Still, I always say that if Howard considers me the "Boss" then he's the "President."

As the producer, I'm responsible for all field production logistics and activity, and for our crew. When we make television programs and IMAX 2D films, I handle all of the arrangements and details myself. IMAX 3D projects are exponentially more complicated, and beyond the scope of what one person can handle.

I'm fortunate to have a talented Associate Producer, Production Accountant, and Production Coordinator at IMAX on my team.

Have you and Howard considered mainstream theatrical films as a next jump? The first film that Howard ever worked on, in 1976, was *The Deep* – a mainstream theatrical film. He was the Shark Wrangler. But we've never seriously considered

1. Michele and Howard with Ultralight in Vorrigo Desert, California, 2005
2. Michele in California kelp bed, circa 1979
3. Bird-woman on the Bahamas Banks, 1992

getting involved in this genre for our productions. We prefer to direct fish rather than people.

In addition to diving, you and Howard also have a passion for flying. What sparked that interest and what equipment do you use? » Howard's interest began in the early 1970s when he began flying hang gliders. When we wanted to film aerials of Cocos Island for *Island of the Sharks* in 1998, the only way to do this was to bring our own aircraft to the island. So we bought an ultralight, sent it by cargo ship from Los Angeles to Costa Rica, stowed it aboard the *Undersea Hunter*, and hired our friend (and Howard's long-time hang gliding buddy) and ultralight-certified-pilot John Dunham to pilot the craft. This worked out so well that Greg MacGillivray repeated the experience in order to capture aerial shots of French Polynesia for *CRA*. But this time the ultralight went by cargo ship from Los Angeles to Papeete in French Polynesia – talk about needing to plan ahead! It almost didn't arrive in time clear customs before the boat headed out with our crew to film! Luckily it made it, and Howard and John

captured some spectacular images flying over Moorea. So, another of his early passions has played a role in his career path!

What will your next film project be? » After the success of *Deep Sea 3D*, Warner Bros. expressed to IMAX that they were interested in funding another film. In early January (2007) we were given the green light to proceed. We've been affectionately calling it *Deep Sequel*. But the working title is actually *Coral Kingdoms 3D*. IMAX's marketing department will test a variety of titles and will most certainly come up with something different.

We've all been around long enough to realize that world's oceans, reefs, and marine life are suffering from severe natural and manmade impacts. Where have you seen the largest impact? » I see changes everywhere I go: diving, hiking, even driving down

Howard Hall

2

Howard Hall

the street. I believe that the strain of our ever-growing population is the core of the problem. More people want to dive the reefs, more people want to explore the outdoors, more people need to be fed, more people are driving the streets. More people, more people, more people... Every time a new traffic light is installed, it's a sign of increased population. Talking about population is not a popular issue. Still, all our other efforts will do little good if we don't get our heads straight about it.

As far as the oceans are concerned, it's probably worse than many have been led to believe. Fish populations are disappearing very quickly. Many of the things we filmed for *Secrets of the Ocean Realm* can't be filmed with any predictability now, just 12 years later. Coral reefs have been hammered in the last decade and the disintegration is accelerating. Indeed, we have seen enormous changes in the ocean.

On a personal note, it's difficult to plan a production when filming is a year or so away and the environment is changing so rapidly. When we were in pre-production for *Coral Reef Adventure*, we scouted Fiji and decided to film coral reef life there. By the time we got to Fiji with the IMAX gear a year later, almost all of the hard corals were dead.

What do think we need to do as a society to arrest this pattern? »Frankly, I'm not smart enough to know. But I do think it will take sacrifices, and I *don't* think that

enough individuals are willing to make the necessary sacrifices on their own. And as much as I hate Big Government wielding a heavy hand, perhaps we'd see some benefit with regulations that forced changes in things like fishing practices, anti-pollution efforts, farming practices, and fuel production and usage.

At this stage, can the ocean environment recover? »Well, if you mean to recover to what we knew 20 or 30 years ago, and during my lifetime, probably not. On the other hand, the ocean will survive, one way or another. It just won't be the ocean we've known.

Does our own U.S. population realize the very real threat that our children may never be able to see the underwater world as we did only three decades ago? »Many people just don't pay attention – they're so busy working to take care of their families' needs that it's difficult to find the energy to think about the environmental issues at hand. Many just don't care.

You've spent years visiting Cocos and diving with its sharks. What's your view on the impact there? »I've been diving at Cocos Island since 1991. There's no doubt that the fishing boats that patrol the waters between beyond Cocos' no-fishing zones have an impact. It's sickening to me to see fishing boats lined up in port at Puntarenas, Costa Rica, their decks covered with sharks, and to watch the fishermen slice off the fins. The Costa Rican government makes an effort to patrol the waters, but they don't have sufficient resources to be terribly effective. I've heard this may be changing though.

I met Hans and Lotte Hass in 1998. I'd read Hans' account of their diving and filming at Cocos in the early 1950s and told Lotte that we were in the midst of making an IMAX film there. With enthusiasm she said, "Oh, then you've seen the Tiger sharks!" I told her, "No, there were no Tiger sharks at Cocos." As she repeated the statement a few times, I thought that possibly she didn't understand what I was saying

Of course!»I went on my first underwater filming expedition with Howard in August 1980. He was producing his first film about the Hammerhead sharks that school in great number over a seamount in the Sea of Cortez, Baja California. Stan Waterman and Peter Benchley were along as hosts for the show. During this expedition I had an experience that changed my life forever.

Returning from a dive on the seamount, I saw Marty Snyderman, one of the show's cameramen, perched on the back of a Pacific manta ray. It was an enormous animal flying over the seamount with wings that spanned more than 18 feet. I couldn't believe my eyes. Marty was trying to cut loose a fishing net that was wrapped around the manta's mandible. As the manta

Bret Gilliam

1

1. Stan Waterman and Michele, 2006 2. Cleaner shrimp doing dental work for Michele, Fiji 2001, *Coral Reef Adventure* 3. Saturday Film Festival Program presenters: Stan Waterman, Bret Gilliam, Wes Skiles, Philippe Cousteau, Jr., Michele and Howard Hall, Boston Sea Rovers, 2006

due to a language barrier. I soon realized, however, that her English is quite good, and that having seen so many Tiger sharks when she was there, she just couldn't understand that I hadn't seen any myself ... that the Tiger sharks could possibly be gone. A lot has happened to the shark population at Cocos Island, and around the world, in the last 50 years.

What has been your most satisfying experience in diving?»My most satisfying diving experience was probably taking the line off the manta while diving on El Bajo in the Sea of Cortez in August 1980. Do you want to hear the whole story?

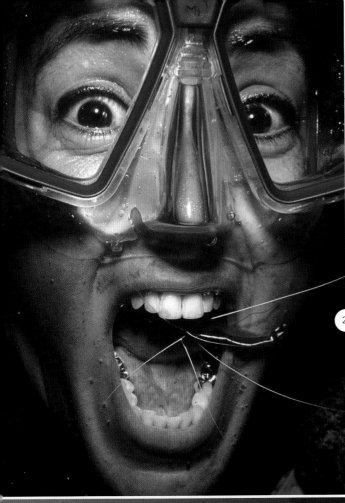

flew by, Marty signaled to me that he was almost out of air and needed to surface. Just then the manta turned in my direction and stalled beneath me. To me, there was no mistaking its intent for me to pick up where Marty had left off. I settled down on the ray's back and succeeded in removing the last tangle of fishing net embedded in its mandible. Whether this behemoth thought me Androcles, or what, I'll never know. But it took me for the ride of my life.

It's difficult to explain what I felt during those moments. Awe, trust, exhilaration, tranquility... these words are barely adequate. With no effort on my part, the ray and I flew around the seamount. My sense of time was confused, as it seemed we were moving in slow motion. Or maybe I just wanted it that way; I didn't want the experience to end. At one point we glided past Howard, Stan and Peter as they returned from a dive. Howard later told me that upon seeing me perched on the ray's back, he'd halted dead in the water, marveling in disbelief as the ray swept me away, helplessly thinking he might never see me again!

When I saw my exhaled bubbles splayed behind me instead of rising directly to the surface I realized how fast we were moving. I was on a magic carpet of my very own, and I was on the ride of my life – I couldn't believe the ride and the view. I felt the need to equalize the pressure in my ears and knew we'd begun to descend. I checked my air pressure and depth gauges and my senses returned. I knew I had to ascend and head for the boat. If the ray had taken me too far away, I could have an impossible swim back. In the late afternoon light, the boat crew might have difficulty finding me. Just as I began to worry, I realized we were at the boat's anchor line. The ray had taken me full circle and was depositing me where we'd started!

For several days following my removal of the net from the giant manta, "Grand Dad" (as he became known to our crew) returned to the seamount. Before the trip's end, he'd taken us all for a "ride" and Howard had added a manta ray segment to the film's storyline. "Grand Dad" had also inspired a new story for Peter, which became his novel, *The Girl of the Sea of Cortez*.

Now, I know that "riding" manta rays is politically incorrect these days. So mind you – this was in 1980, and I was approached by an animal that clearly wanted some attention. Had he not, there's no way that I could have swam fast enough to catch up.

You've got one choice for a fully funded diving expedition. Where would you want to go today? » Well, that would probably be to make an IMAX film in either the Indo-Pacific or the Antarctic. And since we're headed to the Indo-Pacific next, I'd say that dreams can come true!

Neil McDaniel

Who had the most profound influence on you and Howard as filmmakers? » There really isn't one person. In the beginning for Howard, Chuck Nicklin certainly was influential – with Howard working for him at the Diving Locker in San Diego, and then when Chuck recommended him to work on *The Deep*. Then there are Stan Waterman, Jack McKenney, Valerie and Ron Taylor… all have had tremendously positive influences on us.

Who do you see as the next generation of diving leaders in film, still photo, writing? » There's no doubt in my mind that Eric Cheng and Peter Kragh are the new guys on the block. They're both so talented that between them they may end up fulfilling all of those roles before they're through!

If we had a Diving Mt. Rushmore, what four persons should be carved into that cliff face? » Hans Hass, Jacques Cousteau, Stan Waterman, Sylvia Earle

What are your personal recommendations as "don't miss" film releases on diving subjects? » *Blue Water, White Death*, the BBC's *Blue Planet*, and *20,000 Leagues Under the Sea*. The BBC has a recently released a new series called *Planet Earth*,

and I expect once I've seen all the episodes I'll be adding it to this list.

What books? » Hans Hass' *Diving to Adventure* and *We Come From the Sea*; Robert Kurson's *Shadow Divers*; *A Fish Caught in Time* by Samantha Weinberg (not really a book about diving, but a great read about the discovery of the thought-to-be extinct coelacanth); and Stan Waterman's *Sea Salt*.

You have already collaborated on books as companion pieces for your IMAX films. Are you and Howard considering a book about your careers and lives in diving as a stand-alone issue? » We also had a companion book to our PBS series *Secrets of the Ocean Realm*. But no, we don't

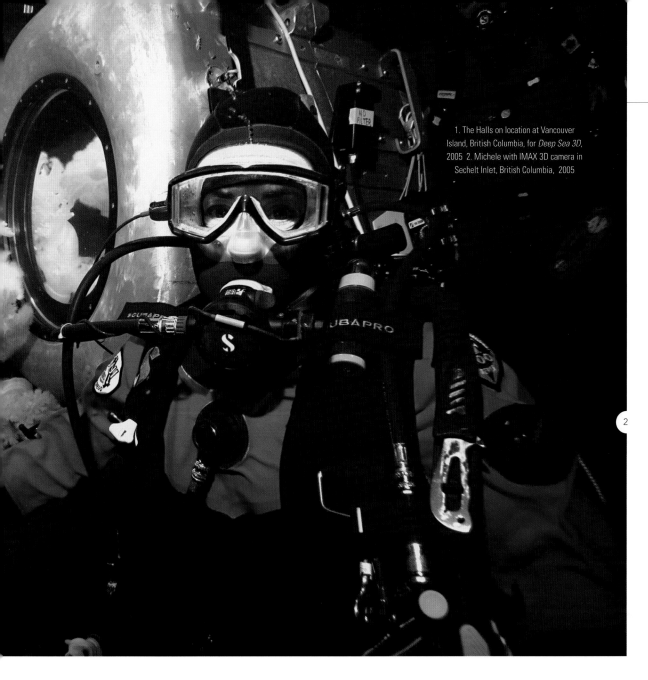

1. The Halls on location at Vancouver Island, British Columbia, for *Deep Sea 3D*, 2005 2. Michele with IMAX 3D camera in Sechelt Inlet, British Columbia, 2005

2

have plans for a book about our lives and careers in diving. Then again, you never know! As we get older and more decrepit, too tired to dive and hike, we may need something to do to pass the time.

Stan Waterman is still diving at 84. I'll bet that you're still going strong past that? »I hope so. He is most certainly a tremendous inspiration. I had the privilege to be on his 80th birthday diving adventure in Tahiti. On one particular dive, as we were exiting one of the passes at the end of a current dive, we didn't stay quite close enough to the wall face, and the current began to sweep us away. We were able to grab the rocks to pull ourselves back around the corner, but the cameras we each held in one hand prevented us from a hand-over-hand maneuver. Kicking and pulling my way along the

bottom, I was having quite a tough time of it. I feared for Stan as I looked back and saw him struggling as well. The next thing I knew he was passing me by, making his way toward the calm water! 28 years my senior, and he could out swim me – in a strong current no less!

We're all about the same age. Okay, you can tell me… is Howard's hair ever going to go gray or fall out? »I love the gray that is replacing the dark brown hair – all over his head!

How about a last word summing up your single most fulfilling or exciting experience in diving? »A single word? "Howard!" If not for learning to dive, I might not have met Howard. And he is the most important thing in my life. ∎

Paul
Humann

LIVEABOARD PIONEER, INNOVATIVE PUBLISHER AND FISH DETECTIVE

BY BRET GILLIAM

PAUL HUMANN IS THE LIVING EMBODIMENT OF THAT OLD JOKE:

"What do you call a thousand lawyers at the bottom of the ocean? – "An awfully good start! He had a perfectly normal and successful career going as an attorney in Kansas and chucked it all to – are you ready for this? – start the first liveaboard dive vessel in the Caribbean. I can almost hear his poor mother wailing. »

But the impetuous career switch led to even more success with the *Cayman Diver* and a long list of publishing projects that followed. His talent as an underwater photographer and his zeal for educating divers about the marine life species they encountered led to a nice anthology of articles and images printed in a slew of diving magazines from the 1970s forward. Eventually, he was serendipitously introduced to Ned Deloach through a period of co-editing *Ocean Realm* magazine. The two men had a vision for a specialized publishing company that would take the subject of fish and coral ID books to an entirely new level. They hocked their homes to finance the first book for New World Publications and now the company enjoys status as the premier publishers of the best marine guidebooks available worldwide. Recently, they expanded their scope to include Stan Waterman's superb book of autobiographical essays called *Sea Salt*. And this book of interviews further widens the net they have cast over diving subjects.

Paul is not just a supremely talented photographer and writer. He's also an unrestrained truth-teller when it comes to the diving industry's foibles and often absurdly ill-advised track record of blunders championed by a segment of archconservatives. He was a vocal champion of divers' rights and one of the first to advocate codifying the practice of solo diving for qualified divers. He also endorsed dive computers, nitrox, applications of technical diving, and enlightened practices for modern liveaboards. At times, his opinions have brought him criticism, condemnation, and harsher reviews from the lunatic conservative fringe. But his vision helped bring all these, initially controversial practices, to the forefront and they are now mainstream.

I like to think of him as a prophet and first-class raconteur who never flinched from speaking his mind and sticking to his principles in spite of the fact that his outspoken wisdom would almost surely have gotten him burned as a witch in an earlier era.

Although our paths had crossed many times over the years, the first chance I had to really spend time with Paul was in 1992 when we were both co-hosting a group of divers aboard a liveaboard in the Bahamas. I taught an advanced diver program and he delivered nightly lectures on marine life. We didn't get one day into the trip before there was an incident.

I surfaced from a dive to find the ship's divemaster/instructor in a total melt-down… pacing the deck, muttering

oaths, threatening reprisals. We were off to a good start. I could only imagine that some diver had committed the cardinal sin of not wearing a snorkel or, god forbid, putting his mask on his forehead while waiting to get out of the water. These were definitely capital offenses in the early 1990s mentality that mandated all divers be treated as manifest idiots… incapable of having a coherent thought about their own diving practices.

I gingerly approached the young man in an attempt to discern the source of his angst. He was fresh out of "instructor college" and had a whopping 50-60 dives under his weight belt. But, by god, the kid was a diving professional; it said so right on his fancy diploma framed on the bulkhead. And he knew what divers should be doing and would not tolerate deviations from the ironclad rules posted right next to his diploma.

Circling him from a safe distance, I managed to get him to gasp out the transgression that had him so upset. "Mr. Gilliam, I can't put up with this. Do you know that Mr. Humann is diving without a buddy? He's all alone down there. By himself. Solo!"

I was shocked and said so… without a trace of revealing sardonic perspective. What would the kid have me do to such a deviant diver?

"Well, we just can't have it. It's against all safety rules. What happens if he runs out of air? Or has a problem? He'll die!"

I gently explained that the likelihood of Mr. Humann experiencing a problem of any sort that he couldn't stumble through somehow on his own was pretty unlikely. I mentioned that Mr. Humann had been

Humann with underwater
camera rig, Caribbean, 1984

doing this, professionally, for a while. Like about three decades. With over 8000 dives, most of them solo. And he'd be just fine.

"Oh, no! We can't be responsible for such bad practices. I'll have to suspend him from diving," our hero trumpeted.

Meanwhile, the amused other divers and I could look over the rail and observe Paul blissfully absorbed with his camera at a coral head about 40 feet down. He was unaware of the furor he had created. I knew I had to act quickly to head off a scene when he finally surfaced and was confronted by diving's equivalent of Dudley DoRight in a wet suit. (In all truth, I feared for the kid's life. Paul was just as likely to snap his neck as listen to a reaming from a neophyte.)

I suggested a cunning plan. "Mr. Humann is an old curmudgeon who's sort of set in his ways. How about if you be his buddy and don't tell him? That way, you can look after him."

The kid thought it over and decided that this was an intervention designed by Solomon himself and agreed. Meanwhile, the rest of the divers fled the dive deck, stifling snickers. They knew full well what was to come, I think.

The next dive began as Paul gathered his camera gear and slipped over the side to take up residence once again at a favorite coral head. The flash of his strobe confirmed that he was happily immersed once again in his photography and largely oblivious to any outside distractions. Our well-meaning instructor lunged into his own gear and splashed in after him, taking up position about 15 feet behind him. Now all was right again in the diving universe. Wrong!

After about an hour, the kid realized he was running critically low on air. I watched with growing amusement as he desperately

tried to stretch his air with breath-holding. A few more frantic glances at his pressure gauge and he was off in a wild scramble of fin strokes and billowing exhaust bubbles. He arrived on the surface about a hundred feet from the boat and then began the "swim of shame" back to the ladder: he had failed to arrive back aboard with at least 750 psi remaining!

He'd also failed to protect the ancient geezer still happily firing away at his fishy subjects. He'd abandoned his buddy. We all gleefully pointed that out. About twenty times. It was a professional failing of biblical proportions. Paul took another 40 minutes or so and calmly swam back to change film. His protector had retreated to the sun deck still mulling over his abdication of duty (and how Mr. Humann could make a tank last so long). In the end, we convinced him to leave Paul alone. Literally. But we suggested that the instructor might want to work on his own self-sufficiency skills and maybe stick closer to the vessel himself where he could be more valuable helping divers out of the water and handling cameras. It was a grim moment in the young instructor's career. Divers weren't supposed to behave like this. He'd bring this to the attention of his instructor agency when he got back to port.

Paul somehow managed to survive a week of unsupervised solo diving and got a bunch of great photographic images along the way. We never told him about the furor over his diving practices… until now. About seven years later, my company Scuba Diving International (SDI) came out with the first industry training agency program to certify divers in solo diving practices. Of course, the recipient of the first card (#00001) was Paul Humann. ∎

You were born in Nebraska and raised in Kansas, not exactly a breeding ground for divers. What sparked your initial interest? »I was always into water sports... on the swimming team in high school and college, lifeguard, Water Safety Instructor Trainer for the Red Cross, coached the swimming team at Washburn University as a part time job while in law school. Between that and *Sea Hunt* it was a natural extension of my water sports interests.

Okay, I can understand that the Midwest has swimming pools, but what existed for scuba training back then? »Nothing, other than driving to Missouri to dive in abandoned pit mines with surprisingly clear water or in murky lakes.

What were the Keys like then? »Live coral and marine life was abundant. You could still see large groupers, even a Jewfish. Whoops, in the new world of political correctness, I meant Goliath grouper. That first dive was off Sombrero Light, and I remember the wonderful lush gardens of Elkhorn Coral. The area around Sombrero is today nothing more than a pile of rocks. However, before I get the Key's operators mad at me, let me interject that in my opinion Key's diving is still some of the best around. Although much of the coral cover is gone, marine life and particularly non-game fish are abundant. I don't know anyplace in the western tropical Atlantic where you can go see schools of grunts even remotely as large as those in the Keys – I mean grunts as far at the eye can see! I still love diving in the Keys.

Where was your first dive? »In 1961 a college friend, who was a diver, and I took a summer vacation to the Keys. My first dive was solo, because being poor college students we only had enough money to rent one regulator. Outfitted with only a mask, fins, snorkel, tank with K-valve and regulator, my friend gave me "comprehensive" dive instructions: "Breathe normal, don't hold your breath, and when it starts to suck hard – come up!" That first solo dive, which lasted 45 minutes before "sucking hard," changed my life. I was so enamored by the marine life and beauty of the reef that diving immediately became an all-consuming passion.

Is that what sparked your interest in underwater photography? Tell us about your first camera system. What kind of results did you get? »I tried to explain to my friends back in Wichita what being underwater was like, but they just didn't get it. So the following year I rented old Brownie Hawkeye 120 film camera, molded into a plastic housing by pioneer underwater cinematographer Jordan Kline, so I could take some pictures to show them. Seeing the results, my friends said I should be in *National Geographic*! Although they flattered my vanity, I knew that was a big stretch. Nonetheless, I was encouraged. Another poor diving college chum and I bought a Calypso/Nikonos

1. Age 8 in Kansas 2. Washburn University swim team, coach Paul at right in dark tee shirt, 1962 3. Three of "Martini's Outlaws" at the First Midwest Underwater Film Festival: Jack McKenney, Dewey Bergman and Humann, 1968

together. We started diving the lakes and quarries of Missouri hoping for some decent visibility. The following summer in the Keys again, with the addition of flash bulbs, I got some surprisingly good results, which fueled my passion even more.

So like many enthusiasts of the era, there was a significant gap between first trying scuba and actually getting certified. When did you get "legal"? And that led to interests in becoming an instructor? Managing not to kill myself diving for five years, I was certified by a YMCA pool course in 1966. I went on in 1968 to become an instructor for the Underwater Society of America's Mid-West Dive Council and, as such, automatically became one of PADI's early instructors, certification #2222.

Share some memories of first getting published? About 10 of my friends and I formed a diving club named Martini's Outlaws. The name came from our

enjoyment of deep diving – remember the old diving "Martini's Law" that was taught to divers in those days? It stated: "Every 50 feet you go down is like drinking one martini on an empty stomach." It was supposedly a way to approximate the effects of nitrogen narcosis. We broke that law a lot. And the fact we also liked martinis didn't hurt either. Anyway, back to your question, Martini's Outlaws put on the first mid-west underwater film festival ever in 1969 and one of the guest speakers was Jack McKenney, then editor of *Skin Diver* and one of the diving world's foremost photographers (Paul Tzimoulis was the publisher). I showed him some of my pictures and he offered to start publishing me in the magazine. And that's how it all started.

Who were your diving heroes then? Well, of course, Jack McKenney. Also Dewey Bergman and Al Giddings, who filmed some of the first shark adventures in Tahiti, and Stan Waterman.

Your path to professional diving was a bit more circuitous than some others. You had an established law career as an attorney in Kansas, how did you decide to take "the road less traveled by"? One winter day while watching the snowfall and wishing I was diving, I simply said to

277

1. The Caribbean's first liveaboard vessel, *Cayman Diver*, 1972
2. Paul with early Nikonos system, 1968

myself "What the hell are you doing with your life?" I knew I eventually wanted to make my living taking underwater pictures, but was realistic enough to know I couldn't make a living at it yet. So the question was how to dive, take pictures full time and still make a living. I thought about buying a dive shop or maybe a resort, but thought I'd just get stuck in the shop or resort. A couple of years earlier several friends and I had chartered a fishing vessel in Cozumel, had it outfitted with tanks and a portable compressor, and sailed to then remote Chinchorro Banks to dive for a week. Although this was a very Spartan adventure, I thought "Now this is the way to go diving – jump in the water anytime you want and be remote enough you didn't have to put up with swarms of other divers." And, that's the way the idea of a liveaboard dive boat was born for me.

What were the origins of the *Cayman Diver*? »I was in San Francisco, on law business, and had lunch with Dewey Bergman, founder of See & Sea Travel and his new associate, Carl Roessler. I told them of my idea and Dewey tells me that Bob Soto in Cayman had the perfect boat for sale. And in fact, Bob bought it with the same idea in mind and actually used the boat for a few trips to Little Cayman, but decided it did not fit into his day-boat operation and wanted to sell it. Next thing I knew I was on an airplane to Cayman and gave Bob a small deposit check. I came home and begged friends, family and, in particular, a wealthy oilman/client for money. I guess my persuasive powers as an attorney were good – because I sold them on the idea – and borrowed with no collateral!

How would you describe its accommodations compared to today's liveaboards? »Spartan! We had a bunkroom for six, three tiny doubles, two heads and one COLD WATER shower. My motto was "Give them the best diving in the Caribbean, the best food, and the best service, and they will ignore the accommodations." Apparently I was right because it worked for eight years.

What other liveaboards were operating anywhere then? »Well, I started the *Cayman Diver* in 1972. The first liveaboard was in Australia, can't remember the name, it has started a couple of years earlier. To my knowledge that was it. Your own *Virgin Diver* started service with See & Sea a few years later. Those were the only two in the entire Caribbean.

How did you market this new concept? »Through See & Sea Travel Service, then owned by Dewey with Carl intending to ultimately buy him out.

278

Any problems back then in navigating the bewildering labyrinth of rules in Grand Cayman for non-resident foreign businessmen who wanted to set up shop? » Well, things were not quite as strict in those days. Bob Soto, who was politically well connected, along with an attorney that he recommended, "greased the wheels." It was done quickly and easily.

How was the diving in the Caymans back in the early 1970s? » Wonderful and basically virgin, especially the north and south coasts of Grand Cayman and Little Cayman. We could sail over to Bloody Bay on the north coast of Little Cayman and dive for a week and never see another person or boat! We had the place to ourselves. Fish abounded, including Nassau groupers, and the visibility was awesome. I'll swear on days it exceeded 200 feet! I haven't seen that in years anywhere.

At some point you saw a serious developing interest in marine life identification for fish and corals from your guests. What books existed then to aid in the ID process? » Jack Randall had a book out on Caribbean reef fishes. This had some living pictures, some dead. In 1976 Gilbert Voss came out with a marine invertebrates book with drawings. Two years later, Pat Colin came out with a bit more comprehensive invertebrate book with pictures, but that was about it.

To meet the cravings of your guests, you began a series of slide shows presented in the evenings aboard the *Cayman Diver*. When did you think that this could be a niche business model itself? » Yes, early on I started giving marine life identification programs in the evenings for guests and they were a big hit. I learned that divers thirst for knowledge about what they are seeing. Then about 1977, I realized that just taking beautiful underwater pictures and selling to magazines wasn't going to catch it. Although the idea for guidebooks was not fully developed, I still thought it would be important to have a comprehensive stock library of marine species. I made a vow to photograph, in a pleasing way, EVERY fish and EVERY marine invertebrate that existed in the Cayman Islands. I came close to achieving that goal before leaving Cayman in 1980. That library of images became invaluable later as the guidebooks idea evolved.

What was your first book? » A small, but large format, pictorial about the Cayman's underwater vistas. That was in 1979. But poor profits reinforced my thought that selling pretty pictures and coffee table type books was not the way to make a living. The real start was with *Reef Creatures*, put out by *Ocean Realm* magazine in 1982. It wasn't really a guidebook in the sense of the books we are doing today. It was written to teach divers what kind of animal they were observing, not so much which specific one. For example, to teach them the difference between an anemone, zoanthid, corallimorpharian or cerianthid tube dwelling anemone.

Others followed? » My first comprehensive identification book was *Corals*, also put out by *Ocean Realm* in 1983.

Did magazine work also step up? » I was working closely with the Ziff publication *Sport Diver* and then with *Ocean Realm* when it started.

I understand that you even hosted *Jaws* author Peter Benchley for a television special. » Yes, it was an ABC hour-long sports special, *The Spirit of Adventure* series. I was Peter's personal guide to see the marine life of the Galapagos Islands and especially the sharks. I had been escorting diving groups to Galapagos for years, and by the time of the special in 1988 had spent cumulatively nearly a years worth of time in the

islands. Howard Hall and Stan Waterman were the cinema photographers. The show was quite a hit as I bumped into re-runs for years.

You also got involved in editing *Ocean Realm* magazine. How did that come about? Richard Stewart, the founder, sold the magazine in the mid-1980s. I was interviewed by the new owner, who by twist of fate, hired both Ned DeLoach and me as co-editors. Ned's claim to fame at the time was his *Florida Divers Guide* and his close association with the cave diving community. Ned and I had become acquainted several years before through a mutual friend and immediately struck up a strong friendship.

You met Ned DeLoach then. Is that what fostered the basis of the *New World Publications* business? Indeed, it was our working together at *Ocean Realm* that made us realize we worked well together and we formulated the idea of a series of guidebooks at that time.

Starting a publishing company from scratch in a decidedly niche market like marine life ID books had to be a challenge. What were your first titles and how did you break into the market? We

needed over $100,000 (in 1978 dollars) to put out the first book so we tried to find a partner. First we approached a printer and then a color separator, but both turned out to be less than desirable partners. We were lucky neither worked out. We didn't want to go to a book publisher because both of us had had bad experiences with other publishers in the past. Besides, we wanted to run the whole show, so we decided to bite the bullet and took a big gamble. We both second-mortgaged our homes to the hilt and lived off of credit cards, hoping to pay everything back within three to five years. Ned was already successfully marketing his *Florida Divers Guide* directly to dive stores, so they easily agreed to start selling our first *Reef Fish Identification* book as well. We are a great example of the American Dream come true, because the book was an instant hit and sold like hot cakes. We paid off our second mortgages in only six months! We have run in the black ever since.

How many titles are in the New World library now? Ten books that we authored and we are working on two more. We also market a number of additional books by other publishers and are starting to publish books by other authors like you and Stan Waterman.

Since your books are about the only comprehensive ones out there, how do you get your identifications? It started back when I was living in Cayman. On a night dive I discovered a fish with glowing light organs under its eyes. Shortly before then I happened to have dinner with Al Giddings and he told me about filming Flashlight fish in the Red Sea. So I thought this was the same thing. One of my passengers told Dr. Bill Smith-Vaniz, a noted ichthyologist, about the sighting. Next thing I knew he was on the phone. It seems the species in the Caribbean was named *Kryptophron alfredii*, and was known only from a couple of dead specimens collected at over 600 feet way back in the early 1920s. My sighting created quite a stir in the world of ichthyology because they were thought not only to be rare, but also to inhabit only deep depths. Shortly thereafter we were chartered for two weeks by the Philadelphia Academy of Sciences, Scripps Institute of Oceanography, and the California Academy of

Sciences to find and collect this little bugger. And, indeed we found and captured the first living specimen at 220 ft. on a night dive. Remember Martini's Outlaws? No, I don't dive that deep anymore and no, I don't think anyone should unless they are on mixed gas – I survived by dumb luck. Ultimately, we found the species as shallow as 40 feet late on moonless nights.

named it in my honor, *Coenocyathus humanni.*

Another result of this work is that many of my pictures are the first ever published of living specimens and, in turn, establish visual identification criteria for many marine animals. This allows scientists to take marine life surveys without the need of collecting specimens –a non-impact plus for the marine world.

REEF FISH
Identification
FLORIDA CARIBBEAN BAHAMAS

PAUL HUMANN
NED DELOACH

(Above) ABC *American Sportsman* film crew: Howard Hall, Peter Benchley, Stan Waterman and Humann, 1988

Finding that fish and getting to know the ichthyologists on the subsequent cruise opened the doors of the scientific community to me. Marine taxonomic scientists around the world and I have developed a good rapport. I freely provide them with pictures of living species *in situ* for their scientific use and they provide me with identifications. Not uncommonly, however, they are unable to make an ID without a specimen. In those situations I go back out, photograph the specimen, and then collect it. Many specimens from this work now reside in the Smithsonian's Natural History Museum's collection. One cryptic species turned out to be a coral unknown to science. Dr. Stephen Cairns with the Smithsonian

You've also collected a few awards along the way? ⟩⟩ In the beginning we sold our books only to dive stores, but realized getting into bookstores was essential to our long-term health as publishers. We quickly found out that bookstores buy almost exclusively from two wholesalers, Ingram and Baker & Taylor. Stores don't want to deal with small one or two product publishers like us. Problem was neither did the wholesalers. We talked to them numerous times and got nowhere. They almost arrogantly would not give us the time of day and "pooh-poohed" potential sales.

Then we heard about a competition run by the American Book Sellers Association in which newly published books can be entered into a number of categories. The winners are published in their trade magazine, which goes to every bookstore in the United States. As a prize for winning you get a free full-page color advertisement in the magazine. We entered the

1. Franklin Publishing Award, 1994 2. Being inducted into Scuba Diving Hall of Fame, Grand Cayman, 2007

second edition of *Reef Fish Identification* and won *The Benjamin Franklin Award* for Best Reference Book published in 1994. All of a sudden we were receiving panicked phone calls from the wholesalers wondering why they were not selling our books as they were getting inundated with orders. Duh! Ingram quickly became by far our largest customer and love us to this day. Then Amazon picked us up, we now receive an award every year as the publisher selling more marine life subject books than anyone else in the world. Not bad for a couple of scuba bums, huh?

What about personal awards?»In May of 2006, I received the *United States Coral Reef Task Force* award for the advancement of public awareness and education concerning marine life environmental issues. Then in November of 2006, the DEMA *Reaching Out Award* for my contributions to the advancement of the sport of scuba diving. And in January of 2007, in Grand Cayman, I was inducted into the *International Scuba Diving Hall of Fame*.

Tell us about the process of creating the Reef Environmental Education Foundation?»In researching for our first fish ID book, we realized that the scientific community knew very little about the abundance of most reef fishes at a given location, and to a degree, their geographical range was unknown as well. We thought, "There's no excuse for that! With so many divers in the water every day, there ought to be a way to put their bottom time to work." We thought of the successful Audubon bird-counting program and concluded divers could do the same thing for fish.

We were very fortunate that both NOAA personnel and the Nature Conservancy bought into the idea early on. With their help and guidance we were able to design a method of taking the surveys that would be fun and interesting for recreational divers and at the same time result in data that would be meaningful and useful to the scientific community.

How far reaching are these collective surveys?» To date, volunteer recreational divers have made over 100,000 surveys of fish species populations throughout the waters of North and Central America, plus Galapagos and Hawaii. It is the largest marine life database in the world. The results of these surveys have been used by marine life scientists and management personnel ranging from NOAA's National Marine Sanctuary program, to Florida's Fisheries Management personnel, to the Cayman Islands Dept. of Environment.

For example, when Florida's fishing commission was asked to take Goliath grouper off the endangered list, they went to the REEF database and armed with that information refused the request. REEF is conducting research on the effect of an artificial reef on surrounding marine populations for the State of Florida. The National Marine Sanctuary program uses REEF to assess the effectiveness of "no-take" marine reserves. And the National Park Service is using REEF to inventory fish species in park waters. The Cayman Department of Environment worked with REEF to study Nassau grouper mass-spawning behavior and the effects of fishing them.

It's wonderful to think that thousands of recreational scuba divers are providing this useful scientific information, and at the same time are having one heck of a good time. Like underwater photography, it is an activity that keeps divers active in diving for years.

In spite of your pioneering efforts in liveaboards and their operation that paved the way for all that followed, you've had your fair share of frustration over the way some of the industry began to evolve. Let's start with solo diving. You've long been an advocate for qualified divers to be left alone in pursuit of photography or other interests. This led to criticism and outright condemnation from the ultra-conservatives. What's your take on all this looking back?》It was and remains stupid. I still consider the buddy system to be more of a danger to divers than a safety measure. I'll try and make this short and to the point. Dive instructors and dive masters dive solo all the time as part of their job. How can they do this safely? Obviously, because the industry thinks their training qualifies them. But to take it a step further, if dive instructors and masters can learn to dive safely without a buddy, why can't other divers take a course and learn to dive solo safely as well?

Buddy diving sounds good on paper, but in reality it often creates a dangerous situation. To be a truly good buddy, you must be aware of your partner's situation at all times. Far too often, if not regularly, a buddy's attention is distracted by the marine life being viewed and the buddy is at least momentarily forgotten. When one is relying on the buddy system for assistance in case of a sudden emergency, this is a formula for disaster! Proponents of the buddy system are simply not facing the reality of what actually happens underwater. I know as an underwater photographer, you cannot concentrate on your picture and keep track of your buddy at the same time. It is impossible. And, as a result, I think every underwater photographer, and more importantly his/her buddy, should be forced to take a solo diving course! No solo diving card, no photography.

Two final side notes on this subject. I do believe in the buddy system for beginning divers, up to say 50 dives. However, their buddies ought to be experienced divers, not another beginner. And, I've been accused of being an anti-social diver, wanting to be by myself. Nothing could be further from the truth. I love having a diving "companion" to share the adventure. I just don't want the responsibility of being charged with his or her safety.

In 1999 you were honored by SDI as the first recipient of a "solo diver" certification when they launched their program. Did you think you'd finally see the day when the practice was accepted?》No, I didn't. I thought the curmudgeons and attorneys would probably see that it never happened. But, I still have forlorn hope.

It seems that change of any kind is met with the harshest dismissal from within a certain segment of the industry. Consider the campaign against liveaboards offering more than two dives a day. What did you think of

that?》Obviously stupid! As I recall that was the Australian Medical Association's idea. When the Tourist Board woke up and realized no one would come to Australia to dive anymore that went out the window fast!

What other industry blunders would you like to share some perspective on? (nitrox, technical diving, dive computers, excessive restriction for depth limits, etc.)》All of the above were, indeed, stupid and irrational blunders. But I don't feel inclined to go further. The ultimate acceptances of these ideas speak for themselves.

It's interesting that these practices all became mainstream within a relatively short time. Is diving a better place now?》In general, yes.

What else chaps you in the category of silly diver rules?》One issue that does bother me today is the "don't touch issue." Let me say from the onset, I do not advocate touching coral, but some of what is currently being taught and advocated is false and a detriment to the dive industry. For example, a single or even a few touches to coral causes absolutely no harm. And certainly one touch does not kill hundreds of polyps and make the colony die as I know numerous instructors have taught their students. Actually coral is tough stuff and quite resilient to damage. Surprising to most people, the primary way new colonies of more fragile branching corals start is from a broken piece. However,

at least from an ascetic point of view, contact hard enough to break the coral should definitely be avoided. In an attempt to hold diver contact to a minimum the pendulum has swung to the neo-conservative side. For simplicity, divers are being taught "don't touch anything; stay at least three to ten feet away from everything!" Even the sand or algae beds. And, blatant falsehoods are being taught to support those rules.

The problem with this approach is that divers do not really get to see a lot. They can't observe many of the smaller animals or study interesting behaviors. For example, how can you observe the interesting interaction between a shrimp goby and its companion blind shrimp hovering three plus feet above the sand? Or watch the interactions between an eel and cleaner shrimp hovering

1. Paul with Jean Michele Cousteau, 1982 2. Humann receiving SDI's first solo diver certification from Bret Gilliam, DEMA, 1999 3. This issue of *Ocean Realm* was the first with Humann and Ned Deloch as editors 4. *Reef Creatures* was Humann's first marine life ID book 5. With DEMA Reaching Out Award, 2006

1

Should the diving industry look to innovation as a growth tool instead of its historical conservatism? In most cases, probably so. I believe one of the biggest reasons growth of diving as a sport is stagnant, at best, is because the dive industry historically and continues today to ignore the single most positive thing it could do to grow. And perhaps more importantly reduce the notorious dropout rate… said by some to be a disastrous 95 percent within three years of learning to dive!

Why do people want to dive in the first place? Asked that question, the vast majority will say, "to see the marine life." What does the dive industry do to nurture this natural interest? Absolutely nothing! How many times have you been on a dive boat where there above the reef? The answer is: you can't! And, you'll never see most of the wonderful cryptic animals.

By hovering three feet or more above things, you're missing a majority of the greatest wildlife show on earth! The result is that many new divers quickly get bored with diving and drop out. We have a huge dropout problem in this industry and our approach to "don't touch" isn't helping. We need to train people how to touch or rest on the bottom without doing damage and observe responsibly. Regrettably, the powers-that-be seem to think that would be too difficult to do or that the average recreational diver is too dumb to understand and learn what might be harmful and what is not. This is too bad, because in the long run it is divers that are most passionate about preserving the reefs. We need more environmentally concerned divers not less.

is a young couple making their 3rd or 4th dive. They come up from the dive all excited about this wonderful fish they have seen and want to know what it is. They describe it to the dive master – far too often the answer is, "Uumm, I don't know." The couple's excitement is tempered. If this happens many more times the couple will become another dropout statistic.

The beginning dive course should include some information about the marine life they are going to encounter and how to enjoy what they are seeing. And the 2nd course should be about marine life, not rescue diver or some other nonsensical specialty that

does nothing toward keeping a person interested and involved in the sport. Specialty courses have captured the "merit badge" concept rather than teaching divers how to enjoy the wonders of marine life. I was telling a high-ranking person in one of the training agencies about this. He said, "You may be right Paul, could you develop a fish identification course for us?" "Sure, I'll start with the Caribbean." He replied, "Oh no! It has got to be international – something we can teach everywhere. That's the way all our courses are designed."

I fumed quietly and attempted to explain what should have been obvious: "But, you can't do that; fish and even their families in Australia, West Coast and Caribbean are all different. A single course for all is impossible." Then, underscoring his ignorance of marine life he responded; "Oh I'll bet I can, I'll work on it." Needless to say he could not, so the whole idea of developing some courses about marine life was dropped.

The dive training agencies would be the logical organizations to develop and market such courses.

However, in general, they have developed nothing meaningful. Consequently, Ned, his video photographer wife Anna, and I have given up. We are currently in the process of developing our own DVD about marine life for beginning divers that hopefully will make their first dives a more meaningful and enjoyable experience. With luck this will be the first of many to come. REEF is also developing the first of several dive store supervised home study fish, identification courses on DVD.

Finally, you have the benefit of 45 years perspective diving in the Caribbean. There have been some devastating changes to the marine environment over that four-decade span. One recent study released their results and noted that nearly 80 percent of the coral in most parts of the region are dead or dying. Is there any hope for the Caribbean? »I think the 80 percent in most parts is wrong – a few parts would be more accurate at this time. Nonetheless, there is no question that hard corals are in decline throughout the region and I don't see any reason this will not continue. It is only a matter of how fast. I think most hard corals will be gone in a matter of 10-30 years as a result of global warming. The full impact of this is not clearly understood at this point, but it is certainly a cause for serious concern.

"Photo-Shopped" right out of the images. Do you think there is any hope at all? »I see two rays of hope. Perhaps the American public will be smart enough in 2008 to elect people that understand the seriousness of the problem and will do something about it, including changing the American peoples' mindset about how we live. Do you drive a SUV? I

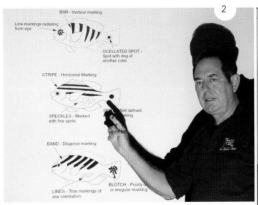

1. Paul and publishing partner Ned Deloach 2. Fish ID lecutre, 2004
3. Sylvia Earle, Eugenie Clark, Humann and Deborah Danner, 2005

The Caribbean is not the only region to be severely impacted. Palau and Fiji have been particularly hit by influences that affected stony and soft corals. This phenomenon can be timed coincidentally with the 1997-98 *El Niño*. Are even these remote areas to be gradually eroded simply due to natural impacts? »Unquestionably global warming is the primary culprit. Anyone who questions the reality of global warming has their head in the sand. Stony corals around the world will be impacted, and again, I think most corals will be gone within the next 10-30 years. We are lucky to have seen them; our children will not be so lucky. It's interesting that you included soft corals, my impression visiting Fiji two years after the most serious bleaching event, was that the soft corals were more plentiful and vibrant than ever, and abounded in areas of dead stony coral.

My impression was based on direct observation of soft corals following the *El Niño* in both areas. In some cases, the soft corals just simply disappeared. I compared it to photos I had taken in earlier years. It was like they had been

don't! And, perhaps evolution will play a role. Darwin was right; I've seen underwater some examples of what is probably "survival of the fittest" in action. After the severe bleaching event in Fiji, I swam over a huge area of dead tabletop corals, but to my surprise for every 15 or so dead ones there was a living thriving colony. Were these genetically superior colonies that were able to withstand the warm water temperatures? Will they spawn to produce less vulnerable colonies? Let's hope so.

In closing, where is the best diving in the world today and why? »Oh, that's an unanswerable question. Every dive destination has its unique charm and I love them all. However, as a final note, I would like to say that I hope my books and photographs inspire people. Divers are fundamentally explorers. We want to go where few people have gone… to discover places that most people only dream of, or only read about from their armchairs. If my life's work has contributed anything to the dive community, I hope it is to inspire people to explore, discover, enjoy, and, ultimately, to preserve marine life. ∎

ALL PHOTOS FROM JOHN CHATTERTON COLLECTION EXCEPT AS NOTED

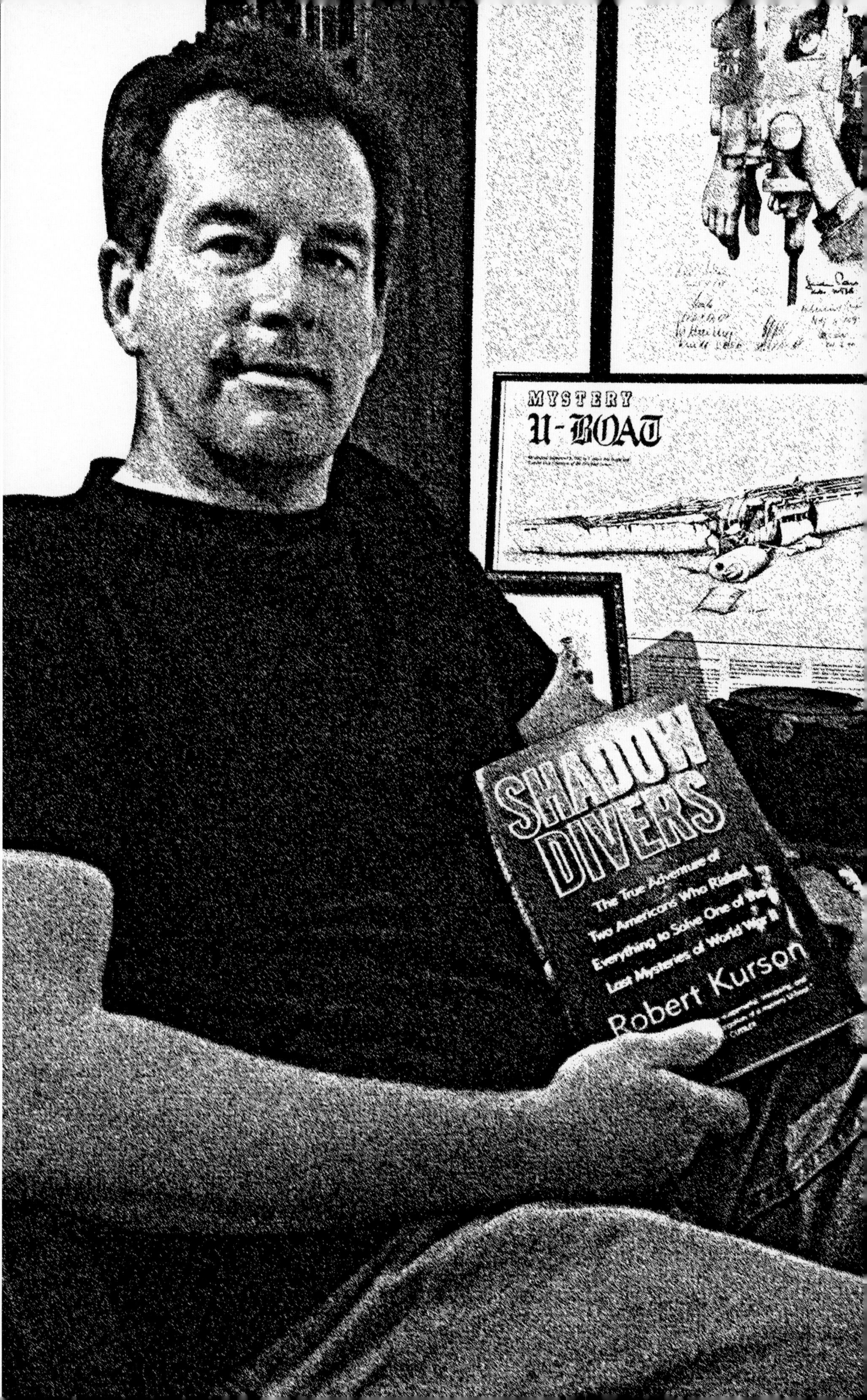
MYSTERY
U-BOAT
SHADOW DIVERS
The True Adventure of
Two Americans Who Risked
Everything to Solve One of the
Last Mysteries of World War II
Robert Kurson

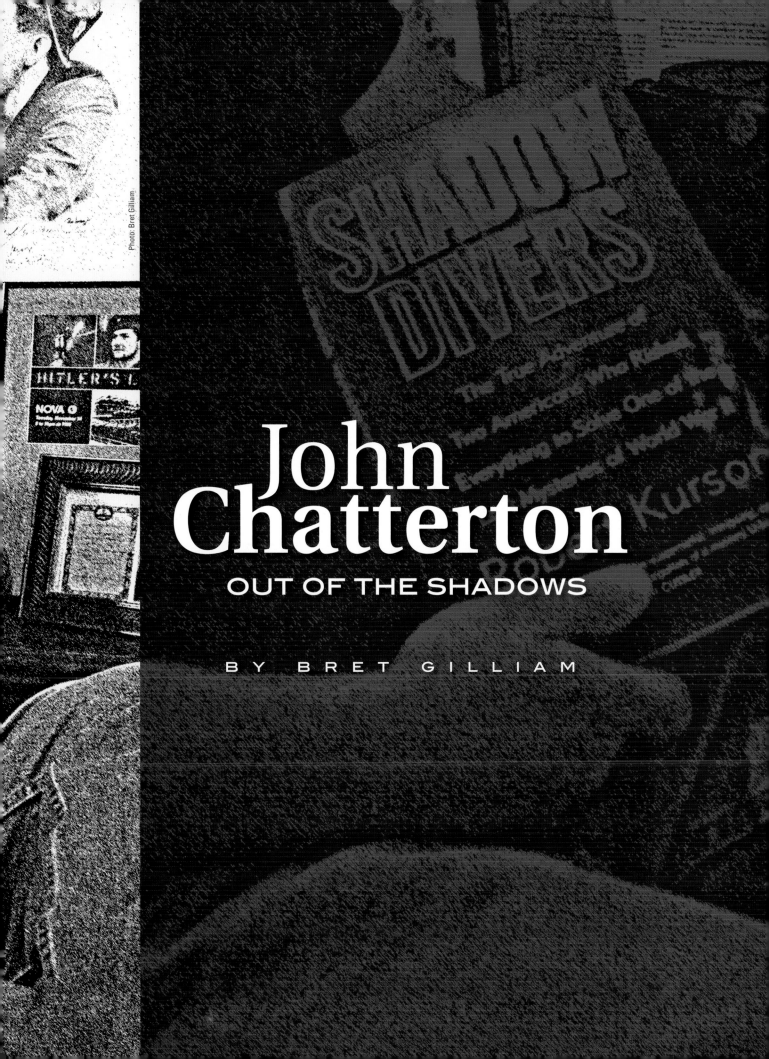

John Chatterton

OUT OF THE SHADOWS

BY BRET GILLIAM

IN MANY WAYS, JOHN CHATTERTON HAS LIVED A CHARMED LIFE.

He saw combat in Vietnam as a battlfield medic and heroically risked his own life to render aid to his fellow soldiers. In spite of repeated exposure to artillery, mortar and rifle fire he emerged unscathed after a year "in country." »

He then put in nearly 20 years as a commercial diver and later came within minutes of being trapped under the World Trade Center towers on September 11, 2001. He lost his car, clothes and wallet when the attacks occurred just as he was gearing up to dive beneath the area on a diving job. He escaped on foot in his wet suit. His cell phone was found in the debris by a fireman who used it to help coordinate rescue efforts. Meanwhile, Chatterton was picked up by a rescue boat that took him to New Jersey desperately hoping to get word to his wife that he had survived.

His passion for shipwrecks and their exploration diverted him from his full time vocation as a commercial diver in the late 1980s. Without fanfare, John established himself as one of the real purists in the north Atlantic wreck diving community as he took part in expeditions to the *Andrea Doria* and scores of other wreck sites in the region. But it was a chance trip to scout a rumored wreck located 60 miles off the Jersey coast in 1991 that forever altered his life.

Chatterton was the first diver to ever lay eyes on an unidentified German U-boat from WWII that had lain undisturbed and undiscovered for nearly 50 years entombed on the silty bottom at 230 feet. This began a six-year commitment to determine the wreck's history and identity. Famously known simply as the "*U-Who*" since all naval archives had no record of any submarine, from any navy, being where it was… Chatterton and dive partner Richie Kohler set out to prove the U-boat's provenance and honor her war dead still contained in her dark hulk. The quest tested their mettle in many ways as rival wreck diving groups attacked with vicious (and undeserved) criticism and attempted to run interference. Meanwhile the wreck itself proved an unforgiving and claustrophobic environment that seemed to defy all attempts to conquer… and ultimately claimed the lives of three fellow divers.

Although a lot of Chatterton's pio-neering wreck dives had been chronicled in various books and magazine articles within the diving industry, ironically it was a non-diving, unpublished author from Harvard named Rob Kurson who finally got his story straight in the runaway best seller *Shadow Divers* released to both critical and commercial success in 2004. Kurson's gripping account of Chatterton and Kohler's exploits in pursuit of the *U-869* attracted a mainstream audience that was fascinated by the story of two men's lives that became intertwined in a naval detective thriller that read with the pace of Clive Cussler novel. But the non-fiction tale of deep wreck exploration, tragedy, sacrifice, and final fulfillment captured the imagination of nearly a million readers and set the stage for a major Hollywood movie to be adapted from the book. Production is scheduled to begin in 2007 with a major studio behind the project, an award winning director, and speculation about which A-list actors will be cast to play Chatterton and Kohler.

With the first proceeds of his royalty stream, Chatterton uprooted himself from New Jersey and planted new roots in Maine. I caught up with my new neighbor and old friend who now lived just across Casco Bay from my own island home. ∎

We're sitting in your waterfront home in Harpswell, Maine, which cracks me up because it's the first interview that hasn't required me to get on a plane and travel. I discovered Maine ahead of you, what brought you up this way? I thought you were a Jersey boy?» My wife Carla and I were living at the Jersey shore, but we were living on the

for years. Chris Newbert moved just across the border in New Hampshire from Colorado, and Mauricio Handler, who's a wonderfully talented photographer from the British Virgin Islands, relocated to Brunswick, right up the road here just this last year. So it's actually become an interesting enclave of divers that have come here and set up shop.» Maine's way of life is something that certain people embrace. Maybe that's the appeal to divers. Divers are so much interested in going their own way, being rugged individualists and that sort of thing, they are less inclined to follow.

1. John at home in Harpswell, Maine 2. On a commercial dive, 1991
3. On dive work barge with World Trade Center in background, 2001

Bret Gilliam

impoverished land side, not the Atlantic side of the street. We decided that we wanted to live by the water, and we wanted to kind of get away from traffic, from rush hour, that sort of thing.

So you moved to Maine to get away from all the urban stuff that drives everyone insane, but had you ever been here before?» We had friends here in business, the Lone-Wolf documentary film group in South Portland. We visited and we fell in love with the place like you did. We had to move.

Maine has become almost an outpost of a lot of diving professionals. You moved here, I came back in 1991, Stan Waterman has been living here since his dad bought a place in Sargentville around the turn of the century. Bill Curtsinger, one of *National Geographic's* long time underwater photographers, has been here

Yeah, the lemmings aren't falling off the cliff here very often, that's for sure. Let's go back a bit. You grew up in Long Island, where did diving come in?» As a kid, I lived at the beach. I was always surfing, snorkeling, diving, spear fishing, that kind of thing. I think I made my first scuba dive with some neighbors. I was ten years old, they made an aluminum tank with no weight, and I just kind of floated around on the surface. I quite literally remember looking down into the water and seeing the light rays penetrating down into the water and thinking "What's down there?" Diving was a sport for me that became a vocation. I guess I got sucked in.

After high school you volunteered for the army as a medic, saw combat duty in Vietnam, and got honorably discharged after four years. What next?» I went to Florida got a job at the local hospital down there working as an arterial blood pulmonary

function technician. But I felt like I wanted to do a little bit more, I wasn't sure exactly what that was, and I moved up to New Jersey. And now I'm a guy with a background in construction, commercial fishing, and respiratory therapy, and I came to the conclusion - almost through an epiphany - that the best course of action for me was to become a commercial diver.

Where did you go to pick up this training? »I went to trade school in Camden, New Jersey, The Divers Academy of the Eastern Seaboard. It's still there. Most of the graduates from commercial diving schools end up going out to the oil patch where most of the work for commercial divers is. But I was going to be much happier working in the underwater construction business as opposed to taking off for the gulf. I was working on dams, bridges, bulkheads, pipeline jobs, all kinds of things, and I remember the first time I put a helmet on and got in the water. My breakout dive was working for a power plant for Con-Edison in NYC on the 11-7 shift.

Trying not to get sucked into the intake? »Yeah. Well, they are memorable dives, and that was certainly one of them. You've got all this phosphorescence in the water, and you have the hum and vibration of machinery all through the plant. It's not an easy job but I kept at it for over 20 years. You start out low, but very quickly I became a diver, and then I was a foreman, a supervisor, and that sort of thing. I enjoyed the work. I liked putting a hard hat on and getting down in the water and figuring out how to get the job done. There were very few downsides.

You began to have some interest in sport diving, motivated by an interest in wrecks. »Well, commercial work slowed down. And I thought what I'd like to do is get in the water and do some fun dives. Some light and easy scuba dives, just to keep my head in it; to keep on top of it as a professional diver. That was in 1982.

You and I came from similar backgrounds... ex-military, ex-commercial, so we were exposed to technologies, methodologies that really were completely beyond the average diver. Did you find a conflict there when all of a sudden you've got guys working in deep, dark, cold water,

and thinking there might be a better way of doing this? I was interested in wreck diving. The thing that really appealed to me was the complexity of it. When I put a hard hat on, I knew I had my job, and the guys in support have theirs. Everyone's working together. It doesn't matter if it's your tender, or the guy on the crane, or the guy working communications, or the other divers, everybody had a job. Not on scuba. On a shipwreck, you're not part of the machine, you are the machine. Everything comes down to your responsibility. It's physically challenging, just to be capable of carrying the equipment. You're in cold water, you're in deep water, and you need to maintain a physical fitness level that will carry you through when things go bad.

At the same time, there's the intellectual aspect. It's not just about understanding diving. A lot of that was what I brought in from commercial diving, studying dive physiology and technology, making your own dive tables, and all that kind of thing. You also want to understand shipwrecks and what it is that you're looking at. You're talking about maritime history in its entirety. So you've got something that is physically demanding, intellectually challenging, and you have to add to psychological stress. You find yourself in intimidating situations. You need a certain degree of mental toughness. You really need to develop the determination to bring all this together. When I looked at wreck diving, I was totally enamored with the complexity of the activity.

What wrecks were you regularly visiting? For me, it centered in two places. The *Andrea Doria* and the Mud Hole in New York, a place that really only got about 200 feet deep. But you are talking about extremely difficult dives. You were in visibility that may be as little as one foot. You're trying to work off a bottom that is extremely silty, confusing just because of the orientation of the wrecks itself, and you're talking about fishing nets all over the place. There was even one wreck where the mast was still intact and there was a fishing net draped across it. A friend of mine got disoriented in 190 feet of water, decides to blow back to the surface. Blows right into the fishing net, and stops. It was an environment about as intimidating as it can get. We used to say we would go to the *Andrea Doria* to tune up for diving in the Mud Hole. Conversely, when you were picking up a lot of dives in the Mud Hole, by the time you got to the *Andrea Doria*, you were ready to go.

1. Carla Chatterton and John at their home in Maine
2. Bill Nagle in with a major score from the second-class area of the *Andrea Doria*, 1991

The *Doria* wasn't so much the depth, wasn't so much the current, wasn't so much the cold water or limited visibility – all those were factors, but thing about the *Andrea Doria* was the vastness of the interior. The *Andrea Doria* was perfectly willing to give you far more rope than you needed to hang yourself.

In the same era, I had contacts for a long time with guys who were doing really pioneering stuff in cave and deep diving. They were always looking for any innovative way to try to give them the edge to come back. In the late 1980s, when I was exposed to wreck divers in the north Atlantic, it struck me that there was little interest in crossing over the technology that these other divers were using and trying to apply some of

that to wreck diving. How did you look at this whole situation? As a commercial diver, you were used to having certain disciplines. How did you feel about guys who were blindly penetrating these wrecks with no comeback protocols? Philosophically, at the time, there was a world of difference between wreck divers and cave divers. I don't mean to say there was an antagonist relationship between the two, but cave diving techniques and technology were being developed for the caves. Wreck diving was a different environment. Now, I'm a certified

that came from the *Andrea Doria* because that was a very well documented wreck. There were extensive, detailed deck plans, and the wreck wasn't very old so you could really identify where you were. But the most important thing was to proceed slowly. That system worked very well for me and most of the divers. But where the system broke down was when divers who came and observed what we were already doing perceived progressive penetration as something akin to "go inside, swim around, but remember the way out!" That is where divers really got themselves in trouble.

cave diver, and I understand what running lines is all about, but in shipwrecks, the problem with a guideline is sharp edges. It is not a line-friendly environment.

That brings us to the discussion of the practice known as "progressive penetration" which entailed studying blueprints and architecture of these wrecks to try to give you the edge of being able to recognize your whereabouts inside the wreck and find your way back out. Unfortunately, this produced a very mixed safety record. All of

There were many fatalities associated with those divers on the *Andrea Doria* – going inside, getting lost, and not being able to find your way back out again.

Eventually we were using lines, but not like they used them in caves. We were running vertical lines on the interior of the wreck, usually very short spaces, maybe 60 or 75 feet of line, something high visibility to denote a particular location of something above. Divers were using strobe lights inside, regular lights to hand carry, bringing other divers to leave them staggered along a particularly deep penetration. By the early

1990s, there was a lot more to technique, especially relating to progressive penetration.

I remember speaking about technical diving at one of the dive shows in 1991, when I happened to suggest that the wreck diving community – which was getting bolder and moving deeper – might want to consider stopping by the main exhibits and checking out the reels that the cave divers use. I suggested that these reels might provide the safety edge when you're inside a wreck that's on its side and suffering some breakdown from age, and all of a sudden silts up and you can't see, maybe that would bring you back out. And I remember that a particularly vocal guy in the back basically shouted me down and told me to mind my own business and not tell the wreck divers how to do things. I found it interesting when I came back to speak the next year and someone came up to me and said, "Remember that guy that was giving you so much crap about the penetration reels?" And I said, "Yeah. I apologize, maybe I was out of line." The guy says, "Well, maybe you weren't, because he got lost inside the *Andrea Doria* and died." When did you start to think that maybe we could take some of the technology from caving and commercial diving or even military stuff, and how can we best apply it to make it safe?» I was grabbing it even in the late 1980s. But what I wasn't willing to do was take something that I was doing, and hold it up to the world and say, "I have the answers. This is the way to dive these deep shipwrecks." I fully understood how dangerous these wrecks were and how far out on the limb I was going. I also had a pretty good handle on my abilities. Just as you discovered in your pioneering deep diving work, I did not feel that what I was doing was suitable for everyone. And therefore, the last thing I wanted to do was encourage someone to do something. At this time, there's no technical diving training, there's no TDI, there's no structure out there to certify, to instruct, to educate anybody. The last thing I wanted to do was to offer tidbits of potentially lethal information. I spent more than half my time by myself and I would experiment with things that I felt would give me insight that would be something that I would learn from. But I also understood that the public could misunderstand what I was talking about. So I did not feel that I was in a position to become an educator.

There were too many guys out there that see something to be gained by being the new messiah and at the same time there's another guy on the next boat with a completely different take on how to do things. And a lot of motivation was centered on bringing stuff up from the wrecks. I don't know whether it's financial,

1. *Andrea Doria* dive, 1992 2. Gearing up for *Doria* dive

or just ego, or what. I've brought up some valuable things from shipwrecks, but I don't think I've ever brought up anything illegal. I don't think I've violated laws. I know there are guys who have done the wrong thing for the wrong reasons, for no apparent gain. A lot of crap has come with the "treasure" label, and some of that stuff I don't get. I don't understand. One man's trash is another man's treasure, I guess.

Sheck Exley, the infamous cave explorer who was tragically lost in 1994, once commented to me that some of these North Atlantic wreck divers were risking their lives for stuff that if it was laying by the side of the road as you drove down the highway, you wouldn't stop your car to pick it up. On the other hand, he admitted that a lot of people couldn't understand his drive to explore the back end of deep cave systems. But the

296

primary difference was fueled by the approach to technology and technique that seemed to be lacking with the wreck divers.》Well, in many ways he was right. The artifact was the trophy. It wasn't so much the thing itself, it's what it represented. What happened on the *Andrea Doria* was there were people who felt that they needed that recognition. That's what got these guys into trouble. There wasn't a lot of long-term perspective and a lot of corners were cut. There should have been more emphasis on experience, technique, equipment methodology. Not all shipwreck divers are mature enough to approach the wreck in that way. They weren't really about the art, weren't really about the diving, weren't really about the wreck, it was about the trophy. They had to have the recognition.

2

If you take a bit of historical perspective and look at the earlier wreck expeditions, you'll see Bob Hollis, Peter Gimbel, Jack McKenney, and these guys that were going out on the *Doria* in 1973. They were such clinicians to a certain degree, they approached it with all the tools they could muster at the time, and then took it one step further by actually going into saturation. Now, all of a sudden in 1991, divers emerged as aggressive in some of their attacks on the *Doria*, but they're just so unbelievably less informed that it shook people up a bit.》When you're starting out that way, I don't think good things are going to happen. At the same time, there were other people jumping in the water who were interested in the art of wreck diving. They were coming back with some sort of insight into the wreck, into diving, into themselves. But they went humbly, as someone who is going to learn as opposed to someone who's gonna go there, grab some loot, and pound their chest about how great a diver they are.

On the speaking circuit in the early 1990s, someone introduced me to Gary Gentile. At the time, Gentile was self-publishing a bunch of books: *Wreck Diver's Guide* and others in a similar theme. As I read through a lot of this stuff it seemed to me that this guy was very well experienced. But I'll never forget one day he called me up and asked me a question about managing oxygen exposure. I presumed that I was talking to someone who was fairly switched on to the subject, so I launched off on a twenty-minute dissertation on oxygen toxicity. At the end of what I thought to be a very basic explanation of the topic, there was silence for about ten seconds, then he replied, "I have to tell you something, Bret, I don't have a clue what you're talking about." I said, "Where did I lose you?" He said, "About a minute and a half into it." At the time, I think Gary was claiming more dives on the *Andrea Doria* than anyone else, yet he didn't have a clue about what was going on with oxygen management. He was unable to even work the essential physics equations, yet he was surviving.》Gary is one of the best natural wreck divers I've ever seen. Intuitively understanding wrecks, being able to get on a wreck, figure out where you are, go to the place that you want to go, and then find your way back out. He has an exceptional gift in understanding wrecks. At the same time, he really doesn't have the technical/intellectual side to his personality. But for some guys, their diving is not about that.

In fact, Gentile published one book shortly after people started being introduced to mixed gas, where his knowledge was so fundamentally flawed that he thought all gasses had a "2" subscript. Since oxygen is O2 and nitrogen is N2, he published a book and listed helium as HE2. I look back now, with 17 years of hindsight from when I first met you, why didn't you step up to the plate and say, "I come from this other technical commercial background, what are you guys talking about here?" »Gary's primary goal was not education. His goal was promoting himself as an author; promoting his business. He still does that. He still writes books, he doesn't have a publisher, he doesn't have an editor, and he publishes his own books. He does it in a vacuum. I'm not saying there's anything wrong with that, but I never assumed he was the spokesperson for me. In the early days, I was not convinced that what we now know as "technical diving" was suitable for the mainstream.

Point well taken, because what we learned was that the more we opened the door to this closet, the more some people stepped through before they perhaps should have. It was a basic lesson in Darwinism because there were a lot of people that got killed or injured, or had unbelievably narrow escapes, that probably never belonged inside that closet door. I think a lot of people became horribly conflicted about whether we were doing the right thing by trying to disseminate the information that, for a long time, had been sealed up and only communicated in private letters. Now, all of a sudden, there was this thing called the Internet, which was beginning to get off the ground, and it was an ideal place for the deliverance of information. Why did the wreck diving community go in a different path than the cave diving community? »The wreck diving community had much more in the way of rugged individualists. The cave diving community had the ability to somewhat control the caves, to control access to the caves: who gets in, who doesn't. If you come in and you behave badly, then we're not going to let you in again. Anybody with a 50hp outboard and a rowboat can get out to a shipwreck, so you don't have that kind of control to accessing the dive sites. When you look at the individuals who were drawn to this in the early days, the divers were very private about what they

were doing relative to what we now know as technical dives and experimentation. It was very much kept within the family, a very small circle of friends. Not the larger wreck diving community. You should tread softly, you go there with all humility, and what happened is some people were moving ahead at light speed with technique, technology and philosophy that were flawed. And they were doing it because they needed to draw a following. It was pure sensationalism and ego.

1. The *Seeker* 2. Capt. Dan Crowell's rendition of *U-869*

At the same time, there was all this other stuff going on. The controversies and the rivalries and, in some cases, the bitterness and acrimony that went on between different boats. I'm thinking now at the unbelievable rifts that developed between Steve Belinda's group on the *Wahoo* and Bill Nagle's group on the *Seeker*. What caused all that? »There were days when I walked around going, "I don't like any of them." It came down to issues about respect and the way they conducted themselves. I think Bill was an incredible diver, and in many ways, he was my mentor from a technical standpoint. When we start talking about the rivalries between Belinda and others, a lot of that is back to this, "I know the way" mentality. New ideas, new concepts, new technology, don't sit well in that environment.

Now you guys were in pursuit of what you were then simply calling the "U-Who." The notoriety that's been achieved by this pioneering search to find the damn thing and then to identify

what it was and what navy it belonged to is amazing. »Yeah, it was Bill Nagel's personal interest in exploring new shipwrecks that led us to it. He traded Loran numbers with a fishing boat captain. They had a wreck offshore; Bill had a little wreck inshore. The fisherman wanted to hang inshore when the weather's crappy, because it's good for business. Bill loved the idea of a new shipwreck. This guy said, "I know there's something out there, I know it's big, I know you guys dive deep, let's trade."

At what depth? »About 200 feet, he thought.

Who went out there and dove it the first time? »I crossed out a date on Labor Day weekend in 1991. Bill put five divers on, and I put five divers on it. Our deal was that we were going to go out and try to find the wreck, and if we don't find it, we keep looking. We made about five passes trying to hook into this thing, but we were having problems with the bottom recorder. One bottom recorder was saying it was up to 260 feet, and the other one said it was around 220. In reality it was about 230 feet, but there was a concern about taking a boatload of guys when we said it looked about 200 feet, and all of a sudden there's a

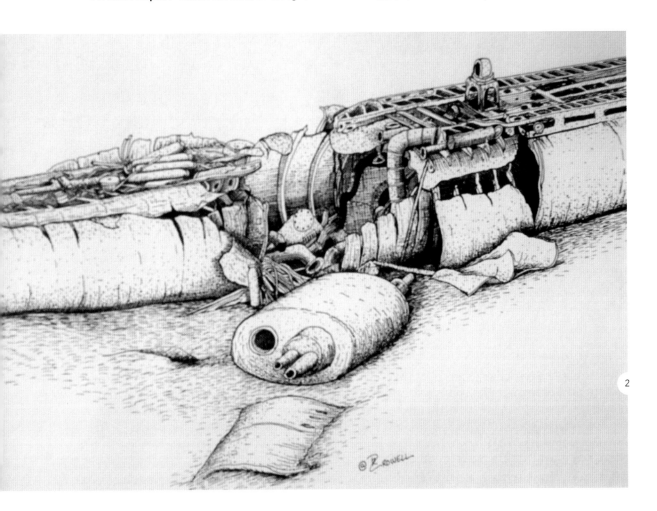

2

How did this fishing guy find it? »He was running a trip out to the canyons, and quite literally stumbled upon it. At this time, I think there were only three fishing boat captains who knew about this site. But they had no idea that this was a WWII submarine, and they certainly – at this point – did not know that this could be a U-boat.

huge difference between 200 feet and 260 feet on air. So our plan was, once we finally got grappled into the wreck, that I would go down and take a look at the wreck. If it was an old trash barge or something in 250 feet of water, that's not where we wanted to spend a day or risk the other divers.

So what did you find? It took me six minutes to get down to the bottom. Literally hand over hand, ripping current. It was a strenuous descent, visibility was about five feet. I'm looking at this wreck and I secure the grapple to keep it from blowing away. I swam up current and saw an angled hatch, very prominent, very much a unique feature. I'm at 230 feet and my mind is racing, and I think I know what this is. I look inside the hatch and I see torpedoes. The hatch is completely blown open.

You know you are looking at a submarine, and you know you're not looking at a submarine from the 1960s. At 230 feet on air, you're kind of stupid. But I know it's a submarine, it appears to be WWII vintage, WWII speaks U-boat, and I am absolutely astounded

1. Crew of *U-869*, after commissioning, January 26, 1944
2. At sea during training 3. Neuerburg (far right) saluting the sub's ensign after commissioning 4. Chatterton on rebreather diving NOAA's saturation habitat *Aquarius*

and mystified. I believe this is a big dive, and I'm taking a moment to appreciate how fortunate I am. During my deco, I'm working over in my mind what I saw, and knowing the history of the area I thought a German U-boat may have been 150 miles away but there's nothing nearby, and I was trying to remember the number… I'm kicking all this stuff around in my head when one of the crew members on board, comes down and gives me the "what's up" sign. I take my slate and write "SUB" and stick it in front of his face. He goes berserk. He goes back up to the boat and tells everybody what it is. Of course at this point, they don't know how deep it is, they don't

know anything. Totally unbridled enthusiasm. Splash by splash, this parade of divers goes past me on the way down to the wreck. I get back on the boat, and Bill Nagel's words were, "I hear we did good."

At this point it's no secret that Nagel had a serious alcohol problem. Was he still diving then, or was he just essentially being a captain and having the enthusiasm that had always driven

4

301

him take him out there? »I guess we all have people that we know have problems with alcoholism. Bill's case was extraordinarily severe. At 43 years old he drank himself to death. In 1991, he still had fantasies of straightening himself out. It hadn't gotten so bad that he had reached a point of no return. He was a very knowledgeable diver, and he understood that he was

not just completely overwhelmed with enthusiasm at the possibilities this wreck offered. So everyone felt they had a shot at identifying the wreck.

We had a buddy team with Steve Feldman, an instructor from Manhattan, with Paul Skibinski. These two guys had a lot of experience diving together. Their plan called for thirteen minutes on the bottom. Pretty

Chatterton and Kohler, *U-869* dive , 1997

not capable of making the dive. At the same time, he felt this was the inspiration he needed to turn his life around. So thought the discovery of the submarine was going to save his life. He wanted to dive it, he wanted to turn his life around.

This wreck turned a lot of people's lives around. How long from the time that this wreck was initially discovered on Labor Day weekend in 1991 did it manage to kill the first diver? »The second trip, two weeks later.

How did it happen? »Everyone on that first trip signed up for the second trip. Everyone on the first trip got at least one dive, some got two. They all understood how deep the wreck was, and they understood the conditions down there. There wasn't anybody who was

conservative, by my standards. They get down on the wreck, do some exploration, get their thirteen minutes, and Paul heads up the line. He turns, and sees Steve is not following. So he stops and waits. He notices there are no bubbles coming up so he swims back down, and finds him on the bottom. He turns Steve over and sees he's wide-eyed and unresponsive. Paul is absolutely shattered. He's over 200 feet deep, his friend and dive buddy could not be in a more severe predicament, and he has to get him to the surface. He starts hauling him up the anchor line. They get up to the point where they see another pair of divers coming down.

Remember, there's a strong current. This means anchor line in one hand, diver in the other. You've got no hand for your BC, nothing for anything. You are at the limit of your ability. He thinks he's running out of gas. It was physically and emotionally demanding, it couldn't have been more stressful. The other divers come down. He grabs the regulator from one and at the same time he lets go of the body. So one stays with Paul while the other one chases the body to the bottom. He's now at 230 feet in the sand with an unconscious, non-breathing diver, and he's not even linked to the anchor line. He doesn't believe there's anything he can do to help Steve. So he ties a line on him, starts up, and miraculously runs back into the anchor line. He ties off the line he'd fixed to Steve's head. But when we went down to try to recover the body, all we found at the end of the line was a mask and a snorkel. Feldman's body was recovered five months later by a commercial fishing vessel. According to their track, they picked up the body at some point greater than a mile away from the wreck. He came up in a net.

We spent the rest of that day trying to recover his body. We used up the bottom time of everyone on board who we felt was capable of going down to search. There were guys that were emotionally distraught and you couldn't ask them to go in the water, and had they volunteered you wouldn't have wanted them to. The last thing you want is someone else getting hurt or killed trying to recover a body.

Later, the diving continued with a different lineup. Not everyone who was on the boat with Feldman wanted to continue. There were guys who gave up diving, there were guys who gave up deep diving, there were guys who gave up diving on that U-boat. And then there were others that wanted to continue.

I credit the Boston Sea Rovers and the Beneath the Seas guys for sponsoring forums and symposiums that made a real effort to bring these groups together, to put together seminars which talked about the new technologies, and it also was a process where a lot of the leading members of different dive communities got introduced to the public for the first time. Sometimes, that was a sobering experience. Back in 1991, I had spoken at the same program with Rob Palmer who'd come over from England. Exley was up from central Florida, Billy Deans from Key West, Jim Bowden flew up from Mexico. We were all introduced to two guys that quite literally scared us to death. It was Chris Rouse and Chrissy Rouse. They babbled in our faces for about ten minutes and then disappeared. The last thing that Chrissy said to Sheck was, "I want to be just like you, but I'm going to be better than you, and I'm going to go deeper than you, and I'm going to be the next Sheck Exley." When they walked away, Rob Palmer turned to me and said, "Those guys are going to kill themselves." And before I ever saw them again, that's exactly what happened. I can understand the reaction of you guys. It was tragic and there were a lot of lessons to be learned. It was the first real public focus on the *U-869*. In 1992, the Rouses had come out and done some *Andrea Doria* trips. They were different, they were unique since they came from the cave diving community. In many ways, they were perhaps better suited for diving on the submarine. Bill kind of liked the Rouses; they were outlandish and wild, but he also thought they were reasonably capable without fully understanding everything they were doing.

The Rouses, if nothing else, had a reputation for a bizarre father-son relationship. It was competitive; it was characterized in some ways as immature. Were they good divers? They seemed to be disciplined; they seemed knowledgeable; and if you pulled out the personality, they were capable. This was Columbus Day weekend 1992, thirteen months after Feldman's death. This was a two day trip; they had been to the U-boat a couple times previously. Chrissy had a spot he was working inside the sub that had German writing on it. He was convinced that he was going to be the guy to identify the sub, much the same way he spoke to Sheck Exley. He had a very high level of confidence and was very vocal about it. He was going to be the one to identify the U-boat.

What happened? Chrissy, the son, was running a reel inside the wreck to a location around the galley where he was trying to dig out this artifact that had German writing on it to bring it to the surface. The father was waiting outside. Chrissy apparently undermined some heavier steel components within the wreck trying to extricate this artifact that turned out to be a rubber life raft. He's trying to pull this thing out, he's digging around, and the next thing you know a large, heavy piece of wreckage lands on him and pins him. He is essentially buried in the wreck, alone, at the end of a line. His father, Chris, was waiting outside. Chrissy does not show up, and he is not going to surface without Chrissy, so he says to himself "I gotta go get the boy."

At this point, we have the elder Rouse – the father – with the horrible realization that his son is trapped inside the wreck, the dive is way behind schedule, what happens next?»The added complexity is that both these guys are on air. Father goes in, finds his son, uncovers him, takes the reel, and heads out, but not the way they came in.

If I remember correctly, they ended up on the surface with explosive decompression sickness.»Right. But all of this stuff was compounded by the fact that they were hammered with narcosis and they had to deal with almost unbelievable psychological stress. Chris, with his son not coming out of the wreck, being buried and having to extricate him… and for Chrissy, the fact that he was buried inside this thing for a long time before his father even showed up. So

1. Chris Rouse and son Chrissy 2. One of the Rouses's scuba tanks, still lying on the wreck after their fateful dive

So the supposition is that as they exited the wreck, they were disoriented as to which direction they were facing. They were only about forty feet from the anchor line.

This is significant because they didn't come up on the anchor line, but free ascending. They had spent more time on the wreck searching for the anchor line. They couldn't find it, they got to the point where they were over 40 minutes into their bottle time, and they had to surface. At this point, they have a huge decompression obligation and they don't have enough gas to do it. They're not coming up on the anchor line or tag line or anything, so this whole scenario is about as bad as it can get before they even leave the bottom.

It's essentially a case of making bad choices, and when things go wrong, you have inadvertently painted yourself into a corner, and that's exactly what happened here. They brought only one of their four stage bottles with them, they did not mark the anchor line with the strobe light, they ran a line inside the wreck, but they didn't run it from their start point, the anchor line. So they found themselves lost with no up-line. After another series of attempts to share the one cylinder of nitrox they had dragged up with them, everything went to hell.

you have this psychological state that is created here, and the straw that breaks the camel's back is Chrissy breathing off of that nitrox regulator and getting water into the mouthpiece. He bolts for the surface. Chris was not going to let his son go anywhere without him. So he comes up, too. The weather was starting to get shitty. I was looking at the water as the two Rouses popped to the surface in front of us. The immediate realization is that they weren't on the anchor line, and they were not on the surface according to the schedule they left with us. We knew there was more than likely a serious problem.

Now you're faced with a bad situation because you're so remotely located offshore, you have to get the guys onboard, and even that is proving difficult.»We're trying to talk to them to get basic information as we're throwing them lines and trying to get them to the ladder on the boat. We're asking if they had a decompression obligation. They indicated they had come directly to the surface and they both looked really scared.

At this point, was any consideration given to trying to adopt some kind of omitted decompression procedure and put them back in?»Yes, but they were not fully responsive, and our policy and procedure has always been if you can talk to someone, you can fix it. But if it's a psychological problem, you can't take someone who is desperate to get out of the water, and put them back down for decompression.

So now you have to extract them. And that means you have to get the equipment off them and get them up on the deck. You're trained as a medic and as a commercial diver, and right away you must have known that the prognosis was very, very grim.》I knew it was grim, but I didn't think it was as bad as it was. We got Chris to the back of the boat. He said, "Take Chrissy first." The son was right behind him. We put a man on either side of the ladder to help him and he said, "I can't make my legs work." We quite literally dragged him up and turned our attention to Chris Sr. He very calmly and specifically said, "I'm not going to make it. Tell Sue I'm sorry." He slumped unconscious with his face in the water. I jumped in, took his knife, cut him out of his rig, and basically did a fireman's carry to get him onto the deck.

At this point, the only tools you had out there were oxygen and basic CPR. How quickly, from the time you got both the guys out of the water onto the deck, did it take them to go from being able to have coherent speech to becoming irrational and passing out? Obviously we're dealing with massive CNS decompression hits here, and it's going to come on pretty quickly.》Chrissy was young and relatively resilient. He was very verbal, expressing his discomfort, he was almost hallucinatory. With very serious CNS, it mimics a stroke. We were not entirely sure how much of what he had to say was true and accurate and how much was delusion. The key was trying to get him calmed down, on oxygen, and trying to maintain as best we could until we could get him air-lifted out by the Coast Guard. Chris Sr. never did have spontaneous respirations. He had a pulse for maybe a minute. We were doing CPR on him and we had a pharyngeal airway that we put in, but you could feel resistance within his body building up. There were so many gas bubbles in his body that, quite literally, his blood was coagulating as we were trying to do CPR. From the time that we pulled him to the stern, Chris Sr. never had a viable chance.

You are faced with what can you do and who can you save, and then you get into an argument with the Coast Guard helicopter during the evacuation?》The Coast Guard swimmer comes down with the rescue basket and said they were going to take the son first. I said, "Take the son. Don't take the father." At this point, we had done CPR on Chris for something close to two hours. I was adamant, "The son has a chance. I know this family. If the father could sit up and have one thing to say to you, he'd say, 'Take my boy.' Chris is not going to make it. The only chance we have is to get the son treated as fast as possible."

And the time element here is absolutely crucial.》We are as under the gun as you can be and we've already kind of resolved on ourselves to the fact that Chris Sr. is not going to make it. We're still doing CPR, but all of our hopes were really with Chrissy.

So how did you reconcile this triage?》I understand the Coast Guard's position that Chris is not dead until he's pronounced dead by a doctor, so we're doing what is procedure, which is to keep doing CPR. But from a practical standpoint, the father was dead and we should expend no further effort in trying to resuscitate him. We should try to focus our efforts on the son. But that's not the way the system works.

Ultimately, the decision was made that both were to go up in the basket and all of you were left behind. The chopper took off with the Rouses to deliver them to the chamber. This presented other treatment issues: the depth capability of the chamber, not to mention the delay.》And you're talking about a significant time lapse now, between four or five hours.

Both of the Rouses succumbed and passed away due to the explosive decompression they suffered. You're left out there on the boat rocking away with your own horrible psychological trauma, and you're facing a long ride back in. This turned off a lot of guys from going back out to this wreck again.》We were absolutely positively traumatized by the accident. Having a fatality is terrible, but having two fatalities is about as much as anyone can imagine dealing with. Having it be a father and son is worse still. There was also a lot of noise from both the cave diving

community and the rival wreck divers. This really caused me, Richie Kohler, and others to question what we were doing. Is deep diving worth these two guys' lives? At the same time, there's multiple fatalities on the *Doria*, there's the Feldman fatality… it's a lot. We had been relatively low key, going out and doing the deep thing under the radar. Now we're not under the radar. We've got a big target painted on our backs.

You never really seemed to waver in your own personal interest in trying to determine the identity of this vessel. You guys called it the *U-Who*. It wasn't where it was supposed to be,

1. Chatterton on dive boat, 2006 2. China off of *U-869*
3. Tag off spare parts box that identified the *U-869*
4. Chatterton, Richie Kohler and Rob Kurson, 2004

out of diving for awhile after the fatalities, then you guys came back in and pursued this common interest. It ended up not only producing an enduring friendship and identifying the wreck through your astounding research, but at some point you were finally able to re-enter the engine room, recover the tag that identified the boat as *U-869*, and put this matter to bed against everybody that had been telling you that you were wrong. Three people have died, unbelievable amounts of finger pointing has gone on, nasty fighting, wild accusations, and you finally unveil the secret. 》We were focused on what we were doing. Kohler and I weren't looking over our shoulders to see if anyone was watching. Richie really felt this was the right thing to do, for the sailors who had lost their lives and were lying in anonymous graves. Being a German-American, he felt a certain empathy to the predicament the families were in. You

nobody could come up with an explanation for why it was there, it had claimed three people's lives in a very short time. How long after the Rouse incident did you resume diving it again? 》That was the last dive of that year, end of October. We were back out there first thing the next summer.

You seemed to react to this with a determination that is almost unfathomable for some outside observers. To think that you dove this first in 1991, and how many years until you identified it? 》Six years, almost to the day.

This was a journey not only for you personally, but also for Richie Kohler. You two didn't get along earlier in your dive careers, Richie dropped

don't stop doing what it is you intended to do simply because it became difficult. The more difficult it became, the greater our personal resolve.

You spent six years of detective work. You've gone through an emotional rollercoaster, your first marriage breaks up, your career is changing, there's a bunch of things going on. In 1997, you unlock the mystery. Now your efforts start to attract some attention. 》We had been involved with PBS and NOVA was doing a documentary on the wreck.

Was this *Hitler's Lost Sub*? 》Yes. And PBS had partners in Germany and the U.K., so while they're building a two hour program in the United States, they put out a half hour program in Germany to find one of

were trying to get across was that this submarine had left homeport in WWII with these 57 young boys on a mission that was doomed. They're in Norway, and they're watching all these U-boats leave, and none of them are coming back. That was the story that interested us: to die anonymously off the coast of New Jersey. That was what we envisioned as the story,

1. Chatterton doing rebreather maintenence, 2004
2. Interior wreckage of *U-869*   3. Chatterton inside the wreck

the veterans from the wreck. The documentary comes out in 2000, and it is seen and reported. Someone comes to Rob Kurson and tells him about the story that they have seen in the NOVA documentary.

What attracted him to the story? I think it was the personalities; he probably was attracted to Richie and me on a very basic level. He went to an agent in New York City, and she made contact with us and asked if we would be willing to talk to him.

Why did Kurson think that it needed to go beyond the documentary, and what was your reaction to meeting with an unpublished author who was not a diver? What made you think he could tell your story? Richie and I had been involved with several attempts at writing a book. In every instance, it just didn't pan out. They didn't quite get it. So when we sat down with Rob Kurson, we felt there was some kind of challenge involved. What we

that's what we spoke to Rob about.

Rob spent all day with us. He brought his pregnant wife, and all of a sudden he said he wanted to leave and start writing. We offered him dinner, and he said no, that he had to write. He's a nut. He has no social grace. He has no concept of anything other than what he's focused on. He made his wife drive home because he didn't want to lose anything in his head. And we're thinking this guy is out of his mind, but at the same time thinking he was perfect for us. He was not a diver; he still isn't a diver. I think that's why the book turned out so well. He had to learn everything about diving from us, and he was in a much better position to then present that information to the reader.

In my case, as both an author and diver, I found that to be true as well. I had read earlier accounts of the Rouse tragedy, and Feldman, and all the other elements that made up the other tragedies like the *Doria* expeditions. Kurson managed to

come in and tell the story so well that I wonder whether anybody could have written it from within the dive community. ⟩⟩The same kind of dedication and focus that we had for our diving, he had for his writing. We understood each other right from the get go. He said, "Trust me. I can make this story a bestseller." And I believed him.

Didn't you also have to tell him that he couldn't go out and dive the wreck himself? ⟩⟩Yeah. You'll love this. He went to his agent and told her he had to go out and dive the wreck with us. She called us up,

So he went to dive class in Chicago. He had to be the instructor's worst nightmare. When it comes time for the pool session, Rob eases himself into the pool and dogpaddles a little bit, and the instructor goes, "You can't swim." And Rob says, "Yeah, you're telling me."

So he asks him what he's doing, and he explains that he just has to make one dive and then he's done. Just one dive to this U-boat sixty miles off the coast of New Jersey, 230 feet down, and then he's done. And the instructor tells him to get the hell out of the pool.

So Rob is now a broken man. He's been thrown out of dive school, and he says that he simply cannot

"Listen, Rob is talking about diving the wreck. You can't kill this guy." We agreed, and when he came to us we told him it was a really bad idea. He said he absolutely couldn't write the book without diving the wreck. We then told him to go to his local dive shop and get certified thinking that would buy us a little time. That once he realized what diving was all about, he would back off. The obvious reality here is that the wreck had claimed the lives of three guys who were experienced divers with many years of diving behind them, and now he wanted to do it in a couple months.

go on writing this book. So we sit down with him and ask him what happened. He explains that if he gets water on his face, he gets all panicky. And Ritchie and I look at each other and just shake our heads. This nut who can't swim and panics when water gets on his face wants to do a deep technical wreck dive? Yeah, right...

So, let me take a wild guess; you don't let him dive the wreck? ⟩⟩Come on, Bret, hell no! He's still a non-diver, a non-swimmer, for that matter.

The book became such an elaborate project, because now the whole thing must be brought to life based on the narrative that you and Richie can supply to him. It is a fabulous book, a runaway bestseller. One thing that is interesting is that you and Richie were smart enough at the outset to know how much work you would be putting into it that you actually negotiated that the royalty be split three ways? »What happened was Rob's agent took Richie and I on as clients of ICM. Like any good agent, they laid everything out. There was no subjectivity. When we signed a contract with them, it was very specific about who was going to get what, who was going to supply what, what would happen if it became a movie, etc. Rob certainly was very generous in sharing with us, and now it's moved on into the movie phase.

You not only secured a movie deal but you originally brought in an A-list director in Ridley Scott. »Actually, FOX and Ridley Scott parted company on this. FOX was adamant that they wanted to shoot this in 2006, but Scott wasn't available in that time frame, so they went looking for a new director. Now they've settled on the great Australian director, Peter Weir. His last film was the epic Russell Crowe movie *Master and Commander*. He also did *Witness* with

Harrison Ford. He knows how to tell a story. Our meetings with him have gone extremely well. He really gets the story and we all like each other.

How you've come from book to movie is interesting. Especially when you compare it to Peter Benchley, who was practically eating cat food when he wrote *Jaws*, and nobody could figure out how that book could possibly be brought to the screen. Peter was the first to admit even he wasn't sure how it could be done because, as you know, sharks don't take very good direction. Do you envision a hands-on role when this thing goes into production? »I think Richie and I will be consulting more on the diving end of things. Bill Broyles has written the screenplay; in fact he's working on the fourth take right now. I saw the second swipe that he took at this, and I have to say it literally made the hair on my neck stand up. I was moved by his script. If nobody screws it up between now and the big screen, it's going to be huge.

Do you have any idea who they might want to cast to play you guys? »They want A-list actors. When I look around at the very talented people they have drawn into this and hear them shooting numbers like a hundred million dollars around, I have the utmost confidence that they will find the right people for the job.

Well, I guess it's safe to say we're not going to see Paulie Shore or Adam Sandler in the parts. »If we're lucky!

How many copies of *Shadow Divers* have been sold? »So far, somewhere just south of a million copies in hard bound and paperback.

and shipwrecks. It's something nobody is doing. *Deep Sea Detectives* they want to call it and initially they wanted eight shows. We figure we can squeeze in two shows before they realize we don't know what the hell we're doing and fire us.

I remember the first day we went to shoot the show, the director of photography asked us what else we had done. We said we had worked on some documentaries. He asked us about dramatic things, and we sort of just sat there. We're at the dinner table when

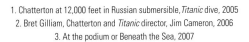

1. Chatterton at 12,000 feet in Russian submersible, *Titanic* dive, 2005
2. Bret Gilliam, Chatterton and *Titanic* director, Jim Cameron, 2006
3. At the podium or Beneath the Sea, 2007

he finally figures out we're not actors. He freaks out.

But now, we've done 57 episodes and we're putting together candidates for the next slate of shows. They're seen all over the world. I get mail from friends in the UK and Yucatan saying, "I saw you on TV last night!"

It's interesting that divers didn't make this a bestseller... the public made this a bestseller and it was ultimately because this is a human story so well told. »The credit really belongs on Rob's plate. I can't tell you how many people have come up to me and said, "I'm not a diver, I know nothing about diving, but I was moved by that book." The way that Rob wrote it was for the reader, and that's the mark of a really good book. People feel like Rob is talking to them. You and I could both read the book and take away completely different things, and that's why people love it.

You guys also parlayed yourselves into television? »While we're working with Rob Kurson and he's researching the book, The History Channel comes to us and asks to do a television series about divers

Any other projects on the horizon? »This past summer Richie and I put together a project on the *Titanic*. We went out, we chartered the Russian support ship *Keldysh*, took the submersibles, we did the whole thing on our own dime, made our own preparations, and then went to The History Channel and sold it as the executive producers. We're still working on *Deep Sea Detectives*, we're producing specials for The History Channel, we're still promoting the book. Twentieth Century Fox and the *Shadow Divers* movie has got us busy and we're consulting with Paramount Pictures on a dramatic television series. The only thing we don't see in our futures is unemployment. ■

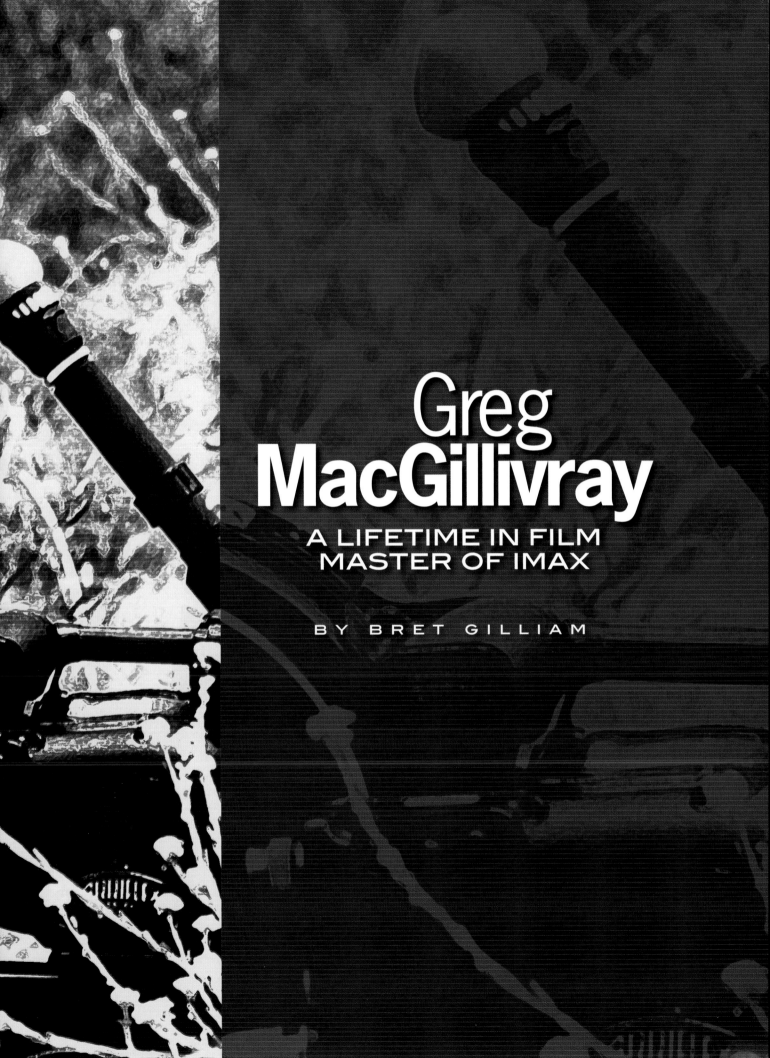

Greg MacGillivray

A LIFETIME IN FILM
MASTER OF IMAX

BY BRET GILLIAM

Bret Gilliam

GREG MACGILLIVRAY MAY NOT BE A GUY WITH INSTANT NAME RECOGNITION FOR A LOT OF DIVERS...

but it's a sure bet that you know his work. As the most successful producer/director of large format films in the world, he has been responsible for bringing a variety of compelling documentary IMAX titles to the 70-ft. screen. »

He got his start as a beach rat making low-budget surf films in the 1960s to success as one of Hollywood's most sought after second-unit directors on features such as *The Towering Inferno*, *Big Wednesday*, *Jonathan Livingston Seagull*, and *The Shining*, he changed course again to pioneer the filmmaking process in a new format called IMAX.

MacGillivray changed the way the world looks at documentaries by celebrating the IMAX format to its fullest potential. Whether he raced through the Rock Islands in Palau by speedboat, strapped his camera to an ultra-light plane to soar over towering breaking waves or mountain peaks, took it underwater to capture the beauty of a coral reef, descended into the labyrinth of intricate cave systems, or captured the stark beauty of the Himalayas from the world's

OUTSIDE THE THIRD DIMENSION, 1964, Cinematographer | COOL WAVE OF COLOR, 1964, Director/Producer
THE PERFORMERS, 1965, Director/Producer/Cinematographer/Editor | **FREE AND EASY**, 1967, Director/Producer/Cinematographer »

FILMS | AWARDS | HONORS

tallest mountain summit, MacGillivray brought back the story on film as none other in the genre.

Whether you were introduced to him through his innovative surf films or stumbled on to his work later through *The Living Sea*, *Dolphins*, *Journey Into Amazing Caves*, or *Everest*, it's unlikely that you escaped without a lasting impression of his ability to bring a nature subject to life as never before. His company MacGillivray-Freeman Films helped create three Academy-Award-winning films and produced two more that were nominated for Oscars. His 1976 film *To Fly!* was the highest-grossing documentary of all time until his 1998 film *Everest* recently surpassed it.

I've been a serious MacGillivray fan since seeing his earliest surf films while in high school. In the mid-1960s I was earning some extra money as a quasi-professional surfer on manufacturers' sponsored surf teams. At the U. S. Surfing Championships in 1967, I arrived in Huntington Beach, CA and had the chance to meet Greg and his partner Jim Freeman as they ran around the beach, into the water, and dived into the waves we rode with their 16mm cameras to capture the action. I was 16 and Greg was an ancient 22 at the time, a really old guy. They were the Stephen Spielbergs of the surf world and we all desperately wanted them to point their lenses at us. To end up in one of their surf films was worth serious bragging rights. No luck in my case. So I had to settle for admiring their craft chronicling

the real stars. Thirty-six years later, we'd get re-acquainted. Funny, he looked older.

I caught up with MacGillivray at his studio offices in Laguna Beach, California. I arrived at his studio and was ushered by various assistants through a virtual museum of old film equipment, cameras, projectors, tripods, etc., all surrounded by a plethora of awards casually decorating shelves, showcases, and coffee tables. A private screening theatre dominated part of the first floor and the halls were decorated with film posters of prior works. A general atmosphere of professionalism and success was inescapable as dedicated staff swirled around me on endless projects. I was shown into MacGillivray's private corner suite and handed a fresh pastry and a glass of iced tea. I guess I expected Orson Welles or Louis B. Mayer to appear at any moment.

Instead Greg arrived in his bare feet and a comfortable pair of khaki pants with a casual shirt partially unbuttoned looking like he might have just come from a beach party. He was trailed by his beloved Corgi dog, Paige, who joined us for the afternoon interview. We settled in for a long rambling afternoon conversation that kicked off by asking about his start in surf films and segued on to his most recent film, *Coral Reef Adventure*, a chronicle of an expedition half way around the world to examine the fate of our underwater environment. A more gracious host than can be imagined, I departed several hours later intrigued by his extraordinary talent and his retiring shy demeanor. ∎

315

MOODS OF SURFING, 1968, Director/Producer/Cinematographer/Editor | **AWARDS 1968:** Best Film Award - Photographic Society of America; Silver Medal - Cortina Film Festival; The Chris - The Columbus International Film and Video Festival; Gold Medal - New York Festivals »   Q+A »

FILMS | AWARDS | HONORS

Q+A

You're remembered for your innovative surfing films in the sixties. Memory serves me that you originally intended to be a physics teacher. So surfing was responsible for diverting you from a path of traditional respectability into the film profession? »I went to college at University of California at Santa Barbara and majored in physics with the hopes of becoming a high school teacher. At the time, I was also making my first commercial surfing film. That film took four years to produce. I'd started it when I was a freshman in high school. I had to hitchhike with my camera to surfing spots until I was old enough to drive and then would borrow my parent's car on the weekends to go shooting the surf – either with a surfboard or, when the surf got big and was good quality, I'd pull out my camera, a 16mm Bolex with a 230mm Century telephoto lens, and a nice wooden tripod. Film was my most costly element (my time was free to me!), so I really had to milk that roll of film. Sometimes I would shoot only two minutes of film in a whole eight hour day of sitting on the beach behind my camera ready for the right wave and the right ride to start happening in front of me. I'd track every one of the rides of the best surfers. So it took me four years to make this film because of my meager budget, but it taught me how to plan well, how to use my time and finances to produce a film. When the film came out four years later, it was reviewed well, so it showed a bit of profit. That's when I said to myself: "Hey, I might be able to make a career out of this." People really liked the movie. It was kind of a beatnik, non-traditional film I called *A Cool Wave of Color*. It featured jazz music and lots of colorful animation and it was original, in that it only featured California surfing – hotdog surfing – the kind of surfing that I felt was the most soulful and artistic. Once my film showed a profit, I decided that I should continue to make films and reinvest the money I was making into more films as I progressed through school.

Jim Freeman became your partner from the outset. How did you two meet and decide to collaborate instead of working independently? »I met Jim Freeman in 1964 after producing two films: A *Cool Wave of Color* and *The Performers*. Jim had made one surfing film called *Let There Be Surf*. We met each other at a screening in Santa Barbara of his second film. It was a very strange film about surfing called *Outside the Third Dimension*. Jim had the wild idea to produce

the film in 3D, 16mm. He shot it in Hawaii and the audience wore glasses. Some of the 3D was actually pretty good but generally the film wasn't a successful artistic endeavor. Jim's effort and perseverance in making this almost impossible-to-produce movie impressed me particularly from a technical standpoint. We soon became friends. As I was finishing *The Performers*, Jim helped me with technical questions that I had about how to work with the laboratory and make good prints. I didn't know at that time how to make dissolves and fades, and titles in the professional way. I was doing all the animation and titles on my

1. Greg with sister Lisa and his first surfboard, 1958
2. Hawaii, 1966 3. Jim Freeman and Greg, 1967

own in front of the camera! So the moment Jim and I became friends, we kept thinking that maybe we could actually make better films, which was our primary goal, if we teamed up. We knew that if we did work together, the profits probably wouldn't be any greater and we'd be splitting them into two pieces rather than just having them alone but we felt that adding quality to the projects was more important than the profits.

In 1966 we took the gamble. We dropped out of college for a year, and traveled for six months through South America with three surfers to tell a story about traveling and surfing in South America. Ecuador, Peru, Chili, Argentina, Uruguay, Brazil and Panama: in most of those locations we were the first people to surf the

WAVES OF CHANGE, 1969, Director/Producer | **CATCH THE JOY**, 1970, Director/Producer/Cinematographer/Editor
AWARDS 1970: Gold Medal - Atlanta International Film Festival; Grand Prize - Sunset Film Festival; Special Jury Award - San Antonio Film Festival; »

FILMS | AWARDS | HONORS

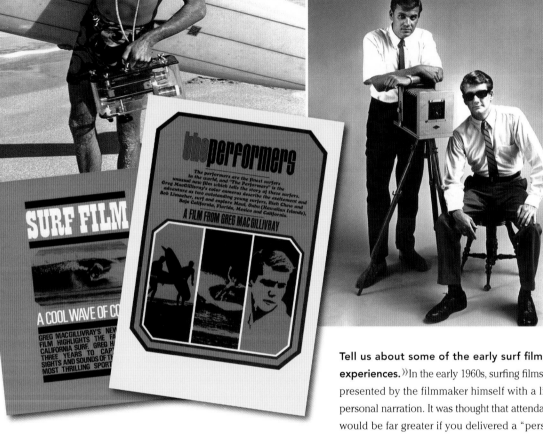

were doing. In the end each of us improved 100 percent as a filmmaker. We loved talking about films that we had seen and ideas that we had about films and new techniques that we thought we wanted to try: special editorial and camera techniques, new kinds of lenses and ways to shoot with cameras in slow motion.

Tell us about some of the early surf film experiences. 》In the early 1960s, surfing films were presented by the filmmaker himself with a live, personal narration. It was thought that attendance would be far greater if you delivered a "personal account." So, at that time you had to be, not only a good filmmaker and be able to shoot and edit well, put good music with your film, and tell good stories, but you also had to be a personality. You had to be able to stand up in front of the audience and hold the audience's attention with your live narration. It was a lot like Vaudeville or being in a play where you either succeeded or failed based on your own performance. You'd have the music on a tape recorder, which you'd start at the beginning of the film and hope that the tape would stay in close sync to the projector. However, that actually never happened, so you'd always have to be either advancing or retarding the tape as you were talking, so the audience wouldn't hear that something

waves. It was a unique experience for us, quite an exciting adventure for a 22-year-old. We could barely speak the language and were looked at by the South Americans as a total novelty. When we'd paddle out on our surfboards, the town's people would come down to watch, rather flabbergasted by our ability to actually ride waves to shore.

There were five of us, initially, Jim Freeman, me, Dale Struble, Mark Martinson and Paul Strauch, Jr. Paul, after traveling with us through Peru, decided that his business obligations back home in Hawaii were too pressing so he had to drop out of the trip. During our six-month trip, Jim and I really pushed each other in terms of technique, storytelling and the art of what we

AWARDS 1970: Cindy Award - Information Film Producer's Association; Golden Eagle - The Cine Golden Eagle Film and Video Competition
SENTINELS OF SILENCE, 1970, Cinematographer | AWARDS 1970: Academy Award for Best Documentary Short; Academy Award for Best Live Action Short 》

Q+A 》

Robert August and Herbie Fletcher, perform for
MacGillivray's camera during *The Sweet Ride*, 1967

was amiss. It was a bit of a trick, something you had to learn through practice. At the first 10 screenings of my first film, I was a stuttering, nervous moron.

Basically, the narration was pitifully unlistenable because I was so nervous. Even with the lights out, it was a terrifying situation. Eventually, timing and delivery did improve. Believe me, if you were a lousy performer or what you said wasn't very interesting, the audience would tell you; surfers are no shrinking violets. They'd yell out their comments, which then would induce everyone else to laugh or hoot or throw things. Wild nights. Kids were ready for you. There wasn't a lot of drinking, not that kind of wild. In a crowd of 300 people you might have two or three people that had a beer, but basically, they were just ready to have a good time. I went to a number of surf film showings where the film was really almost unwatchable and the narrator was irritating. The audience would go bananas! Kids would bring bottle caps that they'd flick with their fingers, sending them sailing like a miniature metal Frisbee, often pinging off the narrator's head. There are countless stories of narrators being pelted by, not only bottle caps, but also paper airplanes and candies. Frisbees and

beach balls would get tossed about during the movie. It was pretty crazy.

Before my first film premiered, I remember worrying about what I would do if the crowd went nuts on me. I didn't want that to happen, so I made certain my film was exciting and interesting and had a lot of funny things in it so the audience would not take it out on me.

Around 1962, at a surfing film showing, Walt Phillips was narrating at the Santa Monica Civic in front of about 2,000 people, and reportedly not doing a very good job. About an hour into the program 10 surfers marched down to the front of the auditorium, went up onto the stage, picked him up in his seat, carried him down the steps to the side exit and pitched him outside. The audience clapped and hooted and watched the rest of the film without any narration. That's the kind of crowd at a surfing movie. It was a huge motivation to me to make a really good first film. The fear factor!

Many would say that the 1960s were the golden age of surfing. You had the chance to interact with some of the sports' greatest characters. ⟩⟩I finished my first surf film in 1964 when I was just 18. This was the same year Bruce Brown released *The Endless Summer.* His film was light years ahead of all the other films that had come out before, including mine, and changed the way that the audience looked

SKI MOVIE ONE, 1970, Producer, Producer with Summit Films | THE SUNSHINE SEA, 1970, Director/Producer, Producer with Summit Films
FIVE SUMMER STORIES, 1972, Director/Producer/Cinematographer | ABOVE SAN FRANCISCO, 1973, Creator/Producer ⟩⟩

FILMS | AWARDS | HONORS

at surfing films. My film premiered three months before *The Endless Summer*, and it was different, too. The two films kind of complimented each other. Mine was much more personal and different artistically. Bruce's film was much more of a story, much less of a photographic or artistic exploration, but a story with humor and characters. *The Endless Summer* set tremendous records at the box office in its first and second run. By the next summer, Bruce and Paul Allen had blown the film up to 35mm and were testing it with "normal" film audiences. The film had done that well.

In 1964 there were three main surf filmmakers. Bruce Brown was at the lead. John Severson, who previously was number one, produced films every year from 1959-62. He created a weak film in 1963 called *The Angry Sea*. He dropped out of making surfing films at that stage to devote time to *Surfer*, the brilliant magazine he founded. Bud Browne, who was also a wonderful cinematographer, and had great films, produced the first surfing film in about 1955-56, and then had a film out every year from 1958-62. Bud became a close friend and remains one today. We worked together on *Five Summer Stories* and *The Sunshine Sea* in 1969, 1970 and 1971. Those were the kingpins, the three main surf filmmakers.

Before you and Jim Freeman got into the act, surf films were pretty much a product of long lenses on cameras shot from the beach. What made you decide to try filming from the water, from surfboards and even underwater? » Jim and I were continually challenging one another. Our teamwork allowed us to concentrate on shooting from the water, which was my specialty. Jim would be on shore with a telephoto lens getting what you would call "coverage" of the good surf and the good rides and whatever else was happening on shore while I was in the water with the surfers trying to get new camera angles either by riding a surfboard next to them or by swimming to keep in position and getting the surfers coming by.

It's always a struggle to get the water shots. Your chance of success is about 10 percent in comparison to shooting from the beach. The result is worth it because you end up with an angle that obviously is completely different and more involving than shooting with a telephoto lens from shore. When you're shooting with a 10mm lens in 16mm, you're getting about a 90-degree view and so you really feel like you're out there

swimming or surfing with your stars. We were able to experiment a lot with shooting from the water, getting new camera angles and editing with two cameras so that essentially the ride had more dimension than previous surfing films. With two cameras, obviously, you're able to edit much more interestingly.

How did you get the specialized housings to work with? » The first camera housings that I had to work with, I built myself. In fact, I built all of our housings from 1960 through 1972. Basically, I got a book from a dive shop that Mart Toggweiler had published, a little pamphlet showing how to use Plexiglas, how to cut it, how to form it with a blow torch, how to bend it, how to glue it, how to use the Plexiglas cylinders. I built probably 10 to 15 waterproof housings all in my garage with actually no fancy tools, just whatever I could find at the store. I didn't have any electric saws, so it took me a long time to build these housings. It was a lot of trouble. Oftentimes they leaked and I'd have to modify them. I lost cameras to water damage, so I had to just throw them away.

My final camera housing that I built had a high-speed camera and eight pounds of batteries inside of it. We'd found a military 16mm camera that ran 200 frames per second, still only shooting with a 100 feet of film. For our film, *Waves of Change* which came out in 1969, I shot some slow motion water shots with a 10mm lens, which were the first super-slow motion (200 frames a second) shots done in the surfing world. About the same time George Greenough did some slow motion shots with a camera mounted on his back, shooting inside the curl at Rincon. But I believe that we were the first to shoot with a 200-frame per second camera in the surfing world, which really gave a completely new perspective on surfing because water droplets were now hanging in the air catching the light, undulating and moving around in a really interesting way. It gave surfing the kind of beauty that Jim and I always felt that it had.

Although you produced a series of fondly remembered surf films, most everyone would agree that *Five Summer Stories* was the pinnacle of your efforts. Many would say it's the best surf film ever. How did it come about? » Jim and I had decided that we really had done all we could do in the surfing world. We were ready to move on to produce and direct and shoot other kinds of films either for us or

319

HONORS 1973: selection for the permanent film library of the University of California Archives, the Museum of Modern Art in NY and the Paris Cinematheque
GOING SURFIN, 1974 | Co-Producer with Bud Brown | **JONATHAN LIVINGSTON SEAGULL**, 1974, Academy Award nomination for Best Photography »

FILMS | AWARDS | HONORS

Q+A »

for Hollywood. We wanted to make one last surfing film: our tribute to this sport, which we both loved so much. The difficulty for us, though, was that in 1969-71, Jim and I were already working on films with Hollywood studios so our time was limited. We were commissioned to make four 10-minute films for United Artists that were shown with the James Bond films as short entertainments. We were also making films for the educational market like *Catch the Joy*, a dune buggy film. We'd already shot a few television commercials and had some assignments on feature films, such as *The Sweet Ride* for 20th Century Fox and a host of other movies.

In order to make our final surfing film, I came up with the idea of doing a series of stories so that we could spend three weeks working on one story and complete it—and then go off on a Hollywood assignment. We'd then come back later and make another film story. I sat down and wrote out five stories that I thought would be interesting. The thrust of the film was the idea that surfing is almost a religious experience and that the spiritual side of surfing is significant to people who surf. The film started with the creation of Earth and waves and people and the final sequence was, what we call, "The End of the World." *Heaven's Gift to Man: The Tunnel of Love* was the film's epilogue filmed at Pipeline inside the tube. It was a paean to our love of the ocean. We used the "tunnel of love" as a metaphor for our personal love of the ocean.

It took us more than two years to complete the film. We worked on it with Bud Browne, who, because of our obligations with other films, would go to Hawaii for two or three months at a time and shoot film and send it back to us. We'd look at his footage, make suggestions and he'd just continue on. He was doing water shots with that same 200-frame per second military camera that he then put into a special rubberized, waterproof housing. He could actually swim it out at Pipeline and get great, super-slow motion shots. That was one big innovation for the film: shooting in 10 to 15-ft. surf at Pipeline, which is probably the most treacherous surfing area with the most lethal impact zone of any surfing spot in the world. Bud got amazing shots in horrendous conditions. It's amazing to me that he wasn't killed or seriously injured.

Five Summer Stories premiered March 24 and 25th, 1972, at the Santa Monica Civic on a Friday and Saturday night. It was an amazing event. It was the first surfing movie released with stereophonic

Greg at Makaha Beach, Hawaii, 1966

synchronous sound. We equipped the theaters with special speakers – huge full-range speakers – and the film soundtrack was played on a 100-lb. piece of equipment that we'd lug up into the projection booth. It ran in sync with the projector, if you punched the projector and the tape recorder start buttons at exactly the same time. Otherwise, you had to try to adjust as the film started screening. The sound for every performance was unbelievable. It was far superior to any sound in any movie theater at that particular time, comparable or even better than the 70mm six-track sound reproduction that was done in Hollywood and New York City. It was something special to watch this movie when it was shown with stereophonic sound, which was the case in the majority of the screenings for the seven-year period that the film ran.

So Jim and I produced this 92-minute film, which was released in 1972 and it became an instant classic. All the attendance records which were established

THE TOWERING INFERNO, 1974, Academy Award for Best Photography | TO FLY!, 1976, Director/Producer
AWARDS 1976 (TO FLY!): National Film Registry - Library of Congress; IMAX Hall of Fame - Voted in by members of the Giant Screen Theatre Association; »

FILMS | AWARDS | HONORS

previously by *The Endless Summer* in 16mm eight years earlier, all the records that were established by *Free and Easy* or by *Waves of Change*, all those records were broken by *Five Summer Stories*. It was a knockout of a film. After our first run of the movie, which was from March 1972 through September 1972, we continued to re-release the film every six months or every year for the next seven years the demand for the film was so great. In 1974, in its re-release, we added a new sequence, a new story, and then in 1976, we added a couple of new sequences including one of the last films that Jim Freeman worked on called *The Magic Rolling Board*, a film about skateboarding. In 1977, I released the film with a sequence on Shaun Tomson who at that time was the world champion and one of the greatest ambassadors to the sport of surfing.

The film was innovative, it was artistic, and it was controversial. One of our main objectives was to leave the surfing world with a few things to think about. We were very critical about environmental issues, the way that the public was treating the ocean, and we also were critical about the way surfers were treated, particularly by surfing contests and advertisers who would use surfers to their own advantage and not really compensate them in any way. The film was also the first, or one of the first surfing films to pay surfers, not only to be in it, but also gave surfers 15 percent of the profits of the film. The surfer profit was actually divided in a very carefully orchestrated formula between the 60 surfers who were in the movie. Every year, each one of those surfers would get a check in the mail for his or her participation. That was new. Other surfing movies had paid surfers in the past (including our films), but this is the first time that every surfer who was in the film got a paycheck in relationship to the number of seconds that he or she was on screen.

Our criticism of surfing contests, for example, produced quite a reaction at the Huntington Beach Surfing Championship and prompted Huntington to begin paying surfers prize money. Our actions were well appreciated by the surfers and gave them the opportunity to ask other surf film producers to at least help them out in some way during the production of a film.

You ended up releasing several editions of that film over the years and its popularity has achieved almost cult status. Was it your best surf themed film? ⟩⟩ Sure, I think *Five Summer Stories* was our best

surfing film. It was insightful, interesting, entertaining, accurate and provided the audience with a new way technically to look at surfing. The stories were good and contained interesting, real-life characters – all non-fiction. The photography was unique, particularly the slow motion and close-up photography. Also, the music and the sound reproduction were both very high quality. Regarding the film's music, we were fortunate to have a friendship with Bruce Johnston, who is in the *Beach Boys* and who also is a surfer. We'd announced the fact that we were going to make *Five Summer Stories* as our last surfing film, in fact it was subtitled *The Last Surfing Movie*, kind of as a takeoff on *The Last Picture Show*. When Bruce heard about the film coming out he talked to the other *Beach Boys* and offered us their entire library if we wanted to use it. That was incredible. Even though some of the early *Beach Boys'* hits were exploitative of the surfing genre, the music that the *Beach Boys* were doing in the 1970s was just as creative and more interesting than their early work. It was a wonderful opportunity to use their brilliant music particularly from the Surf's Up album, the songs *Feel Flows* and *Surf's Up*, and from the *Holland* album, the song *Sail On Sailor*. Beautiful music.

The success of the film, as well as the success of our previous surfing films and the films that we were making for Hollywood, really built a sturdy foundation for our company, benefiting us in a number of ways. Not only do we have no debt and no big concerns from a financial standpoint, we also own all of our own film equipment free and clear. We can make sure it's the finest equipment and is maintained in the very, very best manner so that when we go out and shoot, we can rely on the lenses and the cameras to be performing to an A-plus level. That's why in our IMAX theatre films, all of the scenes are absolutely crystal-sharp and steady. Quality of the image on screen is hugely important to us, and we're able to achieve that because of the strong foundation that the surf films built for our company.

By the early 1970s, you had widened your horizons beyond the surf genre to include work for mainstream Hollywood. How did you make that connection, and what kind of work did Hollywood push your way? ⟩⟩ Beginning in 1970, Jim and I decided to get more involved with Hollywood film productions. We began shooting *Jonathan Livingston Seagull*, the Paramount feature film from Richard Bach's

321

AWARDS 1976 (TO FLY!): Best Film of the Decade Award - The Information Film Producers of America ; Golden Eagle - Cine Golden Eagle; Best Film Award and Special Jury Award - International Film Festival, Chicago; First Place - Berlin Inforfilm Festival; Grand Place - Bicentennial Festival of Films on Aeronautics and Space; ⟩⟩

Q+A ⟩⟩

FILMS I AWARDS I HONORS

book, which was the biggest selling book of the year. Our company was in charge of shooting all the scenes of seagulls in the air while Jack Couffer was the Director of Photography and was responsible for shooting all the beautiful images of the seagulls walking on the ground and talking to one another. The reason that Jim and I wanted to do films outside of surfing was that we felt that we'd done, by 1970, just about everything that we possibly could do. Any future films would be going over the same ground again. We were more interested in challenging our artistic abilities with new subjects and new ways to express ourselves in film. Working with Hollywood was a good way to learn and a great way to challenge ourselves.

Big Wednesday came along in 1978 as Hollywood's attempt to capture the surf lifestyle in an authentic script instead of the usual Gidget garbage. How did you get involved? »Big Wednesday, which we photographed in 1977 and 1978, was a film with Warner Bros. and John Milius as the director and writer. Another surfer, Denny Auberg was John's co-writer. I was asked to produce and direct all of the surfing sequences, which were sprinkled throughout the screenplay. So for over a year, I drove back and forth, once or twice a week, to Hollywood to have meetings with John Milius and his A-Team Production Company to plan and shoot the surfing sequences. Milius brought a lot to the project, including interesting ways to compose the surfing shots and together we designed the storyboards for each of the surfing sequences.

What was John Milius like to work with? »John was really a lot of fun to work with because he is such an encyclopedia of historical knowledge. He loves to expound with story after story about Teddy Roosevelt and the Roughriders, Jack London, and stories about filmmakers and films. Through the production, John and I became good friends. John Milius, at the time, was coming off of a big success with *The Wind and the Lion*, (starring Sean Connery, Candice Bergen, and Brian Keith), which was a beautifully written film with brilliant cinematography, great editing and a beautiful score by Jerry Goldsmith. Because of that, John had quite a bit of clout with the Warner Bros. studio, so when I needed to stay in Hawaii for an extra five or six weeks to get the best footage possible, he was able to

push the issue with Warners to get their approval. This allowed us to jointly make the surfing sequences better than they were budgeted to be and better than the studio would have normally approved.

I have to say that John really stuck by the project even though he was so heavily involved with other productions that were ongoing with his production company, including Steven Spielberg's film, *1941*, which was going into production at A-Team about the same time. John's a great guy and a brilliant writer.

Were you given carte blanche to create the live surf scenes using real professional surfers? »We used real surfers to act as stunt doubles, but John did find main characters that actually had surfing experience. Jan-Michael Vincent and William Katt were good surfers and became cast in the leading roles. Gary Busey, who played the third main character, was from Oklahoma and had never touched a surfboard in his life. We sent him more or less to surfing school for about two weeks and then took him to El Salvador when we were shooting for seven weeks down there. He was a total trooper. He tried his hardest to learn to paddle, catch waves, stand up, ride to shore, just so we could intercut his face with the backgrounds and the stunt double work, which was being done with surfers who looked like him. The surfers that actually rode the biggest waves were: Bill Hamilton, Jay Riddle and Jackie Dunn rode for Jan Michael Vincent. Bill Hamilton, who is one of my favorite people in the world, traveled with us everywhere, to El Salvador, to The Ranch, and to Hawaii. He surfed brilliantly in all locations. To stunt double for Billy Katt was Peter Townsend who looked almost identical to Bill Katt and was just a perfect stunt double. Doubling for Gary Busey was Ian Cairns. All of these surfers were completely enjoyable to work with and we really bonded over the 20 weeks we had to shoot all of the sequences for the film.

Getting the shots, however, was nothing but a lot of trouble. In order to get the coverage, I had to have a group of photographers, some of whom, frankly, just did not match up to the job. The guys who really came through for the production and who shot 95 percent of the surfing shots used in the film were five: George Greenough, who shot brilliantly from the water; Spyder Wills who shoots with a telephoto lens better than anyone else in the world; and Bud Browne

AWARDS 1976 (TO FLY!): Special Jury Award - Festival of the Americas; Chris Bronze Plaque Award - The Columbus International Film and Video Festival.
NOTE: To Fly! was screened at President Reagan's 1981 Inauguration Ceremonies and later presented as a gift to the Soviet Union's General Secretary Gorbachev. »

who can get the camera inside the curl deeper and in the impact zone better than anyone else alive; and Jack Willoughby and Roger Brown, each who shot brilliantly from the helicopter.

The film followed the lives of three surfers from high school to Vietnam and into adulthood culminating in the legendary big surf conditions that reunited them after difficult separations and personal failures. It was simultaneously rowdy and immature yet sensitive and hopeful. Did it capture the soul of surfing as you might have written it? »I loved the script and particularly loved the idea of the four periods of growth and maturity of each character. There were sentimental moments which may have been too exaggerated, which is kind of a Milius trademark, and which became heavily scrutinized by film critics across the country. For me, the film captured the freshness and spontaneity of the early 1960s surfing scene. It had that naive, "we will live forever" attitude, which I think surfers believed in the '60s. *Big Wednesday* premiered in May 1978. It was two years after Jim's death and, for me, it was kind of a sentimental reflection on the time that Jim and I spent together shooting surfing in the 1960s and the early 1970s. It gave me a chance to say goodbye to surfing films and to Jim.

Enter the world of IMAX with *To Fly!* How did that film evolve? »In 1974, the Smithsonian Institution's National Air and Space Museum called us to say they were building a new museum in Washington D.C. on the mall. They were putting an IMAX theatre into the museum and wondering if we were interested in producing and directing a film for that theater. In our view, the Smithsonian called us because we had co-photographed *Jonathan Livingston Seagull*, which earned an Academy Award nomination for Best Photography. We also just worked on the aerial photography for *The Towering Inferno*, which in 1973 was the biggest box office hit of the year. So they came to us because of our experience with shooting from helicopters and airplanes. We had heard about the IMAX film format through technical journals, which we read with relish every month and were delighted to be able to be involved in an IMAX theatre film.

The Smithsonian and their consultants, Francis Thompson, Inc., had written a short treatment for the

film which Jim and I read and felt was workable, but not perfect. We took the treatment and shaped it into a chronological story that contained humor, comical fictitious characters, and mixed it with a little bit of flight history. At that time, the director of the Air and

Space Museum, Astronaut Mike Collins, told me that even though the film was to premiere in America's Bicentennial Year of 1976, celebrating 200 years of American government, he did not want the film to be a historical journey through flight with dates and facts and people like the Wright Brothers and Charles Lindbergh. He said to us, "I have plenty of historical plaques on the wall of my museum; please give me a film that entertains, and allows the audience to be amazed by flight."

We took that suggestion and ran with it. It fit perfectly with the way that we had been making movies all through our surfing years: enthrall an audience with great entertainment and photography, inventive music, and images the audience had never seen before. Put the audience through the experience of flying. Give the audience the thrill of taking to the air.

So for the next two years, Jim and I devoted ourselves, and our miniscule team to *To Fly!* Cindy

THE MAGIC ROLLING BOARD, 1976, Director/Producer | AWARDS 1976: Grand Prize - La Jolla Film Festival; Grand Prize - Sunset Film Festival; AWARDS 1976 (THE MAGIC ROLLING BOARD): Gold Medal - Festival of Americas; Golden Eagle - The Cine Golden Eagle Film and Video Competition »   Q+A »

FILMS I AWARDS I HONORS

1. Actress Lee Purcell and actor Jan Michael-Vincent greet Greg, during a scripted party scene filmed for *Big Wednesday*, 1978
2. Jim Freeman and Greg on location, 1974

Huston, who was Jim's girlfriend, acted as the camera assistant; Barbara Smith, who was my girlfriend, became the production assistant, craft service specialist, still photographer and behind the scenes cinematographer; Bill Bennett came along as a production manager with Jeff Blyth, who was the unit production manager; Brad Ohlund, was the second assistant camera-person; and Phil Schwartz was our first assistant camera person. That was our team. We traveled for a period of about 20 weeks to shoot *To Fly!*

When Jim and I had the film completed, I remember us both sitting on the curb, outside the Todd-AO mixing facility in downtown Hollywood, at eight o'clock on a summer's evening. We talked endlessly about what we should do after this IMAX theatre film was released. We talked about the string of television commercials that we were contracted to do for Kodak and how exciting they were. We talked about ideas that we had for feature films, even films in a revolutionary, new 3D technique called Stereovision. We were swimming with ideas of what to do with our future. In one week we were set to premiere *To Fly!*,

probably the best film that we'd worked on together in our 11 years as partners.

As Jim left for Bishop, California to scout locations for the Kodak commercials, I flew back to Washington D.C. to run the film and check the soundtrack one last time before the major premiere. With me were Jim's mother and his sister, my parents, Jim's girlfriend, my girlfriend, our helicopter pilot and several other friends. We were all there to celebrate this new episode in our life, a new direction for us in the IMAX theatre format. On our second day in Washington I got a telephone call from Bill Bennett, who was there in Bishop. Jim had crashed in a helicopter with three other people, high in the mountains while scouting for those locations that we had planned to film in the coming week. Jim and the agency producer were killed and the pilot and the agency co-producer were able to crawl away from the helicopter before it burned.

I thought my life had ended too. It took me weeks before I could really even talk about the tragedy and it took me months before I even cared to face work. With the strength of my girlfriend Barbara, who is now my wife, and with the help of close friends like Bill Bennett, and Cindy, Jim's girlfriend, I was able to get through the pain of the loss and continue to make films. After his death, I dedicated myself to creating films in Jim's

SKYRIDERS, 1976, Directed and photographed the action sequences | BIG WEDNESDAY, 1978, Producer of the surfing sequences
THE SHINING, 1979, Directed and photographed the American scenes including the opening sequence | KOYAANISQUATSI, 1982, Second Unit Aerial Photography »

honor and I decided to leave his name, the Freeman name, on our company as a tribute to his artistry and his contribution to what our company had become. I often reflect on what a loss Jim's death has been and wonder what brilliance and artistry he would have brought to our films had he lived.

To Fly! set a few box office marks along the way. » Thankfully, *To Fly!*, the final film that Jim worked on, became an enormous critical and financial hit. At the Smithsonian, the first year running, over a million people saw it in one theater alone. It was producing

2

huge attendance numbers and ran 14 times per day. Through that entire year, the theater was filled to over 80 percent capacity. After the end of that year, it is said that every museum in the world wanted an IMAX theatre because of the potential for profit and good educational communication, because of the huge success of *To Fly!* Today, 25 years after the premiere, *To Fly!* has been seen by over 15 million people at the Smithsonian Institution alone and has grossed over $110 million worldwide. It has been said that in all its versions, 15/70, 35mm, 16mm, and videocassette, as well as its television exposure, *To Fly!* has been seen by over 100 million people. Up until this past month, when *Everest* overtook *To Fly!* in box office receipts, *To Fly!* has been the highest grossing documentary film of all time.

What brought you into Kubrick's production of *The Shining* and what was he like to work with? » In 1975, Jim and I worked for Twentieth Century Fox on the production of *Skyriders*. We directed and shot hang gliding and stunt sequences in Greece for this feature film with James Coburn and Robert Culp. My assistant director for that feature film was an Englishman named Brian Cooke. Brian, Jim and I worked together closely with our 25-person second unit crew for over nine weeks in Greece under very, very trying conditions. I'd known that Brian was also the assistant director for Stanley Kubrick on many of Kubrick's films, but in the last week of shooting in Greece, Brian came to me and asked if I'd mind if he told Stanley Kubrick about us and wondered if we were interested in working on Kubrick's next film. I was knocked over because Kubrick was my favorite feature film director. *A Clockwork Orange* and *2001: A Space Odyssey* were two of my favorite movies and *Barry Lyndon*, I felt, was a photographic masterpiece. I, of course, said that I'd love to be able to contribute in any way that I possibly could.

Well, about a year and a half later, after Jim had been killed in the helicopter crash, one afternoon our company secretary called up to me and said that a man by the name of Stanley Kubrick was on the phone and wondered if I wanted to talk to him. I thought it was probably a joke, that it was some friend of mine calling. I never imagined it was really Stanley Kubrick. But it was. Evidently he was the kind of man who would make all of his own calls, night or day, and who produced his films with a very small crew, with very little overhead but worked exceedingly hard and long to make the films as brilliant and innovative as possible. He must have liked what I said. In fact, he told Brian that he thought that I sounded humble and well versed in cinema and the technical side of filmmaking and that he wanted me to be the second unit director and cinematographer for all of the scenes that would be shot on *The Shining* outside of London. Well, for me, this was a tremendous opportunity because I not only would be working with one of my filmmaking idols, but I would be working with him directly, and be able to learn from him while I worked.

The actual production was even better than I expected. Our first assignment was to try to develop the opening of the film, which was to establish Jack Nicholson and his family driving in a yellow

325

THE WONDERS OF CHINA, 1982 | Cinematographer/Producer, A Circle Vision Feature | FLYERS, 1982, Producer
BEHOLD HAWAII, 1983, Director/Producer/Cinematographer | SPEED, 1984, Director/Producer »

Q+A »

FILMS | AWARDS | HONORS

Volkswagen Bug through the mountains up to the Overlook Hotel. We decided to shoot in Glacier National Park and went there in September for a two-week shoot. Once a week, I sent the raw footage, undeveloped, to the Technicolor Lab in London where Kubrick would

Filming first IMAX Theatre feature, *To Fly!*, 1976

have it processed and then he would look at the work print of every foot of film that we shot. After one week, he called me and complimented me and said he loved the footage, he loved the photographic techniques that we were utilizing, including the helicopter mount where you looked forward from the helicopter rather than out the door with a side view and that he felt that these images would match really beautifully with the Steadicam, forward moving shots that he was using elsewhere in the film.

Kubrick was shooting the film in London on incredibly complex and enormous sets depicting the expansive Overlook Hotel, all built on sound stages in Borehamwood, England. It was the Elstree Studios Lot and Kubrick had essentially taken over the entire studio. He planned to shoot there for more than a year. He was, at that point, probably three months into shooting in England. Getting these dailies showing actual outdoor locations was probably a breath of fresh air for Kubrick and for his technical staff. He

called me after one week, and then again after one and a half weeks, and then two weeks. I kept begging him for more time because the location was absolutely stunning but the lighting wasn't good enough. Kubrick trusted me, and he allowed us to stay a third week, then a fourth. On our final day in the fourth week we got the day I had been waiting for.

We'd practiced at least 20 times a very complicated one and a half minute shot from the helicopter where the helicopter comes over a ridge and then down a mountain, the Volkswagen being almost a speck on the horizon. The helicopter then flies up quickly behind the Volkswagen, tucking in behind it. As the Volkswagen makes a right-hand turn on a curve in the road, the helicopter continues out over the lake. As you take in the beautiful scenery, you've almost completely forgotten about the Volkswagen, when it comes into view suddenly from behind some trees. This shot required perfect second-by-second timing, beautiful sunrise lighting, and glassy conditions on the lake. We finally achieved it on the last day of the last week at 10 minutes after sunrise. The lake was glassy smooth and the fall colors were turning all of the aspen and maple trees in the region a bright yellow. It was probably the single most beautiful motion picture shot that I had ever done in my life. When Kubrick saw it, he was ecstatic. He called me and wanted me to rush over to England to see the shot and to meet the rest of the crew, Jack Nicholson, Shelley Duvall, legendary cinematographer John Alcott and to bask in the glory of what we had done in Glacier National Park.

So I did that and had a wonderful time over a two-week period, being with Kubrick, having lunch and having dinner with him almost daily, spending 12-to-14 hours a day on the set with him and getting to know the way that he made films. I've often said that I probably learned more in the year that I worked on *The Shining* than I learned in any five years through the rest of my career. One thing most people forget about Kubrick is his terrific sense of humor. He loved to laugh as much as he loved filmmaking. For a filmmaker who used words so sparingly in his films (like *2001: A Space Odyssey*), words came very easily and quickly to him, revealing his active, alert mind. It was fun to be around him and conversation with him was delightful. Stanley was intensely interested in nearly everything. Because I knew filmmaking, we talked about emerging film systems, like IMAX, film emulsions, lenses that we each

DANCE OF LIFE, 1984, Director/Producer/Cinematographer | **ISLAND CHILD**, 1986, Director/Producer/Cinematographer
TIME CONCERTO, 1988, Producer | **TO THE LIMIT**, 1989, Director/Producer/Cinematographer »

FILMS | AWARDS | HONORS

owned, recent films we'd seen, and what was going on in Hollywood. Our love of film was what we shared throughout our entire association.

Months after I finished working on *The Shining* I got a call from his executive producer, Kubrick's brother-in-law Jan Harlan, who said that Stanley wanted to give me more credit on the film than I'd requested. He loved the work I did for him and he wanted to give me a credit at both the beginning and ending of the film. I was astonished. In Hollywood, it's common to fight for your credit when you negotiate your deal beforehand. Then, later, you have to fight when the producer or director wants to rob you of your credit so it'll appear as if he's done everything with no one else's help. Here, the world's most famous director wanted me to have an additional credit, over and above what my contract called for. I was honored and humbled by his generosity. (This was also from a director who had conducted a very public fight with Douglas Trumbull, because Kubrick felt that Trumbull was over-promoting and stretching his credit on *2001: A Space Odyssey*.) He did this but it sounds petty!

I was very sad when he died at age 70 a couple of years ago. A month after his death, I attended a "Tribute to Kubrick" at the Director's Guild Theatre in Hollywood. As part of the tribute, they showed a collection of classic Kubrick moments in film. Our long and beautiful helicopter shot for *The Shining* was the first image they showed. It made me feel so fortunate to have worked with him. Kubrick's films and personality were so unusual, outstanding and thought provoking that they caused everyone to re-evaluate – to search further within themselves and to improve. You could not meet him, even casually, without sharing at least one laugh and without him providing one remarkably insightful comment. What set him apart was that he was alive with and tuned in to all possibilities. Working with him was an exploration through a forest of ideas and visions, always seeking a solution that was not only best, but also most original. Millions of fans, including me, miss him and his inventive films.

How about Jack Nicholson? I first met Nicholson in London on a Saturday night. It was 8 p.m. on the studio sound stage. The film crew had just finished 28 takes of a scene of Nicholson removing a vacuum tube from the Overlook Hotel's two-way radio. In the film, Nicholson takes the tube out so that Shelley Duvall, Mrs. Jack

Torrance, can't call for help when Jack becomes a little deranged. After 28 takes and it was only a close up of Nicholson's hand. Jack kept making jokes about how Stanley should use a "hand double" and Jack could go out on his Saturday night date, as he had planned. Stanley said, "No, the audience would notice – and, anyway, only you, Jack, could remove a tube so villainously." Then, they'd all laugh.

Actually, Stanley did not want to pay a hand double (he was a very frugal filmmaker), and felt that if he could stay late, Jack could too. Both Jack and Stanley seemed very respectful of each other, knowing that they each wanted to push the limits on his craft in sometimes invisible or less-than-obvious ways. Recently, I was pleased to notice that Nicholson's *The Shining* performance was included in a film magazine's list of the "50 Best, but Un-Awarded Performances" of 100 years of cinema history, no doubt because of the hand close-up shot. (laughing)

Three months later, on my second visit to *The Shining* stage in London, Nicholson immediately asked me about all the up-to-date news about the Lakers, the football teams and whatever else I knew about Hollywood films. He was hungry for any news from America. The crew had been isolated, pre-CNN, for half-a-year. It was great fun talking with Nicholson, Shelley Duvall and Danny Lloyd, who was playing the boy with "the shining." We all knew we were working with a master. It was long, difficult work, but we all recognized that we could learn something valuable from the experience and from Kubrick, and that the film would be beautiful and have a lasting quality.

Other films like *Jonathan Livingston Seagull* and *Towering Inferno* kept your hand in Hollywood films. Did you like that work as much as the documentary films? The first Hollywood film that we became involved with was in 1967 just after Jim and I had taken a three-week, nine city tour of the East coast showing our film, *Free and Easy*, a 16mm, 90-minute surfing documentary featuring four main characters and their surfing exploits on three islands in Hawaii and in California. Right after we got back from that trip, we had a call from the offices of the head of production at Twentieth Century Fox, Richard Zanuck. He was in charge of a production called *The Sweet Ride*. The screenwriter had written in several short surfing sequences that would be taking place somewhere near the Malibu, Southern California area. They'd seen our film, *Free and Easy*, when it was showing in Santa Monica earlier in the summer and they felt that we would be the best two people to manage, direct and shoot the surfing sequences of about five minutes total for their feature film.

We discussed the show with the production manager, a wonderful man of great experience, Chico Day. Chico was the brother of the famous Hollywood actor, Gilbert Roland, and had run the production on probably over 100 big Hollywood movies and so Chico was very well known. He wanted to make sure the experience that we'd have with the Hollywood studios would be a pleasant one for us. We drove up to Hollywood, which was always an ordeal because it was at least an hour and a half on the road and the traffic was horrendous to the Twentieth Century Fox Studios in Century City.

We went to the production offices, in this incredibly beautiful old Hollywood studio and were ushered into Zanuck's main office. He was sitting behind an enormous desk, a small man, probably five-foot-five, but with a tremendous amount of confidence because his father, Darryl Zanuck was one of the founders of the studio. To say the least, we were very intimidated by the surroundings but Chico tried to make us feel comfortable. Chico ran the meeting and explained what the film was and what they wanted us to do and they asked how much we would charge for the two to three week job. Without flinching, because Jim had obviously prepared for this question before we went to Hollywood, Freeman said, "$7,500." Now, $7,500 at that time was like $750,000 today. In other words, this would have been more than 10 times what we'd ever made for that period of time working as hard as we'd been working over the past seven or eight years.

Richard Zanuck cleared his throat and said, "$7,500?" And Chico gave us kind of a sharp look like, gee, maybe you're reaching too far. But Freeman said, "Yes, $7,500. We feel that we can do the best job of anyone and we also feel that we'll end up saving you at least $7,500 because we'll do everything right the first time." Zanuck shuffled around papers on his desk and he looked up at us and said, "Boys, I just don't think we have the budget for that kind of expenditure. Thank you very much for driving all the way up here, it's been pleasant meeting you, and I hope we can work together on some future project, but thank you."

Well, Jim and I were completely devastated because we'd really needed the $7,500 and we thought that we'd completely blown it with Zanuck. We left the office not really knowing what else to do. Just as we made it to our car in the parking lot down below Zanuck's third-story office, Chico came running from the building yelling at us to wait. When he came up, he said, with a big grin on his face: "Nice work, guys. I've never seen anyone get the best of Zanuck before, but he's gone for it. After you left, he said, well, I like those guys. They stick to their guns. I think they can save us at least what we're going to pay them. Chico, go tell them they have the job."

So that was our first experience with the big Hollywood studios. What made the story even more fun is that we talked Chico and his staff into renting the Hollister Ranch, particularly "Rights and Lefts" which is a beautiful peak wave surfing spot. The Hollister Ranch is a private community and to be able to get in there to surf is next to impossible. It has some of the best waves in California. Jim and I and the rest of the surfers had a great time. I have to say that the people at Twentieth Century Fox, particularly Chico Day, were enormously helpful and professional and taught the two of us a lot about the way movies are made. Though the Hollywood films continued to lure us away from Laguna Beach, our real heart was in making documentary films about subjects that we cared about. On each one of the Hollywood shows, we would learn many new things, both technically and artistically. It was clear that Jim and I really wanted to make films that would treat the audience to real experiences that were much more involving than the artificial and phony Hollywood moments. So, when IMAX opportunities came knocking and the Smithsonian decided that they wanted us to make a film in this large format, our sights were set.

IMAX theatre films continued to beckon and became your personal arena of excellence. Tell us about what makes an IMAX film special. It's reality filmmaking to the extreme! As a filmmaker, to be able to see your images big, beautiful and crystal clear is very, very rewarding. I wouldn't want to film in any other format. Also, it's about the positive messages that IMAX theatre films contain. Because this genre grew up in the museum world, our films are designed for families who are spending the day together wanting to have fun and to learn something along the way. It's

AWARDS: (At Sea): Alfred Thayer Mayan Award - Navy League; Bronze Plaque Award - Columbus International Film & Video Festival; Gold Award - Worldfest Houston
YAMPA – THE UNTAMED RIVER | Producer/Cinematographer »

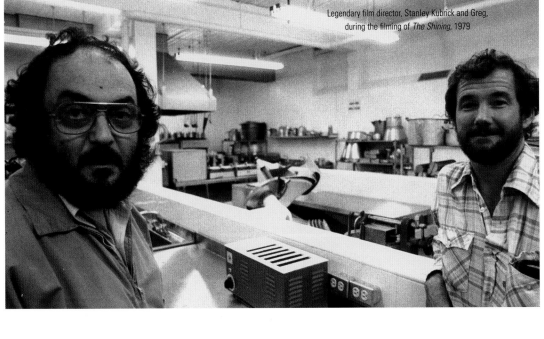

Legendary film director, Stanley Kubrick and Greg, during the filming of *The Shining*, 1979

a real pleasure to work in a format that is so positive. These big, beautiful images are educational and inspirational tools. Our world is an amazing place and this format reveals that like no other can.

How did the format originate? »The format began because of a need at a World's Fair. In the late '60s, World's Fairs were the rage and every pavilion tried to develop a new way to entertain and educate the audience. One of the main factors was that perhaps as many as 3,000 people would go through a pavilion every hour over the 16 hours a day. Film formats became an important way to communicate and entertain because they are repeatable and require only a small staff to run 20-to-40 times a day. So, the World's Fairs in New York in 1964 and Montreal in 1967 had all kinds of lavish and creative film formats utilizing many screens, and formats like CircleVision and 3D that gave the audience a completely new way to experience film. One of the filmmakers who had become expert in making these films was Graeme Ferguson, a Canadian who had a big hit at the Montreal Fair. He was then asked to produce an unusual film for a 1970 Fair in Japan. He sold to the Japanese the idea that it would be a one-film, huge-format experience, projected onto a screen six-to-sever stories tall and over 100-feet wide. In order to fill this large screen with an image of clarity, sharpness and steadiness, a complete new projector and camera would have to be constructed. Bill Shaw,

a bicycle maker from Canada, was chosen to build this new projector. That's the way IMAX was initially started.

By 1974, when Jim and I got the call from the Smithsonian, there were three theaters in existence. One of those theaters was a dome theater in San Diego and the other two were flat-screen theaters, one in Toronto and one in Spokane. When we started *To Fly!* in 1974, there was only one camera available. We were concerned that if that camera broke, both our film and another IMAX Theatre film being produced for the Bicentennial, *American Moments* would be compromised. *American Moments*, produced by Francis Thompson Inc., was to be part of Philadelphia's Bicentennial celebration. It would premiere in an enormous 800-seat IMAX theatre, which was destined to be torn down after one year. Jim went to Canada and discussed the camera situation with Graeme Ferguson and Bill Shaw and their partner, Robert Kerr. Jim proposed to them to produce three new cameras with a list of improvements based on our experience owning and operating various other cameras. Six months later, IMAX Corporation delivered three cameras, which we and the Philadelphia film used for the next year and a half of production.

Producing and directing *To Fly!* was a new and interesting experience for Jim and me. We were given such a small budget ($590,000) and told that we couldn't go over that budget by even a dime. We carefully constructed a script and storyboard and set out to

329

THE DISCOVERERS, 1993 | Director/Producer/Cinematographer, AWARDS (The Discoverers): Golden Eagle - Cine Golden Eagle; Gold Award - US International Film and Video Festival | HOMELAND, 1995 | Executive Producer

Q+A »

1. Water angle view from the IMAX camera from *The Living Sea,* 1995
2. Chasing tornadoes in 1994's *Storm Chaser*

shoot only the scenes that related exactly to what we had drawn in the storyboard, the template for the film. It worked, because the script that we had written was tight, comprehensible, filled with exciting moments and new camera tricks that would engage the audience, and had a style similar to the carefree surfing films that Jim and I had created over the previous 10 years. Our style made *To Fly!* a film that was different from any other film released at that time. There were at least 10 significant films released as a tribute to the Bicentennial, each having a budget far surpassing our $590,000.

To Fly! was completely different than any of the other IMAX theatre films that we would ever produce.

In 1976, when the film premiered, very few people had seen an IMAX Theatre film before. So what we wanted to do is to give the audience a treat to the size, the clarity, the dimension of sound, the visceral involvement and thrilling moments that can be felt when watching this kind of a film. Only an IMAX theatre image, with clarity derived by shooting film that is 10-times larger per frame than conventional 35mm motion pictures, gives the audience a true-to-life, you-are-there sensation. Probably no other film format, except for Cinerama, which was a huge hit between 1953 and 1960, can deliver this kind of exceptional involvement in the image.

Jim and I designed ways to thrill the audience with the big screen, including having a train, an 1890 steam

THE LIVING SEA, 1995 | Director/Producer/Cinematographer **AWARDS** (The Living Sea): Academy Award Nomination for Best Documentary/Short Subject; Gold Award - Worldfest Houston; Gold Camera Award - US International Film and Video Festival; Certificate of Merit - International Film Festival, Chicago »

FILMS I AWARDS I HONORS

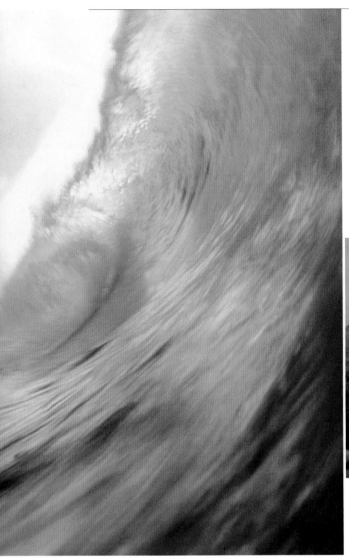

decided to make the film fun. We took what we knew from our surfing films and we wrote a film that revolved around characters who were fictitious, but humorous representations of real aviators in history.

From the first one and a half minutes of the film, the audience realized that this film was a comedy and that they didn't have to take notes. They could sit back and relax and laugh all the way through the film. Even though this movie was projected inside the hallowed halls of the Smithsonian Institution, we were creating a fun film, not a dry, historical drama. The film became

such a success that filmmakers like Keith Merrill who created the IMAX Theatre hit film, *Grand Canyon*, said that, "Without *To Fly!*, there may not have been an IMAX Theatre industry." I don't know if that is really true, but *To Fly!* certainly helped the industry grow.

locomotive, roar headlong, straight into the audience, landing in its lap! We filmed the scene by putting a mirror on the track, and shooting with two cameras into that mirror, as the train roared down the tracks and it plowed into the mirror, breaking it into a million pieces. With Nelson Tyler's help, we also built two new helicopter mounts, which would enable us to get steady and smooth helicopter shots from two positions. To get the audience in the air, we made mounts to go on to the 747, and also on to Art Scholl's chipmunk monoplane. In addition to the technical innovations, I think the central reason that the film became such an enormous hit was the charm of the storytelling. Because the audience would be in Washington D.C. on vacation, sitting in a theater, in a museum with a million facts, we

How many theaters are there? »Today there are 235 IMAX-branded theaters using IMAX projectors, and about 100 additional large format theaters utilizing other projectors. All the theatres are owned independently, by museums, cities, national governments, or private concerns.

How many IMAX features have you produced? »I have produced 29 large format films and directed 20.

What is your favorite? »Though I spend at least two years making each one of my films and therefore, have a deep affection for each, I think my mission-driven films, like *The Living Sea*, *Dolphins*, *Everest*, and *Coral Reef Adventure* are the most important to me. If I

STORMCHASERS, 1995 | Director/Producer/Cinematographer | AWARDS (Stormchasers) : Gold Award Worldfest Houston; Gold Camera Award - US International Film and Video Festival, SINGAPORE: A NEW DAY, 1996 | Executive Producer/ Cinematographer »

Q+A »

FILMS | AWARDS | HONORS

had my wishes, I would make no other films except conservation-based movies. Also deep in my heart is *To Fly!*, because it was the last film that Jim and I worked on together. In every frame of that film, I see the artistry and perseverance that was Jim Freeman.

You've been particularly adept at matching your films to what seems to be the perfect music soundtracks. How did you get Sting to do the score for *The Living Sea*?»When I was envisioning *The Living Sea* back in 1991, I felt that it would be important with this film to enlarge its mission and attract a greater audience. I felt that to do so, I'd need better, more emotive music. So early on, I wrote down a list of five composers whose music I felt I could use in significant ways artistically in the film. We sent letters to these five composers and within a three-week period, Sting's manager called us back, asking for more information.

You have to understand that people like Sting or Stevie Wonder or Paul Simon make more money per year than nearly anyone and that each of these artists is very protective of his compositions and the way that these important songs are used. Though it helps enlarge their fan-base amongst our audience members, they get involved because they believe in our film's mission.

Sting and his wife Trudie Styler are ardent conservationists and are very concerned about communicating conservation messages to the public. Because *The Living Sea* was all about understanding and protecting the ocean, our film was a good match for them. The song *Fragile*, moreover, was the ideal theme song because of its tone, sensitivity and poetry. At the time that we were making this film, using pop music in an IMAX Theatre film was nearly unheard of and basing a soundtrack completely on one composer, someone such as Sting, had never been done before. I had a tremendous amount of resistance from all kinds of people who were working on the film with me, and from theater managers who felt that a more traditional score, done by a Hollywood composer, would be more powerful and more significant. I didn't agree. I knew that we could take Sting's songs, such as *Fragile*, *One World* and *Why Should I Cry?* and make a very impactful soundtrack and film.

For one early test screening of *The Living Sea* in 35mm at our office, we inserted Sting's lyrical soundtrack in a very, very rough assembly. I gave our

staff a questionnaire after the screening and asked them whether they felt that Sting's music added or subtracted from the movie. Only one person agreed with me that the film was far better with Sting's music. So even though there was a tremendous resistance and we were trying something completely new in our industry, I felt convinced that it was the right way to go and pushed hard with my staff to make it happen. With persistence and artistry, particularly from Steve Judson and Alec Lorimore, we were able to raise the bar a bit higher.

I felt that because each one of us has heard *Fragile*, *One World* and *Why Should I Cry?* at least a thousand times on the radio and at home, these pop standards hold memories for each one of us that, in most cases, are extremely positive and emotional. Some songs are so memorable that people can recall exactly where they were when they first heard them. I felt in making *The Living Sea* that if we could tap into those emotional memories that each audience member has that we would have a film that meant more personally to the audience than just a documentary with yet another orchestra score. Filmmakers like Steven Spielberg have never taken this direction in their film scoring. They choose instead, to use a completely fresh and original symphonic score, and in the case of Spielberg, from composers like John Williams. From my position, I felt that we would derive a more emotional result by using melodies the audience had heard before. This was new ground for a documentary with a heavy narration component.

You continue in that vein with *Coral Reef Adventure* by incorporating the music of *Crosby, Stills and Nash*. How did you get them involved?»I knew that *Crosby, Stills & Nash* each have an affinity toward the ocean. Crosby and Nash are both surfers and sailors; Stills is a sailor and lives on an island. All three have a deep concern for the environment and for conservation of the ocean. I felt that their music, lifestyle and beliefs were completely in tune with *Coral Reef Adventure*.

I called David Crosby when he was on vacation in Hanalei, Hawaii, one of my favorite spots for surfing. He answered the phone at the house that he was renting on the beach, and I could hear a child playing in the background as we chatted. I told him about the film and he was enthusiastic about working on it with us, and then he had to interrupt and say, "You know, I

THE MAGIC OF FLIGHT, 1996 | Director/Producer/Cinematographer
ADVENTURERS IN WILD CALIFORNIA, 2000 | Director/Producer/Cinematographer »

FILMS | AWARDS | HONORS

promised my son who's now eight, that I'd take him out front and show him how to surf. So, I've gotta get going, but give me a call when I return to Santa Ynez and we can take this further." I thought at that point, boy, this guy's great. Not only is he talented, but also his priorities are right on.

The music by *Crosby, Stills & Nash* would do the same thing that Sting's music did for *The Living Sea* and that is, tap into the emotional well-spring of past memories for each member of the audience. Steve Judson, the editor and co-writer and I decided to use ten different songs from *CS&N* and base the score on those ten. Because each member of *CS&N* is a writer, instrumentalist, and vocalist, we also wanted to get the representation from each one of these enormous talents. I think their music lifts the film to a new level and will help bring our message of conservation and sensitivity to the ocean's needs to far greater numbers of people around the world.

There is an element of "extreme" in virtually all of your work from the ocean depths to subterranean caves to soaring flight sequences and even the summit of Mt. Everest. How did a surf guy carve so broad a niche? » I think my films are broad in their subject base, going from a quiet, artistic documentary of *Dance of Life*, all the way to a brash and comical *To Fly!*, to a sensitive four-character climbing allegory

in *Everest*, because surfing teaches you one thing – adaptability. You have to be adapting instantly to the conditions of the surf. I think because there are so many variables in surfing, a surfer has a much more fluid look at the world; things never seem rigid and confined, but expansive with all their possibilities. Every time a surfer looks out onto the ocean, the conditions are different; the wind is blowing one day, it is absolutely calm and glassy the next. One day the ocean is completely flat, no surf at all, and the next day the waves are thundering. Each wave a surfer rides is different by perhaps 50 percent from the wave that he just rode 10 minutes ago. With a mindset that conditions change instantly and that life's possibilities, whether they are themes for films or challenges to take on, are as wide, broad and diverse as the conditions of the surf, a person is ready for everything.

This is the way that I look at filmmaking. I never want to repeat myself. Like Stanley Kubrick, I'm most interested in working on new problems, not problems that I've solved in the past. This gives me an eagerness to take on the challenge of *Everest*, or the mission of communicating to the public the importance of coral reefs, or finding a way for a sky surfer to fall through the air with an 80-lb. IMAX camera strapped to his chest, when everyone has said it was impossible. It's my makeup to cherish the different, to relish the biggest and newest challenge. It's what keeps me alive.

Tell us about some of the challenges presented in getting an IMAX camera to the top of *Everest*, to nearly 400-ft. depths underwater, and hung on a stunt plane? » I approach every film I work on with fresh eyes, always looking for new ways to use the camera, new experiences for audiences, new stories to tell. So, in every film there are challenges that I can't wait to try to tackle. As a producer of the film, the toughest challenges are those where I feel a bit like a general sending my troops into battle. We hire the very best people to conduct specialty filmmaking, whether it's jumping out of airplanes with a camera strapped to your chest or sending a climbing team to the top of the tallest mountain in the world. Filming on Mt. Everest, of course, is fraught with danger, from killer altitudes to dangerous icy crevasses. Sadly the year we went was when so many died. Our film team became involved in the rescue efforts; it was just an awful, difficult time. We'd not yet tried to summit Everest with our camera when the tragedy on

EVEREST, 1998 | Director/Producer **AWARDS**: (Everest) WorldMedal - New York Festivals; Grand Prize for Best Film - La Géode Film Festival Award; Gold Angel Award - The International Angel Awards; Golden Eagle Award - Cine Golden Eagle; Platinum Best of Show (Documentary) - The Aurora Awards; »

the mountain occurred. I did not want to push our crew to take the risk of going back up. They'd been through so much already. But they wanted to go. In their minds, there was no other choice. It was an agonizing few days for me as we waited to hear their progress. When our team called me via satellite telephone from the top of Everest, they sounded upbeat and very happy. I felt like I was on the top of the world! These films that we work on add to my list of personal heroes. Our film crews are very smart, courageous, hard-working individuals. I get a lot of strength and inspiration from them.

You forged a successful alliance with Howard and Michele Hall. How did you hook up with them originally and what other films have you collaborated on together? »I first came to know Howard and Michele from their reputation. For many years I'd been a fan of Stan Waterman, an underwater documentary filmmaker. I'd heard that Stan had said, "Well, there's a new man on the scene and I feel that he's the best underwater cinematographer in the world, and that man is Howard Hall." I had either seen this quotation or heard it from Stan and I thought, boy, if I ever do an underwater film, I've gotta call this guy Howard Hall. At that time, I didn't even know where Howard Hall lived, and assumed that he was from the East Coast, where Stan Waterman resided. When we started to work on *The Living Sea*, I knew that I wanted to have some of the most beautiful underwater sequences that had ever been photographed for large format. So Alec Lorimore tracked down Howard Hall. Lo and behold, he lived in Del Mar, just 30 miles away, and was also a surfer. We got together and talked about the film, and Howard went with us to shoot the underwater sequences in Palau with Bob Cranston, Mark Thurlow and Brad Ohlund. We had that production divided up between my unit, which was the aerial and the ground unit and Howard Hall's unit, which was the underwater team. Each day after shooting, we'd get together at eight o'clock at night for a debriefing over dinner.

It was over those dinner meetings that I began to appreciate and deeply admire Howard Hall for his story telling ability, his humor, his humanity, and his ability to lead. Furthermore, he possesses one of the most important attributes, and a rare attribute once you've worked in Hollywood, that of honesty. He'll tell you his opinion directly and without spin, and he'll give you

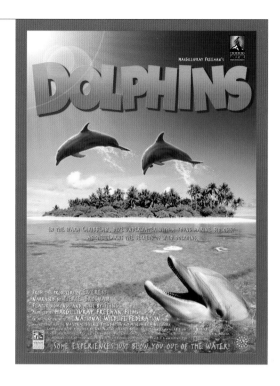

advice regardless of the consequences. Michele wasn't able to come on that trip with us because of our limited budget, but I got to know her very well and deeply respect her abilities after that trip. Somewhere around the latter part of the 1990s, I thought that it would be a good idea to make a movie about coral reefs and to have as the main characters, Howard and Michele Hall, a husband and wife team whose partnership is not only one of love, but one of mission. They're concerned about the oceans; they are dedicated to showing marine habitats and marine animal behaviors, and are true partners in adventure.

How did *Coral Reef Adventure* come to be? »In 1998, El Niño hit and almost 30 percent of the coral reefs in the world became bleached and many died. People concerned about the oceans were completely devastated by this news, including Howard, Michele, and I. I became determined to make a movie that would bring to the audience the news of these coral deaths and the work that had to be done to prevent future demise. It was at that time that I committed not only my resources but also the resources of my company to funding this conservation film, *Coral Reef Adventure*, and laid out the plan to photograph it over the next two-year period. At first, Howard and Michele were uncertain they should be on-camera in this film. They didn't want to be portrayed as heroes. It was my

AWARDS: (Everest) Chris Award - The Columbus International Film and Video Festival; Grand Award - The Worldfest Flagstaff; Best Picture, Best Cinematography and Best Score - Maximum Image Awards; IMAX Award for Outstanding Achievement and Excellence in Large Format Filmmaking » idea though that by looking at the reefs through their eyes and through their camera's lens, that the audience could not only see the love and concern that they share, but also see their dedication for saving the reefs of the world. After several months of persuasion, they agreed not only to photograph the film, but also to be, as you would say, reluctant stars of the movie. I think today, having gone through the experience with me that they feel completely comfortable with their role and are proud of the way that the film portrays them and their adventure across the South Pacific.

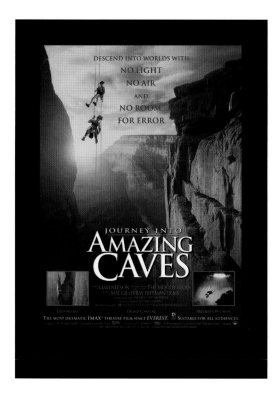

Why did you feel compelled to make an IMAX adventure film about coral reef systems? » The beauty of coral reefs is so unexpected and so spectacular, they're hard to resist. Diving among corals is like being in the middle of the greatest flower show ever – you're just floating in a blaze of color and your eyes are dazzled by shades of yellow and blue so brilliant it's hard to believe nature created them. Then, when you start to study the corals more deeply, more scientifically, and begin to understand how they make up this whole little village, this teeming community hidden from those of us who live up here on land, they really start to get fascinating. Once you learn that life in coral reefs is even more abundant than in the rain forest, you

also realize just how important they are to the planet.

So it was my own love of coral reefs that inspired me, but it was also my alarm at reading scientific reports about the decline of the reefs. I felt that this was something the public should know more about right now, because I know that once you fall in love with coral reefs you can't imagine losing them. This film also has become part of my personal mission, which is to impart my deep passion for the ocean and to convey the importance of the sea and all its creatures to everyone in the world.

As a surfer, naturalist and filmmaker, you've spent a lot of time in the ocean. How have you seen coral reefs change? » In just 20 years of diving, I've seen tremendous, devastating changes. I can recall shooting a diving sequence in Indonesia 20 years ago in a coral reef that was just bursting with health and life and now has been severely damaged by over-fishing, dynamite fishing and a local population explosion that has had tremendous impact on the reefs. I'm not the only one who has witnessed the change. Anyone who has been diving for the last five years has probably seen it. Not only are the corals themselves being bleached and dying, but bio-diversity has been visibly reduced. That's why I think we really have a responsibility to learn more about the reefs scientifically so we can learn how to stop the damage and how to live in balance with them. I feel very strongly that there are workable solutions out there. Human beings are unique on this planet in being able to intellectually adapt to different situations and to solve problems. We just need to apply our scientific reasoning to the issues surrounding the survival of reefs. We can find smarter ways to fish and get rid of our wastes and live with the ocean in better harmony. But first we have to learn more about the reefs and their life systems.

What does the IMAX theatre image bring to underwater photography that you just can't get from regular film or video? » An IMAX theatre film takes you there so you feel like you're under water with the divers. You can almost sense the pressure on your eardrums, and it's as if you're being cooled by the water. We've discovered that the IMAX image fools the brain so well that audiences watching our underwater movies actually experience a drop in body temperature – they literally cool off. That's part of the reason that we

DOLPHINS, 2000 | Director/Producer/Cinematographer **AWARDS** (Dolphins) : Academy Award nomination for Best Documentary Short Subject; International Documentary Association Award nomination for Best Documentary Short; Silver WorldMedal - New York Festivals; »

Q+A »

FILMS I AWARDS I HONORS

think films such as *The Living Sea* and *Dolphins* have been so popular. But it's more than refreshing – it's also awe-inspiring because it's a chance to really see and feel what the most expert divers see and feel, even if you don't know how to swim.

What's it like shooting an IMAX film underwater? »It's both a lot of fun and a tremendous challenge. When you're working with big cameras underwater, it's physically strenuous and you're always trying new things to balance yourself, to conserve air, to swim faster and that kind of challenge to your skills is always fun. Another wonderful aspect of shooting underwater is that you're always working in a team effort that leads to camaraderie and friendship that is unique and very emotional. For me, it's also a wonderful creative challenge – as I look for ways to meld innovative

photography with dramatic, human storytelling to give audiences an experience they can't get anywhere else. But the flipside to this is that there is always danger, there is always an edge to working underwater. It's not just the critters – the sharks and the stingers and biters – that are going to get you. There are also things that can go wrong with gear or ocean currents that are out of your control. It's not an ordinary job but the rewards are so tremendous.

Were you ever scared that Howard Hall was taking too great a risk doing deep dives with the IMAX camera for this film? »I felt very similar to the way I felt when we sent out our teams to the top of Mt. Everest – a little bit like a general sending my troops into battle. I knew the dangers were high and I also knew that the Halls wanted passionately to take the

AWARDS (Dolphins) : Gold Camera Award - US International Film and Video Festival; Special Gold Jury Award - 34th Worldfest Houston; Lifelong Learning Award - Giant Screen Theatre Association Achievement Awards; Grand Prix du Public - La Géode Film Festival Award »

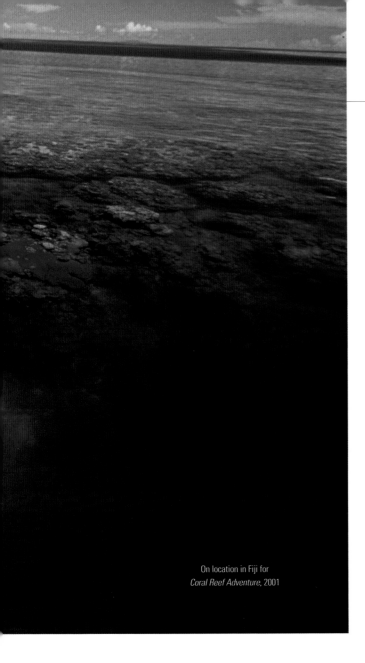

On location in Fiji for
Coral Reef Adventure, 2001

astronauts – very courageous, charismatic and deeply caring, with a tremendous amount of knowledge, a great couple to travel around the world with.

Tell us about your favorite moment during the making of *Coral Reef Adventure.*》Even though I didn't do them myself, the deep dives were probably the most exciting part for me personally. Frankly, I'll never do that kind of diving myself. Going 350-feet down is for the most expert of the experts. And it is so technically demanding and the consequences are so severe, I won't do it. But watching our team do it time after time with so much courage and curiosity was really an inspiration. They have a deep understanding of the ocean and themselves, which is something I admire.

What is your personal vision of the future for coral reefs?》I'm an optimist. I have heard some scientists talk about doomsday theories of where the human population expansion is leading us, but it's my nature to believe we can figure out ways to limit our impact and solve some of the problems we are creating in the ocean. I look at it as a challenge that has been set before us – a big one, but one I think we are up to. One thing that excites me is that we are increasingly finding out more and more reasons why we must save the reefs. For example, pharmaceutical companies are discovering that there are very exciting medicinal cures among the plants and life forms of the reefs and they've only just scratched the surface of what's there. This is an incredible living resource – and I think that as our desire to keep the reefs healthy grows, we'll also find new ways to save them.

You're obviously comfortable with the ocean, and the sea has been a predominant theme in your films from the outset, but you came to scuba diving a bit late in your career. How so?》I became certified as a scuba diver in 1983 in preparation for an underwater sequence that I was going to shoot and direct in Indonesia for an IMAX Theatre film called, *Island Child*. My wife, Barbara, had researched and had written the story of seven individual children, boys and girls, from the age of infancy through to 18 years, each child growing up in a different culture and region on one of Indonesia's 3,000 islands. One of those stories, the final episode, was about a boy named Sandy who was studying to be a marine biologist at the university in Ambon. To photograph Sandy's story, we would

risks, but I still felt responsible.

It was especially hard for me when Howard got the bends. We had a month break after that, it was real soul-searching time for all of us as we questioned whether to continue, especially knowing that if Howard got the bends a second time it could be considerably worse, causing paralysis or even death. We had long talks about whether he really wanted to do it again and the answer was always the same: he felt very strongly that he must.

I had to trust Howard's instincts. He is such an intelligent, self-aware man and he convinced me he could dive back down to those severe depths with a reasonable amount of safety. I just insisted that they stay in close touch with me and gave them all the logistical support that I could. In the end, Howard and Michele have become two of my personal heroes. They really remind me of the kind of people who become

337

JOURNEY INTO AMAZING CAVES, 2001 | Producer **AWARDS**: (Journey Into Amazing Caves) Best Soundtrack- Giant Screen Theatre Association Achievement Awards; Merit Award for Excellent Cinematography - International Wildlife Film Festival; Gold WorldMedal - New York Festivals; 》

Q+A 》

FILMS | AWARDS | HONORS

travel over a three-week period aboard a dive boat all through the Java and Banda Seas. These seas have the most diversity of species of any location in the world.

We had a six-person crew: me as director and co-cinematographer; Ron Taylor as co-cinematographer; Valerie Taylor, who would be on-camera talent and still photographer; Ron and Valerie's nephew, who would act as boat and equipment supervisor and would run the generator to power the underwater lights that I wanted to use; Brad Ohlund, who was the camera

to communicating the importance of all of Indonesia's 50 or more cultures, languages, and histories. The film was a tremendous success, showing to almost a million people per year at that theater.

I was privileged to see the rough-cut of *Coral Reef Adventure* last June when you were testing its appeal with trial audiences. You've since reacted to input. What changes did you feel were necessary and why?》With *Coral Reef Adventure*, we

1. Greg with kids, Shaun and Meghan, in Palau shooting *The Living Sea*, 1995 2. Greg and wife Barbara 3. MacGillivray still surfs his local home break over 45 years later, 2002

assistant; and Sandy, the on-camera talent.

We made two and three dives per day over a 21-day voyage and visited some of the most exquisitely beautiful coral reef locations anywhere in the world. We were able to shoot some of the most original underwater scenes yet to be done in the IMAX theatre format, and came away with an original sequence about this Indonesian student. The film was produced and shown for a five-year period at the Jakarta IMAX Theatre, the largest IMAX theatre in the world, which is located in a cultural park dedicated

did something that no other producer has done before. I decided that, because the issue of coral reef survival is so important to me and so important to many others, that we'd conduct almost a political campaign early, nearly nine months before the premiere of the film itself. We completed an early version of the movie and projected it in IMAX Theatres to more than 3,000 people in 10 locations in May and June 2002. The idea was to try to build support among all kinds of diverse elements: conservation groups, politicians, high school and college educators, civic leaders, corporate public relations departments who have an interest in conservation, and individual conservationists. Moreover, as a film artist, I would be able to show my film and get the audience's

AWARDS: (Journey Into Amazing Caves) Silver Screen Award - US International Film & Video Award; Silver Statuette - Telly Awards; Gold Special Jury Award - WorldFest-Houston; Intermedia-Globe Gold - World Media Festival 》

response to the film so that I could make improvements to it before it premiered. This is much like trying out a play off-Broadway before it hits the big-time. From a creative standpoint, I learned a tremendous amount from the screenings and we were able to change quite a few elements in the film in order to improve our communication, the story's entertainment value, and to deliver better science and information. This effort is not one to be taken lightly though, because it is costly and it takes an enormous amount of time. In my opinion, it's worth this expenditure ten times over because of the additional impact that the film will have when it premieres on February 14th, Valentine's Day, as our tribute to the reefs in 2003.

What's next on your film agenda? ❯❯ We're now finishing a film called, *Top Speed*, featuring Tim Allen and Marion Jones, which is a comedy for the IMAX Theatre market. We're beginning work on these films: *Greece - Secrets of the Past*, *Space Journey*, *Ocean Planet*, *The Nile*, *India*, and *Return to Everest*. All these films will take us out to about 2008. We've also just incorporated a not-for-profit side of our business to enable us to continue making educational conservation films, museum exhibits and books. It's called MacGillivray Freeman Films Educational Foundation.

What's your dream project? ❯❯ I'm living it! I have the most talented, efficient and enjoyable staff in the whole world – and a great family – and they all make me very happy!

Finally, I know you still surf regularly. Where's your favorite spot and do the locals really know who the old guy is sharing the break? ❯❯ I did a few smart things in my life. Number one, I followed my heart and became a filmmaker. Number two, I married my best friend, my wife Barbara. Three, I bought a house right at a surfing spot. This allows me even today to roll out of bed, walk to the window, check the surf, and if it's good, paddle out and get a quick surf in even before work. Moreover, my idea of a perfect day is to go to work, make films for eight hours, come home at 5:00 and sit on my surfboard riding waves until 8:00 at night, with the beautiful sunset sinking beyond Catalina Island and my son, daughter and wife sitting on surfboards next to me, kinda feeling the rhythms of the waves, talking to each other about the comedy of life and about what film we would see that night after dinner. That's my idea of the perfect day.

It just so happens that the surfing spot where I live, called North Reef, is a very, very mellow and friendly spot. There are about ten surfers who frequent the place and each one of us gets along exceptionally well, which is the way I feel it is in Laguna and should be everywhere. Because I ride an 8-ft. long board, I'm looked at as a geezer in the water, but it doesn't really bother me because others who are there are there to laugh with me. In fact, many of the surfers who share the break with me also eat breakfast with me at our favorite, small, funky health food sandwich store, Orange Inn, which is about 100 yards away from the surf break. Even at the age of 57, I still try to stay as active as possible, probably surfing 60 to 80 days a year, and skiing, playing volleyball, Frisbee golf or mountain biking 40 to 60 days out of the year. You can't get locked to a desk or even an editing machine. You have to keep moving both mentally and physically, keep pushing yourself in all kinds of different directions, taking off on waves of new styles and themes. I think that only in this way will you become original and creative in your artistry and enthusiastic about what you do. ■

Bob Hollis

FOUNDER OF OCEANIC, ANDREA DORIA PIONEER AND RESORT INNOVATOR

BY BRET GILLIAM

BOB HOLLIS
IS DECIDEDLY
OLD SCHOOL.
HE BUILT
UNDERWATER
CAMERA HOUSINGS
AND STROBES OUT OF
NECESSITY...

there were none in the mid-1950s that met his needs. He created the most popular underwater strobe of all time and over 30 years later scores of photographers are still using the Oceanic 2001 series without a glitch. »

He designs equipment for divers and tests it on himself. He builds the finest eco-resort in the middle of the remote Papua New Guinea jungle because he liked the diving so much on his frequent visits and thought the area deserved a proper facility. He buys a 120-ft. liveaboard vessel to add diversity to the resort without ever even seeing the ship himself firsthand. And he's spent more

time on the infamous wreck of the *Andrea Doria* than any diver in history.

He's a throwback to another era when his peers have long since retired or passed away. There are none of the original manufacturing founders left running diving companies except him and Oceanic has continued to set new marks for cutting edge products. It might have something to do with the fact that he still dives when most companies are run by tight-assed accountants whose hair only gets wet in the shower. And he lives life with a passionate wild abandon that belies turning the corner on his 70th birthday. Motorcycles, fine wine, semi-religious herbs, crazy diving: bring it on!

Bob is one of the great personalities of diving. Last to leave the party, first to explore the new dive site, and not afraid to step across the line into the wild side… with a deadpan sense of humor that catches a lot of folks off guard. In short, he's my kind of guy and we've spent more than a few rollicking nights out on the edge of the envelope over the years.

I met him back in the early 1970s when I took on the Oceanic line in my diving operation in the Virgin Islands. Bob was barely dry from saturating on the *Andrea Doria* in the most challenging exploration of the wreck ever attempted. His expedition stunned the industry and their adventures became the stuff of legend. He followed the first sat mission with another on an even larger scale in 1981 when he teamed up with *Blue Water, White Death's* Peter Gimbel and penetrated the interior to recover the First Class purser's safe and other key artifacts.

He released the best selling professional camera housing of all time called the Hydro-35 in the early 1970s. In 1975 he introduced the Oceanic 2001 strobe and just about every underwater pro photographer embraced it as the most durable product ever built. The list of shooters included Chris Newbert, Howard & Michele Hall, Carl Roessler, Marty Snyderman, Paul Tzimoulis, Jack McKenney, Doug Faulkner, Dave Doublilet, Al Giddings, Geri Murphy, Phillipe Cousteau, and countless others who made a living counting on Hollis's product in the field. The damn things were bulletproof. I even fended off a shark that bit one right off my camera housing metal arm and swam away with it. I recovered it six days later and it worked fine. I've still got it, teeth marks and all… and 22 more carefully hoarded in my equipment locker. No one ever built a better strobe.

At a time when most men his age are considering retirement, he turned his attention in a whole new direction and built the Tawali Resort in Milne Bay, Papua New Guinea. Following on that success, he has just introduced a new luxury liveaboard to the area called *Spirit Of Niugini* that started operations in March 2007. Because PNG is isolated and far flung between islands, he's now contemplating a seaplane to simplify access. Never mind that he's not a pilot. He'll probably build it himself anyway and like the Wright brothers, he'll figure out how to fly when he's finished.

I'm crazy enough to fly with him. Because I know if he built it, it will work. And, no matter what happens, we'll have a good time along the way. ∎

1

Diving wasn't a part of your youth. I understand that you didn't get into the sport until you dropped out of college and moved to the Bay area around San Francisco. Tell us about the early days for you. »I was born in Chico, (northern) California. Later I lived in Orland, 20 miles west until I moved to the bay area in 1955. It was a small town of 3,000 people with 400 students enrolled in high school. Growing up in a small town has merit, especially one that is close to creeks, rivers, mountains. You learn about the outdoors, hunting, fishing and girls.

I graduated from high school and got married two months later. I was working in the summer saving money for college and was injured on a job. We were harvesting English walnuts. To do this you use a tractor with a spool of cable with a hook on the end. You run out the cable, put the hook in major areas of the tree high up, the tractor makes the cable taut. I'm in the process of putting the hook in a crotch of the tree 14 feet up, and this clown is operating the tractor screws up and he yanks me out of the fucking tree. I fall face down onto a branch, knock my front teeth loose. The impact flips me over and I land flat on my back. Split two vertebrae, crushed a disk. I'd had enough of the farm life.

We were expecting a child in December. I'm 18, out of cash, without a job, a back injury, and a baby due. A good friend from school had moved to the bay area and said I could stay in his apartment if I came down. So I filled my tank with gas, packed a few shirts, jeans, and left Orland. My wife moved in with my parents while I looked for a job.

I landed a job working nights, got a little apartment in Point Richmond with a small view of the bay, moved Joann and our new daughter, Debbie, in and started attending classes at Contra Costa Junior College.

So what sparked your interest in diving? »During high school I came across *Diving to Adventure* by Hans Hass. The memories remained with me and one evening in the early part of 1956 I was reading *Popular Mechanics* and came across an article on how to build an underwater scooter. I was intrigued by the design and the thought of using a vehicle underwater. A couple of weeks later I was reading the "for sale" section in the newspaper and there was an ad selling a two-hose regulator, twin tanks and other equipment. I called this guy, set up a time to see the equipment. As it turned out, he had bought the equipment and never used it. It was a Healthways two-hose regulator, converted 38 cubic foot military cylinders with bushings to accept tank valves. So I bought the equipment.

He told me about Steele's Sporting Goods in Berkeley. I went there the next weekend, met Howard Steel, and proceeded to buy everything else… mask, fins, a wetsuit. Howard also told me that I should start by learning to free dive and then move onto SCUBA. I followed his advice and took up spearfishing and diving for abalone on the northern California coast. I was up there every weekend. There were damn few divers then but I met some others and developed some great friendships. Within a few months I started scuba diving in Monterey. I had yet to take any classes. One guy said, "Diving is easy; you need to see, breathe and move." How true it is.

After the initial dives you headed off to Mexico, right? »In the fall of 1956, a couple of friends and I drove to Guaymas, Mexico and dove in the Sea of Cortez. It was my first dive trip beyond Monterey and Carmel. We went there in a pickup with a camper and stayed at the bay of San Carlos. There was a small compressor to fill tanks and small boats for rent. For the trip I built a housing for my first 8mm movie camera.

I lucked out to meet Ken Smith, a contractor from Santa Rosa. Ken spent three months every year at San Carlos. He had a 26-ft. boat for fishing and he was a free diver. He offered to take me diving. The following morning we traveled north to San Jose Island. Ken had several large Nemrod spear guns and told me to use one of his, telling me that the small single band gun I

1. Testing camera system, 1955
2. Early designs for underwater strobes, 1960

had was not enough for the fish here. My free diving skills were good, but I had never speared a big fish or a game fish. My spearfishing was for Ling Cod and other bottom fish on the northern California coastline.

We jumped off the boat and I was in the clearest water that I had ever experienced. And there were lots of fish. Ken said to follow him down. I did, and at 40 feet, I saw my first Yellowtail. Ken speared one and we swam back to the boat. He told me, "We will spear only a few fish, therefore take your time, wait for the bigger ones." We made many free dives that day, to depths up to 70 feet, and I speared three nice fish. After that I made dives with my new 8mm camera in its housing. This was a decision-making day… I thought then about being professionally involved in diving.

When did your interest in underwater photography take hold?》After my first dive I started reading any book or magazine on diving. Hans Hass's books continued to be the inspiration for underwater photography, adventure, and he steered us to develop rebreathers. I thought about taking pictures of the adventures, the animal life I was seeing to share with others. Everyone wanted to hear the stories but I wanted to show them what I was seeing.

Who was shooting underwater then in your area that influenced you?》I started diving with Helmut and Karl Stellrecht from San Jose. Helmut was still in college and Karl worked in a camera repair center. Both were avid underwater photographers, they designed and built all of their underwater housings, flash bulb units and other accessories. We continued to develop newer equipment; it was an exciting period of time for me.

Considering the primitive underwater systems available then, how long did it take to realize that you were going to have build a lot of the equipment yourself?》The early issues of *Skin Diver* magazine had articles about building housings for cameras. I started to learn about o-rings, and how to work with Plexiglas. In the early part of 1956 I began working for Standard Oil. I was offered the opportunity to go into an apprenticeship program, learning to be a Boilermaker Welder. This was a three-year program providing classroom education half days and the other half you worked the trades. These shops were huge and had tools allowing you to build anything. Personal projects were called "government jobs". During the nine years I worked at Standard Oil, I had a continuing stream of "government jobs" building underwater photographic and diving equipment. That's where it all started.

My first camera was an Argus C-3 35 mm with a 50mm lens. I don't know why I picked this camera. It was difficult to use above the water, let alone the controls needed to operate it underwater. But it worked. I built a flash bulb unit, started to learn about open water connections and the difficulty to make electrical things work consistently in salt water.

Did you have any engineering training then? »I had natural mechanical skills. I built my first motorbike when I was 12, bought my first car when I was fourteen. You could get a driver's license at 14 in those years. My father was an engineer and during my Boy Scout years he helped me with a lot of the merit badge projects; the more you learn… the more you want to learn. In high school I developed skills to do custom work on cars, rebuilding the engines, making hot rods. I bought my first Triumph motorcycle in my senior year.

How did the early designs you tried out work? »There were many trips back to the Sea of Cortez and I continued to spear fish, but my focus was on exploring and taking pictures. We were doing a lot of diving at Point Lobos State Park at the south end of Carmel. This park is famous in that it has the oldest protected marine reserve in the USA. In 1958 we housed the first commercially available electronic strobe lights. Developing connectors for strobes was far more difficult than connectors for flashbulbs. We used Amphenol connectors and filled them with grease. We would then enter Whalers Cove in Point Lobos, swim on our floats to the outer edge of the cove or over into Blue Fish cove, tie off the floats to a piece of kelp and make our dives hoping that the strobe connection would work. It did on most occasions but there were many times that I would need to swim back in, re-grease, and swim out again. We would swim out a minimum of two times per day.

There were few divers but those that came as well as normal tourists that were visiting the park would marvel at the various pieces of underwater photographic equipment we had on the tables, changing film or greasing up connectors. Divers that were interested started asking where they could buy camera housings and flash units. A diving buddy, Helmut Stellrecht, was excellent at building housings. I began to take on work building housings or other pieces of equipment. My "government jobs" at Standard Oil were increasing. Its funny how word spreads. I started getting calls from people that I never met asking me if I would build this housing or that.

There were no commercial dive boats in those days. How did you access the dive sites? »Back in 1961, I'm on 60-ft. fishing boat called *Privateer*, heading out for a dive trip. There were 18 divers on board and we were heading to the Farallon Islands, 26 miles off the coast of San Francisco. Some of us were members of the Littoral Society, an environmental organization concerned about the issues in the littoral zone, that area on the beach between low and high tides. The group in northern California was affiliated with the department of Fish & Game. I'm not sure how I got involved, but I knew there was going to some trips to the Farallons and other places, and I wanted to be there.

The diver makeup was from all over. I knew Dan Gotchall from the Department of Fish & Game, Ed Kelly a good diving buddy and still a good friend today, a few people from the Central California Council of Diving Clubs, and a person that had defining influence on my future, Dewey Bergman.

We anchored on a reef off the main island. The assignment on the first dive was a fish count. We did our count and then spent the balance of the dive exploring. We had heard stories of Great Whites but I can't remember it being a concern to us then. Back on board we started to talk about the dive, fish life and I then discovered that Dewey had brought back a good-sized octopus. I asked what he was going to do with it and he said eat it. That was something different for me.

We moved the boat for the second dive, a large bay on the west side. During this dive some of us discovered what appeared to be a cave or an opening of sorts. Two divers discovered two small amphorae among other debris and it was reported by one diver that he saw a large encrusted chest in the area. The six of us that were involved in this discovery did not talk about our find on the way back. Those involved had visions of treasure, riches… and we were not going to discuss it with anyone, even ourselves.

A month went by and one by one we started talking about what our plans were to go out again, to find the chest. We got together and chartered a boat to take our smaller group out. The seas to the Farallons can be treacherous; that's why wrecks are there. We spent two rough days trying to rediscover the area where the others found the amphora. With seas picking up we pulled anchor on the second day and headed for home empty-handed. We made 13 trips looking for the mystery location where the amphora were found and the reported site of the chest. But sand had covered the opening to what could have been an old ship. Never did find anything.

Then I purchased a converted double-ended lifeboat equipped with a DA Buda diesel and a small cabin. A very seaworthy boat, small, 26-feet long, but adequate space for four to five divers and numerous tanks. It was fine to travel to the Farallon Islands. I also owned a 12-man UDT rubber boat. Our normal trip to

Working on camera and strobe housings, 1960

the islands was to leave Richmond around 10:00 PM at night, towing the rubber raft. A four-hour trip for my boat, getting there early morning, allowing for a couple of hours of sleep prior to our first dive. We always anchored in Fisherman's Bay; this was protected most of the time by prevailing winds and currents. It's a

habitat for the hundreds of sea lions and elephant seals. And, we found out, the lurking White sharks.

On the last trip we made with this small boat we arrived at the islands under fog. The sea conditions were picking up and I was concerned that we could slip anchor at night and wind up on shore. So I chose to move out of the cove and tie up to the main buoy on the south end of the main island. That was a very large buoy used by the Coast Guard and anchored by chain to a thirty-ton cement block on the ocean floor. I put out our anchor and tied the stern off to the buoy. Our little boat was like a cork in a rolling sea, five of us were wedged into this small cabin. During the early morning, the seas calmed, and we woke to discover that our anchor had broken during the night, but we were still tied to the buoy. We saw another boat on the horizon. We recognized the other boat as being from Sausalito and it had a group of divers on board. We suited up and made our first dive. The water was exceptionally clear. We were diving on a solid granite ocean floor, a good number of fish in the water.

On surfacing we saw that the other boat had pulled anchor and moved past us to the small island south of the main island. We noticed that the divers had spear guns and this was a concern. They anchored and were preparing to make a dive. We were starting to get ready for our second dive, I told everyone then to be careful and be in eye contact with others. During our second dive, I was swimming along the edge of a shelf at 90 feet. At one point I swam out over the edge to look down. Below me was a Great White shark… so large his dorsal fin seemed to list to one side. Must have been nearly 20 feet long.

I immediately backed onto the shelf like a schmoo looking for the other divers. When I came in contact visually, I motioned that we were to ascend to the boat "now". We didn't really have shark signals; the only signal was to go up. When we got onboard, the other boat was gone. It was strange… how did this boat pull anchor and leave so quickly? I told the guys about the big shark. They laughed. I pulled out a bottle of whiskey and said, "We're not diving again today!"

We had no radio on board and the compass worked some of the time. It was our practice to pull up a crab pot on the way home, fill the boat with enough for a good neighborhood feed, and head for port. No exception this trip. Pulling into the harbor, I noticed more lights than normal. Then we saw a large group of people on the end of the wharf. As we approached they yelled, "Is everyone OK, who was hit by the shark?" I didn't need the harbormaster to see the hundred or so crabs on board so I yelled that all was okay. We off-loaded the crabs under the cover of darkness and headed for home.

The following morning we learned that one of the divers on board the other boat was attacked by a Great White on the second dive and it took over six hundred stitches to sew him up. He was in the hospital for six months. I suspect that the shark that swam under me was the one that attacked this diver. This was the second diver in two years to be hit by a White shark at the Farallons. Leroy French was severely attacked the year prior and Al Giddings, his partner, pulled Leroy back to the boat and saved his life.

We made a few more trips to the Farallons, for fishing and a few dives, a great place for diving but we had our fill and it was time to move onto other adventurers. On the way back in one time, Dewey and I struck up a conversation and he told me about his shark experiences diving in the Tuamotu Islands, specifically Rangiroa and diving the pass. Dewey, an ex-naval officer, had dove all over the world. He was one of the first divers to dive Bikini after the atom bomb tests and had spent most of the last three years diving the south pacific including the Tuamotu Archipelago. His zeal for exotic diving would affect both us profoundly in the near future.

Al Giddings is one of your old friends. How did you guys hook up originally? » I met Al in the early 1960s. We became good friends. We worked together on some early films about diving. We have other common interests like riding motorcycles. That's one of my passions. I was very much into off-road, hill climbing in my early years. I remember Al coming along on his bike one weekend. He had lights, mirrors, all of the bells and whistles. My bike was built for off-road terrain. On one run I was coming back down a hill and here comes Al up this steep face and all of sudden the front end of the bike goes up in the air and he begins to summersault to the bottom. Now Al is a very aggressive competitor. He's doesn't want to be beaten in anything and it was so funny to watch his look at all of the broken lights and bent mirrors knowing that he was finished for the day. We're still riding bikes together. In 2002 my wife Ronda and I,

Bill & Bee Mitchell rode up through Wyoming, through Yellowstone and to Al's ranch that is 40 miles from one end of the park. He joined us and we rode to Sturgis in South Dakota and spent a week exploring.

You were one of the founders of the Underwater Photography Society of Northern California. What sort of activities did that spark? » Ed Cummins and I formed the Northern California Chapter of the Underwater Photographic Society in 1962. Dewey became a member, others joined including Giddings and Leroy French. We had a great group of underwater photographers, a lot of egos. Some of the meetings were held in Dewey's home overlooking San Francisco Bay. This was during a time when Philippe Cousteau traveled through the bay area and he was always invited to Dewey's home. The NCUPS is a very active group today.

At some point you were involved with leading early trips for See & Sea Travel. Where were you headed? » While attending UC Berkeley, Dewey did a thesis on how to start a travel agency. The professor gave him a low grade but he used his plan to start Eur-Cal travel and later owned Don's Travel Service in Berkeley. He managed a very successful travel business. Dewey had connections and dive friends everywhere. He set me up with passes on airlines to destinations I had only read about and I met many of his friends who took me diving in the Bahamas, Andros, Cozumel, and the Virgin Islands. These trips were in the very early 1960s.

In 1964, I organized a group of 14 divers to take a trip to Cozumel. To the best of my knowledge this was the first organized dive group to go there. This was also the first and founding trip for See & Sea Travel. The tickets were issued by Don's Travel but

doing trips to the Yucatan, overnight in the bay of Chalau, diving the wreck of the *Manticerous*. Then on to Akumal and the ancient grounds of Tulum. We were the first diving group to do this. Akumal then was nothing but a copal plantation. On our second trip there, I negotiated with the manager of the plantation to take us to a ceynote that we learned about from the locals. Using a tractor and a flat bed trailer, we traveled north to access the site. The local people told us that the inland cave connected to the sea. When we dove in the ceynote, we discovered a tunnel and swam this connection to the ocean.

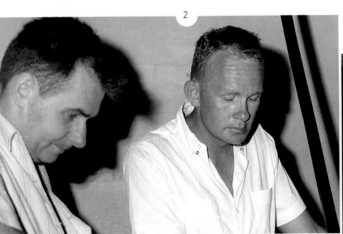

1. Hollis and Al Giddings, 2005 2. Paul Tzimoulis and Hollis, at Anchor Shack, 1959 3. Together again, 2002

Dewey's intent was to sell Don's and to specialize in dive travel from then on. The following year I led both See & Sea trips to Cozumel. One of the divers on the trip in the second year was a paying guest, Carl Roessler, a computer expert from Yale University.

We stayed at the Cabana's Del Caribe, one of three hotels then in Cozumel. On the first trip we brought with us a compressor for the hotel, 80 dive cylinders, and lots of equipment for the resort. I look back and remember this staggering amount of equipment sitting in the San Francisco airport along with our diving baggage and photographic equipment. It was unbelievable.

Our dive boat to Palancar was the *Pez Vela*, a 36-ft. boat with a small cabin that could carry eight divers maximum with tanks. Captain Melisio became our favorite guy. There were no diving rules... a beer following a dive was the norm. We used two more boats, equally enjoyable. From Cozumel we started

Didn't you have some sort of run-in with the Mexican government over cannons on the Chinchorro Banks? »Exploring the Yucatan was a great experience; I was intrigued by the charts and the offshore islands. I started to ask fishermen in town about Bank of Chinchorro, a long archipelago with three islands inside the reef. Rumors were that modern day pirates were in the area, ships were running aground, and importantly, there were ancient shipwrecks to be found. I was interested and negotiated with the harbormaster in Cozumel to allow one boat in our group to explore Chinchorro. The other two boats of divers would do the trip to the mainland. Dewey was upset about my decision to split the group and he led the group to the mainland while six of us went to Chinchorro.

When we were exploring the shores of Monterey, Carmel, and down to Big Sur in the late 1950s, we used a planning board build by Karl Stellrecht. The board had handles with a viewing window and a chart on the side. We towed the board using signal corps wire from World War II. The wire towed us and allowed us to communicate using our own Morse code system to identify reefs, fish, pinnacles, wrecks, interesting sites. We had 20 different signals listed including "help!" This was our first underwater vehicle. It was fantastic. During the early years we explored almost every part of Monterey Bay, Carmel and south to Big Sur.

We used this method to locate the best dive sites on Palancar. Some of the sites we named and the locations became favorites from then on. We took the planning board with us to Chinchorro. Prior to the trip we were told about a potential area on the outside of Cayo Norte where remains from a wreck were found by fisherman. We spent a day trolling the area; there were lots of sharks following or nearby. While I was being towed, I spotted something in shallow water that appeared to be man-made. I signaled for a stop to look closer and within the next 30 minutes we discovered six breach loader cannons from the 15th century. Time was against us to really explore the area, so we loaded the cannons on the stern of the *Pez Vela* and then spent another day of tourist diving before heading for Cozumel.

Back on the island I arranged to have the cannons boxed up and planned to take them on the plane home. I knew nothing about preservation of artifacts, nothing about taking antiquities from foreign waters. As far as I was concerned, I found 'em, so they were mine. Dewey was reluctant, but said, "okay, go for it". Rumors from the crew were running rampant in town and the word spread fast. The house next to the Cabanas del Caribe was owned by Pablo Bush Romero, the President of CEDAM, a new organization dedicated to conservation and protecting the environment. I knew Pablo… I was interested in what he was doing, but not interested in talking to him about our find.

Well, Pablo heard about the cannons and our intent. He came to my room asking about our trip, where we had gone, and if we found anything. I was vague about everything but he persisted. He told me that the laws of Mexico were strict about taking any antiquities out of the country. I quickly deduced that he knew something. In the end we negotiated a reasonable deal. He agreed to take possession of the cannons and give Dewey and I credit for finding them on a CEDAM Expedition. He, in turn, would preserve them, put them in his museum or others, and we

would be free to leave Mexico. I later heard that two of the cannons wound up in Smithsonian and CEDAM received a nice grant for a future expedition. I didn't get squat, but I didn't go to jail either.

You finally got into the retail dive store business in the mid-1960s. How did that come about and was this a successful path? » In the latter part of 1964 I made the decision to open a retail dive store and surf shop, the Anchor Shack. I had done a little surfing and thought this would be a nice addition to diving equipment. My partner was Ray Collins, a neighbor who was a non-diver at that time, but a great guy. We rented a building in Hayward, designed the interior, and opened in March of 1965. We obtained a line of products from US Divers, White Stag, and a couple of others. I set up a small machine shop in the back end of the store to maintain the production of custom built photographic equipment. The dollar volume on custom photo work was sufficient enough to cover the overhead and pay us a meager salary until the retail store developed a clientele.

What were the training programs you ran back then like? » I hired instructors to teach. I did very little teaching myself although I wrote a couple of instructional programs for the local communities and the store. We offered NAUI and NASDS certifications. We also wrote our own advanced course, along with courses on underwater photography, marine biology, spearfishing, and gold dredging. The gold panning and dredging classes were held on the American and other rivers in the Sierras. By year three we were teaching two classes every night of the week and on Saturday with Sunday for ocean checkouts.

During the Anchor Shack days, you started selling underwater photography equipment. Tell us about those products. » I developed a metal housing for the Honeywell strobe lights in 1967. The Hydro Strobe was an immediate success. I put advertising in *Skin Diver* magazine to promote the stuff. With articles by editor Paul Tzimoulis, more interest was generated and established a growing market for our product line. I continued to expand and built our travel department. We were selling three trips a year by the end of 1968. In 1969 we opened our second location in Concord. Another product we introduced that evolved over time was the ball joint arms to connect strobes, flash bulb units and movie lights to all types of camera housings. We started building metal housings for the Kodak K-100 16mm camera; this was the most popular system for several years.

When did you transition from shooting stills to movies? »Actually I was into shooting film early on with my first attempt in the Sea of Cortez in 1956. I have always been into stills and film and thought about producing films or publishing books. I developed a large collection of stills in my early years. The collection was

On the beach Rolleimarine, 1961

lost in a fire in 1974 and this event had an effect on my future direction. I've had a lot of great photographic expeditions and was paid well for some of the work, but my primary focus has been the design and manufacture of equipment. I continue to take lots of pictures and maybe someday I'll re-think doing a book.

I remember a CBS television special that you and Giddings worked on with Bob Croft. Tell us about that. »In 1968 Carl Roessler introduced me to Bob Croft, a Navy diver. Croft's goal was to set a new depth record holding his breath. Sponsorship was in place and I negotiated with Croft for the film rights. I needed partners in this deal and contacted Dewey and Al Giddings. Toward the latter part of 1968 we joined Croft's dive team in Ft. Lauderdale. Five weeks later Croft set a new record… 241 feet on a single breath of air. We recorded the dive on film, Al edited it and we co-produced *Deep Challenge*. The film was sold to CBS for a special.

How did Oceanic Products come about? »By 1971 the camera product line was taking most of my time. Ray decided to leave the business and I hired a manager to run the retail operation. There was good growth in diving during the early 1970s. My stores were operating on their own and we added swim instruction to the program. I was running out of room in the machine shop and was eager to expand the manufacturing division. I decided to spin it off and form a new company. In 1972 the product range became known as Oceanic. I brought in a partner who had owned and operated a large machine shop in Berkeley. We expanded our machining business for customers such as Dow Chemical, General Electric and others but my focus continued to be diving products.

You produced the iconic Hydro-35 aluminum housing for Nikon and Canon cameras that became the best-selling housing of its era. What year was that and how long a run did the housing enjoy? »I started the engineering for the Hydro 35 in 1971. Nikon and Cannon were the primary choices because of the large viewing systems and their selection of lens. This product coupled with the Hydro Strobe and various connectors kept us moving forward. We added housings for popular super 8 format cameras, movie lights & housings for 16mm cameras. A significant portion of the line was accessories for the popular Nikonos cameras.

Meanwhile, Oceanic was growing. When did the company become a full line manufacturer? »We definitely had growing pains. We were behind in deliveries and the business was not generating the projected cash flow. A fire in 1974 destroyed Oceanic. We picked up our pieces and moved to a temporary location while our building was rebuilt. We learned years later that an arsonist set fire to the building. I started making long road trips, traveled through every one of the 48 states except North Dakota. I made sales calls to every retailer that would take the time to look at the product line. In the later part of 1974 I bought out my partner.

I knew that I needed to do something fast, my cash reserves were running low. So I sold my interest in the Anchor Shack stores and then embarked on a product design using injection tooling. My objective was to design a tool that would allow me to use the parts for a number of products. By mid 1975 we introduced the Ocean Pro lights and they became the best selling diving hand lights in the country. I entered into an agreement with Scubapro to produce the light on an OEM basis for them in Europe. My next focus was to design the electronics for a new strobe light. The same parts used for the light were used to produce the new strobe product line, the 2001 and 2003 strobes. The strobes coupled with ball joint arms were an instant success.

Who were the major players in dive manufacturing then? »The top three were US Divers, Scubapro and Dacor but there were lots of other companies such as Sportsways, White Stag, Bailey Suits; diving was still a very small industry.

How did you do competing against them? »We focused on niche products such as the photographic line, then lights, and began moving into electronics. Most of the larger companies were not selling products that we were designing so this allowed us to begin developing a brand and a customer base. The diving industry had its greatest growth from 1975 to 1990. Paul Tzimoulis at *Skin Diver* magazine promoted dive travel and underwater photography. This fueled our growth. We were a small company, profitable, and with a staff of people who wanted to expand. The bulk of the customers for our products were divers that came to a retail store and asked for the products; the store would order them, sell to the customer and keep a nice profit. But dive stores in general did not

promote and inventory underwater photographic equipment. We decided that future growth would require us to have a core product line.

At some point, you took over your friend Ralph Shamlian's company Farallon. How did that come about? I met Ralph when we were producing the Anchor Shack products and we developed a life long friendship. Ralph, a brilliant inventor attracted the eyes and pocket books of investors to fund his new company Farallon Industries in 1971. Farallon became the buzzword in diving, introducing new products at a rapid pace. Innovation has its rewards but the downside is the continuing requirement for money. You can only go to the well so many times. By late 1975 Ralph was on the outs with his investors. Within a few months we learned that Norm Moore, the new CEO and largest investor, was negotiating to sell the product line to Scubapro. They wanted to buy the assets and leave Norm with the liabilities. Farallon was in the process of a major product recall and Norm didn't want to be stuck with this liability.

You can learn a lot by going through trash! We were diving into the Farallon dumpsters at night. Getting access to their current financial info and other correspondence provided us a picture of what Farallon was all about. I entered into discussions with Norm. He thought I was interested in buying the tooling for a movie light. This allowed me to begin discussions about his pending offer and to begin influencing him that we might be a better fit. Four weeks later I bought the whole company. I was in the office when he told Scubapro the deal was off. They were pissed! Especially when he told them it was me. I moved Oceanic

from San Leandro to San Mateo across the bay and the new company was known as Farallon Oceanic until 1980 when we dropped the name Farallon and carried on with the name - Oceanic.

Farallon was the first company to invest in electronics. They were building digital depth and pressure gauges. Because of many issues, I stopped producing a number of the products and wanted to go back and re-engineer them to eliminate the returns. Half of the cash flow was coming from analog instrumentation but they were buying the movements from other suppliers and installing them in plastic parts produced by Farallon.

Oceanic continued to expand. What came next? I thought we would be better served if we could engineer, design, and manufacture the analog movements. I hired an employee away from one of the suppliers and put one of our engineers on the project. My son Mike, a commercial diver for Taylor in the North Sea and the Gulf of Mexico, agreed to come home and work in the company. Mike had learned a lot in the three years he was employed by Taylor. I asked him to be a part of the new instrumentation program we formed called Pelagic Pressure Systems. Pelagic became an OEM supplier of products to Oceanic, our sister company Aeris, and a number of dive companies in the world. Pelagic manufacturers OEM products for the industrial life support markets as well as aircraft instrumentation. Mike is the president of Pelagic.

In 1979 we also moved Farallon Oceanic back to San Leandro. Our machining division was getting larger and the customer base was growing. We formed another company in 1981, ROMI Enterprises. Today ROMI machines and produces the regulator lines for Oceanic, Aeris and other companies.

You were also involved with one of the first dive computers, right? One of the products that Farallon developed was an early dive computer. This product was going through a recall with the Consumer Protection Agency. We assumed the liability and managed the recall. I continued the engineering effort to allow us to re-introduce the product. I finally determined that the future dive computer needed to be an electronic product and not the type we were engineering. In 1979 I entered into an agreement with John Lewis, a physicist. John was a diver and had

353

developed an algorithm for a dive computer. We began a development program to test the algorithm and, in parallel, to develop the electronics. We had our first operational dive computer at the end of 1979. We continued to test the unit and made a presentation to US Divers in early 1980. They were impressed and this led to an agreement for Pelagic to be the OEM supplier of instrumentation beginning in 1984. Pelagic produced all U.S. Divers instruments and computers through 1995. We first introduced the

2

1

1. 2001 series strobes 2. Hollis with his complete camera system, 1975
3. Hydro-35 camera housing

Data Max gauge, a depth gauge with a bottom timer. This instrument gained in popularity and paved the way for our first commercial dive computer. We were the first company to have an air-integrated computer that provided remaining air time as well as no-decompression and deco information. This product was introduced in 1984.

We entered into an agreement with Johnson Engineering, one of the companies associated with NASA. The project was to develop a stand-alone dive computer that could receive pressure information from a transmitter attached to the regulator. The product was delivered to NASA in 1987 and this became a commercial product the following year. Pelagic has continued to develop dive computer technology and is an OEM supplier to a number of companies. Oceanic and Aeris have a secure position in instrumentation and computers worldwide.

What became of the venerable Oceanic photo products line? To make the advancements needed to secure a solid position in instrumentation, regulators, and buoyancy compensators required our entire R&D budget. We were losing ground in lights and the photographic product line. To my disappointment, we decided to stop the funding of the Oceanic photo line in the early 1990s. This had been my passion, and photography still is, but we needed to make long term decisions that would best serve the growth of the company. Consider that we had invested in developing our own amphibious 35 mm camera complete with a large format viewing system and the ability to couple standard Nikon lenses encased in a lens housing. This was years before the Nikon RS model. To satisfy the growing requirement for 16mm photographers, we modified the Arriflex 16S camera by replacing the 100-ft. spools with 400-ft. coaxial spools. We then added new lenses to the optics and increased the viewing screen. A special housing was developed and this system was the standard for a number of underwater cinema photographers. I later developed a state of the art self-contained 16mm system with 400-ft. spools and through the lens viewing system. We only sold a couple of these units and the remaining unit is in my home. That was the end of the photo line, an emotional time to shut the line down.

You had a few issues in management as well. »I hired Mike Chapman to be the president of the company in 1995. Mike had a long tenure at US Divers and we developed a good relationship over the years. Mike was a good leader but left a couple years later to form his own company, Body Glove. I then hired Rich Mitchka, the former president of Dacor. Rich was not a good fit with our company. I continued to look for the right person. In 1996 we decided to start a new brand for instrumentation and called it Aeris. This was introduced in 1997. Dan Emke, our sales manager on the east coast, moved back to California and was appointed the position of COO for Aeris. The company developed into a full line manufacturer and Dan is now President.

I remember the old building from the early 1970s. You've moved up a bit since then. »In 1994 we bought our current building on Davis Street in San Leandro. This 110,000 square foot building houses the current operation. We are adding more office space and will move Aeris into the building in April 2007. One thing that separates us from most dive manufacturing companies is the fact that we manufacture the product from raw materials to the finished product. Some of our manufacturing is now offshore in our own plants located in China and Taiwan.

How about military work? »In the last five years Oceanic has won three government contracts to develop products for military applications. We designed and developed the CDDM, Combat Divers Display Mask. We are currently working on integrating the display mask portion into a full-face product made by DSI, a Bev Morgan product. The Data Mask, including a dive computer in the display, is in the Oceanic and Aeris product catalogs for delivery in July of 2007. The second contract was to develop a PDA that can be used by tactical swimmers and be the heart of a swim board. We're also developing CO_2 sensors to be used in rebreathers. The most recent contract is to develop the ATUBA – Advanced Tactical Underwater Breathing Apparatus, a new fully closed rebreather.

What's next? »We have new company on the launch pad simply called Hollis. The Hollis product line will have a technical division including dry suits, flotation jackets, plates, canister lights including HID, Quartz and LED lamp heads. We are finishing a new line of underwater vehicles that will include features - long-duration, speed and thrust. We are designing an instrument for the vehicle that will provide speed and distance traveled and it will adjust for current movement. We will put the full-face mask with the HUD using a dive computer software program, not the military software. Coupled with underwater communication this product will be excellent for film teams and search and rescue teams. Pelagic is finishing a swim board that includes a depth gauge that allows you to program in your compass heading and return with swim legs and timers. This product, in combination with a compass, will provide better information than current military swim boards. We have a new Hollis regulator that will be introduced by mid 2007 and we will introduce a commercial rebreather by mid 2008.

One of the great epic stories in diving is the saturation project on the *Andrea Doria* in 1973. How did you get involved? »Some friends of mine, Don Rodocker and Chris Deluchhi, Navy divers who

355

had set some of the deep saturation records, were planning a new business when their enlistments were up in 1972. The first project was to design and build a portable saturation complex. The objective was to tow the complex 50 miles northeast of New York, to the wreck site of the *Andrea Doria*. They wanted to anchor a support boat to the *Doria*, lower the complex, secure it to the side of the wreck, swim down, and live in the complex. From saturation, they could then make dives from the complex, use cutting torches to create a hole in the port side, find the safe, and remove it. They wanted me to invest in the deal, have the contract for the film documentary, and help in the construction of the complex. I bit… hook, line and sinker.

In 1973 the diving system left San Diego on a flat bed truck… 20 tons of diving equipment bound for Fairhaven. Don and Chris had secured a support vessel, a stern haul fishing trawler, 65 feet in length named the *Narragansett*. Our support systems were installed on the deck and we slept in cloth bunks located in the fish holds. First class, huh? After establishing a down-

line to the foyer doors on the port side, we lowered the complex, all 10 tons, and tied her off over the doors. Don and Chris swam down, entered the habitat and went into saturation. Two days later I went into saturation. Cutting torches were lowered and we cut the first entry into the *Doria*.

Describe the habitat itself. » We called it simply *Mother*. It was a pressure vessel like a recompression chamber, thirteen feet in length and five feet in diameter. The inside of *Mother* was designed to accommodate three saturation divers, a gas mixing panel and canisters for removing the CO_2 gas in our breathing loop. A hatch on the bottom of the chamber provided an entry and exit to the ocean. The hatch could be closed and sealed during descents and accents and sleeping periods.

The breathing gas inside of *Mother* was a mixture of 92 percent helium and 8 percent oxygen, varying with depth. The chamber was contained in a large frame with 40 large storage cylinders of gas: 8,000 cubic feet of helium, 1,200 cubic feet of oxygen and 4000 cubic feet of heliox. Under the chamber was a cage for in-water storage of our diving equipment including our hot water suits and all tools necessary for the project. The Kirby Morgan band masks with communication pods were kept inside *Mother*. The system displaced 21,080 pounds.

2

4

1. *Andrea Doria* underway prior to collision with *Stockholm*
2. Support vessel *Narragansett* anchored over wreck, 1973
3. *Andrea Doria* heels over following the collision that sank her, 1956 4. Loading the saturation habitat *Mother*

The chamber and dive system was connected by an umbilical to the master control van sitting on the deck of the *Narragansett*. The umbilical provided hot water for heating the chamber and for our hot water suits. It also had hoses for breathing gases, communication, video links and other life support systems. The umbilical to the surface support ship was the lifeline to *Mother* and the dive team in saturation.

There were several mishaps and close calls. Give us some insight on the hazards? » Just to get *Mother*

secured to the side of the *Doria* was a formidable task in itself. We shackled a cable to a porthole opening close to the main foyer doors. Supporting the cable topside was a five-foot diameter metal buoy we nicknamed *Big George*. This cable was our down-line for *Mother*. The dive system had three ballast tanks on the top. To lower *Mother* required us to move the down-line into a guide system with a braking mechanism on the side of the habitat.

Using the principles of a submarine we would jettison air from the ballast tanks, take on water, and achieve negative buoyancy. This allowed *Mother* to sink. To slow the sinking, the gas operator would use compressed air to blow the water from the tanks

357

and we could achieve positive buoyancy in a short period of time. The objective was to create negative buoyancy, slide down the down-cable, and then secure *Mother* to the wreck.

On the morning of July 25, 1973 seven of us pulled *Mother* alongside the topside buoy. Fighting a one-knot current, we finally managed to get the down-wire cable into the guide system. We then recharged our cylinders, needing all of the air possible for the upcoming dive. This was to be one of the most physically demanding dives any of us had ever made, seven divers on scuba gear lowering 21,000 pounds of steel onto the side of the *Andrea Doria*, 170 feet below. I thought at the time, "I'm away from my new business, in the North Atlantic, 43 degree water temperature, and were going to swim down an entire saturation diving system and tie it off on the *Doria*. This has to be one of the most hazardous dives ever attempted." About then, I figured I was just a little bit nuts.

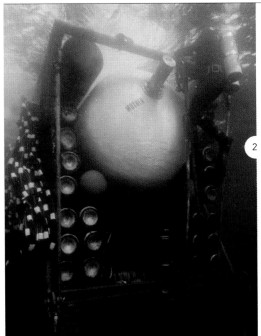

target. Each corner of the system had a rope 100 feet in length with a come-a-long. Four divers were now on the corners pulling the tie-down ropes out to their maximum length, finding a location tie off to and then using the come-a-long to pull *Mother* into position. Gary used the ballast tanks and locked *Mother* in a buoyant attitude, holding the four-point mooring in a tightly fixed position. *Mother* ended up next to the main foyer doors and hovering 10 feet off the port side.

Seven tired divers ascended to our decompression stop at 30 feet with second stages waiting for us with 100 percent 02. Our schedule on all surface dives

1. Hollis gears up for dive aboard *Narragansett* 2. *Mother* is lowered over the side to the wreck 3. L to R: Chris Deluchhi, Hollis, Jack McKenney and Don Rodocker discuss dive plan, 1973 expedition

You were nuts. How did the set-up operation go? » Ballast tank control was critical. To allow too much water to enter would sink *Mother* like a rock. The one-knot current could push it off target, meaning we could be over the side of the ship and land in 240 feet of water. Gary Gada, the diver manning the ballast tanks did a great job. He controlled the descent and we were floating about 20 feet off the side deck on

was to equal our bottom time at 30 feet on oxygen. George meanwhile had fired up the hot water system to begin heating *Mother*. The habitat needed to have an inside temperature of 105 degrees because the saturation divers would be breathing helium. That gas accelerates loss of body temperature so we needed to live about thirty-five degrees above what was a normal room temperature to be comfortable.

The morning of July 26th all systems were finally operational. Don and Chris had a meeting with George Powell, the diving supervisor, and Dr. McMillian, our medical diving officer. Four of us swam down with Don and Chris; they entered *Mother* and went into saturation. It was a major historical moment. Our next assignment was to get the cutting torches ready. We were going to cut a hole through the foyer doors to provide entry to the First Class area and the Bank of Rome.

1. McKenney and Hollis ponder upcoming difficult dive
2. Hollis cuts the main access hole into the wreck while in saturation at 160 ft., 1973 expedition

One incident stands out in my mind particularly. Jack McKenney and the wet pot transfer. Give us the gory details. »Late afternoon July 26, 1973, Powell told Jack and me that we had a problem. He said that *Mother* had lost buoyancy and had taken on water. Water entered the canisters of our Sofnolime, the chemical we were using to remove the CO2 from our breathing system. George said, "Guys, we have two choices, take new canisters down to *Mother* or bring *Mother* up." Well, bringing that thing back up was a huge task so we knew we had to get the canisters down ourselves.

McKenney and I, along with 24 members of our Saturation Systems dive team, had just spent the last seven days securing an anchor line from our support vessel to the port side of the *Andrea Doria* and then getting *Mother* tied next to the main foyer doors, our target to enter the ship. Inside *Mother* were Chris Deluchhi and Don Rodocker, the designers of our saturation dive system. Well, everyone is exhausted from the non-stop diving work and heavy exertion. Jack and I had already done a long dive that morning

taking Chris and Don down to the habitat and then we went forward to film the *Doria's* name on the bow plate. So we were pretty well done in when this new crisis raised its head.

George lights a big cigar and gives Jack and I our assignment: take the transfer pot to *Mother* containing two canisters with hot meals for the guys in sat and the needed tools for *Mother*. George wants the transfer pot brought back to the surface once its contents are delivered. And while I'm down there, he asks me to open two oxygen cylinders for gas mixing.

The evening of July 26th, Jack and I walk down the ramp on the stern of the *Narragansett* and get into the small boat that will take us over to the anchor line. It's now 8:45 PM at night. Wearing wetsuits, twin 72s, and Fenzy vests we're ready to descend. During the daytime decompression stops we had lots of Blue sharks swimming close, and this was a concern. In addition to the transfer pot, we're taking two lights and a rope to tie off to the lifeboat davit and then secure the other end to *Mother* on the side of the Promenade deck.

George told us the transfer pot would weigh about four pounds in water. My adrenaline was running high. They handed Jack the pot and it was a good thing that he was holding onto the side of the boat. Instead of weighing four pounds, it was closer to 30 pounds in water. Jack and I made a quick decision to inflate our Fenzy vests, each of us would sling one arm under the rope attached to the pot and use a free hand to hold onto the down-wire.

The phosphorescence was our only light for the first hundred feet. I yelled into my mouthpiece for Jack to turn on the dive light. He did and then turned it off. I yelled again and he left the light on. There was nothing to see on this descent into blackness but the light gave me a small degree of comfort. Our first contact was the large boat davit. One rule for me when diving shipwrecks is to become familiar with the area, memorize the location of everything. I talk to myself about where this is and that is. I want to minimize the chances of making a wrong decision and on dives like this it is easy for things to go wrong. I don't like the unknown, especially at night.

The initial plan was to tie the rope off on the davit, however things changed when Jack let go of the rope and it drifted off in the current. I signaled to Jack, "Stay there with the pot". I knew the location of another line and swam off in darkness to find it. I brought back

the line and secured it to the davit. Now we needed to carry the pot across the beams on the promenade deck. A misstep here and one of us with the pot would fall into the open area of the promenade and then into the opening of the ship. A bad situation.

We were only 50 feet from *Mother;* we continued this balancing act, working the pot to the solid hull. *Mother* came into view. She was really eerie at night, giving off a glow from the small outside lights and a

the habitat, and I knew he was breathing the helium mix inside. Jack was coherent but not thinking all that clearly due to narcosis from our own tanks breathing air. I grabbed his legs and yanked but it was another precious minute before he left the habitat. He handed me the pot, it was almost as heavy as before. I wanted to leave it but he insisted we needed to take it.

Time was critical; we were into serious decompression at this point. I looked at my pressure

1. Lowering dive bell 2. *Sea Level II* anchored over wreck, 1981 *Doria* expedition 3. Elga Anderson, Peter Gimbel and Hollis discuss dive plan 4. Saturation system deployed on aft deck of support vessel

humming sound from the system. With narcosis coming on, I felt like we had entered another zone. We lifted the pot into the cage. I used a tool to hit the entry hatch of *Mother* to let Don and Chris know we were there and it opened up with a hiss of escaping gas.

I left Jack with the task of getting the pot up into *Mother,* removing the canisters and getting the pot ready for the return trip. I went to the main gas bank, opened two cylinders of gas that were needed and checked the pressure on the outside panel. A quick glance at my watch determined that we were way beyond our planned bottom time. We needed to get the transfer pot back across the promenade and begin our ascent. I looked for Jack, his head was up in

gauge: 900 PSI left; Jack showed me his gauge: only 500 PSI left. We're at 170 feet in the dark... I thought, "Damn, we're in trouble."

We started our ascent, Fenzy's filled, pulling our way up the anchor line. Our decompression regulators with 100 percent oxygen were waiting above us but it seemed like miles at this point. Jack always ran low on air first and I was worried that he wouldn't make it. A moment later the worst happened: Jack let go of the pot and started to go up the line by himself. I'm frantically kicking with all the dead weight myself now and reaching out to grab the line. I dropped more than 40 feet before I locked my hand onto the anchor line. I was frantic at this point. I needed to get the damn pot to 30 feet before I run out of gas or ditch the thing and we might lose it forever.

I could see lights above me. I pulled hard on the line, bubbles racing past my head. I'm beginning to

over-breathe the regulator as my air supply is going when a hand from another diver reaches out and takes the pot from my hand. I let go and began rocketing to the surface. Before I can release the gas in my Fenzy my head hits the bottom of *Big George*. Support divers were telling me to get back to the decompression stop at 30 feet. Totally wasted, I stripped myself of my tanks and pulled myself into the small support boat. I grabbed the oxygen line that Jack was on and pulled hard. At the same time I yelled at George to fire up *Big Blue*, our topside decompression chamber.

You have only a few minutes to get your ass into a chamber from a decompression dive. Jack hit the surface and I said, "Get rid of your tanks now, we're going into the chamber." We ran up the ramp on the back of the *Narragansett*, scrambled into the chamber with our suits on, and collapsed. I told George on the way in to pump it down fast. Ten minutes had passed since I hit the surface and I was worried.

Gas flowed, the door sealed, and we were on our way back to pressure. It was foggy inside, night outside with flickers of light coming through the chamber windows. None of us talked for the longest time. Jack and I had made a lot of dives together. This was a close

one. An hour later we were on oxygen at 60 feet and we came out clear and symptom-free. We took a day off but we were back at it the next. I went into saturation the following week with Don and Chris and we cut the first entry hole in the side of the *Doria*.

What do you feel was ultimately accomplished? »
The experience of living in a chamber tied to the *Doria* at 180 feet for six days was surreal. The three of us made lengthy excursions as far as our 250-ft. umbilical would allow us to travel. We were saturated on helium inside the chamber but our excursions were on air. Therefore we were saturated on both gases. Because Chris had some skin abrasions, Don and I did most of the cutting. I had never cut metal underwater before but my training as a welder at Standard Oil paid off. Imagine, cutting a hole through the doors of the *Doria* at night: hundreds of fish attracted by the light formed an igloo over me and Blue sharks were swimming through feeding on them during this operation.

Following a couple of hazardous dives inside the first class area we made the decision that we did not have the resources to finish the job. It was

363

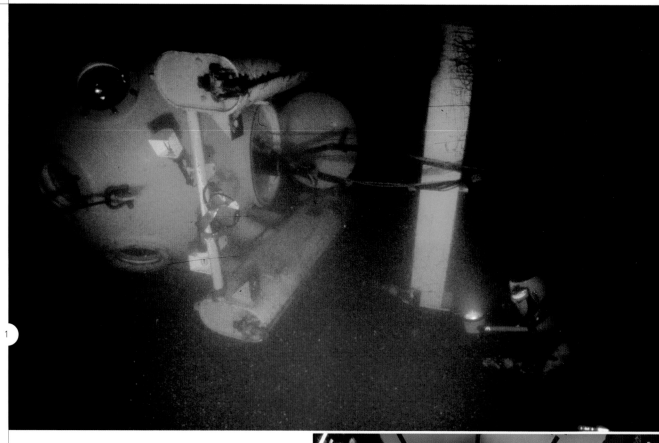

1. Dive bell supporting diver on umbilical hose along side wreck at 160 ft 2. Peter Gimbel, Hollis and Ted Hess inside saturation living compartment 3. The First Class Purser's safe is winched aboard after over a quarter century entombed in the wreck, 1981 4. *Doria* expedition Silver platter recovered from First Class dining room 5. Dishes recovered

simply too dangerous to continue beyond this point. A decision was made to bring the complex up and head for shore. We shot a lot of film but a good film needs a beginning, middle and an end. We didn't have an ending. We needed something, some treasure. We sold an option to the film early on. The option financiers paid me to be in New York for three weeks for post editing but in the end they passed.

Almost eight years later, Peter Gimbel raised money to go back to the *Doria* for another assault to try to find the first class safe and other potential riches. How did you feel about going back?»I received a call in 1980 from Gimbel; he was a good friend. The Gimbel name was synonymous with business on the east coast and Peter was famous for his underwater films and being the first person to dive on the *Andrea Doria* following its sinking. He also was the producer, cameraman, and star of the breakthrough documentary *Blue Water, White Death* that brought sharks to the public in a real way for the first time about a decade prior.

Peter told me that he had a final quest, to determine if the watertight bulkheads on the *Doria* were secure when the *Stockholm* hit her and to find and remove the safes from the wreck. "Was I interested in going back?" he wanted to know. Like he had to ask me if I was

4

3

5

for every possible event and product.

We boarded the *Sea Level II* at Long Island and spent six weeks over the *Doria*. I spent 17 days in saturation on this dive. Jack and I made excursions to every area of the ship that our 250-ft. long umbilicals would allow. We were there to remove the doors, find the safe, and cut it free. We'd then bring it to the surface. Peter also wanted to penetrate the ship to see if the watertight doors were in place to further determine why this ship sank.

Ted Hess, the lead diver for Oceaneering, cut the doors free and we brought those topside. This allowed a giant entry into the first class area. The inside of the ship was a junkyard, most everything fell from the port side to the starboard side piling 10-15 ft. of junk in the area where the safe was located. To remove the all this crap and a lot of great artifacts included, we built a giant sling using wire fencing. The topside winch operator would lower this big sling through the doors, and then down to the port side of the ship another eighty feet deeper. We spent days and nights, around-the-clock "weather permitting" piling everything in our way into this giant sling and taking it up through the opening. Jack and I were on all of these dives working and filming.

We had a basic layout of the ship to find the safe. I suggested that we use the plan we had since it was to scale, and it provided us basic indicators of the safe's location. We used a line on a spool with distance marks and this provided us the range transects as we looked for the damn thing.

Another piece of equipment we used was an eight-inch vacuum device that sucked debris from the starboard side and lifted it to the outside of the ship...

interested… just give me the date! Peter's plan was to engage Oceaneering International and one of its large saturation dive systems along with a 200-ft. ship designed for operations in the North Sea. It could not get any better than this. Peter had the finances to back an expedition of this type and he accepted nothing less than the very best system and team possible to ensure success.

Peter, Jack McKenney, Nick Caloyianis and I were to be the four underwater photographers. The four of us went through a saturation-training program at Commercial Diving Center in southern California. From there we assembled at Peter's family home back east to inventory and pack all of the photographic and dive equipment needed for the trip. One thing about Peter, he was big on contingency planning. He had multiples of nearly all the components and redundancy

the first people who ever made a night dive on the *Doria*. Even though we dove more during the day, I spent more than 50 hours at night on the wreck cutting the hole in 1973, removing debris and filming inside the foyer and first class compartments in 1981. You're right; no

1. Hollis on *Doria* expedition, 1981
2. Chris Newbert with Ronda and Bob Hollis, 1999
3. "A fool and his money are some party!"

eight feet overhead. Drew Rudy, an Oceaneering diver, and I were sucking our way through a ton of debris one night. He'd run the vacuum for a while and then let the silt settle to see what we uncovered. I was filming him while he was moving things around and when the silt settled on this dive I saw the knob of the safe. We just looked at one another with disbelief! I'm not a skeptic usually, but there were times that we thought we were not going to find this damn safe. The following day we lowered the cutting torches and cut it free.

We accomplished both objectives and Peter produced *The Andrea Doria, Final Chapter*. The film was a major hit; Peter recovered all of his investment and in the end made money on the production.

A lot of today's divers, who seem blissfully uniformed, lay claim to having more dives on the *Doria* than others. Your team spent time on the wreck that will never be equaled. »This was an incredible diving operation with a great group of divers. It was an experience I will never forget. I spent a total of 12 weeks on the *Doria*, including 81 surface dives and a total of 21 days in saturation. Jack and I were probably

diver traveling from the surface for bounce dives will ever come close to the time I spent down there. I figure I've got nearly 300 hours of time on the old girl. For those guys like Gary Gentile who trumpet their hundred dives or so of about 20 minutes bottom time each... well, they're about 250 hours or so short of my bottom time.

Your team went after the *Doria* with well-trained and highly experienced divers using then state-of-the-art systems. How did you feel about the surge of popularity that followed and interest among other divers who wanted to dive the wreck? »Just because you're an excellent diver doesn't qualify you to dive the *Doria* or other deep wrecks. Some of the divers on our 1973 trip became nervous and after a couple of dives chose not to make any more. There are many factors: weather, currents, visibility, and cold water. The *Doria* is a big ship; it's easy to lose your orientation on the outside of the ship... let alone inside. There are psychological issues to deal with as well. Getting to the wreck is one thing; peering through the big hole is an eye-opener. On the inside you need to be trained and if you're not in the right frame of mind... well, things happen.

There was a rather astounding amount of accidents and fatalities that began in the mid-1980s and continued until recently. What are your thoughts on that era and the methodology a lot of those divers used? »Problems come from the lack of training and/or preparation. I'm of the opinion there is a lot of peer pressure that leads people to do things they should not be doing. Diving on the *Doria* is a good example.

Technical diving came out of the closet in the early 1990s and with it the use of mixed gas, accelerated decompression procedures, penetration techniques, etc. and still these mid-Atlantic wreck divers were knocking themselves off with regularity. Were you ever tempted to make comment based on your own expertise? »Of course, as you'll remember from your own experience back years ago, we didn't use the term "technical diving" during the 1960s thru the 1980s. The term came into use later to distinguish what was going on from the every day sport stuff. Our groups rigorously planned each and every dive… and even then things went wrong. Without a strong support group topside, we could not have made the dives we did. I tend not to make public comments about what others were doing but I've offered personal opinions to divers who planned to dive the *Doria*. You'll have no trouble guessing what I told them. You were telling them the same thing.

Nitrox and dive computers became hotly debated topics in the same period. What were your opinions then about these innovations? »We were a forerunner in the development of electronic dive computers building our first unit in 1979. Properly used a dive computer today provides all divers extended time and more freedom underwater. The electronic dive computer is one of the great inventions for diving.

Nitrox came into full view in 1995 when DEMA put out a notice that they were not going to allow the term nitrox to be used and that exhibitors could not market nitrox training at the DEMA show. That was just plain stupid. It was a knee-jerk reaction reflecting their lack of knowledge on the topic. And the storm of protest that followed led to a swift decision to rescind that policy. The show went forward with nitrox vendors from all sectors. Oceanic was one of the first companies to acknowledge that their products could be used with nitrox mixtures to 40 percent O2. NOAA divers had been using nitrox for 20 years at that point.

In many ways, the arch-conservatives of diving's old school seemed absolutely dead-set against just about every innovation that came along from BCs to single hose regulators to submersible pressure gauges. And this was way back in the late 1960s. How did you fit in to that group considering your engineering interest and desire to expand the sport? »I didn't share those perspectives. My focus is and has been to make diving safer and more enjoyable. Our tag line is innovation. Small and lighter products, easier breathing regulators, dive computers built into the mask. We were one of the first companies to announce and have a commercial rebreather at the DEMA show. This was 1995. I love to explore; I always want to swim deeper and stay longer. To satisfy that desire requires innovation and lots of engineering.

You've served multiple terms on DEMA's Board and as its President. What's your vision of the future for the sport? Will it regain its growth and attract more people to diving? »I was elected to the DEMA Board of Directors in 1993 or thereabout. I enjoyed being the president of the board in 2001 and 2002. During my tenure we made progress but we could have done more. There are political issues in DEMA. There will always be political issues, personal agendas, etc. and that prevents opportunity. One project was a major disappointment for me.

Diving had rapid growth in the late 1960s through the 1980s. Diving had exposure with the *Sea Hunt* series and regular Cousteau specials. This fueled growth. When these programs went off the air, popularity dropped. During the 1990s we witnessed an evolution of new sports, mountain biking

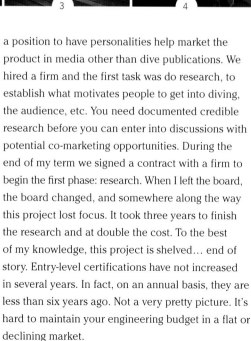

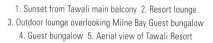

1. Sunset from Tawali main balcony 2. Resort lounge
3. Outdoor lounge overlooking Milne Bay Guest bungalow
4. Guest bungalow 5. Aerial view of Tawali Resort

with hi-tech features, roller-blading, skateboards, snowboards, kite boarding. These sports and others now compete directly with diving for time and discretionary income. In the mid 1990s people began to learn about computers and today every household has one or more. People are addicted to e-mail and Internet content.

To rekindle growth in diving requires exposure: marketing dollars are required and lots of them. DEMA and the diving industry does not have the resources required. My focus was to hire a marketing and communications firm to develop a means to do that. I am of the opinion that you need to develop partnerships with large companies and to be in

a position to have personalities help market the product in media other than dive publications. We hired a firm and the first task was do research, to establish what motivates people to get into diving, the audience, etc. You need documented credible research before you can enter into discussions with potential co-marketing opportunities. During the end of my term we signed a contract with a firm to begin the first phase: research. When I left the board, the board changed, and somewhere along the way this project lost focus. It took three years to finish the research and at double the cost. To the best of my knowledge, this project is shelved… end of story. Entry-level certifications have not increased in several years. In fact, on an annual basis, they are less than six years ago. Not a very pretty picture. It's hard to maintain your engineering budget in a flat or declining market.

Photos: Bret Gilliam

What do you think will be the largest area of growth in the next decade?》In terms of products, it will be tied to electronics. We are going to start shipping our Data Mask in mid-summer 2007. Other similar products will follow. You will see advancements made in dive computers offering more data along with information as to where your buddy is or where the boat is and how far away. Electronics will be included in BC's, regulators and, for sure, in rebreathers. We will see more rebreathers in the market place. Yeah, they're expensive and not as user-friendly as open-circuit SCUBA but this product will find its level in the market place.

In terms of new divers, dive travel is the attraction. Family vacations on liveaboards or specialty dive resorts are key. People are traveling more than ever and the thirst is there to dive in exotic locations.

Let's look back a bit. You had the chance to go out and visit a lot of the most exotic diving regions back when diving travel was fairly primitive. Any hairy experiences to share.》Beyond the *Doria* and wrecks in Bikini

and Truk lagoon, my stressful experiences are minimal. The ones I do remember are drift dives in the Galapagos and areas of the South Pacific. I got on the wrong side of Wolfe Island in the Galapagos one time and the current was taking me taking me south… next stop Antarctica. The pick-up boat finally came around and saw my arm flapping away. I never dive without safety sausages any more. I love drift diving but I remember that it's very difficult for boat operators to see you if you're not visible due to water conditions, location of the sun, and distance from the boat.

Somewhere along the way, you stumbled into Papua New Guinea. When was that and what impression did the region leave with you?》I had the opportunity to dive most places on the planet; there are a lot of great places, Truk Lagoon, Palau, Galapagos, Cocos, Sulu Sea, Red Sea, Sudan and shipwrecks like the *Doria*. But my favorite location is Papua New Guinea. My first trip there was with Bob Halstead on the *Telita*. I went back two years

1. The 120-ft. vessel, the *Spirit of Niuguini*
2. Guest state room 3. Ancient skull cave, near Tawali Resort

later on the *Chertan*. The owner, Rob van der Loos, and I became good friends. I wanted to explore the southern islands, the Engineer Group, the Conflicts, Misima and the Louisiade Archipelago. Rob agreed and we spent two to three weeks a year for several years doing these trips and discovered some fabulous diving. The waters of Milne Bay have to be some of the best on the planet. The biodiversity does not get any better than here.

So that sparked the vision you had for your new Tawali Resort? »My wife Ronda and I talked to Rob about buying a big live-a-board boat in PNG. We later talked about buying a piece of land on the north coast and building a small eco-dive resort. We have done both.

How did you ever locate that remote property and manage to acquire it? »It took seven years to secure title to the land and build Tawali. The resort is at the mouth of Hoia Bay; on a limestone bluff 60 feet off the water. The main lodge with a dining room seats 50 people. A front veranda with a breath-taking view of Milne Bay and its outer islands is perched on the high bluff. There are now 14 bungalows along covered walkways. We put in two main wharfs for our boats. We built our own home at the base of the bluff just 15 feet off the water. We also have staff housing where 40 people live that are employed at Tawali. We have an instructors' house with four bedrooms over the dive shop, a compressor building with 25,000 cubic feet

of gas in storage including 32 percent Nitrox. We just installed our hydro machine to keep tanks date current along with a new workshop for repairing motors and other equipment. A 60-ft. dive boat for our day trips was added four months ago. We are currently building a scientist workshop. Other projects include showers off the wharf including additional rinse tanks for cameras after getting off the day boats. At the top of the stairs we are going to build a big room with tables for working on camera systems, charging outlets and lockers to allow individual storage of camera equipment. It's a very special place and provides immediate access to some of the world's best diving that was previously virtually inaccessible except by a handful of liveaboards.

You've recently thrown some more chips into the pot by buying a 120-ft. luxury liveaboard

vessel. **Tell us about the ship and how that came to be?** »The *Chertan* is a great liveaboard but it has limitations for big trips to the Louisade Archipelgo and the chain of islands and reefs on the way. We also want to begin trips to Egum Atol and other reefs in that area. With this in mind we started looking for a boat. In October of 2006 we entered into an agreement to buy the *Aqua One*, a liveaboard that has operated in Thailand and Indonesia for the past five years. The vessel is now at Tawali and will begin operation in March of 2007. We call it *Spirit of Niugini*.

You and I both have been around long enough to see what used to be pristine marine systems decimated by natural and manmade influences. What can we do to preserve what's left of the world's great diving? »Education and we need to limit the pressure on fragile eco-systems. Bonaire and a few other islands in the Caribbean are doing just that and it's working. The Red Sea is a different story… the pressure there is such that they are destroying reefs. On a recent trip, our day boat with 20 divers was moored to a small reef structure in open water off the coast of Hurgada. The problem was there were seventeen other boats moored or tied to each other or us. There were no less than 400 divers underwater during those dives! Beginning divers holding onto anything they could hold onto. It was funny: they gave you the number of the boat you're on. That number is also painted on the bottom of the boat and you can more easily find your way back to the right one.

Do the Third World governments have the will and financial resources to act independently to save their ocean habitats? »Diving tourism in the Red Sea is a big business. They have the resources and someone with political power needs to step to the plate. The Ecuadorian government is financially poor but they control the Galapagos. The Asian fishing fleets are after the sharks and the governments tolerate illegal fishing. If the government ever issues a permit to fish the sharks, that would kill dive tourism in that region. Asian fishing fleets have severely reduced the shark population in the Pacific and it will continue until action is taken.

You've got one choice as the single place to go for the best diving in the world. Where and why? »That's easy: Papua New Guinea… 1400 islands, five million people, 700 cultures and that many languages. PNG has the best biodiversity of marine life on the planet. The waters are clear and warm and, for the most part, unspoiled. We built our second home there. Granted, it's a long way to travel but we wanted a place for our children and their children to be able to travel to one of the last unspoiled destinations on the planet.

Those of us who started diving in the 1950s had Lloyd Bridges, Cousteau, and others to inspire us in diving. Finally, who do you see as the next emerging leader/hero/role model? »We currently have several role models: Jean-Michele Cousteau, others in the Cousteau family, Giddings, Howard Hall, Stan Waterman, and James Cameron. But none have the media appeal like Lloyd Bridges did in *Sea Hunt* or the original Cousteau series. We need a role model, a Tiger Woods of diving. A basic problem with our sport is that

it's not conspicuous. A diver goes underwater and there is no real-time activity for the audience to follow.

You've had a lifelong passion for motorcycles. Didn't that nearly do you in back a few years ago? » I grew up on motorcycles; they have been a part of my life forever. I ride my bike to and from work on sunny days. I did a lot of off-road riding, hill climbs, trails and even entered a few amateur races. I fell off many times, too, but was never hurt until January 2, 1995. My son Mike and I were riding our trail bikes and climbing this shale rock hillside, hopping over

1. Hollis ready for dive at Tawali, 2007
2. With motorcycle, 2004

boulders, pretty wild stuff. I remember telling myself I need to turn this damn bike around. The next thing I remember was lying on the ground with the bike on top of me. I was in serious pain. Mike came back and helped me get the helmet off. I could move my head; that was a good sign. I tried to get up but the pain in my legs was excruciating. That was a bad sign. Mike basically dragged, half-carried me down the hillside to a trail. Another bike came along and Mike sent him off to get the rangers. They wanted to bring in a chopper to take me out but I said no. So Mike loaded me and the bikes into the pickup. Jon Hayes, my son-in-law, kind of held me into a sitting position during the one-hour drive to the hospital.

My wife, Ronda, met us there and she was frantic. I got wheeled into the emergency room and this Indian doctor is over me asking me questions, keeps repeating the same question. I'm asking for a shot of morphine or something to reduce the pain. They finally determined that I needed to be moved into the emergency trauma room next door with its own set of doctors. Following x-rays, and checking all vital areas, they put me out. I woke about eight hours later; Ronda was there. The head doctor from the trauma unit told me that I broke all the ribs on one side, fractured the scapula into four pieces, broke my collarbone, and cracked my pelvis in three areas, and had a slight bruise to my heart. Not bad for the second day of a new year.

I hate bedpans! So I was determined to get out of bed in the next two days. They put me on a morphine drip, allowing an extra drop if needed but it would allow you only one extra drop every 15 minutes. I woke early the second morning and started adding the drops. Ronda arrived a bit later. I was on a major high and told her to get a walker. She flatly refused. I insisted and she finally said okay. I pulled my legs around onto the floor and began to lift myself to try to stand. Even with the flood of morphine, the pain was too intense and I had to admit defeat. On day three, with the help of Ronda and a nurse I managed to get to the bathroom. I endured the pain, used the toilet, hurdle one was behind me. Ten days later I was out.

During the ten days I was hospitalized, DEMA put out a notice to the industry for whatever reason that led people to believe I was dying. Ask Ronda sometime how many plants and flowers we received; it was overwhelming. The deliveries continued; we filled all of the rooms in the ward and the nurse station. A nurse asked one day, "You must be a very important person, who are you?" I told her I was a Senator but not to tell anyone. In a short while all the nurses and doctors were poking their heads into the room saying hello. What a week!

You're 70 years young. Any thoughts of retiring? » I'm into putting this new Hollis line together, my twin sons, age 22, are now in the business and I'm having fun watching them grow into normal adults. Ronda and my daughter Debbie are marketing Tawali and the new boat. So, no, I'm not ready to retire yet but I look forward to my trips to Tawali.

"There is much to do and so little time" – my favorite line. ■

Al Giddings

DEAN OF UNDERWATER HOLLYWOOD

BY BRET GILLIAM

DURING THE LAST FOUR DECADES, AL GIDDINGS HAS EARNED A REPUTATION AS ONE OF THE MOST CREATIVE AND TALENTED FILMMAKERS...

in the entertainment industry. His diversified roles have included that of director, producer, and cinematographer. Never settling for off-the-shelf technology, Giddings is constantly designing innovative camera, lighting and optical systems in all film and video formats to High Definition TV. »

He is well known for his underwater directing and shooting of such highly acclaimed films as *The Deep* and the James Bond series *For Your Eyes Only* and *Never Say Never Again*. But what many don't know is that Giddings was also a pioneer in technical diving out of necessity for his film projects. He was the first to dive with mixed gases on the *Andrea Doria* in 1969, the first to discover, dive and penetrate the Japanese *I-169*

submarine in Truk Lagoon in 1973 and he's been incorporating innovative gear, such as rebreathers, in his projects for years. Giddings also pushed underwater film techniques and technology for *The Abyss* and the film went on to capture an Academy Award nomination for Outstanding Cinematography. More recently, he served as co-producer and director of underwater photography on Jim Cameron's spectacular *Titanic* released in 1997. The film, of course, broke all box office records in film industry history as well as dominating the 1998 Academy Awards.

Giddings has directed and filmed dozens of works for television, including his specials on the *Andrea Doria*, as well as films on the North Pole, deep-sea volcanoes, great whales and sharks. In 1996 he did *Galapagos: Beyond Darwin* for the Discovery Channel, one of the highest rated shows in its 10-year history. Three television specials, *Blue Whale*, *Shark Chronicles*, and *Mysteries of the Sea* each earned him Emmys. He also produced and directed *Ocean Quest*, a five-part NBC ocean adventure series that captured the number one slot in prime-time ratings.

For Giddings, like many other filmmakers from Cousteau to Howard Hall, technical diving has been a means to an end, whatever it takes to get the shot. Much of the technology Giddings developed, both in diving and film-making, opened the door for the modern diver to follow in his virgin footprints. Still, it has been his talent behind the lens, along with his willingness to push the edge of diving, that has won him great success and acclaim.

This interview actually began in 1997 and portions were used in the old Garth/Gilliam magazine *Deep Tech*. At that time I was dispatched to track Giddings down at his lavish Montana ranch and production studio. We first met on the *The Deep* over 30 years ago then, and had continued to exchange information on emerging rebreather technology. On my first visit, Al told me that I might have trouble finding his place even with good directions, so he'd meet me at a place called the Old Saloon just off the main highway in Emigrant, Montana, about 30 miles out of Yellowstone.

It was a nice fall day about 70 degrees and, of course, I'm in shorts and a T-shirt.

So I stroll into this bar and it's like stepping back in time into the Wild West. There are guys in Stetsons sipping beer who look like they just finished a cattle drive and some very friendly women eagerly attending their needs. I figured Miss Kitty was in the back somewhere. The bartender takes one look at me and says, "You gotta be looking for Giddings. He'll be coming in shortly. Sit down and have a drink." Whether a suggestion or a command, it seemed like good advice. I climbed onto a stool and he shoved over a beer mug roughly the size of Rhode Island.

Al arrived and escorted me across the Yellowstone River in front of towering mountains to his new 20,000 square foot studio. Just up the hill at his house, a friend was preparing a gourmet meal of fresh salmon and pasta. We watched a herd of elk grazing in the high pastures from his back deck while a Montana sunset of impossible beauty wrapped the valley and mountain range in warm light. Over a glass of fine Chardonnay, we caught up with each other and let the tape recorder run.

Then about to celebrate his 60th birthday, Al is the consummate hard-driving professional who hasn't lost a step. We had spent some time at DEMA 1997 getting him set up with closed-circuit rebreathers and now he was eager to show me some footage from his upcoming Discovery Channel special on whales. As the sequence unfolded in the studio, I sat speechless. He had captured over 30 humpback whales in one frame as they congregated for their migration to Alaskan summer grounds. Nothing had changed. Al was still the king. ■

You've been in the business for nearly 40 years.
When did you start diving? »Mid to late 1950s. I
really loved the water. I grew up in Northern California
with a fly rod in my hand, fishing and hunting. I started
off shooting with a speargun as do so many people
from Gustav to Cousteau. I got excited about diving
and, I thought, somehow I'm going to make my living in
the diving world. Probably two years into it, I became
more interested in shooting with a camera. I bought
an Argus C3 Matchmatic Camera and I put it in a '46
Ford oil filter with a screw down top. Then I cut some
holes and came up with lens ports. I sold two pictures
to *Motorland* magazine. Now I could see the possibility
of earning my keep diving, but photography, that
would really be the high tech way to go. So I started
the retail diving operation, Bamboo Reef. Sal Zammitti
got involved later, Leroy French was my partner. Al
Santmeyer bought my interest out years later.

What year was that? »We started Bamboo Reef
in 1961. I was teaching diving at Drake High School
that I did for three or four years. So at the age of 21
or 22 I sat down and wrote this paper on "diving's
physiology & practical aspects" or some zany title
like that. I don't know who reviewed it, but soon I
had a state teaching credential, three or four years
out of high school, no college. I was back at my high
school as an accredited teacher.

With Bamboo Reef you guys were classic dive
retailers. But later on you went into building
customized cameras. »Leroy French and I got $600
of home-improvement loans and bought $1,000 of
inventory and then we took all of our personal gear
and displayed it in the store. We took no salary for the
first two years, then $25 a week for the second year
or two. This was 1961. So I started building camera
housings on the side. I was already doing stills, I could
buy $20 worth of Plexiglas and a bunch of surplus store
fixtures and build an underwater housing fashioned
after Jordan Klein's, who was building them at the time.

I remember when you came out with the Giddings
Felgen line of underwater camera gear. »That was
in 1969, seven or eight years into my career.

That was really top of line. I still have a Nikomar
housing and a Seastar III strobe. »You were our

first dealer in the Caribbean. Because of my personal
interest in photography, I would develop these systems
for my own use and then spin off a product. We really
popularized motor drives and some of the first dome
ports. My personal and professional interests were
growing so I partnered with Mike Felgen. Even then,
around '69, when I announced to the world that I was
going to really earn my living just shooting underwater,
they thought I was crazy. The first year I made $40,000
to $50,000 and I couldn't believe it because I had no
overhead, no inventory. When I started shooting, the
volume money wasn't there, but the take home money
was. I would get a check for $3,000 and I didn't have to
pay US Divers for all the tanks I had ordered.

1. Filming humpback whales in Alaska
2. Giddings' production studio in Montana

What were your first underwater jobs? »I started
getting involved with *National Geographic*. There was
an oil spill in San Francisco Bay; I shot some stuff there.
Then I shot an article for the *Geographic*, also about
this time, on plankton with Bill Hammner in Bimini. I
started to do motion picture film. Al Tillman had the
first big underwater festival in Southern California, so
I started selling some of that material. I did films with
AMF Voit and US Divers: *Painted Reefs of Honduras*
and *Twilight Reef in Cozumel*. There was just enough
work to sort of pay the rent and 10 years later an event
happened that really accelerated things.

Cornel Wilde (the actor) approached me and
had this feature called *Shark's Treasure*. That was
a real Hollywood pot-boiler. I think his budget was
about a $1.8 million. So we shot on 16mm and blew
it up to 35mm. I took Cornel and a bunch of people

to Australia, set up cages and strategically baited the sharks. I had really great results and although it was a B-picture, a lot of people saw it, the shark material specifically, and thought it was pretty exciting. That led to *The Deep*. Columbia called me a few years later and they brought up *Shark's Treasure* and I initially backed off a bit embarrassed. But they said, "Why are you backing off? The picture did $11 million dollars gross but cost only $1.5!" At the time that was real money and they loved the images so I partnered with Stan Waterman to shoot *The Deep*.

I built the camera systems for *The Deep*, three 35mm models. That really was a remarkable project in so many ways. I was involved for eight or 10 months before we pulled the trigger. We built the housings and ran around the world trying to find the sites — Bermuda, Virgin Islands, Australia. I think that was the first time anyone hat shot underwater material in any other way than the "set-it-and-forget-it" wide angle lens approach. With three cameras, my approach was to shoot it as a creative topside Director of Photography would: with different focal lenses, three cameras shooting simultaneously, and give the editor something

really dramatic to cut. Lighting was another issue. We brought in not one or two 1Ks, but 5Ks and dozens of 1Ks and built an enormous underwater set. We shot all of the master shots in open water on the 1867 wreck of the *Rhone* in the British Virgin Islands and then went to the underwater set in Bermuda. We laced the set with live eels and live fish so as the camera panned around, you really felt that you were there.

Many people have said that they can't tell the difference between the *Rhone* and the set. 》Right, the biologists complimented us to no end saying they didn't know where the scene transitioned between the set and the open sea. It really made the movie. I could actually go: "stand by, roll camera one, roll camera two, and feeder." Somebody would then sprinkle the set with fish food. We wouldn't feed them for a day or so; the fish would be all over the place. There are shots of Robert Shaw lighting a fuse to blow up the wreck and as the camera backs off, fish are looking at the burning fuse. That created a production value that no one had ever seen before. Imagine too, we would shoot an extreme wide-angle lens master plus a medium close-up on Jackie Bissett or Robert Shaw or Nick Nolte or Lou Gossette and somebody else would be running tight on the burning fuse, so the editing was really

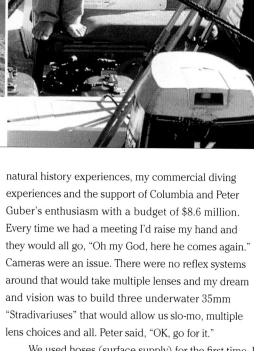

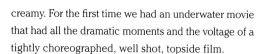

1. Spear fishing in 1959
2. Directing Sean Connery in *Never Say Never, Again*, 1983

creamy. For the first time we had an underwater movie that had all the dramatic moments and the voltage of a tightly choreographed, well shot, topside film.

I remember when the movie first came out, many people critically hailed it as the most ambitious underwater project that had ever been done since *20,000 Leagues Under the Sea* some 25 years before. How did Columbia react to this whole thing when you guys pitched this and said we are going to do this thing with 60 percent of it under water? That must have been a daunting sell. »They were really nervous, and for Peter Guber, 29 years old. His first picture was *The Man Who Would Be King* with Sean Connery. Peter was a very persuasive, very high-voltage guy. We got along very well and the core and fiber of our relationship was my endless excitement over what we had set out to achieve. Peter gave me full backing and support and Columbia deferred to him as the producer. Peter Yates (the director, who had also done *Bullit* with Steve McQueen) was really excited about the ideas that were brought to the table.

It was an incredible challenge and I mixed my

natural history experiences, my commercial diving experiences and the support of Columbia and Peter Guber's enthusiasm with a budget of $8.6 million. Every time we had a meeting I'd raise my hand and they would all go, "Oh my God, here he comes again." Cameras were an issue. There were no reflex systems around that would take multiple lenses and my dream and vision was to build three underwater 35mm "Stradivariuses" that would allow us slo-mo, multiple lens choices and all. Peter said, "OK, go for it."

We used hoses (surface supply) for the first time. I took the first stage from a dozen regulators and hooked them up to a master manifold and ran a dozen hoses in the water – 60, 70, 80 and 100-ft. hoses. We would go in and of course, we could stay on the bottom forever since the depth was only 30 feet or so. We covered the whole set so that it was dark as night and then we would light the interiors of the set. It was amazing, I remember, for the first time ever, looking through the viewfinder and thinking it looked like that vision of the shipwreck that I had when I first started diving. You know, you close your eyes and you think someday I'll be on a shipwreck like this. It was absolutely perfect.

BLACK WIDOW (Fox) Director, U/W Photography | DAMIEN: OMEN II (Fox) Director, U/W Photography | NEVER SAY NEVER AGAIN (Warner) Director,U/W Photography »

In addition to the technology challenge, this was the first time that anybody had really tried to put the actual actors in the water and shoot them. You had all of these non-diving actors, how did you do that?》The studio guys talked constantly about doubles. I wanted to approach this a little bit differently. I wanted to sit down with Shaw, Bissett, Nolte and Gossette, all of these people, and teach them how to dive. Of course it was, "Oh no, use doubles for that." I said, "Wait a minute, we're going to get a production value. We'll get voltage, we'll get excitement out of these people that you could never get with doubles and I'll be able to shoot all of the close ups and pull-backs and all of this on the actors and I think they are really going to love it."

You know Nolte is a very physical guy. But Jackie Bissett was a little different. She said to me, "I want to get something straight at the beginning of this conversation, not only am I not going to dive but I don't even like to put my face in the water." I took a deep breath and waded in and said, "Well, then you are going to miss a most incredible experience. Perhaps, one of the most exciting experiences of your career." I heard her groan. She was trying to figure me out, where is this guy coming from, but I was totally serious. I left *National Geographic* magazines with her when I was finished. I did the same thing with Shaw and Gossette and all of those guys. I have never, in my career, ever worked on a film that had the unique spirit of those people. All of those people learned how to dive. They were challenged by the diving as well as their first discipline, acting and doing a movie.

Bissett was the largest name at the time with Shaw who had just finished doing *Jaws*. He had something of a notorious drinking habit. How did you handle that?》Bless him, I loved him. He was a great man and a wonderful artist but he did have a bit of a drinking problem, as you'll remember. In fact, on the last day of the last hours of *The Deep*, he was too much into the sauce to do his scene. I know you remember that scene where the giant eel grabs Lou Gossett by the head and drags him back into the wreck. Shaw's character is also tied up in the line from a spear gun and is being dragged toward the eel's hole. Well, Shaw showed up to the set pretty bombed, actually more than bombed. In fact, Peter Yates took one look at him and said, "Forget it, no way!"

Shaw came down, took me aside and said, "Al, I know you can get me through this."

So I went back to Yates and said, "It's going to be okay, we're going to do it." Then I got Chuck Nicklin and the rest of the crew and told them to get in the water and light the set. They couldn't believe it after watching Shaw stagger around. But in we went. Shaw somehow made it to the edge of the platform and I got in facing him. I grabbed him by the tank straps and hauled him into the water. I had to put the regulator into his mouth for him, all the while I'm looking into his eyeballs trying to read him. He just smiled, he was feeling no pain. So down we went to the underwater set, the lights came on, the cameras were ready and I jammed him into position then wrapped the line around him to set the scene. He was so out of it he kept spitting out his regulator too soon since he thought we were rolling and I'd keep jamming it back in his mouth. I'd go, "No, not yet!" and he'd just grin at me.

Finally, I had him in position and all tied up and ready for the eel to drag him away. I grabbed my camera and had him hold still, then focused on his face. I nodded and he came alive and started acting. He spit out the regulator and I'm shaking him for effect with one arm, and he's fighting back looking pretty heroic for a guy who could barely walk, much less swim. We did about five takes, then I handed the camera back to Nicklin and swam Shaw back to the surface. I had to lift him out of the water he was so gone. Then he puts his arms around me and said, "We got her, boy!" Meanwhile Yates, the director, is in the parking lot doing laps around his limo shaking his head.

You look at *The Deep* today and you see that shot and it all worked. It looks like Shaw is in pain and struggling for his life in mortal combat with the eel. But in reality he's smashed and half-laughing at the crap he's putting us through. In hindsight I guess it was pretty funny, but at the time no one thought he was capable of getting through it.

The Deep was in 1976, but you did some definitive stuff years before on the *Andrea Doria* wreck that was really some of the first technical diving of the era.》It was 1969 and I had met Bruno Vailatti at a film festival and he was interested in doing a film project on the *Doria*. This was deep stuff, especially back then, and he talked me into joining the project. It was only about a dozen or so years since the ship went down and it had

BOYS (PF Productions) Director, U/W Photography | GALAPAGOS (IMAX) Producer, Director, Cinematographer | WHALES (IMAX) Director, Cinematographer》   Q+A 》

THEATRICAL FEATURES I DOCUMENTARIES I HONORS AND AWARDS ::

hardly been dived at all. We chartered this 85-ft. trawler *Narragansett*. In those days we were using the old SOS deco meters and we were doing two dives a day. I ended up doing 21 dives, all on air and using pure oxygen for the decompressions. I'd never done that kind of deep repetitive diving and it was pretty hairy at the time. One time Bruno and another diver got lost on the wreck, we all had less than 150 psi left in our tanks and our meters so far in the red zone that I thought we'd never come out. A year later Elgin Ciampi, got bent when a Pegasus DPV had a failure, he ended up unconscious in the boat's chamber, barely survived.

But it was an exciting time. Later we used trimix for the first time. I had the wheel of the *Doria* in my hands on dive six. I was in the chart room with all the stuff spread out all over the place and the ship's compass was still in place although it was smashed. It was the first real serious exploration of the wreck and we had a ball. But we were definitely out there on the edge at the time.

Hollis. I remember rigging a camera on the line. The first dive he made with the camera on the slide was a disaster because the balance was off. It wouldn't run right, so I ended up being the guinea pig. I had Hollis go to 100 feet. After we tinkered with the slide I rode to about 140 feet.

1. Bissett, Shaw and Nolteon, the underwater set of *The Deep*, 1976
2. The funeral pyre ceremony for the Japanese crew of the *I-169*

Speaking of going over the edge, you did an amazing project in the 1960s with Bob Croft. » I did Bob Croft's 240-ft. breath-hold dive and, in fact, that was the first network show I ever sold. Bob Hollis and I worked on that with Dewey Bergman.

This was a revolutionary dive for breath-holders. » Totally unbelievable at the time! Bob was doing bottom drops, 110, 120-ft. deep breath-hold dives. Croft was a chronic smoker – two or three packs a day – and I remember Doc Schaeffer told him to back off on the smoking. But Croft said his tolerance for carbon dioxide was very high when he was smoking and he didn't want to change his routine. When he quit smoking, his breath-holding capability was far less. Don't ask me to make any sense of this.

Where was the diving done? » We were in the Gulf Stream off of Fort Lauderdale. Carl Rosseler was there at the time doing stills. Dewey Bergman, myself, and Bob

Croft was entering a zone that had the doctors concerned. They actually predicted that he was going to have a residual volume lung collapse. » Right, they were concerned about hemorrhaging and I remember Doc Schaeffer set him up with an electronics package that would give him a readout. I remember gulping because we could watch his heart rate as he left the surface. It was a bit frightening because it looked like his heart was shutting down. Schaeffer said something about shunting blood to the extremities and at that time, a lot of this was really unknown territory. Anyway, Croft eventually got to 240 feet! I was down below him filming, slightly out of my mind from narcosis because I'm kicking like mad in the Gulf Stream trying to get the shot. At the time, his breath-hold dive just seemed impossible.

You followed that up with one of the first expeditions to Truk Lagoon. » Sometime around 1973 Paul Tzimoulis of *Skin Diver* called me and said

DREAM WEST (CBS) Director, Cinematographer | ON THE EDGE (Alliance Films) Director, U/W Photography | THE DEEP (Columbia) Director, U/W Photography »

THEATRICAL FEATURES I DOCUMENTARIES I HONORS AND AWARDS ::

he was trying to locate a Japanese submarine, the *I-169*, that was sunk in the Allied strike *Operation Hailstorm* in 1944. So we started systematically looking for the sub among the 60 or so known wrecks at that time. But until we actually put out the word through the Fishing Department that we'd pay $100 for any information on the *I-169*, we weren't making any headway on finding her. About three days later a man came aboard and said he had lived on the island as a child, remembered the whole attack and knew where the sub had gone down.

So we took off making passes with this little profile fathometer. Stan Berman was actually the first to see it and he came up almost choking because he was so excited to tell us about what he'd seen. I remember jumping in the water and going through that murky upper layer, my eyeballs popping out of my head, then all of a sudden, boom, the bottom opens up and there's the *I-169* stretching into infinity. It was about 140 feet to

the bottom. We had a little come-along and jacked open the hatch over the engine room. The hatch opening was too small for a big American in doubles, so I had to take everything off to squeeze in. Tzimoulis passed a single tank to me along with a big light. I remember turning it on and actually hyperventilating. There were human remains on top of the engine. It was like something out of a horror movie! The clocks had stopped at 8:02 in the morning and there were personal effects and skeletal remains everywhere!

It was damn spooky. I'm walking around in the cramped compartment of the sub with no fins and about 40 pounds of weight on. I'm sinking into the

muck and silt. At one point I'm nearly up to my waist in the stuff, crew remains and white skulls looking back at me everywhere. Then my light went out! I'm way in from the hatch and it's totally black. I remember talking to myself saying, "Okay, cool it, don't get excited, keep it together." I managed to turn the damn light on and turn around. Black silt pouring off me and I'm bumping into skeletal remains. Talk about a rush! It was like entering a time capsule.

Few people have even seen it since. I dove it in 1994 it was just exactly the way you left it, untouched. »After we left, other sport divers managed to find the wreck several months later. One diver ended up getting caught inside and drowned. It was a real tragedy and it scared off others. In 1974, the Japanese raised $240,000 to recover their war dead and I was invited back to film the effort. It was an incredibly moving experience that became the basis of my film, *Search For the Shinohara*. It was nominated for an Emmy.

You had a *National Geographic* cover story on Truk as well, didn't you? »Yeah, they sent me back again and a huge article was published, almost 50 pages in length. It turned out to be one of the most popular articles ever published for them. It seemed to strike a chord for everyone with ties to WWII, including the Japanese.

I remember seeing pictures of the Shinto ceremony, the funeral pyre, and the religious rites that you recorded. »Yeah, that was part of the film. It was all I could do to hold it together emotionally and shoot the ceremony. There were two survivors of the *I-169* there, a Mr. Maki and a Mr. Eura, along with a throng of family members of the dead crewmen. The salvage crew brought up newspapers and magazines that were still readable after 30 years submerged. There were personal photos that hung on the bulkheads along with letters home that were never mailed. There were wooden tags from foot lockers and other personal effects that had been brought up. The image of mothers of the dead sorting through this stuff and crying was so compelling that all of us were moved to tears. At one point in the funeral ceremony Mr. Maki stepped forward and played taps, the U.S. version. Everyone was so overwhelmed by the emotions and loss of those brave men.

Following your success with the Truk expeditions, you produced another hit for ABC, *Mysteries of the Sea*. »This was the second time I had worked with Peter Guber and I really wanted to do a chronicle of undersea history and indeed that is what it became. We traveled all over the globe in 1979-80 looking at the different developments and progresses in diving techniques over the centuries. We built full-size models of gear and equipment and even did period wardrobes for the re-creations. We filmed things like treasure hunting, predators and sharks, diving research and submersibles. I wanted the film to really have wonderful moments and remembered that *National Geographic's* first grant for $1,000 was to Admiral Peary. I knew that Gilbert Grosvenor, (*Nat'l Geo's* President) had sat on Peary's knee as a young man. So I called him up and said, "Gil, I'm going to the North Pole to do this film. We're going to dive in Peary's footsteps and I'd really love to have you come." He said, "Oh my God, that all sounds incredibly interesting." He had some reservations though and wanted to think it over. I didn't know if he was going to join us. On the third day I called and I got his secretary. She said, "Al, Gil is not here, but he told me to tell you that he was at Abrocrombie & Fitch and you would know what that meant!" So Gil committed. The film team went up to meet our Canadian expedition crew. We had chartered a vintage DC3 airplane and I remember this pilot had a roll of toilet paper hanging in the cockpit between the two windows so he could wipe the frost away while searching for the Pole. It all seemed totally bizarre.

Mysteries resulted in an Emmy Award winning film, and also as a wonderful book. »That's right. We were flying back after a wonderful expedition to the North Pole. Gil and I were very excited. We had shot some great stuff and had dived through nine feet of ice. Gil had walked upside down in Peary's footsteps. I was telling Gil about *Mysteries* and about how we were going to do a book and he said, "Let's do it together." In fact, at the time I was headed for my connecting point in Seattle and Gil was going east, but he said, "Don't go to Seattle, let's talk further about this."

So I changed planes and we went on from Yellow Knife in the Yukon to Washington. We talked all the way back on the plane and the result was the book, *Exploring the Deep Frontier*. Sylvia Earle was my co-author. Initially, they didn't think it would

1. Giddings and Shawn Weatherly in ice cave filming *Ocean Quest* series, 1985 2. Actor Ed Harris in special helmet designed for *The Abyss*, 1988 3. Giddings in the ice at the North Pole

find much of a market. But the first year it did about 250,000 copies in hardback. It was a runaway bestseller for the *Geographic*.

Tell us about some of the projects that you did between that and when you jumped in with both feet to do *The Abyss*. »I have had an interesting career working in two camps, the theatrical camp and the natural history camp. So in between theatrical projects, I was doing natural history and vice versa. I went on to do *Gentle Giants*, the first real film on whales. I spent a lot of time in Hawaii and then went on to Alaska to film the first bubble-net feeding behavior on humpbacks. In fact, we were just on a piece shooting widescreen digital in Alaska last month, revisiting one of the places that I worked years ago.

I am also excited by Hollywood projects, particularly working with Jim Cameron, because I'm just so impressed with his work. That is an incredible challenge. I have really always been challenged by

FOR YOUR EYES ONLY (EON Productions) Director & Cinematographer, U/W scenes | THE END (Burt Reynolds) Cinematographer, U/W sequences »

THEATRICAL FEATURES | DOCUMENTARIES | HONORS AND AWARDS ::

challenges posed when you did *The Abyss* were unheard of at the time. Tell us how you conceived shooting *The Abyss,* as well as the site you chose.》*The Abysss* will be historic. It was one of those special projects that only comes along once in a lifetime. Jim Cameron was committed to doing something that was totally believable. Cameron is really an excellent diver and a consummate filmmaker. He is unlike any other director with whom I have ever worked. We used 10,640 dive tanks in 90 days on *The Abyss.* Cameron was in the water, shoulder to shoulder with me for all of it. I never expected that. My respect for him, not only as an artist, but as someone who would invest that much personal and physical effort into a project, was immense.

You weren't doing this in some small-scale set. Describe the set you were working on.》Well, like all Cameron projects, they are just sort of bigger than one's imagination and this was no exception. We went to view a turbine pit at an abandoned nuclear power plant in Gafton, South Carolina. I remember being excited about the turbine pit and the possibilities of doing shoots underwater. About a half mile away was the main containment vessel. So Cameron, young, tough, rugged, brilliant, and I climbed this abandoned crane that had been sitting there for seven years. And now we're looking down on this massive structure: four foot thick walls, 200 feet across, 55 feet deep. This great bowl would make the ultimate superset.

Anyway, about three million dollars later, we had scarfed all of the metal out of this concrete bowl that had held all of the reactor stuff and painted the entire thing with black dye. I wanted a totally black environment. Things were now set in motion for the largest, most extensive underwater set in the world. Eight million gallons of water, filled, filtered and heated to 81 degrees. We then shot for five months.

You were using full size submersibles and habitats, right?》As soon as I read the script and spoke with Cameron I knew the elements from this picture were not coming from the props department at Fox. They were coming from the commercial diving world so I called Phil Nuytten. Soon after that Phil came to LA. We talked about everything from the helmet-like masks to beam splitters that would give some of the light on the actor's faces. Once again I took the same approach that I had on

the natural history projects. In fact, each discipline benefits from the other. Working underwater and doing all of these natural history programs gives me a real take on how to approach theatrical programs and underwater lighting. I take those lessons and disciplines back to the natural history world.

As big of a challenge as working with natural history can be, where you have an uncontrollable "actor," if you will; the technology-driven

SHARKS TREASURE (United Artists) Cinematographer | LIVE FROM A SHARK CAGE (Discovery) Producer, Director, Cinematographer 》   Q+A 》

THEATRICAL FEATURES | DOCUMENTARIES | HONORS AND AWARDS ::

The Deep years earlier. I wanted to teach Mary Elizabeth Mastrantonio, Ed Harris and Michael Biehn how to dive, how to use rebreathers and all the sophisticated gear. The approach was really going to be commercial diving. When production started we would enter the tank at 6:00 in the evening and work on the bottom from 6:00 until 1:00 in the morning. We were shooting nights so we had no light leakage, no daylight. We would come out at 1:00 in the morning, have lunch, jump in a hot tub right next to the set, warm up, jump back in to the set and finish at dawn.

That movie was a success and, of course, Cameron's prior successes with *The Terminator*, established him as the leader of this film genre. You both have recently gotten back together again on a very ambitious project which will be premiering shortly. Tell us about that. »I did a show with the Russians in 1992. I went out on the *Titanic* with Emory Kristoff and Joe McInnes to shoot *Titanic: Treasure of the Deep*. Walter Cronkite hosted the show and we had a premier screening in Burbank at the Academy with about 700 people and I called Cameron and said, "Jim you should come and see this." He said, "Okay, I'll be there." He was a very busy guy, I wasn't sure he was going to make it. But that evening just before the lights went down, I looked back and standing in the doorway to the theater was Jim and his brother.

They came down and sat with me and we talked and watched the film. When the lights went up everybody was applauding, it was a very nice moment. Jim was so excited because he had been thinking about the *Titanic* and had seen *A Night to Remember*, the old black and white *Titanic* film weeks earlier. That historic night I think he saw unbelievable possibilities in the actual wreck as part of the story. Probably six months after his initial excitement at the screening, Cameron called up and said, "I've got to finish *True Lies* but then I want to dive *Titanic*." I said, "You've got to be crazy, but I love it."

So off we went to Russia to investigate the submersibles and support vessel. We spent 10 days and had some wonderful parties with the bottomless vodka-bottle tradition and all. Later we rendezvoused

with the Russian ship at Halifax for the expedition. We set up one submersible and nine HMIs. The Russian submersible *Mir I* was the gun-ship and carried a 35mm deep

1. Abandoned nuclear containment tank became the set for *The Abyss*, 1988 2. Full-scale operating submersibles were used in *The Abyss*.

water system with pan and tilt, and a black and white monitor inside the submersible. Our dives were 17 to 21 hours at 12,460 feet! If you really pinned me down and asked what is the most high-voltage underwater feature film ever done, I would certainly have to say *Titanic*.

The ROV footage went to Fox's prop department and they recreated the interiors of the wreck along with a 90 percent scale model of the ship. Looking through the viewfinders while shooting in the underwater set was like looking at the *Titanic*. I mean I would look through the viewfinder at night, we would have it lit, the ROV would come around the corner, into the room, flickering light off the mirrors in the Astor suites, the main ball room, the promenade decks. The set was so good. Once again, you are going to see something like

CUBA'S FORBIDDEN DEPTHS (Discovery) Producer, Director, Cinematographer | SECRETS OF THE HUMPBACK WHALE (Discovery) Producer, Director, Cinematographer »

THEATRICAL FEATURES | DOCUMENTARIES | HONORS AND AWARDS ::

The Deep years ago, where it's a seamless setup. The audience will just freak because you are seeing the master super wide shots of the *Titanic* and we move up to the doorway, down the hall and around the corner and the set is so beautiful.

Around the corner, you enter the first-class cabin; it is the core and fiber of the story. The fireplace, the wreckage, the safe that they eventually get to. All of these things are as if I was in a wreck swimming with scuba at night. It magically transported me to the real wreck. I wouldn't really know the difference. So Cameron once again championed a whole new watermark and *Titanic* will carry a look and authentic fabric that has never been done before.

How many directors do you know who would go to the *Titanic* itself and jump into a 23-ft. long submarine with a seven foot diameter interior space, along with three guys then log 150-200 hours on the bottom two miles down?

***Titanic* will be released just before Christmas 1997. In spite of the fact that you have had a presence in Montana for a number of years, you have recently made a major commitment to this area with the film studio and production facilities.** »Well, the Montana facility is a dream come true. I have had the ranch here for 15 years; it was always my getaway place. Years ago, fax machines, Fed-Ex, UPS, all of those great services finally came into this wonderful valley 20 miles from Yellowstone and I thought, "Could I really run my business from Montana?" I had a wonderful studio in Northern California, central to the real action in LA, just down the road. At this point in my career I sort of know all the players, with these new super ways to communicate, I took a deep breath and designed this building.

This coincides with the practical reality of high definition film systems. How do you feel about this technology? »Just recently, new standards were finally realized and established internationally for high definition television. High definition has six or seven times the smack of the finest television image you've ever seen, of any size. With high definition, a little shutter dialed into the camera can capture any one of those frames and be printed on the cover of *Geographic*. I believe that the average set in America five years down the line will be 60 inches. High definition is so dramatic; a feature film in HD will be something akin to going to the theater. The marriage of images and sound in the future will be such that we are going to see a shocking new and wonderful change in home entertainment.

It is a very exciting time. Most of my friends are saying this revolution is going to be something like the change from black and white to color. I disagree. I think the change is really going to be more like to the change we realized going from radio to television! ❑

THE LIVING EDENS: PALAU (ABC/Kane) Producer, Director, Cinematographer | TRUK LAGOON: UNDERWATER ODYSSEY (Turner) Producer, Director, Cinematographer »   Q+A »

TRAFFIC-STOPPER IN YELLOWSTONE

FRED GARTH, TETON MOUNTAINS

BRET GILLIAM © 2002

Back in 1997, I concluded the interview with Al and eagerly awaited the premiere of Titanic. *We stayed in touch and I made a couple more trips back to his Montana house and studio. Later in 2002, I went back and re-read the original interview and was amazed at how accurately Al had predicted the blockbuster success of* Titanic *and the emergence of HD film systems and the popularity of home theatre including the DVD format that has replaced the VHS video tape. I thought it would be interesting to pick up where we left off and resume the interview.*

This time I brought along my publishing partner, Fred Garth. I had introduced him to Al before but he'd never had the chance to visit. After I filled Fred's noggin with glowing accounts of how beautiful Montana is in the fall, he eagerly committed to the trip. After all, an invitation to visit Gidding's private sanctum is one not offered to many persons. So we grabbed a flight from Las Vegas at the end of the 2002 DEMA show in late October and landed in Jackson Hole, Wyoming to begin the scenic drive through the south entrance to Yellowstone Park up to Al's place just over the border in Montana. I told Fred to expect hospitable fall weather and maybe to bring a jacket in case it got cool at night. Wrong!

We landed in a driving snowstorm and had to renegotiate our rental car for an upgrade to a four-wheel drive vehicle. We got the last one in town. When we informed them that we were driving up to Montana, the clerk just kind of chuckled and said, "Have a nice trip."

We then embarked on an ethereal trip into America's wilderness. A little more than two hours north of Jackson Hole, we were detoured by a herd of snow-covered buffalo that decided to have some sort of Bison World Congress smack in the middle of the only road. After sorting ourselves through that little mess, we toured through a premature winter wonderland of snowy roads, moose, a few more buffalo who hadn't apparently heard that their convention was a bit further south, and finally an endless herd of elk feeding in the lush pastures next to the hot springs and geysers that turn Yellowstone into a spectacle of indescribable beauty. After nearly 10 hours of transit over 11,000-ft. mountains, descents through water-carved canyons, and a display of wildlife that rivaled any zoo, we arrived at Gidding's estate just as it began to snow again. We settled in at his plush log home (on the market for a cool six million as he builds something a bit grander) and grabbed a drink before touring the studio facilities just down the hill.

As always, Al was the perfect host and eagerly took off on an excited account of the system he had acquired that allows him to "up-convert" his invaluable library of film and video to the new widescreen 16x9 HD format. We sat there for hours entranced as he previewed sequences he shot decades before that now were magically transformed into images with such depth and clarity that you felt you could reach into the screen and touch a whale, a shark or actually feel the warmth of a sunset. It was mind-blowing and more than a bit surreal. Once again, Al had not only anticipated the new technology but was leading the implementation process. At 65, he had managed to turn the clock back and re-birth film he'd shot in his youth. He was as excited as if he'd been given a time machine.

We had to begin somewhere, so I figured a good shark story would get Fred's attention. That's where we started. »

Your partner, Leroy French, was involved in a shark attack that is worth sharing. »It was the early 1960s and we were new to the dive business. We chartered a fishing boat to the Farallon Islands about 25 miles out from the Golden Gate Bridge. We had about 12 people on the boat and it had a very high gunnel making it awkward to dive from. We were in double 90s, which were the order of the day in that era. I was wearing a set of those doubles; Leroy had a set of triples on a la Cousteau... you

GALAPAGOS: BEYOND DARWIN (Discovery) Producer, Director, Cinematographer | BLUE WHALE: LARGEST ANIMAL ON EARTH (ABC/Kane) Producer, Director, Cinematographer »

THEATRICAL FEATURES | **DOCUMENTARIES** | HONORS AND AWARDS ::

know, those skinny 40s or whatever. We were both taking pictures and others were spearing fish. I was on the surface at the boat that had this very high ladder and an eight-foot climb straight up the side. Suddenly a woman started screaming. And I thought, oh my God, somebody's caught in the current.

Where were you when all this started? » I was getting out of the water. I had come back to the ladder and was awkwardly handing up my camera when this woman started screaming. So I turned and looked and it wasn't a woman! It was Leroy, about six octaves above what is humanly possible. I couldn't understand what was going on. I was a competitive swimmer all through school, so I took off swimming overhand with those awkward doubles, face down with my mask around my neck. I got about halfway to him and looked up. Leroy was about 30 feet away in a huge pool of blood. A very riveting moment. There was a 12-ft. circle of blood around him. We had no sense of what was going on. We couldn't even spell White shark in those days and really knew very little about them.

Leroy later said this was his worst moment, this huge tail went up behind him and he's staring at me but hearing the rush of water. He's already been hammered terribly once (receiving 470 stitches or something later), and the shark was so huge, maybe a couple thousand plus pounds. I first thought it was a killer whale. Again, we were green young kids just getting into it, but then I knew it's no killer whale, it's a huge shark! And it took him by the legs and "glump" he disappeared - silence.

So I guess I was on automatic, as people do under those circumstances. I dropped my face in the water again, then swam to close the distance and stopped. I'm treading water and frantically looking around in the middle of this big blood ring. All of a sudden he popped up, maybe 10 feet away, screaming out of his mind. And I remember thinking this will be a total mess unless I can get him turned around. We both had on these outrageous tank systems so I sort of manhandled him so I could get a grip on the manifold. Those triples were just right. I could really grab the bar. He was just out of his mind. I mean, literally just primal sounds, as I towed him to the boat, basically waiting for the next jolt.

About three years earlier a woman had been hit at Monterey. Somebody was swimming with her and the shark continued to hit her, so I was waiting for that. The other people were climbing up anchor chains and scrambling out of the water any way they could. A guy named Joe Michato still had his tanks on and was going up the anchor chain hand over hand. People had just never experienced anything like it - total mental chaos. Anyway, Don Josslyn jumped in the water and swam to us, which I thought was unbelievably ballsy, considering what he'd seen happening. With everyone else scrambling by whatever means to get out of the water, Don jumped in to come help. What a guy, and was I glad to see him! Ironically, later on he was a victim of a White shark attack himself, less than 10 miles away. How many people have been in two incidents of that magnitude? Anyway, we towed Leroy to the boat. Then we had to get him up that ladder straight up the side of the hull.

Where had the shark gotten Leroy? » The first bite took most of the calf muscle from one leg and part of his buttocks was hinged back and flapping. The second time the shark took him by the arm and pulled him down about 20 feet. A little sidebar, he had a SportsWays vest on with the little CO2 cartridge thing. At about 10 or 15 feet down Leroy pulled that. We thought later maybe the explosive nature of the cartridge sort of startled the animal and it released him. Anyway, we were trying to get him up this ladder

THE SECRETS OF UNDERWATER VOLCANOES (Kurtis) Director, U/W Photography | TITANIC: TREASURE OF THE DEEP (CBS/W. Cronkite) Producer, Director, Cinematographer »   Q+A »

THEATRICAL FEATURES | DOCUMENTARIES | HONORS AND AWARDS ::

and I remember trying to keep my cool so that the rest of the people would not completely give way to panic. So I'm trying to hoist Leroy out of the water before the shark hits him again. People told me later it was raining blood. You can imagine. He was cut wide open and I could see blood vessels and tissue hanging. I remember this because they looked like telephone lines that had slipped through the shark's teeth.

Finally, with blood pouring all over me, we got him on the deck and radioed the Coast Guard to send a helicopter with a basket. He was then lifted to the Letterman Hospital. He was there for about two weeks then went through a long period convalescing. That experience kind of broke his spirit. Anyway, Leroy recovered and dealt with the dive shop for a while. Eventually I went to San Francisco to pursue filming and Leroy went off to the Caribbean and sort of disappeared.

How old were you guys then? What year was that actually? ⟫I was about 25. It was 1962 or 1963 maybe.

And Josslyn? ⟫I don't know how many years later but Don was in water 15 or 20 feet deep diving for abalone and all of a sudden, "this great head came off the bottom" and Don fended it off. The shark took his leg and lifted him completely out of the water. Don is a big, tough, focused guy, and realizing he had the abalone bar in his hand, he gripped the handle and punched it into the side of the shark's head once or twice, really hammered it, and the shark let him go. Luckily the boat was right there so he got out of the water with much less damage than Leroy. But still, to be involved in two major moments within five or six years was amazing.

Another interesting incident following that was in San Francisco when the Southern Pacific Scuba Club guys came in to the store. They were renting gear to go to the Farallons, and I said, "Listen, I'm in this business and I want to promote it, but don't go to the Farallons. It's a major breeding area for White sharks, don't do it." And this guy said, "Yeah, yeah, we know, it will be fine." That Saturday I was in the shop when all of a sudden the radio crackles with a news bulletin: a group of divers was being attacked by a school of White sharks at the Farallons. Anyway, it was another guy, Jack Rochette, who was hit under similar circumstances.

So 12 years later when you were put in touch with Peter Benchley to preview the *Jaws* film, how did you react to the movie? ⟫Stan Waterman and I went to the premier in New York. There were only a dozen of us attending. I thought, there was no way this film will ever approach the voltage of the real thing, so I'm going to have to think of some discreet response after this film was over. You know, "Gee, wonderful, terrific, I loved it", whatever. I remember being into the Spielberg magic when the young woman was hit at night in the sea, watching through my clenched fingers and covering my face. When it finished, my thought was how could they release this to the public? It's going to rock like Hitchcock's film *Psycho*. I thought, there's no way they can show this because filmgoers will pass out in the aisles.

One of the interesting things Spielberg did that was so effective was never showing you the shark until the third reel. That made it scarier. ⟫It was the dramatic and skilled management of those scenes. The anticipation, the leaning eight inches forward in your seat, and just not knowing. He sold that very well in a dramatic sense. It was quite remarkable. I think it *was* the third reel when the shark came up off the back of the boat and Roy Scheider is pitching chum out the back, that's the first time you really ever got a good look at the head, and he says, "I think we'd better get a bigger boat" or something like that. And the whole audience at that point had just gone, "huhhhhhhhh!" It was crazy.

Give us some reflection on *Titanic*. Did you ever think that that film could do what it did? ⟫No one anticipated *Titanic's* success. I think everyone agreed that it would be a remarkable film. Jim Cameron called me during the edit and said, "You must come over." I went over to a sort of inner sanctum in his house where thousands of cables literally took over like a postproduction facility. We went into the inner chamber where he had his screens and playback systems and he showed me elements, unedited but assembled, where the stern came up and people are dropping like flies and hitting stanchions. It was five times as severe as what you saw in the film. I mean, once again sort of like Spielberg, I thought, "Jim, how can you..." and

IN CELEBRATION OF TREES (Discovery) Producer, Director, Cinematographer | VISIONS OF THE DEEP: THE UNDERWATER WORLD OF AL GIDDINGS (Nova/BBC) Cinematographer ⟫

THEATRICAL FEATURES | DOCUMENTARIES | HONORS AND AWARDS ::

Jim Cameron and Giddings
during *Titanic* shoot, 1997

he stopped me and said, "Al, I've got to cut about 80 percent of this." And he did. But if you saw six or eight shots that were originally 10s on the on dramatic scale, there were 30 shots, 50 shots, I mean again and again. I was impressed! This film would be another one of those shockers in that sense.

We anticipated a very successful film. But I didn't feel that anyone had any sense of what it would end up doing - a billion, $700 million. Unbelievable. The next closest film is probably *E.T.* at $400 or $500 million, and I'm not sure that's accurate. Something that no one anticipated was the fact that legions of people, tens of thousands of people, saw it four, five, six times.

The studio had to argue with Jim on the money to complete the film, right? » Well, at one point in time I sat at the Golden Laurel Awards with Jim and he leaned over and said, "Fox reinstated my deal." Because before the film was completed, the budget was running wild, $200 million plus, Jim gave up his director's fee and his points and said, "You must stay with me and back this. I'm glued to my convictions and to my excitement over this film. Here's my money, take it." It was an extraordinary gesture for a director to do that. I really respect that

kind of conviction in Cameron. He is an unbelievably capable director and will leave, in the truest sense of the phrase, no stone unturned to deliver. So the deal ultimately was reinstated. They gave it back to him, and the amount of money that represented was unbelievable. I think I said at the moment, "Jim, they love you." And he said, "Baloney, they don't want me across the street."

Earlier when we worked together on *The Abyss*, I anticipated that film doing much more because I saw so much of that material on the screen. It was really something riveting. And I thought *The Abyss* would go to the moon. I think Fox made a mistake. They pressed Jim in the end to deliver under any circumstances because of the money and interest on the money and all of that. And so Jim more or less mailed in the end because he was sick and tired of arguing with the bean-counters over the budget. I think you can make some mistakes early on in a film, but if you make them at the closing of the film, people leave with a negative impression. So *The Abyss* floundered around and did not go over the horizon financially. But no, *Titanic*, I thought wouldn't do anything like *The Abyss*. And so as Bill Goldman says in his book about Hollywood, "nobody knows anything."

391

THE ETERNAL SEA (Disney) Circlevision, Director & Director of Photography | MYSTERIES OF THE SEA (ABC) Producer, Director, Cinematographer »   Q+A »

THEATRICAL FEATURES | **DOCUMENTARIES** | HONORS AND AWARDS ::

in the first release because they pressed him, so it stumbled a bit. How about this? When they came to Jim to do the DVD version he said, "I'll do it if you strike 20 release prints. I'll cut it in my long version." He added 25 or 30 minutes to the film. And when it was released, there was a reviewer in *The Chronicle* in San Francisco who wrote, "Never in my career did I think I would say the following: the film to see this weekend is not a new release but Jim Cameron's director's cut of *The Abyss*, at 30 minutes longer. It is brilliant."

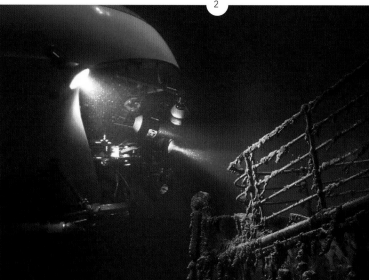

1. Giddings on film set, 1979 2. *MIR* submersible hovers over *Titanic,* 1997 3. Giddings and film crew on the underwater set for *The Abyss,* 1988

How was *The Abyss* supposed to end? It was a fascinating film anyway because of all the technology you guys had going. » Technology and the pace of the film. It did not let up for a second. That's right. Just as you said, the ending originally was incomprehensible.

When they finally did release the director's cut, I know scores of people who went out and got it just to see what it was all about. And everybody had the same reaction: How in the world did they not release it this way the first time? » As it was shot and released, frankly it didn't make any sense. And when they put the extra scenes back into it on the director's cut, now all of a sudden you realize that this is an alien presence that's coming here to destroy the earth because we can't get along with each other. Jim's wonderful vision was not realized

I went to the Galaxy Theatre, which is the nicest theatre in San Francisco, and couldn't get in. I thought I'd go and there would be a handful of people. Forget it. I was there with a date and couldn't get through the door. So I came a couple of nights later on Wednesday, the second showing or something, and watched it. People stood up and applauded. I think the Fox executives blew it the first time around. Had it come out of the chute in its full-length form, it would have done a few hundred million dollars at the get-go. Cameron is the most remarkable force to ever grace the halls of Hollywood.

When is he coming out with his next masterpiece? » Well, I'm curious. He's so taken with the undersea world that he's snorkeling around. That's my way of saying, he's playing around with all sorts of other things and not, I'm sure, making real money

DIVE TO THE EDGE OF CREATION (National Geographic) Co-director, Cinematographer | WATER, GIFT OF LIFE (Music Video) Producer, Director, Cinematographer »

THEATRICAL FEATURES | **DOCUMENTARIES** | HONORS AND AWARDS ::

393

OCEAN SYMPHONY (MCA Music Video) Producer, Director, Cinematographer | OCEAN QUEST (NBC) Producer, Director, Cinematographer »

Q+A »

THEATRICAL FEATURES | **DOCUMENTARIES** | HONORS AND AWARDS ::

as it relates to his day job. He's driving Hollywood crazy because they would all like to see him do *Terminator XII* and *Alien VI* and *Titanic II*, you know, billion-dollar deals. But Jim is really enamored with the underwater world and would like to be Jacques Cousteau, I think, or somebody of that ilk in the historic sense.

Let's talk a bit about high-definition technology. I think it was 1997 when you shot the Truk Lagoon HD program. Give us your perspective on how that went and what it was like to shoot in that format the first time. »Well, in my opinion, high-definition television is not an upgrade. I hear people make that reference all the time. It is a new form of entertainment with seven times the resolution. I anticipate when the dust settles, considering the American appetite for entertainment, the average home will have an 80 to 90-inch screen. The images will be very refined. HD is such a visceral experience that lights will dim, the family will gather, phones will shut down, and people will be entertained by this incredible technology. This ability to give you an almost three-dimensional image will be there in a way that will make tears flow and emotions soar. Right now you can watch fantastic films like *Titanic*, on your square 19 or 20-inch television, but the film wasn't shot in a 4 x 3 aspect ratio, you miss part of the picture. And with speakers only four inches in diameter there's no horsepower behind it emotionally. So, people don't respond as they do in a theatre. When HD is full up, transmitted to everyone's home, those experiences will be unbelievable. There are people concerned now on a number of fronts over HD and its resolving powers as it relates to say a Mike Tyson fight. Its clarity combined with such graphic and brutal sights could really blow people away.

There are also concerns about models or aging actresses and how to handle that since the HD image is dead-on real. The cameras now have diffusion ability so that you can deal with skin tones to manage that. But HD is magic. What Sony, Panasonic and others are pioneering is unbelievable. Nobody, in my estimation, has a clue as to what's coming. It's an unbelievable format. And "frame-grabbing," the ability to capture a single image off the motion picture stream, is unbelievable! You really can't do that with the old technology of film or even modern digital

1. Hutton and Giddings at Bret Gilliam's annual DEMA dinner, 1999
2. The equipment and camera workshop
3. IMAX 3D camera rigged with DPV drive units, Galapagos, 1999

stuff. But if you shoot with that HD camera, you dial in an electronic shutter, you're producing 30 frames a second, 108,000 frames an hour, any one of which could be frame-grabbed and printed on the cover of *National Geographic*.

What tool would be more exciting for someone in the nature world - whether it's Jane Goodall or me - than an HD camera shooting a breaching whale and having the ability to go in at the apex of the breech and extract the most dramatic frame. Imagine model calls in the future where a model like our dear mutual friend Lauren Hutton walks in, does a shoot for 15 minutes then while the camera is still running, we're able to go through those 40,000 frames and extract only those that Revlon wants for their new magazine. Whoa, the whole photographic universe just changed!

I gave a presentation at Jackson Hole a year ago, and at the end, all of it was at this voltage. Then I said there's only one downside, and the audience got set to hear the second shoe drop. The downside is, I'm not 30 and beginning my career with this new format. Cameron is experimenting with something that the two of us looked at very carefully, and he really is pioneering this. He went to Japan and talked to Sony. Out of that came a couple of the newest F900 cameras reconfigured to allow the cameras to be close enough, that is, the two lens centers to be close enough to shoot 3D. If you shoot 3D high-definition, two cameras, you then have a universal format. You can go in any direction. You could go to IMAX and expose 70mm film for display in Japan and all over the world, Paris, Tokyo, wherever. You can go to 35mm, you can go down to television, you can go over to 35mm theatrical, anyplace, any of those entertainment formats from one

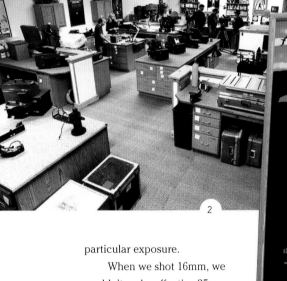

particular exposure.

When we shot 16mm, we couldn't make effective 35mm slides and we certainly couldn't do IMAX. You had one relatively myopic format. An HD camera as we know them today and the HD camera that I'm talking about has three chips, part of the recording system, and each chip has about 2,200,000 pixels, bits of information. Those three chips create an imaging system, the base of which is about seven million pixels. Sony will show a new camera in Las Vegas next year. Each chip is the size of a 35mm frame, so each chip might carry 10 million pixels. I just said that the best HD cameras today that blow my mind have a total of 7 million bits of information plus. This camera will be 10 million pixels per chip for a total of 30 million bits of information. Now, do you think you can extract stills from that?

Oh, I think so. 》You could – I mean they'd be the quality of something shot with a 500C Hasselbladd. Remarkable. So HD is a new form of entertainment of the most provocative nature. Imagine a format that allows you to shoot, surface and then view it.

For my whole career we've shot and then shipped film out for processing. Then we get a telex back in Tahiti or Galapagos or wherever we are, from the lab in LA saying, "no apparent technical difficulties." Well, that doesn't really tell us anything about the artistic nature. Did you like it? Was it great? Watch what this change to HD does to the shooter. Like Howard Hall, who's already a brilliant filmmaker, jumps in the water to shoot a sequence and when he comes out he can play back his material in the field! Everybody, the lighting guy, you, everybody that supports him can look at it. With the old film cameras you have two-minute and four-minute loads. IMAX is a three-minute or 16mm is a nine-minute load. I now load 40 minutes of tape!

If HD is the obvious future, let's step back to 1999 and talk about your film, *Galapagos in 3D*. You're talking about pushing an IMAX camera system so huge that you actually had to mount DPVs on it to fly it around. Do you think that's over with now? 》The 3D IMAX camera system that Howard Hall told me about had my knees turning to jelly initially. I ended up putting four DPVs on the back and came up with a series of bolts that I could walk the propulsion package up and down on this master plate until I found the sweet spot. Then I could fly that system. Once I had it up to speed, it was very effective. I'd literally launch it, disappear for an hour

Bret Gilliam

Giddings in high definition editing
suite, Montana studio, 2002

with a one-ton, multi-million dollar system and come back with smiles usually. We sort of pioneered a new approach to using a blacksmith system. It was the total opposite of my comments on HD in the sophistication level. We'd shoot, store the stuff, and ship it once a week. We wouldn't hear anything for a month, so if we were out to lunch on exposure or the camera had a problem, we were effectively screwed.

And now with the two-camera HD system that, in essence, will simulate 3D, what are we talking about in size for that compared to this 3D IMAX 2,000-lb. monster? » Probably a package that would weigh 125 pounds in air that is relatively small, might be 25 inches long, 18 inches wide, 20 inches high and load 40 minutes of material. And you have the use of zoom lenses, beautiful primes - all matter of things that any creative Director of Photography would demand in any creative film project.

But HD and IMAX - and I love the IMAX format - both have their place in film. Remember, I have walked in two camps throughout my career. Half of it has been natural history nonfiction and the other half has been Hollywood. One of them is the pure art of documenting real-time, exciting natural history, and the other is the art of illusion. Here at our studio, we have all sorts of formats from 70mm to HD from HMI lighting to Motordrive Nikon still camera, all those different formats. And the reason that they're here is I don't know whether the next call is going to be 70mm IMAX or theatrical or natural history nonfiction HD. So that's really been an exciting and challenging adventure and experience, and I've carried the best of both worlds across the line. Learning theatrical techniques and approaches in lighting has really done wonders for the sort of shooting that I do underwater in a natural history sense.

That's a very good point, so much of your natural history stuff is shot with a theatrical slant. » Well, when you looked at the HD material here today, down in the editing suite, all of that was borne of an approach that nobody uses. I would go to the bottom with a couple guys at midnight in Palau with a camera that had a super-zoom ability and diopters, as well as the ability to fill a frame with a macro subject or back off to wide angle and manage it all on the bottom. So whatever we encountered we could cover. We don't use fins in 50 - 60 feet of water or with 60 - 80 pounds

of weight so we could literally tiptoe around the bottom. Your breathing rate is way down, believe me, much below what it is with fins and your balance is unbelievably enhanced.

People very often say, "Come on, this was shot in an aquarium." I mean it's too dead still perfect.

Steve Burns was here a couple of weeks ago with four executives from *Discovery,* and they said, "Nobody uses zooms like you do. Nobody racks focus and zooms at the same moment or moves in and pans to the right with focus clicked on. That's a dramatic move." I realized early on that in making images with a wide-angle, "set-it, forget-it" system is not enough because people had already been exposed to all of this. I felt we had to fill a frame with a whale's eye. We had to make it dramatic. We had to tell a story with the camera. Those are the approaches to dramatic storytelling.

I was reading that CBS is filming some of their new shows in HD and some of them in film, and some of the people were commenting that HD is still not at the level of film with certain light situations, similar to digital photography. Do you agree? » No, they're totally incorrect. I think those people are classic Hollywood or classic film people who are perhaps a little intimidated by the technological jump, the move to high definition, the move to computer systems, so to speak. All this means is that they are more comfortable with older technology. I made the move 15 years ago to tape. The criticism then was, "Al, how could you?" At the first Jackson Hole symposium, Mark Shelley was there. He was the only other tape guy and was on a panel. I walked in and Mark said, "Oh, my God, I'm saved. Al is here." And he knew that I had a hot new tape. So I screened that tape for those people, and the place went stone quiet. After I finished the first hand shot up. A guy said, "I'm really upset with you." And I thought, okay here it comes. Then he said, "You just cost me $120,000. I just bought a film camera, an Arri SR and I bought this and that. It's not going to do what you're able to do with tape."

I'd seen the handwriting on the wall 15 years ago and migrated to tape for a dozen obvious reasons. Again, playback in the field, how can you put a price on that? Forty-minute load. And it goes on and on. Today, I'm really vindicated. I sit downstairs with today's latest imaging technology, pioneering a process once again as I did with Sony's cameras, changing the black levels, changing the chromo levels and really getting into those cameras, which is a part of history. When I started with video, Sony couldn't spell "natural history." They had no market there. And I said, "Listen, there's a whole other market. It's not huge, it's not like the news market but it's significant." So when Jeff Cree prevailed, put a video camera in my hand and we started shooting in Cocos, I discovered that I loved the entire system but didn't like the image all that well. Jeff just kept saying, "I can change that, I can change that", so in the field I would look at it and say, "It's not a Kodachrome look, where are the blacks?" Jeff would then get into the camera with a plastic screwdriver, open the side, and take my breath away.

You're talking about a Betacam. »Yeah, Betacam 300. He would dump the black. He had the ability to go to a part where he could back it off. Then I would shoot and say, "Oh, that's much better, a much better contrast, more like Kodachrome." Then I'd carry on about something else. I remember the third or fourth day in Cocos the camera was so dialed in that I wanted to take it to bed with me for fear the electrons would fly off in the night. They used to drift with the old tube camera. Those guys would have to dial those cameras in every day sometimes in the early news broadcast usage. I took Sony's cameras and radically changed them.

About an hour ago you said you love this new HD format, your only regret was that you're no longer 30 years old. »Right.

So, now you *really are* 30 years old again because you're taking your entire library and transferring it to this 16 x 9 aspect. Tell us about that. »It goes back to what I said previously. My first innovative technological adventure in the electronic world was to establish the black parameters of cameras. Today, Sony's cameras are delivered factory setup, but you can get into the menu and set it to your specifications. It's really wonderful. I've made deals where I would say, "Listen, I'll shoot this project for $8 instead of $10 but I want stock footage rights. I want the ability to use this natural history nonfiction material that is not dated by cars, clothes or period dress, there is no architecture, there are no straight lines, no buildings, all of that. I want to be able to store this and I want to be able to

see income from the library sales. I saw natural history stock early on as something to treasure, something historic, something wonderful, the first whales, the first White sharks in slow mo, all of that stuff.

Now let me back up a little bit. Three years ago I said, "I'm a little nervous, more than a little nervous about what's going on with HD." The digital world is coming on and all of the tape that I shot over the years was analog. So my library is going to be antiquated, 18th Century Fox. All these wonderful images are not going to be applicable. So I said, "I'm either going to sell it bargain basement or I'm going to contemporize." So I started running around the world talking to everybody; and fortunately I've met the most wonderful tech people, Larry Thorpe from Sony and Michael Brinkman, president of Panasonic. I started chatting with all these guys asking, "Is there an

instrument or magic box in existence that will allow me to take an analog electronic image and up-convert it to digital tape?"

It seemed logical to me, and I'm not a super tech. Could all of these millions of hours and tens of thousand of projects on tape be up-converted to digital? I'm not going to leave all of this stuff in the vault. They're going to convert it into the digital world somehow, right? I not only wanted to go to the digital world but to go to the HD world. So while in Japan with Jim Cameron, I started talking with Larry Thorpe, then with Michael Brinkman. Everybody had a neat box. Everybody said yes. I looked at the results and was not impressed. I'm really more of a nut over definition than the image. Look at the Emmys on the

GALAPAGOS: BEYOND DARWIN, Gold Medal, New York Film Festivasl | WATER, GIFT OF LIFE, six Gold Medals | SHARK CHRONICLES, Emmy, (ABC)»

THEATRICAL FEATURES | DOCUMENTARIES | **HONORS AND AWARDS** ::

1. Forty years of film library archives
2. Sylvia Earle in JIM-Suit prior to record deep dive beyond
2,000 feet, chronicled in Giddings' special *Mysteries of the Sea*

wall. None of them are for programming. They're all for cinematography and the art of film.

So everybody who knows me said, "Al, you'll never find anything that will satisfy you. Equipment that will effectively up-convert to HD doesn't exist." Enter Barry Clark and a couple of people said, "Are you aware of the Teranex company?" I soon found the company and talked to the various people there. They volunteered to do a demonstration. That demonstration, which included about half a million dollars worth of equipment, took place here in Montana. Sony had the feed and record machines. Teranex had the magic up-conversion boxes. My vision is to have a system that would allow me to take my tape images, at least, the last 15 years of my career and all those titles, *Blue Whales*, *Titanic*, *Galapagos*, etc., and up-convert that square image to wide-screen HD. The Teranex guys said, "We can do it." The Sony guys said, "You're not going to be thrilled. The resulting conversion will not be brilliant, at least to your standards."

So, anyway, the Teranex guys felt confident

and came here. I gave them a copy of *In Celebration of Trees*. They put it through the process on that now-famous Wednesday two years ago, and I was speechless. The Sony guys came into the room seconds later and slumped in their chairs in total disbelief. The Teranex system had come out of the U.S. Government surveillance world. The Teranex box not only does an up-conversion to HD but it will up-convert and down-convert from any format in the world. It doesn't make any difference. Any tape will go in and out of that and make anything else. The box also deals with electronic noise reduction and refinements. I'm using five percent of its capability to do a magic process, and the machine is incredibly more capable. Anyway, that was the second innovative and ground-breaking moment, at least in my personal world. First was a camera

OCEAN SYMPHONY, American Film Institute, Best Video of the Year, Nature & Science | GRIERSON AWARD, Photographic Excellence | THE LIVING EDENS: PALAU, Emmy, (ABC) »   Q+A »

THEATRICAL FEATURES | DOCUMENTARIES | **HONORS AND AWARDS** ::

re-management and all that I shared with Jeff Cree, a brilliant guy at Sony, and the second is happening right here right now.

I'm here in Pray, Montana, population 63 or whatever it is, with a system that is really space-age. I'm taking analog square images in today's formats and up-converting to HD with seven times the pixel count resolution. The results are stunning. I have had people from NHK and the *Discovery Channel* to *National Geographic* here to see this process. I can't tell you how pleased I was with their response. I am able to take all of these titles representing the whole history of my career along with a lot of the history of the undersea world and its animals and convert it all. It's a thrill to go into the vault and take the 287 hours I shot for *Blue Whales* and convert it. Imagine the process. I went out, shot it, shipped it, viewed it briefly in the field to make sure all the parameters were technologically online and forgot about it. They cut it, sent the material back and we put it in a vault. I did that title after title after title. It's so exciting to go through the material, up-convert, color-correct and reformat. I can't tell you what a good thing it is, and in thousands of shots I'm saying, "I cannot believe this."

And so this year we will up-convert 20,000 to 30,000 scenes. They represent about a 6 to 1 ratio, so within the original material is another 200,000 beautiful scenes. At the end of the year we'll have 110 or 120 categories for the library. Each one will be meticulously organized by subject matter. For instance; one tape will consist of nothing but White sharks, the next tape, all blue whales, the next, all sunsets or rattlesnakes (because I've also done a lot of topside stuff). The library will include both underwater and topside shots.

So to wrap it up, the second exciting, innovative, ground-breaking, pioneering effort goes on downstairs. We now have the only suite of its kind in the world (*Editor's note: as of late 2002*), although other people are coming up to speed. We're taking all of that analog video 4 x 3 and converting it to widescreen, and no information is lost because of the anamorphic process whereby the image is squeezed, top and bottom slightly, to create the wide-screen format. The pixel count, the information recorded, is there in total. The Teranex system is so refined that it extracts from the tape more information than probably any other processing super box on the planet. So these

Bret Gilliam and Giddings at his Montana home, 2002

Fred Garth

are exciting times. In the end, we will take all of the HD tapes, newly rendered with seven times the resolution and frame-grab maybe 75,000 stills from the best selects to add to our still library.

SMPTE Fellowship | BLUE WHALE: LARGEST ANIMAL ON EARTH, Emmy, (ABC) | MYSTERIES OF THE SEA, Emmy, (NBC) | SEARCH OF THE SHINOHARA, Emmy »

THEATRICAL FEATURES I DOCUMENTARIES I **HONORS AND AWARDS** ::

400

Tell us about when you showed Howard Hall, who made a business decision to sell his 16mm library, the results of your magic box system. »Well, you know, Howard is a wonderful character. He and Michele were in Jackson Hole when Sony asked me to anchor their tech panel consisting of all Sony people more or less and me. It was a 90-minute panel where all the Sony guys had different facets of HD technology. At the end, they said, "Al will now blow a few minds with something that everybody has said you can't do. I spoke for 20 minutes about my up-conversion, commenting again that there was only one downside - that I wasn't 30 and starting my career. I then finished by showing projected images in HD, up-converted images on a Panasonic HD projector and people sucked their breath in. I mean how could you take material 13 or 14 years old, Betacam SP, analog square and in 2001 project it onto an HD wide screen 16 x 9 format image? It was unbelievable.

What was Howard's reaction? »He said to Chuck Nicklin, "I could throw up. Goddam. Giddings comes flying out of the weeds with another outrageous approach to video." I believe Howard knows that I have tens of thousands of hours of really well-shot material. I had Paula Lumbard in here, a very innovative pioneer in stock footage who's opened a stock footage house in Los Angeles dedicated to HD. She heard about us from the video world. We got together, made a date and she came up about six weeks ago. I know that she would agree with this word: speechless. She sat down in our suite and said, "How can this be? How can you put a cookie in and get a chocolate éclair out?" Within a week we had a contract and she's going to represent us in LA. She's really brilliant and we're sending her beautiful up-converted HD material.

So I am bumping these images, refining them, creating a HD master, while simultaneously creating a digital 4 x 3 master for today's market. In other words, when I push go on a shot, it records it in two formats simultaneously. I would bet big money in the next five years there will be refinements in the up-conversion process. I will then take my newly up-converted tapes and refine them yet again. Teranex already has the ability to double or triple the resolution of HD.

I've always felt that any way you cut it, no one is going to leave all of the archives unused. Howard Hall's wonderful stuff and Stan Waterman's wonderful stuff, and all of the material that has been shot historically over the last 40 years in any format will be beautifully up-converted. There ain't no way *NHK* is going to leave a million hours of material in the vault and sign off on it. It's their history; it's culturally important. Every country in the world has such an archive. Are they going to leave it there? No. It's rendered in the contemporary sense, the last 30 or 40 years, in a resolution that's totally up-convertible by machines that are not even on the market yet. Do you know what I'm saying?

Absolutely. It's an amazing technological break. »That also applies to stills. *The Geographic's* fabulous collection will not be left on the table. I'm early in making this move, taking images to wide-screen HD, but now I'm smiling because I know that at some point there will be yet another more sophisticated box that will take what I've done and refine it again.

Fred and I left the next morning after a meal of excesses at a nearby restaurant that caters to the jet set who fly in for the food experience. We promptly drove into another premature blizzard that ultimately closed the Yellowstone roads due to the intense snow and forced us to backtrack from Wyoming to Montana through the western exit. We then slogged across the state to the other side of the Rockies and turned south in Idaho. The storm intensified and we gradually reduced speed to less than 20 mph. As we turned east again to summit the Teton Pass that would require us to climb above 10,000 feet over a road that twisted and turned next to precipitous drop-offs, the full fury of the blizzard came on us. Cars were sliding off the mountain, accidents were everywhere and when we reached the top a local cop advised us not to even attempt the descent. We shifted into the lowest four-wheel gear and fearfully creeped down the mountain while rodents passed us making rude gestures. Fred kept his door ajar and his seat belt off in case I blundered and he was forced to bail out before we plummeted to our deaths. Nearly 15 hours after we bid Al farewell, we crawled into Jackson Hole and in weary relief, began drinking… heavily. The trip was worth it. But next time we'll visit in the summer. ■

401

American Express | Energizer | Chevrolet | Starkist | Squibb | Exxon | McDonald's | Chevron | Pacific Telesis | General Electric | Dream Quest | At&T ▦   Q+A ▦

THEATRICAL FEATURES I DOCUMENTARIES I **COMMERCIALS** ::

Ernie Brooks

MAKING A STATEMENT WITH IMAGES

BY MICHEL GILBERT
& DANIELLE ALARY

Danielle Alary

Michel Gilbert runs tape
with Ernie Brooks, 2006

THE YEAR WAS
1975 OR WAS IT 1976...

time flies and I cannot relocate that copy of the
late *Skin Diver* magazine. The issue included
a portfolio of images from a California-based
photographer. Contrary to most color-addicts, he
was shooting exclusively in black and white. »

I was addicted to color too, the cheap
GAF-brand slide film I was using cost less
than $0.10/image, processing included!
My images were so bad that it made a lot
of sense to use it.

But the b&w portfolio left an imprint
in my mind and some 20 years later, I
decided I would try to do a bit of work
in black and white… I quickly learned
that mastering that media was far more

complicated than splashing a colorful fish
on a slide… and went back to color.

Fast forward: the year is 1999, Danielle is a member of the still photography
jury at the World Festival of Underwater
Images in Antibes, an event where the
attendees list looks like the Who's Who of
the underwater imaging world. Officially
they say they attend because of the inspirational flavor of this unique gathering.

After a few Pastis, a drop of Rosé over patés and cheese they candidly confess that it is an addiction: the food, the wine, the French Riviera's relaxed atmosphere and topless beaches or the fact that they can play Rolling Stones songs in the impromptu u/w photography band that rocks the night, at the Festival's improvised bistro. Any excuse, including photography, is a good reason to be there!

Let's get back on track here: Danielle was a member of the stills jury chaired by the black and white portfolio man: Ernest H. Brooks II. Besides being the quintessential gentleman – a title that he shares with Stan Waterman – Ernie, as he likes to be called, exudes calmness second only to what is required from micro-surgeons. Instructions were straightforward: Pick the 10 images you prefer. Danielle was anxious beyond belief – cramps and cold sweat included thinking: "I am not a bad photographer and managing our photobank provides me with kind of an eye but how will he react to my choices?"

The jury later met and, as expected, there were discrepancies; mixing an American, a Canadian, two French and an Italian in a jury is asking for trouble: North Americans tend to agree whilst the European fight each other and shout like crazy! As jury members were quarrelling over composition, lighting and whatever other Cartesian arguments, the soft-spoken Chair simply said: "Pick the image that has the strongest message."

All of a sudden, there were not twenty different choices - it took less than five minutes to pick the winners! And Danielle was relieved since her ten initial picks matched Ernie's for all images but two… She was even more relieved when Mr. Brooks whispered her name to the President of the Festival as a good choice for jury Chair. Coming from a man of his stature, this was the best recognition she could receive. As a teacher, a mentor for generations of photographers and more so for underwater trigger-happy up and coming image-makers, Ernie loves to share, stimulate, recognize and promote what others do.

We had wanted to interview him for so many years without finding the time or the right occasion. Finding Mr. Brooks is not a simple task. He is a secret man who surfaces once in a while at DEMA, Our World Underwater, the Boston Sea Rovers, or in Antibes… only to disappear again. So we made arrangements for an interview in March 2006 at Beneath the Sea … and conducted it at DEMA the following November. Oh yes, we are still working on some black and white underwater images… ∎

405

Was photography always your career? »I was born to be an image-maker. My grandmother was a portrait photographer, my uncle was a landscape photographer, both in black and white. My father turned the corner in color; he became a world-famous flower photographer before founding a photography institute. Photography was in the conversations. I loved the process, it was time consuming but beautiful. Being in the dark was also a very important part of it. It took a lot of time so it gave you time to think, time to be with yourself. And I think a lot of my work is that way; it is very peaceful, at peace with itself.

All the work we have seen from you is done in black and white. Has it always been like that? »Definitely. My father was colorblind; I can't see how he accomplished what he did. Black and white has always been in my life. This is how I have seen everything. Coming from a photographic school later in my life, the black and white process was just fantastic; having complete control of everything, starting from the light up to the finished product. It also has to do with my mentors, the people that I studied: Ernst Haas, Ansel Adams, Edward Weston, Alfred Stieglitz and Edward Steichen. I just love the quality of black and white, and the color.

You mean the absence of color? »No, the color of black and white; it has its own color. Grey is beautiful; and black; and white.

Did you want to emulate what Ansel Adams has done in land photography? »Only his light. I tried to learn and apply the way my mentors were seeing the light; the way they were capturing it… the details in the highlight and the details in the shadow. You have to know where to put the exposure and you have to know in what range you want to process it. It needs to fit the emulsion, the range of the film. That's the way we were raised. That curve has to be there. Today, it is possible to falsify that a bit with computers and software, but the joy then was getting that on the negative and into the darkroom making the print. That was an important part of my work and so was the importance of the statement.

And what about underwater photography? » Portrait, landscape, nature and flowers were already taken so, I was left with very little to explore: I turned to the sea.

When did you start diving? »1949, that was very early skin diving.

Did you start in underwater photography at that time? »It was around; Dr. Hans Haas was my hero. He and his wife produced beautiful black and white images. I would show those pictures to my parents and they would say, "Their blacks and their whites are not that great." But for me it was the discovery of a whole new world. In the late 1940s and early 1950s there were some great underwater photographers that produced wonderful work. Jerry Greenberg and Luis Marden, for example. The latter even presented me with the NOGI Award in 1975.

You were also part of an emerging breed of great photographers? »We can say so. People like Ron Church. He and I used to enter competitions and it was great. He was good and so was I. He had the advantage of photographing turtles and corals in all these exotic places. I would have kelp and sea lions. Al Giddings, then a still photographer, along with Bob Hollis were just starting. We founded the Academy of Underwater Photographers at the time.

What was your first underwater camera and how did it evolve from there? »My father had an old Exakta, a very primitive camera. I built a housing for it. It leaked miserably. I took one or two photographs with that rig and decided that 35mm was not for me. Remember, the only film we had was Panatomic X, ASA 40 – try to push that one some place… it didn't work. So 2x2 and 70mm became my style.

Which camera did you use then? »The Rolleimarin, a Hans Haas-designed housing manufactured by Franke and Heidecke that enclosed their twin-lens Rolleiflex camera. It was housing number 107. I had an f2.8 Rollei lens.

Many of your published work was done with a Hasselblad; when did it come into action? »I went from the Rolleimarin directly to the Hasselblad SWC. The former was too limiting for me. I like wider angles and I didn't like macro. I don't care for close-ups. I like the vista, the feeling… the great expanse of the ocean. I liked the wider view, the sunlight, the "landscape".

Haven't you done macro photography underwater? »In 1975 I made two rolls of 35mm macro pictures and the resulting images created an exhibit later that year in Beijing. For me there was no challenge in underwater macro photography.

Your father founded the Brooks Institute of Photography; did you introduce underwater photography in the program? »My father founded the Institute back in 1945. I came along and assumed the presidency in 1971. I turned the school into a four-year university-level program. I introduced the audio-visual, the undersea technology, the high science end of it, physics and optics. I brought it into more of a liberal education and created a graduate school for master degrees in art and science. But the undersea program gave me my birth, everything I ever wanted in life. It was the students that made it.

Was the underwater photography program always your favorite at the Institute? »Definitely, without it I wouldn't have stayed! As divers know, there is a calling into the ocean. We wanted our students to make a statement on what they felt about a subject and publish their work. This made the program different.

Was the underwater photography program profitable? »It never made money. It was the costliest one. I would meet with my board of directors and tell them, "Let's see how much publicity this underwater photography program can create for us, how much energy it can generate for the institution."

You later sold the Institute but I think that they still have an underwater photography program, don't they? »The have a smaller underwater photography program than what it used to be. Had I stayed there I would have made it into a four-year program.

North Americans tend to talk too much about equipment and/or technique. Was it hard for you to tell students that equipment and technique are part of the work but there is far more to it? »F-stops and shutter speeds don't work! You learn technique early in school and you are right, photographers tend to concentrate too much on technique. You see it so much in the portraiture field and also in other aspects of photography. It's all about optics, physical optics, shutter speeds. It has nothing to do with what I wanted to say. I learned my craft very well. I could walk outside, look at the sun and tell you exactly what exposure I need in the deepest shadows, in the brightest highlights. So, what else do you want to talk about? Let's talk about how we will light the subject, this is important. How will we separate it from the background so it comes forward? Or do you want it to come forward? What is the most important thing you want to say with your image? Those are the important issues.

How do we tell or teach someone to go beyond the f-stop question, start seeing the light and use it effectively? »Today, with the technologies that drive the profession and the amateur field, they are slowly learning what it took us years to absorb. They are realizing that digital photography cannot record the highlights and shadows on the same exposure like film did. They are thus using techniques like masking, adjusting it, fine tuning it. In other words, getting a foundation probably without even knowing it. This is almost a self-taught process today. Also, everyone must get continuing education. I personally love to go to school and to continue to learn. You cannot stop learning. I opened up a book today and I looked at some of the images where I found new scenes, new ways of looking at things. There are also new media created and all of this is very exciting.

Wouldn't it make us better photographers if we started in black and white? It imposes an approach where one has to concentrate on contrast, shapes, texture and composition. Isn't it the best school to learn the basics? »I tend to agree with the statement. Black and white is like starting with a blank piece of paper. It is one tone and you create something on it. The 21 or 8 steps of grey create such delicate transitions. I definitely would not be where I am, had I had just color in my background. Some of the best photographers in the business today started that way. This is all we had then.

However, when I look at Chris Newbert's work or at your work for example, so much of it has to be in color. It is nature's way of living. My work takes some of that away. In my case, I love the way highlights and shadows fall on the subject. Also, it is easy today to turn a color picture into a black and white one. In the end, it depends on the subject.

As photographers, we found that the learning curve is not straight. It starts slowly and then, over the years, there is a dramatic improvement. Has this been the case for you as well? »One becomes more selective. You know what you want to do, which statement you want to make with your images. Your eye becomes more selective. In my case, since I only had 10 exposures to work with, I would take just one or two photographs during a dive. I was searching for light first and then for the subject or, conversely, if I found a subject, I would search for proper light and try to bring the subject into this light. The idea is to make a statement with light. I had a rule on my boat, Just Love, which I used to teach underwater photography. I told my students that they had to control their index finger. They did not have to come back from a dive with a full roll of exposed film. The selective eye is a key notion in photography and there were many books written on this concept.

In the case of your imagery, were most of the images made in your mind before entering the water? »No, it was not the case. A few maybe, but not the majority. An image that comes to my mind is the three sea lions perfectly positioned, shot

against bright sunlit background from 60-ft. deep that became my signature. I squinted and saw that they were in the ideal composition and made only one picture. Each time I would go in the water with sea lions afterward I would try to make a similar photograph and it never happened.

Your book, *Silver Seas*, contains incredible images. Tell us how it came to be? ❯❯ I never even thought about doing a book. I had always promised to myself that at 65 I would retire and do something else. A good part of my life was spent as an administrator and this was not my favorite type of work. I loved the students and the teaching though. So, when I was preparing to retire, my Vice-President and former

students convinced me. They found a publishing company and told me that I simply needed to pick the negatives and they would do the rest of the work. The name *Silver Seas*, a natural, came up from Media 27, those involved in the publishing. Also, the proceeds, when they come, will go to organizations like Ocean Future and when they are exhibited, it should also benefit the kids.

There are many images in the book, which one is your favorite? ❯❯ It has to be "Spot" the harbour seal because there is a story behind the image, an interesting story. It is 6:30 one morning in August, 12 students are aboard Just Love. We are anchored off Anacapa in the Channel Islands near a sea lion and

harbor seal rookery. I am alone, snorkeling, looking through the kelp. Here comes this harbor seal. I think it is a boy since it is fat. It comes up, grabs one of my fins, spits it out and leaves.

I swim back to my boat with one fin as the students are getting up. They ask, "Mr. Brooks, how come you only have one fin?" My answer, "Don't talk to me, get me my Hasselblad." The students add, "Isn't it early to go snorkeling?" I said, "That's enough, can I borrow your fins?" Someone hands me those very long blade fins – I hate them. I get my snorkel, look down, it's 7:15 and I say to myself, "I am diving down to 15 feet, he's going to be 1/125th at about f/8, ISO 800, and I'll nail him!"

I dive, snap one image, and come back up. The seal leaves and, as I swim back to the boat, the guy tries to grab my snorkel with its mouth - a terrible character. We photographed Spot many times over the years but I never got the same image again. Also, one year, we get there and Spot had a little one… this is when I realized that the seal was female. She comes forward and pushes her pup towards me… this brought tears in my eyes as I realized the bond that existed between us. Spot is my favorite picture because of the story.

Tell us a bit about your technique? I know how to read light and here's an interesting story. I got my Hasselblad in 1961 and gave it up in 2000 without ever changing an O-ring! Some water would creep in and, eventually the shutter got stuck at 1/125… Of course, I wouldn't tell my students… Since the shutter and the aperture were coupled together, I ended up with a fixed combination, it was either 1/125 at f/8 or 1/250 at f/4 and so on… those became my settings. I would go and find a subject to fit them.

And you never seem to use a strobe? I only used a strobe once with my underwater work. The image is in my book. It is called "Magnificent Blue"; a Blue shark lit from underneath. This is the only picture I lit with a strobe.

What would be your first advice to someone who would like to take up underwater photography, as a hobby or a profession? First, education is really important. You need to understand today's craft. Not so much what I was raised with but today's technologies and techniques.

You need to perfect that up to a point where the person comes up with a realistic image. Then the person needs to find an outlet for what he or she wants to say. It does not need to be a magazine; it can be through books, the Internet, etc. There needs to be an audience, an outlet for what you need to say. If I was starting today I would go see the Hemisphere magazine people or the American Way magazine publisher, En Route magazine editor and bring them my story, my statements. I would tell them, "Here's what I want to say to your customers, here's my story." It needs to be done more. You need to go beyond the obvious.

And where should underwater photographers go for inspiration? This is a good point. I would go to a library, a hardcopy library. I'd look at books. I'd look at the pages, the paper they were printed on, the beauty of the images and the statements that are made by the artists. It could be pictures from years ago. Look at them like you do with all art. You cannot go "www.photography.com" and find it. You find those things under Library of Congress number XYZ. Look at Adams, Steichen, Stieglitz, Weston and others. Look at those who influenced the earlier people. Who did they look up to? You have to go way back in history as well as exploring contemporary photographers and artists.

Is it easier to make a photographer out of a diver or a diver out of a photographer? Good question, because they are mixed techniques. But I'd rather work with a photographer. First, because we speak the same language. And I think that if you do a cross-section of today's underwater photography it is done by someone who truly loves photography and wants to do something with it. There are exceptions but someplace, there is land-based photography in their blood.

How does someone learn to see in an artistic way like you do? It is hard to say; some of those things are in your genes. For whatever reason, I have always been able to see the little ants walking on the ground. My uncles and my parents have always been visual people. They would look at people differently; you have to have that. Language creates the vision; the words create the vision.

What is the most overlooked aspect of underwater photography in what you see from contemporary photographers? »What we need yet to do is to make statements that are significant and that make some changes within the ocean environment to a positive stance. That's easy to do with shark-fining or whaling, for example. What is much harder to do is to make pictures that will help in reducing water pollution. There is a need to do more visually to show to the world what is happening when we use cyanide to capture fishes for aquariums. The same applies to the dynamite use in fishing. Also, we need to show the true aspect of bleaching. We have a responsibility with our craft to do something. We see artists doing it and we are artists. This is one of the reasons we created the Ocean Artists Society.

What do you see in the coming years in the underwater photography field? »It is now global; it is an international subject. Many photographers from all around the world are making statements. This is healthy. I see more and more documentary work about what is happening in the ocean and how we can contribute. We need to publish more in foreign languages, not only in English.

Is digital a blessing or a curse for photography? » It is truly an incredible blessing because it allows more people to do it, with the help of modern technology, in their homes. It is healthy.

Should someone start by learning the craft using film or digital? »I think that you do not need to learn with film. It won't be long before you won't see much film around. I don't look for Fuji or Kodak to continue this foolish polluting process that is chemical photography. I have seen too much chemicals go down the drains.

Is there an image that you would want to make but have never been able to achieve in your lifetime? »Not really. I love my craft and the joy of making images fulfilled my dreams. Something interesting: many times I would not realize how good the image was until I started working on it in my lab. I would watch the image materialize on the paper and see how much better it was than when I tripped the shutter.

So, on many occasions, the print would be better than what you thought it would; was it the case more often than the opposite? »Yes, and there is an image in particular in the book; it is called California Gold. You are looking up at the kelp on the surface and just where the bubbles are on the kelp there is a little starburst. I did not see it when I was making the picture. I saw the whole kelp but not that detail. I happened to make my test strip just in the middle of the image where this starburst is located. When I saw that I felt lucky; to me this came as an extra.

If you had to relive the past, would it be the same or would it be different? »I wish I had been more of a shepherd, to bring more young people into the program; help more those who could not afford it. Education is expensive and I wish I had gone to other schools and found ways to attract more students through scholarships. I did as much as I could but I could have done more. ■

421

ERNIE BROOKS'S MAGNIFICENT BOOK *SILVER SEAS* MAY ORDERED THROUGH:
Media 27 Inc., 3030 State St., Santa Barbara, CA 93105-3304 | ph: 805-563-0099 | www.media27.com

Q+A ▥

Howard Hall

MASTER OF DOCUMENTARY UNDERWATER FILMS

BY BRET GILLIAM

Michele Hall

HOWARD HALL HAS ENJOYED HUGE SUCCESS AS A FILMMAKER. THAT MAY BE THE BIGGEST UNDERSTATEMENT...

I've ever made. And even that concise praise would probably make him wince. Because, in spite of being blessed with an innate talent and instinct for creative filming that perhaps is only shared with an iconic figure like Al Giddings, Howard is the epitome of reticence... »

a seemingly shy, almost reluctant hero. Having been privileged to share stages with him over the years and to spend time in the field with him on an IMAX shoot, I can attest to both his striking intelligence, as well as his private gracious generosity. And he possesses a delightful sense of ironic and understated humor. Like Stan Waterman, an evening spent with Howard over dinner and

wine is both entertaining and profound.

He got his start in film by spearing fish for Giddings on *The Deep* back in 1976, Howard has forged ahead to be recognized as one of the finest and most creative underwater cinematographers in the world. As a team, he and wife Michele have received seven Emmys for television specials. And they are considered the best to use the IMAX format underwater. Back in the summer of 1998, I caught up with them when we rendezvoused off Cocos Island where they were on their fifth three week expedition filming a new IMAX production, Island of the Sharks. They had chartered the 90-ft. *Undersea Hunter* while I had the 120-ft. Sea Hunter with an eager crew of rebreather divers aboard for the month.

I invited Howard's crew over for dinner and drinks on our ship and a good time was had by all. Howard agreed to sit down with me and let the tape recorder run later in the week. So a few nights later I braved a typical Cocos downpour to drop

impossibly nice. As attractive a couple as you'll ever want to meet, they're also incredibly patient and gracious. I watched Howard get backed into a corner the night he visited us aboard *Sea Hunter* by an over-eager tech diver who interrogated him without letup for nearly an hour. Poor Howard couldn't even eat his dinner. Finally, Michele and I interrupted Howard's cross-examination and banished the offender to the upper deck on the promise that he could bend a technician's ear about reconfiguring his rebreather unit.

I apologized to Howard for being subjected to such a barrage of questions.

in for the interview. All of us had spent about seven hours underwater that day thanks to the rebreathers and with the help of a few memorable bottles of red wine, I got Howard to talk about his work and how he got started.

In a world that is frequently populated with more than its fair share of pretentious, arrogant, pain in the ass, "I'm so important" types… Howard and Michele are almost

He replied that "it wasn't a problem with the volume of questions, it's just that he wasn't listening completely to my answers." How's that for a complaint? I love this guy. Even Michele threw her hands up and told him to finish his dinner already.

So on the promise that I would listen carefully and completely to all responses, the interview began while the rain deluge splashed occasionally into our wineglasses. ∎

Chuck Nicklin

Bob Cranston

1. Black sea bass trophy circa 1973 2. Filming Hammerheads at
Cocos Island for *Secrets of the Ocean Realm*, 1993
3. Howard on location for *Seasons in the Sea*, 1988

426

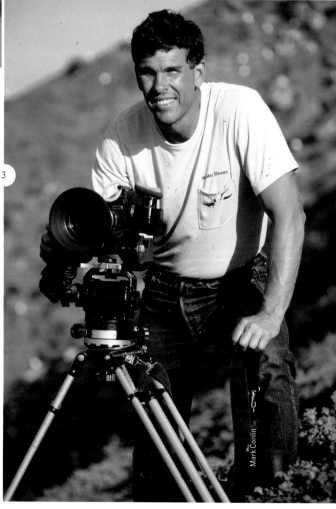

Mark Conlin

Okay, the obvious first question, when did you start diving? »When I was six, my parents took a trip to Guaymas Mexico and we would go snorkeling. I didn't know how to swim, but I learned to snorkel dive. I had one of those full-face masks with the pair of attached snorkels with the little cages holding ping-pong balls. I remember using that before I could swim and my parents watching over me from the pier while I tried to catch starfish in six feet of water. I snorkeled often after that. When I was in high school I took up competitive swimming and in my junior year took a LA County Scuba class.

When did you start to work in diving? »Almost immediately. I got a job at LA County Skin Diving Schools in Whittier and got my instructors certificate when I was a senior in high school. Then I went off to college in San Diego and found job at San Diego Divers Supply. Working as a diving instructor paid my way through college. I later moved over to the Diving Locker and worked there from 1972 through 1978.

When I started at the Diving Locker I was inspired by Chuck Nicklin who was supplementing his living by selling underwater photos as well as film assignments. A lot of pros came from the Diving Locker, Marty Snyderman, Steve Early, Flip Nicklin, Mark Thurlow – a bunch of guys got their start there. I started taking still photographs, writing stories for diving magazines and by 1978 I was able to make it a full time job.

I remember that one of you first jobs in professional film was on *The Deep*; you went on from there to do other things. Tell us about the progression of projects that you got into from there. »After the NBC Shark Special with Waterman, I went to work with Stan on several *American Sportsman* episodes. I produced a couple myself, one of which popularized the Marisula Seamount in Baja where Stan and I filmed schooling hammerheads and people riding manta rays. I then directed 16 episodes of *Wild Kingdom* over the next five or six years.

Marlin Perkins was with us on about half of those shows. Tom Allen who was a rep for Scubapro was with us on the other half. Marty worked on many of them as second cameraman. I was with Marlin on his last dive during the winter off Catalina Island for a film about squid. He was 80 years old. He was a great guy.

Jack McKenney was also instrumental in my career progression. He was very generous with his advice and support. He also recommended me to Hardy Jones for a film about dolphins on the Bahamas Banks. Hardy had already made one film out there using Jack. But Jack was already booked when Hardy called him the second time. So Jack suggested me. I got the call from Hardy and we eventually did a whole series of important films together. He was the first person to produce a film about the spotted dolphins of the Bahamas Banks. Hardy later went on to become an accomplished filmmaker and an important marine mammal conservationist.

Both Stan and Jack were important as far as getting me started, making it easy for me to get jobs, promoting me as a young cameraman. I worked with Stan on many different things and Jack recommended me on a variety of projects. I learned a great deal from both men. I learned a lot about professionalism from Stan, how to work with people and keep everything in proper perspective. Stan once said, "Every time I see someone else achieve something great, a little piece of me dies." Then he laughed. He was making a joke, but there was a lot of truth to the statement. It's easy to envy another's success, but it's a laughably stupid emotion. Stan handles it better than anyone I know. What I learned from Jack was much different. I studied Jack's camerawork. Jack was doing things that even today most underwater cameramen can't begin to figure out. He was a genius with an underwater camera.

Such as? »Jack was the first guy I ever saw to use a tripod and bright surface powered lights to do macro cinematography underwater. I remember seeing one of his films at a film festival in San Diego and there was this spectacular close up shot of a nudibranch crawling across the reef. It was full frame, unbelievably colorful and rock steady. I'd never seen colors like it. So I learned how he did it. It was done with tripods, heavy weights, and lots of light and special macro lenses. He went to a great deal of trouble. Most underwater photographers would have just hand held the shot, but Jack was a perfectionist. Jack was doing the most sophisticated underwater wildlife work of his time.

Speaking of state of the art camerawork, you went from 16mm to larger format to IMAX. What was it like to do the first underwater IMAX 3D production? »Graeme Ferguson, one of the founders of IMAX, called me up one day. He had seen *Seasons in* *the Sea*, a film I produced that won best of show at the Wildscreen International Film Festival. Graeme wanted me to do the first ever IMAX 3D film underwater. I couldn't believe it. At first I thought it was a joke. He wanted me to write the script, set up the logistics, go where ever I wanted to go, just do it. It wasn't until after Michele and I met with him that I really began to believe it was going to happen. The problems were almost overwhelming. The camera was just being finished at a cost of 3 million dollars. Bob Cranston and I booked a trip to Toronto to see it and to create the concept for the underwater housing. The camera itself weighed 340 pounds with a full load of film. The housing was going to come in at around a ton. To our surprise IMAX did a fabulous job of building the housing based on our design concept. Of course, it should be a good piece of work, the cost was $350,000. It was possibly the most expensive underwater housing that was ever produced.

Let's talk just a minute about the dimensions and the weight of this thing. »The housing weighed about 1,300 pounds depending upon how it was rigged. It was loaded with two 2,500-ft. rolls of 70mm film. That's 5,000 feet of film. The weight of the film load alone was 50 pounds. By the time you purchased the film, processed it, and printed it to IMAX, that single load cost $25,000! And that single load of film ran for only seven minutes. It cost $60 a second to run the camera and it took five seconds for the camera to come up to speed and another five for it to ramp down. That's about $600 just to pull the trigger to see if it will run. The whole thing was just about half the size of a Volkswagen beetle.

So how did you move it around underwater? »Slowly. If there was any kind of current at all, it was impossible. We couldn't work in current. Surge was problematic too. We made the film in California where surge is a given. If you got caught between the camera and a rock, it could crush a hand or break ribs. Usually, we took the thing down and mounted it on a tripod. In some cases where there was dead calm, two of us would handle the camera and do slow moving shots. There were some shots where we pushed it through a kelp forest. But once you got it going, it was pretty much out of control. We spent over $50,000 building a thruster system to propel the camera. But I simply didn't have time to learn

to fly the thing. We made one dive with it, crashed a few times, and gave it up.

We worked at Anacapa, Santa Cruz, Catalina, San Clemente, San Miguel, and even off La Jolla. The nice thing about it was I figured I was fail-proof. The film was being made for a single theater in Osaka, Japan. I never dreamed the film would be shown in the United States. But by the time it was done, there were 12 IMAX 3D theaters in the US and all of them had booked the film. It debuted at the new Sony IMAX Theater on Broadway at Lincoln Center and it sold out! It was the highest grossing single screen in North America during Thanksgiving of 1994. It was still playing on Broadway four years later and highest grossing IMAX 3D film ever made at the time. Incredible. Today it still ranks in the top three or four highest grossing IMAX 3D films and is still playing.

There are very few couples that have been able to make their careers work as well as you and Michele. When did you guys meet? »Michele and I met in May of 1975. She had decided to learn how to scuba dive, found Chuck Nicklin's Dive Locker in San Diego and signed up for lessons. Marty Snyderman signed her up and put her into my class. I started at the Diving Locker in 1973. *The Deep* came along in '76. That was probably my first big break. I had already been shooting still photographs, recently published my first photos in *National Geographic* magazine, which was a major milestone for me. Chuck Nicklin got me involved in *The Deep*. I was basically a gopher, my job was to spear fish and attract sharks in order create the shark sequences for the movie. I was a very minor player.

You worked on one of the best action sequences in *The Deep* out in the Indian Ocean or the Coral Sea, right? »It was the Coral Sea and that is the only part of the production in which I was involved. I was there only to do the shark work; I never met Jackie Bissett, Robert Shaw or any of the other actors.

Did you know Al Giddings prior to *The Deep*? »I had never met Giddings, Stan Waterman or Jack McKenney. I met all those people in the airport as we departed for Australia. Jack and Stan became incredibly important in the years that followed, in developing my career. Stan has been a mentor

The massive IMAX 3D camera and housing in the California kelp, *Into the Deep*, 1994

for me. I learned a great deal about underwater cinematography technique from Jack McKenney, he was way ahead of his time. Both of those guys bent over backwards to help me get started in this business. During *The Deep* I learned a lot about leadership from Al. And, of course, Chuck Nicklin was my original inspiration and got me the job in the first place.

and shoot a three-minute load of film and then return to the mainland would be out of the question.

Almost any helicopter or float plane that flew to Cocos would have to refuel by landing on a boat or on floats, weather permitting. I considered all of these options and in the end an ultralight presented itself as the most practical solution to the IMAX

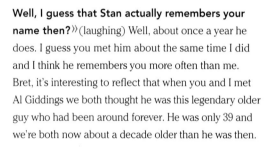

1. Ultralight aricraft used for aerial sequences at Cocos Island during *Island of the Sharks*, 1998 2. Mark Thurlow, Bob Cranston and Hall aboard *Undersea Hunter* with IMAX camera

Well, I guess that Stan actually remembers your name then? (laughing) Well, about once a year he does. I guess you met him about the same time I did and I think he remembers you more often than me. Bret, it's interesting to reflect that when you and I met Al Giddings we both thought he was this legendary older guy who had been around forever. He was only 39 and we're both now about a decade older than he was then.

Back to technology advances, we are sitting here talking to you underneath the wing of a specially designed mini-plane on floats. Well, the ultralight is a solution to a difficult problem. Giant format films typically contain aerial photography; there is almost no IMAX film that has been made without this type of photography. Producers of large format films tend to feel that aerial shots are sort of a must. Everyone, myself included, wanted aerials but to get a conventional aircraft to Cocos Island is not practical.

When we were in the pre-production stages of the film there was a float plane that flew out to bring passengers to a sportfishing operation in Cocos. That organization has closed business and the float plane is no longer in Costa Rica. A round trip flight from the mainland to Cocos Island is 600 miles. So, therefore to fly from the mainland to Cocos with the IMAX camera

camera problem. Obtaining, testing and the shipping of an aircraft of this caliber to Cocos would not be easy. To make the project happen we recruited John Dunham, a good friend of mine, to help collaborate on the preparation plans. John is qualified to operate a wide variety of aircraft including the ultralights. This Cocos film was an opportunity to get John involved in productions, so I commissioned him to buy an aircraft, rig and test it for the handling of IMAX aerial camerawork. It was an expensive production to get the aircraft to Cocos, but it has worked out great. We have shot ten rolls of film to date and have had no technical problems to speak of.

In addition to the aircraft and the very technical camera systems utilized in this project you were one of the first crews to embrace the use of rebreathers. We became interested in rebreathers when we completed a film on the Sea of Cortez in the late 1980s. The film contained an important

sequence on hammerheads, these sharks will spook at the sound of scuba bubbles and were extremely difficult to approach. I had been down there many times before, filming hammerheads, for programs such as *Wild Kingdom* and *American Sportsman*. For all of those films, I had free dived to get into the schools of hammerheads, which was tough. Swimming down sixty or seventy feet, with a 50-lb. movie camera, and remaining long enough to get a usable shot of twenty to thirty seconds is very hard. Swimming back to the surface after taking the shot is much more dangerous and difficult. For this film I wanted to find a way to get into the school of sharks and remain filming for a while.

The film we were making was called *Shadows in a Desert Sea*, which was made for the PBS series *Nature*. Anyway, I dreamed of having a closed circuit rebreather for getting into the schools of Hammerheads without spooking them. I remembered seeing the Electro Lung advertised in *Skin Diver* magazine back in 1969 and wanted one ever since. Of course, Electro Lungs were not on the market long, a half dozen divers were killed almost immediately and the lawyers shut the product down. In the late 1980's, there were no rebreathers available to civilians so I began to look for ways of getting my hands on a Navy Mark 15. Unfortunately, at the time one could only obtain a Navy Mark 15 by stealing it from the U.S. Navy and that was not going to work.

I began working with Bob Cranston who had some military contractor experience from his days working for DUI (dry suit manufacturer). Bob knew some individuals involved in the Mark 15 program and it just so happened that our timing was perfect. Biomarine (manufacturer of the Mark 15) had just lost their bid to build the new Mark 16. As part of their bid for the Mark 16 contract they had built a prototype called the Mark 15.5 or Mark 155. When Biomarine lost the contract for the Mark 16, that left the prototype rigs in limbo. We started out by leasing a pair of 155s from Biomarine for use during the filming of the *Shadows* project. Later we managed to purchase two of the units. Initially, we were terrified of the things; everyone told us that we were going to kill ourselves. During each dive we made a dive, the list of people who had died on the Electro Lung ran through my mind. We memorized the manual, developed our own equivalent air depth tables, and taught ourselves along the way. It took about 50 hours underwater before we began to feel comfortable. But eventually, we got great schooling hammerhead footage including the first record of mating hammerheads ever filmed.

Have you modified the rebreathers for your use since then or are you basically using them the way they were? »Our Mark 155s are now highly modified. It would be easier to list the parts that we haven't changed rather than list the modified parts. We've modified the plumbing to provide low-pressure diluent

Howard and Michele Hall with IMAX
camera, Cocos Island, 1998

and oxygen for BC inflation and emergency open circuit. We've created a mounting system, modified the mouthpiece design, and dramatically altered the static balance. We've altered the counter lung size, changed the primary electronic logic circuit, and gone to LED displays. Mark Thurlow is now working on a new secondary display that will incorporate an alarm system. The 155 is not an easy system to use right out of the box, there is no facility for BC inflation and no open circuit back up. With our system, if you need to go to open circuit, you have about 20 cubic feet of diluent to breathe and then you can switch a valve and breathe about 20 cubic feet of oxygen. The units are now working extremely well; I personally have logged just over 715 hours (as of 2007 more than 1900 hours) and feel more comfortable and safer on my rebreather than I do on standard scuba.

How much of your shooting are you doing on rebreathers as opposed to open circuit? »We are doing almost all of our shooting on rebreathers now. About 95%. The primary reason we are using rebreathers would probably surprise you, it surprises everyone else. The silence of bubble-free rebreathers is not the major advantage in wildlife film work. Certainly, there is a difference between the way animals react to you when using a rebreather as opposed to open circuit, but the difference is not so great that it justifies the huge additional logistical hassles that come with rebreathers.

The reason we use closed circuit rebreathers is because we get an optimized gas mix at any depth we go to. Our decompression is minimized, and the life support capacity is essentially unlimited. We can potentially stay down up to twelve hours on any dive we make. That's a really big deal. We no longer determine what we are going to photograph based upon how much air we have in our tanks. We simply stay down until we get the shot or until we are physically exhausted. The air supply clock no longer runs against us. Unlimited dive duration – for natural history film work, that's a giant advantage!

What was your typical working bottom time on this shoot? »Typically, it takes us an hour and a half to shoot a single roll of IMAX 2D film. That may seem surprising since each roll is only 3 minutes long. But the shortness of the running time is balanced by the

cost. Those three-minute rolls cost over $3,000 to buy, process, and print. It takes a long time to set up each shot and we try to wait until everything is perfect before we press the run switch.

Depth of field is a big problem in 70mm photography, so we do much of our camera work from a tripod. The tripod weighs 65 pounds and we usually anchor it down with an additional 50 pounds of lead weight. When things are going well, Cranston, Thurlow and I will often stay underwater while our surface crew recovers and reloads the camera. We have had mornings when things happen much faster, one time we shot five rolls on a single dive and stayed underwater for nearly four hours. To date, we've shot 242 rolls of film here at Cocos (some of which was above water wildlife and aerial photography) and I've logged 271 rebreather hours and 197 dives. And we have one more 22-day trip to go.

I understand you have had some vision problems, »I accumulated more than 90 hours underwater during our first 22 days of shooting out here in Cocos. Towards the end of that trip I began to notice significant problems with my eyes and by the time we were on our way home, I couldn't see well enough to get around the airport terminal. Michele called DAN as soon as we got home and no one knew what the problem could be. Finally we found a doctor in Pensacola, Florida who knew what was causing my vision problems. Dr. Frank Butler, a Captain in the Navy who works a lot with the SEAL Teams, said I had hyperoxic-induced myopia. It's a condition that is not uncommon among patients treated for burns or skin disorders in hyperbaric chambers under high partial pressures of oxygen for long periods. Although it had never been seen in divers, to his knowledge, he was sure it was induced myopia.

Hyperbaric patients are generally treated daily for 90 minutes or so at oxygen pressures well over 2 atmospheres, much higher exposures than we are getting on our rigs. But 22 days at four hours a day at 1.3 atmospheres of oxygen was enough to cause my vision problems. He suggested that hyperoxic induced myopia has not been seen in divers because nobody has put in so much time at 1.3 atmospheres for so many days straight. The good news is that it usually goes away after a few weeks once out of the water. It took three weeks for my eyes to normalize after that first trip.

Tell me about the film you are making now. »
The film we are doing now will be titled Island of
the Sharks. It is being produced by Michele and
is directed by me. It's a Howard Hall Productions
endeavor and our diving crew includes Bob
Cranston, Mark Thurlow, Mark Conlin, and Lance
Milbrand. We're also getting some diving help from the
Undersea Hunter's dive master, Peter Kragh and from
Avi Klapfer. We are making the film for WGBH Nova
Large Format Films; they produce the PBS series
Nova and have made a number of giant format films
including Special Effects that received an Academy
Award nomination. Susanne Simpson was the
director of Special Effects and is now our Executive
Producer. We began discussing this project with Nova
about four years ago and received the contract to
make the film about two years ago – long before El
Niño began to raise its ugly head.

**Had you done anything with *Nova* or is this a
new company that you are working with?** » No,
I have never done anything with *Nova* before, although
Susanne and I discussed the idea of making a large
format film as far back as 10 years ago. It has actually
taken us this long to make it happen which is typical
in the film business. Our projects usually take
several years of development and then six months
of pre-production followed by a couple of years of
production before they are finished. We actually
began building the IMAX camera housing for this film
before we started production of our recent television
series, *Secrets of the Ocean Realm*.

1. Mark Thurlow tends Howard in the current at Alcyone pinnacle at
125 feet, Cocos Island, 1998 2. Howard shooting from the top of the bird
rookery at Manuelita Island, off Chatham Bay, Cocos Island, 1998
3. *Undersea Hunter* anchored in the lee of Manuelita, 1998

What's the budget on this film? » It's in the
neighborhood of five million dollars. It's a little hard
to be specific because there are a variety of parts
to the budget including promotion and educational
outreach. To do the actually filming and post-
production, we will spend about four million dollars.

**Is that a pretty large budget for a documentary
film or is that standard?** » That would be a really
big budget for a television documentary; large format
film budgets typically run between three and six
million. If the film were to be shot in 3D, the budget
would be more like about $8 million. Island of the
Sharks is a 2D film; our budget is right about in the
middle for a project of this dimension. Typically,
what people do is not create a script and then cost it
out to come up with the budget, instead an average
budget amount and what the market will bear will
determine the cost. On *Island of the Sharks*, we will

434

spend over 130 days in the field, most of which will be diving at Cocos Island. I could probably get by with less time out here, but because I have so much time, the film should be terrific. If it's not terrific, I have no excuse.

In this case you are doing this entire film at Cocos. Tell us why you picked Cocos as a spot for production and how you picked your support facilities. » Obviously, Cocos is a great place to dive and there are some spectacular animals here. But really the decision to make a film

just film; we bring 800 pounds of 70mm film with us on every expedition!

We'll spend nearly a million dollars on film, processing and printing and the boat cost is also substantial… but we needed a substantial vessel. It was crucial to have a crane that can lift a 250-lb. camera system into the skiff, and skiffs that could hoist the camera on and off-board. We couldn't do it from inflatables. Logistics was a big part of the decision to work at Cocos. If the *Undersea Hunter* were stationed in the Galapagos, we would be making the film there.

Avi Klapfer

3

435

at Cocos is a combination of what the site has to offer and the logistics available. The logistics are incredibly important whether I'm doing a television film, but especially, if I'm doing a giant format film. What Cocos had to offer was good diving, good marine life, and an excellent logistical support. Our support vessel, the *Undersea Hunter*, is ideal for this operation. Avi Klapfer's operation is very slick and professional, the vessel is capable of handling the huge IMAX camera equipment and there is space for crew and all our stuff. And we bring tons of stuff, literally. We fill up one entire cabin on the boat with

But here in Cocos you pretty much have the whole place to yourself, don't you? » Well that's partly true. Other divers seldom get in our way. Mostly, everybody has been quite courteous about diving where we were trying to work. The disadvantage to Cocos is that there is not a lot on the reef, very little invertebrate growth and not many small animals. It has been hard to get a lot of color and variety into the film.

You have ex-military rebreathers, an ultralight aircraft, and state of the art camera systems. What else do you want? If you could look into your

**wishing ball, what would take your filming another
step forward?** »My life is already over-complicated. The
older you get, the more of this stuff you accumulate. I
look back on the days when I would go spearfishing with
fondness. I would put on a weight belt, mask, fins and
snorkel and go diving. It was so simple; it could be done
in an afternoon not an entire month. Now, my diving is
always a major logistical production.

**Of course, you didn't get $4 million to go out
spearfishing either.** »No that's true. I'm not knocking
it. Anybody who feels sorry for me is completely
crazy. I might say that I would really like to have a
120-ft. ship with a submersible on the back. But the
truth is, I don't want that. Things are as complicated
as I want them to get now. Having said that, my next
film will probably be an IMAX 3D film. I've already
directed one of those and it's considerably more
difficult than what we are doing here.

**You also did some IMAX work with humpbacks
on the Silver Bank; tell us a bit about that
experience.** »It's been my experience that the
only way to get close to whales is if it is their idea.
Typically, what we do is go out in our boat and
approach the whales as close as we can without
disturbing them. We put the boat in idle so they knew
where we were and would wait to see if they get
friendly. Usually, they move off on their way. In order
to get anything good, the whales have to cooperate.
During the weeks we were on the Silver Bank, we had
one or two very good days. On one day the whales
followed us around all day. We used open circuit to
film the whales on the bottom at ninety feet. Anyway,
we went through two tanks of air and four rolls of film
each, Cranston and I. When we went back to the *Coral
Star*, our liveaboard, the whales followed us and we
dived with them the rest of the afternoon right under
the big boat. You couldn't scare them away. Michele
shot some terrific stills. The whales were having a ball.

**You have how many trips scheduled on the
Undersea Hunter out here to Cocos?** »Each trip
is 28 days long and we get 22 full days of diving
at Cocos. This is spread out from January through
October so that gives us time for the seasons to
change. Bait balls tend to occur at one time of year
versus another, birds tend to nest seasonally. By

The sun sets between Cocos and
Manuelita over Chatham Bay, 1998

spreading out the expeditions it gives us a chance for
best weather and our best chance at the marine life.
If we get skunked on one trip, then we have a chance
to catch up.

**This year in particular because of the El Niño,
you must have had some fairly twitchy moments
when you didn't have marine life that you might
normally have expected.** »We picked the worst year
in meteorological history to make this film. There is
no question about that. When I saw you at the Boston
Sea Rovers in March you were asking me about the
prognosis for your own rebreather expedition coming
up for the month of August. At that time I hadn't even
seen a shark. In fact, until this week when you showed
up I still hadn't seen a hammerhead. Now they're all
over the place again.

436

Bret Gilliam

Timing is everything. I must be your good luck charm. »Yeah, I guess so. But our advantage is the type of scheduling we do when we make a film; spreading it out over a period of a year or a year and a half with very long expeditions in evenly plotted spaces throughout the year. Even in a really bad year, like this one, we are bound to get some good stuff. We were here sixty-six days before I saw my first hammerhead! But they're back now and the stuff we got when the hammers were gone is all good material. This is going to be the best film we've ever made. Hammerheads are important to the film, but there are many other things in the film besides hammerheads.

After 110 days of diving you are going to accurately depict diving at Cocos, even though you have had some slim pickings in the beginning due **to El Niño.** »I think we are going to get everything that Cocos has to offer. We may not get the whale sharks or manta rays. They may not come back in time. But we will certainly get the hammerheads, they are back now and we have a lot of other very good stuff that even people who have dived here for years haven't seen. We have a bait ball sequence that will completely amaze you.

How much time have you allowed yourself to cut and edit this film. Are you going to spend a lot of time in a dark, air-conditioned studio somewhere? »We have allowed from October 20 until April 1 of next year to cut the film. Fortunately, our studio is in our home. We're walking distance from an excellent reef break in Del Mar and when editing I almost always start the day with two hours of surfing. That's how I stay sane.

Bob Cranston

Many people would say that you have an ideal job. You basically had an unlimited budget, you've picked one of the best film and dive crews and you're working from the best support vessel available maybe in the world. Where else could you go to hope to do better? »Cocos is a special place. There is no question about that. But I'm happy making films almost anywhere where the ocean is natural and there are not too many people. I suspect that our next project will be a coral reef film, shot substantially in the Caribbean. Probably much of the work will be done in the Bahamas. I'm happy diving the Caribbean but I am actually just as interested in the small animals as I am the big stuff. It's great to see a school of hammerheads, but I get as big a thrill out of seeing some unusual small animal behavior. That stuff fascinates me and I get a real charge out of seeing something new and unusual even if it's small and the behavior is very esoteric. My films tend to reflect my passion for the small and the weird.

What about terrestrial stuff? »We climbed all over the island, on Manuelita and completed work on nesting birds. The plan is to do more in October when the brown boobies are nesting, we have already filmed red-footed boobies nesting and we did a fabulous sequence on fairy terns.

Any of the wild pigs? »No pigs. The pigs, deer, cats, and rats on the island are feral and we're trying to keep the wildlife as natural has possible. Basically, that leaves birds and crabs.

Do you know what your next film will be? »Well, it won't be pigs. I'll do us all a favor and stick to fish.

I concluded that interview back in 1998 and waited until 2001 to pick up again. In the last three years Howard had managed to indulge every diver's dream with a trans-Pacific itinerary that included just about every atoll and island James Michener ever thought

Bret Gilliam

Howard most people haven't seen and you'll appreciate his candor and informed perspective on a slew of topics pertinent to divers... including his frustration at finding a parking spot at the beach.

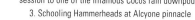

You started out in San Diego as an instructor and dive store employee. How has the area changed since 1969 from a diving perspective? I came to San Diego in 1969, got a job teaching scuba diving and enrolled at San Diego State University. Dive instruction financed my college education and I have been diving in San Diego waters ever since. How has the diving changed? For the most part there is simply less of everything. There are less lobsters, abalone, moray eels, schooling fish, Blue sharks, Mako sharks, and just about everything that swims, floats, or crawls on the bottom.

1. Bait-ball stimulates wild feeding activity, Cocos Island, 1998
2. Howard and Michele with Bob Cranston, surface from lengthy dive session to one of the infamous Cocos rain downpours
3. Schooling Hammerheads at Alcyone pinnacle

Bret Gilliam

1. IMAX film crew descends over Fiji dropoff during *Coral Reef Adventure*, 2001 2. Howard and Valerie Taylor with wild pig friends, circa 1978 3. Sea turtle admires his reflection in the camera dome as Howard films *Coral Reef Adventure*, 2001

There are some major exceptions. A moratorium on killing giant sea bass seems to have worked wonders. Now we often see giant sea bass where we almost never saw them 30 years ago. Harbor seals and sea lions seem more plentiful since people began expressing displeasure with fishermen for shooting their heads off every time they took a fish off a line.

But for the most part, wildlife populations are in steep decline. Everywhere. Water quality is also in decline. Visibility averages much less here than it did a few decades ago. Perhaps as disturbing as wilderness decline is the reduced access to our beaches. Today getting a parking place on a weekday is a major achievement. Forget about it on the weekend. Traffic congestion getting to the beach is so bad it's often more fun to stay home and watch a *Sea Hunt* rerun. Almost all beach parking is now metered. In the summer you have to walk over the bodies of sunbathers to get to the water. With all your diving gear on you crush a few in process, but it doesn't matter much because there are so many no one really notices.

What is the most serious environmental problem threatening San Diego waters? »Almost any winter day within a week of the most recent rainstorm you can find "Polluted waters. No swimming" signs posted on numerous California beaches. The list of environmental problems and their severity becomes larger every day. Pollution, beach erosion, over-fishing, introduced alien species, all impact diving here as they do in virtually all ocean environments. Anyone who has been diving longer than 10 years can attest to the fact that the ocean wilderness is in decline. In general, all environmental problems are related to one single factor. Population. As long as global human population continues to increase, all other efforts to save our environment is just pissing against the wind. Ironically, population would be the easiest environmental problem for governments

environmental pollution. Then look ahead 500 years and try to imagine half a millennium of today's rate of environmental impact. That certainly produces a horrible mental image! Sure, everyone says, "Well, something will happen to solve these problems by then." Well, certainly they're right.

Michele Hall

to solve. With tax incentives, social pressure, and education, governments could affect population reduction. But no one dares talk about that very much.

Religion is a wonderful thing, often corrupted by greed and stupidity. Many people questioned whether the planet could handle six billion people when we reached that level a few years ago. When the Earth didn't implode immediately as population passed six billion, conservatives said, "See, no problem." But when you get a terminal disease you don't necessarily die immediately. Sometimes years may pass before you feel symptoms. I believe Earth cannot support our present population, let alone continued population growth. Imagine today's rate of deforestation, global warming, decline in natural resources, loss of biodiversity,

Something will happen, but I doubt anyone will like the solution when Mother Nature decides to dish it out. The stupidity of ignoring population growth as the number one most critical environmental problem amazes me. It's unequivocal proof that there is no intelligent life on this planet. Well, except for you and me, people who agree with me and, of course, the dolphins and whales.

How has California diving changed from a business perspective? » I'm not really tuned into the sport diving business today. But I sense that there is a decline in the spirit of adventure that seemed to inspire our generation. I think young people stay at home watching TV and playing video games and explore their natural world much less then our

generation was compelled to do. Certainly, there is less exploration left to be done. Hell, now they're leading tours for the blind to the top of Everest! That's great for blind people, but it does take some of the romance out of mountain climbing for young people. As for diving in San Diego, there seem to be fewer dive boats, dive shops, and beach divers. But maybe I just haven't been looking. I can't get a parking place at the beach.

One reason young people are less interested in nature is that their parents don't let them out of the house. Television media has completely terrorized parents by sensationalizing every horrible child abduction and abuse case. The media is commercializing these sordid tales, selling soap using other people's misery and their audience's fear. Certainly these terrible things happen. But they are not happening with any greater statistical frequency than when you and I were growing up. But the effect is that parents are terrified to let their children out of their sight. Even those parents not terrified by the

media would today be ostracized if they "neglected" their children by letting them go outdoors to play. A recent study showed that children who have unsupervised wilderness experience grow up to be much more environmentally concerned than those whose wilderness experience is either limited or supervised. So in addition to everything else, we are producing a generation that won't care about environmental issues as much as we do.

Do you still like southern California life style or do you long for a 4,000-acre ranch in Montana or to live on an island in Maine? I occasionally fantasize about "going Giddings." Al has a fabulous ranch hidden away in Montana somewhere. You live in splendor in Maine. Anyway, I'd like either location. But I have to be near the water. I like to dive locally and I surf several times a week. Southern California is great for both. When the crowds eventually threaten our sanity, Michele and I may move northeast. But for now life is still great in Del Mar.

Chuck Nicklin

1. Fiji reef scene on *Coral Reef Adventure*, 2001
2. Preparing for shark dive on *The Deep*, Coral Sea, 1976
3. Howard in the Philippines, 1985

After starting as a still photographer, what led you to film? » Money. Back when I worked at the Diving Locker, owner Chuck Nicklin could often be heard saying, "You can't make a full-time living as an underwater photographer." He would sell photos to dive magazines, general interest publications, occasionally *National Geographic* and it seemed true

that this income only represented a nice supplement. But then he'd get these three-week gigs to go off filming something in 16mm making real money. The potential was obvious. So after developing a reputation as a still photographer and photojournalist, I began setting my sights on 16mm assignment work – where the money was. The trick was breaking into the tiny fraternity of underwater cameramen.

Chuck provided me with the opportunity. He got me a position as "shark advisor" during the filming of Peter Benchley's *The Deep*. "Shark Advisor" was my credit in the film. But I didn't advise any sharks. I speared fish to attract them. And I did whatever else Al Giddings asked me to do. I earned $125 per day and made a total of $2,500. When I got back to San Diego I commissioned a machinist to build me an underwater 16mm camera fashioned after the old Cousteau torpedo cameras. It took a year to get the camera ready to go in the water. I had almost no money and couldn't justify just shooting tests in a pool because 16mm film was and is extraordinarily expensive to purchase, develop and print. So, along with my friend Larry Cochrane, I went out and shot three rolls of Blue sharks. That was 1977. The test was successful and I had about 30 minutes of shark footage in the can as a bonus.

A few months later I was talking to Stan Waterman on the phone. Stan had been co-director of underwater cinematography on *The Deep* along with Giddings. He complained that he had been offered a contract to make a film about sharks but couldn't think of anything new to do. I asked if he had ever seen footage of Blue sharks before. When he said he hadn't, I offered to send him my three rolls. "Oh, I didn't know you were a film cameraman," he said with surprise. "Oh, sure I am," I said, deciding that this was not technically a complete bald-faced lie. Anyway, the long and short of it is that the footage had some really new and exciting things on it – people hand feeding sharks, which was completely new then. Stan showed the footage to his clients in England and was awarded the contract. He hired me as second camera and never asked about my film experience. The film was shown on prime time and my film career was off and running.

Doing assignment camera work is one thing, producing and directing your own films is quite another. When did you start making your own films? » The best way to learn an art is to study

443

someone else's work. If you want to learn underwater film work, just watch television. If you don't understand a specific technique, write it down and ask someone. But most of the answers are obvious by just watching other films. I used to do that all the time. I would watch animal behavior films made in Africa by Des and Jen Bartlett or by Alan Root and sit on the couch as say. "I could do that underwater." Or, "Why doesn't anyone do that underwater?" Or, "I could make great behavioral films underwater." Blah, blah, blah. Michele finally got

sick of it and one evening said, "Well, why don't you just shut-up and go do it?"

So I wrote a one-page letter to the executive producer at PBS *Nature* suggesting I do a film about the kelp forests of California. I never expected to get a response, but figured that would get Michele off my back. As it turned out, I had recently been underwater cameraman on a very popular episode of *Nature* called The Coral Triangle. David Heely, then executive producer for *Nature*, decided I was worth taking a risk. His two-page letter in response to mine said basically, "Ok." I almost went into shock. I spent two years making the film on a budget of $135,000 excluding post-production costs that I traded out for distribution rights with a company in England. The film, *Seasons in the Sea*, was the first true underwater animal behavior film. It won a Golden Panda award for best of show at the Wildscreen film festival which is, for natural history film producers, just like winning best picture at the Academy Awards. Winning that was like being given a credit card with no credit limit or obligation to pay the money back. My career went from pushing a load of bricks uphill in a wheel barrel to flying a jet.

1. Howard swimming into position at Cocos Island, *Island of the Sharks*, 1998 2. IMAX crew, Fiji, *Coral Reef Adventure*, 2001 3. Filming top side sequences in French Polynesia, 2001

2

3

You obviously made a brilliant film. » Actually, let me tell you how that works. I came along with the right idea at the right time. I didn't evaluate business demand and say to myself, "the market is primed for a good underwater behavior film." I just happened to have a talent for capturing good behavioral stories on film. Just like a frog has a talent for catching flies with its tongue. No genius to it. I didn't know I would be any good at it until I saw the film's success. I also had a coincidental passion to make a behavioral film that had nothing

Your wife, Michele, has obviously played a huge role in the success of your company. How do you keep work and play separate and who handles what duties in the business? » Well, that "shut up and just do it" comment certainly had something to do with kick-starting my filmmaking career. Actually, our talents and strengths complement each other almost perfectly. I do the creative work and she handles the business operation. She now produces the films we make and I direct them. I select a filming location;

John Dunham

whatsoever to do with market demand or timing. I just wanted to do it. It just turned out that I made my film at that single best moment in history when it was most in demand. No one was more amazed by its success than me. I can't compare myself to Bill Gates, but imagine if Bill were 10 years younger and started his career 10 years later. What do you think he would be doing for a living? Running Microsoft? I suspect he would be just another computer geek writing programs for someone else's operating system. He came along with the right idea at the right time. *Seasons in the Sea* was the right film to make at the right time to make it. I was very damn lucky!

she constructs the logistical plan for getting there and handles all the details. I create and oversee the film budgets. She writes the checks and balances the books. I edit the films; she handles the incredibly complicated business of post-production. When we finally get out on the boat to start filming (which is the easiest part of the filmmaking business) I do most of the camera work and Michele shoots most of the production stills. She has now become a more prolific still photographer than I.

If she wears the pants in the business side of things, how do you look in a dress? » Actually, I am not forced

Michele Hall

Bret Gilliam

2

3

1. Michele and Howard, 2005 2. Howard working on
Deep Sea 3D, Bahamas, 2005 3. Shark school at Cocos Island, 1998

office help. It's just Michele and me. Most IMAX films are produced with a staff of 20 or more.

How has the nature film business changed in the last five years? As I mentioned earlier, I got started in the natural history film production business at just the right time for an underwater animal behavioralist. If I went fishing with my proposal to do *Seasons in the Sea* today, no one would be biting. Pure animal behavior films, where you only see the natural wilderness and rarely see humans, are called (in the natural history business) blue chip natural history films. A few years ago, blue chip fell out of favor. Now, *Crocodile Hunter* is in. This change in audience demand is probably a result of over-production in blue chip natural history and the proliferation of animal channels. Just over 10 years ago we only had the *Nature* series and *National Geographic* specials. Now we have numerous channels dedicated to natural history. I guess people got tired of seeing lions catching zebras and eagles feeding their young. Like any other business, however, I think this one is cyclical. I think blue chip natural history will come back. I hope so because, like the frog and his tongue, I'm not sure I have any talent for doing anything else.

We're familiar with your incredible IMAX work but understand that you are shooting a lot now with the HD format. How do you like this and is it the wave of the future or simply the next fad? I

to become that submissive. Well, not often anyway. We almost never question each other's decisions. We almost never argue. Even I find that incredible when you consider that we produce IMAX films entirely in-house with multi-million dollar budgets and without any additional

have about a quarter million dollars invested that says High Definition Video is more than a fad! I'm invested up to my neck. The gear is phenomenally expensive. The camera is about $90,000. If you want a lens that's another $25,000. How about a battery? $800. And, gee, you want to look at what you shoot? Better get a monitor - $15,000. But don't worry. It won't take up much space. It's only a 14-inch monitor. You want a big monitor? Belly up! How about a tape deck? Don't even think about it! So yeah, I think HD is more than a fad.

Is that why you recently sold off all your old 16mm library? »Certainly, that is part of the reason. I believe that footage originated on 16mm won't measure up when HD goes mainstream. Michele and I didn't want to watch all our magnificent wildlife footage

depreciate. So we sold it and are now starting over in a format with much higher resolution. We had also produced *Secrets of the Ocean Realm* largely from our library footage. Producing our own series was one of our reasons for building the library. Now that was done. We were offered a great price. And frankly, I now really look forward to revisiting all those locations and animals with my new camera. Between film contracts Michele and I will be running trips all over the oceans capturing sequences.

***Island of the Sharks* got great reviews and everyone who saw it was impressed. Did IMAX do as good a job as you would have liked in promoting it and getting it in as many theaters as possible?** »Ah, politics! The answer is no. It was

Capturing aerial sequences over Tahiti
for *Coral Reef Adventure*, 2001

Hollywood feature and, yet, to be profitable IMAX films had to be made with a fraction the average Hollywood budget. Making "Hollywood" features in IMAX is like trying to win the Indianapolis 500 with bicycle! I admire IMAX's ambition, but they came to a gunfight with a pee-shooter. Earlier we were talking about "the right idea at the right time?" Well, I think IMAX simply had the wrong idea at the wrong time. Anyway, the upshot is that *Island of the Sharks* sat on the distributor's shelf while IMAX's feature attempts were promoted. Actually, the film is now beginning to play more widely and perhaps it will emerge as a sleeper. It's not a perfect film. The writing is poor and the story jumps backwards in some places. But it was reviewed very well and filled theaters where it was shown.

What happened? I didn't think the writing was that bad? It wasn't good. Still you would think that if you spent five million dollars you would always be able to make a good film. You may wonder why so many Hollywood films are so bad. Well, it's perfectly clear to me. Money often creates more problems than it solves. When you have a budget of five million, you have lots of people involved in positions of influence. All of them think they are writers and directors. And they have rights of approval. I don't wonder how Hollywood films (or other IMAX films for that matter) get to be so badly made. I understand that completely. What I don't understand is how a large budget film ever manages to be good. That's a miracle and I don't have a clue how it happens. Few people do.

449

probably a mistake selecting IMAX as a distributor. Especially at that time, a couple years ago. At that time IMAX stock was selling at over $30 and they were riding high on the promise of the IMAX format being accepted as the new Hollywood format for narrative films. Within a few short years, there were as many commercial IMAX theaters (usually in feature film megaplexes) as there were institutional theaters (like at natural history museums and aquariums). There was talk of major film directors making their next films in IMAX. IMAX preferentially promoted and distributed their Hollywood style films over their educational library. *Island of the Sharks* was not promoted well by IMAX.

Making narrative films is extraordinarily difficult even with mega-budgets. IMAX is a much more expensive production process than the typical

Tell us about your role in the IMAX *Amazing Caves* project. Did you enjoy working with Wes Skiles? That's a funny story. Greg MacGillivray, producer of *Journey Into Amazing Caves*, wanted the best underwater crew he could get. He wanted Wes because he was the best at filming in caves. He wanted me because Wes had no experience with IMAX cameras and because I own the best IMAX camera housing for the job. When Wes learned that I was coming along as cameraman, I think he was worried. Maybe horrified is a better word. Because I was already a big-time IMAX director, he figured I might want to run the show. Because I had no experience in caves (hell, I'm not even cave certified), he figured my insisting on running the show would be a very bad idea. I think Wes also felt he needed to prove himself with the camera. He wanted to be "the cameraman." Wes and I had never worked together before, so his trepidations were justified. Anyway, I didn't run the show. I did just what I was told by the underwater director, Mr. Wes Skiles. In the real world of major film production, the director has all the talent, makes all the decisions, composes the image, and outlines all the camera moves. The cameraman pushes the "on" button when the director says, "Roll camera," and pushes the "off" button when the director says, "Cut." Get the picture? When you see *Amazing Caves*, you're looking at Wes' work despite the fact that I held the camera.

So, did Wes quickly settle into his role as Director? »It took Wes a few days and I'm not sure he ever was happy not holding the camera. But it did work very well. Wes dove with an AGA mask and the rest of us used Buddy Phones to hear what he was saying. I had an OTS mouth mask I could use when I needed to ask Wes a question or tell him I had screwed up and we needed to do a shot over. But most of the time Wes did all the talking. Sometimes he never stopped. During our 1/5 of a mile swims in and out of the Dos Ojos cave system, he would regal his mute crew with jokes and his philosophy on life. You could take your Buddy Phone off, but then you'd risk putting it back only to find Wes screaming, "Hey stupid, I'm talking to you."

Did Wes ever handle the camera? »Yeah, and that was a major point of irritation to me. After years of experience handling the IMAX system, I knew that it took a practiced talent to do good work with it. Then Wes insisted on doing a couple shots where there simply wasn't room for both of us in the hole. Instead of botching the shots or being overwhelmed by the camera, he did the shots gracefully and perfectly the first time, completely validating his premise that my presence on the project was entirely unnecessary.

Is he really a relative of that guy from *Deliverance* or does he just sound that way? »Wes carries around a set of artificial teeth that he inserts when addressing his crew during less serious moments. The teeth and his associated manifestations make him seem like someone deprived of oxygen at birth and raised by the guy from *Deliverance*. It's both funny and terrifying. Without the teeth, he becomes a completely normal guy - for a backwoods hick from the Florida swamp.

So, how did you like cave diving? »Actually, I had no appetite for cave diving whatsoever until I saw a television film Wes had made showing how beautiful some of these caves are. If I hadn't seen that show, I might not have taken the job when Greg offered it to me. Anyway, I found cave diving disorienting at first, but then I began to become accustomed to the protocols and then it started to be fun. During my first day I began a cave dive class with Dan Lin. We never finished and I never got certified. Wes decided we all had more pressing obligations than teaching me enough to know what I was doing. While taking the class, I watched Dan put a line arrow on backwards. That scared the hell out of me. He caught the mistake a moment later, but I can see how easily cave diving can get spooky. After a few days, I was doing the long swims in and out of the cave unsupervised. I really enjoyed it.

And do you think cave divers are crazy? »Of course, they're completely nuts. But they're not stupid. In that element, they are superior divers. In the ocean I almost never see someone with better buoyancy control than me. In Dos Ojos, all of the divers had better buoyancy control than me.

Tell us about your most recent project that took you across the Pacific including Fiji? »The film will be called *Coral Reef Adventure*. It's another IMAX film and is produced by MacGillivray Freeman films, producer of *Amazing Caves*. Michele and my roles in this film are a bit unusual for us. I directed the underwater sequences and Michele was the line producer. We will also appear in the film. In fact, the film is largely about us and how we make underwater IMAX films. Greg MacGillivray is the director and has the unenviable task of trying to make us look good on film. Despite the questionable on-camera talent, I think it's going to be a great film.

Yes, but will it be an "adventure?" »You know, "adventure" might be defined as an exquisite balance between the passion for exploring the unknown and the fear of it. In fact, this film was more an adventure than most of the films we've made. We wanted to justify the *Coral Reef Adventure* title by legitimately pushing our personal limitations and the limits of underwater film production. We did both. We pushed the envelope way out there.

For example? »A lot of our filming was done with air diluent below 200 feet. And we went deeper than that. Below 250 feet we went to trimix. And believe me, shooting IMAX below 300 feet is really out there.

What were you filming down there? »We did one sequence on Gray Reef sharks at the mouth of the Rangiroa pass. Those were all air dives to between 200 and 250. But our deepest dives were in Fiji filming

MacGillivray Freeman's
CORAL REEF
ADVENTURE

Richard Pyle capturing undiscovered species of fish in what he's calls "the twilight zone."

Richard Pyle is the ichthyologist who dives a Cis-Lunar rebreather? » Right. Richard's logged over 50 dives deeper than 350 feet where he has discovered numerous new species. With us, he logged a few more. On one of his dives he descended below 400 feet.

Did you follow him down to 400 feet? » No. I made several dives below 350 and my deepest was just over 370 feet. But keep in mind these were not simple technical dives (if trimix dives can ever be simple). Not only were we carrying trimix rebreathers and emergency bailout gas, but we were also carrying not one but two IMAX camera systems! One IMAX camera weighed over 100 pounds and the other was over 250 pounds. We also were equipped with special experimental OTS underwater communications, underwater lights, and all of Richard's capture gear. As you know, over-exertion can be a serious problem doing deep trimix dives. Well, try swimming around with a 250-lb. camera system and a few bailout tanks along with an 80-lb. rebreather! Try it in a current!

Who were the other divers? » I carried the larger IMAX camera with Mark Thurlow assisting. Bob Cranston carried the second camera with Dave Forsythe. And, of course, Richard was in front of the cameras. That makes five.

I didn't know your IMAX housing could go that deep. » Well, it can't! In fact, the other housing, the 100-lb. system, was housed in a 1/16-inch thick aluminum splash housing. Both would have crushed like

paper cups if we took them below 200 feet. The splash housing was only rated to 10 feet!

You did take them down, didn't you? » Yeah, but we modified them first. We attached air tanks to the housings and pressurized them during descent. That's how we shot IMAX at 350 feet using a splash housing. The camera was always at ambient pressure.

Well, that seems like a simple enough solution. It seems to have worked? » Not without problems. These cameras were not designed to work surrounded by gas at more than 10 atmospheres. That's pretty thick stuff. The smaller camera nearly always jammed below 300 feet. It just couldn't move the film through gas that

1. Dr. Richard Pyle with collected specimans, 2001
2. Yosy Naamen and Howard launch IMAX camera from *Undersea Hunter*, 2001

dense. The larger camera failed to run 50 percent of the time, but the problem was electrical. We spent months trying to figure it out. The camera would simply not ramp up to speed when at depth. But would then run fine as we ascended to shallower water. After 21 trimix dives, we finally solved the problem before our last deep dive of the project. It turned out to be a small cork clutch that was compressing and causing the electrical switch failures. Ironically, on this last deep dive with the problem solved, the camera jammed anyway for an entirely unrelated reason.

That must have been massively frustrating? Yes, but it was also great fun making the dives. Still, dedicating an entire day and obligating a crew of five deep divers to four hours of decompression only to have both cameras jam as soon as they were switched on did cause some jaw clenching. Fortunately, for each dive the camera jammed, we made a dive where it ran flawlessly. We did get the footage we needed to make a great sequence. Certainly, that is the deepest divers have ever used IMAX cameras.

Did Richard catch any new species? Actually, he did. He caught a beautiful new species of wrasse about six inches long. It was pink and yellow. And when he caught it the camera was running and it didn't jam. It makes a great sequence.

How did you like diving in the "twilight zone?" I loved it. Funny, earlier we were talking about the lack of places to explore for young people. Well, below 200 feet almost every reef is unexplored. The potential is spectacular. And it is different down there. You see animals you've never seen before and many are undescribed. No one has ever seen them before.

What was the most exciting thing you saw on a deep dive? Well, there were two spectacular encounters. We saw a Thresher shark swim by 20 feet away at about 300 feet. The camera jammed on that one, for sure. And on one dive we saw an enormous school of Hammerheads - more than 200 sharks. As far as I know, schooling Hammerheads were not known to occur in Fiji. Well, they do below 300 feet! I was out of film for that one.

You chartered the *Undersea Hunter*, your support vessel from the Cocos film project. How did you convince Avi Klapfer to send it half way around the world and back? Money. No, actually, Avi loves this kind of challenge. Given the choice, he would use the *Undersea Hunter* full-time for film production all around the world. Unfortunately, these mega-budget underwater documentaries are few and far between. I've been fortunate to be able to bring two to Avi. But it could be a long time before there is another project that can justify such expense. I'd love to do it again and will keep my eyes open for any opportunity. Working with Avi and the *Undersea Hunter* has been a superb experience. The boat is extremely well

run and well maintained. Avi is also quick to make major modifications in order to accommodate IMAX equipment and even the ultralight aircraft we used for shooting aerials.

Why not charter locally in each region?》Well, we did that too. We also used the *Nai'a* in Fiji. Rob Barrel and Cat Holloway were our guides and the *Nai'a* supported some of our crew on one of the expeditions. *Nai'a* is a beautiful vessel and a more comfortable boat than *Undersea Hunter*. But it is not configured

well for IMAX production. Launching, recovering, and maintaining the IMAX system and all the other IMAX gear would have been difficult on *Nai'a*.

What do think of all the recent shark hysteria?》 Ouch! That's a loaded question. Personally, I think it's stupid and tragic. Professionally, as an underwater filmmaker, it's great for business. Certainly there have been a few spectacular attacks this year. Due to those unique cases, however, every shark encounter is now major news. The number of shark bites in Florida was

Howard films reef scene for
Coral Reef Adventure, 2001

Has the Discovery Channel's *Shark Week* **series degenerated into a freak show of bad science in pursuit of a reality show audience?** No, definitely not. It has *always* been a freak show of bad science in pursuit of a reality show audience! This is largely due to the poor budgets most of the film producers have to work with. But Discovery doesn't always limit their production to low budget programming. Occasionally, there are some real gems on Discovery's *Shark Week*. The high-budget shows made by talented professionals can be really well done. I watched several of the *Shark Week* shows and thought they were excellent. Unfortunately, you never know which you're going to see when you tune in. More unfortunately, the audience may not always be able to tell the difference.

What is your dream film project? A dream project? Well, I'd like to get a film contract to make 10 high definition films in the locations of my choice... California, Cocos, British Columbia, the Tropical Pacific. The budgets would be enormous allowing me to bring all my friends along on only the best boats. The contract would specify that I own all the footage rights for my library. I would have 10 years to do the work and would not be obligated to deliver anything worth a damn.

What person or persons have been your greatest influence? As an underwater cameraman, two individuals stand out. Stan Waterman and Jack McKenney. Stan taught me a lot about the business and professional attitude. Jack was the best technician I've ever seen. I fashioned my photographic style much after Jack's work. As a filmmaker, Des and Jen Bartlett, Alan Root, and Hugo van Lawick taught me much about capturing animal behavior sequences on film and making that into a compelling story.

no greater this year than last. But this year, get bit by a halibut on your big toe and you're on prime-time news! It's good for underwater photographers, but it's bad for the dive business and it's bad for sharks. And don't you think there's something fishy about the story of the little boy who tragically lost his arm to a Bull shark in Florida? Do you know any human being powerful enough to wrestle a healthy seven-foot Bull shark to shore barehanded? I don't. I sure couldn't do it. I suspect there is more to that story than we are being told.

You've been doing this a long time, what advice can you impart to the next generation of aspiring underwater filmmakers? The best advice I can give may be not to take any advice too seriously. Natural history filmmaking is a passion. The odds of being successful at breaking in are enormously against you. Still, if the passion is overwhelming, the odds don't matter. Go with your heart and enjoy the process. It's the process that really matters. The true reward is finding justification for being out in the wilderness appreciating beauty purely for the sake of beauty itself, not in seeing your pictures in print or on television or in cashing a check. ■

Bret Gilliam

BAREFOOT RENAISSANCE MAN OF DIVING

BY LINA HITCHCOCK

:: bret gilliam

Cathryn Castle

BRET GILLIAM
IS ONE OF
DIVING'S MOST
ENDURING
PERSONALITIES
AND ALSO
ONE OF THE
INDUSTRY'S
MOST SUCCESSFUL
ENTREPRENEURS.

A self-made millionaire by the age of 34, he has invested in nearly every phase of the diving business from resort owenership, liveaboard vessels, cruise ships, training agencies, publishing manufacturing, and filming. »

He holds multiple licenses as a USCG Merchant Marine Master, aircraft and deep submersible pilot, and recompression chamber supervisor. Since beginning diving, at the age of eight in 1959 in Key West, he has logged over 17,000 dives.

He began his professional diving career in January 1971 with a special Navy team working with fast attack nuclear submarines in the Caribbean. That led to other commercial diving work before starting V.I. Divers Ltd., Southern Exposures (a publishing business), and a luxury yacht

charter company in the Virgin Islands. After selling out his Virgin Islands holdings in 1985, he spent two years on filming and consulting projects while cruising aboard his yacht *Encore* before being recruited as an executive to run the diving and ship operations with Ocean Quest International. Their 500 ft., 24,000 ton dive/cruise ship *Ocean Spirit* would become the world's largest sport diving operation in history.

He was elected to NAUI's Board of Directors in 1991 and became Chairman and President in 1994. The same year, he formed

Hitchcock and Gilliam, 1978 aboard dive boat.

Bill Walker

Technical Diving International (TDI) and that company quickly grew into the world's largest training organization for nitrox, trimix and other tech programs. In early 1996 he became President and CEO of UWATEC, the dive instrument manufacturer, and took over *Deep Tech* magazine. His work has been published in everything from *Playboy*, *Vogue*, *Outside*, *National Geographic*, *Wired*, *Sports Illustrated*, *Time*, *Life*, as well as most of the diving magazines in the world. He has had over 600 articles published and authored or contributed to 26 books. He founded *Fathoms* magazine in 2001 with long-time magazine collaborator, Fred Garth, and that publication quickly gained critical review for the highest quality in diving publications.

Considered one of the pioneers of technical diving, he held the world depth record for scuba on compressed air at 490 feet and drafted most of the original training standards and practices for mixed gas, rebreathers, deep diving, nitrox, and other segments of the booming tech market. He was elected to the prestigious Explorers Club as a Fellow National and is a member of the Boston Sea Rovers. He also served as a diving consultant for the U.S. Navy, U. S. Coast Guard, Naval Criminal Investigative Service (NCIS), Federal Bureau of Investigation (FBI), and the Central Intelligence Agency (CIA) as well as working as an expert witness for the U.S. Marine Corps in general court martial proceedings.

His business success defied conventional paradigms and his disdain for the trappings of corporate "style" was legendary, especially his loathing for suits and shoes. He wore tee shirts and shorts to his office and employees were encouraged to bring all their pets to work. His dog accompanies him everywhere and woe betides the person who might dare to object. He once compared having to wear a tuxedo to speaking engagements and formal social affairs as akin to sticking pins in his eyes. Not exactly IBM or General Motors executive practice. But over the years, two of his companies were taken public and the others sold to private investor groups. The total value of these sales exceeded $80 million. Not bad for a barefoot guy who steadfastly refused to believe that diving was a "real job"…

I met Bret in 1977 when I ventured into V. I. Divers Ltd. in St. Croix to sign up for dive lessons. I was 22 and right out of college. I later joined the staff and eventually became Vice President & Operations Manager. Bret engaged me in his filming projects as well and we ended up traveling around the world together. I especially enjoyed the role as his model that took us to the Red Sea, the Solomon Islands, Micronesia, Indonesia, Cocos Island, Vanuatu, the Bahamas, and throughout the Caribbean spanning 30 years now of exciting and challenging diving. It's been a wild ride. I guess I'd hung around him long enough to give me some perspective on handling an interview. Now if I could only get him to talk… ■

459

Let's start this a little differently. At the top of your business career when your companies were enjoying huge successes, you decided to walk away from it all. Why?》I had an epiphany brought on by a sudden event that just sort of stunned me. On Labor Day weekend 2003, our mutual friend Bill Turbeville was diagnosed with a terminal brain tumor at the age of 44. He was one of the healthiest guys I knew. He was a prominent attorney and we worked together on dozens of cases defending the diving industry. Initially, his doctors only gave him about three months. We talked a lot about life, the things he wished he had the time to do… not in a negative way, but more philosophically.

1. Turbeville and Gilliam in Maine, 2004
2. Cdr. Gill Gilliam and Bret, Bimini, 1959

All Bill's friends rallied around him and we dragged him around doing all sorts of things he'd put off doing. He made it into the New Year when we almost lost him due to a mistake his medical people made while he was on a trip with family to London. You may remember, you and I were in the middle of the Banda Sea in Indonesia in January 2004 when Gretchen, my wife, called me aboard the ship on the Sat-phone to tell me his time was up and I needed to come back. That was impossible but when we made port in tiny Bandaneira, the Indonesian captain (who had been aware of my conversations in the wheelhouse) expressed his sympathy.

He invited me to go with the crew to perform a Hindu ritual that celebrated life and was supposed to send Bill some positive energy or karma or whatever. We trekked over to a beautiful garden, burned some incense (at least I think it was incense!), sniffed some flowers, and poured water all over ourselves while lounging in this makeshift fresh water pool by the old fort. We drank a couple of Bin-Tangs (Indonesian beer) as well; I figured they couldn't hurt, although that might have been a departure from the regular ceremony. It was nice day in the midst of terrible looming tragedy.

But when we got back into Bali ten days later, I found out that, almost to the hour of that little Hindu session, Bill started to get better. He was alive and well. I couldn't believe it. Must have been the Bin-Tang… He outlived every prognosis. We had a lot of time to talk. I brought him up to Maine that summer and we enjoyed fine wine, great music, and stimulating conversations between boat trips and touring the country. I told him that he had made me focus on what was really important. I was 53. Bill survived the whole year and passed away peacefully on January 2, 2005.

I changed my priorities. I had been lucky enough to make more money than I was probably going to spend, so my lifestyle wasn't going to suffer if I changed directions. I decided to sell all my companies and concentrate on a lot of stuff that I hadn't had time for. So I sold everything. Now I almost exclusively limit myself to the friends whose company I most enjoy, like you… and, of course, Gretchen, and my dog, Pete. I cut out trips that took me away from Maine from July to October because this is the most beautiful place in the world for me. Islands, mountains, forests, lakes, wildlife, the most glorious fall colors imaginable. No crime, no hassles, little traffic, no pollution, great boating, thousands of islands, and a wonderful climate with four distinct seasons. When I'm not in Maine, I'm traveling to places unrelated to diving that I didn't have time for in the past.

Okay, back to the beginning. Where and when did you learn to dive?》I began in 1959 in Key West, Florida. Back then diving really was not a recognized sport and I was eight years old. My father indulged my interest in learning to use scuba gear. I was already free diving as deep as 40 feet or so and I think he and his navy buddies regarded me with a certain amusement. They hooked me up with a small oxygen cylinder that they cleaned out and rigged a harness to. The double hose regulator hung nearly down to my knees. But I just adored being underwater and it began a lifelong passion for me. I finally got certified in 1960 and later ran a very successful fish collecting business, supplying specimens to the local municipal aquarium and one in Miami. At the age of eleven I had my own boat and outboard and was making over a hundred bucks a week diving for fish. That was a fortune in those days.

Why diving and shipping as a career? I don't really think I ever had much choice when you think about it. I was born at the U.S. Naval Academy. As a baby, my first word was "boat" and I learned to swim before I could walk. My father was a senior naval officer who indulged my passion for snorkeling and diving by letting me go through an early YMCA program after watching the first episodes of *Sea Hunt*. That year my family had moved aboard an 80-ft. motor yacht named *Argo* and when my dad was transferred we simply moved our boat to his next duty station. By the time I was in high school we had covered the entire Atlantic seaboard from Maine to Key West, Florida twice. So diving and boats were my whole life. The only time I lived ashore was when I went off to college. Ever since then I've either lived on an island or commanded a ship somewhere. What else was I going to do for a job? Sell insurance?

You got involved with the Navy in some pretty crazy diving projects. How did that come about? Complete blind good luck. When I graduated from high school, the Vietnam War was at its peak. Basically, you either got a college deferment or got sent to Southeast Asia for your "senior trip". I had no idea how long the war was going to last but knew that I'd get nabbed eventually when college was over. I figured if I had to serve, I'd rather do my time as an officer so I applied for and won a National Army ROTC scholarship. This came with a six-year active duty obligation but paid all tuition costs, housing, food, books, transportation… everything to attend any university in the country. It even paid me a modest salary while in school. It was actually a hell of a deal. And I hoped the war would be over by the time I graduated. By late 1970, it was showing no signs of ending and guys that I had served with were rotating back from Vietnam and coming to visit with real horror stories. It was sobering.

To make a long and circuitous story short, because of my diving background I ended up working with the U.S. Navy on some projects with submarines. This kept me out of the army and negated my six-year

Jeanne Gilliam

2

obligation. At the time, all of their sub operations for this project were based in Puerto Rico and later in St. Croix in the Virgin Islands. I worked directly with one of the contractors who operated the Navy support ships and coordinated with the P-2V and P-3V aircraft and subs. Our work was classified at the highest secrecy levels and considered to be extremely hazardous duty. So I even got paid more. Since we worked on the ships with other civilian technical contractors, we didn't even get hassled about haircuts. From my point of view as a 20 year old that had just escaped duty in Vietnam to go work underwater in the Caribbean… well, I thought I'd died and gone to heaven.

What were you actually doing? This was at the height of the Cold War and the threat of Soviet missile submarines launching an undetected attack on the U.S. These big Russian subs carried ballistic missiles and a perpetual "cat and mouse" game was being played out by the Navy's fast attack subs that hunted the "boomers". A basic tactic was for an attack sub to spend hours simply waiting and listening underwater to track their enemy counterparts. But eventually, the U.S. subs had to speed ahead and reposition themselves before going back into silent running, listening for the Russians to approach. The attack subs were just about undetectable when lying silent or cruising at slow speeds. But when they leaped ahead at high speed, they created acoustic noise signatures that could give them away.

Our mission was to film the visible wake vortex that was created by the sub's propeller, struts, dive planes, etc. By studying the film we shot, the Navy's experts found ways to reduce the noise signature and make the subs less likely to show up on the Russians' sonar and listening devices.

We worked in three man dive teams and positioned ourselves in a triangular formation that the attack subs would drive through at varying speeds. As they passed between us, sometimes there was only about 25 feet or so between the sub and us. We'd get in position, as deep as 300 feet or more sometimes, and wait hovering with our camera gear. They would give us a ping to let us know they were starting their run and we'd hold position and start filming. The subs went by us starting at crawl speed, then up to 10 knots or so. That was pretty tame. But eventually they were making passes at flank speed. This was in excess of 50 knots. It's a pretty hairy experience to be a diver in the water with a 300-ft. nuclear submarine buzzing past you. You get tossed around.

We were working about 15 miles offshore in the Virgin Islands Trench that's over 10,000 feet deep. The visibility in the open ocean depths is fantastic, over 200 feet at times. But even then, we rarely saw the subs coming. The human eye couldn't pick it up fast enough, coming out of the blue. The sub would be on us and by us so quickly that you couldn't react. Then the wake would hit us. You'd be thrown to the right or left, or up and down depending where you were in the triangle. It was just crazy, but we got good results.

The captain on our support ship used to watch our diving operations and just shake his head. He liked to say, "Ya know, the Navy has a really good retirement program. The key is living long enough to collect the benefits."

This was really new ground and our dive team was given extraordinary latitude to improvise if we felt we could be more efficient. We quickly took wide departures from standard Navy diving procedures at the time. We had a reputation as mavericks but we were so productive it was hard to rein us in. We were getting better film and were able to work far deeper than any of the divers that preceded us.

Sharks were actually the key to our independence since none of the regular Navy diving supervisors wanted responsibility for us or even to visit to evaluate our methods. One time, we had a very uptight officer sent over from the naval station on Puerto Rico because he was pissed off at all the non-standard stuff we were doing and wanted to "straighten us out". When it came time to enter the water from the ship's aft deck, the crew had to push the dozens of Oceanic Whitetip sharks away from our entry point with boat hooks just to make a hole we could jump into. The guy took one look at this mayhem and said, "No way!" After that, we were pretty much left alone.

Eventually you were involved with a fatal attack, weren't you? 》That actually came about a year or so later. We had a lot of problems in the open ocean with these pelagic sharks. Sometimes we'd have scores of them around us at a time and they could be nasty. They were naturally inquisitive but they were really stimulated by the low frequency sound signatures that the ship was putting in the water. These trials simulated submarine noises when we were testing the hydrophone listening devices dropped from the aircraft. This seemed to agitate the sharks into a frenzy of unpredictable behavior. Once the low frequency sound generators went active, the sharks just lost it. They'd bite our cameras, our fins, the ship's props and rudder, and even the boat hooks used to push them out of the way when we made our entries. We had to watch each other's backs all the time. Our entries and exits from the water were the most dangerous so everything we did was focused on getting quickly down to about 25-30 feet where the foam cleared and we could stabilize below the ocean waves. Not being able to see when you jumped in was very stressful. At the conclusion of our dives when the deco was over, we'd try to time our exits to use a big wave to sort of throw us up on to the deck with the crew scrambling to grab us. It was not for the faint of heart.

In 1972 a friend of mine, Rod Temple, was killed while we were working on a scientific project on the north shore of St. Croix. On that particular day, two Oceanic Whitetips simply swam up to him in about 180 feet depth and attacked him. There were three of us on the dive. I sent the diver who was low on air up and I went back to try to save Temple. The sharks had hit him several times and when I got to him, I grabbed him and tried to swim up. But they kept coming back, biting him, and were pulling us deeper over the drop off wall. I was hanging on to one side of him and we were both trying to beat them off, but it was no use. He eventually passed

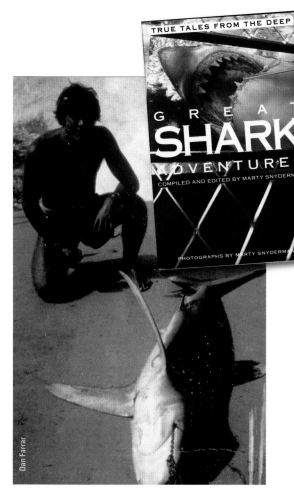

Gilliam and Oceanic Whitetip, hooked during diver's decompression, aboard Navy ship in Virgin Islands, January 1971

out from blood loss and trauma and the sharks pulled him away from me. He was dead by then. I was out of air and had to do a free ascent from well over 300 feet and ended up badly bent. I was evacuated by the Navy and the Coast Guard to Puerto Rico to the chamber there and treated. I was extremely lucky to survive.

You were cited for heroism for trying to save Temple during the attack. What went through your mind at the time? Certainly nothing heroic. When I went back for Rod, I didn't initially realize that he was under attack. He was below me on the bottom and everything was all stirred up and murky. In fact, I thought he had an equipment problem and would need to buddy breathe. It was only after I swam into the mess and grabbed him that I realized the sharks were hitting him and that's why everything was chaotic. So I sort of got sucked in unwittingly.

To me, a hero is someone like Al Giddings who actually jumped out of a boat where he was safe and swam to rescue Leroy French who was under attack

by a Great White shark some years earlier in northern California. Al dragged Leroy out of the shark's mouth, swam him back to the boat and pulled him in. He survived. There should be a statue of Al somewhere as an example of selfless courage. That's a hero. Later Al and I became good friends and I remain in awe of him.

Your attack got a lot of publicity didn't it? Understandably so. It happened right off a popular swimming and snorkeling beach area and involved pelagic sharks that most people weren't even aware were present in those areas routinely. This was before *Jaws*. It shook people up pretty badly. The local newspapers splashed it all over the headlines and it was written up in a lot of articles about shark behavior. It was something I just wanted to forget. But it was always being recounted and after *Jaws* came out as a movie, it generated new interest. In 1992, a producer from the BBC was doing a series of documentaries called *Dead Men's Tales*. It was about people who had survived extraordinary accidents against all odds. He met with me and bought the rights to the story. So I was in the BBC series with people who had fallen out of airplanes with no parachute, got trapped in caves that collapsed, dodging volcanoes that erupted with lava streaming down on them, all sorts of bad situations. It was interesting to meet some of these characters. The survival instinct is phenomenal in some circumstances.

Some years later, Marty Snyderman edited a book called *Great Shark Adventures* and had me write the first hand account of my incident that was included with other chapters from Howard Hall, Mike deGruy, Stan Waterman, Rodney Fox, Leroy French, Carl Roessler. A couple other books including *Mark of the Shark* bought the story later as well.

Moving on... how did your time with the Navy end? ⟩⟩Ironically, our rather gonzo methods produced results way ahead of the Navy's projected time frame. We finished their project; I was assured that I had no further obligation for service and I was almost immediately recruited for some commercial projects. The first one was a massive underwater blasting job to prepare a ship channel for super tankers going into the Hess Oil refinery on St. Croix's south coast. We were working with strings of 80-lb. TNT shaped-charges linked in series, probably a couple thousand pounds of explosives. We were diving in about zero visibility most of the time doing everything by touch and feel. Once you fired off the rack, it blew a column of water about 30 feet in the air and rained down sediment, coral, dead fish all over the place. We had issues with sharks there too, but they were mostly Reef and Lemons that weren't as crazy as the Whitetips. A few big Bull sharks would occasionally swim through and we'd have to get out.

But that was a great job and taught me a lot. This was the summer of 1971 and I was making as much as $500 a day. I saved my money and that nest egg let me launch into sport diving later.

That same year had you involved in your first film didn't it? ⟩⟩That's a funny story. A crew came to the Virgin Islands to shoot an early X-rated movie. They needed some local site support and got steered to me for a boat and suggestions for where to shoot some outdoor sequences. At first I didn't know what the nature of their film was. I thought it was a travel piece or something. They had hired Harry Reams, the male star from *Deep Throat* that had just been released and was doing great box office sales. There really wasn't a porn industry then and the guys that were doing this were mainstream directors and producers trying to capitalize on the phenomenon that *Deep Throat* had created.

Their movie was called *Pleasure Island* and after I saw a couple of the rudimentary storyboards, I quickly figured out that we weren't shooting a sequel to *The Sound of Music*. They had a female lead actress named Nancy Kool and about a dozen other professionals from the adult film genre. But before the first week was out, some sort of money misunderstanding took place and everyone but Harry and Nancy left. So the film investors decided to hire local people as replacements. It was hilarious. Nowhere else but St. Croix in 1971 could you have had a casting call for a porn film

1. On the set of *Pleasure Island*, 1971 2. On film set, 1976
3. Smithsonian Project crew: Dr. Mendel Petersen, George Tyson, Dr. Alan Albright, Gilliam, Dave Coston, 1973 (with early proton magnetometer over wreck site)

and have nearly a hundred mainstream people try to sign on. There were real estate agents, lawyers, bar tenders, waitresses, pilots, insurance salespeople, even schoolteachers who showed up. These were people already living in the tropics… tanned, athletic and in good shape. They moved to the islands in the first place probably because they were a little non-conformist by nature. Well, this movie production unleashed their inner "wild-child" streak.

Once the film managers promised them that they would never allow the film to be released or shown in the Virgin Islands, the last of whatever inhibitions that remained went out the window. One girl who taught the sixth grade in a local elementary school actually surpassed Nancy Kool as the star. She was this drop-dead gorgeous blond, built like Pamela Anderson, without a trace of modesty. I remember one day, shooting had to stop because she said she needed the afternoon off. She had to coach her school softball

464

team in a game. So the whole movie crew went with her and filmed her. It was surreal. We were all cheering and going nuts as the kids ran around having a great time while wondering why their game attendance had just shot through the roof. The filmmakers wanted to work it into the story line of the film but she drew the line at that. She said she thought it might not be appropriate. For once, the voice of reason prevailed.

We also went over to Virgin Gorda in the British Virgin Islands and decided to shoot a graphic scene in the natural rock pools at The Baths. In those days, Virgin Gorda was a sleepy little island with practically no visitors. It was fabulously beautiful on these south end beaches and we figured we'd have the whole place to ourselves. Wrong! Right in the middle of the "action" a group of about 20 elderly bird watchers from the Midwest

3

heartland wandered right into the scene and got an eyeful. We found out later that we wrapped up filming and got back on my boat for St. Croix only minutes before a couple local policemen came down to check out the birdwatchers' excited report. The mystery porn crew was the subject of urban legend in the BVI for years afterward.

After that you decided to get into the sport diving business. »Diving was really in its infancy then. I figured if I wanted to stay in the Caribbean I might as well try getting people to buy gear, take lessons, and run some tours. So with my own meager savings and a $3,500 loan from my mother, I rented some retail space

It must have been quite different on your next project for the Smithsonian Institute? »Yeah, just a bit. We were working on the excavation of a 17th century shipwreck called the *Santa Monica*. It was a joint venture with a local archeologist named Dr. Allan Albright and the legendary Mendel Peterson, Curator of Historical Archaeology at the Smithsonian. It entailed work with airlifts during the underwater excavation, mapping the wreck that had been covered in sand and coral for a couple centuries, and recovery of the artifacts. Absolutely fascinating. We also did a lot of work with some of the first towed proton magnetometers that allowed us to search for and locate several other old wrecks including the *Wye*. The *Wye* was the sister ship of the *Rhone* that sank in the same storm in 1867. It was a great experience.

in Christiansted, St. Croix and jumped in. I called the company V. I. Divers Ltd. That was in 1973.

How did a 22 year old with no prior formal business training possibly survive? »Common sense got me through a pretty steep learning curve about business and management. Since no bank would loan me money in those days, I was playing with my own chips in the ultimate poker game. If I failed, I was doomed to getting a real job that would require me to wear shoes and get a haircut. Maybe that was my best motivation. But my philosophy was quintessential 1970's "Hippie-Zen-Karma": treat your customers like you'd want to be treated yourself, and give them a good value for their dollar. Sort of an entrepreneur's "golden rule." And I never hesitated to

left he let me take the Scubapro line with me. I owe him a lot. Everything I did in business later started from that first success at V. I. Divers Ltd.

1. V.I. Divers LTD retail facility, St. Croix, Virgin Islands, 1977
2. Bill Walker and Gilliam training Coast Guard Rescue teams, Puerto Rico, 1977 3. Gilliam shooting documentary film, Virgin Islands, 1975

expand in order to have the largest vessels, the best equipment, and the widest variety of services. It paid off. I was lucky to find some really great staff like manager Bill Walker who was key to our success until you took over in 1980. Over 35 years later, I still had customers with their grandkids coming back to me that had been with me in various operations before.

Who was the biggest influence on your career? »

Well, without the enthusiasm of my parents I would never even have gotten started. For the life of me, I still can't believe that I convinced them to let me take up diving when the other kids were worrying about getting their first bicycle or baseball glove. But they were great and forked over the dough for my first set of gear and helped me manage my money from the fish collecting business to buy my own boat. I think by the time I was a teenager they realized that diving might become part of my professional life. But I don't think they ever thought that it would make me wealthy as it ended up doing. I think they just hoped that I would eventually come to my senses.

I also could never have gotten started without the support and faith of Dick Bonin, the founder of Scubapro. He took a chance on me and gave me the Scubapro franchise over the protests of a big company that sold a little dive gear along with hardware and commercial gas supplies. I had managed their diving division for a year and when I

How did things go with your new business? »

Pretty slowly, at first. Initially, it was just me since I couldn't afford to hire anyone. I sold gear, stocked the shelves, did repairs, filled the tanks, taught courses, and basically starved a lot. I had become an instructor for NAUI in 1972 but they actually didn't approve of dive stores, something about perverting your ethics if you sold gear. But I taught their program and simply ignored their weird ideas about business. When I got my first boat, I finally had to hire someone to watch the store so I could go run the dive trips. I knew the only way I was going to succeed was to overwhelm my customers with service. It paid off and word of mouth steered a lot of business to the place. And gradually we grew.

A turning point came in 1975 when I decided to move to a waterfront location in the town's classiest retail section called the Pan Am Pavilion. The rent was $500 a month for a massive two-story space with two entrances. I thought, "$500, that's a fortune, I'll never be able to pay that kind of money." But I knew "location" was going to be key to our growth so I choked back my horror at the price and moved in. And I was smart enough to sign a 10-year lease. Within a year or so, we broke a million in sales for the first time - a huge benchmark. We ended up with over 30 employees, a bunch of big dive boats, contracts with marine science labs, a commercial diving division, a luxury yacht charter fleet, and a film support division as well.

How did you get into the filming end of things? »
A production company had hired one of my boats for
some second unit sequences for a movie. I wanted to
make a good impression so just about anything they
asked for, I'd agree to. "Can you back your 50-ft. boat

1. Michael York, Gilliam and director Don Taylor on set
of *Island of Dr. Moreau*, St. Croix, 1977 2. Gilliam in lower right
holding boat steady for Michael York sequence 3. Barbara Carrera
taking direction from Don Taylor 4. Actors in full makeup
5. Burt Lancaster and Michael York on set

in through the breaking waves so we can work right off
the beach?" And I'd go, "Yeah, sure!" and then have to
figure out how to do it safely with a bunch of yahoos
on board who could barely dress themselves without
getting into trouble.

    Anyway, they also asked me to arrange a helicopter,
a local carpenter to build some sets, an electrician for
lighting, and even the catering service. Before I knew
it, I was providing just about everything including stunt
people. "We need someone to dive off that cliff into the
ocean between these coral heads. Can you arrange that?"
Hey, no problem. And I'd go find some crazy friend who
would do it and we'd split the hefty fee I negotiated. Once
I figured out that film crews on location, outside their
comfort zone back in Hollywood, would pay virtually
anything to get things done smoothly and without a lot
of logistical hassles, I had the keys to the kingdom. We
did good work and the referrals just poured in.

What type of films did you work on? »You name
it. Television, big budget movies, documentaries,
nature films, travel destination specials, shark stuff,
advertising shoots, soap operas, it never ended. For
TV, we did things like *Miami Vice*, *Greatest American
Hero*, *Days of Our Lives*, *Caribe Force*, *The Young
and the Restless*, *American Sportsman*, a bunch of
stupid shark tagging contests. Most of it was tedious
and pretty lowbrow but it paid well.

What was your favorite movie production? »No
contest! In 1977 we started work on *The Island of Dr.
Moreau* and it was the most fun I ever had. I'd briefly
done some work for Columbia when *The Deep* was
being shot in the BVI. But it was mostly advance stuff
for compressors, boats, specialized gear. And the entire
budget for *The Deep* back then was only about eight
million. When AIP decided to shoot *The Island of Dr.
Moreau* six months later, they had twice the money to
throw around. They spent money like it was going
to burn their fingers if they held on to it. I was serving
as the marine coordinator since a lot of the movie was
filmed on the ocean or in remote beach areas.

The movie was based on H. G. Wells' novel about a mad doctor who experiments with turning wild animals into humans on this isolated South Seas island where he's created his own idea of paradise. Burt

Lancaster played the lead role with Michael York as the castaway sailor who washes ashore after his ship sinks. He falls in love with a young beauty played by Barbara Carrera whom he wrongly assumes must be the daughter of his reluctant host. The catch was, she's not human. She's a panther or some other predator cat and is dependent on the good doctor's regular injections to keep from reverting back to her original form. Yeah, it was a pretty preposterous premise but it posed all sorts of morality questions and set up the characters for lots of conflicts.

Richard Basehart played the leader of a group of mutant animals who didn't quite make it all the way to fully developed human status and lived in the jungle

under Lancaster's domination. Watching these guys get into the makeup for these roles was amazing. It took hours each day. What really made the movie different was working with all the wild animals. They brought in tigers, lions, bears, hyenas, buffalo, panthers, leopards, giant wild boars… all aboard a specially designed freighter and then moved them ashore to what amounted to a private zoo near the sets built at Davis

Bay. There's a giant resort hotel on that property now, but back then it was just a beach and jungle.

I remember those days. Were the animals a problem to work with?》Sometimes. Mostly we could leave the professional handlers to manage them but these were not circus performing beasts and they really weren't very tame. The cats and boars were temperamental and hated being anywhere near the water. Of course, that's where my crew always had to interact with them. One time they tried a sequence where the tigers, lions and a panther were supposed to be fleeing the fire that burns the village down at the movie's conclusion. The animals were supposed to run out of the burning jungle and into the ocean. Bad idea. They hit the beach where we had our floats and boats moored in close with the first unit film crew and director all running five or six cameras with lights and cables strung all over the place as the sun was setting. The handlers let them go and they were supposed to be trained to go part way into the water and stop. Instead

See & Sea Travel Service Inc.
Newsletter

ANOTHER RECORD-BREAKING YEAR

It's been another smash year for See & Sea, as our carefully-crafted diving adventures draw an ever-increasing audience. The Cayman Diver continues to be the yardstick by which other dive boats are measured; the new Virgin Diver has drawn fantastic turnout since its April debut; our new 102-foot dive boat Seaquest in the Philippines had a great inaugural cruise and promises to be a new star on the diving horizon; our new combination of Truk Lagoon with beautiful Ponape Island is an excellent match; and now the lovely Fijian islands of Taveuni and Mana join our roster. Not only do we offer all these trips of great beauty—See & Sea's Great White Shark program will operate in February. For those who remember our famed inaugural this is a thrilling revival!

Meanwhile our long time favorites Cozumel, Australia/Coral Sea, Tahiti, the Red Sea and the Galapagos reliably provide divers with the finest in comfort, service and incredibly varied diving.

1978 looks even better, but we're not resting on our laurels. Four new destinations are being re-

The Virgin Diver can sleep up to ten divers, ranges widely among these beautiful islands, and offers some extraordinary diving. The wreck of the Rhone, site of filming for the movie "The Deep" has an unparalleled profusion of fish swarming about it. And one of the Virgin Diver, with sea horses, dives is a feature of the world's most unusual night batfish, lizardfish, sponges and octopus in abundance.

The Virgin Diver is available for group charter for dive shops and clubs during free weeks between regularly-scheduled See & Sea programs.

they made these wild leaps from the sand directly into the boat. Everyone scattered, total pandemonium. It took most of the evening to round them back up.

The animals were really pampered though. In many ways, they had a better deal than some of the actors and stuntmen. The handlers had strict rules about how long the animals could work, what they ate, how long they could be out in the sun. One incident sort of summed up the pecking order between animals and people. We were shooting another of the fire sequences and one of the stuntmen who was in full makeup and costume was required to go into the burning building and release his fellow animals so they could escape. A leopard drops on him through a breakaway skylight and chews on him a while before he falls about thirty feet to the floor. He then gets charged by a bear that knocks him through a burning wall and out into the courtyard. The two of them wrestle around with sparks flying and finally the director yells, "Cut!" When the smoke and dust settles, here's this three or four hundred pound bear sitting on the guy. His costume is still on fire in places, he's all cut up, and totally beat.

Don Taylor, the director, surveys the whole scene and says, "Set it up again. We need another take." The stunt guy can't believe it. He's go to go through this torture again but he gets up and starts pulling himself together. Then Taylor says, "And get me a fresh bear. This one's tired and all dirty." We just cracked up.

What were the actors like? »They were the nicest people I ever worked with. We took Michael York scuba diving sometimes and Barbara Carrera would go out to Christiansted bars and to parties with us. Burt Lancaster was in his mid-sixties then and a Hollywood legend. I spent a lot of time with him and we became very good friends. I stayed in touch with him right up until he passed away years later. He was real gentleman and an amazing actor.

We really got on well with the actors and stuntmen that had to play the animal parts. By the time they got through for the day, they were ready to get crazy. Sometimes I'd go down to our dock in town to move the boats over for the morning shoot and we'd find them passed out on deck. They knew the boats would

1. Bill Walker, Geri Murphy, Paul Tzimoulis and Gilliam aboard *Virgin Diver*, Cane Bay drop-off, St. Criox, 1977 2. 130-ft. Westport motor yacht

take them back to the set that was way out of town on the north shore. So they'd just collapse on board when the bars closed and we'd wake them up for makeup and costuming when we got to the beach.

You also expanded into luxury yacht charters? What took you in that direction? »In the mid-1970s, I met Carl Roessler who was running See & Sea Travel in San Francisco. He came down and went diving with us and thought the British Virgin Islands would be a perfect venue for his next dive vessel. He had conceived the "liveaboard" unlimited diving idea and was having great success with Paul Humann's *Cayman Diver* over in that part of the Caribbean. So he talked me into looking for a suitable vessel to start service. I went to Florida and must have looked at 50 boats before finally settling on an 85-ft. motor yacht that needed a lot of work but was affordable. After six months in the shipyard, the *Virgin Diver* was launched and began operation.

We could host up to twelve divers. Back then Carl was charging $600 per person for a week of unlimited diving on both *Cayman Diver* and *Virgin Diver*. He took a one third commission off the top for marketing leaving Humann and I a net of $400 per person. That worked out to about $50 a head a day and we had to house them, feed them, take them diving, pay for fuel, everything. We could make a little money if the boat was full but sometimes he'd send down three or four people and we had to run for a week to only make $1200 or so. It was a losing proposition so I got out of it after the first year.

But it opened my eyes to where the real money was: in big luxurious motor yachts that concentrated on accommodating three to five couples in total decadence. So I bought a 96-ft. Benetti and it was an immediate success since most of the charter yachts in the late 1970s were sailboats with minimal creature comforts. We offered air conditioning, private

staterooms with big queen beds, formal dining with a trained culinary chef, water sports, great entertainment systems including the first onboard VCRs with a movie library. That yacht led to contracts to manage others for wealthy owners who wanted to charter but didn't want the hassle of running their own operation. So we handled crewing, maintenance, provisioning, emergency services, marketing, the whole nine yards. At one time, we had 13 vessels in operation ranging all the way up to 280 feet. It was great fun and a hugely successful business model.

Any memorable clients? ⟩⟩We appealed to a wealthy clientele and, frankly, most of them were older and a little stuffy. But we got a call one day from a charter broker in Los Angeles who had some special clients and wanted to know what "rules" we had on our charters. Rules? About all we cared about was getting paid and that nobody fell overboard. Our mainstream customers went to bed after dinner shortly after sunset. They were

pretty much a Scotch & soda bunch, very pedestrian.

So I told the broker that her clients would be free to do as they pleased. Well, they came down in a private jet and turned out to be a bunch of famous crazies in a rock & roll band with their girlfriends. Their lifestyles were just a bit different on charter than what we were used to. Let's just say that they weren't Scotch drinkers. They also seemed to have forgotten to pack their bathing suits. Well, we had a great time. They loved our kicked-back attitudes and a whole new element of clientele came our way from the music and entertainment business. These people were rich and could afford just about anything but mostly wanted to get away without being recognized or bothered. Big yachts offered the escape and anonymity they desired while still wrapping them in luxury. And since we let them indulge a few other eccentricities, we had a great pipeline of referrals.

Pipeline of referrals? That's the worst pun you've ever used. ⟩⟩Ya think so? Well, it was accurate. One famous rock star used to say, "I only use these semi-religious herbs as part of my faith-based rituals". Yeah, right… like "sunset appreciation." I probably should have just inscribed "Gimme That Old-Time Religion" on our stateroom towels. When Jonathan Edwards played at my wedding years later, he ended up dedicating "Lay Around the Shanty and Put a Good Buzz On" to the old days in the Caribbean.

Any juicy stories? ⟩⟩Are you kidding? But discretion really has to stop me. In a lot of ways, we sort of had a doctor/patient relationship and I'd be out of line to pull the curtain away. But for pure unadulterated craziness, it's a tie: Keith Richards (*Rolling Stones*' guitarist) or Hunter S. Thompson (*Fear & Loathing In Las Vegas*). That's the varsity team. I couldn't keep up with them; didn't even want to try.

Hunter is dead now, but I think Keith is going to live forever, like some millennium cockroach. Remember in 1999 when we were introduced to that woman in the Solomon Islands who was supposed to be 102 years old? I told her she didn't look a day older than Keith Richards. Hey, she didn't.

Any other guests worth noting? ⟩⟩Another great experience was when we were chartered by Bruce Sundlun who had just sold his radio and television conglomerate for mega-bucks. His last act under the old company structure was to charter one my of my big yachts *North Star* to come to Newport for the 1983 America's Cup races. This was about a half million dollar deal for me... and I had no expenses since they paid for everything from dockage, fuel, booze, catering, even a guaranteed tip for my crew.

So the new owners inherited his contract with us and had to pay for "Bruce's Excellent Adventure" as we entertained him and his clients from June to October that year. One of the television stations he owned was

WJAR, the NBC affiliate in Providence, RI. He arranged for the *Today Show* to do a segment on us and we hosted Willard Scott onboard. Great guy! Bruce was a major sailing enthusiast and when the finals came down to the U. S. versus Australia, he asked if we could coordinate a film crew aboard and we'd work with the Goodyear blimp to send the final race live around the world. It had never been done before. I did some live commentary during the broadcast to explain the racing strategy to a TV audience that probably didn't understand 12-meter sailing tactics. Of course, that turned out to be the defining moment in America's Cup history as the Aussies upset the New York Yacht Club's defender. We were right there at the finish line when *Australia II* took the Cup. What a day!

Bruce was also well connected politically and we had all sorts of celebrity guests aboard including then Vice President Bush and a regular stream of Senators, Congressmen, Governors, and the like. He reveled in inviting politicians who couldn't stand each other and

not tell them who was going to be onboard in advance. It made for some hilarious standoffs. One time Bruce invited about thirty local legislators out for one of the first final races. Most had never been on a boat before. It was rough as hell and we were getting tossed around from the weather and the wakes from the thousands of vessels in the spectator fleet. Bruce used to always like to ride in the wheelhouse with me and when a race was going, he was oblivious to his guests.

My first officer, Dan Farrar, finally came into the wheelhouse to tell us that a lot of the guests were seasick and terrified. They wanted to go back in. Bruce inquired, "How many are really sick?" and Farrar replied, "About 20 are prostrate and puking on themselves. The rest are glued to the rail with white-knuckle grips and think we're going to sink."

The America's Cup finals are about to start the first race in minutes and we're at the starting line. I asked, "Do you want me to head in?" He paused for about ten seconds and said, "Hell no, those are acceptable losses." He went on to be elected to two terms as governor of Rhode Island. I doubt if any of those people on board that day voted for him.

By 1985 I was worn out and looking to take some time off. I sold the diving operation, the yacht business, the film support company, and a bunch of real estate I had accumulated in the Virgin Islands. It was a monster payday, a ridiculous figure. I was only 34. My timing couldn't have been more perfect.

Why? »I sold out at just about the top of the Virgin Islands market. Less than two years later, there was the disastrous October 1987 stock market crash. It killed the high-end charter business for nearly a decade. Then Hurricane Hugo blew through in

ended up in Maine. Along the way, I did a lot of diving and exploring in some really remote places. And I also had a nice series of filming contracts and some photography assignments to keep me busy.

How did you get involved with *Ocean Quest*? »In 1987, the original partners contacted me with their idea for a ship that would cater specifically to divers. They were boundlessly enthusiastic but really didn't have any experience at what they were trying to do. They'd raised a little funding but nothing close to what they'd need. I figured that was it.

Later they got back in touch and I went to New Orleans to meet with them. They now had some cash but were still locked into ideas for operation that simply

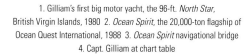

1. Gilliam's first big motor yacht, the 96-ft. *North Star*, British Virgin Islands, 1980 2. *Ocean Spirit*, the 20,000-ton flagship of Ocean Quest International, 1988 3. *Ocean Spirit* navigational bridge 4. Capt. Gilliam at chart table

Tom Mount

1989 and leveled St. Croix with winds over 200 knots. There was rioting, looting, total anarchy for a while. They had to send in the U. S. army and navy to restore order. Tourism went in the toilet and has never really come back to this day. Meanwhile, I had cashed out and was long gone. It was the single best business decision I had made up to that point.

What then? »I went cruising in one of my smaller motor yachts for a couple of years. Just me, no crew, and a revolving door of handpicked friends. I ended up going from South America, through Central America, along the Mexican Yucatan, back across to Trinidad and up the eastern island chain from Barbados to St. Maarten. Then I took off for the Bahamas and

wouldn't work in the real world of ocean operations. They were paying me handsomely as a consultant and I figured I owed it to them to give them the cold reality, not what they wanted to hear. I think this was the first time that they realized I held a Master's License as well as my diving expertise. I was there for two days and basically shot down nearly every element of their proposed operation while pointing out why their misconceptions would not work. I gave them a quick list of alternative suggestions as they took me back to the airport. I never expected that they would ever want to talk to me again.

But they called back to ask me to join the operation as a hands-on senior member. This was a lot different from consulting and I initially didn't want to get involved. But it looked like a challenge and I finally agreed to sign on. I had moved them away from thinking they could run this type of company with a small coastal vessel launching little floats to dive from. We acquired the original flagship of Norwegian Cruise

Lines, the *Sunward I*. It was nearly 500 feet in length and over 20,000 tons. When we made the deal it was in the Suez and in terrible cosmetic and mechanical condition. We sent it to Singapore for a nine-month complete refit. When it was re-launched and commissioned *Ocean Spirit* she was better than new.

Over 110 feet high, with ten deck levels, a casino, four bars, three restaurants, two main entertainment lounges, gift shops, a movie theatre that showed first run films, a pool, and even a "sky bar" top deck lounge. She accommodated 360 passengers in 180 private staterooms and suites, 198 officers and crew, and up to 32 members of the professional diving staff. I even installed a state of the art recompression chamber. We carried ten of our own 32 ft. dive boats that we launched with a special high speed overhead crane out of the back of the stern.

We had some growing pains in the beginning while we worked through problems with a foreign officer contingent that didn't share my zeal for excellence and customer service. When I finally fired the captain at sea and replaced him, there were no doubts as to my expectations for professionalism. It shook up the operation from the top down and the partners upped my equity and I became Vice President. I was the only Board member who actually had ship and diving experience. The rest of the partners were bankers and marketing types.

This was the largest diving operation in the world, wasn't it? It was then and probably always will be. The ship was so ahead of its time that the diving industry had a hard time even beginning to understand how big it was. People would ask with all seriousness, "Is it as big as the *Cayman Aggressor*?" And we'd have to explain that we could lift that vessel on board our ship and put it on the back deck like a dinghy. We

routinely did as many as a thousand dives a day in Cozumel, Belize, and the Bay Islands of Honduras. We covered over 2500 miles a week roundtrip.

One funny thing always happened to a lot of the guests that came on board: they got lost. The ship was so big and had so many decks and corridors, that we'd find people wandering around completely disoriented. We finally had to install red phones in strategic places so guests could call the main hotel desk on the entrance deck and we'd send someone to find them.

What was it like to do business back then in Central America? In addition to breaking completely new ground with our diving operation, we were the first to ever bring a cruise ship to Belize and Honduras. That led to some surreal negotiations. At the time, Belize had just elected a new president and I went down to meet with him. He was insistent that we had to offer shore tours and "shopping" for our guests. I diplomatically tried to explain that our clientele were divers and primarily interested in the offshore atolls. I didn't bother to explain that Belize in 1987 was still fairly primitive with really only one decent hotel and no such thing as tourist shops. I think he read my mind because he said he was going to send me out the next day with his assistant director of tourism to show me the various "sights" that he thought we'd want to include for our guests.

So the next morning I get picked up by this nice fellow who admitted that he'd never been on a cruise

about an hour from town. He arranged a local Indian guide who spoke no English but would lead me into the interior to these great old stone temples. The next morning I'm up at dawn to go on my trek. My guide is this little man about 5 feet tall, long dark hair down his back, and about 100 pounds. Not a trace of body fat, looked like he could walk up mountains all day and not break a sweat. So he leads me through the jungle up this scenic trail. Monkeys are screaming at us, we get a glimpse of a jaguar and some great parrots, and I'm thinking, "Maybe this might be a worthwhile tour after all if the ruins are interesting."

After about an hour and a half, we come to this stream and I signal him that I've got to stop and rest. It's about a hundred degrees and I'm dying in the

1. Aerial view of *Ocean Spirit* 2. Main dining room
3. Main entertainment lounge 4. Gilliam operating recompression chamber
5. Dive boats coming along side *Ocean Spirit*, Roatan, 1989

ship and had only been out of Belize once before in his life. He then proceeded to take me on his idea of a great tour to offer. It included going down to the center of Belize City and watching a chain gang of convicts hand-crank a bridge open over a river that runs through the city. Then we stopped in to a place where the local amputees and lepers congregated to beg. That unique experience was followed by a "shopping tour" to sample the local hardware store, an appliance store, and a supermarket. Of course, it was ridiculous but, at that time, they were actually quite proud of these new shopping opportunities and couldn't understand why I thought the convicts and lepers wouldn't be major attractions.

Finally, he suggested I visit a remote Mayan ruin

humidity. I plunk down on a log and he sort of squats on his haunches nearby. He's not even breathing hard. I dangle my feet in the cool water and take it easy for about 10 minutes. When I push off the log to stand up, it shifts and a big snake comes shooting out and proceeds to strike my guide twice in the calf of his leg. It then spirals off into the brush but I got a quick look at its triangular head and it matches up to several of the deadly venomous species in Belize.

I'm trying to be cool about the situation and figure there's very little time to try to do some field first aid and then throw the little guy on my back and haul him back down the trail for medical help. I reach into my pack and dig out a Swiss army knife and a lighter. He watches with interest as I run the flame over the blade and indicate that he should sit down and pull up his pants to show me the bites. He does and I reach over to make incisions to draw out the venom and he goes

1. Doug MacDonald and Mutley, the diving dog, for
television series *Mac & Mutley*, Cozumel, 1989
2. Gilliam during shooting of *Mac & Mutley* television special, 1989

absolutely nuts. He's having none of it, kicking and
fighting, babbling in a dialect I can't understand. But
he's less than half my size and I figure that I have to
save his ungrateful butt in spite of his resistance. So I
sort of pin him down under me and aim the knife at
his bites while he struggles. I'm cutting him in a dozen
places because he won't hold still and we're rolling
around the ground when this group of people come
down the trail from the ruins and pull us apart.

It's a Baptist missionary with some tourists and
I hastily explain what happened and that I need their
help in subduing this guy to save him. Meanwhile, my
Indian guide unleashes a torrent of dialect as well.
The missionary waves me to shut up and listens to
the guy since he understands his language. I'm frantic
and tell him to explain what we have to do and that
I'm not trying to attack the little guy. The missionary
has a brief exchange with my wounded partner and
starts laughing. I go, "What so funny? He's going to die
if we don't treat him!" The missionary chokes back his
mirth and tells me, "The Indian says he's been trying to
explain to you that the snake is not poisonous."

That's it. I'm back down the trail to my hotel. No
more damn discussions about shore tours and shopping.

**You did some television and movie work aboard
as well, right?** ≫We had some incredible adventures
and great times. One trip we were chartered to be
the host "hotel" for the 1989 Miss Universe contest
being held in Cancun. Several movies were made on
board including an absolutely horrible comedy called
Going Overboard. It was the first role for a young guy
named Adam Sandler. Billy Bob Thorton was in the
cast as well. Don't waste your money at Blockbuster, it
was terrible. That film company was so sleazy that we
denied them permission to use any of the public areas
when the passengers were around. So they had to grab
their shots in the dining rooms, bars, pool, casino when
they were closed at night or when the passengers were
off the ship diving or shopping. So to fill out the places
that had to look lively, they hired a lot of the onboard
staff to be the extras. My staff loved it.

We did specials for network television, The Travel
Channel, HBO. We did a series with a great host named
Doug MacDonald for *Discovery* called *Mac & Mutley*. It
was about this dog that did all these incredible sports…
surfing, skiing, skateboarding, hang-gliding, toboggan,
you name it. We rigged him up with a plastic dome

helmet and a tiny pony tank. And the little guy went scuba diving as deep as 50 feet with Olympic swimming champion Matt Biondi.

I heard some stories about a toga party that went awry. 》That was all my fault. We were on our last night out before getting into New Orleans from Cozumel and disembarking our passengers. We were showing *Animal House* that afternoon in the movie theatre and, since it was raining, the place was packed. Later that night in the main lounge I was thanking the guests for a great week and thought, "Why not do something a little different?" We had this little "sky lounge" way up on the top deck that had a neat bar, dance floor, and was all glass with a great view. So I invited anyone who wanted to stay up late and we'd have a toga party beginning at midnight.

So I climb out of my formal white uniform and hunt up a sheet from the ship's laundry. My girlfriend then, Lynn Hendrickson, whips up two barely decent togas for us and we go strolling up to the sky bar expecting maybe a dozen people might show up. Wrong! There were nearly 200 crazies jammed into a bar that was supposed to handle fifty or sixty people… maybe. And they're all in togas of some sort. The music is grinding, the bar is doing thousands of dollars in business, and the guests are having the time of their lives, screaming "Toga! Toga! Toga!" at me as I walked in.

Right in the middle of all this, I get a panicked call from the hotel manager who needs to see me right away. "Captain, the guests have torn up all the bed sheets, towels, and covers to make costumes for your party. We don't have enough replacements clean to make up their beds tonight and we have all new guests coming aboard tomorrow afternoon. What am I to do?"

Well, I never thought of where the resourceful guests were going to get their toga materials from. It cost about three grand to get new linen the next morning but the party was worth it.

What finally happened to *Ocean Quest*? 》After nearly three years I was really ready to come ashore. I had been at sea at that point for over a decade. We were having some internal power struggles and I got sick of refereeing. Especially since I was the only member of the Board that actually rode the ship and was responsible for day to day operations, dealing with the U. S. Coast Guard inspections, trying to schedule shipyard maintenance around our calendar of sailing

Lynn Hendrickson

2

dates, running the recompression chamber, staying in compliance with U. S. rules for Public Health. It was very involved. Right in the middle of all this, we were approached by Sea Escape Cruise Lines who wanted to buy us out and use the ship for gambling out of Ft. Lauderdale to the Bahamas. They made an offer that couldn't be refused, nearly $26 million. It was a no-brainer. Our group only had about five million invested. So the company was sold with more than a little rejoicing. I was 39 and decided to move to an island in Maine. It was the first time I'd lived in the U.S. in more than twenty years.

In the nineties, you've been regarded as one of the leaders in technical diving. How did you get into that part of diving originally? 》I guess the best answer is that I was already in it since the early seventies but we didn't have a name for it then. Some of the stuff we did for the Navy during the deep submarine filming projects was so out at the edge of the envelope that I don't think anyone ever went back and tried it after we finished in 1971.

Who else was around in those days doing early tech dives? 》Well, we sort of operated in our own little vacuum until late 1972 when I met Tom Mount and he was hooked up with Dr. George Benjamin doing some amazing deep Blue Hole explorations in Andros. Hal Watts was real active in both cave and deep diving. And then Sheck Exley bumped into me in Florida in 1973 and found out we had a lot in common. Sheck didn't do much ocean diving because he got seasick and

1. V.I. Divers' 52-ft. dive vessel *Sundance II*,
Marina Cay, BVI, 1979 2. Gilliam blowing air-ring during extended
decompression following dive to 350 feet, St. Croix, 1976

really loved cave exploration, but we kept up a running correspondence on various deep diving techniques that continued right up until his death in 1994.

A lot of the definitive stuff on all sorts of procedures, gear configurations, special tables, and cave diving innovations came out of this period. But it was a pretty closed community. There was not a lot of shared information back then except among the cave guys and even then it was limited. We didn't have the communications systems and publications then that are commonplace today. In 1974 I published one of the first formal papers on techniques for deep air diving and I had people tracking me down from all over wanting more information or with new ideas to share. About the same time Sheck published something on oxygen for decompression and all of a sudden there were a lot of divers coming out of the woodwork wanting to share ideas for the first time.

About this time I met Dr. Bob Dill. He was a Ph.D. in underwater geology and had a reputation as something of a gonzo scientist. Bob would do anything if it advanced his research and he couldn't have cared less about critics who questioned his methods. He

hired me for a whole series of projects that spanned about five years while he was director of Fairleigh Dickinson University's West Indies Laboratory in St. Croix. He was also a fund raising genius who brought the Hydrolab saturation habitat program to the Virgin Islands. Just before I met Bob, Cousteau had taken him as a scientific advisor for the *Calypso* when they explored the great Blue Hole in Belize. Bob would go blasting off on some pretty deep stuff and scare the hell out of the *Calypso* team but they loved his passion for exploration and the samples he brought back. He was one hell of a guy.

So deep diving was controversial even thirty-five years ago? Yeah, to some. But mostly those involved were professionals and not much of what we were doing got out into the sport diving public. A lot of the real deep air work that Sheck, Mount, Frank Martz, Jim Lockwood and others did was basically kept in the closet. Primarily we were concerned about unqualified and inexperienced divers getting themselves in trouble.

I think the controversy really got started up again in the early 1990s when there was more publicity focused on technical diving. Accidents have a way of making headlines. Never mind that most accidents were predictable and usually involved divers that were not properly trained or prepared. But a lot of divers were really not well informed as to the academic and medical physiology side of things. Many of these folks went charging off and didn't come back. Common sense goes a long way. There were a lot of lessons in Darwinism.

Diving deep on air was controversial but you and a handful of others worked astounding depths. Why? » First of all, in the early days we simply didn't have access to helium. Even when I worked on the navy projects, we routinely went to 300 feet before we even considered heliox. A lot of people don't realize that the

Paul Tzimoulis

ability to work deep on air has applications in mixed gas diving as well. For instance, in some extreme trimix diving the equivalent narcosis depth may be equal to 400 feet on air. This is because the nitrogen in the mix still has narcotic properties. Although helium is essentially non-narcotic, trimix still has nitrogen in it for several reasons: first of all, it makes the decompression

less lengthy and, secondly, nitrogen buffers the effect of high pressure nervous syndrome (HPNS) caused by breathing helium below about 500 feet. So... deep air diving in many ways was part of the process for me on commercial and science diving projects back then. We were going to go even deeper on other gas mixtures.

It's important to remember: we weren't doing this diving for fun. We were being extremely well paid for commercial inspections and scientific work. It was a job and the ability to dive deep got us to the job site with our cameras and tools.

Also, in many exotic remote places it was impossible to obtain helium mixes and air was the only choice. The alternative would be to simply cancel some of the explorations. For me, I function quite fine on air and have been doing so for over 35 years now. And in many applications, air is a "friendlier" gas to breathe with regard to decompression schedules for shorter, deeper dives. For most divers, 220 feet is good place to stop on air since they will have reached the 1.6 bar partial pressure of oxygen. But in my case, I have had no problems going deeper.

What about narcosis? At these extreme depths how did you avoid being incapacitated? » Narcosis is very subjective to each individual. It affects each diver differently. I have a very high tolerance for narcosis as well as developing a certain "adaptation" to its effects from a long history of deep diving. I also had the benefit of operating my own hyperbaric chamber facility and could perform test experiments in that environment. Probably most critical is developing dive techniques that minimize carbon dioxide (CO_2) in the diver's system. This means staying relaxed, keeping exertion to a minimum, using high performance regulators, and using good "whole lung" breathing cycles.

CO_2 is known to accelerate the onset and severity of narcosis and oxygen toxicity. So every effort is made to simply do things slowly, calmly, and with as little hard effort as possible. When I set the depth record in 1990, even at 452 feet, I was still quite capable of performing higher math problems as well as a series of questions requiring analytical thought process. Some people may well have been incapacitated, but for me, I was able to operate. But again, we're talking about being specifically trained under controlled circumstances and with a constant schedule of diving deep each day. I had just turned 39 when I broke the record and in really

good shape since I was diving daily and cranking over 750-800 dives per year then. When I went to 490 feet in 1993, I was 42. Now I'm 56 years old. So you make adjustments with age.

You did most of your deepest work without a buddy. Why? »I dove alone but had assistance from other divers on the surface. Like Sheck Exley, I'm more comfortable with just myself to look after. I tend to worry about other people.

Your book *Deep Diving: An Advanced Guide to Physiology, Procedures and Systems* became the best selling book on the subject of all time. How many copies are out there? »I really have no idea, tens of thousands. When it was first published in 1992 it sold out its first press run in less than a year. The timing was right for a book that took very complex subjects and explained them so the average person could understand the physics and operational methodology. The 2nd edition came out in 1995 and is still selling. I think it has been translated into five languages. As long as the checks keep coming, I'll keep cashing them.

Over the years you've written everything from medical texts, engineering handbooks, formal scientific papers, instructional manuals, dive magazine articles, etc. as well as editing the works of others you published. What did you enjoy most? »Well, I loved writing in general and tried to always do the best I could for the audience I was writing for. But my favorite time as a writer was when I could indulge my own sardonic perspective and sense of humor. Most of diving journalism is pretty uptight and serious. I used to say that most diving writers had their sense of humor surgically removed at birth. I loved the stuff that Dick Anderson wrote in the 1960s and early 1970s. He had a unique gift for poking fun at things that people in diving took too seriously. Dick always

cracked me up and one of the highest compliments I ever got was when a reviewer compared me to him. Obviously, I couldn't incorporate humor into a medical piece or a guide to mixing breathing gases, but I loved to give the readers a laugh when I could in more general articles.

It's funny, people really seemed to get a kick out of some lines that I'd toss into an article and think they wouldn't be remembered. But readers would come up to me and quote them to me at dive shows and speaking engagements. That's validation, I guess.

Give us an example. »Oh hell, there was a lot of nonsense. One line that folks seemed to remember was the time I said that the 1998 El Niño was causing a lot of peculiar weather. The ocean was warming, the northeast was buried in rain, but out west it was so dry that squirrels were putting moisturizer on their nuts.

Another time I commented on some dipstick critic of nitrox back in the early 1990s by saying that I couldn't dignify his ignorant comments with a reply because my mother said it wasn't sportsmanlike to engage in a battle of wits with an unarmed man. Needless to say, he didn't get the joke.

What inspired you to set up Technical Diving International (TDI) in 1994? »Originally I was involved in founding IANTD with Dick Rutkowski, Tom Mount and Billy Deans but I had become a bit disillusioned over the quality of materials that were badly written and really didn't handle the subject matter thoroughly. I also felt that the prices were overly high to the instructors. But I was a minority shareholder and didn't want to get into a big deal with the Mounts at the time. My basic failing is that I'm a perfectionist. I was also President and Chairman of the Board of NAUI at the time and wanted to see a serious professional quality technical training agency get going. So I put together a new corporation called International Training Inc. to operate the nucleus of the TDI program and it just took off.

But I vividly remember the early days when, once again, it was just me in the office. I typed the c-cards, laminated them, answered the phone, did the mail, edited the training manuals, wrote the standards, designed the ads, everything. In April of 1995, I finally hired Lynn and Lauren Hendrickson as the first full time staff. Those two ladies were a big part of our success and really

Bret Gilliam

1943 WWII Japanese aircraft wreck in Solomon
Islands, one of Gilliam's scores of magazine
covers. His wife Gretchen is the model, 2005

understood the total commitment to customer service. Lynn is still with the company… and so are her three Jack Russell terriers. Now the company is the largest tech agency in the world with offices in over twenty countries.

Ironically, as Chairman of NAUI, I tried to get them to implement a nitrox and technical program within that agency. Trying to lead that bunch was like herding cats. They were still arguing about dive computers and buddy breathing… in the 1990s! They flatly rejected any move in that direction. Well, they gave up millions. Even though I was elected to a second term on the NAUI Board in a landslide, I resigned in 1997 when I could no longer deal with banging my head against the wall trying to get them to innovate and be proactive in training revisions.

Later in 1998, our TDI instructors asked us to put together an entry-level training program so they could do all their training within one agency. We quickly responded and had the curriculum and training materials in place within six months. I called this division of the company Scuba Diving International or SDI. We sort of re-wrote the book on training divers by expanding open water training, teaching dive computers from the outset of class, and using full color textbooks and computer-based interactive training methodology. Now SDI is one of the top three training agencies for sport divers with PADI and SSI. Those three companies totally dominate the certifying business now.

NAUI is really no longer even a player; it's kind of sad in a way. When I became an instructor for them in 1972 they had nearly an 80 percent market share. They pissed it all away by not being able to evolve and see where the industry was going. To this day they have refused to join the RSTC and so they flounder around in a vacuum and continue to shrink. They'll eventually go the way of NASDS and the YMCA program. A handful of diehards will cling to it forever though.

The group that bought International Training Inc. from me in 2004 has continued to innovate and grow. Brian Carney is now the President. He came to work for me at UWATEC when he was about 25, right out of college, and then followed me to TDI. I must have taught him something. They're doing very well with double-digit growth annually. I love it when my successors do well.

You were always a proponent of innovation in spite of criticism from diving's conservative element. Do you feel vindicated that nearly

all of your positions evolved into mainstream practice? I guess I'm proud to see what I was doing at SDI and TDI have a positive affect on how new divers get trained. We were certainly criticized for being the first to suggest that dive tables had outlived their usefulness in favor of computers. But I'm used to controversy. Back in the 1970s it was considered heresy when I suggested that one dive was not enough

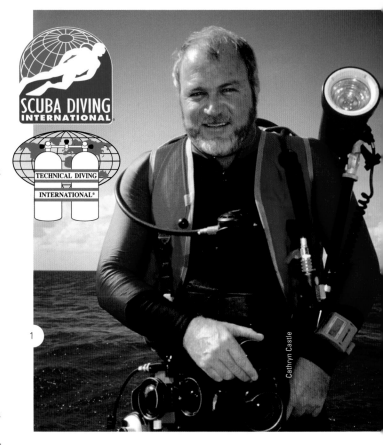

1. Geared up for dive computer test dives, Belize, 1992
2. Accepting *Diver of the Year* award at Beneath the Sea, 2004

to qualify a new diver. Later I advocated the use of modern BC's, inflators and submersible pressure gauges. Incredibly, there were conservatives who didn't like that. When we started some of the first liveaboard dive vessels in the Caribbean with unlimited diving, the neo-Nazi element suggested that we were going to be responsible for bending everyone since no one should ever make more than two dives a day. Nonsense! Who makes these stupid rules? You should hear me and Paul Humann with a couple of bottles of wine in us about how nuts the industry can be!

Of course, dive computers met with skepticism when first introduced as well as nitrox. But both are standard practices of the sport today. So I guess I've always been a little ahead of my time. Sooner or later, the industry catches up but there's always a lot of griping along the way.

What led to your involvement in UWATEC?》I was a firm believer that diving computers would make the sport more convenient and safer. So beginning in 1988, I educated myself on the subject of decompression models, algorithms, how the various manufacturers were handling ascent rates, off-gassing, oxygen toxicity, repetitive dives. I published several formal papers on the subject and was in demand as a speaker for the Undersea and Hyperbaric Medical Society as well as other diving medicine forums. In 1993 the UHMS invited me to be on the faculty of a special workshop on dive computers they sponsored in Halifax. It was quite a lineup of the top docs, physiologists, and professional divers with medical expertise like me. Even the great Swiss physiologist Dr. Albert Buhlmann was there; he was doing the special technical work on algorithms for UWATEC. I had the best hard data from the field along with chamber records and was beta-testing a lot of the stuff myself in the ocean. I was teaching doctors to treat diving patients with Dick Rutkowski, NOAA's retired Deputy Director of Diving. Between the two of us, we had some of the most extensive treatment backgrounds of any two guys in the country. We both passionately advocated for nitrox and computers.

I really believed that dive computers were the future and that the critics were both uninformed and more interested in advancing their own agendas than looking at the available technology with an open mind. Eventually my articles and public speaking reached the attention of the two Swiss guys who owned UWATEC. At the time, they were only doing OEM production, building stuff that other manufacturers put their name on. But they were about to change direction and come out under their own name and greatly expand the line. They called me up and hired me as a consultant to make recommendations on design features for their new nitrox models. I was already using their stuff and it was a perfect match. A year later, they fired all their U. S. management and handed me the company as President and CEO.

How long did it take for the company to take off?》When I stepped in, I brought my own sales and marketing people in that shared my ideas of service and commitment to the customer. Within a year, we had raised sales about 500 percent and began to dominate the market. When we took the company public in 1997 to Johnson Worldwide Associates, we had a 74 percent world market share in computers and instruments. The sale brought over $40 million to the stockholders. We all had a very nice day.

I'm surprised you stuck around after the sale. How did you fit into a classic "white bread" corporate system?》I didn't. It was a classic mismatch of entrepreneurial style versus constipated accounting types. But I actually continued to run things for nearly two years out of loyalty to the original founders. I was 100 percent behind the sale as it was the perfect time, once again, to sell out at the top of the market. We

Stan Waterman

2

were about three years ahead of our competitors on technology but they were going to catch up. That would have eroded our profits and made the company less valuable down the road.

But I knew when we sold out that there would be a bad match between our people and the new owners. They weren't divers and their managers for their other diving company (Scubapro) were not exactly setting records like Dick Bonin did when he made Scubapro the number one brand in the world. At UWATEC we were all hardcore divers and most of our management were self-made millionaires already. Independence and

483

non-conventional thinking was encouraged in my team. That's what built the company in the first place. So we were hard to control; certainly no one could be bullied by corporate stiffs who made only a fraction of what we did. We pretty much were going to do things our way. And they needed us, not the other way around. There were some memorable confrontations. It wasn't *Ozzie & Harriet*, that's for sure.

By the end of 1998 I was ready to leave. Everybody was ready to go. There was a mass exodus. Most of our top people in sales, engineering, product development, and senior management went to competitors who welcomed them with open arms. I stayed on as a consultant until mid-2000 to fulfill my contract. I think the last report I saw recently had UWATEC's market share in computers and instruments down to eight percent, a rather astounding slide. But predictable.

I'm surprised you were able to juggle all the things you had going in 1998. ⟩⟩ Well, it was hectic at times. In addition to running UWATEC, I was President of International Training Inc. (TDI & SDI), and partners with Fred Garth in the publishing business. And I had one of the busiest years ever as a legal consultant. So leaving the day-to-day obligations of UWATEC was welcomed. Then another serendipitous business event fell out of the sky.

Fred called me up in mid-December to say that Petersen Publishing had contacted him and they wanted buy *Deep Tech* and *Scuba Times* magazines from us. We both figured it was yet another ploy to find out our circulation base, ad revenues, and insider details of our company. We'd been through that before. So I said, "Throw some seven figure number out at them and they'll go away." I just couldn't see wasting our time on the same song and dance. But Fred called back a few days later to say, "Bret, they screwed us. They took our offer!"

We were both floored. Petersen didn't really even try to knock our price down. It turned out that they were simultaneously selling their company to British publishing giant, E-Map Ltd., and they needed our circulation numbers to prop up the struggling *Skin Diver* magazine in the diving market. So we took the money and ran.

Wasn't 1998 when you started taking Lauren Hutton with you on a lot of trips? ⟩⟩ We were introduced in January of that year. She came to Maine and stayed longer than originally planned due a massive snow and ice storm that pretty well shut down the east coast for about a week. She ended up cooking dinner for all my friends that came over for the Super Bowl. She started diving back in the late 1960s when she first went to New York and became the first "super model". I was about to head off for a month or so in Fiji and she decided to come along. After that we went to the Bahamas, Truk, and then a month at Cocos Island off Costa Rica. She even came along when I went to see Al Giddings in Montana that fall and they became friends

1. Lauren Hutton in Fiji, 1998 2. Gilliam, Hutton and Fred Garth aboard *Sea Hunter*, Cocos Island, 1998 3. Gilliam and Garth aboard *Sea Hunter* with rebreathers, Cocos Island, 2002

as well. Lauren is one of the nicest, easy-going people anyone could meet. Absolutely no pretense. And a radiant natural beauty, especially that gap-toothed smile!

I seem to remember that her attempts at Spanish in Costa Rica led to some interesting exchanges. ⟩⟩ Well, Lauren tends to like to immerse herself in local culture wherever she goes. She really had no Spanish skills at all. But she was always willing

3

to give it a shot. Once when we were on the *Sea Hunter* passing a prominent headland, she asked the name of the place. Fred Garth told her it was called Punta Maria. Later when we were off the west end of Cocos Island, she again wanted to know the name of that part of the island. This time Fred told her that it was unnamed. "Aha, then we'll name it after me. How about we call it Puta Lauren?" Everyone immediately agreed that would be a perfect name. And Puta Lauren it has remained.

Unfortunately, she got the nuance of Spanish a little wrong. The word "Punta" means, "point". The word "Puta," which she had prefaced her name with, means, "whore". So Puta Lauren is remembered fondly.

But our favorite Spanish lesson came between trips when we killed a few days on the mainland by visiting the Costa Rican rain forest in the high mountain region known as Monte Verde. We grabbed a local taxi right out of *Romancing the Stone* to bounce over ill-tended roads for about six hours before arriving at the small village that serves as the business and cultural center of the region. We shook the dust off and strolled into the first bar we saw to toss down a few beers.

The local currency in Costa Rica is known as "colones" and Lauren had neglected to get a supply before we left San Jose. So she ambles up to this local teenage kid behind the counter. She's wearing a sweat-soaked halter-top and a pair of super short cut-off jeans. She's going to buy a round of drinks. She slaps a $100 bill on the counter and asks the kid if he can get her some beer and "cojones".

The guy couldn't believe his luck as he stared at the seductive beauty in front of him. "Si, senorita, I can get you all the cojones you need!"

Fred intervened before Lauren caused a major desta-bilization to the local currency. We got our beer, the kid had his fantasy, and Lauren picked up a bit more Spanish.

Now that you have retired, what is going to occupy your time?》I'm doing some books that are already underway that will be on diving subjects and a two part novel for a mainstream publisher. I'll still do some legal consulting work because the trial process is both ridiculously lucrative and very challenging. Of course, I'll continue diving and will still put together some expeditions to the best places for my loyal trip customers. But mostly, right now I'm enjoying the fact that I don't have to do anything! I just bought a 48 ft. motor yacht and I'm enjoying cruising around Maine. I'll probably take her down to the Caribbean in a year or so and noodle around there. And I may indulge myself in another large ship project again, something in the 200-250 ft. size range, but for private use.

What do think has had the most effect on diving as a sport? 》Two things. First, diving computers liberated us to plan dives on the fly with active

1

calculative devices that freed divers from static rigid tables and eliminated the human error factors in timekeeping and depth recording. Now you can program mixes, change mixes during a dive, run

1. Gilliam's home waters are summer feeding grounds for North Atlantic Humpback whales. Here singer Jonathan Edwards is introduced to a 55-ft. female in the Gulf of Maine, 1992 2. Working with wild dolphins, Bahamas, 1976 3. With seal, 1982

simulated profiles, and electronically store all the data for log-keeping, accident review, and forensic evaluation. It made diving easier, more efficient, and dramatically safer. (To Dr. Carl Edmonds, Peter Bennett, and the rest of the mindless dipsticks that tried to condemn and thwart this technology, including nitrox… please bite my ass, thank you!)

Secondly, nothing changed the way divers access the best diving more than liveaboard vessels. When Paul Humann and I started the first popular liveaboards in the 1970s, it allowed us to routinely take people to sites and areas that previously were simply unreachable by any day boats. The places we could get to and stay on top of were just too far away from main tourism centers. When

things became more refined later, the vessels added real comfort features, photo labs, onboard specialized training opportunities, and private accommodations that, in many cases, exceeded those of land-based hotels. You can credit the *Aggressor* fleet for getting the ball rolling in the modern era. But you can thank Peter Hughes for bringing a standard of luxury to diving that set the bar to a new level. Peter put the sizzle and style in the mix and raised everyone's expectations for sheer ambiance and comfort. God bless him.

Other visionaries like Avi Klapfer applied a standard of excellence and professionalism to his *Sea Hunter* fleet that made places like Cocos Island and Malpelo safely accessible. Lenny Kolczynski's *Odyssey* in Truk is the most comfortable and spacious dive ship in the world. And what Rick Belmare has done with *Bilikiki* in the Solomons is remarkable. It combines a reliable first-rate ship that really understands how to handle divers with perhaps the best diversity of marine life, corals, big animals, and interesting local culture. I'm going on Bob Hollis's new *Spirit of Niugini* soon in PNG and I suspect that will be top end as well.

You've followed whales and dolphins all over the world and also worked as a photographer for a bunch of aquariums. How do you feel about captive marine mammal parks? »Personally, I'm horribly conflicted on the subject. I've had occasion to work with several facilities dating back over 25 years now with mixed results. Some U. S. and Canadian based operations have done a very good job of providing a reasonable home, good safety and medical support. And they have undoubtedly raised the awareness of the general public about the real threat to these wonderful creatures in the wild due to netting, hunting, pollution or loss of habitat. Good facilities have inspired people who first came into contact with dolphins, orcas, seals, etc. through such exhibits to open their wallets and cast their important votes to protect marine mammals. That's great and I can swallow my knee-jerk aversion to placing such intelligent species in captivity by recognizing that these animals are well cared for and help bring hundreds of thousands of our own species closer to understanding how important it is for us to preserve their wild habitat as well.

However, it seems that for every good exhibit or park, there are just as many horror stories that include facilities that are too small, improperly designed, lack proper medical care, or fail to meet any kind of standard for sanitation and safety. Some of these "parks" that exist beyond the U. S. and Canada are nothing short of concentration camps for marine mammals and the death toll is beyond any acceptable level. Many lack even the most rudimentary oversight from legitimate marine biologists who specialize in

we have today. Imaging systems for motion picture and still photography have simply jumped over the horizon.

The problem is the decline of the world's oceans and marine habitats. When I look at slides I shot in the early 1970s in the Red Sea, Caribbean, Bahamas, Palau... it's sobering. I don't need to dwell on the fact that we will never again see that vitality and diversity.

1. Gretchen and Bret, Boston Sea Rovers 50th Anniversary program, 2004 2. Gilliam's 48-ft. yacht *Encore* anchored off Stan Waterman's house, Sargentville, Maine, 2006

such species. And the conditions in which the animals are kept would make most of us sign on to aid in their *Great Escape*. For me, nothing can justify this horrible exploitation and I am diametrically opposed to this cruelty. I'm just as pissed off at a lot of the diving press that has given them a pass since they buy expensive ads and pay for flattering articles that encourage the continued bad practices. Shame on everyone involved.

It doesn't take a huge amount of intellect to reasonably differentiate between the two types of exhibits. So I swallow hard and say okay to the ones who do their utmost to run responsible operations. And I wish an enduring curse of pestilence on those who exploit marine mammals solely for a quick buck. For me, my most memorable and dramatic encounters have always come in the wild where species can independently decide for themselves whether they want to interact. Then again, I feel the same way about half the people I meet at cocktail parties.

Any thoughts on the future of diving? »Diving has never had better equipment and support for whatever people may want to do. I can only imagine what we might have done 35-40 years ago with the technology

There are still some wonderfully pristine places that are like rolling the clock back forty years but they're sadly limited to the Solomon Islands, Papua New Guinea, and the remotest areas of Indonesia. Cocos Island remains an outpost to see massive shark populations but they are still fighting a constant battle over poaching. Everyone should wake up to what is being lost.

What can an individual do to make a difference? »You can have an immediate effect by supporting conservation groups like Seacology. This organization spends their money to do things like build schools in Third World island regions in exchange for agreements to protect adjacent reefs from dynamite fishing and other exploitive non-sustainable uses. They protect wetlands, forest lands, and establish marine preserves all by making direct deals with the local inhabitants who derive tangible immediate benefits in the form of schools, medical clinics, elderly homes, etc. There's no wasteful bureaucratic structure within Seacology. Your money goes to accomplish a direct immediate protection of the marine environment. They're good people. Talk to their Executive Director, Duane Silverstein (islands@seacology.org, phone: 510-559-3505). They've done great work in the Solomons, PNG, Fiji, Indonesia… Check them out at www.seacology.org

Who do you think made the biggest impact on diving? »Cousteau is an obvious choice but he really wasn't a hands-on guy. He was more of a producer. Within the same first generation of diving, guys like Stan Waterman, Hans Hass, Bob Hollis, and Al Giddings brought the gift of visual impact to people. Their

telegenic, great speakers, and they're wonderful ambassadors. They're impossible not to like. Spending time with them is always uplifting for me. How many people can you say that about?

You are credited as one of the most influential pioneers of modern diving, what do you think? »There have been a lot of good folks who helped move diving ahead. I'm just one who wasn't afraid to speak up and articulate more progressive perspectives. I saw opportunity in embracing new technology and innovations. It was good business. (Now I sound like some mafia don… "It was only business, Fredo, not personal. Never go against the family.") Although the

Bret Gilliam

films and photographs brought diving to the public in a very personal way. And they did it in a time of inferior equipment, both diving gear and cameras. Yet it grabbed the viewer and drove a lot of folks to try diving. The late Paul Tzimoulis did so much for the sport through his stewardship of *Skin Diver* magazine back in the 1970s especially to promote new and exotic diving locations, liveaboards, and equipment breakthroughs. (This was before the magazine whored itself out to became the worst example of "advertorial" crap.) Manufacturers like Dick Bonin and Hollis really changed the way gear was built and brought to the consumer. They each had a huge influence on me and I'm proud to know them as friends. Sadly, Paul passed away in 2003. We had some great times together.

Diving needs some new heroes. If the industry was smart, they'd latch on to Howard and Michele Hall in that role. Their work is superb, they're

conservative lunatic fringe frequently savaged me, eventually all the controversial positions that I took proved to be correct and helped move the sport forward. Look at liveaboards, computers, nitrox, rebreathers, technical diving, solo diving, changes in how training is done. That's very satisfying.

But it's worth remembering that old expression: "You can always tell a pioneer… he's the one with arrows in his back." »Well, if that's true, then at times I must have looked like a veteran of Custer's Last Stand. But hey, that's life. Diving was very good to me. I made a fortune doing exactly what interested me most and enjoyed every minute of it along the way. If I contributed, even in a small way, to innovation and progress, then I'm glad I gave something back. At this stage, I'll borrow my own perspective on life from Bob Dylan, "I was so much older then, I'm younger than that now." ∎